Historical Dictionary of Napoleonic France, 1799-1815

Historical Dictionaries of French History

This five-volume series covers French history from the Revolution through the Third Republic. It provides comprehensive coverage of each era, including not only political and military history but also social, economic, and art history.

Historical Dictionary of the French Revolution, 1789-1799
Samuel F. Scott and Barry Rothaus, editors

Historical Dictionary of Napoleonic France, 1799-1815
Owen Connelly, editor

Historical Dictionary of France from the 1815 Restoration to the Second Empire
Edgar Leon Newman, editor

Historical Dictionary of the French Second Empire, 1852-1870
William E. Echard, editor

Historical Dictionary of the Third French Republic, 1870-1940
Patrick H. Hutton, editor-in-chief

Historical Dictionary of Napoleonic France, 1799-1815

Edited by
OWEN CONNELLY

HAROLD T. PARKER,
PETER W. BECKER, *and*
JUNE K. BURTON,
Associate Editors

JANICE SEAMAN BERBIN,
Editorial Assistant

Greenwood Press
Westport, Connecticut

Library of Congress Cataloging in Publication Data

Main entry under title:

Historical dictionary of Napoleonic France, 1799-1815.

Bibliography: p.
Includes index.
1. France—History—Consulate and Empire, 1799-1815—Dictionaries. 2. Europe—History—1789-1815—Dictionaries. I. Connelly, Owen.
DC201.H673 1985 944.04′5 83-22754
ISBN 0-313-21321-6 (lib. bdg.)

Library of Congress Catalog Card Number: 83-22754
ISBN 0-313-21321-6

First published in 1985

Greenwood Press
A division of Congressional Information Service, Inc.
88 Post Road West,
Westport, Connecticut 06881

Printed in the United States of America

10 9 8 7 6 5 4 3 2 1

Contents

Contributors

Geoffrey Adams, Concordia University (Montreal, Canada)
Eric A. Arnold, Jr., University of Denver (Colorado)
Janos Bak, University of British Columbia (Canada)
Richard J. Barker, Montclair State College (New Jersey)
Vincent Beach, University of Colorado
Thomas Beck, Chapman College (California)
Peter W. Becker, University of South Carolina
Helmut Berding, Justus-Liebig-Universität, Giessen (West Germany)
Claude Bergeron, Université Laval (Quebec, Canada)
Hugh Bonar, California State University at Los Angeles
Gordon Bond, Auburn University (Alabama)
Ulane Bonnel, Commission d'Histoire Maritime (France) and Library of Congress
June K. Burton, University of Akron (Ohio)
Francis Lawrence Butvin, University of Akron (Ohio)
Melanie Sue Byrd, University of Akron (Ohio)
Jack Censer, George Mason University (Virginia)
Susan P. Conner, Tift College (Georgia)
Dawn L. Corley, University of Akron (Ohio)
Robert R. Crout, Princeton University (New Jersey)
Ray E. Cubberly, University of Hawaii, Manoa
Conrad Donakowski, Michigan State University
Geoffrey J. Ellis, Hertford College, Oxford (England)
Robert Epstein, U.S. Army Command and General Staff College
Milton Finley, Louisiana State University at Shreveport
Robert Forster, The Johns Hopkins University (Maryland)
Wallace Fowlie, Duke University (North Carolina)
Francisco A. de la Fuente, Florida State University
John Gallaher, Southern Illinois University at Edwardsville
Reed Geiger, University of Delaware
Richard Glover, Carleton University (Ottawa, Canada)
Jacques Godechot, Université de Toulouse (France)
James N. Hardin, University of South Carolina

Fred E. Hembree, University of South Carolina
Jean Henry, University of New Haven (Connecticut)
Brigitte Holl, Heeresgeschichtliches Museum, Wien (Austria)
Robert B. Holtman, Louisiana State University
Gerlof D. Homan, Illinois State University
Donald D. Horward, Florida State University
Walther Hubatsch, Universität Bonn (West Germany)
Lynn A. Hunt, University of California-Berkeley
Stanley Idzerda, College of St. Benedict (Minnesota)
Gerda Jordan, University of South Carolina
Yolita Kavaliunas, University of Akron (Ohio)
John Keep, University of Toronto (Canada)
Emmet Kennedy, George Washington University (Washington, D.C.)
Michael L. Kennedy, Winthrop College (South Carolina)
W. Ben Kennedy, West Georgia College
Lee Kennett, University of Georgia
Paschalis M. Kitromilides, Centre d'Etudes d'Asie Mineure (Athens, Greece)
Rainer Koch, Johann-Wolfgang-Goethe-Universität, Frankfurt (West Germany)
Domokos Kosáry, Academiae Scientiarum Hungaricae (Budapest, Hungary)
Enno Kraehe, University of Virginia
Siegfried Erich Kraus, Pädagogische Akademie Österreich (Austria)
Miriam R. Levin, University of Massachusetts
Helen P. Liebel-Weckowicz, University of Alberta (Canada)
Colin Lucas, Balliol College, Oxford (England)
Leonard Macaluso, University of South Alabama
Frances Malino, University of Massachusetts, Boston Campus
Kenneth Margerison, Southwest Texas University
Jack Allen Meyer, University of South Carolina
William I. Miller, University of Akron (Ohio)
Leslie G. Mitchell, University College, Oxford (England)
Michael Müller, Institut für Geschichtliche Landeskunde der Rheinlande an der Universität Bonn (West Germany)
Linda J. Nelson, University of Akron (Ohio)
Joachim Niemeyer, Baden-Baden (West Germany)
Cora Lee Nollendorfs, University of Wisconsin
Nancy Nolte, University of Akron (Ohio)
Jeanne A. Ojala, University of Utah
Peter Paret, Stanford University (California)
Harold T. Parker, Duke University (North Carolina)
Reinhard Patemann, Staatsarchiv Bremen (West Germany)
Kenneth J. Perkins, University of South Carolina
Uwe Puschner, Institut für Neuere Geschichte, Universität München (West Germany)
Hugh Ragsdale, University of Alabama

Matthew Ramsey, Harvard University
Margit Resch, University of South Carolina
David C. Riede, University of Akron (Ohio)
Alexander Roland, Duke University (North Carolina)
Steven T. Ross, U.S. Naval War College
Gunther E. Rothenberg, Purdue University (Indiana)
Herbert H. Rowen, Rutgers University (New Jersey)
Rachel R. Schneider, University of Akron (Ohio)
Dieter Schwab, Universität Regensburg (West Germany)
Jesse Scott, University of South Carolina
John K. Severn, Florida State University
Thomas F. Sheppard, College of William and Mary (Virginia)
John M. Sherwig, State University of New York at New Paltz
Joseph I. Shulim, Hunter College, City University of New York
Michael D. Sibalis, University of Ottawa (Canada)
John Stanley, Toronto, Canada
Martin Staum, Paris, France
John Stine, Military Campuses, University of South Carolina
Viktoria Strohbach, Institut für Neuere Geschichte, Universität München (West Germany)
Reinhard Stumpf, Militärgeschichtliches Forschungsamt (West Germany)
M. J. Sydenham, Carleton University (Ottawa, Canada)
Peter G. Thielen, Universität Bonn (West Germany)
Eckhardt Treichel, Institut für Europäische Geschichte, Universität Mainz (West Germany)
Jean Tulard, Ecole des Hautes Etudes, IVe Section, Sorbonne (Paris)
Hans Tümmler, Universität Köln (West Germany)
Horst Ueberhorst, Institut für Sportwissenschaft, Ruhr-Universität Bochum (West Germany)
Eberhard Weis, Institut für Neuere Geschichte, Universität München (West Germany)
Carolyn A. White, University of Alabama at Huntsville
John Charles White, University of Alabama at Huntsville
George Winton, University of South Carolina
C.H.E. de Wit, Oirsbeek (The Netherlands)
Joseph F. Zacek, State University of New York at Albany

Preface

The emphasis in this dictionary is not on Napoleon the man or on Napoleonic warfare but on Napoleon's Empire, which at its height comprised most of Europe. France is not neglected, but the civil endeavors of the Napoleonic regime have been stressed. On both scores, we are in line with recent trends in Napoleonic historiography—of concentrating on the history of the era rather than the man, Napoleon, about whom perhaps too much has been written, and too often the same things, generation after generation.

More coverage might have been given to warfare, nevertheless, since Napoleon was, before all things, a general; however, David Chandler's relatively new *Dictionary of Napoleonic Warfare* (New York: Macmillan, 1979) is readily available and superbly done. It seemed unnecessary to try to duplicate Chandler's work. Thus this dictionary includes only brief articles on the major campaigns and more famous battles, together with essays on the French army and opposing armies. To aid readers, there is also a "list article," CAMPAIGNS, which lists them, in sequence, with dates, under the names applied in this Dictionary (where, for example, AUSTERLITZ CAMPAIGN is preferred to Campaign of 1805).

My fellow editors and I have included articles on those subjects (including persons) that seemed most important to an understanding of the Napoleonic period. Topical articles were commissioned (or written by us) to cover—for France and the rest of Europe—the events, politics, the economy and economic developments, society and its evolution, and the institutions and culture of the era. Biographical articles were produced for persons judged to have had a significant impact on events and also (for certain writers, artists, actors, and the like) simply because of their fame in the period and/or later influence. Thus the members of Napoleon's family and those who smoothed his path to power are included. His ministers have a collective "list article," and each has a separate article; only a few lesser civil officials get notice. The most eminent scientists have articles; others are mentioned under SCIENCE or MEDICINE. Napoleon's marshals all have individual articles (albeit short), but only those generals are included whose roles were particularly heroic, tragic, or notorious (for example Desaix, Dupont, Junot, and Moreau) or who strikingly represent a type (Colbert) or were later famous (Ségur). A few persons are identified only briefly, such as

General César Berthier, brother of Napoleon's famed chief of staff. Finally, there are those who are given space because readers seem insatiably interested in them; examples are Jerome Bonaparte's American wife, Betsy Patterson, of Baltimore, and Desirée Clary.

Dealing with Napoleonic Europe made it mandatory that the satellite kingdoms (Italy, Naples, Holland, Westphalia, and Spain) be included, as well as the lesser states created by Napoleon, such as the Grand Duchy of Tuscany and the Duchy of Warsaw. It followed that the rulers deserved articles, as did the more important ministers, such as Gogel in Holland, Agar in Naples, and Potocki in Warsaw. For Spain, the outstanding ones are discussed under *AFRANCESADOS* (followers of King Joseph Bonaparte). Full lists of ministers are included for each kingdom; thus SPAIN is followed by SPAIN: MINISTERS. Similarly, Napoleon's most constant allies—Bavaria and Württemberg, among others—had to be covered, along with their rulers and some ministers. So did the French emperor's "reluctant allies," Prussia and Austria, and with Prussia the great reformers, such as Stein, Hardenberg, and Scharnhorst. To balance all that, articles were included on the persistent enemies of Napoleonic France: GREAT BRITAIN, (rebel) SPAIN, the GUERRILLAS in Spain and Naples, the papacy, and certain intellectuals. Such, generally, were the considerations on which we based our selection of topics. None would justify UNITED STATES, or BRAZIL, or ANDORRA, which are included. The first two were markedly influenced by the events of the period. ANDORRA is "my fault." The *National Geographic* in 1982 asked me if it should be "colored French" on a map of Napoleon's Empire. I thought readers might like to know that the answer was "No" but that Bonaparte did not overlook this tiny republic. There are a number of very short entries that are included for similar reasons, and for which I take full responsibility.

I am proud of this dictionary. Some of the articles are revisionary; a great many represent the results of original archival research. None, in my opinion, fails to present the state of our knowledge on the subject. The book represents the work of the most renowned scholars in the field—men and women of many nationalities—and of promising younger scholars. I will mention none here but simply refer readers to the list of Contributors. In all cases, the opinions expressed in signed articles are those of the author, whether the editors concur in them or not. Unsigned articles were written by me.

A word on cross-references may be in order. For full articles, they appear under "Related Entries," at the end. For very short, identification articles, the system is simpler; ACT OF MEDIATION, for example, is followed by "See SWITZERLAND," where the act is more fully explained and put into context. And since there are many possible alphabetizing schemes, all equally logical, many one-liners appear such as "FRENCH ARMY. See ARMY, FRENCH."

My heartfelt thanks go to all the contributors, whose only reward will be academic "glory," and that only if the dictionary receives wide circulation. They have been unfailingly generous, cooperative, and tolerant of my editing efforts. My special appreciation goes also to my associate editors, Harold T. Parker, Peter W. Becker, and June K. Burton, all of whom labored with the strength of ten. As their by-lines will show, all three wrote articles by the score (though Harold Parker did the most), and, which will not be evident, found expert authors for more. Peter Becker, moreover, corresponded at length with the German and Austrian contributors and in most cases translated their articles into English. Louise Salley Parker is hereby appointed Honorary Editor for her help to Harold and the rest of us, especially on the proofs. I am much indebted as well to Herbert H. Rowen of Rutgers University, who translated the articles from the Dutch, and to that amiable genius, Janos Bak, who translated Kosary's article from the Hungarian and contributed one (in English) of his own. Translations from the French are mine. The English versions of all articles, in whatever language written, were approved by their authors. I must express my profound gratitude, as well, to Janice Seaman Berbin, without whose skill, industry, and critical sense this enormous tome would have been even longer in taking shape. Finally, my associates and I want to thank, most sincerely, our most patient, understanding, tactful, and knowledgeable Greenwood editor, Cynthia Harris, for all that she has done to help us.

Owen Connelly

Abbreviations of Journals in References

AHR	*American Historical Review*
AHRF	*Annales Historique de la Révolution Française*
BSBN	*Bulletin de la Société Belge d'Etudes Napoléoniennes*
CRE	*Consortium on Revolutionary Europe (Proceedings)*
EHR	*English Historical Review*
FHS	*French Historical Studies*
JMH	*Journal of Modern History*
REN	*Revue des Etudes Napoléoniennes*
RHMC	*Revue d'Histoire Moderne et Contemporaine*
RHq	*Revue Historique*
RIN	*Revue de l'Institut Napoléon*

The Dictionary

A

ABDICATION, FIRST (4 and 6 April 1814), forced on Napoleon by the Allies and his own marshals at the end of the Campaign of France. Following the triumphs of the Battles of Five Days, ending with the defeat of Prince G. L. Blücher von Wahlstatt at Vauchamps (14 February 1814), Napoleon mauled Prince Karl zu Schwarzenberg, his other major opponent, at Montereau (18 February). But after that, Napoleon lost steadily—not every battle or skirmish but in men and the resolve of his marshals and generals. His outlook brightened in March when Blücher and Schwarzenberg marched on Paris, and he was able to drive east into their lines of communication. But to his surprise the Allies continued their march on the capital, and Napoleon also marched for Paris.

On 31 March he was at Fontainebleau and received the news that Marshals A.-F.-Louis Marmont and Joseph Mortier had surrendered Paris the day before. He blamed Joseph Bonaparte, his lieutenant general in Paris and head of the Regency Council, which advised the Empress Marie-Louise: "He lost me Spain, now he has lost me Paris!" Joseph, responding to Napoleon's repeated orders not to let his son fall into enemy hands, had sent the empress—over her protests—and Napoleon's son, the king of Rome, to Rambouillet on 29 March and then followed himself after authorizing Marmont to treat with the Allies if the situation became impossible. From Rambouillet the party went to Blois. Joseph had made serious errors. With Napoleon at their backs, the Allied commanders (accompanied by Czar Alexander) might have withdrawn if Paris had resisted stubbornly. If the Allies had entered anyway and the empress and little king had been in Paris, she might have persuaded the czar to accept her son as Napoleon II. As it was, the traitor Charles-Maurice de Talleyrand had the ear of the czar, whose choice was crucial.

At Fontainebleau, Napoleon decided to march on Paris anyway, and his troops cheered his decision. While he prepared, however, Talleyrand formed a provisional government in Paris (1 April) and persuaded the senate to depose Napoleon (3 April). On 4 April, Napoleon's marshals refused to march. (Marshals present were Michel Ney, Jacques Macdonald, Nicolas Oudinot, Jeannot de Moncey, and François Lefebvre.) Napoleon reluctantly abdicated in favor of his son, Napoleon-François-Charles-Joseph, the three-year-old king of Rome, Napoleon

II. He dispatched Armand de Caulaincourt, his foreign minister, and Marshals Ney and Macdonald to Paris to safeguard his son's rights. On their arrival, however, they heard that Marshal Marmont, with his corps, had gone over to the enemy (3 April). The czar shortly gave in to Talleyrand, rejected the candidacy of Napoleon II for the French throne, and backed the Bourbon, Louis XVIII, brother of Louis XVI guillotined in 1793. The treason of Marshal Marmont, duke de Raguse, enabled the restoration of the Bourbons, identified by the French with the Old Regime, which had provoked the Revolution. Despite all the wars, Napoleon was still popular. In the nineteenth century, *raguser* meant "to betray" to the French.

Napoleon's delegation brought to Fontainebleau the demand of the czar that he renounce the throne. Bonaparte angrily vowed to march on Paris, but the marshals again refused. On 6 April, Napoleon abdicated unconditionally. In return, by the Treaty of Fontainebleau (11 April 1814), Napoleon was given sovereignty over the island of Elba, with an income of 2 million francs a year from France. The Empress Marie-Louise was to be duchess of Parma, Piacenza and Guastalla, and generous pensions were provided for all the Bonapartes.

Napoleon was very depressed, however, particularly because Marie-Louise had not come to him. Nevertheless, he had refused to order her brought to him when it was still possible—before the Allies reached Blois. Instead, on 10 April, he wrote to his secretary, C. F. Méneval, who was with the empress, to try to determine whether she wanted to accompany him into exile. He seemed unable to believe that she cared for him now that he had fallen, but her letters indicate that she did—but also that she expected him or her father, the Austrian emperor Francis I, to decide her fate. It was her father who did so, taking her and her son away to Vienna. Napoleon would never see them again.

The ex-emperor's world seemed totally destroyed. On the night of 12–13 April, he tried to poison himself. He used a capsule, however, which he had carried for over two years, and it did not kill him. By 15 April he had recovered and tried to arrange for Marie-Louise and his son to join him. All he got was an ambiguous note from Francis I, which left some hope that they would be allowed to come to Elba later, for now they were en route to Vienna. Nothing was left but for him to proceed to his tiny new empire.

On 20 April 1814, Napoleon bade farewell to the Old Guard in the White House Court of the château of Fontainebleau:

> Adieu, mes enfants! Would that I could press you all to my heart; at least I can embrace your banner!...General Petit, seizing the Eagle, came forward. Napoleon...kissed the flag. The Silence was broken only by the sobs of the soldiers.

Shouting that they must carry his love in their hearts, Napoleon hurried to his carriage and was driven away. On 4 May he was installed on Elba. It all seemed dramatic and final, but in ten months Napoleon would be back in France, emperor again.

R. Christophe, *Napoléon, empereur de l'Ile d'Elbe* (Paris, 1959); G. Godlewski, *Trois cents jours d'exil: Napoléon à l'Ile d'Elbe* (Paris, 1961); P. Gruyer, *Napoléon: Roi de l'Ile d'Elbe* (Paris, 1936); H. Houssaye, *1814* (Paris, 1888); H. Lachouque, *Napoléon en 1814* (Paris, 1959); F. L. Petre, *Napoleon at Bay, 1814* (London, 1977).

Related entries: ALEXANDER I; BONAPARTE, JOSEPH; ELBA; FIVE DAYS, BATTLES OF; FOREIGN POLICY; FRANCE, CAMPAIGN OF; MARIE-LOUISE; MARMONT; TALLEYRAND.

ABDICATION, SECOND (22 June 1815), made by Napoleon at Paris after his defeat at Waterloo (18 June 1815). On Napoleon's arrival in Paris on 20 March 1815 after the famous "Flight of the Eagle" from Elba, he found the people so riotously happy to see him that they carried him on their shoulders into the Tuileries Palace. It had been the same with the people along his march route, though there were royalist areas in France. The politicians, however—noble and bourgeois—many of whom owed him their careers, received him dispassionately. He had to make a choice between the masses and the notables, "men of substance" who dominated their local areas. He said, "I do not care to become a king of the *jacquerie*." He sided with the politicians, who could form a government for him quickly, a necessity with the Allies sure to make war against him. It was a fatal decision, however, in terms of his survival as emperor after Waterloo. The notables were willing to support him only for a short, victorious campaign, one that would bring peace and secure their positions, influence, and fortunes. If the struggle proved long, they would turn on Napoleon, and he knew it. He gambled further by the "Additional Act" to the constitution, which made him responsible to the legislative branch and created a chamber elected more directly than before. The hastily held elections for the chamber brought into it liberal nobles, such as the Marquis de Lafayette, no friend of Napoleon, and ambitious republicans, such as Bertrand Barère. To add to his jeopardy, he recalled former ministers, all of great talent but some of questionable loyalty, notably the minister of police, Joseph Fouché.

After his defeat at Waterloo (18 June 1815), Napoleon hurried to Paris, arriving 21 June. His brother Lucien and Marshal L. N. Davout, minister of war, recommended that he declare the nation in danger, dissolve the legislature, and establish a dictatorial government to carry on the war. (Napoleon had 120,000 troops readily available and many more in reserve.) Outside the Elysée Palace, where Napoleon was lodged, great crowds gathered, shouting their support. "You see them," he said to Benjamin Constant, "They are not the ones I loaded with honors and stuffed with money....But the voice of the Nation speaks through them. If I wish, in an hour, the chamber will be no more." At the same time, however, the chamber met and passed a decree making it treason for Napoleon to dissolve the body.

On 22 June Napoleon abdicated in favor of his son: "I offer myself in sacrifice to the hate of the enemies of France." He asked that the Senate proclaim Napoleon II and that the Chamber appoint a regency council for him. (Napoleon

II, age four, now called the duke von Reichstadt, was in custody of the Austrian emperor in Vienna.) The Senate vacillated and finally voted against Napoleon II. The Chamber, led by Lafayette, appointed a provisional council of government, headed by J. Fouché. On 24 June, Davout, whose offer of the army to Napoleon had been refused, placed it at Fouché's disposal in the interest of peace. That was all Fouché needed to embolden him to contact Charles-Maurice de Tallyrand, the arch-traitor of 1814, regarding the restoration of Louis XVIII, who reentered Paris on 8 July.

Meanwhile, on 25 June Napoleon went to Malmaison, where he bade farewells to members of his family and, one suspects, the ghost of Josephine, whose home it had been from 1809 until her death in 1814. From there (29 June) he went to Rochefort, where his brother Joseph, who had chartered a ship, urged him to flee to the United States. Napoleon refused to sneak away like a thief, but instead surrendered himself boldly to Captain Maitland of H.M.S. *Bellerophon*. He appealed to the prince regent of England, "the most powerful, constant, and generous of my enemies," for refuge. This was denied, however, and he was exiled to Saint Helena. The result of the second abdication was Bourbon restoration in France with a partial return to the Old Regime and the return of the Old Regime, in greater or lesser degree, to Europe, together with the legitimate rulers of the major European states.

A. Brett-James, ed., *The Hundred Days* (New York, 1963); R. E. Cubberly, *The Role of Fouché during the Hundred Days* (Madison, Wisc., 1969); J. Duhamel, *Les cinquante jours de Waterloo à Plymouth* (Paris, 1963); H. Lachouque, *The Last Days of Napoleon's Empire* (London, 1966); G. Martineau, *Napoleon's Last Journey* (London, 1976); M. J. Thornton, *Napoleon after Waterloo, England and the St. Helena Decision* (Stanford, 1968).

Related entries: BONAPARTE, JOSEPH; BONAPARTE, LUCIEN; CONSTITUTIONS; FOUCHE; HUNDRED DAYS, THE; JOSEPHINE; LAFAYETTE; NAPOLEON II; TALLEYRAND; WATERLOO CAMPAIGN.

ABENSBERG, BATTLE OF. See WAGRAM CAMPAIGN.

ABOUKIR, BATTLE OF (24–25 July 1799). See EGYPTIAN CAMPAIGN.

ABOUKIR, NAVAL BATTLE OF. See NILE, BATTLE OF.

ABRANTES, DUC D'. See JUNOT, J.-A.

ABRANTES, DUCHESSE D'. See JUNOT, L.

ABRIAL, ANDRE-JOSEPH, COMTE (1750–1828), an able jurist, studious, cautious, and grave; minister of justice (1799–1802). Born in Annonay in the Languedoc, Abrial after completing his studies in Paris at the college of Louis le Grand was admitted to the practice of law before the Parlement of Paris.

Declining to continue practice before the reformed courts of Maupeou, he migrated to Senegal where he managed an office for the government. With the coming of the Revolution, he served in Paris as commissioner of the central government before the tribunal of cassation from 1791 to 1799. As minister in title, Abrial participated in the reorganization of the judicial system (new tribunals of first instance, of appeal, and of cassation), in the nomination of a multitude of new judges, in counseling the new judges on what ancient and revolutionary laws said, and in the formation of a single clear civil code (the code Napoléon). Abrial was continuously supervised by the second consul, J.-J. de Cambacérès, who reviewed his reports and nominations before transmitting them to the first consul and who was the de facto minister of justice until 1814. When N. Bonaparte combined the ministries of justice and police, he dismissed Abrial on 4 September 1802 but made him a senator and grand officer of the Legion of Honor. In 1813 he appointed his son prefect of Finistère.

J. Bourdon, *La réforme judiciaire de l'an VIII* (Rodez, 1942); R. Boulind, ed., *Cambacérès and the Bonapartes: Unpublished papers of Jean-Jacques-Régis Cambacérès* (New York, 1976); J.-J. de Cambacérès, *Cambacérès: Lettres inédites á Napoleón*, vol. 1: *1802–1807*, vol. 2: *1808–1814*, ed. Jean Tulard (Paris, 1973); Napoléon, *Correspondance, six cents lettres de travail (1806-1810)*, ed. M. Vox (Paris, 1943).

Harold T. Parker

Related entries: CAMBACERES; LAW, CODES OF.

ACADEMIE FRANCAISE (French Academy), France's oldest scholarly and honorific body, abolished during the Revolution and restored by Napoleon, if not for the noblest reasons. The academy had been founded in 1635 by Cardinal Richelieu, first minister of Louis XIII. In 1795, the National Convention created the Institut National to replace it and the other royal academies (sciences, inscriptions and belles lettres, painting and sculpture, architecture, and music). The Institut had 144 members (fewer than half the number in the royal academies), divided into three classes: Physical and Mathematical Sciences, Literature and Fine Arts, and Moral and Political Sciences.

The Third Section was populated heavily by vocal *idéologues*, for example, Benjamin Constant, who opposed Napoleon's moves toward authoritarian government and empire. In 1803, to deprive these opponents of a forum, Napoleon dissolved the Institut and reorganized it into four classes, to none of which his major enemies were reappointed. The new divisions were: Physical and Mathematical Sciences; French Language and Literature; History and Ancient Literatures; and Fine Arts. The second class was the old Académie française, unofficially referred to as such and comprising, as tradition dictated, forty members—the "Forty Immortals"—as it does today. A number of former academicians were appointed, such as Louis de Fontanes, future head of the Imperial University, and the poet Jacques Delille. New members included Lucien Bonaparte, Louis-Philippe de Ségur (the elder count), and Vivant Denon, director general of Museums.

Napoleon had the artist Jacques-Louis David design a uniform for the Immortals and showered pensions and honors on the members, but he would not allow them freely to fill vacancies in their ranks, which discouraged dissent. Chateaubriand was elected in 1811, for example, but was not allowed to take his seat. Nevertheless, Napoleon revived the Académie française, which persists to this day, performing its time-honored function of preparing and repreparing the official French dictionary.

L. Aucoc, *L'Institut: Lois, statuts, réglements* (Paris, 1889); Baron de Barante, *Souvenirs du Baron de Barante (1782–1866) de l'Académie française* (1890); C. M. Biver, *Le Paris de Napoléon* (Paris, 1963); D. M. Robertson, *The French Academy* (New York, 1910).

Related entries: FONTANES; INSTITUT NATIONAL; *IDEOLOGUES*; UNIVERSITY, IMPERIAL.

ACRE, SIEGE OF. See EGYPTIAN CAMPAIGN.

ACT OF MEDIATION (19 February 1803), instrument by which Napoleon formed the Swiss Confederation (Confédération Helvétique), which allied with France. The confederation replaced the Helvetic Republic, formed in 1798, which had never been peaceful. Under the Diet of the confederation, nineteen virtually autonomous cantons coexisted well until 1813. See SWITZERLAND.

ADDINGTON, HENRY (1757–1844), Viscount Sidmouth. He succeeded William Pitt as British prime minister in 1801, which made possible peace with France under the Treaty of Amiens. He was replaced in turn by Pitt in 1804. See GREAT BRITAIN, DOMESTIC.

ADMINISTRATION. Napoleon as administrator may be termed the originator of modern centralized bureaucracy in France. He carried to fruition the long struggle of the French kings to bring their subjects under the administrative control of the central government. For centuries the French monarchs had dispatched from Paris a variety of agents (*baillis, intendants, sous-intendants*) to govern the outlying provinces and had developed standard operating procedures to handle the administrative routine. But the kings had left standing many older conflicting circumscriptions, intermediate bodies, and privileges, which curtailed their ability to act directly and uniformly on their subjects. The Constituent Assembly of 1789–1791 substituted for the crazy-quilt of multitudinous privileges, personal and local, the equality of everyone before the law and the rational, uniform division of France into departments, districts, cantons, and communes. It placed these circumscriptions under local elective officials, however.

Bonaparte, as first consul, by the Law of 28 Pluviôse Year VIII (17 February 1800) accepted the principle of equality before the law and the rational division of France into departments, districts (which he enlarged and renamed *arrondissements*), and communes. He appointed officials to administer the will of the central government uniformly: prefects for departments, subprefects for *arrondissements*, and mayors of cities (those with over 5,000 people directly; the smaller ones through the prefects). These officials reported along well-defined channels of communication and command to ministers in Paris who were organized on functional lines: ministers of finance, of police, of the interior, of war, of the navy, of foreign affairs. These in turn reported, usually in writing, to Napoleon, who oversaw and ran everything. Parallel to this administrative structure was a series of advisory councils: a municipal council for each mayor, an *arrondissement* council for each subprefect, a departmental council for each prefect, a *conseil d'administration* for nearly every minister, and a Conseil d'Etat for Napoleon himself. But these councils were appointive too and served only for information and consultation.

The features of Napoleon's administration were those of a modern bureaucracy: hierarchical organization; stability of positions and of personnel; written, well-defined procedures of operation; promotion through the ranks based on seniority and merit; increasing professionalization of personnel and of code of conduct; and a system of training new personnel. The training, devised and instituted by Napoleon himself in the Law of 19 Germinal Year XI (9 April 1803), adroitly combined theory (the study of public law) with practice (the observation of senior administrators and the performance of minor missions). It was Napoleon's most original contribution to the science of public administration and was decades ahead of its time. The chief weakness of Napoleon as an administrator was his inability to delegate authority and responsibility. His tendency to take everything unto himself sometimes delayed decisions and damped initiative. Yet in this process of daily attentiveness to administrative strategy and detail, he established for France an administrative structure that has endured.

C. Church, *The French Bureaucracy, 1770-1850* (New York, 1981); J. Clinquart, *L'administration des douanes en France sous le Consulat et l'Empire* (Paris, 1979); O. Connelly, R. Holtman, F. Markham, and H. Parker, "Napoleon: Civil Executive and Revolutionary," *Proceedings (1972) of the Consortium on Revolutionary Europe 1750-1850* (Gainesville, Fla., 1973); C. Durand, *Le fonctionnement du Conseil d'Etat napoléonien* (Gap, 1954), *Les auditeurs du Conseil d'Etat napoléonien* (Aix-en-Provence, 1959); J. J. Petot, *Histoire de l'administration des ponts et chaussées, 1599-1815* (Paris, 1958); E. A. Whitcomb, *Napoleon's Diplomatic Service* (Durham, N.C., 1979), and "Napoleon's Prefects," *AHR* (1974).

Harold T. Parker

Related entries: CONSTITUTIONS; LAW, CODES OF; MINISTERS OF NAPOLEON.

ADMINISTRATION, MILITARY. Napoleon was his own minister of war, but he inherited from the Directory a Ministry of War that conducted the administrative routine of military recruitment and supply. He placed it first under Alexandre Berthier (11 November 1799) and Lazare Carnot (2 April 1800), before returning it to Berthier (8 October 1800) and then Henri Clarke (9 August 1807). Marshal L. N. Davout was minister during the Hundred Days. On 8

March 1802 it was divided into a Ministry of War and a Ministry of Administration of War. The first was responsible for conscription, muster inspections, pay, nominations for promotions, personnel and materiel of the artillery, movement of troops, and pensions. The Ministry of Administration of War was responsible for provisions, uniforms, transportation, and hospitals. The latter was successively headed by J.-F.-A. Dejean (12 March 1802), J.-G. Lacuée (3 January 1810), and P.-A.-N.-B. Daru (20 November 1813). Parallel to the war ministries was the war section of the Council of State, which drafted the laws and executive orders that the ministries were to administer and defended them before the legislature when legislative approval was required. The head of the war section to 1806 was Lacuée.

Efficient administration of conscription was essential if Napoleon was to have the soldiers his enterprises required. Bonaparte also inherited from the Directory an able civil servant, Antoine-Audet Hargenvilliers, aged thirty, who in 1798 took charge of the conscription bureau within the Ministry of War and administered it for sixteen years. Then in 1806 Napoleon created a manpower branch under a director general, but within the War Ministry. From 1806 to 1810 the director was Lacuée, who was succeeded by Mathieu Dumas and then the baron d'Hastrel. During the Consulate and Empire, the staff of the two war ministries in Paris burgeoned. In 1802 there had been about 500 employees in the Ministry of War; by 1814 some 1,500 were employed in the two ministries together. Out in the field the supply ministry of the administration of war worked through an intendant general with each army. But when the war with Prussia came on quickly in October 1806, the intendant general of the Grand Army, J.-P. Orillard de Villemanzy, could not cope. In desperation Napoleon appointed Daru, his ablest administrator, as intendant general. Daru brought some systematic order to chaos, but despite his effort and efficiency and the loyal work of Dejean and Lacuée in Paris, supply (or logistics) always remained the weakest element in Napoleon's military organization, as it was one of the strongest in Wellington's.

C. H. Church, *Revolution and Red Tape: The French Ministerial Bureaucracy 1770-1850* (Oxford, 1981); W. S. Moody, "The Introduction of Military Conscription in Napoleonic Europe, 1798-1812" (Ph.D. dissertation, Duke University, 1971); H. de la Barre de Nanteuil, *Le Comte Daru, ou l'administration militaire sous la Révolution et l'Empire* (Paris, 1966).

Harold T. Parker

Related entries: BERTHIER, A.; CLARKE; CONSCRIPTION; DARU; DEJEAN; LACUEE.

AFRANCESADOS, Spaniards who were loyal to or served King Joseph Bonaparte of Spain (1808–13). At first they were more generally called *Joséfinos* (Josephists) and by rebel-patriots also *traitors* and less polite names. The term *afrancesados* gradually came to mean all who collaborated with the French and was used pejoratively by the rebels and after 1813 by the Spanish generally. Before the French invasion of Spain (1808), *afrancesado* referred to someone who aped the French, or overly admired French culture, or (among intellectuals) was taken with French ideas meaning those of the Enlightenment. Thus it could have applied to Pedro Campomanes, Spain's most famous statesman-economist-historian of the eighteenth century (d. 1802).

Joséfinos seemed to abound at the time of the junta of Bayonne (May–June 1808), which, prompted by Napoleon, named Joseph king. Ferdinand VII, just forced from the Spanish throne by Napoleon, wrote to express his best wishes for Joseph, his "brother," and "Most Catholic Majesty." The inquisitor Don Raymondo Ettenhard y Salinas promised in person that the Spanish would give Joseph "affection and fidelity." The duke d'Infantado promised the fidelity of the Spanish army. Melchor de Jovellanos, the dean of Spanish liberals, sent the Bonaparte king a letter of support. So did the cardinal de Bourbon, the cousin of the deposed Charles IV of Spain. The city swarmed with liberals who had served Charles III; the nobility was well represented; the heads of the Franciscan and Dominican orders were there (the pope had abolished the Jesuits), along with numerous bishops.

Joseph was crowned (7 July 1808) by the archbishop of Burgos and proceeded to Madrid accompanied by the prince del Castelfranco and the duke d'Infantado and the duke del Parque, members of his household, and an all-Spanish ministry of eminent liberals—Pedro de Cevallos, General Gonzalo O'Farrill, Sebastian Peñuela y Alonso, Miguel José de Azanza, Admiral José de Mazarredo y Salazar, Mariano Luis de Uriquijo, Manuel Romero, and Francisco Cabarrus. Only Jovellanos, appointed minister of the interior, had failed to appear. He had seen the strength of the grass-roots uprising against the French and had decided that to have a voice in Spain he must side with the masses—though his dreams for Spain had nothing in common with the field leadership of the rebellion—reactionary nobles and clergy, largely friars. He would have found many fellow spirits among the members of the Cortes later called by the rebel government, but he fell victim to the rebellion he had favored and never reached Cadiz.

After Joseph's inglorious retreat from Madrid before rebel armies two weeks after his entry, he found that the grandees of his household, along with Peñuela and Cevallos, had joined the rebels. The other ministers remained loyal, however, and became the best remembered of the *afrancesados*, except perhaps for certain "marginals," notably the artist F. José de Goya, whose role in the period is still argued.

There were, however, thousands of people who at one time or another collaborated with the French. Their numbers varied with the fortunes of war and thus were limited in 1809, expanded greatly in 1810–11, when the French fairly subdued Spain, and shrank again in 1812 and 1813, as Joseph lost his kingdom. Most were ordinary people, from those who did the work of Joseph's ministry, government, and court to local officials—city and town mayors, tax collectors, police, judges—who continued their normal careers in French-controlled areas. Others were recruited and trained by the French, especially in Aragon, where Marshal Suchet eradicated guerrilla activity and successfully organized Spanish administrative and judicial corps. One reason for Joseph's poor performance as a military commander in 1813 was his reluctance to concentrate his forces, which meant evacuating whole provinces and leaving his erstwhile followers at the mercy of the *guerrilleros* (whose numbers multiplied as French defeats increased). When Joseph left Spain, at least 12,000 families also sought refuge in France. At that, the vast majority stayed behind to face the "purification" procedures of the cruel Ferdinand VII. Only the most wily escaped some punishment.

Still, it is the ministers who appear the archetypical *afrancesados* to modern scholars. They had in common that they were old (the average age was sixty; Cabarrus, Mazzaredo, and Romero died during Joseph's reign). All were eighteenth-century liberals who had been favored by the reforming Charles III and had their hopes for Spain dashed after a brief honeymoon by Charles IV. Some had been in prison or in exile. All had genuine faith that they were serving Spain, which they believed would fare better under Joseph than it had under the degenerate Bourbons. (There were, of course, young *afrancesados* with the same belief. G. Lovett celebrates Colonel Francisco Amoros, who, after Joseph's fall, introduced calisthenics into France and amused himself by penning insulting letters to Ferdinand VII.) Beyond their common convictions, however, the ministers were quite various. Gonzalo O'Farrill, a Spaniard of remote Irish ancestry, soldier, diplomat, and ex-minister of war, accepted the portfolio of war from Joseph. Charming, efficient, and honest, he was one of the few officials whom the rebel Cortes continually tried to win over, to no avail. O'Farrill went into exile with Joseph in France in 1813. To justify their conduct, he and Azanza wrote a memoir, which is important for understanding Spanish attitudes in the period. Azanza had been viceroy of Mexico and had held several ministerial positions. He served Joseph as minister of the Indies, and then foreign minister, where he battled gamely against Napoleon's schemes to annex part of Spain to France. Mazarredo, former general, former admiral, and late minister to Paris, was given the Ministry of Marine (Navy, Ports). Francisco (François) Cabarrus had been born a Frenchman (at Bayonne) and, incidentally, was the father of the notorious Madame Tallien. Drawn to Spain by economic opportunities, he had served Charles III and founded the Bank of San Carlos (in effect the central bank of Spain). Charles IV had made him a Spanish count and then condoned his imprisonment by the Inquisition as a dangerous radical (the French Revolution was in progress). He was Joseph's finance minister, bent on freeing the economy (the progressive thing at the time), divesting the crown of its monopolies, and the like. Urquijo had been first minister of Charles IV more than once; he had been frustrated in his attempts to reform Spanish land tenure and promote industry. His fulminations had landed him in prison, from which he was released just before Joseph took the throne. His faith in the Bourbons had been destroyed. He served as Joseph's minister secretary of state throughout the reign and followed the king into exile. Don Manuel Romero's promising career in Bourbon service had been ruined by the perennial first minister, Manuel Godoy. As minister of the interior, he emerged as Joseph's chief planner, producing blueprints for a new public school system, a departmental administrative system, and much else.

In short, the leading *afrancesados* were among the most progressive and talented men in Spain. In retrospect, as evidenced by the testimony of the count de Toreño and other ex-rebels, it is unfortunate that the liberals of the Cadiz Cortes and those who served Joseph could not have worked together. The leaders, surely, were patriots, on both sides. The principles elaborated by Joseph's Constitution of Bayonne (1808) and the Cortes's Constitution of 1812 differed largely in semantics. But the Cortes group helped to bring down Joseph, making an end of his plans for liberating Spain. And when Ferdinand VII returned (1814) he rejected the constitution and views of the Cadiz liberals. Spain was doomed to more of absolutism—and revolution.

M. Artola, *Los Afrancesados* (1953); O. Connelly, *The Gentle Bonaparte* (New York, 1969); M. Defourneaux, *Pablo de Olavide ou l'Afrancesado, 1725–1803* (1959); G. Demerson, *Don Juan Melendez Valdes et son temps* (Paris, 1962); G. Lovett, *Napoleon and the Birth of Modern Spain* (New York, 1969); C. Martin, *José Bonaparte I, 'Rey Intruso' de Espana* (Madrid, 1969); D. J. Mercader Riba, *José Bonaparte, rey de España* (Madrid, 1972).

Related entries: BAYONNE, CONSTITUTION OF; BAYONNE, JUNTA OF; BONAPARTE, JOSEPH; CADIZ, CONSTITUTION OF; CADIZ, JUNTA OF; GOYA Y LUCIENTES; GUERRILLAS; PENINSULAR WAR; SPAIN, KINGDOM OF; SPAIN, KINGDOM OF: MINISTERS.

AGAR, JEAN-ANTOINE-MICHEL (1771–1844), comte de Mosbourg. Born at Mercais, near Cahors, Agar was a Gascon compatriot of Joachim Murat, an accident that had much to do with his career. When he finished his schooling in France, he went to Santo Domingo (Haiti), where his parents owned property, arriving just as the Revolutionary upheavals began that lost France the colony. Captured by the British, who were aiding the black rebels, he was soon freed and returned to France via the United States in 1795. After taking a turn at conservative journalism in Paris, he returned to Cahors (1797), where he practiced law and entered politics and renewed his acquaintance with Murat, by then a general and a favorite of Napoleon. After the Marengo campaign (1800), Napoleon, now first consul of France, left the pacification of Italy to Murat, who called Agar to be commissioner to Tuscany, where he helped usher in the short-lived Kingdom of Etruria (ceded to Spain for Louisiana and then in 1807 converted into the Grand Duchy of Tuscany under Elisa Bonaparte).

Agar returned to Cahors, where he became head of the departmental council of Lot and in 1804 was elected to the Corps Législatif of the Empire. In 1806, when Murat became duke (later grand duke) of Berg, he called Agar to Germany to manage his finances and shortly to administer the state. In 1808, Agar bought the tiny state of Mosburg (Mosbourg), which carried with it the title of count. Also in 1808, he was called to Paris by Napoleon to audit the accounts of the

Kingdom of Naples—in which King Joseph Bonaparte was being replaced by Murat and his wife, Caroline Bonaparte, as king and queen. Agar preceded Murat to Naples and served him until 1815 as minister of finance. There, despite Murat's army building, he gradually reduced deficits, regularized taxation, and centralized banking (in all of which he owed much, as to plan, to Joseph's minister, Pierre Louis Roederer). In 1814, he reluctantly followed his monarchs into treason against Napoleon. In 1815, when the kingdom was toppled by the Austrians and British, he left Naples for Vienna with the queen. In Germany, he was able to get his title confirmed by the king of Prussia, to whom the Congress of Vienna had returned Rhineland territories, including Mosburg. In 1817, he was allowed to return to France but stayed out of Restoration politics. In 1830, however, after the revolution, he was elected to the Chamber of Deputies from Lot. In 1837, Louis-Philippe made him a peer of France. He died in Paris in 1844.

Agar was among the European civil servants whom Napoleon created—men such as Pierre Roederer, Miot de Melito, and Karl Friedrich von Reinhard—men devoted to the Empire and capable of serving in France or abroad. He differs from the others named in that his foreign appointments were all at the behest of Murat, which to some degree explains his disloyalty to Napoleon in 1814.

U. Caldora, *Calabria napoleonica* (Napoli, 1960); O. Connelly, *Napoleon's Satellite Kingdoms* (New York: 1965); H. A. L. Fisher, *Studies in Napoleonic Statesmanship* (London, 1903); A. Fugier, *Napoléon et l'Italie* (Paris, 1947); C. Schmidt, *Le Grand-Duchy de Berg, 1806–1813* (Paris, 1905); A. Valente, *Gioacchino Murat e l'Italia meridionale* (Turin, 1961).

Related entries: BERG, GRAND DUCHY OF; MURAT, J.; NAPLES, KINGDOM OF.

AGRICULTURE. See ECONOMY, FRENCH.

ALEXANDER I (1801–25), czar of Russia. Son of Paul I and Sophia Dorothea of Württemberg (b. 1777), Alexander I was educated by the Swiss philosophe, F. C. de La Harpe, under the supervision of his grandmother, Catherine II, with whom his parents were in constant conflict, which confused Alexander's loyalties. In 1801, he assented to the coup against his father, stipulating only that Paul's life be spared (it was not). The Russian nobility rejoiced at his accession but was soon again disgruntled. The political program of Paul's assassins is not entirely clear, but many prominent nobles wanted constitutional guarantees of their status and a predictable legal order. Alexander seemed amenable, but when he overcame his initial fear of the court politicians, he declined to surrender any of his power.

After Russia's defeat of 1807 and the Treaty of Tilsit, talk of constitutional reform of a different kind was inspired by Alexander's confidant, Michael Speransky. He was a moderate progressive whose proposals did not threaten the stability of the empire. Many nobles, however, were suspicious both of Alexander's French alliance and of Speransky. In 1811 the czar was forced to dismiss him. After the war of 1812, though Alexander granted a constitution to the Poles, as he had earlier to the Finns, he gave no serious consideration to political reform in Russia.

In foreign affairs, Alexander initially decided to deal impartially with both Britain and France. However, the affair of the duc d'Enghien (March 1804) and Napoleon's assumption of the imperial title (May 1804) offended him, and he determined to oppose French expansion. At the Battle of Austerlitz (2 December 1805), Alexander was in command of the Austro-Russian army, which met disaster because of his vanity and his rejection of the cautious advice of M. Kutuzov. Austria made peace, but Alexander allied with Prussia to continue the war. The battles of Jena and Auerstädt (14 October 1806) destroyed the Prussian army, and the French victory at Friedland (14 June 1807) the Russian. Alexander sued for peace. Napoleon's panoply of power and flattery of the czar on the raft in the Niemen led to the alliance of Tilsit (7 and 9 July 1807). Russian scholarship shows that Alexander was eager to make peace but reluctant to make an alliance, which was, however, Napoleon's price for peace. The alliance was unpopular notably because French principles were anathema to the nobility; the continental system ruined Russian commerce; and Napoleon showed no inclination to partition the Ottoman Empire with Russia, which he had promised. By the end of 1810, when Alexander withdrew Russia from the continental system, war was a foregone conclusion. After Napoleon's retreat from Moscow (1812), Alexander anchored a coalition to liberate Europe. In 1815, he brought forth his last, and perhaps most dubious, contribution to the history of Napoleonic Europe, the Holy Alliance.

A. McConnell, *Tsar Alexander I* (New York, 1970); A. V. Predtechenskii, *Ocherki obshchestvenno-politicheskoi istorii Rossii v pervoi chetverti XIX v* (Moscow-Leningrad, 1957); H. Ragsdale, *Détente in the Napoleonic Era* (Lawrence, Kan., 1980); A. Trachevskii, ed., *Diplomaticheskiia snosheniia Rossii s Frantsiei v epokhu Napoleona I*, 4 vols. (St. Petersburg, 1890–1893); A. Vandal, *Napoléon et Alexandre I*, 3 vols. (Paris, 1893–1896); P. A. Zhilin, *Gibel' napoleonovskoi armii v Rossii*, 2d ed. (Moscow, 1974).

Hugh Ragsdale

Related entries: AUSTERLITZ, BATTLE OF; DIPLOMACY; ERFURT, INTERVIEW AT; RUSSIA; RUSSIAN CAMPAIGN; TILSIT, TREATIES OF; VIENNA, CONGRESS OF; WARSAW, DUCHY OF.

ALI (real name LOUIS ETIENNE SAINT-DENIS) (1788–1856), Frenchman who became Napoleon's second Mamluk in 1811 (the first was Roustan). He followed Napoleon to Elba and St. Helena and was at the emperor's bedside when he died.

Related entries: MAMLUKS; ROUSTAN RAZA; ST. HELENA.

ALVINCZI, JOSEPH OF BORBEREK, BARON (1735–1810), general in the Habsburg Imperial Army. Grandson of a famous Transylvanian lawyer and civil servant, Joseph (Jozsef) Alvinczi joined the army as a youth and served for nearly sixty years. He was made a baron in 1763 for his bravery in the Seven Years War, the defense of Prague (1757), and service in Silesia (1761). He received the Order of Maria Theresa for his coup at Habelschwerdt (1779) where he captured the duke of Hesse-Philippsthal. Alvinczi was the military instructor of Archduke Franz (the future emperor Franz II). In 1790 he commanded Habsburg armies against the Belgian revolution and in 1792 against the French under Charles Dumouriez. In 1793–1794 he fought at the sieges of Condé, Valenciennes, and at the relief, on 16 June 1794, of Charleroi, and was awarded the Grand Cross of the Order of Maria Theresa. In 1795 he became a member of the Vienna Hofkriegsrat. He was detached, however, to relieve Mantua, under siege by Napoleon. At the battles of Arcola (15 November 1796) and Rivoli (19 January 1797), he sustained defeats that, in effect, terminated his active career. Thereafter the aged general was given the supreme military command of Hungary, where he worked hard on reforms and also kept in touch with literary efforts of the Transylvanian Enlightenment. His last brief active service was on the side of Palatine Archduke Joseph, who rallied the Hungarian nobility to oppose Napoleon in 1809. He died childless; the family became extinct.

B. Ivànyi, "Bàrò Alvinczi József tàbornagy Ievelei," *Hadtörtènelmi Közlemènyek* 23–24 (1922–23).

János Bȧk

Related entries: HUNGARY; ITALIAN CAMPAIGN, FIRST.

AMIENS, TREATY OF (27 March 1802), which established peace between France and Great Britain for the first time since 1793. It followed on the collapse of the Second Coalition and the fall of the Pitt cabinet in Britain. The negotiators were Joseph Bonaparte for France and Lord Cornwallis for Britain. France pledged to respect the integrity and independence of Naples, Portugal, and the Batavian Republic (Holland). Britain agreed to restore all conquests of possessions of France or its allies, except Ceylon (formerly Dutch) and Trinidad (Spanish), and to evacuate Elba and Malta. Malta was to go to the Knights of St. John (or of Malta). The Ionian Islands were to become an independent republic. There was no commercial agreement, however, a large factor in the failure of the peace, which lasted barely a year.

Related entries: FOREIGN POLICY; GREAT BRITAIN.

ANDORRA, state in Pyrenees Mountains between France and Spain, with an Area of 191 square miles and elevations of 6,000 to 10,500 feet. Andorra was under joint suzerainty of the counts of Foix (France) and the bishops of Urgel (Spain) from 1278 and under the kings of France and bishops of Urgel from 1589. Its status became uncertain during the Revolution. Napoleon regularized its government by granting a republican constitution in 1806.

ANGLO-PORTUGUESE TROOPS. See ARMY, PORTUGUESE.

ANNEXATION POLICY, republican policy inherited by Napoleon. In 1792, the French Convention pledged "fraternity and aid" to peoples who desired to "recover" their liberty. Under that rubric, responding to the desires of native republicans, France annexed the Austrian Netherlands (Belgium), the left bank of the Rhine, Savoy, and Nice. French possession was affirmed by the treaties of Basel with Prussia (1795) and Campo Formio with Austria (1797). Napoleon Bonaparte, as first consul (1799), thus inherited conquered territory and the policy of retaining it. In fact, it fulfilled a dream of French kings to expand France to its natural frontiers. The possession of Belgium and the Rhineland, however, was a standing affront to the Holy Roman Emperor.

E. Bourgeois, *Les Révolutions, 1789-1830*, vol. 2 of *Manuel historique de politique étrangère*, 4 vols. (Paris, 1893–1926); Colloque de Bruxelles, *Occupants-occupés, 1792–1815* (Brussels, 1969); H. E. Deutsch, *Genesis of Napoleonic Imperialism.* (Cambridge, Mass., 1938); R. B. Mowat, *The Diplomacy of Napoleon* (London, 1924); S. Ross, *European Diplomatic History, 1789–1815.* (Garden City, N.Y., 1969); A. Sorel, *L'Europe et la révolution française*, 8 vols. (Paris, 1885–1904).

Related entries: AUSTRIA; CAMPO FORMIO, TREATY OF; EMPIRE, FRENCH; FOREIGN POLICY; LUNEVILLE, TREATY OF; PRESSBURG, TREATY OF; SCHÖNBRUNN, TREATY OF (1805); TILSIT, TREATY OF.

ANTOMMARCHI, FRANCESCO (1780–1838), Corsican physician to Napoleon during the last eighteen months of his life on St. Helena. Born at Morsiglia and educated in Italy and France, Antommarchi had a reputation as an anatomist and pathologist. He was not experienced at treating living patients, however. Apparently Cardinal Fesch, Napoleon's uncle, had chosen him (at the request of Napoleon's mother) because he was Corsican and considered brilliant by his peers. Napoleon did not like him. He considered Antommarchi a child (though he was thirty-nine on arrival) from the wrong part of Corsica and made jokes about him. Antommarchi could dissect his horse, Napoleon said, but he would not let him treat his big toe. The doctor was not amused and refused to take Napoleon's illness seriously until the last weeks before his death. Even then, what he prescribed (for example, a laxative in the last hours), may have hastened the ex-emperor's death. Consulting English physicians approved, however.

After Napoleon's death on 5 May 1821, Sir Hudson Lowe ordered that a "public" autopsy be performed. Napoleon had requested one in order that his son know what had killed his father, he said, and be able to guard against it and also, perhaps, hoping to show that the English had poisoned him. Lowe wanted an autopsy to prove that neither he nor his government had done anything to hasten the death. Antommarchi performed the autopsy, assisted by three English doctors and observed by four more. (Representatives of Lowe and Napoleon's household were also present.) The autopsy reports, signed by Antommarchi and English physicians A. Arnott, C. Mitchell, T. Shortt, and F. Burton, stated that Napoleon had died of stomach cancer (the same as probably killed his father).

Antommarchi later gained notoriety by publishing a book, *Les derniers moments de l'Empereur* (1825) in which he stated that Napoleon might have been killed by hepatitis, induced by the climate, though his stomach was cancerous. He thus implied that the English had killed Napoleon by "chaining the Eagle to the rock" of St. Helena, thus contributing to the martyr image Napoleon had so desired and to the Napoleonic legend.

Antommarchi's later years were undistinguished. He died in Cuba in 1838.

F. Antommarchi, *Mémoires ou les derniers moments de Napoleon*, 2 vols. (Paris, 1825 and 1898, 1975); J. Kemble, *St. Helena during Napoleon's Exile: Gorrequer's Diary* (London, 1969); L. Marchand, *Memoires de Marchand, premier valet de chambre... de l'Empereur*, 2 vols. ed. J. Bourguignon (Paris, 1952–55); G. Martineau, *Napoleon's Saint Helena* (London, 1968); C. F. T. de Montholon, *Récits de la captivité de l'Empereur Napoléon à Sainte Hélèna*, 2 vols. (Paris, 1847); A. P. Primrose, Lord Rosebery, *Napoleon, The Last Phase* (London, 1900).

Related entries: LEGEND, NAPOLEONIC; LOWE; ST. HELENA.

ANTRAIGUES, EMILE-LOUIS-HENRY-ALEXANDRE DE LAUNAY, COMTE D' (1754–1812), a French *émigré* and professional spy who masterminded the inept espionage apparatus of the comte d'Artois. He was assassinated in London in 1812.

Related entries: ARTOIS; FOUCHE; POLICE, MINISTRY OF GENERAL; SAVARY.

ARC DE TRIOMPHE (Arch of Triumph). See ARCHITECTURE.

ARCHITECTURE. While very little is known about private construction in Napoleonic France, a good deal has been written on the works in which Bonaparte was personally involved. His building activity was concentrated almost exclusively in Paris, although he founded two new towns in the west of France (Pontivy and La Roche-sur-Yon) and for a long time contemplated building an imperial palace in Lyons, which he finally decided to erect in Paris (Palais du Roi de Rome). This demonstrates the policy of centralization by which Napoleon, through his minister of the interior assisted by a Conseil des Bâtiments Civils, exerted his authority on every work of civic architecture. Three of the six architects making up the Conseil were also among the six architects of the Institut whom Napoleon regarded as advisers. In 1811, centralization became even stronger with the appointment of Louis Bruyère as directeur des Travaux Publics de Paris who paid little attention to either the Conseil or the Institut. Napoleon's most customary adviser on architectural matters was Pierre Fontaine, whom he appointed architect of his palaces, along with Charles Percier, as early as 1800. Fontaine was officially made the emperor's first architect in 1813.

Although Napoleon commissioned numerous constructions and showed a definite interest in them, he did not have a grasp of architecture. Suspicious of architects, afraid they would cause extravagant expenses, he is said to have preferred to deal with the engineers, and the architects complained about that situation. Except for his own residences, it was only after 1806 that he regularly assigned contracts to architects. But from that time up to 1812, not only commemorative monuments (Arc du Carrousel, Percier and Fontaine; Arc de Triomphe de l'Etoile, Jean-F.-T. Chalgrin and J. Arnaud Raymond; Colonne Vendôme, Jacques Gondouin; Temple de la Gloire, P. Vignon) and public buildings (Bourse, Alexandre Brongniart; Palais de l'Université, Joseph Peyre and Alphonse Gisors; Palais des Archives, Jacques Cellerier), but also some fountains like the Elephant on place de la Bastille by Cellerier, and even purely utilitarian buildings such as markets and slaughterhouses (among them, the Halle aux Blés, F. Joseph Béllanger; Halle aux Vins, Béllanger and Francois Gauché; and Marché Saint-Germain, Auguste Molinos and J.-B. Blondel) were all commissions given to architects.

One of Napoleon's main objectives in commissioning these monumental works was to make Paris "not only the most beautiful city that has ever existed, but the most beautiful city one can imagine" and, by the same token, to proclaim the grandeur of the French Empire. Convinced that "what is big is always beautiful," he conceived excessively ostentatious projects such as an immense colonnade in front of the château of Versailles in order to outdo Louis XIV. In 1806, riding the wave of enthusiasm after his military victories, he commissioned a monumental Temple de la Gloire (the Madeleine) he did not know what to do with a few years later. The birth of his heir inspired him to build in Paris a Palais du Roi de Rome that would have surpassed any other royal residence in Europe. The decline of the Empire after 1812 caused a sharp slump in building activity, which had hitherto been largely financed by war compensations imposed on defeated enemies.

The emperor's megalomania, which made him dream of a "colossal Paris," was accompanied by an obsession with antiquity. To the sculptor Antonio Canova he had confided his ambition to resuscitate Rome. Through his ardent desire to present himself as the successor of the Roman emperors and through his declared intention to erect in his capital monuments "as there used to be in Athens," Napoleon largely contributed to the spread of neoclassicism; and in this respect as in several others his architecture carried on trends begun in the second half of the eighteenth century. Most of his architects were eighteenth-century men who wound up their careers under his regime, and the Empire gave them the opportunity to erect colossal buildings and colonnades such as they had designed before 1800 but had never built. Also inherited from the eighteenth century was the practice of setting monumental buildings in the midst of vast empty spaces, necessitating extensive demolitions (between the Louvre and the Tuileries and in front of the churches of Notre-Dame and St. Sulpice). At the same time, Napoleon encouraged more progressive trends that had also originated in the previous century, such as the use of iron (Pont des Arts and Halle aux Blés) and a functionalist approach to architecture largely influenced by the growth of the profession of civil engineering after the foundation of the Ecole des Ponts et Chaussées in 1747.

These opposite trends were also echoed in the teaching of architecture, which followed an evolution that can be traced back to the eighteenth century. On the one hand, the abolition of the Academies by the Convention and the housing of artists and architects in the Louvre brought closer artists and architects who, later during the Empire, were trained in the same school. Under the supervision of the Fourth Class (Fine Arts) of the Institut, where the artists were much more strongly represented than the architects, the teaching of architecture at the Ecole des Beaux-Arts fell under the influence of the artistic disciplines and emphasized an archaeological approach. On the other hand, since 1795 architecture had been taught also at the newly founded Ecole Polytechnique. There, Jean-Louis-Nicolas Durand, an influential proponent of rationalist theories, stressed the principles of solidity, commodity, and economy, rejecting the decoration of the classical orders. Former pupils of Durand's later studied architecture at the Ecole des Beaux-Arts, and in fact such a fervent supporter of Durand's ideas as J. B. Rondelet became a professor there in 1806. Nonetheless, it was only very slowly that this more progressive trend influenced nineteenth-century French architecture.

M. L. Biver, *Le Paris de Napoléon* (Paris, 1963) and *Pierre Fontaine, premier architecte de l'Empereur* (Paris, 1964); L. Hautecoeur, *Histoire de l'architecture classique en France*, vol. 5 (Paris, 1953).

Claude Bergeron

Related entries: ART; FONTAINE; HERALDRY; PERCIER; SCULPTURE.

ARCIS-SUR-AUBE, BATTLE OF (1814). See FRANCE, CAMPAIGN OF.

ARCOLA, BATTLE OF (15–17 November 1796), between the French Army of Italy under Napoleon Bonaparte and the Austrians under General Josef Alvintzi (or Alvinczi) who attempted to relieve the blockaded fortress of Mantua. To defeat Alvintzi's divided army of 58,000 men, Napoleon moved to cut his communications at Villanova, seize his supply train, and prevent a union of Austrian forces. On 14 November, Generals André Masséna and Charles Augereau crossed the Adige at Ronco and the following morning attacked the Croat regiments defending Arcola and the wooden bridge over the Alpone three times, without success. Napoleon's attack was also turned back, but General Jean Guieu seized Arcola temporarily from the rear. Alvintzi's troops, however, escaped through the Villanova defile. That night the French were inadvertently withdrawn from Arcola so two days of additional fighting and a fake charge of cavalry in the rear of the Austrians were needed to gain control of the village and bridge. In the three-day battle, the Austrians lost 7,000 men and 11 guns; French casualties reached 4,500. As a result, the Austrians were unable to relieve Mantua, Alvintzi's army was defeated and driven back to Montebello, and Napoleon reoccupied Verona.

F. Bouvier, *Bonaparte en Italie, 1796* (Paris, 1899); R. G. Burton, *Napoleon's Cam-*

paigns in Italy 1796–1797 and 1800 (London and New York, 1912); G. J. Fabry, *Histoire de l'armée d'Italie, 1796-1797* (Paris, 1900–1901); W. G. Jackson, *Attack in the West* (London, 1953); R. W. Phipps, *The Armies of the First French Republic and the Rise of the Marshals of Napoleon I*, 5 vols. (Oxford, 1926).

Donald D. Horward

Related entries: ALVINCZI; ITALIAN CAMPAIGN, FIRST.

ARIPLES, BATTLE OF (22 July 1812), victory of Wellington over Marshal Auguste Marmont at Salamanca, also called First Battle of Salamanca. See PENINSULAR WAR.

ARMY, BRITISH. At the outset of the Napoleonic Wars, the British army was poorly prepared for the conflict. Military administration was confusing, needlessly complex, and cumbersome. The secretary of state for war and colonies developed general strategy; the secretary at war, not usually in the cabinet, regulated troop movements and finances and ordered weapons. The commander in chief supervised the line infantry and cavalry with the assistance of the adjutant general. The artillery and engineers, however, were controlled by a cabinet-level official, the master general of ordnance, who also provided the weapons and munitions for the entire army. The quartermaster general handled the movement and quartering of troops and intelligence. The treasury appointed the commissariat, which furnished rations and supplies; the home office supervised the auxiliary forces—volunteers and militia.

British officers came almost exclusively from the aristocracy and middle class because they were literate and could supplement their meager army pay. Most commissions were purchased. Artillery and engineering officers came primarily from the graduates of the Royal Military Academy at Woolwich, and their commissions were not for sale.

The British common soldier did not represent the population at large. Recruited from among the lowest elements of society, he was bluntly called, by the duke of Wellington, the ''scum of the earth.'' Enlisting to escape troubles at home or lured by bounty, he signed (before 1808) up for a lifetime of service; after 1808 he had the option of a renewable seven-year term. Volunteering from the militia was authorized after 1805, and for the remainder of the war almost half of the troops raised were militiamen. By 1815 the British army numbered more than 200,000 including the King's German Legion, the most respected of the foreign troops in British service.

The basic unit of infantry was the regiment—two battalions of (ideally) about 800 men (500 in combat was common)—broken down into ten companies. Each battalion had one company of light infantry and one of grenadiers. The cavalry was organized by regiment also, each with four squadrons of two troops of 80 men; thus the regiment at full strength numbered 640 troopers. Cavalry was light (Dragoon Guards; Light Dragoons) and heavy (Horse Guards; Life Guards). Artillery was organized in troops (about 120 men) of three divisions, each with two six-pound (later nine-pound) guns and one 5 1/2–inch howitzer. Early on, brigades were formed according to mission with a varying number of units of each arm. In 1809 Wellington introduced the division, composed normally of two brigades, but it was not uniformly used.

The standard weapons of the British soldier were the flintlock, muzzle-loading, India Pattern musket, a modified version of the famous ''Brown Bess,'' with a 17-inch bayonet. The Baker rifle with a longer bayonet was carried by detachments eventually known as the Rifle Brigade. In order to maximize infantry firepower, British tactics emphasized the two-rank line formation perfected by Wellington in the Iberian Peninsula.

British light cavalry were equipped with a sabre and a carbine; heavy cavalry were similarly equipped but with longer weapons. The carbines were generally of little utility, and standard drill called for the charge, sword in hand.

British field artillery was normally made of brass and included three-, six-, nine-, and twelve-pound guns and howitzers. The six-pounder, with an effective range of 1,200 yards, and the nine-pounder, with a range of 1,400 yards, were the most popular. Siege guns, eighteen- and the twenty-four pounders, were of iron and had a range of 2,400 yards. Ammunition consisted of round shot, canister, common shell, and a modified version of the latter, shrapnel. The light, mobile Congreve rocket was often erratic, but was occasionally useful during sieges.

Much of the success of the British army during the Napoleonic Wars has been attributed to the military reforms of Frederick, duke of York, who as commander in chief (1795–1809, 1811–27) also assisted in the establishment in 1802 of the Royal Military College at Sandhurst.

G. Davies, *Wellington and His Army* (Oxford, 1954); J. W. Fortescue, *History of the British Army*, 13 vols. (London, 1899–1930); R. Glover, *Peninsular Preparation: The Reform of the British Army, 1795-1809* (Cambridge, 1963), and *Britain at Bay: Defence Against Bonaparte, 1803-1814* (London, 1973); C. W. Oman, *Studies in the Napoleonic Wars* (New York, 1930); G. E. Rothenberg, *The Art of Warfare in the Age of Napoleon* (Bloomington, IN, 1978).

Gordon Bond

Related entries: ENGLAND, ATTEMPTED CONQUEST OF; GREAT BRITAIN; CASTLEREAGH; PENINSULAR WAR; WELLINGTON.

ARMY, FRENCH. Napoleon inherited much from the armies of the Old Regime and of the Revolution. From the Bourbon armies came the weaponry—the .69 calibre Charleroi musket and matching .69 carbine and pistols—the field artillery of Comte J.-B. V. de Gribeauval—four-, six-, eight-, and twelve-pound guns and six-inch howitzers. From the Revolutionary armies came the basic tactical formations: for the attack, the battalion column (840 men with 60-man front, eleven to fourteen ranks deep), or the *ordre mixte*, combining the column and line (of two or three ranks) and for the defense the line or square of three or four ranks. Napoleon made essentially no change in either. His forte was organization, detailed staff planning to concentrate the greatest possible number of men at the probable site of battle, and personal tactical plans, evolved during battles, which were different for every battle. His superior use of artillery has often been exaggerated. He did mass fires better than earlier commanders, but the guns (average range one-half mile) did not change, nor was his gun-soldier ratio (3 per 1,000) much better than that of the Old Regime.

The tactics of Napoleon defy analysis, one reason for his incredible string of victories. His rule was "*s'engage et alors on voit.*" He engaged, held back a large reserve, and waited for the enemy to make a mistake or expose the weak point in his line. Then he would strike with devastating force, infantry followed by massed cavalry, the way prepared by concentrated artillery fire. His genius lay in knowing where and when to strike. This art, he said, could not be learned; great commanders were born with instincts others lacked.

From 1805 onward the standing army numbered 500,000 to 600,000. Napoleon usually took to the field, however, with 200,000 French, who were reinforced as they marched by increasing numbers of foreign contingents. In 1812, the Grande Armée of 611,000, which marched into Russia, was two-thirds non-French. The ranks of the army were filled out, as required, by military conscription. The basic system was inherited from the Revolution: the *levée en masse* of 1793 and the Jourdan-Delbrel law of 1798. All male adults eighteen to twenty-five years of age had to register, creating a pool of over 1 million eligibles. Of these, Napoleon called on average only about 73,000 per year between 1800 and 1810, but with the buildup for the Russian campaign in 1811–1812 he called up 500,000, and in 1813–1814, 1 million. Throughout, officers and noncommissioned officers were regulars, though many had begun in the National Guard or as conscripts (draftees).

Napoleon made the corps standard, his greatest organizational innovation. It was the basic unit-of-all-arms, numbering 20,000 to 30,000 men, usually commanded by a marshal, and capable of giving battle alone. It comprised two or more infantry divisions of about 12,000 men, a brigade of cavalry (2,500 men), six to eight companies of artillery, one company of engineers, plus headquarters, medical and service units, and train. The division, commanded by a major general, comprised (ideally) two brigades of two regiments of infantry, one or two companies of artillery, and a company of engineers. The infantry regiment (after much experimentation) had four battalions of six companies of 140 men each or 3,360 infantry (at full strength), but it numbered nearer 4,000 with its headquarters, medical detachment, train, and, always, a band. The battalion (840 men) had four companies of *fusiliers*, one of *grenadiers*, and one of *voltigeurs* (or *tirailleurs*). The *grenadiers* were shock troops, composed of the tallest men; the *voltigeurs* were skirmishers, who preceded the battalion in attack.

The artillery company (battery) had 100 to 120 men with six cannon and two (six-inch) howitzers. The guns (cannon) were generally twelve-pounders at corps level, eight- and six- and some four-pounders at division (with six-pounders gradually phased out to almost none by 1812), though all calibres appeared at all levels. (Between 1809 and 1812, regiments had companies with four-pound guns attached, but they were withdrawn because they impeded movement and after 1813 there was a shortage of horses to move cannon.)

The cavalry was of two basic sorts, heavy and light. The heavy, *cuirassiers* and *carabiniers à cheval*, wore metal breast and back armor (the cuirass) and metal helmets. They were armed with the .69 calibre carbine, .69 pistol, and straight, heavy saber tapered to a point. The light cavalry wore no armor but were similarly armed, except that their swords were curved and had a cutting edge. They were the dragoons, hussars, and *chasseurs à cheval*. Dragoons wore a light helmet, resembling that of the *cuirassiers*. Cavalry regiments numbered 1,200 to 1,800 men, with light cavalry divided into four squadrons of two companies each and heavy into three squadrons of two companies each. The heavy cavalry had the more ponderous horses, such as the French Norman and Bavarian Berberbeck; the light cavalry had faster saddlehorses, usually European stock bred with Arabians, like the present-day hunters and thoroughbreds. Regiments aspired to have matched horses and before 1812 usually did—surely in the Imperial Guard.

The Imperial Guard was not a bodyguard for the emperor but a small, elite army. It had infantry, cavalry, artillery, and its own service troops, medical personnel, and trains. It was multinational, especially in the cavalry, which had proud units of Egyptian Mamluks, Italians, Poles, Germans, Swiss, and others, as well as French. It was Napoleon's ultimate reserve, made up of veterans and (except for the artillery) almost never committed in battle. The most honored were the Old Guard, regiments formed between 1800 and 1806; next was the Middle Guard, formed between 1806 and 1809; and finally the Young Guard. Its numbers grew from 8,000 in 1805 to 80,000 in 1812 (60,000 marched into Russia). At Waterloo, the guard had 18,000 men; the twenty-three infantry battalions, however, averaged 500 effectives. When Napoleon committed the Old Guard battalions and they were thrown back, he had lost the battle.

G. Blond, *La Grande Armée, 1804-1815* (Paris, 1979); A. S. K. Brown, ed. *The Anatomy of Glory: Napoleon and His Guard* (Providence, R.I., 1962); E. Bukhari, *Napoleon's Cavalry* (San Francisco, 1979); D. Chandler, *The Campaigns of Napoleon* (New York, 1965); H. Lachouque, *Napoleon et la garde impériale* (Paris, 1957); O. von Pivka, *Napoleon's German Allies* (London, 1978); H. C. B. Rogers, *Napoleon's Army* (London, 1974).

Related entries: CONSCRIPTION; SOLDIER, FRENCH, LIFE OF; TACTICS, NAPOLEONIC.

ARMY, HABSBURG (Austrian). Permanently embodied since 1648, it was reorganized on Prussian lines after 1744. During its 108 months of war against France between 1792 and 1815, it retained an *ancien regime* character with an aristocratic officer corps and a long service rank and file. Except for a short-lived militia (*Landwehr*) experiment in 1809, it made no appeal to nationalism. Its field service regulations dated to 1769, slightly modified by Archduke Charles

(1771–1847) in 1807–8. With a strength fluctuating between 250,000 and 425,000 men, organized in some sixty foot, thirty-five to forty mounted, and three to four artillery regiments, it relied primarily on linear close order tactics and a magazine-based strategy. From 1809 on it began to employ corps formations and the tactics of line and column supported by massed artillery. Frequently led by elderly and incompetent generals and hampered by interference from the Court War Council (*Hofkriegsrat*), it frequently was defeated but showed remarkable recuperative capacity. In 1813–14 it provided the largest allied contingent.

C. Duffy, *Austerlitz 1805* (London, 1977); O. Criste, *Erzherzog Carl*, 3 vols. (Vienna, 1912); Kriegsarchiv Wien, *Kriege unter der Regierung des Kaisers Franz*, 10 vols. (Vienna, 1905-12); G. E. Rothenberg, *The Art of Warfare in the Age of Napoleon* (Bloomington, IN and London, 1978), and *Napoleon's Great Adversaries: The Archduke Charles* (London, 1982).

Gunther E. Rothenberg

Related entries: AUSTERLITZ CAMPAIGN; FRANZ II; KARL VON HABSBURG, ARCHDUKE; WAGRAM CAMPAIGN (1809).

ARMY, PORTUGUESE, often called Anglo-Portuguese during the 1808-14 period because of the large number of British officers and noncommissioned officers (NCOs) serving in the army. Reorganized along Prussian lines in 1763 by Count Wilhelm von Schaumburg-Lippe-Bückeburg, the Portuguese army had steadily declined since that time, especially during the reign of the mad Queen Maria and her son, Prince Regent John. The indiscriminate sale of commissions, neglect of duty, habitual laziness, and fraud were common. By 1808 the army was virtually useless. The few good units were sent to France by General Andoche Junot after his conquest of the country. The remaining Portuguese commanders were patriotic but jealous of one another and uncooperative.

In February 1809 the Portuguese junta asked the British government to provide a general to reorganize the army. They wanted Sir Arthur Wellesley (later duke of Wellington), but he refused the appointment, and William Carr Beresford was selected instead. Although a junior major general, Beresford was a friend of Wellesley and a man of known organizing ability, though stubborn and uncompromising. He also was familiar with Portuguese, having been the governor of Madeira for a year. Overall he proved to be the near-perfect man for the job, although he was not a good field commander. Beresford found the army in a state of chaos, with the few promising officers totally inexperienced and the rest useless. The men were mostly raw recruits. Short of time, he arranged for volunteer officers and NCOs from the British Army to train the Portuguese in British drill and tactics. The drill manual of "Old Pivot," David Dundas, was translated into Portuguese, although all commands were given in English (since most British officers knew little Portuguese) to avoid confusion on the battlefield.

With few competent Portuguese officers, it soon became clear that British officers would have to be used on a regular basis. To encourage volunteers, all officers who entered Portuguese service were given the next higher rank on their Portuguese commission. This caused some resentment when it happened that an officer in Portuguese service found himself commanding officers in British service who were senior in British rank. Although most Portuguese units were commanded by British officers, Beresford was careful to assign capable Portuguese officers as second in command and mixed British and Portuguese officers at the lower levels. To provide for future growth, all of the subalterns were Portuguese. In all, over 350 British officers and a number of NCOs accepted commissions in the Portuguese army. On paper the reorganized Portuguese regular army consisted of 56,000 men, although in September 1809 there were only 42,000 present or accounted for. There were twenty-four infantry regiments, each with a nominal strength of 1,500 men in two battalions. In addition, there were variously eight to twelve light infantry battalions, the *cacadores*, who were partly rifle armed. The infantry was generally very good. The cavalry, twelve regiments of dragoons, was not very reliable and was frequently used for garrison duty because of the shortage of horses. The four regiments of artillery were excellent.

While some units served in the Oporto campaign, the first real test of the Portuguese army came at Bussaco, where nearly half of Wellington's army was Portuguese. The Portuguese fought very well and took losses exactly equal to those of the British. From Bussaco on, the Portuguese army served with distinction in every battle in the peninsula and the south of France. As early as the end of 1809, Wellington recognized its potential when he recommended that it be evacuated to England should the British be forced to leave the peninsula. He paid it a far higher compliment in 1815 when he wrote Beresford from Vienna at the beginning of the Hundred Days and asked him to send 12,000 to 14,000 Portuguese infantry to his army in Belgium. The Portuguese army did not serve at Waterloo, but had they done so, they would have again given good service.

C. Ayres de Magalhaes Sepulueda, *Historia organica e politica do excercito portuguez* (Lisboa, 1896–1932). J. W. Fortescue, *History of the British Army*, 19 vols. (London, 1899–1930); J. C. F. Gil, *A Infantaria Portuguesa na Guerra da Peninsula*, 2 vols. (Lisboa, 1912–1913); Sir Andrew Halliday, *Observations on the Present State of the Portuguese Army, as Organized by Lieutenant-General Sir William Carr Beresford. . . .* (London, 1811); C. W. C. Oman, *A History of the Peninsular War*, 7 vols. (Oxford, 1902–30).

Jack Allen Meyer

Related entries: BERESFORD; PENINSULAR WAR; PORTUGAL; PORTUGUESE CAMPAIGNS; SOULT; SPAIN, KINGDOM OF; WELLINGTON.

ARMY, PRUSSIAN. The army of Frederick the Great (1740–80) made Prussia into a great power. The army retained his organization and tactics, resting on discipline, precise linear evolutions, infantry fire, and cavalry shock during its campaigns against the French Revolution and in its war against Napoleon in 1806–7. Badly defeated by superior generals and flexible tactics, the army, though restricted by the Treaty of Tilsit (July 1807), underwent a fundamental reform. It pioneered in the creation of a powerful general staff and created new tactics combining skirmishers, columns, and lines supported by cavalry and artillery. In addition, political and social reforms created a strong patriotic feeling. In 1813 the reconstituted Prussian army numbered 100,000 regulars supported by 120,000 raw but highly motivated militia troops (*Landwehr*). Led by charismatic leaders such as General Gebhard Blücher, it took a prominent part in all major battles and by 1815 had regained much of its former prestige.

Germany, Great General Staff, *Das preussische Heer der Befreiungskriege*, 2 vols. (Berlin, 1912–14); C. Jany, *Geschichte der königlich-preussischen Armee*, 4 vols. (Berlin, 1928–33); P. Paret, *Yorck and the Era of Prussian Reform, 1807–15* (Princeton, N.J., 1966); W. O. Shanahan, *Prussian Military Reforms, 1786–1813* (New York, 1945).

Gunther E. Rothenberg

Related entries: GNEISENAU; GERMAN WAR OF LIBERATION; HARDENBERG; JENA-AUERSTÄDT-FRIEDLAND CAMPAIGN; PRUSSIA, KINGDOM OF; SCHARNHORST; STEIN.

ARMY, RUSSIAN. The military force that did most to defeat Napoleonic France owed much to the Corsican's example, as it did to other Western influences, but its strength derived principally from the native Russian tradition of universal state service. Officers, almost exclusively noblemen (*dvoriane*), as well as peasant soldiers, saw themselves as fighting for "Czar, Faith and Fatherland." The "Patriotic War" of 1812 fostered a national mood of unity and exalted self-sacrifice. As supreme commander of the armed forces, Alexander I (1801–25) took a close interest in military affairs, but his personal assumption of command at Austerlitz was disastrous. In 1812 he wisely left major strategic decisions first to his war minister, General M. B. Barclay de Tolly (1761–1818), and then to the elderly Fox of the North, General (later Field Marshal) M. I. Golenishchev-Kutuzov (1745–1813).

Disputes at the top and the lack of an effective general staff seriously impaired the decision-making process. As war minister from 1808 to 1810, A. A. Arakcheyev (1769–1834) reformed its cumbrous bureaucracy, especially the Artillery Department, but he was a crude disciplinarian and generally unpopular. From 1806 on the division, not the regiment, became the largest tactical unit. By 1811 there were twenty-nine infantry and one guards divisions. As a rule each division comprised three brigades and each brigade two regiments. There were thirty-three cavalry brigades, most of them grouped in nine cavalry divisions; they included cuirassiers, dragoons, hussars, and uhlans. The artillery, organized into twenty-eight field and fourteen other brigades, disposed of about 1,600 guns (twelve to a company). From 1802, army strength was built up determinedly, reaching 430,000 in 1805 and about 600,000 in 1812. Of these, however, only approximately 230,000 were available to confront the invaders. The rest were held in reserve or manned rear garrisons, the Caucasian army, and internal security or training units. Among the irregular forces, the Cossacks, skilled horsemen from the Don, and other ''hosts,'' who in 1812 were organized into sixty regiments, had a well-deserved reputation for ferocity. A militia (*opolchenie*), some 200,000 strong, was raised in 1806-7 and again in 1812-14, when it participated actively in the fighting at home and abroad. Civilians also joined in the fray as partisans (guerrillas), but the high command gave them only lukewarm support, and their importance in expelling Napoleon's armies has been exaggerated.

Three persistent problems afflicted the Russian army. First, the supply of arms and ammunition was inadequate for this enormous force. Although Russia manufactured 110,000 rifles in 1812, some had to be imported from Britain, and calibres were not standardized. Second, chronic maladministration, plus (in 1812) the loss of forward magazines, led to an acute shortage of provisions. Third, most officers were poorly trained; although there were 3,000 places in various cadet schools, the training emphasized parade ground skills and discouraged initiative. Noncommissioned officers received scarcely any formal training, and the mass of soldiers was both untrained and illiterate. Recruiting was normally by annual levy, but there were three levies in 1812, which brought in 420,000 men. Service was for twenty-five years. Despite the introduction of recruiting depots (1808), losses, mainly from disease, were very heavy. Medical care was minimal, even for officers. Total military casualties amounted to 420,000 between 1805 and 1814; the Battle of Borodino alone cost 42,000 men out of 120,000 committed. Discipline was strictly enforced, and men were beaten for the slightest infringement of regulations. Despite atrocious conditions, few soldiers deserted to the enemy. Their physical endurance under fire was legendary.

Tactical training stressed use of the bayonet rather than firepower, but joint maneuvers involving all arms were held, and infantry learned to fight in column and extended order formation. Strategic decisions were often arbitrary. In 1806-7 General L. L. Bennigsen wasted his forces in a campaign of attrition and at Eylau failed to exploit a breakthrough in the French center. At Austerlitz the Russian troops were strung out over too wide a front. This was partly due to poor inter-Allied cooperation, but in 1812 the mistake was repeated: the First and Second Western armies were stationed too far apart and could be driven back in turn; there was no overall strategic plan. After the retreat from Smolensk, Kutuzov's decision to stand at Borodino was taken too hastily for proper defenses to be constructed, but afterward he wisely decided to abandon Moscow to the enemy, despite the psychological shock, in order to save his army, and then executed a brilliant secret move to Tarutino, southwest of the city, where he barred Napoleon's access to more fertile regions and forced him to retreat the way he had come. Although Kutuzov was criticized for slowness in pursuit, he was short of vital supplies and could not afford to overstrain his men; he also realized that the invaders' destruction could be left to nature (and the irregulars). The Russian troops' subsequent advance into Europe was a political necessity but cost the country dearly: in 1813 67 percent of the state budget went to the armed forces.

General Androlenko, *Histoire de l'armée russe* (Paris, 1967); L. G. Beskrovny, *Russkaia armiia i flot v XIX veke* (Moscow, 1973); C. Duffy, *Borodino: Napoleon against Russia, 1812* (London, 1972); A. A. Kersnovsky, *Istoriia russkoi armii*, vol. 1 (Belgrade, 1933); A. N. Petrov, ed., *Russkaia voennaia sila*, (Moscow, 1892); F. von Stein, *Geschichte des russischen Heeres*. . . (Hanover, 1885, reprinted Krefeld, 1975).

John Keep

Related entries: ALEXANDER I; AUSTERLITZ CAMPAIGN; FRANCE, CAMPAIGN OF; GERMAN WAR OF LIBERATION; JENA-AUERSTÄDT-FRIEDLAND CAMPAIGN; RUSSIAN CAMPAIGN.

ART. The tension between classical and romantic elements in Napoleon's enigmatic personality was exactly reflected in the artistic impulses of his age and saved the Empire style from sterile adherence to rigid neoclassicism, a style rooted in seventeenth-century French classicism but that evolved as a reaction to the excesses of baroque in the rococo. Napoleon's interest in art was not aesthetic, however, but social. Emigration and the financial ruin of the nobility during the Revolution had deprived artists of patrons, and their advocates demanded that the government should either subvent them or supply commissions to provide them with a livelihood. Napoleon was highly conscious of the propagandistic potential of the visual arts for serving the authoritarian state. Thus, between 1804 and 1814, he exploited the preexistent art style of the Directory and Consular periods so ably that the title *Empire* is applied to the art of about a twenty-year period, which was characteristically grandiose, heroic, and imperial.

Napoleon was the central figure in Empire art, not only in terms of patronage and direction but in inspiration as well. While he passed through the Louvre without pausing anywhere for a closer look and could not comprehend why anyone could become enthused about a painting or a statue merely copied from nature, he did appreciate immensity and equated big with beautiful. His conquests opened up new fields of art for study, specifically Italian paintings looted from Italy during the campaigns of 1796–97 and the additional knowledge of Egyptian art brought back in 1801 that led to the cult of Egyptomania. In addition, Napoleon's physical appearance, especially his facial structure, delighted the antique taste of friends and enemies alike, providing inspiration for portraitists, history painters, and sculptors who tried to capture his rational and romantic qualities.

Painting was the art form Napoleon exploited best for personal glorification, and Jacques-Louis David became chief celebrant of the emperor in paint. Although David had established his reputation by glorifying Republican moral virtues, as in the *Oath of the Horatii* (1784), Michael Levy has pointed out that Napoleon became his own private emotional solution to the reason and passion that also warred within him. Napoleon sought out the former Jacobin political activist, famous artist, and respected teacher and made him *premier peintre de l'Empereur* (1804) under his protection. The school of David included some of the most important painters of the day: Jean-Auguste-Dominique

Ingres, who defended neoclassicism until the 1860s; David's favorite pupil, the ''romantic classicist'' Antoine Gros; the rebellious romantic, Anne-Louis Girodet; François Gérard, who excelled at painting ladies; and the innovative miniaturist-lithographer Jean-Baptiste Isabey. While David encouraged their individuality, their art reaffirmed the value of superb draftsmanship, displayed idealism, the eternal quality of art, plasticity of form, and precisely delineated space according to sensory perception.

Ranking beside David in importance as a powerful figure in the world of art was the dynamic Dominique Vivant Denon, who had won everyone's admiration for galloping ahead and dodging bullets in Egypt and elsewhere while surveying battlefields and making drawings during Napoleon's campaigns. As director general of museums, Denon exerted a great influence over artists, as well as all the collections, salons, mints, and state porcelain, carpet, and tapestry works.

The minor arts benefited greatly from the fact that Empire art became a unified style, largely due to the inspiration and leadership provided by the architectural team of Charles Percier and Pierre François Fontaine. As Napoleon commissioned them to renovate and decorate royal residences, they became the arbiters of taste, being guided by their love for timeless, classical design, which they set down in their handbook *Recueil des décorations intérieures* (1812). Despite the ostentation and vulgarity of some of the throne rooms and royal suites, Empire at its best left an enduring legacy of severely restrained, solid, dignified, well-proportioned furnishings with graceful lines, contributing to an atmosphere of calm and privacy. The finished products were masterpieces of craftsmanship in rich fabrics, precious metals, wood, stone, leather, glass, and clay.

E. Bayard, *Le Style Empire* (Paris, 1913); C. Blanc, *Ingres: sa vie et ses ouvrages* (Paris, 1870); Etienne Jean Délécluze, *Louis David, son école et son temps: Souvenirs*, 2nd ed. (Paris, 1863); P. Francastel, *Le Style Empire* (Paris, 1939); L. Hautecoeur, *L'Art sous la Révolution et l'Empire en France, 1789-1815* (Paris, 1953); V. Malamani, *Canova* (Milan, 1911).

June K. Burton

Related entries: CANOVA; DAVID; DENON; FONTAINE; GERARD, F.; GROS; GUERIN; ISABEY; VIGEE-LEBRUN.

ARTOIS, CHARLES-PHILIPPE, COMTE D' (1757–1836), brother of Louis XVI; *émigré*, 1789–1814; king of France as Charles X, 1824–30. Poorly educated, he married at sixteen and commenced a career as a playboy. His relationship with Marie Antoinette helped discredit the monarchy, and in the Assemblies of the Notables of 1787–88 he opposed double representation for the Third Estate in the Estates General. Artois' extravagance, his irresponsible indulgences, and opposition to any modification of legal privilege made him archetypical of the leadership that provoked the Revolution of 1789.

In exile, after July 1789, Artois displayed blind determination to restore totally the *ancien régime* in France. His and the comte de Provence's negotiations with foreign powers, military projects, proclamations, and conspiracies gave the Bourbons visibility. But their activities also caused the Revolutionary assemblies to enact extreme measures against the *émigrés* and nurtured the Revolution by offering no choice between it and the Old Regime.

The acceptance of Napoleon by the French was a terrible blow to the *émigré* princes. Artois' agents attempted to assassinate Bonaparte on 24 December 1800 and failed. When a second plot to eliminate Bonaparte miscarried in 1804, the first consul ordered the duc d'Enghien (the Bourbon prince nearest at hand) seized in Baden and taken to Vincennes, where he was summarily executed. The *émigré* princes in exile were convened in Sweden by the comte de Provence (the future Louis XVIII), to consider new means of disposing of Bonaparte, but this came to nothing. The princes were bitterly discouraged by the Concordat of 1801, which deprived them of papal support (until 1809, at least) and spelled the end of royalist-clerical rebellion in the Vendée.

Oblivion seemed the sure fate of the Bourbons until the defeat and abdication of Napoleon in 1814. Following in the wake of the Allied armies, Artois, as lieutenant general of the kingdom, was the first of the princes to reach Paris. The count's leadership of the ultraroyalists during the reign of Louis XVIII forecast his performance as king (1824–30); as Charles X, his reactionary programs led to his overthrow in 1830.

Archives du Ministère des Affaires Etrangères, *Fonds Bourbon*, vols. 558, 623, 624, 625, 626, 627, 647; Archives Nationales, *Assemblées des Notables, 1787-1788*, C 7 11, and *Pièces relatives a l'émigration*, 34AP-3A12; V. W. Beach, *Charles X of France: His Life and Times* (Boulder, Colo., 1971); British Museum, Windham Papers, added MSS. 37859 to 37868; Public Record Office (London), *Papiers de Calonne*, 1/124, 1/126, 1/127, 1/129, 1/131; J. Turquan and J. d'Auriac, *Monsieur Comte d'Artois* (Paris, 1930).

Vincent Beach

Related entries: CHURCH, ROMAN CATHOLIC; *EMIGRES*; ENGHIEN; FEDERAL CITIES; LOUIS XVIII; VENDEE.

AUERSTÄDT, BATTLE OF. See JENA-AUERSTÄDT, BATTLES OF.

AUERSTÄDT, DUC D'. See DAVOUT.

AUGEREAU, PIERRE-FRANCOIS-CHARLES (1757–1816), duc de Castiglione, marshal of France. Born in Paris, he was the son of a mason and sometime servant. He enlisted in 1774 with the Royal Cavalry, gained a reputation as a brawler and swordsman, and advanced to sergeant. He served in the Russian army against the Turks and then in the Prussian army, from which he deserted. He reentered the French army through the National Guard and under the Terror (1793–94) advanced to major general.

He and André Masséna were Bonaparte's chief subordinates during the first Italian campaign—heroes again and again. Although in 1799 Augereau refused to support the coup d'état of 18 Brumaire, Napoleon made him (with Masséna) one of the original marshals (1804) and, later, duc de Castiglione, after a victory of 1796. In 1807, Augereau was badly wounded at Eylau but recovered to serve in Spain (1809–10), Russia (1812), and Germany (1813).

In 1814, Augereau's faith in Napoleon was gone. Ordered to defend Lyons, he abandoned the city and retired to the country. During the Hundred Days, nevertheless, Augereau offered his sword to Napoleon, but it was refused.

J. Colin, *Etudes sur la campagne de 1796–1797 en Italie* (Paris, 1900); G. Fabry, *Histoire de l'armée d'Italie en 1796–1797,* 3 vols. (Paris, 1900–1901); W. Jackson, *Attack in the West: Napoleon's First Campaign Re-read Today* (London, 1953); R. Lehmann, *La vie extraordinaire de Pierre Augereau* (Lille, 1945); A. Masséna, *Mémoires*, 7 vols. (Paris, 1849–50).

Related entries: ITALIAN CAMPAIGN, FIRST; MARSHALS.

AUGUSTA AMALIA LUDOVIKA GEORGIA (1788–1851), Princess of Bavaria, wife (vice-reine) of Eugène de Beauharnais, viceroy of Italy, later duchess of Leuchtenberg and princess of Eichstädt. The childhood and youth of Augusta were directly affected by the wars of the French Revolution and Napoleon and the fortunes of her father, Prince Max Joseph. With the outbreak of the Revolution in 1789, the family was forced to flee from Strasbourg, where her father had commanded the French regiment d'Alsace. In 1799, when Max Joseph became elector of Bavaria, the family moved to Munich, only to flee French troops again in 1800 and return in 1801 after the Peace of Lunéville. At sixteen, Augusta was considered ready for a dynastic marriage. Several prospects were explored, and she finally was engaged to Prince Karl von Baden. In 1805, however, Napoleon forced the Bavarian court to dissolve the engagement and proposed that Augusta marry his adopted son, Eugène de Beauharnais. Max Joseph was violently opposed, but Napoleon changed his mind by making Eugène viceroy of Italy and elevating Max to king of Bavaria. The marriage (1806) for the first time connected Napoleon's family with an established dynasty.

In Milan, Augusta lived a retiring life, read Italian books, and was liked for her charitable work. Although she had married Eugène for reason of state, the marriage was a happy one; there were six children. After Napoleon's defeat, Augusta and her husband returned to Bavaria, where in 1817 Eugène was granted the titles of duke of Leuchtenberg and prince of Eichstädt. After his death in 1824 and that of King Max I Joseph in 1825, Augusta was engaged chiefly in educating and arranging marriages for her children. She also devoted time to the promotion and support of artists and scientists and helping people in need.

C. Amery, *Prinzessin Auguste und Eugène Beauharnais* (1980); A. von Bayern, *Eugen Beauharnais, der Stiefsohn Napoleons. Ein Lebensbild* (1940), *Max I. Joseph von Bayern. Pfalzgraf, Kurfürst und König* (1957), and *Die Herzen der Leuchtenberg. Chronik einer napoleonisch-bayerisch-europäischen Familie* (1963); F. Melzi d'Eril, *Ricordo di Monaco. Eugenio Beauharnais e Augusta di Baviera* (1897); L. von Montgelas, ed., *Denkwürdigkeiten des bayerischen Staatsministers Maximilian Graf von Montgelas 1799–1817*

(1887); M. Probst, *Die Familienpolitik des bayerischen Herrscherhauses zu Beginn des 19. Jahrhunderts* (1933).

Uwe Puschner

Related entries: BAVARIA, KINGDOM OF; BEAUHARNAIS, E.; ITALY, KINGDOM, OF.

AUSTERLITZ, BATTLE OF (2 December 1805), decisive victory of Napoleon over a Russo-Austrian army under Czar Alexander I, which abruptly collapsed the Third Coalition. On the eve of the battle, Czar Alexander I, accompanied by the Austrian emperor, Frances I, moved 85,700 men into position just west of Austerlitz. Napoleon deployed 66,000 troops on the west bank of Goldbach Brook, which ran north and south through the middle of the battlefield. The center was dominated by the Pratzen Heights, occupied by the Russians. The southern extremity of the battlefield was marked by lakes and marshes. The Allied strategy was to concentrate half of its forces on its left flank, between the Pratzen Heights and the lakes, in order to drive back and turn the French right. To do so would mean weakening the Allied center, but if the maneuver were successful, it would cut off the French line of retreat south along their lines of communication to Vienna. Napoleon, anticipating the Allied strategy, made his plans accordingly. On the morning of the battle, the Allied left, commanded by General F. W. Buxhöwden, crossed the Goldbach in heavy fog and attacked the weak French right. L. N. Davout, supported by one of Marshal N. Soult's divisions, fought a fierce battle throughout the morning with the greatly superior Allied left.

In mid-morning, the Allies began to move General J. C. Kollowrat's corps south off the Pratzen Heights to support Buxhöwden's attack against Davout. Napoleon waited until the Russian general had committed himself to his maneuver and then sent two of Soult's divisions (St. Hilaire and Vandamme) up the Pratzen Heights. Heavy fighting raged throughout the morning and early afternoon, but by 2:00 P.M. the French had gained the upper hand at every point. While Marshals J. Lannes and J. Murat drove back the Allied right and Davout held the French left, Soult swung south on the Pratzen Heights and took the Allied left on its flank and rear. The Allied center retreated through Austerlitz. Buxhöwden's force was shattered. Two divisions laid down their arms, while the remainder of his command fled between the lakes and over the frozen marshes. The victory was complete. The Allied army no longer existed as a fighting force. Allied casualties were 27,000; the French suffered some 1,300 killed and 6,940 wounded. Napoleon also captured 180 guns and 50 colors and standards.

C. Manceron, *Austerlitz* (Paris, 1962); K. von Stutterheim, *La Bataille d'Austerlitz* (Paris, 1806); J. Thiry, *Ulm, Trafalgar, Austerlitz* (Paris, 1965).

John Gallaher

Related entries: ALEXANDER I; ARMY, FRENCH; ARMY, HABSBURG; ARMY, RUSSIAN; AUSTERLITZ CAMPAIGN; DAVOUT; TACTICS, NAPOLEONIC.

AUSTERLITZ CAMPAIGN (26 August–2 December 1805), Napoleon's first campaign as emperor, in which he won swift and decisive victories over Austrian and Russian armies. France was at war with England in the summer of 1805. By the end of August, the government in London was able to bring together Austria and Russia to form the Third Coalition. The war aim of the coalition was to restore the Continent to its 1789 territorial conditions. With English gold to help finance the Austrian army, the Aulic Council formulated the Allied grand strategy. The principal theater of operations would be in Italy. The Archduke Charles, with an army of 95,000 men, would march to the Po and conquer northern Italy. His brother, the Archduke John, with 23,000 men, would hold the Tyrol and provide a link between the armies in Italy and Germany. The Archduke Ferdinand, the youngest brother, would nominally command an army of 70,000 in southern Germany. Ferdinand's chief of staff, General Karl Mack, actually commanded and was to be reinforced in Germany by the Russian army of 95,000 men that was marching westward in three widely separated parts.

Napoleon, meanwhile, had abandoned his plan to invade England, and transforming the Army of England into the Grand Army marched seven corps to the upper Danube. This brilliant maneuver was marked by great quickness made possible by excellent staff work, which laid out the lines of march arranged for supplying the columns. The French arrived on the Danube between Ulm and Regensburg by 7 October, less than six weeks after breaking camp on the Channel. Mack, who had taken up a position at Ulm facing west, was completely outmaneuvered, and his line of retreat was severed as the French moved south to Augsburg and Munich. Napoleon then sent the corps of Marshals M. Ney and J. Murat, later supported by L. Marmont and N. Soult, west to attack the Austrians from the rear. While Marshals J. Bernadotte and N. Davout faced east to receive the Russian army should it arrive, the other corps encircled Ulm and forced Mack to lay down his arms. The Battle of Ulm marked the end of the Austrian army in Germany and opened the road to Vienna.

Napoleon quickly regrouped his army corps in Bavaria. General Mikhail Kutuzov, with 36,000 Russians, had joined an Austrian army of 22,000 men commanded by General Maximilian Meerfeldt in the vicinity of Braunau on the lower Inn. The Allied commanders began to retire to the east as the superior French forces advanced. Napoleon hoped to catch Kutuzov south of the Danube and force him to give battle. But the wise old Russian was determined to fall back along his lines of communications into Bavaria in order to join with General F. W. Buxhöwden's 30,000-man Russian army. Despite Austrian demands that Kutuzov retire on Vienna in order to defend the threatened city, the Russians crossed the Danube at Krems and Stockerau on 8–9 November. On 11 November he turned on Marshal Joseph Mortier, who was marching alone along the north bank of the Danube, and nearly destroyed his corps. The timely arrival of General Pierre Dupont's division prevented a disaster. Kutuzov made good his escape, however, and linked up with Buxhöwden and Austrian units to form an Allied army of 86,000 men.

Napoleon now found himself in a precarious position between the Allied army to the north and 90,000 men under the Archduke Charles, who was marching across the Alps from Italy pursued by Marshal André Masséna's Army of Italy but not pressed. Furthermore, Prussia was preparing to join the Allies in December. Napoleon, although he had captured Vienna, could not remain long in Austria without a decisive military victory. He therefore marched north into Bavaria to attack the nearest Allied force, now commanded by Czar Alexander. The Russian was lured into attacking Napoleon at Austerlitz where the Allied army was destroyed on 2 December. The czar, with the remnants of his army, retreated into Russia. The Austrian emperor, Francis I, asked for an armistice, which Napoleon granted, bringing the campaign to an end. The Peace of Pressburg (27 December) ended the war with Austria and broke up the Third Coalition.

P. C. Alombert-Goget and J. L. A. Colin, *La campagne de 1805 en Allemagne*, 3 vols. (Paris, 1902–04); C. Manceron, *Austerlitz* (Paris, 1962); C. von Schönhals, *Der Krieg 1805 in Deutschland* (Vienna, 1873); K. von Stutterheim, *La Bataille d'Austerlitz* (Paris, 1806); J. Thiry, *Ulm, Trafalgar, Austerlitz* (Paris, 1965).

John Gallaher

Related entries: ARMY, FRENCH; ARMY, HABSBURG; ARMY, RUSSIAN; AUSTERLITZ, BATTLE OF; ENGLAND, ATTEMPTED CONQUEST OF; MACK VON LEIBERICH.

AUSTRIA (Oesterreich), the most determined foe of Napoleonic France—next to Great Britain—despite the Austrian emperor's forced alliance with Napoleon during 1809–13 and Napoleon's marriage to the Austrian Archduchess Marie-Louise (1810). The antipathy began with the onset of the French Revolution, and the War of the First Coalition (1792–97) began when Louis XVI declared war on Francis II, naming the ancestral titles of the Habsburg and avoiding use of his highest title, Holy Roman Emperor, in the hope of not involving the German states, which constituted the Empire. The plan failed. Prussia and most of the smaller states allied with Austria, together with almost all of the Italian states (with the pope providing subsidies). Defeats in the war led to the overthrow of Louis XVI, the establishment of the French Republic, and the execution of the king (January 1793), after which France also had Britain, Spain, and Holland (the United Provinces of the Netherlands) against it. The French Republic built massive armies, however, and promoted young generals—Napoleon was one—to lead them. In 1795 Spain and Prussia made peace, and the French conquered Holland and established there the Batavian Republic. In 1796, Austria was the only major continental power still fighting; Britain confined itself to the seas. In 1796-97 young General Bonaparte finished the coalition in the first Italian campaign. By the Treaty of Campo Formio (October 1797), the Austrian emperor ceded Belgium (the Austrian Netherlands) and (as Holy Roman Emperor) the west bank of the Rhine to France and recognized the Batavian (Dutch) and Cisalpine (north Italian) republics established by the French. He received in return principally Venice and Venetian Dalmatia-Istria. Moreover, he had to agree to a conference at Rastadt that would allocate lands in Germany proper to princes who had lost territory on the Rhine; Austria and the German states of the Holy Roman Empire were to make the basic decisions, but French influence was inescapable.

The great French diplomatic historians of the nineteenth century, led by Albert Sorel, considered that from 1797 Austria was perpetually committed to war against France whenever the odds were favorable because Austria could not accept the permanent loss of Belgium and the Rhineland—and, secondarily, because of the Italian secondogenitures. Thus, the wars of Napoleon were defensive, at least initially. The mood of the Austrian emperor was not improved by the establishment in 1797 of the Ligurian Republic (Genoa) and in 1798 of the Helvetian (Swiss) and Roman republics, all sister republics of France.

In 1798, when Napoleon seemed trapped in Egypt, Austria allied with Great Britain, Turkey, and Russia (the Second Coalition) against France. By the end of 1799, however, Austria again stood alone on the Continent, and Napoleon had returned from Egypt to seize power in France. In the second Italian campaign, after a spectacular crossing of the Alps, Napoleon again defeated the Austrians in Italy; Jean Victor Moreau beat them in Germany, and Austria affirmed the loss of Belgium and the Rhineland and agreed to a commission to remap Germany. The outcome was the *Reichsdeputationshauptschluss* of 1803, which generally enlarged the pro-French states and eliminated almost all ecclesiastical states, free cities, and imperial cities (112 states disappeared). The Holy Roman Empire was already a shadow of its former self, since the states most loyal to the emperor were the smaller ones, those incapable of independent action.

Meanwhile, Britain, placated at Amiens (1802), had resumed war with France in 1803. Napoleon immediately occupied Hanover, possession of George III as hereditary duke, putting French troops in central Germany. Meanwhile he had annexed Piedmont and Elba to France, seized Parma-Piacenza (an Austrian secondogeniture), and made himself president of the Italian (formerly Cisalpine) Republic. In 1804, Napoleon had the duc d'Enghien, a Bourbon prince, shot as a warning to the monarchs of Europe and then proclaimed the French Empire. At his coronation on 2 December he used the regalia and crown of Charlemagne, by tradition the first Holy Roman Emperor, thus challenging the title held by the Austrian Habsburgs. Moreover, he made himself king of Italy (the former republic), a challenge to Austria, Russia, Naples, and the pope. In 1805 the Third Coalition was formed, with Britain, Austria, and Russia as the major members. The alliance was destroyed by Napoleon's lightning campaign, ending in the Battle of Austerlitz (2 December 1805).

Despite contrary advice from Charles-Maurice de Talleyrand (soon into systematic treason), Napoleon punished Austria severely. By the Treaty of Pressburg, Austria lost Venice and Venetian Istria and Dalmatia; more destructive of Habsburg pride, Bavaria got the Tyrol, Vorarlberg, Brixen, Trent, Burgau, Eichstädt, Passau, Lindau, and Augsburg. Württemberg and Baden got what remained of Austrian lands west of the Inn. To add insult to injury, the dukes of Bavaria and Württemberg, Napoleon's allies, were made kings. Austria put its top general, the Archduke Charles (Karl), at the head of the War Office and began preparing for further conflict.

In 1806, Napoleon created the Confederation of the Rhine, comprising most of the German states (ultimately all) except Prussia. The French emperor assumed the title protector of the confederation. Francis II, shorn of power over Germany, abdicated as Holy Roman Emperor and became Francis I of Austria. In 1806–7, Napoleon defeated Prussia and Russia (with Britain a Fourth Coalition that Austria was too weak to join), and by the treaties of Tilsit strengthened his hand in Germany making Saxony a kingdom (and ally) and by creating the Kingdom of Westphalia, the Grand Duchy of Berg, and the Duchy of Warsaw. Napoleon then turned to Iberia, sending armies into Portugal in 1807, Spain in 1808, and making Joseph Bonaparte king of Spain, which provoked popular uprisings and led to French defeats. Napoleon took command in Spain for three months in 1808–9, taking with him most of his troops from Germany.

Austrian warhawks saw a golden opportunity. Clemens von Metternich, ambassador to Paris, assured them that Talleyrand believed Napoleon was doomed. A swarm of literary-political exiles and pan-German nationalists beat the drums for war: Friedrich von Gentz, Baron vom Stein, August and Friedrich von Schlegel, Pozzo di Borgo, and Madame de Staël, among others. The chancellor, Philip von Stadion, led the war faction, seconded by the beautiful young empress Maria Ludovica (Francis's third wife), the Baron Hormayer, and the archdukes Johann and Ferdinand. Only the Archduke Charles held out, and not for long. Austria developed a surprising nationalistic spirit based on the mutual hatred for (or distrust of) the French and loyalty to the Austrian emperor of the noble leadership of the various nationalities—Germans, Hungarians, and various groups of Slavs.

Convinced by the German exiles (Gentz, Stein, the Schlegels) that all Germany would rise to support Austria, the Archduke Charles proclaimed the War of German Liberation and on 9 April 1809 invaded the Confederation of the Rhine. But the Austrians had misjudged the Germans and underestimated Napoleon. France's German allies remained loyal; not a single German state sided with Austria. Moreover, Napoleon appeared in Bavaria on 13 April with 170,000 troops. He drove the Austrians steadily back, defeating Charles at Abensberg, Landshut, Eckmühl, and Regensburg (19–22 April); the archduke retreated into Moravia. On 13 May, Napoleon was in Vienna. Charles had kept his army intact, however, and massed it north of the Danube, and Napoleon's first attempt to cross the river failed (Battle of Aspern-Essling, 21–22 May 1809). Austrian chances looked good since it appeared that before the French could attempt another crossing, the Archduke John (Johann), who had attacked Eugène in Italy, was marching to reinforce Charles. Eugène caught John at Raab, however, sent him flying eastward, and marched to reinforce Napoleon. On the night of 4–5 July 1809, Napoleon crossed the Danube and battled for position on 5 July. Early on 6 July, Charles seemed to have the advantage. (He was the most skillful commander to face Napoleon, surely save Wellington, in the entire period.) But the French emperor countered with a massive thrust, led by Marshal Jacques Macdonald, in the center and another by Marshal L. Nicolas Davout on the Austrian left. At nightfall the Austrians were in retreat. The war was over.

The Austrian emperor, Francis I, finally seemed to accept French preponderance on the Continent. He replaced his hawkish chancellor, Count Stadion, with von Metternich, who at this time represented accommodation with France. By the Treaty of Schönbrunn (14 October 1809), he ceded parts of Galicia to the Duchy of Warsaw and to Russia (the czar's price for neutrality), gave Austria's remaining Balkan territory to France, and Salzburg-Berchtesgaden to Bavaria (France's ally). Further, he sanctioned the creation of the Grand Duchy of Tuscany (formerly an Austrian secondogeniture) for Elisa Bonaparte and the division of the Papal States between France and the Kingdom of Italy. (Pius VII had already been imprisoned again.)

Most astonishingly, however, by separate agreements, resulting from delicate negotiations involving Metternich and Talleyrand, Francis I agreed to the marriage of his daughter, Marie-Louise, to Napoleon. Napoleon secured a civil divorce from Josephine in December 1809, an annulment of their marriage by the archbishop of Paris in January 1810, and in March 1810 took his new Austrian bride. His dream, realized the following March, was to have a male heir by an empress from the oldest royal house in Europe. Such a prince, he believed, could inherit the French Empire without opposition from the monarchs of Europe.

In 1810, with the child (the king of Rome) expected, Napoleon annexed Holland, and the Hanse cities of Lübeck and Bremen, northern Hanover, other north German territories, and the Illyrian Provinces to the empire and provided sufficient forces (he thought) for the final subjugation of Spain and Portugal. He seemed indeed to be the emperor of Europe. Every state was either a satellite or allied with him, at least to the extent of cooperating in the Continental Blockade (System). On 31 December 1810, however, the czar issued a *ukase* breaking with the Continental System, and in 1811 Napoleon began to prepare for war.

Austria contributed only 30,000 troops to the Grande Armée of 1812, paltry considering that it had raised over 500,000 in 1809. (Napoleon's marching force totaled 611,000, two-thirds non-French). Nevertheless, Napoleon was satisfied that Francis I, his father-in-law, whose grandson would inherit the French Empire, would not betray him. In 1813, however, following the retreat from Moscow, he found that Austrian forces under Prince Schwarzenberg (who had fought very little) had been ordered to assume a neutral posture. Metternich shortly proclaimed that Austria would act as armed mediator between the Allies and France. In August 1813, Austria went over to the Allies, swinging the balance in numbers against Napoleon. It was the Austrian army of Schwarzenberg and the Prussian of Blücher that beat Napoleon in the Campaign of France and forced his abdication in April 1814.

Napoleon had expected that Francis I would at least support Napoleon II, the king of Rome, for the throne of France and initially abdicated in his favor. When he did not, the ex-emperor expected that the Austrian emperor would be humane enough to allow his wife and son to join him on Elba. Francis denied such permission. Instead he took the king of Rome, retitled the duke von Reichstadt, to Vienna to be educated. Further, he sent the charming Count Adam Neipperg to escort Marie-Louise to Parma, her new domain, and to look after her there. He soon became her lover and after Napoleon's death married her.

In 1815, Austrian forces had no direct part in defeating Napoleon at Waterloo but were available in Germany—200,000 strong—if Napoleon had prevailed. The Congress of Vienna did not return Belgium or the Rhineland to Austria, but Austria was handsomely compensated in Germany and its Italian and Balkan lands and secondogenitures restored.

Throughout, Austria had remained a land of the Old Regime, touched only briefly, in 1809, by currents of nationalism and the dimmest flickering of a liberal movement. The emperor, the aristocracy, and the church remained supreme in 1815. The economy remained overwhelmingly agricultural. Only in mid-nineteenth century would the problems of the nationalities and liberalism begin to trouble the imperial court at Vienna and only in the twentieth century become acute.

F. Gentz, *Osterreichisches Manifest von 1809* (Wien, n.d.); H. A. Kissinger, *A World Restored* (Boston, 1957); H. Kohn, *Prelude to the Nation States: The French and German Experience* (Princeton, 1967); E. E. Krache, *Metternich's German Policy*, vol 1: *The Contest with Napoleon, 1799-1814* (1963); W. C. Langsam, *The Napoleonic Wars and German Nationalism in Austria* (New York, 1930); A. Robert, *L'idée nationale autrichienne et les guerres de Napoleon* (Paris, 1933); H. Rössler, *Oesterreichs Kampf um Deutschlands Befreiung*, 2 vols. (Munich, 1945); H. R. Srbik, *Metternich, der Staatsmann und Mensch*, 3 vols. (Munich, 1925–54).

Related entries: COALITIONS AGAINST FRANCE; COBENZL; DIPLOMACY; FOREIGN POLICY; FRANZ II; KARL, ARCHDUKE; MARIE-LOUISE VON HABSBURG; METTERNICH; STADION; TALLEYRAND.

AUSTRIAN ARMY. See ARMY, HABSBURG.

AUSTRIAN CAMPAIGN (1809). See WAGRAM CAMPAIGN.

AUXONNE, town on Saône, near Dijon, and site of the Royal Artillery School attended by Napoleon Bonaparte during 1788–89. Napoleon was the prize pupil of the commandant, General Jean-Pierre de Beaumont, chevalier du Teil.
Related entries: ARMY, FRENCH; NAPOLEON I.

B

BACCIOCHI, FELIX (1762–1841). See BONAPARTE, ELISA.

BACLER D'ALBE, LOUIS-ALBERT-GUISLAIN, BARON (1761–1824), Napoleon's map expert who from 1805 until 1814 was always with him on campaign. Chief of the Bureau Topographique in 1804, he was made a baron in 1809 and promoted to brigadier general in 1813. He did not join Napoleon during the Hundred Days. He served the Bourbon kings in 1814 and from 1815 to 1820.
Related entry: NAPOLEON I.

BADAJOZ, SIEGE OF (1812). See PENINSULAR WAR.

BADEN, Rheinbund ally of Napoleon. The ruling Zähringer dynasty traced its line to the Carolingian era. The first margraves date from the eleventh century. The territory was divided along religious lines between Baden-Baden and Baden-Durlach in 1535. The Protestant margrave Karl Friedrich reunited Baden, however, when he succeeded to Roman Catholic Baden-Baden in 1771. Karl Friedrich (1728–1811), was an outstanding enlightened absolutist ruler. Although a pietist, he was influenced by the French Enlightenment and by physiocratic ideas. He created an independent judiciary but did not revive the Baden estates. He willingly accepted compensation for left bank losses from the Reichsdeputationshauptschluss in 1803 when he was made an elector and acquired the Bishopric of Constance and parts of the bishoprics of Basel, Strasbourg, and Speyer. In 1806 he joined the Rheinbund alliance, which was cemented by the marriage of the crown prince Karl to the Empress Josephine's cousin, Stéphanie de Beauharnais. Karl Friedrich became grand duke and acquired the Austrian Breisgau with Freiburg and the cities of Heidelberg and Mannheim from Kur-Pfalz (Palatinate). The enlarged duchy was organized into an absolutist system by Karl Friedrich's chief minister, N. F. Brauer (1754–1813), responsible for reorganization edicts of 1803 and 1807–8. He also introduced the Code Napoléon (civil code), directed foreign policy in 1809–10, and served in the cabinet. The state was administered according to four regions divided according to geography and historic origin. In 1818 a Parliament was introduced; in 1848 Baden was a hotbed of liberalism.

R. G. Haebler, *Badische Geschichte* (Karlsruhe, 1951).

Helen Liebel-Weckowicz

Related entries: CONFEDERATION OF THE RHINE; KARL FRIEDRICH; KARL LUDWIG FRIEDRICH.

BAGRATION, PJOTR IVANOVICH, PRINCE (1765–1812), Russian general who was a major opponent of Napoleon in the Russian campaign and died of wounds sustained at Borodino (7 September 1812). A descendant of the noble Georgian family of the Bagratids, Bagration entered the Russian army in 1782 and served for a number of years in the Caucasus. He participated in the siege of Ochakov (1788) and in the Polish campaign of 1794, being involved in the capture of Warsaw. His abilities were recognized by Alexander Suvorov, whom he accompanied in the Italian and Swiss campaigns of 1799 in which he won distinction by the taking of Brescia. Suvorov said of him that he had a spirited presence, skill, courage, and good fortune. Tall, thin, with a hawk-like nose and slanting, piercing eyes, Bagration became an excellent tactical commander with a charismatic effect on his men, who nicknamed him "God of the Army." Many regarded him as Suvorov's heir.

He had an opportunity to prove his skill in the Danube campaigns of 1805–7. His rear guard of 6,000 men skillfully held off 30,000 men led by Joachim Murat, securing M. Kutuzov's main army's escape, even though he lost half of his men in the process. At Austerlitz Bagration commanded about 13,000 men on the allied right, and at Preussisch-Eylau, Heilsberg, and Friedland he fought with similar courage. After the Treaty of Tilsit, he conducted a daring march across the frozen Gulf of Finland, capturing the Aaland Islands, and thus helped to wrest Finland from the Swedes. He was promoted to full general and in 1809 commanded Russian forces in Bulgaria in the war against Turkey.

In 1812 Bagration was in command of the Second West Army, based on Volkovisk on the Russian-Prussian border and consisting of about 60,000 men. He advocated a counterinvasion, advancing up the Bug and Vistula rivers to Warsaw, but instead, with his customary skill and courage, became engaged in evading French forces under L. Nicolas Davout and Jérôme Bonaparte and united his army with that of Mikhail Barclay de Tolly at Smolensk.

Bagration was personally jealous of Barclay who, though junior in seniority, commanded the much stronger First West Army. Czar Alexander I, unwilling to relinquish any authority, had failed to appoint a supreme commander. Bagration once had been close to Alexander's favorite sister, Grand Duchess Catherine, and Alexander therefore treated him cautiously, yet was not prepared to do more than divide command between Bagration and Barclay.

Bagration was outspoken in his criticism of Barclay, whose strategy of retreat he interpreted as traitorous. Prior to Smolensk he barely spoke to his nominal commander and resorted to written notes, some extremely vicious. At Smolensk, though, he tempered his behavior and acknowledged Barclay as commander in chief of both armies. Gradually he even began to espouse a strategy very similar to Barclay's and to understand the rationale for the past conduct of the campaign.

At Borodino, Bagration's Second Army, with about 25,000 men, was responsible for holding the bulk of the center and the left. Part of his defenses were three arrow-shaped entrenchments with embrasures, known as the Bagration *flèches*. It was this sector against which Napoleon directed his main attack. The *flèches* changed hands several times in bloody hand-to-hand combat. Bagration and Barclay overcame their personal animosity and, motivated by their desire for victory, cooperated fully.

Before the end of the battle, Bagration's left shinbone was shattered by a bullet. Aware of the effect his departure would have on his men, he protested his evacuation from the field. Three weeks later he was dead at age forty-six, having taken part in 20 campaigns and wars and more than 150 skirmishes and battles. Twenty-seven years later Czar Nicholas I had the remains of this valiant officer returned to Borodino and buried there.

D. Chandler, *The Campaigns of Napoleon* (1966); C. von Clausewitz, *Campaign of 1812 in Russia* (1843); C. Duffy, *Borodino and the War of 1812* (1972); R. Holmes, *Borodino* (1971); A. Palmer, *Napoleon in Russia* (1967); R. Parkinson, *The Fox of the North: The Life of Kutuzov, General of War and Peace* (1976); J. J. Polosin, *Pjotr Ivanovich Bagration* (1948).

Peter W. Becker

Related entries: BARCLAY DE TOLLY; KUTUZOV; RUSSIAN CAMPAIGN.

BANK OF FRANCE, central financial institution of France, created in 1800 by Napoleon and still functioning. Established by a statute of 6 January 1800, it was a private stock company, organized by a group of Paris bankers headed by Jean Frédéric Perregaux. Capital was 30 million francs, in shares of 1,000 francs. The bank was operated by a board of fifteen directors, elected by the 200 largest shareholders, of which the government was one (though not the majority stockholder). In 1803 the bank was given a monopoly on the issuance of paper notes (of 500 francs and 1,000 francs), and its capital was increased to 45 million francs. The war of 1805 put the bank in jeopardy because it lacked funds; its stock fell 10 percent. Napoleon reorganized the bank in 1806, however, increasing the capital to 90 million francs, assuming the right to appoint a governor and two subgovernors and placing it generally under the supervision of the new minister of the treasury, François Nicolas Mollien. The bank came back stronger than ever. In 1808 it was granted permission to establish branches, and by 1813 it had three—at Lille, Rouen, and Lyons. In 1814 and 1815, Louis XVIII had little choice but to retain the Bank of France, and it became a permanent institution. It was nationalized in 1945.

L. Bergeron, *Banquiers, Négociants et Manufacturiers parisiens: Du Directoire à l'Empire*. (Paris, 1978); R. Bigo, *La caisse d'escompte et les débuts de la Banque de France*. (Paris, 1927); J. Godechot, *Les institutions de la France* (Paris, 1968); G. Ramon,

Histoire de la Banque de France (Paris, 1929); R. Szramkiewicz, *Régents et Censeurs de la banque de France nommés sous le Consulat et l'Empire* (Geneva, 1974).
Related entries: BARBE-MARBOIS; ECONOMY, FRENCH; FINANCES; FRANC; MOLLIEN.

BARBE-MARBOIS, FRANCOIS, MARQUIS DE (1745–1837), minister of the treasury (1801–6) and president of the Court of Accounts (1807–14, 1815, 1816–34), known to Americans for negotiating the sale of Louisiana for Napoleon. Born in Metz into a family of lawyers, Barbé-Marbois first followed a diplomatic career. He was successively secretary of the legation at Regensburg, then Dresden, chargé d'affaires to the elector of Saxony and to the elector of Bavaria, and finally (1780) consul general to the Congress of the United States in Philadelphia, where he married the daughter of the governor of Pennsylvania. Appointed in 1785 intendant of San Domingo (Haiti), the richest island of the French Antilles, he restored order to its fiscal affairs by incorruptible administration. On his return Louis XVI entrusted him in 1792 with delicate fiscal-diplomatic missions to Vienna and the diet of the Holy Roman Empire. Elected in 1795 to the Council of Ancients of the Directory and eventually chosen its president, he participated actively in the discussion of financial legislation until the leftist coup d'état of 18 Fructidor (1797) deported him to Guiana for his alleged royalist connections.

He returned to France after Napoleon came to power. On the advice of Third Consul Charles F. Lebrun, Bonaparte named him first director, then (1801) minister of the treasury, responsible for paying the bills of the new government. Honest, incorruptible, an experienced administrator, and a strict disciplinarian dedicated to economy, Barbé-Marbois seemed just the man for the job of keeping down expenses. To bring order into the fiscal disarray left by the Directory, he established within the ministry three administrative sections, the first charged with receiving all funds disbursed into the treasury, the second responsible for punctually paying expenses on duly formulated requisitions, and the third, which kept the books of the treasury and reported daily on its situation. To these sections, each under an experienced clerk, Barbé-Marbois added fifteen inspectors general to check on their activity.

There were still problems in the total operation of Napoleon's financial administration, however, and Barbé-Marbois became involved in a complex financial, monetary, and economic crisis that was not entirely his doing. There was the problem of cash flow. The expense outgo of the French government continued steadily throughout each year, and with the resumption of war with England in 1803, the expenses of rebuilding the army and navy greatly increased, but the treasury's income from direct taxes came in only during the closing months of the year. Since Napoleon refused to finance his wars by floating new public loans, the French treasury financed its outgo during the early lean months by borrowing first from its own collectors of taxes and then from an association of financiers, the Négociants réunis, who were also chief suppliers of the French military forces. The transaction was facilitated through issuance of Bank of France bank notes, ultimately redeemable in bullion.

The bank imprudently issued far more notes than its bullion store could support. To secure more silver, Gabriel Julien Ouvrard, a leader of the Négociants réunis, a fiscal wizard, and a shady operator, devised, with Napoleon's approval, a speculative scheme to bring Mexican silver through the British blockade to France. The silver reached the Bank of France more slowly than the bank notes were being issued, however. The Négociants réunis in their many transactions found themselves owing the French treasury over 100 million francs. A commercial depression caused several large Paris banks to fail. By November 1805, after the defeat of Trafalgar and before the victory of Austerlitz, confidence in the imperial regime and especially in its financial soundness was dissolving. The price of government securities declined; there were runs on the Bank of France; public credit was tottering. Barbé-Marbois, clear-sighted and honest, had been quite aware of the hazards of the financial operations. Napoleon nevertheless, on his return from the Austerlitz campaign in January 1806, made him the scapegoat and fired him as minister of the treasury.

Napoleon then shifted personnel and introduced institutional reforms to prevent such a crisis in public credit from arising again. He replaced Barbé-Marbois with Nicolas F. Mollien, who required collectors of taxes to place tax proceeds at the government's disposal immediately on receipt. Emmanuel Crétet was appointed governor of the Bank of France, and he reorganized it to ensure greater governmental control. Contributions were levied on conquered regions in central Europe to support the French army. Then, the fiscal storm past, Napoleon in 1807 appointed Barbé-Marbois president of the Court of Accounts, which audited the bookkeeping of treasury agents, both receivers of taxes and payers of expenses. There the inflexibly upright Barbé-Marbois functioned very well and served the successive governments of Napoleon (except during the Hundred Days), of Louis XVIII and Charles X, and of Louis Philippe until he retired at age eighty-nine in 1834.

A. Duchene, *Guerre et finances: Une crise du Trésor sous le Premier Empire* (Paris, 1940); P. Escoube, "Faut-il rehabiliter Barbé-Marbois?" *RIN No. 131* (1975); M. Marion, *Histoire financière de la France depuis 1715*, vol. 4: *1799–1818: La fin de la Révolution, le Consulat et l'Empire, la liberation du territoire* (Paris, 1927); U. Todisco, "Le personnel de la cour des comptes sous l'Empire," *RIN, No. 109* (1968).

Harold T. Parker

Related entries: ADMINISTRATION; BANK OF FRANCE; CRETET; DIPLOMACY; FINANCES; FOREIGN POLICY; MINISTERS OF NAPOLEON; MOLLIEN; OUVRARD; UNITED STATES.

BARCLAY DE TOLLY, MIKHAIL ANDREAS, PRINCE (1761–1818), Russian field marshal, minister of war (1810–12), and a major commander against Napoleon. Credited with a plan for strategic withdrawal that resulted in Napoleon's defeat in Russia, Barclay was a fourth-generation Russian whose Scottish forebears had settled in Livonia in the seventeenth century. Throughout his life, he spoke Russian with the German-Baltic accent of his youth. In addition to German and Russian, he also became proficient in French. As was customary in Russia at the time, young Barclay was inscribed in a regiment at the age of six, though he did not enter active service until he was fifteen. Ten years later, he was commissioned lieutenant. He was tall and well built, had a high-domed forehead and a long, rather pale face, with a strong straight nose and dark brown eyes. Unlike most other Russian officers, he was interested in ideas and read a great deal.

Barclay saw his first action in the Turkish War of 1787–91, participated in several engagements, notably at Ochakov, and ultimately, as a major, led a cavalry regiment. As a result of the Swedish attack in 1788, Barclay in 1790 was transferred to Finland but saw little action before peace was made. He then participated in the Polish campaigns between 1792 and 1795 and advanced to lieutenant colonel. Czar Paul promoted him to full colonel and, in 1799, to major general. In the war against France, he was in command of the advance guard of Bennigsen's army, which failed to reach Austerlitz (December 1805) in time for the battle.

In the subsequent Battle of Pultusk, Barclay distinguished himself, and his exploits received special mention in Bennigsen's report to the czar. During the retreat of the Russian army, Barclay commanded the rear guard, and his detachments struggled against the French at Frauendorf and Hof. During the 1806–7 campaign against Napoleon and just before the Battle of Eylau (February 1807), Barclay was severely wounded and evacuated to Memel. He remained an invalid for the next fifteen months but was promoted to lieutenant general.

It was in Memel that Czar Alexander called on him, a visit that established an immediate and lasting rapport between the two men. Barclay was always given to honest assessments, and after the disaster of Friedland (14 June 1807) he concluded that only a Fabian delaying strategy would be successful against Napoleon. It consisted of luring Napoleon deep into Russia and attacking him in strength only after he had used up his supplies. The Treaty of Tilsit (7–9 July 1807) placed such plans in abeyance.

More immediately Barclay took part in 1808 in the campaign against Sweden. Finland was gained, but the war continued. The Russians decided to take the war into Sweden, and in a daring crossing early in 1809 across the frozen Gulf of Bothnia at the Kwarken Straits Barclay took the city of Umea. Barclay was promoted to full general, and Alexander appointed him both commander in chief and governor-general. Within a short period of time, Alexander learned that in Barclay he had appointed an extremely able administrator who succeeded in inducing many Finns to be loyal to Russia.

In 1810 Alexander appointed Barclay minister of war, a post he held until 1812. Convinced that war with Napoleon was inevitable, Barclay reorganized the ministry and almost doubled the size of the army from 200,000 to 380,000 men. A major aspect of his work was the revision of Peter the Great's Army

Regulations, which had been in effect since 1716. Barclay's revision simplified the chain of command and defined the functions of the fifteen branches of the army. (Barclay's regulations remained in force until the 1860s when the emancipation of the serfs called for another revision.) The revisions were put into effect only half a year before Napoleon invaded Russia. Barclay's contingency plan for such an event consisted of defensive operations until the enemy had been weakened through attrition and his supply lines became vulnerable.

With Napoleon's invasion imminent, Alexander decided to place Barclay in command of the First Western Army of 100,000 men with headquarters at Vilna. Outnumbered by almost four to one and convinced that what Napoleon desired was another Jena or Friedland, followed by a quick peace treaty, Barclay put in operation his planned withdrawal. Sensible as this strategy was under the circumstances, it was very hard on those who disagreed with it or failed to understand it. There were some in Barclay's immediate environment who went so far as to suspect a sinister foreign influence at work (reinforced when they heard Barclay and Wolzogen converse in German). Alexander, always wavering, was not strong enough to withstand the vituperations of Barclay's critics; he began to call for an offensive stance and, giving in to the ultranationalists, decided to appoint Kutuzov, indubitably a Russian, as supreme commander in chief.

Barclay remained in the field as the commander of the First Army, with which he fought resolutely at Borodino. His performance convinced most of his erstwhile critics that he was neither a coward nor a traitor. Yet friction continued between him and Kutuzov, and in September Barclay decided to go on leave for reasons of health. There were many who attributed not only the loss of Smolensk to him but that of Moscow as well.

By February the czar recalled him and entrusted him with the command of the Third Western Army. When Barclay seized the fortress of Thorn on the Vistula a month later, the czar responded by awarding him the Order of St. Alexander Nevski together with 50,000 rubles. Advancing farther into Germany, Barclay in May fought the Battle of Bautzen, following which Alexander appointed him commander in chief of the Russian and Prussian armies. After the battles of Dresden and Kulm, Barclay received the Order of St. George, First Class, Russia's highest military decoration, from Alexander and the Commander's Cross of the Knighthood of Maria Theresa from the Austrian emperor. After the Battle of Leipzig, the czar raised him to count.

Barclay continued to lead his forces into France and to Paris, where he was promoted to field marshal. With Prince Blücher von Wahlstatt giving up command of the Silesian army, Frederick William III placed these troops under Barclay's orders. Barclay accompanied his sovereign to the victory festivities in London and then led his troops back to Russia.

Napoleon's return to France also saw Barclay active again. Leading a Russian army of 200,000 men toward France, he had reached the Rhine when news of Waterloo was received. When he arrived in Paris for the second time, the czar bestowed the title of prince (*kniaz*) on him, a rare honor, as Peter the Great had bestowed it only once and Catherine the Great only twice. He died three years later, still the supreme commander of all Russian forces.

Barclay was most responsible for Napoleon's defeat in Russia. He set in motion the strategy of planned withdrawal, a plan that, except for Borodino, was also followed by Kutuzov. Alexander Pushkin immortalized him with his poem, "The Commander."

C. W. Barclay, *A History of the Barclay Family* (1924); C. von Clausewitz, *Campaign of 1812 in Russia* (1843); C. Duffy, *Borodino and the War of 1812* (1972); M. Josselson, *The Commander: A Life of Barclay de Tolly* (1980); R. Parkinson, *The Fox of the North: The Life of Kutuzov, General of War and Peace* (1976); F. W. Von Weymarn, *Barklay de Tolly und der vaterländische Krieg* (1914).

Peter W. Becker

Related entries: FRANCE, CAMPAIGN OF; GERMAN WAR OF LIBERATION; JENA-AUERSTÄDT-FRIEDLAND CAMPAIGN; RUSSIAN CAMPAIGN.

BARRAS, PAUL-FRANCOIS-JEAN-NICOLAS, VICOMTE DE (1755–1829), one of the most powerful members of the Directory (1795–99) and a pivotal figure in the frequent coups of the 1790s, was born on 30 June 1755 at Fox-Amphoux (Var) and died 29 January 1829 at Chaillot, near Paris. The eldest son of the Provençal nobleman François Barras, Paul refused a position as page to the duc d'Orleans in order to enlist at the age of sixteen as a *cadet-gentilhomme* in the regiment of Languedoc. He resigned his military career in May 1783 and took a lodging in Paris, where he married Mlle de Saint-Rémy, sister of Jeanne de La Motte-Valois.

The unemployed Barras welcomed the outbreak of the Revolution in 1789 and joined the Jacobin club almost as soon as it was created. He took part in the storming of the Bastille (14 July 1789), the march of the women to Versailles (5–6 October 1789), and the attack on the Tuileries (10 August 1792). Barras was elected in 1792 to represent the department of Var in the National Convention, and at the trial of Louis XVI he voted for immediate execution without appeal to the people. As commissar in the French Army of Italy, Barras helped liberate the Var and Nice from royalist forces. In the autumn of 1793 Barras and Louis Fréron, as representatives on mission, condemned to death about 200 counterrevolutionaries at Marseille.

Barras then hurried to the last of the federal cities in revolt, Toulon, where he was to be much more severe in his punishments, and also where he met for the first time Captain Napoleon Bonaparte, commander of the artillery of the French army. Toulon fell in December 1793, and Barras, along with Joseph Saliceti and Augustin Robespierre, mercilessly ordered the execution by firing squad of 1,000 or more royalists and Girondins. Napoleon had played a leading role in the capture of Toulon, and Barras and his fellow representatives on mission saw to it that Bonaparte received credit for the victory and a promotion from the rank of captain to brigadier general.

At the height of the Terror, Barras feared for his life. He sought to escape from the Law of 22 Prairial (10 June 1794), a new Law of Suspects, by working to organize the Convention against Maximilien Robespierre and his Reign of Virtue. Barras, Joseph Fouché, Louis Fréron, Jean Tallien, and others succeeded in convincing the deputies that their lives too were threatened by the "dictator" Robespierre. On 9 Thermidor (27 July 1794) the Convention voted the arrest of Robespierre, and Barras' climb to power began.

During the Thermidorian period, Barras won command of the Army of the Interior and the police, and he held a number of important positions in the Convention, on the Committee of Public Safety, and on the Committee of General Security. It was also during this period that Barras began his affair with Josephine de Beauharnais. A revolt by the Parisian populace against the Convention presented Barras with an opportunity in the autumn of 1795. Charged with the defense of the Tuileries, he enlisted the ruthless skills of Brigadier General Bonaparte, then with the Bureau topographique. Napoleon's "whiff of grapeshot" of 13 Vendémiaire (5 October 1795) allowed Barras to engineer elections to the Directory, and Barras quickly became the most popular of the five directors, "le roi du Directoire." Of the original five, only Barras held office uninterruptedly for the duration of the Directory.

In 1796 Barras joined Charles M. de Talleyrand, Joseph Fouché, Benjamin Constant, and Madame Germaine de Staël in "Le Cercle Constitutionnel," an antiroyalist group that supported the authoritarian structure of the Directory and the Constitution of 22 August 1795. Barras respected the opinions of Madame de Staël, and following her advice he sponsored Talleyrand's appointment to the Ministry of Foreign Affairs. Royalist victories in the elections of 1797 compelled Barras once again to call on Napoleon, who had just defeated the Austrians in the first Italian campaign. Bonaparte dispatched to Paris General Pierre Augereau, who aided the triumvirate (Barras, Louis M. de La Revéllière, and Jean-François Reubell) in the coup of 18 Fructidor (4 September 1797). This coup purged the royalists from the Assembly and brought Barras to the apex of his career.

Barras fell from power in Napoleon's coup of 18 Brumaire (9 November 1799). Even before 18 Brumaire Barras had sought indemnity from Louis XVIII, and Bonaparte's suspicion of Barras' conspiratorial activities resulted in his exile to Brussels in 1801. Barras was allowed to return to southern France in 1805 but in 1813 was exiled to Rome due to his secret meetings with the former Spanish king, Charles IV. Following the second abdication of Napoleon, Barras returned to spend the remainder of his days at his Chaillot estate, where he finished his much-quoted *Mémoires*.

J. P. Garnier, *Barras, le roi du Directoire* (Paris, 1970); G. Lefebvre, *Le Directoire* (Paris, 1958); M. Lyons *France under the Directory* (1975); A. Mathiez, *Le Directoire* (Paris, 1934), and *The Thermidorian Reaction* (1931); M. Reinhard, *La France du Directoire*, 2 vols. (Paris, 1956); A. Soboul, *Le Directoire et le Consulat* (Paris, 1967).

Fred D. Hembree

Related entries: BRUMAIRE, COUP OF 18 YEAR VIII; CONVENTION; DIRECTORY; FRUCTIDOR, COUP OF 18 YEAR V; TERROR, THE; VENDEMIAIRE.

BASSANO, BATTLE OF. See ITALIAN CAMPAIGN, FIRST.

BASSANO, DUC DE. See MARET.

BASTILLE, PLACE DE LA. The fall of the fourteenth-century fortress of the Bastille on 14 July 1789 marked a turning point of the early Revolution. The fortress was dismantled stone by stone beginning the same day, a job begun by the people but finished by the workers of the entrepreneur Palloy. Napoleon inherited a vast, empty square, for which he commissioned (1803) a gigantic elephant, some fifty feet high, to stand in the center. A full-sized model in wood and plaster was erected but was never completed in metal. The model stood until 1846, when it was demolished. The *carrefour* has remained empty since that time.

BATAVIAN REPUBLIC (1799–1806), sister republic of France created in 1795, which became the Kingdom of Holland in 1806. The Republic of the Seven United Provinces, known in the seventeenth century for its commercial power, diplomatic influence, and contributions to art and science, was only a second-rate power during the eighteenth century. It was torn by internal strife in the 1780s and poorly led by the last Orange *stadholder*, William V (1766–95). The French Republic declared war on the Dutch Republic, an ally of England, in February 1793.

French armies invaded Dutch territory in 1795, and a new regime, the Batavian Republic, was established. Henceforth the Netherlands was tied to France by the Treaty of the Hague (May 1795). With French assistance, a new constitution was finally accepted in 1798, which provided for a government similar to the French Directory. At the time of the coup d'état of 18–19 Brumaire (1799), many Dutch citizens had become disillusioned with the revolution and wanted a more conservative government.

First consul Bonaparte considered the Batavian Republic of considerable strategic and economic importance and demanded, much to the dismay of the Dutch, strict enforcement of the treaty obligations. In 1801 Bonaparte did approve a constitutional change, which established an authoritarian form of government, the so-called *Staatsbewind*. In 1802 it successfully rejected Bonaparte's request for a substantial loan to support a new war but was forced to implement French trade regulations against Britain and its allies. In 1805 Bonaparte made Rutger Jan Schimmelpenninck councillor pensionary of the Batavian Commonwealth. His regime proved to be progressive, but in 1806 the emperor replaced it with a monarchy, the Kingdom of Holland, under his brother Louis.

H. T. Colenbrander, *De Bataafsche Republiek* (Amsterdam, 1908); G. D. Homan, *Nederland in de Napoleonische tijd, 1795-1815* (Bussum, 1978); S. Schama, *Patriots and Liberators. Revolution in the Netherlands, 1780-1813* (New York, 1977).

Gerlof D. Homan

Related entries: CONTINENTAL BLOCKADE; HOLLAND, KINGDOM OF; NETHERLANDS ENTRIES; WARFARE, ECONOMIC.

BAUTZEN, BATTLE OF. See GERMAN WAR OF LIBERATION.

BAVARIA, KINGDOM OF, previously an electorate, made a kingdom by Napoleon in 1806, and allied with France until 1813. Bavaria was the largest and most influential state of the Rheinbund (Confederation of the Rhine). King Max and his minister, Count Montgelas, instituted far-reaching reforms modeled on those of the French Empire. It was due chiefly to Montgelas' influence that in the war of 1805 Bavaria switched from the Austrian to the French side. Other members of the future Rhenish Confederation followed suit, driven by the desire to survive under the prevailing power relationships. Bavaria had earlier lost the Wittelsbach territories on the Rhine (Jülich, Berg, Zweibrücken, and Electoral Palatinate); in 1806, thanks to Napoleon, Bavaria received extensive areas in Franconia and Swabia to round off its territory.

Bavaria, however, backed by Württemberg, prevented the Rheinbund from becoming a federal state, as Napoleon had wished, but remained a military alliance of sovereign states. Bavarian troops had to participate on the side of France in the campaigns of 1805, 1806–7, 1809, and 1812. In the Russian campaign 30,000 Bavarians lost their lives (out of a population of 3 million).

In 1813, before the Battle of Leipzig, Bavaria, in a timely diplomatic move, allied with Austria, which guaranteed Bavaria territorial integrity. Once again, the other south German states followed Bavaria's example. In 1816, in exchange for Salzburg and the Inn River area, Bavaria received the Palatinate on the left bank of the Rhine.

Domestically, Montgelas' principal objectives were the creation of a modern, unitary, and centralized administration similar to that of the French Empire and the adoption of such reforms of Revolutionary and imperial France as seemed beneficial to Bavaria, considering its condition and traditions. In fact Montgelas succeeded in fashioning modern Bavaria. He welded together a multiplicity of secular and ecclesiastical principalities, as well as free cities, and breathed life into the new state. He also developed the economic power of his state, restored its finances, and saved its political independence.

Montgelas instituted equality before the law, the obligation for all to pay taxes (including the nobility), equal access for all citizens to state offices, and universal compulsory military service. In the more conservative period after 1809, exceptions were made again, just as in France, but the principles continued to be honored throughout the nineteenth century. After 1815, the middle class dominated the upper echelons of government and military (excepting ministerial posts) in Bavaria and Württemberg, whereas in Prussia the role of the commoners diminished. The Imperial Recess of 1803 (*Reichsdeputationshauptschluss*) empowered German states to dissolve monasteries and confiscate their property. Bavaria under Montgelas exploited this opportunity ruthlessly, which contributed to the disappearance of many art treasures, manuscripts, and books. The most valuable objects, however, were gathered in state collections.

After the end of the Holy Roman Empire in 1806, the estates were dissolved, and until 1818, when a new constitution was introduced, Bavaria was an absolute monarchy. Montgelas' reforms were simply decreed by the king, including the abolition of noble privileges, the beginnings of the emancipation of the peasants, toleration and equality of religious denominations, emancipation of the Jews, abolition of internal customs fees, a new and more humane penal code, a judicial system modeled on the French example, and administrative units that ignored historical boundaries. Moreover, there was reform of academies, high schools, and other educational institutions, which made Bavaria a center of scholarship in Germany. Additionally, significant steps were taken to promote trade, mining, agriculture, and commerce. For this purpose the government employed a new civil service, which was required to meet high standards of honesty as well as ability and performance.

Montgelas went too far, however, in centralization and the destruction of communal autonomy. After his dismissal in 1817, both errors were corrected. The constitution of 1818 transformed Bavaria, thirty years earlier than Prussia, into a constitutional monarchy.

K. O. von Aretin, *Bayerns Weg zum souveränen Staat. Landstände und konstitutionelle Monarchie 1714–1818* (Munich, 1976); M. Dunan, *Napoléon et l'Allemagne. Le système continental et les débuts du royaume du Bavière, 1806–1810* (Paris, 1942); H. Glaser, ed., *Krone und Verfassung. König Max I. Joseph und der neue Staat* (Munich, 1980); K. Möckl, *Der moderne bayerische Staat. Eine Verfassungsgeschichte vom aufgeklärten Absolutismus bis zum Ende der Reformepoche* (Munich, 1979); E. Weis, "Die Begründung des modernen bayerischen Staates unter König Max I," in M. Spindler, ed., *Handbuch der bayerischen Geschichte,* vol. 4 (Munich, 1979).

Eberhard Weis

Related entries: AUGUSTA; BEAUHARNAIS, E., CONFEDERATION OF THE RHINE; MAX I JOSEPH; MONTGELAS.

BAYLEN, BATTLE OF. See PENINSULAR WAR.

BAYONNE, CONSTITUTION OF, constitution of the Bonaparte Kingdom of Spain, approved by a Spanish national junta (Assembly) convened by Napoleon at Bayonne, France (8 June–7 July 1808). The constitution was very liberal for Spain except that it declared the "Catholic, Apostolic, and Roman" religion to be that of the "king and the nation" and allowed no other. Joseph Bonaparte was named king (Don José Napoleón, king of Spain and the Indies). Succession was to be to his male heirs (he had none), then those of

Napoleon (who could adopt), then those of Louis Bonaparte, then Jerome Bonaparte. The legislative branch was to be a single-chamber Cortes, with the majority of members elected, indirectly, by universal manhood suffrage. Those elected had to be landed proprietors. Seats were allocated, moreover, for nobles, clergy, and businessmen, who were to be appointed by the king. The king was also to appoint the senate, which could suspend the constitution in an emergency, but whose duty otherwise was to "maintain freedom of the individual and the press."

Freedom from arrest without warrant and imprisonment without court order were guaranteed, as were prompt trial and equality of punishments. Torture was forbidden except by judicial warrant. Taxes were to apply equally to all classes. Titles of nobility were authorized, but feudalism was abolished and the principle of "careers open to talent" was stated. The constitution had 144 articles, which specified precisely how the new government would function—for example, providing for a Senate commission to hear appeals from prisoners held over thirty days without trial, outlining the structure of the judicial system, and providing how entail was to be abolished. Provision was made for the extension of the king's government to the Spanish colonies ("the Indies") and for their representation in the Cortes and other bodies. For the time, it was an admirable document. Unfortunately, it was never really put into effect in Spain or the Indies—in Spain because of the continual war, in the colonies because the authorities rejected Joseph's (Napoleon's) authority out of hand.

P. Conard, *La Constitution de Bayonne, 1808, essai d'édition critique* (Paris, 1910); O. Connelly, *Napoleon's Satellite Kingdoms* (New York, 1965); G. de Grandmaison, *L'Espagne et Napoléon*, 3 vols. (Paris, 1914–32).

Related entries: BAYONNE, "INTERVIEW" OF; BAYONNE, JUNTA OF; PENINSULAR WAR; SPAIN, KINGDOM OF.

BAYONNE, "INTERVIEW" OF (4–6 May 1808), forced abdication of the Bourbons of Spain by Napoleon. In March 1808 at Aranjuez, the Spanish crown prince had overthrown his father, Charles IV, and proclaimed himself Ferdinand VII. Napoleon's troops were already moving into Spain, an ally; Joachim Murat shortly occupied Madrid. Both Ferdinand and Charles (and Queen Maria Luisa) sued for the support of the French emperor, who was at Bayonne on the border. Napoleon offered to mediate their differences and invited them to join him. The monarchs came, together with all possible heirs to the throne. On 4 May, Charles IV abdicated in favor of Napoleon, and on 6 May Ferdinand VII did the same; all the *infantes* renounced their rights. In return all were provided with residences and incomes in France. Charles went to the chateau de Chambord, Ferdinand to Valençay, there to remain until 1814.

Related entries: CHARLES IV; FERDINAND VII DE BOURBON; PENINSULAR WAR; SPAIN, KINGDOM OF.

BAYONNE, JUNTA OF (8 June–7 July 1808), Spanish National Assembly summoned by Napoleon at the French border city of Bayonne. It approved a new constitution for Spain that recognized Jospeh Bonaparte as king and thus tacitly accepted the end of Bourbon rule. Napoleon had ordered 120 deputies elected (May 1808) by the three estates of the realm (clergy, nobles, commoners), but most of the ninety-one who appeared had been appointed by Marshal Joachim Murat, who had occupied Madrid, the junta of Madrid (which served him), or Napoleon himself. Nevertheless it was such an Assembly of Notables that it affirmed Napoleon's belief that Spain would not resist him. Among those present were the prince del Castelfranco, the duke de Frias, two archbishops, the vicars general of the Franciscan and Augustinian orders, former royal ministers such as Pedro de Cevallos, General Gonzalo O'Farrill, Sebastian Piñuela y Alonso, José de Azanza, and others, plus eminent liberals, such as Francisco Cabarrus, Luis de Urquijo, and Manuel Romero. The junta adjourned after hearing King Joseph's oath to the constitution on 7 July 1808. Although it had, in fact, represented the approval of Bonaparte rule by a large part of the establishment, the Spanish people responded with a grass-roots rebellion.

Related entries: BAYONNE, CONSTITUTION OF; BAYONNE, "INTERVIEW" OF; PENINSULAR WAR; SPAIN, KINGDOM OF.

BAYONNE SUMS *(Sumy bajonskie)*, total debt owed to France by the Duchy of Warsaw, set by convention signed at Bayonne in 1808. It was the sum of balances due on mortgages on lands in the duchy held by the Prussian government, which mortgages Napoleon claimed by right of conquest. The amount agreed on, 25 million francs payable within four years, deranged the duchy's finances from the beginning. Because of depressed grain prices, the noble landholders, from whom the government had to collect, had no cash. The government, composed of nobles, was not disposed to foreclosure, which would have netted little in any case. Thus the debt to France was never paid. The default caused great resentment among the Poles, however, who felt that Napoleon had sold them mortgages on their own territories. The term *Bayonne sums* entered the Polish language as a synonym for enormously high amounts.

T. Mencel, "Sumy bajonskie," *Roczniki historyczne R. 19* (1950).

John Stanley

Related entry: WARSAW, DUCHY OF.

BEAUHARNAIS, EUGENE DE (1781–1824), viceroy of Italy, French prince and general. He was the son of the Empress Josephine by her first husband, the vicomte Alexandre de Beauharnais, who was guillotined during the Terror. When his mother married Napoleon Bonaparte, Eugène became his loyal follower, and remained so despite the divorce of 1809. He was Napoleon's aide-de-camp in Egypt and served as a captain in the Marengo campaign. In 1805 he was named viceroy of Italy at age twenty-four and in 1806 was married to Augusta of Bavaria, who became a model queen. Perhaps the most capable satellite ruler, he gave Italy efficient and enlightened government and also served Napoleon as a general.

In 1805, with André Masséna, he occupied the Austrians in Italy while Napoleon triumphed in Germany. In 1809 he assured Napoleon's victory at Wagram by defeating the Archduke Johann (John) at Raab and preventing his juncture with the Archduke Karl (Charles), and also appeared to fight at Wagram. In the Russian campaign of 1812, Eugène distinguished himself, particularly during the bloody retreat from Moscow. He won the Battle of Maloyaroslavets (25 October 1812) by committing his valiant Italian Royal Guard, which was almost destroyed. He rescued Marshal Michel Ney and the rear guard at Smolensk. After Napoleon left the remnants of the army under Marshal Joachim Murat, who abandoned his post to return to Naples, Eugène assumed command of the army. Eugène organized all available effectives, drew in units that had not marched to Moscow, and conducted a brilliant retreat across Germany to the Elbe River. He held the line of the Elbe until Napoleon appeared in April 1813 with a new army. He then departed for Italy and during 1813–14 while Napoleon fought in Germany and France, Eugène held the kingdom against assault by Austrian forces reinforced by those of the turncoat Murat, king of Naples. He was still fighting, and well, on 16 April 1814, when he heard of Napoleon's abdication at Fontainebleau (6 April). He then concluded an armistice with the Austrians, who considered allowing him to retain his kingdom but did not. Eugène retired to Bavaria at the invitation of King Max, his wife's father. In 1815 he did not rally to Napoleon because it would have endangered his family. He lived out his life as duke of Leuchtenberg and prince of Eichstädt, titles granted by his father-in-law. His children—two boys and three girls—all married into European royal families.

Prinz A. von Bayern, *Eugen Beauharnais, der Stiefsohn Napoleons* (Munich, 1940); F. de Bernardy, *Eugène de Beauharnais 1781–1824* (Paris, 1973); O. Connelly, *Napoleon's Satellite Kingdoms* (New York, 1965); C. Oman, *Napoleon's Viceroy: Eugène de Beauharnais* (London, 1966); C. Zaghi, *Napoleone e l'Italia* (Napoli, 1966).

Related entries: AUGUSTA; BEAUHARNAIS; ITALY, KINGDOM OF; RUSSIAN CAMPAIGN; WAGRAM.

BEAUHARNAIS [BONAPARTE], HORTENSE DE (1783–1837), queen of Holland, daughter of the Empress Josephine by her first husband, the Vicomte Alexandre de Beauharnais. By arrangement, she was married in 1802 to Louis Bonaparte, brother of Napoleon. In 1806 they became king and queen of Holland. They had three sons: Napoleon Charles (1803), Napoleon Louis (1804), and Louis Napoleon (1808), who became Napoleon III. As a young woman, Hortense was beautiful, vivacious, and genteel, as befitted a graduate of the school of Madame Campan. She did not get along well, however, with Louis Bonaparte, who by 1802 had become something of a hypochondriac. They were often apart, and even when living in the same palace in Holland, they kept separate apartments. They separated at about the same time Louis was driven into exile (1810) and never saw each other again. In 1811 Hortense gave birth to an illegitimate child by the comte de Flahaut. Under the Second Empire he was created duc de

Morny. During the Allied occupation of Paris in 1814, Hortense became the favorite of Czar Alexander I at whose request she was given the title of duchesse de Saint-Leu. During the Hundred Days she returned to Malmaison but after Waterloo again went into exile. She died at Arenenberg, Switzerland in 1837.

C. d'Anjezon, *Hortense de Beauharnais* (Paris, 1897); Hortense, reine de Hollande, *Mémoires*, 12th ed., 3 vols. (1927); C. Wright, *Daughter to Napoleon* (New York, 1961).

Related entries: BONAPARTE, LOUIS; CAMPAN; HOLLAND, KINGDOM OF; JOSEPHINE.

BEAUHARNAIS, JOSEPHINE DE. See JOSEPHINE.

BEAULIEU, JOHANN, BARON VON (1725–1819), first Austrian general to oppose Napoleon during the first Italian campaign. Defeated in a series of battles, including Lodi (10 May 1796), he was replaced by Field Marshal Dagobert Wurmser.

Related entry: ITALIAN CAMPAIGN, FIRST.

BELGIUM, part of France between 1794 and 1814. The French conquest of Belgium began in 1792 as the first act of war against the Austrian Emperor Francis II and was completed by the victory of Fleurus, 26 June 1794, which gave France all of modern-day Belgium: the Austrian Netherlands, Liège, Stavelot-Malmédy, and the duchy of Bouillon. The Committee of Public Safety treated liberated Belgium as a conquered territory, pillaging and extorting to such a degree that economic disaster resulted in 1794 and 1795. The rationale for exacting heavy taxes from the nobles, priests, and privileged classes was to recover the cost of the campaign of 1792. Afterward, without consulting the people, the Belgian provinces were annexed to France by the Convention (decree of 1 October 1795).

Belgium was divided into nine departments: Lys, Escaut, Deux-Nèthes, Meuse-inférieure, Ourthe, Forêts, Sambre-et-Meuse, Jemappes, and Dyle. While French law was supposed to be applied, it was modified by centralization and military rule, and popular sovereignty was an empty phrase because government *commissaires* interfered in elections. The principle of equality, which was better applied, manifested itself in equal taxation, religious equality, the cessation of venality of offices, and the abolition of primogeniture, the last thereby diminishing the influence of the nobility. A new general code of simple laws unified the contradictory customary laws, and registration of births, deaths, and marriages became civil matters. Torture and cruel punishment were abolished, along with arbitrary imprisonment, and a new judicial organization was improvised, all of which resembled the enlightened reforms proposed but unrealized by Joseph II. The abolition of internal tariff barriers meant that the potential commercial market of Belgium, which became France's most advanced industrial region, swelled from 3 million customers to 30 million. These gains of the Revolution benefited the people overall and stimulated the birthrate.

Still, the Directory imposed extraordinary contributions on Belgium, exploiting the wealth of the state, private persons, and, especially, the church. In 1797 the Directory suppressed all nonproductive religious orders not maintaining schools or hospitals. Blatant religious persecution began after the coup d'état of 18 Fructidor Year IV, after which external signs of religion (crosses, images, and clerical robes) were outlawed and about thirty recusant priests who refused to take the required oath of hatred toward royalty were deported to Guyana. New elections showed a swing to the left as, for example, a communist and partisan of François N. "Gracchus" Babeuf, was elected in Liège. "Blind masses" were held clandestinely in houses during this *Gesloten Tyd* or ("time of closure") of churches when the observance of the *decadi* was made obligatory. Even the University of Louvain was closed for not conforming to republican principles. The Belgians' largely silent resistance to the Directory's harsher measures was evident in the poor response to republican fêtes and refusal to use the republican calendar. In 1798, resistance to conscription turned into the flare-up of the so-called Peasants' War in the Hageland, Kempen, and in the Ardennes. It ended in pitiless repression of the brigands; those who escaped death on the field were shot. The insurrection then became the pretext for further oppression of the clergy. This time 7,500 priests were condemned to deportation although only 400 to 500 were actually arrested and of these 300 sent to the isles of Ré and d'Oléron. The Directory terrorized the countryside under martial law for a year. Yet unlike the French, Belgians emerged from the period of poverty, brigandage, and economic stagnation morally intact, and there was nothing there comparable to the Vendée revolt in western France.

The coup of 18 Brumaire was greeted indifferently; former nobles were cautious because they expected the Consulate to be ephemeral. But the government of Bonaparte endeavored to restore order and to reorganize the administration using more tact than did its predecessors. Prefects were all foreign, but they were supposed to select officials from among the former opposition as well as from among loyal French supporters. By this and other means, public security and civil peace gradually were restored. In contrast, the church, under the leadership of a priest named Corneille Stevens (1747–1828), continued to resist French rule until the Concordat of 15 August 1801 brought a truce. Catholic worship was reestablished throughout Belgium on Pentecost Day 1802 (6 June). Thereafter the bishops appointed by Napoleon adulated and served him with devotion. Nevertheless, the emperor's attempt to modify the Concordat by the "organic articles" led to the formulation of a schismatic group, *la petite église* (sometimes erroneously referred to as Stevenists), which opposed the feast day of Saint Napoléon (15 August) and the emperor worship included in the imperial catechism. Because Napoleon imposed the French language on the Flemish districts, intellectual activity in Flanders continued to be limited to the aristocracy and the bourgeoisie.

From 1804 Belgium was treated on an equal footing with France, and Napoleon was, perhaps, at the peak of his popularity there. Thereafter the majority of former nobles consented to participate in public affairs. The emperor's policy was full assimilation into France, and since equality of rights implied equality of obligations, he called up successive levies of troops, from 1807 on even before their time of service was due. Belgium's harbors offered Napoleon a maritime base for use in an attack on England. In 1809, after Jean-Baptiste Bernadotte's forces scared off the English expedition that occupied the island of Walcheren, Napoleon ordered construction of defensive works at the port of Antwerp, and when he visited them in 1811, he was pleased at the semblance of bustling commercial activity.

But passive hostility never ceased to exist in Belgium for several reasons. Along with the economic stress, the clergy obstructed Gallicanization, particularly after the breach between Pius VII and Napoleon (1809). Once the emperor suppressed the temporal power of the pope and annexed the Papal States, Belgians regarded him as a persecutor. This hostility was expressed notably by the count de Mérode-Westerloo and the bishops de Broglie, Hirn, and Troyer. In the Werbrouck case, the emperor annulled a judgment acquitting the mayor of Antwerp of committing fraud against the customs. Conscription was a further reason for the seething hostility, so much so that the fall of Napoleon was greeted joyously, and many Belgian volunteers took up arms against him in the campaigns of 1814 and 1815.

On 1 February 1814, Brussels was evacuated while Lazare Carnot defended Antwerp. The secret Treaty of Chaumont (1 March 1814) stipulated that Holland should receive the additional territory of Belgium, whose population exceeded its own by three to two, and this was confirmed by article 6 of the Treaty of Paris (30 May 1814). On 11 June 1814 the Allies established a provisional government for Belgium under the duke of Beaufort. The secret Treaty of London (23 June 1814) further provided that the union of the Dutch and the Belgians be internal and thorough under the existing constitution of Holland and ruled by the Prussian prince William I of Orange-Nassau. The Battle of Waterloo (18 June 1815) secured the final deliverance of Belgium, yet the territory, where the French conquest had begun and ended twenty-one years later, did not receive its independence. It became, instead, part of the buffer state created by the Great Powers to thwart French imperialism.

R. Devleeshouwer, *L'Arrondissement du Brabant sous l'occupation français 1794–1795* (Brussels, 1964); L. DeLanzac de Laborie, *La domination française en Belgique, 1795–1814* (Paris, 1895); H. Pirenne, *Histoire de Belgique*, VI (Brussels, 1926); P. Puraye, *Liège sous l'Empire* (Paris, 1954); S. Tassier, *Histoire de la Belgique sous l'occupation française en 1792 et 1793* (Brussels, 1934).

June K. Burton

Related entries: ADMINISTRATION; ANNEXATION POLICY; CARNOT; CHURCH, ROMAN CATHOLIC; CONCORDAT OF 1801; CONSCRIPTION; FOREIGN POLICY; PIUS VII.

BELLEGARDE, HEINRICH VON, COUNT (1756–1845), Austrian field marshal and statesman. Bellegarde, son of the Saxon minister of war, entered the Austrian army in 1778 and after 1792 distinguished himself in eighteen campaigns against Revolutionary France. In 1796 he became Archduke Karl's chief of staff, and in 1797 he negotiated the preliminary Peace of Leoben with Napoleon. During 1799–1800 he safeguarded the lines of communication between Russian forces in Italy and Austrian armies in Germany. From 1806 to 1808 he was governor of Galicia. In 1809 he fought at Aspern and Wagram and after Austria's defeat was made president of the Imperial War Council. From 1809 until 1813 he supervised the reorganization of the army and the levying of troops. In 1813 he became commander in chief in Italy, where in 1814 he negotiated the capitulation of Viceroy Eugène de Beauharnais. From 1814 to 1816 he was governor of Lombardy and Venetia. His forces defeated those of King Joachim Murat of Naples in 1815. In 1816 he was appointed seneschal of Crown Prince Ferdinand and from 1820 to 1825 was state and conference minister and president of the Imperial War Council.

K. von Smola, *Leben des Generalfeldmarschalls Heinrich Graf von Bellegarde* (Vienna, 1847).

Eckhardt Treichel

Related entries: BEAUHARNAIS; ITALIAN CAMPAIGN, FIRST; ITALIAN CAMPAIGN, SECOND; ITALY, KINGDOM OF; KARL VON HABSBURG, ARCHDUKE; LEOBEN, PRELIMINARY PEACE OF; MURAT, J.; NAPLES, KINGDOM OF; WAGRAM CAMPAIGN.

BENNIGSEN, LEVIN AUGUST THEOPHIL VON, COUNT (1745–1826), Russian general of great tactical ability who is unfortunately best remembered because of his defeat by Napoleon at Friedland. Born at Braunschweig into an old noble German family, Bennigsen at ten became a page at the court of Hanover and at age fifteen an ensign in the foot guards. He participated in the campaigns in Westphalia and the Rhine until 1762, leaving the service with the conclusion of peace in 1763. For the next ten years he administered his estate, but owing to the death of his wife and financial pressures entered Russian service with the rank of major. He fought in the Turkish wars of 1778 and 1787–92, distinguished himself at the siege of Ochakov, and emerged with the rank of brigadier general. In the Polish campaign he participated in various battles and was rewarded with large estates confiscated from the Poles. In 1796 he took part in the war against Persia, where he was instrumental in the capture of Derbent. He spent several years in the Caucasus, and Czar Paul promoted him to lieutenant general.

In 1801 he played an important part in the conspiracy against Paul. Although Bennigsen's precise role in the assassination is not quite clear, there is no doubt that he was the guiding spirit and backbone of the coup. Czar Alexander I in 1801 named him governor of Lithuania, in 1802 promoted him to general of the cavalry, and in 1805 placed an army of 50,000 under him to assist other Russian forces in Germany.

In the following war in 1806, he commanded another army of 50,000 men and achieved a signal success at the Battle of Pultusk. He then became commander in chief of all Russian and the remaining Prussian forces and encountered Napoleon at the Battle of Preussisch-Eylau, for which Alexander rewarded him with the order of St. Andrew and a pension of 12,000 rubles. The outcome of the bloody battle was inconclusive, but Bennigsen earned the fame of being the first to breach Napoleon's aura of invincibility. He was equally successful at the battles of Guttstadt and Heilsberg. His fortune changed, however, at the Battle of Friedland (14 June 1807), where he was disastrously defeated by Napoleon, losing 25,000 of 60,000 men; the rest were scattered and demoralized. The czar immediately bid for peace, which was made at Tilsit. Benningsen withdrew to his estate near Vilna and remained there until 1812.

When the French invaded Russia, Bennigsen at first served on Alexander's personal staff and then participated in the battles of Borodino (for which success he claimed credit) and Tarutino. For the latter he received the order of St. Vladimir, First Class, and the sum of 100,000 rubles. Still, he resented having to serve under M. Barclay de Tolly and Mikhail Kutuzov, feeling that he should have been given supreme command. He favored a battle in front of Moscow, but Kutuzov ignored Bennigsen's advice in this matter as much as when he advocated hot pursuit of the retreating French. Intriguing against Kutuzov, Bennigsen was forced to retire from active military service, but after Kutuzov's death in 1813, he was placed in command of the Russian Army of Poland, arriving just in time to fight during the final phase of the Battle of Leipzig. Alexander conferred the title of count on him. Subsequently his army engaged the French at Torgau and Wittenberg and besieged Magdeburg and Hamburg, thereby preventing L. N. Davout from uniting the remaining French forces in northern Germany.

After the war Bennigsen was entrusted with the command of the Second Army in Bessarabia where he remained until 1818. He then retired and spent his remaining years on his native estate in Germany, writing his memoirs.

Of tall stature and equally great ambition, Bennigsen was an able tactical commander; his strategic understanding was limited, however.

C. von Clausewitz, *Campaign of 1812 in Russia* (1843); C. Duffy, *Borodino and the War of 1812* (1972); E. R. Holmes, *Borodino, 1812* (1971); M. Josselson, *The Commander: A Life of Barclay de Tolly* (1980); A. Palmer, *Napoleon in Russia* (1967); R. Parkinson, *The Fox of the North: The Life of Kutuzov, General of War and Peace* (1976); F. Petre, *Napoleon's Last Campaign in Germany, 1813* (1972).

Peter W. Becker

Related entries: BORODINO, BATTLE OF; FRIEDLAND, BATTLE OF; GERMAN WAR OF LIBERATION; JENA-AUERSTÄDT-FRIEDLAND CAMPAIGN; RUSSIAN CAMPAIGN.

BERESFORD, WILLIAM CARR, VISCOUNT (1768–1854), British commander in chief of the Portuguese army, 1809–20. An illegitimate son of the first marquis of Waterford of the Irish nobility, Beresford chose a military career as a means of advancing his fortune. In the period 1793–1808, he participated in campaigns on four continents. Although ambitious, Beresford failed to establish the reputation he sought as a military commander. He achieved recognition, however, as an able administrator and a strict disciplinarian. It was these qualities that recommended him when the Portuguese regency requested that a British officer be named to take command of its armed forces.

In March 1809, Beresford assumed the position of commander in chief of the disorganized Portuguese army. He instituted a reform of the Portuguese officer corps, introduced British junior officers to facilitate the imposition of a strict discipline and drill on the army, and reorganized the army's recruiting, logistical, and judicial systems. As a result of Beresford's efforts, the Portuguese army attained a level of competency approaching that of the British. Despite this accomplishment, Beresford's unsuitability for active field command was confirmed by his controversial role in the Battle of Albuera on 16 May 1811. His active involvement in the army declined after this bloody encounter, but he continued to exercise considerable influence in the Portuguese government until his ouster by the liberal revolt of 1820.

Arquivo Historico Militar, Lisbon, *Beresford, Marshall Sir William Carr. Correspondencia para Forjaz, caixa 17-33*; W. C. Beresford, *Colleccao das Ordens do Dia*, 6 vols. (Lisbon, 1809–14); J. W. Fortescue, *A History of the British Army*, 13 vols. in 20 (London, 1917); Sir A. Halliday, *Observations on the Present State of the Portuguese Army, as Organized by Lieutenant-General Sir William Carr Beresford, with an Account of the Different Military Establishments and Laws of Portugal, and a Sketch of the Campaigns of the Last and Present Year, during which the Portuguese Army Was Brought into the Field against the Enemy, for the First Time as a Regular Force* (London, 1811); C. Oman, *A History of the Peninsular War*, 6 vols. (Oxford, 1902–22); S. E. Vichness, "Marshal of Portugal: The Military Career of William Carr Beresford, 1785–1814" (Ph.D. dissertation Florida State University, 1976); F. Da Silva Villar, *Atravez das Ordens de Beresford* (Lisbon, 1895).

Francisco A. de la Fuente

Related entries: ARMY, PORTUGUESE; PENINSULAR WAR; PORTUGAL; PORTUGUESE CAMPAIGNS; SPAIN, KINGDOM OF; WELLINGTON.

BEREZINA, BATTLE OF CROSSING OF. See RUSSIAN CAMPAIGN.

BERG, GRAND DUCHY OF (1806–13), established 1806 as a duchy from Berg and Cleves, possessions of Bavaria and Prussia ceded in 1805; a state of the Confederation of the Rhine; Grand Duchy 1807. The Grand Duchy of Berg provided a perfect object lesson of Napoleon's cavalier disposition of German territories. In 1806 Napoleon bestowed the new principality on his brother-in-law, Marshal Joachim Murat. In 1807 he added to it Nassau territories and Münster (by the Treaty of Tilsit) and made it a grand duchy. In 1808, however, Napoleon raised Murat to king of Naples and ruled Berg himself until March 1809 when he installed his four-year-old nephew, Louis Napoleon, as nominal ruler. In 1810, Berg lost approximately one-fourth of its territory when the emperor annexed Holland and the North German territories to France.

At its largest, the Grand Duchy had 880,000 inhabitants and was divided into four departments: Sieg (prefectory at Dillenburg), Rhine (Düsseldorf), Ruhr (Dortmund), and Ems (Münster). Ems and the northern part of the Rhine department with 213,000 inhabitants were lost in 1810. The duchy's capital was at Düsseldorf, the seat of the imperial commissioner, Claude Beugnot, and after 1810, P.-L. Roederer, who had to report to a secretariat in Paris established for Berg. Germans, predominantly nobles, held prominent positions in the administration. The government established modern, efficient administrative, financial, and legal structures. For the economy, on the other hand, French rule proved disastrous. Trade almost ceased due to the Continental System and Napoleon's customs policy, which protected the French economy from even his allies. Berg businessmen asked for economic integration into France in order to be able to sell their products there. When their pleas went unheeded, Berg manufacturing enterprises moved to the French department on the left bank of the Rhine, contributing to unemployment and the destitution of the population.

In 1813, after the news of Napoleon's defeat in Russia, the people of Berg rose against the French, driven by economic misery, the constant draft calls, and the hated tobacco and salt taxes. The uprising was put down by force, and seventeen leaders were executed. Nevertheless, the end of the artificial creation of Napoleon's power politics was near. In the same year, during the wars of liberation, Prussian and Russian troops occupied the area. In 1815 the Grand Duchy of Berg became part of Prussia's new western provinces.

R. Goecke, *Das Grossherzogthum Berg unter Joachim Murat, Napoleon I. und Louis Napoleon 1806–1813. Ein Beitrag zur Geschichte der französischen Fremdherrschaft auf dem rechten Rheinufer* (Cologne, 1877); O. R. Redlich, "Napoleon I. und die Industrie des Grossherzogtums Berg. Eine historische Skizze," *Beiträge zur Geschichte des Niederrheins* 17 (1902); C. Schmidt, *Le Grand-Duché de Berg (1806–1813): Etude sur la domination française en Allemagne sous Napoléon Ier* (Paris, 1905); K. Schröder, "Ursachen des Aufstandes gegen die französische Herrschaft in den Kantonen Waldbröhl, Homburg und Eitorf zu Beginn des Jahres 1813," *Romerike Berge* 21 (1971).

Michael Müller

Related entries: GERMAN WAR OF LIBERATION; MURAT; ROEDERER.

BERLIN DECREES. See CONTINENTAL BLOCKADE; WARFARE, ECONOMIC.

BERNADOTTE, JEAN-BAPTISTE-JULES (1763–1844), Marshal of France, prince de Ponte Corvo, king of Sweden. Bernadotte, the son of a lawyer, was himself briefly a law clerk. He joined the army in 1780, however, and by 1788 was a sergeant major. He was among the first noncommissioned officers to be commissioned during the Revolution (November 1791). By 1794 he was a *général de division* serving with the Army of the North. In 1797 he was sent to Italy with 20,000 men to reinforce Napoleon and participated in the last phases of the first Italian campaign. In 1798 he was appointed ambassador to Vienna and married Désirée Clary, sister of the wife of Joseph Bonaparte, Napoleon's elder brother.

With the resumption of war in 1799, Bernadotte served poorly in Germany but returned to Paris to become minister of war. A staunch republican, he refused to support the coup of 18 Brumaire. Napoleon nevertheless made him a councillor of state in 1800 and gave him an army command. In 1804 he made Bernadotte governor of Hanover and marshal of the empire. Bernadotte fought well at Ulm and Austerlitz in 1805 and in 1806 was made prince of Ponte Corvo. Later in 1806, however, he incurred Napoleon's wrath for his failure to reach the battlefield at either Jena or Auerstädt but escaped court-martial. By 1809, however, Bernadotte abandoned his position at Wagram and endangered the whole army. Napoleon forced Bernadotte to give up his military career.

Bernadotte, with Napoleon's approval, was elected crown prince of Sweden in October 1810 and was officially adopted by the heirless King Charles XIII in November the same year. Having changed his name to Charles-John and assuming the responsibilities of his new country, Bernadotte in 1813 defeated Nicolas Oudinot and Michel Ney and took part against Napoleon in the Battle of Nations at Leipzig.

By the Treaty of Kiel of January 1814, Bernadotte gained Norway for Sweden and continued in the coalition against Napoleon during the Campaign of France. He aspired to succeed Napoleon, but Frenchmen regarded Bernadotte as a traitor, and the Allies ultimately preferred Louis XVIII. He refused to join the Allied Coalition in 1815 but occupied himself with taking control of Norway. He succeeded to the Swedish throne as Charles XIV in 1818. Before his death at Stockholm in March 1844, he had made a reputation as a reformer.

G. Girod de l'Ain, *Bernadotte* (Paris, 1968); B. Nabonne, *Bernadotte*, 2d ed. (Paris, 1964).

Jesse Scott

Related entries: ALEXANDER I; AUSTERLITZ; BATTLE OF; JENA-AUERSTÄDT-FRIEDLAND CAMPAIGN; RUSSIAN CAMPAIGN; WAGRAM, BATTLE OF.

BERNIER, ABBE ETIENNE (1762–1806), the clever prelate who negotiated Napoleon's Concordat with Pius VII. At the outbreak of the Revolution he was teaching theology at the seminary and University of Angers. Remaining there, in 1790 he was named pastor of Saint-Laud's parish; however, he soon gained notoriety by refusing to swear allegiance to the Civil Constitution of the Clergy. After the Vendée revolt began, Bernier became a de facto leader of the Chouan peasantry because of his great heroism and ability, as well as his skillful intrigues. Bernier eventually became recognized as the head of the royalist supreme council directing the insurrection. He earned his appellation Apostle of the Vendée for his tripartite role of preaching, administering, and issuing military orders. By 1794 Bernier's independent attitude led to trouble with a rival leader, and subsequently he lost the confidence of his collaborators so that when he offered his services to François de Charette, he was not accepted. Thereafter he joined J. N. Stofflet, whom he first forced to make the peace of Saint-Florent with the republican generals but which he later made him break. After the deaths of Charette and Stofflet, Bernier cleverly obtained a safe conduct from General L. Hoche to allow him to go to Switzerland. Instead of emigrating, however, he remained in hiding in Anjou where he continued to arouse the rebels as Louis XVIII's official *agent général* of the Catholic and royal armies. Nevertheless, Bernier realized the futility of the royalist cause and refrained from joining the final uprising in 1799.

Bonaparte's coup d'état provided the opportunity for the unscrupulous Bernier to switch loyalty. In January 1800 he duped the Vendéan leader (we are told by his definitive biographer Jean Leflon) and concluded with General Gabriel Hédouville the treaty that finally granted religious liberty to the Vendéans, the Peace of Montfaucon. After this success Bernier went to Paris, where he preached sermons and was received politely by Bonaparte who listened to his advice and who shared his enigmatic personality traits. Bonaparte used the abbé's talent for intrigue in negotiating the Concordat while holding out the promise of the see of Paris and a cardinalship as incentive. Much to his credit as a churchman, Bernier used his diplomatic skill to defend the interests of Pius VII by playing the role of double agent as intermediary between Jean Portalis, Napoleon's Minister, and papal legate Cardinal Giovanni Caprara. In order to ensure full agreement, he drafted the notes and responses for both parties until the signature of the treaty finally occurred at 2 A.M., 16 July 1801. Unfortunately from Bernier's point of view, his disloyal behavior toward the French government in this regard contributed to his disgrace, and in 1802 he was assigned merely to the bishopric of Orléans instead of the capital.

During his few remaining years, Charles-Maurice de Talleyrand also employed Bernier to negotiate other significant but delicate diplomatic issues: the Italian and German Concordats and the French emperor's coronation. In fact, Bernier succeeded in obtaining Pius VII's acquiescence in the matter of Napoleon's actual self-coronation. Nevertheless, Bernier's desire to rise to the position of nuncio to Germany was frustrated. He had to satisfy his ambition by tending his diocese as bishop until his death at age forty-four. Thus, he joined the ranks of those highly intelligent but crafty men who abandoned monarchism to perform noteworthy services for Napoleon in exchange for somewhat modest reward.

Beauchamp, *Histoire de la Vendée* (Paris, 1820); A. Crétineau-Joly, *La Vendée Militaire* (Paris, 1895–96); J. Leflon, *Etienne-Alexandre Bernier, évêque d'Orléans* (Paris, 1938); C. Port, *Dictionnaire historique, géographique et biographique de Maine-et-Loire* (Angers, 1974); Le Père Theiner, *Histoire des deux Concordats de la République française* (Paris, 1869).

June K. Burton

Related entries: CHOUANS; CHURCH, ROMAN CATHOLIC; CONCORDAT OF 1801; VENDEE, WAR IN THE.

BERTHIER, ALEXANDRE (1753–1815), prince de Neuchâtel et de Wagram, Napoleon's almost indispensable chief of staff. Berthier was born in Versailles, where his father, Jean-Baptiste Berthier, a lieutenant colonel in the topographical engineers, had been placed on detached service to supervise the construction of the buildings for the ministries of war, navy, and foreign affairs and to prepare for Louis XV and Louis XVI a celebrated set of royal hunting maps. Alexandre entered the French army as a cadet in the topographical engineers at age twelve. His advance was rapid for a nonnoble: a lieutenant in the infantry in 1772 and captain of the cavalry in 1777. He served on J. B. de Rochambeau's staff during the American Revolution and was transferred to the General Staff in 1787. During the French Revolution he was chief of staff in 1789 to the baron de Besenval (in Paris), in 1792 to Rochambeau (Armée du Nord) and to his successor, Nicolas Luckner, and in 1795 to F. E. C. Kellermann (Armies of the Alps and of Italy). He was Napoleon's chief of staff for eighteen years, from 25 March 1796, at the opening of the first Italian campaign, until 6 April 1814, the date of Napoleon's first abdication.

In his successive posts Berthier was a model of loyalty, self-effacement, and efficiency. He created a disciplined staff for the production of field intelligence on the enemy, the maintenance of up-to-the-minute records of the locations of French and allied contingents, and above all the rapid translation of the emperor's general commands into precise, lucid, detailed orders for specific army units. Napoleon paid him tribute: "As chief of the staff, Berthier has no equal." He and his associates on the staff constituted an effective flywheel to Napoleon's driving force. Berthier also served as minister of war (11 November 1799–2 April 1800; 8 October 1800–9 August 1807). Yet, as Napoleon recognized, Berthier's ability was a specialized and technical talent, which did not enable him on his own to maneuver army corps and divisions imaginatively across the European landscape. This was Napoleon's gift.

His working relations with Napoleon were necessarily close and in the early years friendly. Napoleon showered on him offices, titles, and revenues: first marshal of the empire, chief of the first cohort of the Legion of Honor, vice-constable, and sovereign prince of Neuchâtel, dignities for which Berthier was grateful. As Napoleon became increasingly despotic, arbitrary, and in policy extravagantly expansionist, however, the friendly feelings of Berthier for his commander in chief cooled. A series of incidents wore thin even Berthier's loyalty. To trick Berthier into abandoning his beloved, Madame Visconti, and marrying royalty, Napoleon had his police falsely report that Berthier's amorata had taken another lover. Momentarily taken in and enraged by the tale, Berthier married Napoleon's choice, the princess Elisabeth-Marie, niece of the king of Bavaria. At the opening of the campaign of 1809, Berthier in strict obedience to Napoleon's orders divided the French army into three widely dispersed contingents, each vulnerable to separate destruction by the advancing Austrian force under the Archduke Charles. When Napoleon arrived, he immediately perceived and retrieved his own error but allowed Berthier to take the blame for the initial dispersion, knowing that his loyal chief of staff could be counted on to keep silent and protect the emperor's image.

As prince of the minuscule Neuchâtel (population 48,000), Berthier took his administrative duties and the welfare of his subjects quite seriously. Although much too busy ever to visit his principality, he methodically read the fiscal, military, and commercial reports and proposals of his deputy governor. He thus approved the enactment of several beneficial reforms: a rationalized fiscal administration, a better administration of forests and the postal service, the organization of a gendarmerie, the construction of badly needed highways, and the abolition of common pasture. Yet in obedience to the emperor, Berthier had to watch his subjects sacrificed to Napoleon's imperial policies, their young men in the battalion (977 men) of Neuchâtel killed in Spain and Russia, their industries (printed calico, lace, and watchmaking) ruined by Napoleon's stonewall protectionism operating for France's benefit.

A victim of Napoleon's ill-tempered outbursts during the Russian campaign, Berthier still indefatigably performed his duties, bound by the bonds of discipline to a commander in chief who had long ago forfeited his friendship. After Napoleon's first abdication and the installation of a new French government, Berthier as an obedient French officer led the marshals to meet the returning Louis XVIII at Compiègne. Loyal to his oath to the new Bourbon government, he declined to answer Napoleon's appeal to join him on his return from Elba. Some think that if he had been at Waterloo, Napoleon would have won. He had died, however, in Germany, on 1 June 1815, of a fall from a window.

J. Courvoisier, *Le maréchal Berthier et sa principauté de Neuchâtel (1806-1814)* (Neuchâtel, n.d.); R. P. Dunn-Pattison, *Napoleon's Marshals* (London, 1909); A. Vachee, *Napoleon at Work* (London, 1914); S. J. Watson, *By Command of the Emperor: A Life of Marshal Berthier* (London, 1957).

Harold T. Parker

Related entries: ADMINISTRATION, MILITARY; ARMY, FRENCH; MINISTERS OF NAPOLEON.

BERTHIER, CESAR, COUNT (1765–1848). Younger brother of Napoleon's famous chief of staff, he served Joseph Bonaparte in Naples. Later he served as governor of the Ionian Islands, of Piedmont, and finally of Corsica which he surrendered to the British in 1814. He was inspector general of infantry under the Restoration.

Related entry: BERTHIER, A.

BERTHOLLET, CLAUDE-LOUIS, COUNT (1748–1822). Under Napoleon, Berthollet was the doyen of French chemists by reason of his seniority, his achievements in both theoretical and applied chemistry, and his genial encouragement of young scientists. Like Paracelsus, Boerhave, and Black, he came to chemistry through medicine. Born in Talloire, a town near Annecy, he came of a French family living in Savoy which since the seventeenth century had furnished members to the local *noblesse de robe*. After studying at the *collèges* of Annecy and Chambéry, he won a medical degree at the University of Turin in 1768. The influence of a near-compatriot, Jean-Robert Tronchin, secured him the favor of the duke of Orleans in Paris and the use of a private laboratory in the Palais Royal. Studying chemistry under Pierre Macquer, Berthollet wrote a series of papers that in 1780 won him membership in the Royal Academy of Sciences. In the lively debate over the relative merits of Georg Stahl's older phlogiston theory of combustion and Antoine de Lavoisier's newer model, Berthollet eventually sided with Lavoisier and collaborated with him and with A.-F. de Fourcroy and L.-B. Guyton de Morveau in the preparation of a *Méthode de nomenclature chimique* (1787) that incorporated the new approach. Aware of certain illogicalities and inconsistencies in Lavoisier's theory, however, Berthollet sought another option that would synthesize the older traditional chemistry and the new. He found the synthesis in his theory of affinity, which he presented comprehensively in his *Essai de statique chimique* (1803), and explained chemical interactions in terms of the attractive forces in molecules.

His membership in the Royal Academy of Science obliged him to appraise allegedly novel industrial projects for their originality and value, an obligation that drew him into practical work. As chemical consultant to successive government agencies (the Bureau of Commerce under the Bourbon monarchy, the Committee of Public Safety and the Commission of Agriculture and Manufactures during the Revolution, and Napoleon himself, who referred to him as "my chemist"), he prepared appraisals that were distinguished for their application of up-to-date scientific theory to technological and industrial problems. En route he discovered (1785) that using chlorine in bleaching of fabrics shortened the process from several months to a few hours. His report (1786), with Gaspard Monge and Alexis Vandermonde, that "the difference between the various kinds of iron and steel is mainly determined by the amount of carbon they contain" (Clow and Clow, 1952) led directly to improvements of manufacture. His standard treatise (1791, 1804) on dyeing lifted an empirical process to one based on scientific principles. Simultaneously, he experimented with beets and other vegetables as sources of sugar to replace that barred by the Continental System.

His relations with Napoleon were friendly and close. He recruited the scientists who accompanied the Egyptian expedition and shared in the military dangers of the venture. Bonaparte appointed him senator, officer of the Legion of Honor, and count. With the emoluments of those posts, Berthollet built a private physical and chemical laboratory at his mansion at Arcueil and in cooperation with P. S. de Laplace supported a private discussion group, the Society of Arcueil, whose older and younger scientists could read papers to each other and have them published.

A. Clow and N. Clow, *The Chemical Revolution: A Contribution to Social Technology* (London, 1952); M. Crosland, *The Society of Arcueil: A View of French Science at the Time of Napoleon* (Cambridge, Mass., 1967); H. T. Parker, *The Bureau of Commerce in 1781* (Durham, N.C., 1979), and "French Administrators and French Scientists during the Old Regime and the Early Years of the Revolution," in R. Herr and H. T. Parker, eds., *Ideas in History* (Chicago, 1965); J. G. Smith, *The Origins and Early Development of the Heavy Chemical Industry in France* (Oxford, 1979).

Harold T. Parker

Related entries: CHAPTAL; EGYPTIAN CAMPAIGN; INSTITUT NATIONAL DES SCIENCES ET DES ARTS; SCIENCE.

BERTRAND, HENRI-GATIEN, COMTE (1773–1844),general, with Napoleon on St. Helena. Graduated second lieutenant from the excellent engineering school of Mézières in 1793, Bertrand advanced through the ranks as engineering officer in the army of the Republic and later the Empire. Napoleon made him general in chief of the engineers of the Grand Army in 1809, governor of the Illyrian provinces (1811–12), and on the death of Géraud Duroc grand marshal of the palace (1813). As loyal servitor responsible for the day-to-day running of the imperial household, he accompanied Napoleon to Elba and to St. Helena, where he and his wife remained until Napoleon's death. His journal of St. Helena, not deciphered until after World War II, is a capital source for the last years of Napoleon.

H. G. Bertrand, *Cahiers de Sainte-Hélène*, ed. P. F. de Langle, 3 vols. (Paris, 1949–1951), and *Commentaires*, 6 vols. (Paris, 1867).

Harold T. Parker

Related entries: GOURGAUD; LAS CASES; MONTHOLON; ST. HELENA.

BESSIERES, JEAN-BAPTISTE (1768-1813), duc d'Istrie, marshal of France. Of the bourgeoisie, born at Prayssac, near Cahors, the son of a surgeon, Bessières had intended to study medicine, but the Revolution changed his plans. He entered the army through the National Guard. He fought in the Pyrenees (1793), under Bonaparte in Italy (1796–97), and in Egypt (1798–99). He returned to Paris with Napoleon and commanded troops during the coup d'état of 18 Brumaire.

In 1800 he headed the Consular Guard at Marengo and was promoted to general. In 1804 he became one of the original marshals of the Empire. Usually in command of the Imperial Guard, Bessières fought in the campaigns of Austerlitz and Jena-Auerstädt-Friedland (1805–7). In 1808 in Spain, he won the Battle of Medina del Rio Seco, which cleared the way to Madrid for Joseph Bonaparte. He marched with Napoleon to Madrid in 1808 and in 1809 was at Wagram. In 1810–11 he was back in Spain commanding an army on the northern coast, which backed up André Masséna and Louis Marmont.

Bessières was the complete Gascon, despite his bourgeois beginnings. He was brave to a fault but neither a tactician nor strategist. In 1811, responding to an emergency call by Masséna for reinforcements (to meet Wellington's assault) Bessières appeared, after much delay, leading not an army but 1,500 cavalry. "I come," he shouted, "like a French knight, at the head of a small band of heroes."

In 1812 Bessières fought in Russia and during the retreat saved Napoleon from capture by Cossacks. In 1813 at Weissenfels, Bessières was mortally wounded by cannonball and died, only the second marshal to be killed in battle. Napoleon wept.

A. Bessières, *Le Maréchal Bessières* (Paris, 1952); A. Rabel, *Le Maréchal Bessières* (Paris, 1903).

Related entries: ARMY, FRENCH; MARSHALS.

BEUGNOT, JACQUES-CLAUDE (1761–1835), one of Napoleon's great prefects, the organizer of the kingdom of Westphalia, and administrator of the Grand Duchy of Berg. Count Beugnot was an *avocat* to the Paris Parlement, and both he and his father had held administrative positions under the monarchy. When France was divided into departments in 1790, he assumed a procurership in the Aube, the department that elected him to the Legislative Assembly the following year. Beugnot earned the reputation of being one of the Assembly's most distinguished orators, and it was he who made the motion demanding an explanation from Austria for the Treaty of Pillnitz. But he also defended refractory priests and supported the movement to condemn Jean-Louis Carra and Jean-Paul Marat before he dropped out of sight after August 10. In October 1792 he was arrested and detained first in the Conciergerie, where he was with Clavière when he stabbed himself, and then in La Force. Beugnot himself survived, however, and was freed after 9 Thermidor.

He stayed aloof from politics until 18 Brumaire when he came forth as a close adviser to Lucien Bonaparte, then minister of interior. Beugnot's role was to organize prefectures, and he personally administered Rouen (Seine-Inférieure) until 1806. The responsible job he performed as Napoleon's prefect for six years led to his promotion to the Council of State, where he participated in the discussion of the decree granting legal recognition of the Jewish religion. Subsequently, due to his administrative and fiscal abilities, Napoleon charged Beugnot with organizing the new Kingdom of Westphalia for King Jerome (12 March 1807). Then in 1808 Beugnot headed the administration of the Grand Duchy of Berg and Cleves. For these yeoman services, he was awarded the title of count of the empire (24 February 1810) and grade of officer of the Legion of Honor.

After the Battle of Leipzig, Beugnot participated in the retreat across the Rhine, arriving in France on 10 November 1813. During the unstable era that followed, he held a succession of posts: Napoleon's prefect of the Nord, minister of interior of the provisional government, Louis XVIII's director of police and minister of the navy, director of posts in the Second Restoration, and finally deputy of the Haute-Marne in the *Chambre introuvable*. His publications mirror his interests during his years in the chamber, primarily in religious issues, fiscality, and promoting freedom of the press.

Beugnot retired in 1824 and entered the Chamber of Peers on 27 January 1830. Louis-Philippe made him a director of manufacturers and commerce. He died at Bagneux, near Paris, 24 June 1835. Besides his admirable service, he is remembered for his lively sense of humor and political quips.

E. Dejean, *Un préfet du Consulat, Jacques-Claude Beugnot* (Paris, 1907); J. Regnier, *Les Préfets du Consulat et de l'Empire* (Paris, 1907); C. Schmidt, *Le grand-duché de Berg (1806–1813)* (Paris, 1905); E. A. Whitcomb, "Napoleon's Prefects," *AHR* 79 (1974); H. N. Williams, *The Women Bonapartes* (New York, 1909).

June K. Burton

Related entries: BERG, GRAND DUCHY OF; WESTPHALIA, KINGDOM OF.

BIGNON, LOUIS-PIERRE-EDOUARD, BARON (1771–1841), French diplomat, resident in Duchy of Warsaw, author of first extended history of Napoleonic period. Bignon entered the diplomatic corps in 1797 and served in minor posts in Switzerland, Milan, and Berlin. He was appointed minister to Hesse-Cassel in 1805 and to Baden in 1808. Napoleon made him baron of the empire and in 1810 resident in Warsaw, removing him before the Russian Campaign of 1812 to flatter the Poles with an ambassador, the Abbé de Pradt. Bignon went to Vilnius (Vilna) as imperial commissioner to the Provisional Government of Lithuania. After the Russian disaster, however, he returned to his post in Warsaw, where he remained until French troops withdrew. In 1815, he returned to serve Napoleon as under-secretary of foreign affairs.

Under the Restoration, Bignon served in the Chamber of Deputies (1817–30). After the Revolution of 1830, he was appointed by Louis-Philippe as interim minister of foreign affairs, then of education. He was reelected to the Chamber of Deputies in 1831 and 1834 and in 1838 joined the Chamber of Peers. Napoleon, at St. Helena, had meanwhile commissioned him to write the history of his reign. The result was *L'histoire de France depuis 18 brumaire jusqu'à la paix de Tilsit*, 6 vols. (1828–30) and *Histoire de France sous Napoléon depuis la paix de Tilsit jusqu'en 1812*, 4 vols. (1838). Volumes 11 through 14, completing the history, were edited by his son-in-law, Alfred-Auguste Ernouf (1847–50), and published after Bignon's death.

L.-P.-E. Bignon, *Souvenirs d'un diplomate. La Pologne (1811–1813)*, 2 vols. (Paris, 1864); A.-A. Ernouf, *Notice sur M. Bignon* (Paris, 1842); M. Handelsman, *Instrukcye i depesze Rezydentów Francuskich w Warszawie 1807–1813*, 2 vols. (Cracow, 1914); M. Handelsman, ed., *Dyplomaci napoléonscy w Warszawie* (Warsaw, 1914); A. Skałkowski, *O cześć imienia polskiego*, (Lwów, 1908); E. Whitcomb, *Napoleon's Diplomatic Service* (Chapel Hill, N.C., 1979).

John Stanley

Related entries: DIPLOMACY; FOREIGN POLICY; WARSAW, DUCHY OF.

BIGOT DE PREAMENEU, FELIX-JULIEN (1747–1825), minister of ecclesiastical affairs, 1808–14. Born at Rennes, son of a lawyer who practiced before the parlement of that town, Bigot in his youth felt a religious vocation and entered a seminary; however, he soon renounced study for the priesthood and took up study of the law. He was admitted in 1767 to practice before the parlement of Rennes and in 1778 before that of Paris. Although with the coming of the Revolution he embraced the cause of liberal reform, he was always moderate in his opinions and his expression of them. Elected from Paris to the Legislative Assembly, he defended royalty when it was unpopular to do so. After the deposition of Louis XVI, he withdrew from public life and reappeared only after 18 Brumaire. Bonaparte appointed him member of the Council of State, president of its section on legislation, and member of the commission that drafted the Civil Code. He was minister of ecclesiastical affairs from 1808 to 1814, during which time Napoleon became increasingly domineering, arbitrary, and tyrannical in his dealings with Pope Pius VII. Bigot, it seems, tried to exercise a moderating influence on Napoleon, but never failed to implement the imperious commands of his master.

A. Latreille, *L'église catholique et la Révolution française*, vol. 2: *L'ère napoléonienne et la crise européenne (1800–1815)* (Paris, 1970); P. F. Pinaud, ''L'administration des Cultes de 1800 a 1815,'' *RIN* 132 (1976); P. Sagnac, *La législation civile de la Révolution française (1789–1804)* (Paris, 1898).

Harold T. Parker

Related entries: LAW, CODES OF; PORTALIS.

BILDERDIJK, WILLEM (1756–1831), Dutch poet and supporter of King Louis Bonaparte in Holland. Bilderdijk became a francophile in the period prior to the French Revolution because he favored reform. He was somewhat taken aback, however, by the policies of the Batavian Republic, created in 1795 by the intervention of French armies. He welcomed the creation of the Kingdom of Holland (1806) enthusiastically, however, and wrote a lengthy ode to Napoleon and personally welcomed Louis Bonaparte to the Hague. He subsequently accepted appointment to and then the presidency of the Royal Dutch Institute created by King Louis. With the return of the House of Orange in 1813, he was forced into retirement. In 1817, he was able to return to teaching at Leiden. He continued to write almost to the day of his death.

Related entry: HOLLAND, KINGDOM OF.

BLAKE, DON JOACHIM (1760?–1827), Spanish general, son of an Irish merchant who had emigrated to Malaga. A professional soldier from 1773 forward, he became a hero of the rebellion against the French in 1808. He continued to fight against the forces of King Joseph Bonaparte until captured at Valencia in 1812, after commanding a brilliant defense. Dispatched as a prisoner of war to France, he returned after the fall of Napoleon in 1814 only to find that he was too liberal for the Bourbon king, Ferdinand VII. His latter years were spent in exile from Madrid.

Related entries: PENINSULAR WAR; SPAIN, KINGDOM OF.

BLANCHARD, MARIE-MADELEINE-SOPHIE ARMANT (1778–1819), foremost balloonist during the First Empire and wife of the aeronaut Jean-Pierre Blanchard. Marie-Madeleine Blanchard was born of Protestant parents in the village of Trois-Canons, near La Rochelle, 25 March 1778. She married Jean-Pierre Blanchard in 1797 when she was nineteen and he was forty-four. Blanchard was one of the early balloonists, having made his premier flight 2 March 1784. He became famous on 7 January 1785 for being the first, with Dr. John Jeffries of Boston, to cross the English Channel in a balloon. After a five-year period in the United States, which included the renowned ascension in Philadelphia on 9 January 1793, he and Marie-Madeleine Armant were married, soon after the death of his first wife, Victoire Lebrun.

After eight childless years of marriage, Blanchard began to accompany her husband on his flights, with their first joint ascension taking place on 27 December 1804 at Marseille. During the next two years, she gave ten performances, six of them solo flights. On 15 January 1809 Jean-Pierre Blanchard was giving a command performance before Louis Bonaparte, king of Holland, when he suffered a stroke, from which he never recovered. He left many debts, and Mme. Blanchard decided to repay them by becoming the first professional woman aeronaut.

She had made fifteen flights when, in 1810, the Imperial Guard asked her to perform at a celebration for the marriage of Napoleon and Marie-Louise. She established her reputation by giving a flawless performance on that important occasion. In March 1811 she was asked to announce the birth of Napoleon's son to the regions around Paris and, while the 101 salvos were still being counted, she was already ascending with the news that the long-awaited heir had been born. In June 1811, Napoleon and Marie-Louise gave an elaborate party at St. Cloud to celebrate the momentous birth, and Mme. Blanchard was asked to be part of the entertainment. For this occasion she created a new spectacle, which became her trademark. After she entered the balloon's basket and the tethering lines had been loosened, a fireworks star was hooked to the bottom of the basket by a thirty-foot chain and a slow-burning fuse was lit. The fuse was calculated to ignite the star when she was high enough that the crowd, estimated at 300,000 on that evening, could clearly see her. The star then showered sparkles for several minutes, brilliantly illuminating the night sky. On 15 August 1811 she again performed for their majesties at the Festival of the Emperor in Milan.

From 1812 to 1819 she was at the peak of her popularity, making ascensions with almost biweekly regularity at Tivoli Gardens. Tivoli was one of the more than 200 new public gardens that, prior to the Revolution, had been the private estates of the aristocracy and had now become parks, dance halls, and places of amusement. Tivoli, on the rue de Clichy near the present-day l'Eglise de la Trinité, had been known as the Boutin Folly. On summer evenings there were horseraces, games, circus acts, often a balloon ascension, and usually fireworks to end the entertainment. Mme. Blanchard had perfected her profession to an art. She had the basket, or nascelle, made of wicker and smaller than usual so that it was light enough for her to manage by herself when necessary. Less weight also made it possible to use less hydrogen in the envelope and still have enough lift. She cut expenses in every way, especially in the beginning when she was paying off her husband's debts, and succeeded in making ballooning a lucrative business.

Despite her perfection, it was not without hazards. Occasionally if there was not sufficient hydrogen to lift both her and the nascelle, she removed the latter and ascended sitting on the ring beneath the envelope. The wind was unpredictable; at times it was so strong that she was thrown against buildings and roofs. She was twice dragged into rivers and on another occasion spent the night tangled in a tree when the wind swept her into mountains far from her destination. Because of her courage and the excellence of her performances, she became very popular throughout Europe, giving performances in Italy, Germany, and the Netherlands. Her popularity was such that, even though she was associated with the First Empire, Louis XVIII named her the "official aeronaut of the Restoration." She was killed on 6 July 1819 at the end of a Tivoli performance, her sixty-seventh ascension. The small envelope she used was necessarily filled to capacity with hydrogen to produce enough lift, and as she rose the expanding gas had to be vented to avoid bursting the balloon. It is speculated that on the night of her death, the valve was not completely closed and that she passed a lighted wick through the trail of gas, igniting it. The balloon burst into flames and descended rapidly. The iron ring holding the basket caught on a chimney, tipping the basket and dumping her onto a roof where she slid to the street.

Archives Nationales, Series F^{1c}III Seine 25, *Journal de Paris* (1805–19); *Le Moniteur Universel* (1805–19); M. Poterlet, *Notice sur Mme. Blanchard, Aéronaute* (Paris, 1819).

Rachel R. Schneider

BLÜCHER VON WAHLSTATT, GEBHARD LEBERECHT (1742–1819), Prussian field marshal, prince. Eager to soldier, Blücher at age fourteen enlisted in the Swedish army at the beginning of the Seven Years War (1756) and four years later transferred to the Prussian army. Insulted by not being promoted, he left the service in 1773. In 1778, he was reinstated and participated in the campaigns against Holland, fought the French in 1793–94, and was promoted to brigadier general.

Chafing from military inactivity after the Treaty of Basel (1795) and soon convinced of the inevitability of a clash with Napoleon, Blücher in 1805 recommended universal conscription and became one of the leaders of the war party in Prussia. His conduct in 1806 at Auerstädt was one of the few bright spots in that disastrous engagement.

After the Treaty of Tilsit, he became military governor of Pomerania and strongly supported Prussian reforms. In 1808, he was ill and depressed, but he revived with the news of the Spanish insurrection. He worked for joint action with the Austrians in 1809, but his hopes were dashed.

In 1813, at age seventy, Blücher was placed in command of the Silesian army, which, though the smallest, became the most active of the armies in the field against Napoleon. After the Battle of Leipzig, he continued to press for an aggressive strategy and the invasion of France, where his performance was a heavy factor in Allied victory. After Napoleon's abdication, he received a tumultuous welcome in England, where Oxford University conferred an honorary degree on him. With Napoleon's return from Elba, Blücher was placed in command of the Prussian forces in Belgium. Defeated by Napoleon at Ligny, he nevertheless arrived at Waterloo to save the day for the duke of Wellington.

The most popular troop commander of the War of Liberation, Blücher was respected and adored by his men for his courage and willingness to share with them glory and hardships alike. Frequently throwing caution to the winds and almost invariably selecting the boldest of the contingency plans prepared for him by his chiefs of staff, he was one of the few who early realized that only audacious warfare would succeed in defeating Napoleon. He was consistent in his suspicion of Napoleon and adamant in his determination to defeat him.

W. Görlitz, *Fürst Blücher von Wahlstatt* (1940); E. F. Henderson, *Blücher and the Uprising of Prussia against Napoleon 1806–15* (1911); R. Parkinson, *The Hussar General: the Life of Blücher, Man of Waterloo* (1975); K. A. Varnhagen von Ense, *Fürst Blücher von Wahlstatt* (1912); W. von Unger, *Blücher*, 2 vols. (1907–8).

Peter W. Becker

Related entries: FRANCE, CAMPAIGN OF; GERMAN WAR OF LIBERATION; JENA-AUERSTÄDT-FRIEDLAND CAMPAIGN; PRUSSIA, KINGDOM OF; WAGRAM CAMPAIGN; WATERLOO CAMPAIGN.

BONALD, LOUIS-GABRIEL-AMBROISE, VICOMTE DE (1754–1840), a leading conservative theorist. Bonald emigrated in 1791, joined the army of the prince of Condé, and settled in Heidelberg. There he wrote his *Théorie du pouvoir politique et religieux* (1796). He returned to France under the Directory and continued to write his conservative treatises: *Essai analytique sur les lois naturelles de l'ordre social* (1800) and *Législation primitive* (1802). As a result of his friendship with Louis de Fontanes, he was appointed counsellor of the Imperial University. During the Restoration he sat in the Chamber of Deputies from 1815 to 1822. Catholic Christian in viewpoint, he found the will of God to be revealed in the Bible and in the immemorial traditions of the people. For France the traditional and hence divine institution was the monarchy, whose king was dutifully served by his nobility and obeyed by his subjects under the sovereignty of God.

Harold T. Parker

Related entries: INSTITUT NATIONAL DES SCIENCES ET DES ARTS; LITERATURE.

BONAPARTE (originally Buonaparte), Corsican family of Napoleon I, emperor of the French. Napoleon changed the Italian name in 1796, when he took command of his first army, to give it a French ring. The family traced its lineage to a Florentine noble of the twelfth century. Gabriele, the first Corsican Buonaparte, had come from Sarzano to Ajaccio in 1567 and was in the service of Genoa, which owned the island. His descendants continued to serve in the government, judiciary, and clergy but were never professional soldiers.

Carlo Buonaparte (1746–85), Napoleon's father, fought under Pasquale Paoli for independence from Genoa, but France, under Louis XV, bought the island and crushed the revolt (1769). Carlo accepted French amnesty, made himself useful to the royal governor, the count de Marbeuf, and converted his Italian genealogical patent into the French title of count. Handsome and elegant, with a law degree from Pisa, Carlo became a prosecutor in the royal courts, was in the Corsican delegation at the coronation of Louis XVI, and was elected to the Corsican estates. His standing was such that Louis XVI financed the education of Napoleon and his sister Elisa, and the church that of Joseph and Lucien. Carlo died prematurely in 1785 at age thirty-nine, probably of stomach cancer (which later killed Napoleon).

Letizia Ramolino (1750–1836), Napoleon's mother, was also of a family originally Florentine and Corsican since about 1550. She married Carlo Buonaparte at thirteen and bore him twelve children, of whom Napoleon was the second of eight to survive. "My mother was as beautiful as love," Napoleon said later. As Madame Mère de l'Empereur, her grace and immense dignity impressed the courts of Europe. As a young wife, she had been spartan and very religious and had ruled the family and ordered finances for Carlo. After his death, she reared the four youngest children with the help of Joseph, her eldest son, who became a lawyer and began a political career. In 1793, Paoli's revolt forced her and the family to flee to France. Under the Empire, as "Madame Mère" (of the emperor), she maintained frugal habits and a devotion to her church. Her laconic "If it lasts..." is famous. In 1814, she visited Napoleon on Elba and returned to Paris during the Hundred Days. In 1815 she retired to Rome, where she died in 1836. She outlived Napoleon by fifteen years. (See genealogical chart).

L. de Brotonne, *Les Bonaparte et leurs alliances* (Paris, 1893); A. Decaus, *Laetizia, mère de l'empereur* (Paris, 1959); W. Geer, *Napoleon and His Family*, 3 vols. (New York, 1927–29); F. Markham, *The Bonapartes* (New York, 1975); F. Masson, *Napoleon et sa famille,* 13 vols. (Paris, 1900–19); G. Sirjean, *Encyclopedie généalogique des maisons souveraines*, vol. 7: *Les Bonaparte* (Paris, 1961); M. Stirling, *Madame Letizia* (New York, 1961).

Related entries: BONAPARTE entries; NAPOLEON I.

BONAPARTE, CAROLINE (1782–1839), queen of Naples; Napoleon's youngest sister. She was ambitious, amoral, and intelligent, as well as pretty. Charles-Maurice de Talleyrand admired her as a fellow spirit. Born at Ajaccio, she married (1800) General Joachim Murat, later marshal, grand duke of Berg, and king of Naples (1808–15). They had two sons and two daughters. She saw to it that Napoleon made her joint ruler of Naples so that she would succeed her

BONAPARTE FAMILY

CARLO BUONAPARTE (1746-85) = LETIZIA RAMOLINO (1750-1836)

JOSEPH	NAPOLEON	LUCIEN	ELISA	LOUIS	PAULINE	CAROLINE	JEROME
(Giuseppe) 1768–1844	(Napoleone) 1769–1821	(Lucciano) 1775–1840	(Marie-Anna) 1777–1820	(Luigi) 1778–1846	(Maria-Paola) 1780–1825	(Marie-Annunziata) 1782–1839	(Girolamo) 1784–1860
m. 1794 Julie Clary (1771–1844)	m. 1796 Josephine de Beauharnais (1763–1814) divorced 1809	m. 1794 Catherine Boyer (1773–1800)	m. 1797 Felice Pasquale Bacciochi (1762–1841)	m. 1802 Hortense de Beauharnais (1783–1837)	m. 1797 Victor Emmanuel Leclerc (1772–1802)	m. 1800 Joachim Murat (1771–1815)	m. 1803 Elizabeth Patterson (1785–1879) marriage annulled 1804
2 daughters		4 children	5 children	3 sons	1 son (d. 1804)	4 children	1 child
	m. 1810 Marie-Louise, Archduchess of Austria (1791–1847)	m. 1803 Alexandrine Jouberthon (1778–1855)			m. 1803 Prince Camillo Borghese (1775–1832)		m. 1807 Princess Catherine of Württemberg (1783–1835)
	1 son	10 children					3 children

husband if he were killed in battle. As queen, she encouraged Murat to be nationalistic, while posing to Napoleon as the protector of French interests. In the interest of her sons, she schemed unsuccessfully (1809) to have Murat named Napoleon's successor if the emperor, then fighting in Spain, was killed. In 1810 she opposed Napoleon's Austrian marriage since she preferred he have no natural heir. In 1813–14 she led her conscience-stricken husband to betray Napoleon and save their crown. In 1815, however, she could not restrain Murat from attacking the Allies in Italy, and he lost their kingdom. She surrendered, with her children, and was taken to Vienna. Murat offered his services to Napoleon for what became the Waterloo campaign. He was ignored and returned to Naples, but the people did not rally to him, and he was shot. Caroline married a Neapolitan general, Francesco Macdonald, and lived in Austria and Italy until her death in Florence in 1839.

H. Cole, *The Betrayers: Joachim and Caroline Murat* (London, 1972); J. P. Garnier, *Murat* (Paris, 1961); J. Turquan, *Caroline Murat* (Paris, 1899); M. Weiner, *The Parvenu Princesses* (London, 1964).

Related entries: BERG, GRAND DUCHY OF; BONAPARTE; HUNDRED DAYS, THE; MURAT, J.; NAPLES, KINGDOM OF; VIENNA, CONGRESS OF.

BONAPARTE, CHARLES (CARLO), Napoleon's father. See BONAPARTE.

BONAPARTE, ELISA (1777–1820), grand Duchess of Tuscany. Born at Ajaccio, she was educated at St. Cyr, France's most exclusive girls' school under the Old Regime. In 1797, before Napoleon was more than a famous general, she married Felix Bacciochi, a fellow Corsican. Napoleon as emperor made them prince and princess of Piombino (1805) and Lucca (1806). In addition, Elisa was made grand duchess of Tuscany (1809). Much like Napoleon in temperament and intelligent, she was an enlightened ruler and drew to her court in Florence the intellectual elite of Italy. The Academy *La Crusca* prospered and produced a Tuscan dictionary, which was widely used to standardize Italian. In 1813–14, her states were occupied by the turncoat Marshal Joachim Murat, but he could not save her crown, and she retired in Italy. She died at Sant' Andrea, near Trieste, in 1820.

P. Fleuriot de Langle, *Elisa, soeur de l'empereur* (Paris, 1947); E. Rodocanachi, *Elisa Bacciochi en Italie* (Paris, 1900).

Related entries: BONAPARTE; ITALY, KINGDOM OF; NAPLES, KINGDOM OF; NAPOLEON I.

BONAPARTE, ELIZABETH PATTERSON (1785–1879), first wife of Jerome Bonaparte, Napoleon's youngest brother, later king of Westphalia. Elizabeth Patterson was the daughter of an American millionaire, William Patterson of Baltimore. A blonde beauty of eighteen, Betsy met Jerome Bonaparte when he visited Baltimore in 1803 without leave from the French navy. After a whirlwind courtship, she converted to Roman Catholicism, and they were married by the ranking prelate in the United States, Bishop Carroll, brother of Carroll of Carrollton, signer of the Declaration of Independence. The marriage was legal in lay and canon law, and the pope later refused Napoleon's request to annul it.

In 1805 Napoleon forced Jerome to return to Europe by cutting off his income but prevented Betsy from landing with him on the Continent. Betsy went to England, where she gave birth to their son, Jerome, but Napoleon detained her husband, and she returned to Baltimore. Napoleon had her marriage annulled by the archbishop of Paris. Jerome then married Catherine of Württemberg (1807), and the two became king and queen of Westphalia.

Throughout her life Elizabeth Patterson's obsession was to have her son recognized as a Bonaparte. Under the Second Empire, she was finally granted her wish by Napoleon III. Jerome, however, preferred to be an American. Elizabeth's grandson, Jerome Napoleon Bonaparte, was a Union officer in the U.S. Civil War. Her great-grandson, Charles Joseph Bonaparte, was successively secretary of the navy and U.S. attorney general under Theodore Roosevelt.

A. Desmond, *Elizabeth Patterson* (New York, 1958); A. Marcel-Paon, "Le mariage de Jérôme Bonaparte et Elizabeth Patterson," *REN* 36 (1933); B. Melchior-Bonnet, "Jerome et 'La Belle de Baltimore,' " *Nouvelle Revue des Deux Mondes* 34 (1979).

Related entries: BONAPARTE, JEROME; CATHERINE OF WÜRTTEMBERG; WESTPHALIA, KINGDOM OF.

BONAPARTE, JEROME (1784–1860), youngest brother of Napoleon, king of Westphalia. Jerome was given princely advantages by Napoleon, fifteen years his senior. Schooled at Juilly, he entered the navy in 1800, saw action in the Caribbean, and established records for high living and indiscipline. In July 1803, without leave, he visited the United States. There he married Elizabeth Patterson, daughter of a Baltimore millionaire, who gave him a son. In 1805, however, Napoleon had the marriage annulled (though not by the pope, who refused). Jerome returned to the French navy, as ordered (1806), then served as a general in the campaign of 1806–7. In 1807 he was made king of Westphalia and married to Princess Catherine of Württemberg. As king (1807–13), though his court was notorious for wild parties ("A Roman circus!" wrote Goethe), Jerome proved an able executive and was not unpopular. Napoleon gave Jerome a constitution, and he respected it insofar as he could. His Parliament took a real part in affairs until 1810, when it balked at Napoleon's financial demands. He abolished feudalism and serfdom, installed the Code Napoléon, and reorganized the administration and courts. Moreover, all this was done by German ministers, officials, and judges. (Their work had its impact; the first revolutions in Germany after 1815 were in areas formerly Westphalian.) In education, two universities had to be closed, but Göttingen, Halle, and Marburg had their curricula expanded. The public schools kept operating, and German and French scholars were brought together in the Societät der Wissenschaften.

Jerome took pride in his army, which benefited from Hessian military tradition but owed much to his administration and personal leadership. It fought well and also helped to break down provincialism and prejudices. Prussians, Hanoverians, and Hessians—Lutherans, Calvinists, Catholics, and Jews—all served together. Jerome's reputation as a ne'er-do-well was strengthened when, it appeared, Napoleon sent him home from the Russian campaign. Actually he had left the army rather than defer to Marshal L.-N. Davout. His loyalty to Napoleon remained strong. He continued to furnish Napoleon with troops and supplies until Westphalia was overrun in 1813. Still, Jerome got no chance to redeem himself as a commander. In 1815, however, Napoleon gave him a division at Waterloo, and he distinguished himself. Though wounded, he was one of the last to leave the field. After Napoleon's abdication, he was given refuge by the king of Württemberg, his wife's father. However, Jerome and Catherine soon settled in Trieste, where she had children, two boys and a girl. (When she died in 1833, he married Giustina Pecori, a widow.) Under Napoleon III, Jerome was a marshal and senator. He died 24 June 1860 and was buried near Napoleon in Les Invalides. Elizabeth Patterson's son, Jerome Napoleon, founded a distinguished American family. Jerome's second son by Catherine of Württemberg, Napoleon Joseph, became the Bonaparte pretender on the death in 1879 of the son of Napoleon III. His grandson, the great-grandson of King Jerome, is the Bonaparte pretender today.

C. de Westphalie Bonaparte, *Correspondance inédite avec sa famille et celle du roi Jérôme* (Paris, 1893); A. du Casse, *Les rois frères de Napoléon Ier* (Paris, 1883); O. Connelly, *Napoleon's Satellite Kingdoms* (New York, 1965); F. M. Kircheisen, *Jovial King* (London, 1932); A. Kleinschmidt, *Geschichte des Königreichs Westfalen* (Gotha, 1893); F. Markham, *The Bonapartes* (New York, 1975); F. von Schlossberger, *Briefwechsel der Königin Katharina und des Königs Jerome von Westfalen*, 3 vols. (Stuttgart, 1886–87).

Related entries: BONAPARTE; CATHERINE OF WÜRTTEMBERG; RUSSIAN CAMPAIGN; WATERLOO CAMPAIGN; WESTPHALIA, KINGDOM OF.

BONAPARTE, JOSEPH (originally, Giuseppe Buonaparte) (1768–1844), elder brother of Napoleon, king of Naples, and later king of Spain. Talented and charming, he succeeded in civil offices but failed as a military commander and was too benevolent to please Napoleon, who judged him "too good to be a king." Schooled at Autun and with a law degree from Pisa, he was rising in Corsican politics when the revolt of Paoli (1793) forced the Bonapartes to flee to France. In 1794 he married Julie Clary, daughter of a rich merchant of Marseille. They had two daughters, Zenaide and Charlotte.

Between 1796 and 1799, as Napoleon's star rose, Joseph was a legislator and diplomat. In 1799, he rallied the intelligentsia to Napoleon during the coup d'état of Brumaire. Under the Consulate he was chief negotiator of the treaties of Lunéville and Amiens and the Concordat of 1801. In 1804 he opposed the Empire

(Napoleon called him "Prince Egalité") but went along. As king of Naples (1806–08), he promulgated a constitution, abolished feudalism, reformed the administration, founded schools, and began modernizing the economy. In Spain (1808–13), however, the nation rebelled, and the French had to battle continuously against Spanish armies, guerrillas, and Wellington's Anglo-Portuguese forces. Joseph labored at enlightened monarchy but had to be a soldier-king. In 1813, he was disastrously defeated by Wellington at Vitoria and lost his kingdom. Nevertheless, in 1814, Napoleon made Joseph the head of government at Paris while he fought the Allies.

In 1815, Joseph returned to serve during the Hundred Days, and then fled to the United States. For seventeen years he was a popular citizen of Bordentown, New Jersey, and Philadelphia. He made friends in high places, was elected to the American Philosophical Society, and was received by President Andrew Jackson. In 1832, he left for Europe to promote the cause of Napoleon II, but the prince died before he arrived. Banned from France, he settled in England. In 1841, he joined his wife in Italy; he died in Florence in 1844. In 1862, Napoleon III had Joseph's remains removed to the Invalides, in Paris, where they rest near those of Napoleon. He left incomplete memoirs, a novel (*Moina*, 1799), essays in defense of Napoleon, and hundreds of letters, most of which have been published.

M. Artola, *Los Origines de la España contemporanea*, 2 vols. (Madrid, 1959), and *Los Afrancesados* (Madrid, 1953); O. Connelly, *The Gentle Bonaparte* (New York, 1968); G. Girod de l'Ain, *Joseph Bonaparte* (Paris, 1970); G. H. Lovett, *Napoleon and the Birth of Modern Spain*, 2 vols. (New York, 1965); J. Mercader Riba, *Jose Bonaparte, rey d'España* (Barcelona, 1971); J. Rambaud, *Naples sous Joseph Bonaparte* (Paris, 1911).

Related entries: BONAPARTE; NAPLES, KINGDOM OF; PENINSULAR WAR; SPAIN, KINGDOM OF.

BONAPARTE, LETIZIA, Napoleon's mother. See BONAPARTE.

BONAPARTE, LOUIS (1778–1846), third brother of Napoleon, born at Ajaccio, Corsica, king of Holland. Louis first became a soldier and accompanied Napoleon as an aide in Italy and Egypt (1796–99) but left service because of ill health. In 1802, he married Hortense de Beauharnais, Josephine's beautiful daughter, who gave him three sons. (Two died young. The third became Napoleon III, 1852–70.) Under the Empire he became (1804) grand constable and commander of reserves (1805). Made king of Holland (1806–10), he enraged Napoleon by becoming a Dutch nationalist. He formed a Dutch ministry and governed with his Parliament, upholding traditional rights and religious freedom, and giving great attention to domestic needs. Among other things, he improved flood control and organized a national health program. At the same time he refused to decree military conscription or institute the Code Napoléon (both were "un-Dutch") or to enforce the Continental System, which he called "immoral." In 1810 Napoleon forced Louis to abdicate and annexed Holland to France. Louis found asylum in Austria but offered his services to his brother in 1813, only to be ignored. In 1815 he sat out the Hundred Days in Rome. Thereafter he lived in Italy until his death at Leghorn in 1846. He left a novel, *Marie, ou les peines d'amour* (1812), books of poetry, history, and the *Documents historiques et reflexions sur le gouvernement de la Hollande*, 3 vols. (1820), which infuriated Napoleon, dying at Saint Helena.

H. T. Colenbrander, *Konig Lodewijk*, 2 pts. (Utrecht, 1909–10); O. Connelly, *Napoleon's Satellite Kingdoms* (New York, 1965); A. Duboscq, *Louis Bonaparte en Hollande* (Paris, 1911); S. Schama, *Patriots and Liberators: Revolution in the Netherlands, 1780–1815* (New York, 1977); C. H. E. de Wit, *Het Onstaan van Het Moderne Nederland, 1780–1848 en zijn Geschiedschrijving* (Oirsbeek, 1978).

Related entries: BEAUHARNAIS, H.; BONAPARTE; HOLLAND, KINGDOM OF.

BONAPARTE, LUCIEN (1775–1840), prince of Canino; younger brother of Napoleon. Lucien was the most willful of the Bonapartes and the only brother whom Napoleon could not control. He was the only member of the immediate family whom Napoleon did not grant a title. (His title came from the pope.) Born at Ajaccio, he attended the Collège d'Autun and entered seminary. When the French Revolution began, however, he returned to Corsica, where he became Pasquale Paoli's secretary but soon alienated him by becoming a fervent Jacobin. In 1793 he denounced Paoli before French Jacobin clubs, which resulted in the family's proscription and flight from Corsica. In 1794 he married Christine Boyer, an innkeeper's daughter, over the family's objections. An outspoken disciple of Maximilien Robespierre, he was imprisoned briefly after the Terrorist's fall (1794). In 1798 he was elected to the Council of Five Hundred and in 1799 was president when Napoleon returned from Egypt. He shortly became the hero of the coup d'état of 18 Brumaire (9 November 1799), which put Napoleon in power. It was Lucien who rallied the troops after Bonaparte, trying to speak in the Five Hundred, either fainted or was knocked unconscious in a crush of deputies. The Republic he had hoped to strengthen and save, he shortly realized, was dead. This fact, his *Mémoires* make clear, bothered him all his life.

As minister of interior (1799) he initiated the systematic collection of statistics, but as ambassador to Spain (1800), he was accused of venality, clashed with Napoleon, and left the government. A widower in 1803, he married Alexandrine de Bleschamp Jouberthon, a lady of uncertain reputation. Napoleon demanded he renounce her, but instead he went off to Rome with her, their child, and both their children by previous marriages. Lucien received no rank in the imperial family (1804), though Napoleon offered him the crown of Italy in 1805 and in 1807 (probably) that of Spain, on condition he divorce Mme. Jouberthon, which Lucien refused to do. They lived on and produced ten children on an estate acquired from the pope, who also made Lucien prince of Canino. Napoleon's power oppressed them, however, and in 1809 they debarked with the family for the United States but were captured at sea by the Royal Navy and taken to England, where they lived until 1814. Lucien was watched but not imprisoned, and British propaganda made it seem he was there voluntarily, which disturbed him. In 1815, when Napoleon returned from Elba, Lucien rushed to Paris to serve him. It was Lucien who prompted the Senate to proclaim Napoleon's son emperor after the second abdication (though to no avail). He spent the rest of his life in Italy and died at Viterbo in 1840. He left many writings, including a book on the Hundred Days and unfinished *Mémoires*.

A.H. Atteridge, *Napoleon's Brothers* (London, 1909); L. Bonaparte, "Lucien Bonaparte et sa soeur Elisa, lettres intimes inédites," ed. Paul Marmottan, *REN* 33 (1931), and *Mémoires secrets sur la vie privée, publique et litteraire de Lucien Bonaparte*, 2 vols. (Paris, 1816); T. Iung (Jung), *Lucien Bonaparte et ses mémoires, 1775–1840*, 3 vols. (Paris, 1882–83); A. Ollivier, *Le Dix-huit Brumaire* (Paris, 1959); F. Pietri, *Lucien Bonaparte* (Paris, 1939).

Related entries: ADMINISTRATION; BONAPARTE; BRUMAIRE, COUP OF 18, YEAR VIII; HUNDRED DAYS, THE; MINISTERS OF NAPOLEON; STATISTICS.

BONAPARTE, NAPOLEON. See NAPOLEON I.

BONAPARTE, PAULINE (1780–1825), French princess and duchess of Guastalla; Napoleon's most beautiful sister, who seemed to enjoy the scandal she created, as when she admitted posing for Antonio Canova's nude sculpture, *Venus Reclining*. She lacked the ambition of her sisters, Elisa and Caroline, but excelled them in wit and compassion. Napoleon had her marry, at sixteen, General Charles Leclerc (her behavior was embarrassing the first consul). She went with Leclerc on the expedition to Santo Domingo, where he died of fever (1802). Their son's death in 1804 almost destroyed her. Meanwhile she had married (1803) Prince Camillo Borghese, an Italian nobleman, from whom she soon separated. In 1806, Napoleon gave her the Duchy of Guastalla in northern Italy, but she did not live there until after she clashed with the new empress, Marie-Louise, in 1810. (She was the only Bonaparte who got on with Josephine.) In 1814 she was the only sister to visit Napoleon on Elba. After 1815 she lived in Italy, where her health began to deteriorate. Her kindness persisted, however. She became the advocate of her American nephew, Jerome Bonaparte, son of her brother Jerome and Elizabeth Patterson of Baltimore, and persuaded her mother, living in Rome, to receive him. She died in Florence in 1825, probably of stomach cancer, which had killed Napoleon in 1821.

J. Kuhn, *Pauline Bonaparte* (Paris, 1963); F. Markham, *The Bonapartes* (London, 1975); B. Nabonne, *Pauline Bonaparte* (Paris, 1964).

Related entries: BONAPARTE; CANOVA; HAITI; JOSEPHINE; MARIE-LOUISE VON HABSBURG.

BORGHESE, CAMILLE (1775–1832), Italian prince, second husband of Pauline Bonaparte. Napoleon gave him nominal governance of the Piedmontese departments of France, which gave him an income but no power.
Related entry: BONAPARTE, P.

BORODINO, BATTLE OF (7 September 1812), climactic battle before Moscow during Napoleon's Russian campaign. The Grande Armée, ultimately 611,000 strong, crossed the Niemen on 24–25 June 1812, with the French emperor in command of the main column of 250,000 men. The Russians, however, under Generals Mikhail Barclay de Tolly and Piotr Bagration (total forces initially 170,000) refused battle until they united at Smolensk (17 August), over 400 miles into Russia, then retreated after two days of sparring. The Russians made for Moscow, with Napoleon, led by Joachim Murat's cavalry, in hot pursuit, losing many men to exhaustion.

At Borodino, the Russians suddenly turned to fight. General Kutuzov, now supreme commander of Russian forces, took command of Barclay's and Bagration's armies. His forces almost matched Napoleon's—now reduced to 130,000—and he was determined to bleed the French. At dawn on 7 September 1812, Napoleon found the Russians in a line beyond Borodino, their positions stretching for four miles along a line of hills, anchored in the north by a great redoubt (an improvised fort) and other fortifications devised by Bagration. Napoleon sent Joseph Poniatowski's corps against the Russian south (left) flank, backed by Murat's reserve cavalry; Eugène de Beauharnais commanded the French left, which attacked Borodino and the great redoubt; M. Ney and L.-N. Davout assailed the Russian center. Poniatowski could not turn the Russian flank, however, and the battle evolved into a bludgeoning match. Eugène captured Borodino and, after bloody fighting, the great redoubt, which changed hands several times. The French center also gradually gained ground, with Murat leading charges again and again against the Russian center and left. As night came on, the Russians had been driven almost a mile from their original positions, but their forces were still intact, and they occupied another line of hills. Murat loudly demanded that Napoleon commit the Guard. But J.-B. Bessières, commanding the Guard cavalry, said softly, "Sire, you are 800 leagues from Paris." The emperor decided not to gamble and ordered only artillery preparation for the next day. Under cover of darkness, however, Kutuzov withdrew.

French casualties were about 30,000 including 10 generals killed and 39 others badly wounded. The Russians had left 45,000 dead and wounded on the battlefield. Napoleon claimed the victory, but so did Kutuzov. He had reduced Napoleon's forces by one-quarter; he had plenty of reserves in the hinterland; the French had only replacements who had to be marched 700 to 1,000 miles. He could supply himself easily; they could not. Kutuzov did not care if Napoleon announced another triumph. He had made his reputation (or recovered it after Austerlitz, which Alexander chose to blame on him) against the Turks and had won repeatedly by making them come to him, stretching their supply lines, depleting their forces. He was doing the same with the French. He declined to defend Moscow, ruling that the important thing was to save the Russian army.

When the czar heard that Moscow had fallen, he wept, but he left Kutuzov, "The Fox of the North," in command. It was a wise decision. After delaying too long in the ancient former Russian capital, Napoleon began a retreat (19 October 1812) during which the Russian winter and Kutuzov's forces destroyed his army. It was the first step toward his downfall.

D. Chandler, *The Campaigns of Napoleon* (New York, 1966); C. von Clausewitz, *The Campaign of 1812 in Russia* (London, 1843); C. Duffy, *Borodino and the War of 1812* (London, 1972); M. de Fezensac, *The Russian Campaign, 1812*, trans. Lee B. Kennett (Athens, Ga., 1970); E. R. Holmes, *Borodino, 1812* (London, 1971); A. Palmer, *Napoleon in Russia,* (New York, 1967); comte de Ségur, *Histoire de Napoléon et la grande armée pendant l'année 1812,* 2 vols. (Paris, 1825); and *Napoleon's Russian Campaign*, trans. and abr. J. D. Townsend, (New York, 1958); E. Tarlé, *La campagne de Russie, 1812* (Paris, 1950).

Related entries: ARMY, FRENCH; ARMY, RUSSIAN; BAGRATION; BARCLAY DE TOLLY; BEAUHARNAIS, E.; DAVOUT; KUTUZOV; MURAT, J.; NAPOLEON I; NEY; PONIATOWSKI; RUSSIAN CAMPAIGN.

BOULOGNE CAMPS, built after hostilities resumed with Great Britain in 1803 upon the collapse of the Peace of Amiens (1802) to train the Army of England, an invasion force of 167,000 men. The largest camp was at Boulogne (near Moulin-Herbert), close by Napoleon's headquarters at the Château de Pont de Briques. Other camps were constructed north and south along the Channel. It was here that the basic organization of the Napoleonic field army was developed, with the corps as the basic unit of all arms. The army never invaded England, nor did it even try. Instead, Napoleon ordered it to Germany in August 1805, where it was tested—with triumphant results—in the Ulm-Austerlitz Campaign. See ARMY, FRENCH; AUSTERLITZ, CAMPAIGN.

BOURGEOISIE, the middle class. See ECONOMY, FRENCH; NOTABLES; SOCIETY.

BOURRIENNE, LOUIS-ANTOINE-FAUVELET (1769–1834), Bonaparte's schoolmate at Brienne and, much later, from April 1797 to October 1802, his private secretary. He had many qualities to recommend him: he could write nearly as fast as Bonaparte dictated, had a prodigious memory, and knew several languages. But he lacked that passion for anonymity that a private secretary should have, and he loved money. In Paris he and his wife began to entertain beyond their means, and he used his position to engage in shady financial transactions. Bonaparte dismissed him in 1802 but gave him another chance in 1805 as minister plenipotentiary to Hamburg. Again, however, Bourrienne corruptly used his post, this time to sell exceptions to Napoleon's Continental Blockade decrees. Toward the end of his life, in the late 1820s, on the verge of insanity, he sold a few notes and his name to a publisher who brought out a ten-volume *Mémoires* under Bourrienne's name but composed for the most part by professional writers. The work is entertaining but extremely unreliable.

C.-F. de Méneval, *Mémoires*, 3 vols. (Paris, 1893–94); J. Tulard, *Bibliographie critique des mémoires sur le Consulat et l'Empire* (Geneva, 1971).

Harold T. Parker

Related entries: FAIN; MENEVAL; NAPOLEON, DAILY ROUND.

BOYEN, HERMANN LUDWIG VON (1771–1848), Prussian minister of war. Orphaned at age six, Boyen joined the army in 1787. He also attended Königsberg University, where Immanuel Kant deeply influenced him. He came to believe that justice, honor, and morality could be realized best in the army because there traditions could be overcome through discipline. Indoctrination, he hoped, could effect better relations between officers and men and between army and people. He also condemned the exemptions of cantonal recruitment and expressed support for universal conscription. These views induced General Gerhard von Scharnhorst, soon Prussian chief of staff in 1803, to make Captain Boyen a corresponding member of his Military Society.

Boyen was severely wounded at Auerstädt in 1806. In 1808 Scharnhorst had him assigned to the Military Reorganization Commission and in 1810 to the War Department. In 1811, Scharnhorst, August N. von Gneisenau, and Boyen were the moving spirits of the Prussian patriots who vainly tried to persuade King Friedrich Wilhelm III to join Russia against Napoleon. When the king refused, Colonel Boyen resigned and joined the Russian army.

Boyen returned to Prussia in 1813. He was named minister of war in 1814 and pursued the objectives of the Prussian reformers. The Army Law of 1814 was, however, the only reform of the Stein era carried to completion. Nevertheless, it subsequently became the model for Germany and Europe. The law incorporated the principle of universal conscription—with service limited to one year for those who qualified by minimal education and property ownership—and created a National Guard. Because of the law's potential for democratization, Boyen was fiercely opposed by reactionaries and was forced to resign in 1819. Under King Friedrich Wilhelm IV, Boyen served once more as minister of war from 1841 until 1847, when he fought to preserve the independence of the National Guard.

H. Boyen, *Erinnerungen aus dem Leben des Generalfeldmarschalls Hermann von Boyen 1771–1813*, ed. F. Nippold, 3 vols (1889–90); F. Meinecke, *Das Leben des Generalfeldmarschalls Hermann von Boyen*, 2 vols (1896–99); J. Ullrich, *Generalfeldmarschall Hermann von Boyen* (1936).

Peter W. Becker

Related entries: FRIEDRICH WILHELM III; GNEISENAU; HARDENBERG; JENA-AUERSTÄDT, BATTLES OF; PRUSSIA, KINGDOM OF; SCHARNHORST; STEIN.

BRAUNSCHWEIG. See BRUNSWICK.

BRAZIL. Napoleon's conquest of Portugal in 1807 sent the Portuguese royal family flying to Rio de Janeiro, ferried by the British navy. With them came 10,000 courtiers and perhaps another 15,000 loyalists, a shock to the primitive colonial city. Rio had over 100,000 people but lacked central water and sewage systems and had no housing suitable for royalty, princes, and grandees. But the refugees arrived with millions in gold. At first the court imposed no financial burdens, spending lavishly.

It was the same with the regent, Dom João, who built palaces, streets, and the public facilities Rio lacked. Eventually he had to levy taxes, but he had an unusual talent for making the affluent classes pay their share—whether natives (Creoles) or recent arrivals from Portugal (Peninsulars). The regent also built an army, but since he had brought very few troops with him, it was manned by Brazilians and not perceived as threatening by the natives. Commerce boomed as a result of the regent's policy of opening ports to the British. Industry grew, especially in textiles, as did agriculture. Communications were improved. The Bank of Rio de Janeiro was created. The regent also created the Royal Institute, Royal Library, a naval academy, and colleges of medicine.

The regent, who became King João VI in 1816, liked Brazil and remained in Rio even after Napoleon's fall. The representatives at the Congress of Vienna felt that this was improper, but he propitiated them by declaring himself emperor of the United Kingdom of Portugal and Brazil. He returned to Lisbon in 1820 when Portugese revolutionaries demanded it. In 1822 his son and regent in Rio, Dom Pedro, probably encouraged by his father, declared Brazil independent and himself emperor. Sixty years later, the Republic of Brazil was formed almost as effortlessly.

Related entries: PENINSULAR WAR; PORTUGUESE CAMPAIGNS.

BRIENNE (Brienne Le Château), town in the Aube department; location of military school attended by Napoleon, 1779–84. It was one of twelve officers' schools established by the crown in the eighteenth century to augment L'Ecole Militaire in Paris. Better students from these schools were allowed to finish their education at the more prestigious Paris academy. This privilege was accorded Bonaparte (Buonaparte, as he then spelled it), who attended L'Ecole Militaire in 1784–1785.

Related entry: NAPOLEON I.

BRIENNE, BATTLE OF. See FRANCE, CAMPAIGN OF.

BRITAIN. See GREAT BRITAIN.

BRITISH ARMY. See ARMY, BRITISH.

BRITISH NAVY. See NAVY, BRITISH.

BRUEYS, D'AIGAILLIERS, FRANCOIS-PAUL (1753–1798), French admiral who commanded the fleet that took Napoleon's expedition to Egypt in 1798. His fleet was attacked by a British fleet under Admiral Horatio Nelson at the mouth of the Nile on 1 August 1798 and, in effect, destroyed. Brueys died in the battle.
Related entries: EGYPTIAN CAMPAIGN; NAVY, FRENCH; NILE, BATTLE OF.

BRUMAIRE, COUP OF 18, YEAR VIII. The events of 18–19 Brumaire Year VIII (9–10 November 1799) overthrew the Directory and put Bonaparte in power. The abbé Sieyès, who disliked the resurgent neo-Jacobins and thought only a new government could obviate the Directory's frequent legislative-executive impasses, initiated the plotting. He and his shadow, Roger Ducos, resigned as directors, and Paul Barras resigned under duress. With only two members of the executive, the Directory could no longer function. For the coup to succeed, a military man was needed, and Sieyès' first choice had been killed. Bonaparte, however, arrived from Egypt and was named commander of troops in Paris.

The conspirators had the support of a majority in the Council of Ancients (upper legislative house), which voted on 18 Brumaire to move the government to St. Cloud so as to avoid action by the Paris populace. On the next day, the Council of Five Hundred (lower house) proved recalcitrant. The real hero among the conspirators was Lucien Bonaparte, president of the Five Hundred. When Napoleon, severely heckled in the Five Hundred, fainted (or was knocked senseless), Lucien rallied the troops, dramatically promising to kill his brother if Napoleon betrayed the Republic. The councils were dispersed.

To give the events an appearance of legality, the two councils were reestablished. Each council chose twenty-five members to serve as a commission to draft a new constitution. The Ancients also named Napoleon, Sieyès, and Ducos provisional consuls. The public generally received news of the coup apathetically.

D. Goodspeed, *Napoleon's Eighty Days* (Boston, 1965); L. Madelin, *L'ascension de Bonaparte*, vol. 2 of *Histoire du consulat et de l'empire* (Paris, 1937); J. B. Morton, *Brumaire: The Rise of Bonaparte* (London, 1948).

Robert B. Holtman

Related entries: BONAPARTE, LUCIEN; CONSTITUTIONS; SIEYES.

BRUNE, GUILLAUME-MARIE-ANNE (1763–1815), marshal of France. Of the bourgeoisie, son of a lawyer, he entered the army through the National Guard in 1789. In 1793 he was a general. He fought in the first Italian campaign under Bonaparte (1796–97) and was promoted to major general. In 1799 he commanded a French army in Holland, which forced the withdrawal of the duke of York, and in 1800 he replaced André Masséna in Italy. In 1802 he was dispatched as ambassador to Turkey and while in Constantinople was appointed marshal of France (1804).

Despite his honors, Brune remained a republican. After 1807 Napoleon sent him into retirement and never recalled him. He welcomed the Bourbons in 1814 but during the Hundred Days volunteered to serve Napoleon and was given an interior command and made a peer of France. He was assassinated by fanatic royalists in 1815.

P. P. Vermeil de Couchard, *Etudes historiques sur le maréchal Brune* (Paris, 1918).

Jesse Scott

Related entries: ARMY, FRENCH; MARSHALS OF THE EMPIRE.

BRUNSWICK, CHARLES WILLIAM FERDINAND, DUKE OF (Ger. Braunschweig, Karl Wilhelm Ferdinand) (1735–1806), Prussian general who was commander of Prussian forces during the Jena campaign (1806). Brunswick, who served as a junior officer during the Seven Years War (1756–63), rose to senior command in the Prussian army prior to the French Revolution. He led a joint Austro-Prussian-*émigré* force in the Valmy campaign (July–October 1792) in an unsuccessful attempt to suppress the French Revolutionary regime. His issuance of the Brunswick Manifesto on 11 July 1792, which threatened the Parisians if they harmed their royal family, drove Paris to frenzy and led to the downfall of Louis XVI. He commanded Austro-Prussian troops at the successful siege of Mainz (March-July 1793). A prominent member of the anti-French faction at the Prussian court of Frederick William III, he undertook a diplomatic mission to St. Petersburg in early 1806 to prepare groundwork for a Russo-Prussian military alliance. Mortally wounded at Auerstädt (14 October 1806), he died at Ottensen (10 November 1806).

John Stine

Related entries: JENA-AUERSTÄDT, BATTLES OF; JENA-AUERSTÄDT-FRIEDLAND CAMPAIGN.

BRUNSWICK, FREDERICK WILLIAM, DUKE OF (Ger. Braunschweig, Friedrich Wilhelm) (1771–1815), son of Charles William Ferdinand, duke of Brunswick; Prussian general in Napoleonic Wars; duke (1813–15). To aid Austria during the Wagram campaign (1809) he founded a free-corps, the "Black Troop" (also called the "Black Hussars"), with which he invaded Saxony, captured Dresden (June 1809) and gave the Westphalian Army under Jerome Bonaparte some anxious moments. Following the Austrian armistice with Napoleon (July 1809), Brunswick and his followers fought their way across Germany to the North Sea whence they were evacuated to England by the British Navy. Brunswick's exploits passed into folk-legend and contributed to the awakening of the German spirit of resistance to the French. Brunswick served under Wellington in Spain (1811–12); commanded a Brunswick corps (1813–15)—under Wellington in the Waterloo campaign—but was killed in the preliminary battle of Quatre Bras (16 June 1815).

H. Lachouque, *Waterloo* (London, 1975), and *Waterloo, 1815* (Paris, 1972); J. Lawford, *Napoleon: The Last Campaigns, 1813-1815* (London, 1977); J. P. Sutherland, *Men of Waterloo* (Englewood Cliffs, N.J., 1966); J. Tranie and J. C. Carmignian, *Napoléon et l'Autriche: La Campagne de 1809: d'Après les Notes et Documents du Commandant Henry Lachouque* (Paris, 1979); J. Weller, *Wellington at Waterloo* (New York, 1964).

John Stine

Related entries: BRUNSWICK, C.; WAGRAM CAMPAIGN; WATERLOO; WESTPHALIA.

BUCHAREST, TREATY OF (28 May 1812), by which Russia made peace with the Ottoman Empire. Although Russia gained only the province of Bessarabia, the treaty had a more important consequence. Because it freed 60,000 troops for use in the north, it aided the czar's preparation to meet Napoleon's invasion force. See also RUSSIAN CAMPAIGN.

BULLETINS OF THE GRANDE ARMEE, the most grandiose of Napoleon's proclamations to his troops. The bulletins, actually written for the French people, were printed in the *Moniteur* and published in the provinces by prefects, mayors, and clergy. The first was issued from Germany at the beginning of the 1805 campaign. The bulletins were numbered consecutively for each campaign. In them Napoleon justified his wars, celebrated the exploits of his troops, designated the heroes of his battles, foisted his version of history on the French, and built his legend. It is ironic that the most famous of the bulletins is the twenty-ninth (6 December 1812), issued during the retreat from Russia, which ended "His majesty's health has never been better."

Related entries: ARMY, FRENCH; LEGEND, NAPOLEONIC; PROPAGANDA.

BÜLOW, HANS VON. See WESTPHALIA, KINGDOM OF; WESTPHALIA, KINGDOM OF: MINISTERS.

BÜLOW VON DENNEWITZ, FRIEDRICH WILHELM, COUNT (1755–1816), Prussian general. As did so many other officers of his generation, Bülow joined the Prussian army in 1768 at the early age of eighteen. He was talented, well educated, of artistic bent, and a difficult subordinate. As captain and aide de camp to Prince Louis Ferdinand, he took part in the campaigns against France in 1793–94. In 1807 he was in the battles at Waltersdorf and Danzig and, after Napoleon's victory in the campaign, was appointed as member of the commission to investigate the events of 1806–7. He served briefly in Pomerania as deputy to G. L. Blücher von Wahlstatt, but their personalities clashed. In 1808 Bülow was promoted to brigadier general and in 1812 made interim governor of East Prussia. In 1813, when Prussia went against Napoleon, Bülow was made a major general and performed well. He won victories at Luckau and Grossbeeren over Nicolas Oudinot and at Dennewitz over Michel Ney, thus denying Berlin to the French. He was awarded the Grand Cross of the Iron Cross and made a count. In 1814 Bülow fought under the command of Blücher against Napoleon, and afterward was made general of the infantry and commander in chief in East and

West Prussia. At Waterloo he distinguished himself as commander of Fourth Army Corps at Plancenoit.

V. von Ense, *Leben des Generals Bülow von Dennewitz* (1853); K. Lehmann, *Die Rettung Berlins im Jahre 1813* (1934); K. von Priesdorff, *Soldatisches Führertum*, vol. 3 (1938).

Joachim Niemeyer

Related entries: FRANCE, CAMPAIGN OF; GERMAN WAR OF LIBERATION; JENA-AUERSTÄDT-FRIEDLAND CAMPAIGN; WATERLOO CAMPAIGN.

BUREAUCRACY. See ADMINISTRATION.

BUSSACO, BATTLE OF (27 September 1810), fought between the French army of Portugal commanded by Marshal André Masséna, prince d'Essling, and the Anglo-Portuguese army of Arthur Wellesley, Viscount Wellington, during the third invasion of Portugal. Wellington posted his army of some 60,000 men on the Serra de Bussaco north of Coimbra to halt Masséna's army of 65,000 men in order to spare Estremadura from devastation and, if possible, turn back the French. Utilizing the topographical advantages of the 1,800-foot high Serra and the ancient walled convent of Bussaco, Wellington interspersed British and Portuguese units in strategic positions along the ridge and reverse of the mountain to await Masséna's attack. Without adequate reconnaissance, Masséna ordered General Jean Reynier to attack up the mountain from San Antonio de Contaro while Marshal Michel Ney advanced directly below the convent. The Allies were able to follow the movements and progress of the French from the top of the Serra and reinforce areas that would come under attack. Although the French succeeded in reaching the top of the mountain, they were met by reinforced units of British and Portuguese troops and driven back down the Serra after bitter hand-to-hand fighting. The French suffered 4,480 casualties; the British and Portuguese lost 626 men. Rather than mount a second attack at Bussaco, Masséna turned the mountain by the Boialvo road, forcing Wellington to resume his retreat toward Lisbon. Bussaco was not decisive in itself, but it weakened French confidence and resolve while demonstrating to the British that the men of the newly formed Portuguese army were courageous, effective, and worthy companions in arms.

G. L. Chambers, *Bussaco: Wellington's Battlefield Illustrated* (London, 1910); M. Glover, *Wellington's Peninsular Victories. Bussaco, Salamanca, Vitoria, Nivelle.* (London, 1963); D. D. Horward, *The Battle of Bussaco: Massena vs. Wellington* (Tallahassee, 1965); S. J. da Luz Soriano, *Historia de Guerra Civil e do estabelecimento do governo parlamentar em Portugal, comprehendendo a historia diplomatica, militar e politica d'este reino deste 1777 ate 1834*, 15 vols. (Lisbon, 1866–1892).

Donald D. Horward

Related entries: PENINSULAR WAR; PORTUGUESE CAMPAIGNS.

C

CABANIS, PIERRE-JEAN-GEORGES (1757–1808), articulate supporter of the Brumaire coup, senator, and *idéologue* leader. In the history of ideas, the physician Cabanis' principal contribution is a monistic (though not mechanically materialist) psychophysiology (*Rapports du physique et du moral de l'homme*, 1802). He led in the analysis of sensations and ideas in the Institut as a member (after the reorganization of 1803) of the Class of French Language and Literature. In politics, Cabanis was a republican moderate elected from the Seine in 1798 to the Council of Five Hundred during the Floréal coup. Hostile to neo-Jacobinism, he became linked to the abbé Sieyès' revisionist projects in 1799 and wrote an address to the nation on 19 Brumaire. Several weeks later, he provided a detailed apologia for the new constitution, including the summary, ''All is done for the people and in their name; nothing by the people or under their ill-considered dictation.''

As an anticlerical and liberal, Cabanis opposed the special tribunals of 1801, the Concordat, the purge of the Tribunate, the reorganization of secondary education (1802), and the reform of the Institut (1803). In the Senate, he was absent from votes approving the life consulate and the proclamation of the empire. Yet Cabanis never openly rejected Bonaparte and thus was hardly an opposition leader.

Archives de l'Institut. Bibliothèque historique de la ville de Paris; P. Cabanis, *Oeuvres philosophiques de Cabanis*, ed. Lehec and Cazeneuve (Paris, 1956), and *Rapports du physique et du moral de l'homme* (1844, reprint Geneva, 1980); G. Gusdorf, *La conscience révolutionnaire, les idéologues* (Paris, 1978); S. Moravia, *Il pensiero degli idéologues* (Florence, 1974); M. S. Staum, *Cabanis: Enlightenment and Medical Philosophy in the French Revolution* (Princeton, 1980).

Martin Staum

Related entries: IDEOLOGUES; INSTITUT NATIONAL DES SCIENCES ET DES ARTS; LITERATURE; SCIENCE.

CABARRUS, FRANCISCO DE. See *AFRANCESADOS*; PENINSULAR WAR; SPAIN, KINGDOM OF.

CABARRUS, THERESE. See TALLIEN.

CADASTRE. During the Consulate, Napoleon directed the prefects of departments to begin a survey of landholdings so that taxes could be more equitably levied. Under the Empire, the cadastre was formally undertaken as of 1802 and made uniform by a law of 1807. At the end of the Empire, nevertheless, the cadastre had not been finished for most of France, and land taxes were being assessed according to records of the Old Regime. The systematic survey of properties was continued under the Restoration.
Related entries: FINANCES; STATISTICS.

CADIZ, CONSTITUTION OF, the constitution of 1812, which became a model for revolutionaries in the early nineteenth century. It was written by the Cortes of Cadiz, which expected Ferdinand VII to abide by it when he returned from exile in France. (In fact, Ferdinand ignored the constitution.) The Cadiz constitution declared the abstract sovereignty of the nation; provided for hereditary parliamentary monarchy (Bourbon); established a single-chamber cortes to be elected by universal manhood suffrage and to meet annually; established ministerial responsibility; separated executive, legislative, and judicial powers; and gave the king a three-year suspensive veto.

A. Argüelles, *Examen. . .de la reforma constitucional*, 2 vols. (London, 1835); M. Artola, *Los origines de la España Contemporanea*, 2 vols. (Madrid, 1959); *Constitución politica de la monarquía Española*, in Colección Documental del Fraile, 762, Servico Historico Militar (Madrid); I. Fernandez de Castro, *De las Cortes de Cadiz al Plan de Desarrollo, 1808–1966, Ensayo de Interpretacion Politica de la España Contemporanea*, (Paris, 1968); R. Solis, *El Cadiz de las Cortes*, (Madrid, 1958–69); J. M. Conde de Toreno, *Histoire du soulèvement de la guerre et de la revolution d'Espagne*, 4 vols. (Paris, 1835–36).
Related entries: PENINSULAR WAR; SPAIN, KINGDOM OF.

CADIZ, CORTES OF, the legislative branch of the rebel government of Spain, 1810–12. See CADIZ, CONSTITUTION OF; PENINSULAR WAR; SPAIN, KINGDOM OF.

CADOUDAL, GEORGES (1771–1804), royalist and counterrevolutionary leader in western France. Born near Auray, Brittany, son of a farmer, Cadoudal was sympathetic initially with the Revolution of 1789, but after the Assembly passed legislation hostile to the Catholic church, he became a bitter opponent. He was one of the first to join the Catholic-royalist rebellion in the Vendée and Brittany in 1793. In seven years of battle, he proved himself as a leader of guerrillas (the *Chouannerie*) and fought against every republican regime. Ultimately supported by English money and arms and endorsed from abroad by the comte d'Artois (the future Charles X), Cadoudal became one of the best known of the *émigrés* of the interior.

When Napoleon Bonaparte became first consul, he undertook to put an end to the fighting. In March 1800, he offered Cadoudal a general's commission or 100,000 francs a year if he would abandon political-military activity. Georges fled to England where the comte d'Artois, acting for his brother, the comte de Provence (Louis XVIII), promoted him to lieutenant general. Meanwhile, however, Napoleon had signed the Concordat of 1801 with the pope, and the guerrillas accepted amnesty and laid down their arms.

Royalist efforts then centered on plans to eliminate Bonaparte. In December 1800 the first consul narrowly escaped death when a barrel filled with powder (the "Infernal Machine") exploded a few seconds after his carriage passed en route to the Opera. Pierre de Saint Réjeant and François Carbon, royalist agents working under Cadoudal, were found to be responsible for the crime (though Georges always denied that he had personal knowledge of it). In late 1803 and early 1804, another conspiracy was hatched involving Generals J.-C. Pichegru and (allegedly) J.-V Moreau, Jules and Armand de Polignac, the marquis de Rivière, and Georges Cadoudal. The plan was to kidnap and kill Bonaparte, open the frontiers to royalist and allied invaders, and make Provence king (as Louis XVIII). Joseph Fouché's police had infiltrated the royalist network, however; all were quickly arrested. Cadoudal was executed in June 1804.

Georges Cadoudal's determined resistance to the Revolutionary regime helped keep the idea of monarchy alive in France during the long years of exile. But to those who had profited from the Revolution, he was a symbol of reaction seeking to destroy their gains and restore the special privileges of the nobility and clergy.

Archives du Ministère des Affaires Ĕtrangères: Fonds Bourbon: vols. 626, 627. British Museum: MS. 37866; Archives Nationales: F⁷6261, F⁷6371, F¹ᶜ124; duc de Castries, *La Conspiration de Cadoudal* (Paris, 1963), and *Les hommes de l'émigration* (Paris, 1979).

Vincent Beach

Related entries: ARTOIS; FOUCHE; POLICE, MINISTRY OF GENERAL.

CALDIERO. See ITALIAN CAMPAIGN, FIRST.

CALENDAR, REPUBLICAN, inherited by Napoleon from the Revolution. After his coronation as Emperor he abolished it in favor of the traditional Gregorian calendar, which again took effect on 1 January 1806. In the Revolutionary Calendar the year I began on 22 September 1792 (the "first day of liberty" of the Republic) and ended on 21 September 1793 (although the calendar was not ready for use until the Year II.) Each month had three weeks (*décades*) of ten days each, making 360 days of a 365 or 366 (leap year) day year; the extra five or six days were holidays (*sansculottides*). Each revolutionary month spanned the last days of one conventional month and the first two-thirds of the next; for example, Vendémiaire, the first month of Year II, began on 22 September and ended on 21 October. The months were Vendémiaire (month of fall harvest), Brumaire (of mist), Frimaire (of frost), Nivôse (of snow), Pluviôse (of rain),

Ventôse (of wind), Germinal (of budding), Floréal (of flowering), Prairial (of meadows), Messidor (of summer harvest), Thermidor (of heat), and Fructidor (of ripening). The calendar was one of many moves by the Convention to break the control of the Catholic Church over the rhythms of peoples' lives. It eliminated Sundays, Christmas, Easter, Saints' Days, and the like. Napoleon had it abolished after the signing of the Concordat of 1801 with Pope Pius VII and the creation of the Empire (1804). His reasons were practical. The Revolutionary Calendar did not work. Most people did not understand it, and hated its clumsy (if poetic) dates; it put France out of step with the rest of Europe. See CONVENTION; TERROR, THE.

CAMBACERES, JEAN-JACQUES-REGIS DE (1753–1824), duc de Parme. As second consul during the Consulate and arch-chancellor during the Empire, Cambacérès was given serious duties and performed them well. He was born in Montpellier into the nobility of the robe, his father being councillor (magistrate) of the *cour des comptes* and later mayor of the town. After attending the college d'Aix, Jean-Jacques-Régis too followed a legal career, first as councillor of the tax court at Montpellier and during the Revolution as president of the criminal court of the department of Herault. Known as a partisan of the new ideas, he was elected to the Convention. Distinguished by his ability to work long hours, his analytical intellectual power, his knowledge of the law, his psychological finesse, and his prudence, he avoided taking clear-cut political positions. He voted for death of the king but also for suspension of execution of the sentence. During the Terror he prudently buried himself in the Committee on Legislation, where he prepared his first trial codification of French civil law. Though he reported a series of articles on divorce, testamentary bequests, and other issues, the Convention was far too preoccupied with more urgent business to deal with them.

After the fall of Maximilien Robespierre, Cambacérès emerged from the relative obscurity and safety of the Plain into the limelight of political activity. In the Thermidorian government (1794–95) he became a member and president of the Committee of Public Safety. Under the Directory (1795–99) he was elected to the Council of Ancients where he proposed (in vain) another codification of French civil legislation. In the closing months of the Directory, he served as minister of justice. In the days after 18 Brumaire, the young Bonaparte, ignorant and inexperienced in the intricacies of French politics, found the sage counsel of Cambacérès so reliable and useful that he appointed him second consul.

Although minister of justice only during the first few days of the Consulate and the Hundred Days, Cambacérès was in reality chief of the administration of justice from 1799 to 1814. The ministers of justice in title were actually his subordinates. The new system of courts of the Consulate was organized under his supervision; nominations for judicial posts were presented to him for approval, either by the titular minister (André Abrial) or by Napoleon who had received them from the minister (Claude Régnier, Louis Molé); much of the ministry's business passed through his hands. In the absence of Napoleon he presided over a majority of the meetings of the Council of State. He also presided over the Senate. As one of France's leading jurists, he participated in the final formulation of the Civil Code and next to Bonaparte himself was chiefly responsible for expediting its completion. When Napoleon was away from Paris, he designated Cambacérès officer in charge of the routine of administration, transmitter of dispatches, receiver of imperial orders, and informant on the state of public opinion. Napoleon, wherever he was, still governed but his commands passed through Cambacérès, whom the emperor relied on to do what was prudent. Throughout his career, Cambacérès courageously gave unpleasant but good advice. He opposed the abduction of the duke d'Enghien, the establishment of the Empire, the Spanish venture, the Austrian marriage, and the invasion of Russia. But once a decision was made, he faithfully and intelligently obeyed Napoleon's orders, devised skillful operational maneuvers to implement them, and built his fortune.

At the time of his death in 1824, his estate was worth 7.3 million francs. Modest until the end of the Directory, his fortune rose thanks to his salary as second consul (270,000 francs a year) and then as arch-chancellor (334,000) and to annual supplements, which increased from less than 100,000 in 1808 to over 400,000 in 1813. He divided his investments among real estate, shares in private companies and government obligations, and funds placed with bankers for loans. His career typified the success of the new elite, the *notables* who would control France in the nineteenth century.

L. Bergeron, *France under Napoleon*, trans. R. R. Palmer (Princeton, N.J., 1981); J. Bourdon, *La législation du Consulat et l'Empire*, vol. 1: *La réforme judiciaire de l'an VIII* (Rodez, 1942); J. J. R. de Cambacérès, *Lettres inédites a Napoleon*, ed. J. Tulard, 2 vols. (Paris, 1973); R. Marquant, "La fortune de Cambacérès," *RIN* 127 (1973); P. Sagnac, *La legislation civile de la Révolution française (1789-1804)* (Paris, 1898); J. Thiry, *Jean-Jacques-Régis de Cambacérès, Archichancelier de l'Empire* (Paris, 1935); J. Tulard, "Le Fonctionnement des institutions impériales en l'absence de Napoleon d'après les lettres inédites de Cambacérès," *RHMC* 20 (1973).

Harold T. Parker

Related entries: ABRIAL; LAW, CODES OF; MINISTERS OF NAPOLEON; MOLE; REGNIER; SOCIETY.

CAMPAIGNS. See (in chronological order): ITALIAN CAMPAIGN, FIRST (1796–97); EGYPTIAN CAMPAIGN (1798–99); ITALIAN CAMPAIGN, SECOND (1800); AUSTERLITZ CAMPAIGN (1805); JENA-AUERSTÄDT-FRIEDLAND CAMPAIGN (1806–07); PENINSULAR WAR (1808–13); WAGRAM CAMPAIGN (1809); RUSSIAN CAMPAIGN (1812); GERMAN WAR OF LIBERATION (1813); FRANCE, CAMPAIGN OF (1814); WATERLOO CAMPAIGN (1815). Also see: CORSAIR WAR; NILE, BATTLE OF; TRAFALGAR, BATTLE OF.

CAMPAN, JEANNE-LOUISE-HENRIETTE GENET, MADAME (1752–1822). *Lectrice* to Marie Antoinette, Mme. Campan became a pioneer in female education and an important chronicler of the last days of the Old Regime. She served as *femme de chambre* and confidante of Marie Antoinette until 10 August 1792 when she was separated from the royal family. Heavily in debt after the Terror, she opened a *pensionnat* at Saint-Germain where Hortense de Beauharnais enrolled. In 1807, Napoleon appointed her *surintendante* of Ecouen, where she instituted a program of useful education for the daughters of the Légion d'honneur. The program, which stressed domestic economy, was patterned partially on the curriculum of St. Cyr (under the Old Regime a royal school for noblewomen). During the Restoration, she retired to Mantes, where she died in 1822 after fulfilling her self-appointed obligation to write memoirs about Marie Antoinette.

J.-L.-H. Campan, *Lettres de deux jeunes amies* (Paris, 1811). *De l'éducation* (Paris, 1824), and *Mémoires sur la Vie privée de Marie-Antoinette* (Paris, 1822); B. Scott, "Madam Campan, 1752-1822," *History Today* 23 (October 1973); B. de Marsangy, *Madam Campan à Ecouen* (Paris, 1879).

Susan P. Conner

Related entries: BEAUHARNAIS, H.; LITERATURE; WOMEN; WOMEN, EDUCATION OF.

CAMPO FORMIO, TREATY OF (17 October 1797), between France and Austria. French possession of Belgium and (secretly) the left bank of the Rhine was recognized. A congress, to meet at Rastatt, was to compensate German princes for losses. France gave Austria Venice, Dalmatia, and Istria but retained the (Venetian) Ionian Islands. Austria also got the archbishopric of Salzburg.

Related entries: FOREIGN POLICY.

CANOVA, ANTONIO (1755–1822), Italian sculptor. The most celebrated sculptor in Europe in his era, Canova was twice called by Napoleon to Paris for extended stays and offered a position at court, but he declined. Nevertheless, his busts and statues of Napoleon and his family made him famous. Canova was inspector general of antiquities and fine arts for the Vatican and Academy of San Luca, Rome, and a leading artist and pioneer of the neoclassical style. In retrospect his work seems to express the ambivalent feelings toward the French of his generation in Italy and its nascent nationalism.

Canova worked not only for Napoleon and members of his family (the Murats, Letizia Bonaparte, Cardinal Fesch, Pauline Borghese, Marie-Louise, Caroline Bonaparte, and Elisa Bacciochi) but also Pope Pius VII, Archduke Albert of Austria, the Bourbons of Naples, British and Russian aristocrats, British patrons, and even Americans. Canova's *Tomb for Vittorio Alfieri* (1803–10) in Florence is the first representation of Italy as a nation-state, done fifty years before unification. Canova's contemporaries saw the monument as a political statement, and it inspired nationalism in later generations. He carried on a crusade, largely in vain, for the return of Italy's confiscated art treasures, which Napoleon had sent to the Louvre, speaking up to the emperor as few others dared.

In his lifetime, Canova created eight major funerary monuments, numerous grave stele, many heroic figures, including *Napoleon as Mars the Peacemaker*, busts of the major figures of the age, and many sensuous pieces. His best-known work is his nude statue of Pauline Bonaparte, *Venus Reclining*.

J. Henry, "Antonio Canova, the *Tomb for Vittorio Alfieri* and Early Italian Nationalism" *Nineteenth Century Sculpture* (Bologna, 1980), "Antonio Canova's Funerary Monuments: A Political Journey," *Modern Art* (Mexico City, 1980); and "Canova, the French Imperium and Emerging Italian National Consciousness," *CRE* (1980); G. Pavenello, *L'opéra çompleta del Canova* (Milan, 1976).

Jean Henry

Related entries: ART; ITALY, KINGDOM, OF; SCULPTURE.

CARL AUGUST (1757–1828), grand duke of Saxe-Weimar-Eisenach, 1775–1828; ally of Napoleon, 1806–13. Educated by Christoph Wieland, among others, Carl August at eighteen received the reins of government from his widowed mother. He quickly brought into government Wolfgang von Goethe and J. G. von Herder and, later, Friedrich von Schiller. After some youthful revelry, he furthered the arts and transformed Weimar and the University of Jena into the spiritual and cultural center of Germany. As minister, Goethe strongly contributed to internal reforms in the small principality (100,000 inhabitants). After 1783 Carl August also strove for fundamental reforms in the decrepit Holy Roman Empire, but the French Revolution ended such attempts. In 1792–93 Carl August fought against France as a Prussian general. In 1796, however, he followed the lead of Prussia and withdrew Weimar from the war. Thereafter began Weimar's decade of high classicism characterized by the friendship between Goethe and Schiller, the flowering of the University of Jena, and the significant literary and scholarly publications by such men as J. G. Fichte, F. W. J. von Schelling, and G. W. F. Hegel.

In 1805 Carl August failed to persuade Frederick William of Prussia to join the Russian-Austrian alliance against Napoleon but served as a Prussian general in the ill-considered war of 1806. His state survived the defeat only because of his close connections to Russia, the influence of Queen Luise with Napoleon, and Napoleon's admiration for Goethe and C. M. Wieland. Thereafter expediency compelled him to join the Confederation of the Rhine and profess loyalty to Napoleon. Carl August was nonetheless an opponent of Napoleon who called him Europe's "most troublesome prince." In the War of Liberation (1813), Carl August joined the Allies and obtained from the Congress of Vienna an expansion of his territory, together with the title of grand duke.

In 1816 he gave his state a constitution; it was the first in Germany and granted complete freedom of the press. His liberalism and his sympathies for the great student movement culminating in the Wartburg celebration of 1817 earned him the enmity of the Holy Alliance. The Carlsbad decrees in 1819 prevented him from continuing his progressive policies. In his latter years, he promoted a German customs union. One of his granddaughters, Augusta, was married to the first German emperor, Wilhelm I.

W. Andreas, *Carl August von Weimar. Ein Leben mit Goethe, 1757-1783* (Stuttgart, 1953); H. Tümmler, *Carl August von Weimar. Goethes Freund. Eine vorwiegend politische Biographie* (Stuttgart, 1978); H. Tümmler, ed., *Politischer Briefwechsel des Herzogs/Grossherzogs Carl August von Weimar*, 3 vols. (Stuttgart, 1954, 1958; Göttingen, 1973).

Hans Tümmler

Related entries: CONFEDERATION OF THE RHINE; GERMAN WAR OF LIBERATION; FOREIGN POLICY; JENA-AUERSTÄDT-FRIEDLAND CAMPAIGN.

CARNOT, LAZARE-NICOLAS (1753–1823), soldier, politician, and scientist; the Revolution's "Organizer of Victory," who gave Napoleon his first big opportunity and later served him. Born in the Burgundian town of Nolay, the son of a well-to-do lawyer who assured each of his eighteen children an excellent education, Carnot after preparatory studies enrolled in the army engineering school of Mézières. As a young officer in the Royal Corps of Engineers, he was posted to the garrisons of Calais, Cherbourg, Bethune, and Arras, where he and Maximilien Robespierre became acquainted with each other. Garrison duties afforded leisure for study, and in 1783 he published his mathematical *Essai sur les machines en général*, "the first truly theoretical treatise" on the subject. "His purpose was to specify in a completely general way the optimal conditions for the operation of machines of every sort" (Gillispie, 1971). In its revised version, *Principes fondamentaux de l'équilibre et du mouvement* (1803), the treatise began to affect the treatment of practical problems in the 1820s.

Meanwhile Carnot had been promoted to captain of engineers by 1789 and with the Revolution had entered politics. He was elected to the Legislative Assembly in 1791, to the Convention in 1792, and to the Council of Ancients of the Directory in 1795. A stern patriot, independent of faction, he placed his abilities and his expert knowledge at the service of France. As member of the Convention's Committee of Public Safety from August 1793 to October 1794, he was in effect minister of war. It was he who had Bonaparte promoted from captain to general after the siege of Toulon. He advanced many other young officers and introduced the *levée en masse* (draft). With Robert Lindet as de facto minister of supply and Prieur de la Côte d'Or as minister of munitions, he organized fourteen French armies of over 600,000 men (1 million men on paper) to repel the invading forces of nine enemy countries and then to overrun Belgium, Holland, and the Rhineland. As a director in the five-man executive of the Directory government, he continued to coordinate the French military effort, appointed Bonaparte in 1796 commander in chief of the Army of Italy, and then in 1797 was himself forced by the leftist coup of 18 Fructidor to flee to Switzerland. After 18 Brumaire, Bonaparte appointed him minister of war (2 April

1800). But Carnot discovered that he had little authority; the generals were independent, even impudent, and crucial matters were referred to First Consul Bonaparte or to the *section de la guerre* of the Council of State. After organizing the armies for the Marengo campaign (1800), Carnot resigned. Appointed to the Tribunate, he, an integral republican, defended the Republic, opposed measures that were leading to monarchy (Legion of Honor, the life consulate, the Empire), and with the abolition of the Tribunate in 1807 retired from politics. However, when France and Revolutionary gains were endangered in 1814, he accepted appointment as governor of Antwerp, defended it with heroism and skill, and surrendered its citadel only after the treaty of peace had been signed. In 1815, during the Hundred Days, he served as minister of interior. As a regicide who had rallied to Napoleon in 1815, he was exiled from France by the Bourbon government. He filled out the remainder of his days in Magdeburg, Germany. During intervals of retirement from politics, including his final years, he devoted himself to scientific studies and made distinguished contributions to the physics of work and energy in engineering mechanics (specifically, the problem of machine motion), to related problems in geometry, and to the foundations of calculus.

C. C. Gillispie, "Carnot, Lazare-Nicolas-Marguerite," *Dictionary of Scientific Biography*, ed. C. C. Gillispie, vol. 3 (New York, 1971); and *Lazare Carnot savant* (Princeton, 1971); R. R. Palmer, *Twelve Who Ruled* (Princeton, 1941); M. Reinhard, *Le grand Carnot*, 2 vols. (Paris, 1950, 1952); S. J. Watson, *Carnot* (London, 1954).

Harold T. Parker

Related entries: ARMY, FRENCH; CONSCRIPTION; HUNDRED DAYS, THE; MINISTERS OF NAPOLEON; SCIENCE; TOULON, SIEGE OF.

CASTANOS, DON FRANCISCO XAVIER, COUNT (1753–1852). The commander of Spanish rebel armies against the French from 1808 to 1814, he won over Pierre Dupont at Baylen in 1808. He served under Wellington at Vitoria.
Related entries: BONAPARTE, JOSEPH; DUPONT DE L'ETANG; PENINSULAR WAR; SPAIN, KINGDOM OF.

CASTIGLIONE. See ITALIAN CAMPAIGN, FIRST.

CASTIGLIONE, DUC DE. See AUGEREAU.

CASTLEREAGH, ROBERT STEWART, VISCOUNT (1769-1822), marquess of Londonderry. An Irish peer born in the same year as Napoleon and the duke of Wellington, he was recruited into government by William Pitt. As war minister (1805–9), he showed great acumen; for example, he made Sir Arthur Wellesley (later duke of Wellington) commander of British forces in Portugal. His one great mistake was the Walcheren expedition (1809). As foreign minister (1812–22) he was guided by principles for a peace settlement set down by Pitt in a dispatch to Czar Alexander I in 1804: no discussion of Britain's interpretation of maritime rights; restoration of France to its ancient limits; expansion of Russia in eastern Europe only if balanced by the expansion of Prussia west and north in Germany and of Austria in northern Italy; establishment of barrier states to hem in France (a Kingdom of Holland enlarged by annexation of Belgium, a Prussia placed by Rhineland annexations in a watch on the Rhine, a Kingdom of Sardinia strengthened by the incorporation of Genoa and by backup support of Austria in Lombardy-Venetia). In return for a settlement promising lasting European peace and British security, Britain would return to France, Holland, and Denmark most of their colonies. In realizing these principles through difficult day-to-day negotiations at the peace conferences of Châtillon with Napoleon's plenipotentiary Armand Caulaincourt (February 1814) and of Vienna (1814–15), Castlereagh found he could work with his Austrian counterpart, Clemens von Metternich, and (at Vienna) with Charles-Maurice de Talleyrand-Périgord. The three men shared the same statesmanlike strategy: to protect the long-term interests of their own countries through a balance-of-power settlement that would hold out the prospect of European peace. The durability of the Vienna settlement, which concluded the Napoleonic age, would seem to testify to the soundness of their calculations based on enlightened self-interest.

H. Nicolson, *The Congress of Vienna: A Study in Allied Unity, 1812-1822* (New York, 1946); C. K. Webster, *The Foreign Policy of Castlereagh, 1812-1815* (London, 1931).

Harold T. Parker

Related entries: CAULAINCOURT; GREAT BRITAIN; METTERNICH; PITT, W.; TALLEYRAND-PERIGORD; WALCHEREN, INVASION OF.

CASUALTIES. In 1930 Albert Meynier computed the number of French soldiers killed or missing from 1800 to 1815 at 1 million. More recently, Jacques Houdaille revised the figure downward to something over 900,000, "of which roughly half were killed or died of wounds in hospital, and half were prisoners of war who never returned and were dropped from the army list." No matter which figure is adopted, the loss was a severe excision from an adult male population of approximately 6.9 million and a total population of 30 million. It was especially hard on the generation of young males born from 1791 to 1795. Called up for service twenty years later, they participated in the desperate ventures of 1812 to 1814: the Iberian war, the invasion of Russia, and the campaigns of 1813–14.

L. Bergeron, *France under Napoleon*, trans. R. R. Palmer (Princeton, 1981); J. Houdaille, "Le problème des pertes de guerre," in *La France à l'époque napoléonienne: actes du colloque Napoléon*, special issue, *RHMC* 17 (July–September 1970); A. Meynier, "Une erreur historique: les morts de la Grande Armée et des armées ennemies," *REN* 32 (1930).

Harold T. Parker

Related entry: POPULATION.

CATECHISM, IMPERIAL (1806), devised by Napoleon, with the help of the abbé Bernier, to inculcate in children loyalty and respect for Napoleon and his regime. In 1806 there were a number of catechisms in use in the several dioceses. Bonaparte standardized them in the form of the imperial catechism, an ecclesiastical reform of the newly centralized Church of the Concordat, which served the political ends of the Empire by placing spiritual authority behind the will and person of the emperor.

The catechism taught the emperor's young subjects that as Christians they owed deference to those who governed them, "in particular, to Napoleon I, our Emperor, love, respect, obedience, loyalty, military service and the taxes ordered for the preservation and defence of the Empire and his throne." The catechism also cited reasons why Napoleon I was especially worthy of devotion: "It is he whom God raised up in difficult circumstances to re-establish the public worship of the holy religion of our ancestors, and to be its protector. It is he who restored and preserved public order by his profound and active wisdom; he defends the state by the strength of his arm." The catechism made it clear that subjects of the emperor owed equal obligations "towards his legitimate successors." The legitimizing principle supporting the catechism was the biblical passage, "Render unto God the things which are God's, and unto Caesar the things which are Caesar's."

Pope Pius VII refused to sanction the imperial catechism, but the compliant papal legate, Cardinal Caprara, did approve it in May 1806, and the French clerical hierarchy complied. The papacy was discomfited by Napoleon's catechism, by his introduction of the Feast of Saint Napoléon every 15 August, by his militarization of the secondary schools (*lycées*), and by the overweening authority of his Imperial University (1808). The imperial catechism was characteristic of Bonaparte's policy of directing religion and education toward national, pragmatic goals.

V. Bindel, *Histoire religieuse de Napoléon*, 2 vols. (Paris, 1940); S. Delacroix, *Documents sur l'organisation de l'église de France après la Révolution, 1801–09* (Paris, 1951), and *La réorganisation de l'église de France, 1801–1809* (Paris, 1962); A. Feret, *La France et le Saint-Siège sous le premier Empire*, 2 vols. (Paris, 1911); E. E. Y. Hales, *Napoleon and the Pope* (London, 1962); A. Latreille, *Le catéchisme impérial* (Paris, 1935), *L'Eglise catholique et la Révolution française*, vol. 2 (Paris, 1950), and *Napoléon et le Saint-Siège (1801-1808)* (Paris, 1935).

Fred E. Hembree

Related entries: BERNIER; CONCORDAT OF 1801; EMPIRE, FRENCH; PIUS VII.

CATHERINE OF WÜRTTEMBERG (1783–1835), born Katharina Sophie Dorothea to Frederick of Württemberg, whom Napoleon elevated to king in 1805. Catherine was a poised, attractive woman who spoke excellent French. In August 1807, Napoleon arranged for his brother Jerome to marry Catherine, even though Jerome had earlier married Elizabeth Patterson of Baltimore, Maryland. When the pope had refused to annul the marriage, Napoleon secured an annulment from the archbishop of Paris. Jerome and Catherine were married in

Paris on 22 August 1807. Jerome, while seeming to love and respect Catherine, could not refrain from amorous adventures and soon was courting a cousin of Josephine, Stéphanie de Beauharnais. Catherine, who loved Jerome deeply, continued throughout her life to ignore all of his extramarital affairs.

In July 1807, the Kingdom of Westphalia was created, and Jerome became its king. He and his bride arrived in the capital on 7 December 1807. Jerome, while always spending great sums of money and often disobeying his brother, was a good king and was respected by his people. Catherine always stood by her husband and Napoleon and did her part to make the court in Westphalia as brilliant as possible. In addition, she was the favorite daughter-in-law of Madame Mère, and Napoleon was exceptionally fond of her and she of him.

Jerome marched with the Grande Armée into Russia in 1812, but because of a mistake he made in command, Napoleon sent him home early in the campaign. He and Catherine continued to live in Westphalia until after the Battle of Leipzig (October 1813), when Catherine was sent to France for safety. Within a week the kingdom was overrun by the Allies, and Jerome fled. His guard accompanied him to the Rhine, got him across safely, and then returned to their homes to await the next rulers.

Jerome and Catherine lived in Paris for a time but fled as the allies arrived, living in Blois until Napoleon abdicated. Wishing to go into exile in the city of Trieste, Catherine appealed to her cousin, Czar Alexander, who was in Paris. She and Jerome were escorted safely to Bern and then on to Trieste. There the couple lived a simple life, with little pomp and little income. In June 1814, their first child, Jerome, was born, seven years after their marriage.

During the Hundred Days Jerome left for Paris where he joined his brother, hoping to reestablish the Empire. Jerome served courageously at Waterloo but again went into exile after the defeat. Catherine, at her father's insistence, reluctantly returned to his court, and in August 1815 Jerome joined her there. Until 1817, the two lived as virtual political prisoners, not allowed to leave the kingdom. Finally, Catherine's father relented and allowed them to move and granted her a pension for life. In addition, Czar Alexander granted her an annuity, and the couple was finally fairly well off. They returned to Trieste, where a daughter, Mathilde, was born in 1820 and a second son, Prince Napoleon, in 1822.

Napoleon's death on St. Helena was deeply mourned by Catherine, but now at least the family was able to move about Europe freely. Soon most of the members of the family, including Catherine, were living in Rome. She and Jerome lived, as usual, beyond their means, in a palace that had belonged to Lucien Bonaparte. Jerome felt this life-style suited his wife's royal ancestry.

Catherine developed dropsy and even a move to Switzerland did not help as her doctors had hoped. She died in 1835, with her husband and children at her bedside. Her last words were, "What I loved most in the world was you, Jerome. I wish I could say farewell to you in France."

A. H. Atteridge, *Napoleon's Brothers* (London, 1909); Catherine de Württemberg, *Briefwechsel der Königin Katharina und des Königs Jerome von Westphalen, sowie des Kaisers Napoleon I, mit dem König Friedrich von Württemberg*. Ed. A. von Schlossberger (Stuttgart, 1886-87), *Mémoires et correspondance du roi Jérôme et de la reine Catherine* (Publies par le Baron du Casse) (Paris, 1861-66); O. Connelly, *Napoleon's Satellite Kingdoms* (New York, 1965); P. W. Sergeant, *Jerome Bonaparte* (New York, 1906); H. N. Williams, *The Women Bonapartes* (New York, 1909).

David C. Riede

Related entries: BONAPARTE, JEROME; GERMAN WAR OF LIBERATION; HUNDRED DAYS, THE; RUSSIAN CAMPAIGN; WESTPHALIA, KINGDOM OF.

CATHOLIC CHURCH. See CHURCH, ROMAN CATHOLIC.

CAULAINCOURT, ARMAND-AUGUSTIN-LOUIS (1773–1827), duke of Vicenza, Napoleon's last foreign minister. Of an ancient noble family with a long military tradition, Caulaincourt was born at the family chateau of Caulaincourt near Saint Quentin. His father, Gabriel-Louis de Caulaincourt, attained the rank of lieutenant general before retiring in February 1792. The young Caulaincourt enrolled in the royal cavalry at age fourteen. Refusing to emigrate from France, he served with distinction in the republican French army under Louis Hoche in the Vendée and with J. V. Moreau in southern Germany. Bonaparte, probably on the advice of Charles-Maurice Talleyrand and perhaps of Josephine, sent him on mission to St. Petersburg in 1801 and on his return appointed him an aide-de-camp. In obedience to Bonaparte's orders, he was involved in the kidnapping of the duke d'Enghien in 1803 in Baden. Although Caulaincourt's primary mission was to transmit to the Baden government Talleyrand's dispatch justifying this flagrant violation of international law, he never could live down the accusation of implication in the subsequent execution of the duke at Vincennes. After the establishment of the Empire, Napoleon named Caulaincourt grand master of horse (1804), duke of Vicenza (1808), ambassador to Czar Alexander I (1807–11), and minister of foreign affairs (November 1813–April 1814 and during the Hundred Days). In December 1812, after the retreat from Moscow, he accompanied Napoleon on a fourteen-day journey across the snowy wastes of Poland and Germany to Paris and left his memoirs of their prolonged encounters.

As ambassador and minister of foreign affairs, he became, under the influence of Talleyrand, a partisan of moderation and peace. Unlike Talleyrand, however, Caulaincourt, honorable and upright, did not intrigue behind Napoleon's back but spoke his mind directly to the emperor. As a partisan of the Russian alliance, he counseled against the invasion of Russia and in 1813–14 tried to secure from the Allies honorable terms of peace for France but never found any Napoleon would accept.

A. de Caulaincourt, *With Napoleon in Russia* (New York, 1935) and *No Peace with Napoleon* (New York, 1936); J. Hanoteau, Preface to *Mémoires du général de Caulaincourt*, 3 vols. (Paris, 1933); E. A. Whitcomb, *Napoleon's Diplomatic Service* (Durham, N.C., 1979).

Harold T. Parker

Related entries: ALEXANDER I; DIPLOMACY; FOREIGN POLICY; MINISTERS OF NAPOLEON; RUSSIA; RUSSIAN CAMPAIGN.

CENSORSHIP. See PRESS.

CEVA, BATTLE OF. See ITALIAN CAMPAIGN, FIRST.

CHAMBRES DE COMMERCE (chambers of commerce), local commercial advisory bodies, created by an *arrêt* of 24 December 1802. The *arrêt* formally organized a number of unofficial local *conseils de commerce* that had replaced the *chambres de commerce* abolished in 1791. Their function was to represent the views and needs of the local merchant community to the minister of the interior. The chambers were composed of fifteen local merchants in cities over 50,000 population and nine in towns of less with the local prefect serving as president. Candidates for membership were screened by the minister. Initially chambers were established in Lyon, Rouen, Bordeaux, Marseille, Brussels, Anvers, Nantes, Dunkirk, Lille, Mainz, Nimes, Avignon, Strasbourg, Turin, Montpellier, Geneva, Bayonne, Toulouse, Tours, Carcassonne, Amiens, and Le Havre. A *conseil-général du commerce*, composed of a representative from each chamber, met at Paris on an annual or semiannual basis. The *conseil* served the same function as the chambers on a national level and also served under the minister of the interior.

Le moniteur universel, 29 December 1802; E. Tarlé, "Napoléon Ier et les intérêts économiques de la France," *REN* 26 (1926).

Robert R. Crout

Related entries: ECONOMY, FRENCH; WARFARE, ECONOMIC.

CHAMPAGNY, JEAN-BAPTISTE DE NOMPERE DE (1756–1834), duc de Cadore. An officer in the French navy from 1771, deputy of the nobility of Forez to the Estates General of 1789, and prisoner during the Terror, Champagny was named by First Consul Bonaparte *conseiller d'état (section de la marine)* and then ambassador at Vienna (1801–04). He succeeded one genius (Jean-Antoine Chaptal) as minister of the interior (1804–07) and then another (Charles-Maurice Talleyrand) as minister of foreign affairs (1807–11). When he indicated his opposition to the proposed invasion of Russia, he was demoted in April 1811 to the intendancy of the domains of the crown but consoled with the title of senator. A conscientious, industrious diplomat of limited views, Champagny prided himself on taking over smoothly running bureaucratic machines in all his posts and making them run more smoothly. Napoleon appreciated his hard work and docility as well as his mediocrity ("I have never had a minister of interior.")

J.-B. Champagny, *Souvenirs de M. de Champagny, Duc de Cadore* (Paris, 1846); J. Savant, *Les ministres de Napoléon* (Paris, 1959).

Harold T.Parker

Related entries: DIPLOMACY; FOREIGN POLICY; MINISTERS OF NAPOLEON.

CHAMPAUBERT, BATTLE OF. See FRANCE, CAMPAIGN OF.

CHAPTAL, JEAN-ANTOINE (1756–1832), comte de Chanteloup, a distinguished chemist whose career illustrates at the level of genius the increasing intertwining of science, industry, and government. Born at Nojaret (Lozère), son of well-to-do small landowners, Antoine Chaptal and Françoise Brunel, Jean-Antoine as a bright youth in the *collèges* of Mende and Rodez attracted the favorable attention of his bachelor uncle, Claude Chaptal, a wealthy and celebrated physician at Montpellier. The uncle supported him while he studied medicine at the University of Montpellier (he was received as doctor of medicine in 1777) and staked him to three and one-half years of postgraduate study in medicine and chemistry at Paris. On his return to Montpellier, he lectured in the university to large audiences on the new theoretical chemistry of Lavoisier. With the capital supplied by his uncle and his wife's dowry, he founded at Montpellier a chemical factory, one of the first in France, where he applied the new chemistry to the manufacture of nitric, sulfuric, hydrochloric, and oxalic acids, sal ammoniac, blue, green, and white vitriol, white lead, and alum. His ingenious application of the new chemistry enabled him to simplify the processes of manufacture, improve the purity of the product, lower the cost, contribute to France's self-sufficiency, and win even a share of the export market.

During the Revolution, he was a partisan of the new, liberal ideas. As a moderate, however, he was outraged by the extremism of the Jacobin Convention and in the summer of 1793 led the federalist agitation at Montpellier against the alleged tyranny of Paris. He might well have been guillotined had not Lazare Carnot, the effective minister of war, and Prieur de la Côte d'Or, the effective minister of munitions, requisitioned his services as industrial chemist. They placed him in charge of the gunpowder factory at Grenelle. Aided by Claude Berthollet, Antoine Fourcroy, and other chemists, Chaptal so speeded the process of powder manufacture that the desperate ammunition needs of the fourteen Revolutionary armies were met. After Thermidor, he was associated with a cluster of young administrators on the Commission of Agriculture and Manufactures (Berthollet, Louis Costaz, and Claude Costaz), who were devising a rational industrial policy for (they hoped) a strong, stable government. They favored freedom of the entrepreneur from government and guild regulation, government encouragement of new industrial initiatives, and promotion of technical education. Unable to accomplish much in the administrative feebleness of the Directory, they came into their own after 18 Brumaire when Chaptal became minister of the interior (6 November 1800–6 August 1804), Claude Costaz chief of its bureau of manufactures, and Louis Costaz one of the founders (with Berthollet and Chaptal) of the Society for the Encouragement of National Industry. They were then able to implement some of their economic policies.

Under Bonaparte Chaptal first served as member of the Council of State. There he drafted the organic law that gave France its enduring administrative structure; the prefects, the councils of the prefecture, the subprefects, the councils of the arrondissement, the mayors, and the municipal councils, their attributions, their interrelations, and the boundaries of their jurisdictions were all instituted and defined in Chaptal's draft. Together with Pierre-Louis Roederer, he secured its passage by the Tribunate and the Legislative Body. As minister of the interior, Chaptal improved everything he touched: the bureaucratic channels of communication and command within the Paris office and with the prefects; the assemblage of statistics; cleanliness and care in hospitals and prisons; construction of canals, highways, and public buildings; and technical education at the Ecole des mines and the Conservatoire des arts et métiers. Knowing from his own experience the fruitfulness of the interplay of theory, observation, and practical application, he insisted that in the technical schools the students know theory, observe equipment worked by able mechanics, and as interns practice what they had observed.

After his retirement as minister, he supervised his chemical factories, turned his property at Chanteloup into a model farm where he experimented with the cultivation of the sugar beet, and continued to be available to the French government for technical advice—for example, under Napoleon as a member of the Council for Commerce and Industry and during the Restoration (after 1818) in the Chamber of Peers. His major books, *Eléments de Chimie* (1790), *Chimie appliquée aux arts* (1807), and *De l'industrie française* (1819), were masterpieces of elegant popularization.

J. A. Chaptal, *Mes souvenirs sur Napoléon* (Paris, 1893); M. P. Crosland, *The Society of Arcueil: A View of French Science at the Time of Napoleon I* (Cambridge, Mass., 1967); H. T. Parker, "Two Administrative Bureaus under the Directory and Napoleon," *FHS* 4 (1965–66); J. Pigeire, *La vie et l'oeuvre de Chaptal (1756–1832)* (Paris, 1932).

Harold T. Parker

Related entries: ADMINISTRATION; BERTHOLLET; MINISTERS OF NAPOLEON; SCIENCE; STATISTICS.

CHARLES IV (1742–1819), king of Spain. Born in Naples (11 November 1742), Charles IV married his first cousin, Maria Luisa of Parma, and succeeded to the throne in 1788. Of mediocre ability and at intervals mad, Charles IV was dominated by his wife and her lover, Manuel Godoy, throughout his reign. He joined the First Coalition in war against the French Republic. Following defeats in Roussillon, he allowed Godoy to end the war by the Treaty of Basel (22 July 1795). Spain then allied with France by the Treaty of San Ildefonso (19 August

1796) and declared war on England. Charles supported Napoleon in the War of Oranges against Portugal, annexing Olivenza to Spain by the Treaty of Badajoz (6 June 1801). Between 1801 and 1808, Charles IV supported Napoleon's political, economic, and military policies.

When he was forced to abdicate by his son Ferdinand VII (19 March 1808), he appealed to Napoleon with every hope that he would be restored. Instead both he and Ferdinand were called to Bayonne and forced to renounce the throne, which went to Joseph Bonaparte. With an annual income of 6 million francs, Charles IV retired with his wife and Godoy to Compiègne and then Marseille before settling in Rome (1812) where he lived until his death (20 January 1819). Charles IV was utterly unprepared and incapable of ruling, and the decline of Spain during his reign clearly reflected this fact.

J. Gomez de Arteche y Moro, *Guerra de la Independencia. Historia militar de España de 1808 a 1814*, 14 vols. (Madrid, 1866-1903), and *Reinaldo de Carlos IV*, 3 vols. (Madrid, 1896); J. Chastenet, *Godoi, Prince de la Paix* (Paris, 1934); M. Godoy, *Cuenta dada de su politica o sean memoiras critica*, 6 vols. (Madrid, 1836–42); M. Ovilo y Otero, *Vida politica de D. Manuel Godoy, Principe de la Paz* (Madrid, 1845); J. Perez de Guzman, *La historia inedita. Estudios de la vida, reinado, proscripcion y muerte de Carlos IV y Maria Luisa* (Madrid, 1908).

Donald D. Horward

Related entries: BAYONNE, "INTERVIEW" OF; BONAPARTE, JOSEPH; CONTINENTAL BLOCKADE; PENINSULAR WAR; SPAIN, KINGDOM OF; TRAFALGAR, BATTLE OF.

CHARLES VON HABSBURG. See KARL VON HABSBURG.

CHARTER OF 1814, constitution promulgated by Louis XVIII on his restoration. It created a British-style monarchy with a legislative branch comprising a chamber of Peers and a Chamber of Deputies, the one appointed by the king, the other elected by limited male sufffrage. A bill of rights was also supplied, which included freedom of religion, of speech, and of the press. The first proved difficult to enforce in the face of the resurgence of the Roman Catholic church. The latter two were shortly negated because of the torrent of abuse levied against the Bourbons.

Related entry: LOUIS XVIII.

CHATEAUBRIAND, FRANCOIS-AUGUSTE-RENE, VICOMTE DE (1768–1848), influential Romantic writer, diplomat, minister and member of the Académie française (1811). Youngest child of poor Breton noblesse, he briefly sought adventure in America among fur traders and Indians. Following Varennes, he returned to France to offer his allegiance to Royalist forces.

Chateaubriand emigrated to England in 1793, where he commenced several of his major works, including the transitional *Essai sur Révolutions*. Returning to Paris in 1800 as a journalist and writer, he published his immensely popular

Indian saga, *Atala*, in 1801. His defense of traditional Christianity, *Le génie du Christianisme*, appeared in 1802 and was praised by royalists and Bonapartists alike.

The Bourbon Restoration brought him honors and positions, if not prosperity: vicount and member of the House of Peers (1815); ambassador to Berlin (1821); ambassador to London (1822); and French representative at the Congress of Verona (1822). Early in the Restoration, Chateaubriand began what is generally considered his most significant work, *Mémoires d'outre-tombe*. The apogee of his government career was achieved under Villèle when he served as minister of foreign affairs until 1824. Chateaubriand was influential in France's intervention in Spain (1823).

Of his many love affairs, his most famous and enduring liaison was with Mme. Récamier. Subsequent generations have given mixed evaluations to his writings, but his influence on the post-Revolutionary generation in France and most especially the youth is undoubted.

R. Bourgeois, *Chateaubriand et la littérature Empire* (Paris, 1972); R. Castries, *Chateaubriand: ou La puissance du songe* (Paris, 1974); F. Chateaubriand, *Memoirs*; selected, translated, introduction by R. Baldick (New York, 1961); G. Godlewski, ''Napoléon et Chateaubriand,'' *Nouvelle Revue des Deux Mondes* 9 (1975); G. Painter, *The Longed-for-Tempests* (New York, 1978).

John C.White

Related entries: IDEOLOGUES; INSTITUT NATIONAL DES SCIENCES ET DES ARTS; LITERATURE.

CHATEAU-THIERRY, BATTLE OF. See FRANCE, CAMPAIGN OF.

CHATHAM, JOHN PITT, SECOND EARL OF (1756–1835), British general, eldest son of William Pitt, and elder brother of the British statesman by the same name in whose government he frequently served. Commissioned in 1778, John saw action at the siege of Gibraltar, (1779–83). By 1795 he was a major general, and he commanded a brigade under the duke of York in Holland in 1799. Promoted to lieutenant general in 1802, he continued to hold the significant cabinet position of master general of ordnance (1801–6, 1807–10), which he performed with little distinction. Given command of the Walcheren expedition in 1809, Chatham's inactivity and indecision contributed to the campaign's dismal failure. His attempt to blame the disaster on the naval commander (Sir Richard Strachan) and the evidence presented at the parliamentary inquiry in 1810 compromised his reputation, and he resigned his cabinet post. A favorite of George III, he was promoted to full general in 1812 and made governor of Gibraltar (1820–35), but he was permanently disgraced by the Walcheren scandal.

G. Bond, *The Grand Expedition: The British Invasion of Holland in 1809* (Athens, Ga., 1979); H. Brougham, *The Life and Times of Henry, Lord Brougham*, vol. 1 (New York, 1871); D. Gray, *Spencer Perceval* (London, 1963); Great Britain, House of Commons, *Parliamentary Papers*, vols. 6–8, *Papers Presented to the House by His Majesty's*

Command, Relating to the Expedition to the Scheldt (London, 1810); Historical Manuscript Commission, *Dropmore Papers*, vol. 9 (London, 1906); T. Picton, *Memoirs*, vol. 1 (London, 1836); Public Record Office, 30/8/260-370, Chatham Papers.

Gordon Bond

Related entries: GREAT BRITAIN; WAGRAM CAMPAIGN; WALCHEREN, INVASION OF.

CHATILLON, CONGRESS OF (5 February–19 March 1814), gathering of top diplomatic representatives of the Allies. Armand Caulaincourt, representing France, was given an offer to Napoleon of the throne of France with the boundaries of 1792 in exchange for peace. The French emperor scornfully rejected the offer, telling Caulaincourt that the Allies were trying to deceive him. Actually he was elated over his recent successes and still thought he could win. As it turned out, he would never have another offer from the Allies. They responded by signing the Treaties of Chaumont, by which they bound themselves not to make peace separately with Napoleon.

Related entries: ABDICATION, FIRST; CHAUMONT, TREATIES OF; DIPLOMACY; FIVE DAYS, BATTLES OF; FRANCE, CAMPAIGN OF.

CHAUMONT, TREATIES OF (9 March 1814), agreement of the Allies to maintain the coalition against the French for twenty years. All parties promised not to conclude a separate peace. See also FRANCE, CAMPAIGN OF; VIENNA, CONGRESS OF.

CHENIER, MARIE-JOSEPH-BLAISE DE (1764–1811), dramatist, author of *Charles IX*, ex-*conventionnel*, regicide. He took an active part in meetings with Bonaparte leading to 18 Brumaire, voted the dissolution of the Council of Five Hundred, and joined the transitional legislative Commission of Twenty-one. Like the *idéologues*, he became quickly disillusioned with the Consulate and as tribune opposed the creation of special courts. Excluded from the Tribunate in 1802, he was appointed inspector general of public instruction. His plays were banned from the French stage after he composed *Cyrus* (1804). His ''Epître à Voltaire'' of 1806 attacked Catholicism and the suppression of free thought. The emperor terminated his inspectorship but soon after gave him a pension. Sometimes reproached for having compromised himself with Napoleon, he was in fact one of his most virulent critics. A member of the National Institute, Chénier was one of the most influential men of letters of his generation.

M. Albert, *La littérature française sous la Révolution, l'Empire et la Restauration* (Paris, 1898); A. J. Bingham, *Marie-Joseph Chénier: Early Political Life and Ideas* (New York, 1939); C. L'Homme, *Les chants nationaux de la France: Poètes et musiciens de la Révolution* (Paris, 1883); A. Lieby, *Le théâtre de Marie-Joseph Chénier* (Paris, 1901).

Emmet Kennedy

Related entries: BRUMAIRE, COUP OF 18, YEAR VIII; EDUCATION; PRESS; UNIVERSITY, IMPERIAL.

CHERASCO, ARMISTICE OF. See ITALIAN CAMPAIGN, FIRST.

CHERUBINI, LUIGI (1760–1842), a dominant Italian composer and teacher in the fifty-year transition period from classicism to romanticism in French music. Born Luigi Carlo Zanobi Salvadore Maria Cherubini in Florence, Italy, 14 September 1760, he was the son of a musician, Bartolomeo Cherubini. His early musical education was in Florence and then in Bologna and Milan where he studied from 1778 to 1781 with Giuseppe Sarti. His early works were primarily sacred music, but by 1782 he had written five operas, of which *Armida* was considered a great success. He left Italy for London in 1784, composing two operas in two years, one of which was a commissioned work for the King's Theatre. In the summer of 1785, he visited Paris, was introduced to Marie-Antoinette, and at the Concert Spirituel in September several of his pieces were performed.

His first French opera was *Démophon*, (1788), which suffered from a feeble libretto by Jean-François Marmontel. In spite of its limited success, he was engaged as musical director at the Théâtre de Monsieur, under the patronage of the future Louis XVIII. His first real success was in 1791 with *Lodoïska*. This opera formed a bridge between the older classical style with its emphasis on arias and the French grand opera of the nineteenth century, which gave new importance to the orchestra and increased the scope of the chorus. He was appointed an inspector of the Institut National de Musique, which in 1795 became the Conservatoire. Although he wrote several republican hymns for the Revolutionary festivals, 1793–98, he had an uneasy alliance with those forces.

The Napoleonic era did not ameliorate the situation because Napoleon's and Cherubini's theories on music did not agree. The success of his next two operas established his reputation. *Médée*, in 1797, was innovative because, although classical in subject, it revealed psychological human traits. *Les Deux Journées*, performed in 1800, was studied by Beethoven before he wrote *Fidelio*; both operas sharing the rescue theme.

An unhappy marriage to Cecile Tourette had left Cherubini depressed and, in 1805, when an opportunity to go to Vienna presented itself, he readily accepted. He was enthusiastically received by the Viennese court and the leading musical figures, including Haydn and Beethoven. While Cherubini was working on his opera *Faniska*, Napoleon occupied Vienna and, in a cordial spirit, asked the musician to direct a series of soirées at Schönbrunn and expressed the hope that Cherubini would return to Paris. He wrote *Pimmaglione* for the Italian opera at the Tuileries in 1808, but it was not favorably received by the emperor, and Cherubini was again subject to depression, vowing to give up music for botany. He was persuaded to return to composing church music but did not entirely abandon the theater.

During the Restoration, he was appointed *surintendant de la musique du roi*. Between 1811 and 1825, he wrote seven masses, including two coronation masses and two requiems. In 1814, he became a member of the Institut and, in 1816, he and J. F. Le Sueur were named directors of the Royal Chapel. When he became the director of the new Conservatoire in 1822, he permanently shaped that institution. In 1841, he was appointed chevalier of the Legion d'Honneur, the first musician to be so honored. He died 15 March 1842 in Paris and, at the state funeral for him, his *D Minor Requiem*, a powerful composition for male voices and orchestra, was performed.

E. Bellasis, *Cherubini: Memorials Illustrative of his Life* (London, 1874, rev., enlarged 1905; 1912, rev. 1971); B. Deane, *Cherubini* (London, 1965); C. G. Parker, *A Bibliography and Thematic Index of Luigi Cherubini's Instrumental Music* (diss. Kent State U., 1972); D. Raoul-Rochette, *Notice historique sur la vie et les ouvrages de M. Cherubini* (Paris, 1843); M. S. Selden, "Napoleon and Cherubini," *Journal of the American Musicological Society* 7 (1955).

Rachel R. Schneider

Related entries: GRASSINI; MEHUL; LE SUEUR; MUSIC; PROPAGANDA; THEATER.

CHOUANS, guerrillas who continued the counterrevolutionary struggle in the Vendée, Brittany, and Normandy after the peasant Royal and Catholic army of the Vendée was destroyed by republican forces during October–December 1793. They were finally suppressed in 1801 by Napoleon, as first consul. Their struggle, termed the *Chouannerie*, had something in common with the Vendéan uprising of 1793. Like the Vendéan royalists, the Chouans resented government measures against the clergy and the enforcement of conscription. Unlike the Vendéans, the Chouans were usually a hated minority in their localities, and they were not so dedicated to the absolutist Bourbon regime as were the Vendéans. Many of the Chouans were smugglers and dealers in contraband salt and were vexed with the republican regime for ruining their illicit trade by the abolition of the *gabelle*, a centuries-old tax on salt. Joining the peasants in the Chouannerie was a group of high-ranking royalists, notably Count Joseph de Puisaye, engaged in clandestine activities with the British.

The Breton word *chouan*, meaning "screech owl," was the nickname of Jean Cottereau (1757–94), a leading spirit of the early Chouannerie. The sporadic warfare of the Chouannerie flourished north of the Loire in Brittany, Maine, Normandy, and northern Anjou. The Chouannerie existed even before 1793, but the passage in that year of the Vendéans north of the Loire no doubt strengthened the Chouan bands. In addition to veterans of the *grande guerre* of 1793, the Chouans enlisted the services of refractory priests, draft dodgers, and deserters from the republican army. The Chouan bands never posed a serious threat to any republican army but played havoc on buyers of national property, republican officials in small towns, and constitutional priests. Following the disastrous *émigré* landing at Quiberon in July 1795, the Chouannerie began to disintegrate, and simple banditry became an essential motivation of the Chouans.

The War of the Second Coalition prompted a revival of the Chouannerie in 1799. The Chouans, under the leadership of Georges Cadoudal, M. Mercier-La

Vendée, René Le Gris-Duval, L.A. Victor Bourmont, and Louis de Frotte, registered initial successes in October at Le Mans, Nantes, Redon, Saint-Brieuc, and La Roche-Bernard. These successes were only ephemeral, however, and General Gabriel d'Hedouville scored telling republican victories before the coup d'état of 18 Brumaire (9 November 1799). Bonaparte, combining force with conciliation, quickly managed to extinguish the insurrection. At the end of 1799 and the beginning of 1800, many of the Chouan leaders negotiated with Napoleon, and after the signing of the Concordat of 1801, the Chouannerie as a legitimate political movement all but vanished.

A. Chaudeurge, *La Chouannerie normande* (Paris, 1982); J.-F. Chiappe, *La Vendée en armes*, 2 vols. (Paris, 1982); A.-M. V. Billaud, *La guerre de Vendée* (Lussaud, 1972); J. Godechot, *La Contre-Révolution: Doctrine et action, 1789–1804* (Paris, 1961); A. Montagnon, *Guerres de Vendée: 1793–1832* (Paris, 1974); T. C. Muret, *Histoire des guerres de l'Ouest, Vendée, Chouannerie (1792–1815)*, 5 vols. (Paris, 1848); C. Tilly, *The Vendée* (Princeton, 1964).

Fred E. Hembree

Related entries: CONCORDAT OF 1801; VENDEE, WAR IN THE.

CHURCH, ROMAN CATHOLIC. Throughout Napoleon's remarkable career, he could never ignore the Roman Catholic church. On the eve of the French Revolution, the church had been wealthy, arrogant, corrupt. Between 1789 and 1791, however, the church had lost its property, the right to collect the *dîme*, and had been subjected to the Civil Constitution of the Clergy. It faced worse trials in the 1790s, including official attempts to supplant Roman Catholicism with new religions. All was overshadowed, however, by the conflicts that followed the schism of the clergy into constitutional (who took an oath to the Revolution) and refractory groups—about equal in numbers. It produced open rebellion among peasants in the West and continual guerrilla war in the Vendée and Brittany. The religious question was therefore the most pressing problem Napoleon as first consul inherited (1799).

After strengthening his hand in northern Italy (Marengo, July 1800), Napoleon opened negotiations with the new pope, Pius VII. The Concordat of 1801 was published in France on Easter Sunday, 1802, along with the Organic Articles, implementing regulations never agreed to by the pope; however, the schism in the clergy was healed. Thereafter Napoleon credited himself with the reconciliation of church and state in France. The Consulate slipped quietly into the Empire in 1804. Pope Pius VII came to Paris for Napoleon's coronation, held in Notre Dame on 2 December 1804.

Napoleon had been anxious to pacify the French peasants, 80 percent or more of the population—who traditionally supported the church—without antagonizing the influential anticlerical elements in France (including many ex-leaders of the republic). Since the Concordat had not reestablished the church (and freedom of religion was still the law) and the document was strongly Gallican in tone, both the secular minded and the clergy seemed satisfied. Meanwhile, however,

Napoleon's growing differences with Pius VII, more political than religious, threatened to disrupt the agreement. In 1808–9 Napoleon seized the Papal States. In 1809 Pius excommunicated Napoleon, who had the pope seized and imprisoned, eventually at Fontainebleau. These events aroused considerable sympathy for the pontiff and, by extension, for his church.

By the time Pius VII left French soil to return to Rome in 1814, the prestige of the church was higher than it had been in a century. This is ironic since it must be concluded that Napoleon managed to solve his religious problem early in his regime and that he had been undone by his harassment of the head of the church.

A. Aulard, *Christianity and the French Revolution*; trans. Lady Frazer (New York, 1966); A. Dansette, *The Religious History of Modern France*, vol. 1: *From the Revolution to the Third Republic*, trans. J. Dingle (New York, 1961); H. Jedin and J. Dolan, eds., *History of the Church*, vol. VII: *The Church between Revolution and Restoration* (New York, 1981); P. de LaGorce, *Histoire religieuse de la Révolution française*; 5 vols. (Paris, 1912–23); A. Latreille, et al., *Histoire du Catholicisme en France*, vol. 3: *La période contemporaine* (Paris, 1962); J. McManners, *The French Revolution and the Church* (London, 1969).

Thomas F. Sheppard

Related entries: CONCORDAT OF 1801; LAW, CODES OF; PIUS VI; PIUS VII.

CIANCIULLI, MICHANGELO. See NAPLES, KINGDOM OF: MINISTERS.

CINEMA AND TELEVISION, NAPOLEON IN. See FILM, NAPOLEON IN.

CINTRA, CAPITULATION OF (30 August 1808). See JUNOT, J.-A.; PENINSULAR WAR.

CISALPINE REPUBLIC. In May 1796, during the first Italian campaign, Napoleon organized the Duchy of Milan (Lombardy) under a civil government dominated by the French military, the Congregation of State, sometimes called the Lombard Republic. In December 1796 delegates from the Duchy of Modena (Modena and Reggio), an Austrian secondogeniture, and the Papal States of Ferrara and Bologna formed the Cispadane Republic south of the Po. In 1797 the Lombard Republic was designated the Cisalpine Republic, and in the course of the year Napoleon added to it the Cispadane Republic, Mantua, Romagna, and part of Venetia, to give it a frontier on the Adige and the Valtelline. This territory was redesignated the Republic of Italy in 1801, with Bonaparte as president, and the Kingdom of Italy in 1805 with Napoleon as king and Eugène de Beauharnais as viceroy.

S. Canzio, *La prima repubblica cisalpina e il sentimento nazionale italiano*. (Modena, 1944); G. de Castro, *Storia d'Italia dal 1799 al 1814*. (1881); A.-L. Forti-Messina, "La legislation du travail en Lombardie a l'époque napoléonienne." *AHRF* 230 (1977); A.

Fugier, *Napoléon et l'Italie*. (Paris, 1947); A. Pingaud, *La domination française dans l'Italie du nord, 1796-1895: Bonaparte, president de la république italienne*. 2 vols. (Paris, 1914); M. Roberti, *Milano capitale napoleonica, la formazione di uno stato moderno*. 3 vols. (Milano, 1946-1947).

Related entries: BEAUHARNAIS, E.; ITALIAN CAMPAIGN, FIRST; ITALY, KINGDOM OF; NAPOLEON, I.

CIUDAD RODRIGO, SIEGE OF (1811). See PENINSULAR WAR.

CLARKE, HENRI (1765-1818), comte de Hunebourg, duc de Feltre, marshal of France, minister of war under Napoleon from 9 August 1807 to 3 April 1814. At sixteen (1781) he had entered the royal Ecole Militaire and by 1784 had advanced to captain. During the Revolution he successfully accomplished a series of important missions, first in combat and then in the administration. For example, in 1795 he served Lazare Carnot as chief of the Ministry of War's topographic bureau, which drafted operational plans for the victorious Revolutionary armies. Under the empire, Napoleon was his own minister of war, but Clarke introduced order, method, consistency and continuity into the paperwork involved in moving personnel and materiel to the armies. Honest, hard working, and well organized, Clarke functioned less as a minister than as an indispensable *premier commis*. He took service with the Bourbons in 1814, and in 1815 followed Louis XVIII into exile and back after Waterloo.

Harold T. Parker

Related entries: ADMINISTRATION, MILITARY; ARMY, FRENCH; MINISTERS OF NAPOLEON.

CLARY, BERNADINE-EUGENIE-DESIREE (1779–1860), reputed fiancée of the young Napoleon and later queen of Sweden. Desirée Clary was born 8 November 1779 at Marseilles, the daughter of a successful silk merchant. Her convent education ended at an early age when the Revolution closed the religious institutions. The Clary and Bonaparte families became acquainted in February 1794 when Desirée went to petition Antoine Albitte, the Jacobin deputy for Marseilles, to release her brother Etienne, who had been arrested. Joseph Bonaparte was secretary to the Committee of Public Safety and apparently was instrumental in securing his release. Joseph became engaged to Marie-Julie Clary, Desirée's sister, and married her on 1 August 1794. When Napoleon met the vivacious Desirée, he was infatuated and talked about marriage, but she was only fourteen, and they did not become seriously involved. Moreover, Napoleon was soon transferred to Paris. Although he tried to initiate correspondence, Desirée responded hardly at all. Meanwhile Napoleon met and fell in love with the sophisticated, aristocratic Josephine de Beauharnais.

In 1797 Desirée met General Leonard Duphot and accepted his proposal, but he was assassinated before they could be married. She had several suitors before choosing to marry General (later marshal) Jean-Baptiste Bernadotte on 17 August

1798. Meanwhile she remained on friendly terms with Napoleon and all of his family, even Josephine. A son, Oscar, was born 4 July 1799, and Napoleon was godfather.

In 1810, with Napoleon's permission, Marshal Bernadotte was elected crown prince of Sweden and became King Charles XIV in 1818. Desirée visited Sweden in 1810 but returned to live in Paris, ignoring even that Bernadotte allied Sweden with Russia in 1812. It was not until 1823, when Oscar married Josephine, daughter of Eugène de Beauharnais, that Desirée went to live in Sweden. Oscar became king in 1844 on Bernadotte's death. Desirée died in Sweden on 17 December 1860.

D. P. Barton, *Bernadotte, The First Phase, 1763–1799* (New York, 1914–25); Baron K. Hochschild, *Desirée, Queen of Sweden* (New York, 1890); T. T. Hojer, *Carl XIV Johan* (Sweden, 1939–60).

Rachel R. Schneider

Related entries: BERNADOTTE.

CLARY, JULIE (1771–1845), wife of Joseph Bonaparte, elder brother of Napoleon, king of Naples and later Spain. Julie Clary was the daughter of a rich merchant of Marseilles and married Joseph in 1794 before Napoleon gained any real fame. She and Joseph had two children, both girls. Her sister Desirée, who married Marshal Bernadotte and became queen of Sweden, is more famous.
Related entries: BONAPARTE, JOSEPH; CLARY, D.

CLAUSEWITZ, KARL VON (1780–1831), German soldier and military writer. Clausewitz entered the Prussian army in 1793, campaigning against the French in Alsace and the Saar. In 1801 he entered the War College recently opened in Berlin, then took part in the campaign of 1806, which proved so disastrous for Prussia. From 1808 on Clausewitz was closely associated with Generals Scharnhorst and Gneisenau and their efforts to rebuild the Prussian army. Clausewitz joined the Russian army in staff capacity during the campaigns of 1812 and 1813, rejoining the Prussian service in time to take part in the Battle of Waterloo. In 1818 he became director of the War College, a post he held for a dozen years. Much of this time was devoted to the writing of works on a variety of subjects, of which the most famous today is his *On War*, left unfinished on his sudden death.

Clausewitz played only a modest role in the Napoleonic wars, but the impact of those wars on his keen mind generated some of the most profound studies of war in modern times. Along with incisive analyses of individual campaigns, Clausewitz offered insights into the psychological factors in war, its varying intensity, and its relation to policy.

K. von Clausewitz, *On War*, ed. and trans. M. Howard and P. Paret (Princeton, 1976); P. Paret, *Clausewitz and the State* (New York, 1976).

Lee Kennett

Related entries: RUSSIAN CAMPAIGN; PRUSSIA, KINGDOM OF; SCHARNHORST.

CLOTHING FASHION, MEN'S. Masculine attire during the Consulate and Empire was heavily influenced by English fashions. British tailoring, which had become popular in the late eighteenth century, survived the wild exaggerations imposed on it by the *incroyables*, and by the Napoleonic era; men's clothing settled into a style that would eventually become the modern suit. The ensemble favored by elegant men, known as the *habit*, consisted of trousers, waistcoat, and coat. Dark blues, greens, and browns trimmed in pea green or tobacco brown were the colors preferred for this costume.

The narrow ankle-length trousers of the early nineteenth century were made from a variety of materials, such as fine cotton, buckskin, and stockinette. Nankeen, a fabric with a soft sheen, was imported from Nanking, China, and trousers made from it were usually buff or yellow. Diagonal or sideseam pockets were often features of trousers from this period. Tight breeches that reached below the knee and buttoned around the calves also were in vogue. Both breeches and trousers had a wide flap closure in the front known as *le pont* or *la patte*. Silk stockings and flat, low-cut slippers or numerous types of boots completed the legwear of the day.

Waistcoats were an integral part of the *habit*. Styles varied because of the different collars used, but the double-breasted, sleeveless vest was generally waist length and cut straight across the bottom. The garment was constructed of two different materials so that the front was made of a finer, more decorative fabric than the back. White piqué or colored percale were frequently used for the waistcoat.

Under the waistcoat was worn a fairly full-sleeved, yoked linen shirt that opened down the front. The opening was trimmed with flat pleating or ruching on the edges. Shirt collars were very high, with points worn flat against the cheeks. A soft neckcloth was wrapped around the throat over the collar. Young dandies often wore the cloth so high that it nearly concealed the chin. A diagonally folded square of black or white silk known as the *cravat* was then elaborately tied over the neckcloth. The practical *col-cravat* consisted of a *cravat* mounted on a collar, which could be easily attached to the shirt with a button or spring pin. For his coronation, Napoleon wore the *royal cravat*, trimmed with cascades of Alençon lace. Senators wore this type of cravat without a collar, while government officials wore muslin *cravats* without visible collars.

Although the types of coats worn with the *habit* differed somewhat, they were generally single- or double-breasted V-necked garments with varying sizes of collars and lapels. The long sleeves were slightly puffed at the shoulder and were turned back in cuffs at the wrist. The coat was waist length in the front with tails in the back. The claw-hammer coat, introduced in 1811, had fairly straight, square mid-thigh-length tails, typical of the period. Napoleon was not a man to follow each whim of fashion, and when the shorter (mid-thigh length) coat tails became popular during the Empire, he stubbornly retained the knee-length tails fashionable in the earlier period. His head valet finally resorted to subterfuge, and each time he ordered a new coat for the emperor, he directed the tailor to shorten the tails an inch, until the imperial coats were *à la mode*.

In addition to the coats worn with the *habit*, the masculine wardrobe included a variety of outer wraps. The ankle-length carrick or garrick of English origin was styled after the coachman's livery and was distinguished by a high collar and a series of capes that reached the elbows. Although they were adopted and modified by women, the long double-breasted redingote and the waist-length, tailless Spencer, both of which came from England, were men's wraps. The long, straight Polish coat with a high stand-up collar and braid trimming reminiscent of the military became popular near the middle of the Empire.

Like their female counterparts, gentlemen of the Consulate and Empire looked to antiquity for inspiration, and the short haircut of the Roman emperors was the prevailing male coiffure. Ends of the hair were brushed over the forehead and cheeks, and the long side pieces in front of the ears were the beginning of sideburns. Near the middle of the Empire, hair curled in loose ringlets became popular. Although some military officers wore moustaches, most men were clean shaven. In the new era of bodily cleanliness, shaving was important, and many men shaved themselves. Even Napoleon, after a few difficult lessons from his valet, learned the art. Although the tall hat of silk or polished beaver appeared in 1803, the flat, felt military bicorne, or *chapeau bras* was the head covering preferred by dandies until the end of the period.

M. S. Bigelow, *Fashion in History* (Minneapolis, 1970); M. Braun-Ronsdarf, *Mirror of Fashion. A History of European Costume, 1789-1929* (London, 1964); L.-M.-P. Debucourt, *Modes et manières du jour à Paris à la fin du XVIIIe siècle et du commencement du XIXe* (Paris, 1957); P. L. Giafferri, *Histoire du costume masculin français 420-1870* (Paris, 1927); R. See, *Le Costume de la révolution à nos jours* (Paris, 1929); G. Squire, *Dress Art and Society* (London, 1974).

Melanie Sue Byrd

Related entries: ARMY, FRENCH; NAPOLEON I; TALMA; THEATER.

CLOTHING FASHION, WOMEN'S. Women's costume in the Napoleonic era provides an excellent example of the impact of political and social change on fashion. The downfall of the monarchy swept away the brocaded hoop skirts and towering powdered wigs favored by the *ancien régime* and, as France's leaders were inspired by Greek and Roman political ideals, the fashionable adopted a toilette based on the ancient style. By the time that Napoleon achieved power, the new mode was firmly established, and the basic features of women's gowns—puffed sleeves, low neck, high waist, narrow skirt—changed little during the Consulate and Empire.

One variation in the costume occurred in 1799 when Napoleon's Egyptian campaign brought sleeves *à la Mamluk* into vogue. Named for the Egyptian military force, the sleeves were composed of a series of gathered puffs extending from the shoulder to the wrist. Sleeves *à l'Anglaise* (English) were short or elbow length and fastened with buttons. Short sleeves were very popular during the Consulate, and under the Empire, long, tight sleeves with a puff at the shoulder also became fashionable.

An important feature of women's costume in this period was the wide, low-cut, square or oval neckline. Often it was adorned with a flat stand-up lace collar known as a *cherusse* or *cherusque*. The collar *à la Gabrielle* was pleated and stood so high that it almost covered the face. The Betsie was a round lace collar derived from the Elizabethan neck ruff, which adorned higher-necked dresses. Although the low neckline was fashionable throughout the period, especially on ballgowns, higher lace-trimmed collars were worn on some costumes during the later Empire.

Classical drapery was imitated in the form of the sleeveless tunics *à la Mamluk* and *à la Juive*, which were worn as overdresses. Cashmere shawls, which increased in popularity after Napoleon's Egyptian campaign, enhanced the draped, antique mode, and elegant ladies took lessons in the art of posing with a shawl.

Since the fashion of the day required that costume reflect the ancient world, sheer, clinging fabrics such as Indian muslin, batiste, lawn tulle, gauze, moire, and cotton were popular. Such materials were not suited to the climate, however. In 1803, an influenza epidemic in Paris was attributed to the wearing of thin fabrics and was therefore given the appropriate sobriquet "muslin disease." Some Parisian guardians of morality were shocked by the fashionable lack of clothing, and the pope issued a bull condemning the transparent nature of women's attire. When Napoleon became emperor, he prohibited the import of cashmere, lawn, and muslin in order to limit foreign competition with the French textile industry. During the Empire, technical advances in the production of cloth allowed opaque fabrics such as velvet, satin, crepe, silk, and taffeta to achieve popularity. As the use of heavier materials increased, the skirts of gowns became more elaborately decorated with embroidery, pleats, ruffles, and lace. In addition to being trimmed, the skirts of mid-to-late Empire costumes became slightly fuller and shorter, revealing the ankles and feet, which were encased in low-cut, heelless slippers.

The wearing of heavier dresses did not diminish the need for a warm outer garment, and many types of coats were fashionable during the Empire. The silk-lined fur coat known as the *witchoura* and the woolen fur-lined *witchoura* first appeared in 1808. The redingote, made of worsted fabric had a short cape around its shoulders, and the abbreviated Spencer jacket was worn unbuttoned with the high-waisted gowns.

The colors that were in vogue during the Consulate and Empire complemented the antique lines of the costume. Pastels were popular, and white was made fashionable by Mme. Récamier, the reigning beauty of the early Empire. Rose was preferred by the Empress Josephine. As heavier fabrics were worn, richer colors such as black, blue, poppy red, purple, marigold yellow, and bright green became popular.

In addition to imitating the ancient past in their clothing, women of the Napoleonic era adopted hair styles reminiscent of classical civilization. The mode of wearing hair clipped short *à la Titus*, which had appeared near the end of the Reign of Terror, continued throughout the Consulate. The fashion was attributed to many causes: the influence of antiquity, a reaction against the towering hair styles affected by Marie Antoinette, and an allusion to the hair that was lost along with heads during the Revolution. This last idea seems to be substantiated by references to coiffures *à la victime* and *à la sacrifice*. Most methods of dressing hair incorporated curls, braids, or chignons, and as hair styles became more complicated, wigs *à la Venus*, *à la Sappho*, *à l'Anglaise*, and *à l'Espagnole* became popular. Switches known as *cache-follies* were also widely used. Hair styles were adorned with combs, hairpins, diadems, ropes of pearls, diamonds, cameos, golden laurel leaves, garlands of artificial flowers, and sheaves of gold or silver wheat. One of the most favored styles of headdress was the satin turban, another mode inspired by the Egyptian campaign. Muslin half-turbans trimmed with red silk and feathers were popular, and broad-brimmed white straw hats *à la Babet'*, decorated on one side with a single flower, were also in vogue.

Since the court of the Napoleonic era was restricted to a few individuals who wore elaborate and expensive costumes designed specifically for ceremonial use, new fashions were premiered at private balls at the theatre and opera. The costumes of style-setting women such as the Empress Josephine, Pauline Bonaparte, and Mme. Récamier can be seen in the paintings of David, Ingrès, Gérard, Gros, Isabey, and Vigée-Le Brun.

L.-M.-P. Debucourt, *Modes et manières du jour à Paris à la fin du XVIII*[e] *siècle et du commencement du XIX*[e] (Paris, 1957); P. L. Giafferri, *Histoire du costume féminin français* (Paris, 1928); G. Squire, *Dress and Art in History* (London, 1974).

Melanie Sue Byrd

Related entries: EGYPTIAN CAMPAIGN; JOSEPHINE; MAMLUKS; RECAMIER; SYMBOLISM AND STYLE; TALLIEN.

COALITIONS AGAINST FRANCE. The First Coalition was begun in 1792 with a nucleus of Prussia, the Austrian crown territories, and most of the states of the Holy Roman Empire (German states), Piedmont-Sardinia, Naples, and other minor Italian states, with subsidies from the pope (Papal States). After the execution of Louis XVI, Spain, Great Britain, and the United Provinces of the Netherlands joined the coalition. Prussia and Spain, however, made peace with France in 1795, leaving Austria and its minor German and Italian allies to fight the war on the Continent backed by Great Britain on the high seas. Napoleon, however, defeated Austria in the first Italian campaign, leaving only Britain at war with France.

The Second Coalition was formed at the end of 1798 following Napoleon's invasion of Egypt (1798) and the aggressive establishment by the French Republic of sister republics in Europe. It comprised Britain, the Ottoman Empire, Austria, and Russia plus minor European states. The coalition dissolved after Napoleon again defeated the Austrians in the second Italian campaign and French armies won victories in Germany. Even Britain made peace, briefly, by the Treaty of Amiens (1802–3).

The Third Coalition was formed in 1805 after the creation of the French Empire in 1804, the establishment of the Kingdom of Italy in 1805, and the annexation of Piedmont, Elba, and Genoa to France. The major powers were Austria, Russia, and Great Britain. It dissolved after Napoleon's victory at Austerlitz (2 December 1805).

The Fourth Coalition was formed in 1806 and comprised Britain, Prussia, Russia, and minor allies. It was prompted by the creation of the Confederation of the Rhine, the dissolution of the Holy Roman Empire, and Napoleon's rough treatment of Prussia, which had been neutral in 1805. It dissolved after Napoleon's victories at Jena-Auerstädt in 1806 and Friedland in 1807. Only Britain remained at war, as it would continuously until Napoleon was defeated.

The Fifth Coalition comprised Austria and Britain, and, in a sense, rebel Spain. Austria had hoped to foment a German national uprising, hoping also to wreak revenge for former defeats, taking advantage of Napoleon's involvement in Spain. The Germans did not rise, however, and Austria was defeated at Wagram.

The Sixth Coalition comprised Russia and Sweden backed by Great Britain and was formed after Czar Alexander I decided to withdraw from Napoleon's Continental Blockade. There followed in 1812 Napoleon's invasion of Russia and the disastrous retreat.

In 1813 a Seventh Coalition formed, comprising at first Russia, Sweden, and Prussia backed by Great Britain. Austria joined in August, and the other German states as the Allies drove Napoleon's armies from their territories. Eugene held fast in the Kingdom of Italy, but Naples under Joachim Murat and Caroline Bonaparte joined the Allies in January 1814. Meanwhile, Joseph Bonaparte had been defeated in Spain by Anglo-Portuguese and Spanish forces under the duke of Wellington who shortly opened up a second front in southern France. This massive coalition finally effected Napoleon's defeat and forced his abdication in April 1814.

The Eighth Coalition comprised the same powers as the Seventh with the addition of the new Kingdom of the Netherlands. Its troops took the field to repel Napoleon's invasion of Belgium, which ended at Waterloo 18 June 1815.

D. G. Chandler, *The Campaigns of Napoleon: The Mind and Method of History's Greatest Soldier*, (New York, 1966); F. Crouzet, *L'Economie britannique et le blocus continental*, 2 vols. (Paris, 1958); H. E. Deutsch, *Genesis of Napoleonic Imperialism*. (Cambridge, Mass., 1938); H. A. L. Fisher, *Studies in Napoleonic Statesmanship*. (London, 1903); R. Glover, *Britain at Bay, Defence against Bonaparte, 1803-1814*, (London, 1973); S. Ross, *European Diplomatic History, 1789-1815*. (Garden City, N.Y., 1969); J.Tranie, *Napoleon et la Russie: Les Années victorieuses, 1805-1807* (Paris, 1980).

COBENZL, JOHANN LUDWIG VON, COUNT (1753–1809), Austrian foreign minister. As administrator in Galicia (1772–74), and as ambassador to Berlin

(1774–79) and St. Petersburg (1779–95), Cobenzl gained the favor of Foreign Minister Franz von Thugut. In 1797 he negotiated the Treaty of Campo Formio; in 1798 he represented Austria at the Congress of Rastatt; and in 1801 he negotiated with the French at Lunéville. Even though he agreed to the cession of the left bank of the Rhine to France without compensation to Austria, the spirited optimist became Thugut's successor as vice-chancellor and foreign minister. Cobenzl was completely wedded to the cabinet policies of the Old Regime, which prevented his developing either an internal reform program or a clear foreign policy. Austria thus failed to meet the challenge of Napoleonic France. Bonaparte's victories of 1805, culminating at Austerlitz, brought about his fall.

K. O. von Aretin, *Heiliges Römisches Reich* (1967); A. Fournier, *Gentz und Cobenzl* (1880); H. Rössler, *Österreichs Kampf um Deutschlands Befreiung* (1945).

Eckhardt Treichel

Related entries: ARMY, HABSBURG; AUSTERLITZ, BATTLE OF; AUSTERLITZ CAMPAIGN; DIPLOMACY; FOREIGN POLICY.

CODES OF LAW. See LAW, CODES OF.

COLBERT-CHABANAIS, AUGUSTE-FRANCOIS-MARIE, COMTE DE (1777–1809), general of brigade, Sixth Corps. Colbert joined the Battalion of the Seine in 1793 at the age of fifteen to avoid being suspected of royalist sympathies. By 1795 he was aide-de-camp to General Emmanuel Grouchy during the first expedition to Ireland. In 1797 Colbert realized his ambition of being assigned to the Army of Italy commanded by Napoleon Bonaparte, whom Colbert greatly admired all of his life. That same year Colbert was appointed aide-de-camp to the flamboyant Joachim Murat. Colbert, as a part of the Army of the Orient, fought bravely at the Battle of the Pyramids and was seriously wounded at the siege of Acre. He returned to France in 1799 and fought at Marengo. Colbert was promoted to colonel of the Tenth Chasseurs in July 1800. Bonaparte dispatched Colbert as emissary to the court of Alexander I in 1803. After completing the diplomatic mission, Colbert and the Tenth Chasseurs were assigned to Michel Ney's Sixth Corps.

Colbert married Josephine de Canclaux in 1804. She was named *dame du palais* shortly after. A son, Napoleon-Joseph, was born in 1805. Colbert was disappointed in his desire for a court appointment, but he was awarded the Legion of Honor in 1804 and promoted to general of brigade in December 1805 after taking part in the victories of Elchingen, Ulm, and Jena. Colbert participated in the Polish campaigns in 1807. As a reward for his services, he was named baron de l'empire in 1808 and received the chateau of Ainay-le-Vieil (Cher). Ordered to Spain in 1808, he voiced flagging enthusiasm for war. During the pursuit of Sir John Moore in the English retreat to Corunna, Colbert was killed by a sharpshooter at Cacabellos. His chasseurs buried him at the side of the road.

Colbert's career covered the periods of the National Convention, the Directory, the Consulate, and the Empire. His loyalty to France and to Napoleon never wavered. Like so many other young officers, however, by 1808 Colbert's energy and ambition were depleted. But better than most others, Colbert seemed to sense the grandeur and magnificence of this period of French dominance.

A. Colbert, MSS (unpublished), courtesy La Baronne d'Aligny; J. Ojala, *Auguste de Colbert: Aristocratic Survival in an Era of Upheaval, 1793–1809* (Salt Lake City, 1979), and "Auguste Colbert: un aristocrate à cheval sur deux mondes," *Carnet de la Sabretache* no. 28 (1975); Gen. Thoumas, *Les Trois Colbert* (Paris, 1888).

Jeanne A. Ojala

Related entries: ARMY, FRENCH; NEY; SOCIETY.

COLLETTA, PIETRO (1775–1831), Neapolitan general who served King Joseph Bonaparte in Naples and later King Joachim Murat. Trained in the Neapolitan artillery, he supported the Parthenopean Republic (1799), established by the French. Rescued from prison by his family, he became a civil engineer. When the French again conquered Naples in 1806, Joseph Bonaparte restored his military rank, and Colletta served at Gaeta and in Calabria. Under Murat he made a reconnaissance of Capri in preparation for the successful invasion of 1808. Afterward the king made him intendant of Calabria Ulteriore and in 1812 director of roads and bridges. A councillor of state in 1814, Colletta remained loyal to Murat through the disastrous campaign of 1815.

The restored Bourbon king, Ferdinand IV, confirmed Colletta in rank. After the Carbonari revolution of 1820, he served the parliament as minister of war until Austrian armies restored King Ferdinand to power. He was imprisoned in Moravia for two years. Released in 1823, he went to Florence, where he died in 1831 after publishing his *Storia de Reame di Napoli dal 1743 al 1825*.

G. Caponi, *Notizie Intorno alla vita di Pietro Colletta* (Milan, 1967); P. Colletta, *Storia del Reame di Napoli dal 1734 al 1825*, ed. N. Cortese, 3 vols. (Naples, 1957); B. Croce, *Storia della storigrafia italiana nel secolo XIX* (Bari, 1929).

Leonard Macaluso

Related entries: BONAPARTE, JOSEPH; MURAT, J.; NAPLES, KINGDOM OF.

COLLIN DE SUSSY, JEAN-BAPTISTE (1750–1818), minister of manufactures and commerce. Under the Old Regime principal collector of customs at Châlons-sur-Marne and Dunkirk for the General Farm, Collin de Sussy was appointed by Napoleon councillor of state, prefect, and then director general of customs (1801–12). When Napoleon wished to sharpen the enforcement of the high-tariff Trianon and Fontainebleau decrees (5 August and 18 October 1810) as part of his economic warfare against Great Britain, he transferred in June 1811 nearly all economic bureaus and councils of the Ministry of the Interior to a newly formed Ministry of Manufactures and Commerce.

The new ministry was geared to execute the Trianon-Fontainebleau system. The former Bureau of Arts and Manufactures was raised to the rank of division and ordered to coordinate the ministry's efforts to make France self-sufficient in raw materials. A new division for the issuance of licenses was set up. Another new division of customs now supervised the operations of thirty-six customs courts established along French frontiers and eight superior customs courts in such cities as Valenciennes, Hamburg, and Florence. A special Conseil Impérial des Prises, formerly attached to the Ministry of the Navy, was shifted to the new ministry. The previously independent Administration Générale des Douanes was brought under the new ministry, and the position of director general of customs was given to François Ferrier, a well-trained customs official and advocate of extreme protectionism. As it proved, only Collin de Sussy, "*le douanier par excellence,*" could direct this multipronged offensive against Great Britain, and he was appointed the first minister of manufactures and commerce (16 January 1812). He worked valiantly (*sans relâche*, he said) to enforce the tariffs and to do Napoleon's will, but the Russian defeat and the ensuing events rendered his efforts unavailing.

R. J. Barker, "The Conseil général des Manufactures under Napoleon (1810-1814)," *FHS* 6 (Fall 1969); F. Crouzet, *L'économie britannique et le blocus continental*, 2 vols. (Paris, 1958).

Richard J. Barker

Related entries: CONTINENTAL BLOCKADE; GREAT BRITAIN.

COLONIES, FRENCH, ultimately neglected by Napoleon in favor of extending his power on the Continent. As first consul, Napoleon dreamed of reviving the French Empire in America. In 1801 he forced Spain to cede him Louisiana (which had been until 1763 a French colony). He proposed to make Louisiana the breadbasket for the sugar-producing islands of the Caribbean, of which the largest was Santo Domingo. In 1802 Napoleon sent an army under his brother-in-law, General Charles Leclerc, to reestablish control of the island dominated by blacks under General Toussaint L'Ouverture. Fever, however, virtually wiped out the French army, killing even Leclerc. Napoleon rejected any plan to retake the island. In 1803 he sold Louisiana to the United States. Slavery had been abolished in the West Indian colonies by the government of the Terror, but Napoleon restored it. The plantation system had continued much as under the Old Regime anyway in the other French possessions—Guadeloupe, Martinique, lesser islands, and French Guyana. The British took over these possessions at their leisure between 1803 and 1810. In Africa Napoleon inherited Senegal, which was taken by the British in 1809. He secured a French station on Madagascar in 1803. France also possessed some of the Seychelle islands, Mauritius and Réunion. The British took Madagascar in 1810 and all the islands in 1811. The British also seized the Dutch colonies, notably Java and South Africa (the Cape Colony), which had passed to the Napoleonic Kingdom of Holland in 1806. Britain kept the Cape Colony after 1815.

A. Cesaire, *Toussaint Louverture. La Révolution française et le problème colonial* (Paris, 1982); S. Daney, *Histoire de la Martinique depuis la colonisation jusqu'en 1815*,

6 vols. (Fort-de-France, 1846); G. Debien, *Les esclaves aux Antilles françaises* (Basse Terre et Fort-de-France, 1975); C. Martin, *Histoire de l'esclavage dans les colonies françaises* (Paris, 1948); P. Pluchon, *Toussaint Louverture: De l'esclavage au pouvoir* (Paris, 1979); J. Saintoyant, *La colonization française pendant la period Napoléonienne* (Paris, 1931); R. Tallant, *The Louisiana Purchase* (New York, 1952); C. F. Tyson, ed., *Toussaint L'Ouverture* (Englewood Cliffs, N.J., 1973).

Related entries: DIPLOMACY; FOREIGN POLICY; HAITI; UNITED STATES; VIENNA, CONGRESS OF.

COMMERCE. See CONTINENTAL BLOCKADE; WARFARE, ECONOMIC.

CONCORDAT OF 1801. In 1800, Pope Pius VII succeeded Pius VI, who had died at Valence in late 1799. Both Napoleon and the new pope, each for his own reasons, concluded that reconciliation between the Roman Catholic church and the French government was in order. Dealing from strength after Marengo (June 1800), the first consul opened negotiations. A concordat with the pope, he believed, would help end the royalist-clerical rebellion in the west of France that had troubled governments since 1793 and reunite the clergy, divided in loyalty to the Republic or Rome. The majority of peasant-farmers, moreover (85 percent of the French population), was still loyal to the church, and a rapprochement with Rome should help win their support for his regime.

The exiled Bourbon pretender (the comte de Provence, styled Louis XVIII) had also bid for Bonaparte's support, but Napoleon had decided that he needed the pope but not the Bourbons. Napoleon was also aware, however, that many ex-revolutionaries, some high in government, the military, and the professions, were opposed to an accommodation with Rome. Consequently negotiations were conducted in secret. Pius VII signed the document in July 1801, but it was not published until Easter Sunday, 1802, in Paris.

The concordat recognized Catholicism as the religion of the great majority of Frenchmen but not as the state religion. (The Code Napoléon later granted freedom of religion.) The pope was assured possession of the Papal States (somewhat reduced) in Italy. The French government agreed to pay clerical salaries. Bishops were to be nominated by the first consul and consecrated by the pope, and the bishops would choose their own lower clergy. Napoleon achieved his aims: the schism in the French church was ended, the refractory clergy were reconciled to the government, and those who had purchased church property had their titles to it validated. The Concordat of 1801 was to be the governing instrument of church-state relations in France for the next century.

S. Delacroix, *La réorganisation de l'église de France après la Révolution, 1801–1809* (Paris, 1962); H. Jedin and J. Dolan, eds., *History of the Church*, vol. VII: *The Church between Revolution and Restoration* (New York, 1981); P. de LaGorce, *Histoire religieuse de la Révolution française*, 5 vols. (Paris, 1912–23); A. Latreille et al., *Histoire du Catholicisme en France*, vol. 3: *La période contemporaine* (Paris, 1962); E. de Pressense,

L'église et la Révolution française. Histoire des relations de l'église et de l'état de 1789 à 1814, 3d ed. (Paris, 1889); H. H. Walsh, *The Concordat of 1801: A Study of the Problem of Nationalism in the Relations of Church and State* (New York, 1933).

Thomas F. Sheppard

Related entries: CHURCH, ROMAN CATHOLIC; PIUS VII; VENDEE, WAR IN THE.

CONCORDAT OF FONTAINEBLEAU (January 1813), a concordat never agreed to by the pope. Napoleon had had Pius VII moved from Savona to Fontainebleau in June 1812. After his return from Russia (December 1812), Napoleon began negotiations with the pope and in January 1813 thought he had gotten agreement to a concordat under which the pope would invest French bishops and live at Avignon. The aging pope, however, repudiated the concordat after it had been printed in *Le Moniteur*. Napoleon was furious, but no other agreement was forthcoming. A year later, in January 1814, Napoleon simply released the pope and allowed him to return to Rome where he hoped Pius would become a problem for the victorious Allies, who now had to decide what part of the Papal States to restore.

Related entries: CHURCH, ROMAN CATHOLIC; CONCORDAT OF 1801; PIUS VII.

CONDE, HOUSE OF, Bourbon first princes of the blood, famous as marshals of France in every generation from the sixteenth century onward. Louis Joseph, prince of Condé (1736–1818), emigrated during the French Revolution with his son Louis Henri (1756–1830) and his grandson, the duc d'Enghien (1772–1804). The old prince formed an army that fought briefly against Revolutionary France. Napoleon had the duc d'Enghien kidnapped from German territory and executed in 1804 as a warning to the Bourbons and other European monarchs. The duke's father, since he had no other sons, was the last of the Condé princes.

Related entry: ENGHIEN.

CONEGLIANO, DUC DE. see MONCEY.

CONFEDERATION OF THE RHINE (Rheinbund) (1806-13). Napoleon's initial intention of recreating Charlemagne's empire by federating France, Italy, Switzerland, Baden, Württemberg, and Bavaria foundered on the objections of the last two states. But after his victories in the Ulm-Austerlitz campaign, Napoleon in 1806 was able to force sixteen south and west German states, among them Bavaria, Württemberg, Baden, and Hesse-Darmstadt, to form the Confederation of the Rhine, with himself as protector. The princes concluded military alliances with France, and Napoleon rewarded most of them by enlarging their territories and some with elevation in rank.

Under the constitution of the confederation, members withdrew from the Holy Roman Empire, and in consequence Franz II laid down the imperial crown.

After the defeat of Prussia (1806) and Russia (1807), the new Kingdom of Westphalia, plus Saxony, Würzburg, and other states, joined—all of "third Germany"—leaving outside only Prussia and Austria. Nevertheless, Napoleon in 1810 violated the constitution of the confederation by annexing the entire northern German coastal region to France.

In 1806, Prince-Primate Dalberg ordered the Diet of the confederation convoked, but it never met. In fact, all moves by Dalberg or Napoleon to promote development of a central government in the confederation foundered on the determination of the states to preserve their sovereignty. Bonaparte's constitutional plans were part of his hegemonial scheme. He envisioned institutions in all of the states based on French models, with similar constitutions and socioeconomic principles. These were to guarantee the internal consistency of the confederation and to facilitate assimilation into the French Empire. Even the Code Napoléon was never enforced in the states of the confederation, however, and Napoleon had violated the principles of the Revolution by the creation of a new aristocracy. After his intervention in Spain in 1808, Napoleon was satisfied with mobilizing the military resources of the confederation.

The particularism of the German states and an incipient German nationalism (which came to the fore during the wars of liberation) both opposed alien French domination and counteracted the coalescing tendencies of the confederation. Following the defeat of the Corsican in 1813, the confederation fragmented, and its members tried to save themselves by siding with the Allies.

The confederation was more than a mere episode in German history. While the northern and central German states experienced no essential changes in their internal or external structures, the confederation served to lay the foundations for a reform of state and society in the western and southern German states.

T. Bitterauf, *Geschichte des Rheinbundes* (1905); E. Fehrenbach, *Traditionale Gesellschaft und revolutionäres Recht* (1974); E. Weis, "Napoleon und der Rheinbund," *Deutschland und Italien im Zeitalter Napoleons*, ed. A. von Reden-Dohna (1979).

Eckhardt Treichel

Related entries: AUSTERLITZ CAMPAIGN; BAVARIA, KINGDOM OF; FOREIGN POLICY; JENA-AUERSTÄDT-FRIEDLAND CAMPAIGN; SAXONY, KINGDOM OF; WESTPHALIA, KINGDOM OF; WÜRTTEMBERG.

CONGRESS OF CHATILLON. See CHATILLON, CONGRESS OF.

CONSCRIPTION, the draft system whereby the Napoleonic armies were assured adequate manpower. The Jourdan-Delbrel Law, enacted by the Directory on 5 September 1798 and expanded by subsequent legislation in 1799, 1800, 1802, and 1806, was the legal basis for drafting men for the French armies until 1814. Estimates of the total number mobilized under the law vary from 1.6 to 3.6 million men; 2.6 million seems reasonable in the light of France's population during the period.

According to the law, all single men who reached age twenty in a given year formed the class of that year and were liable to be called to the colors until age twenty-five. Until 1812–13, however, far from all eligible men were inducted. The law fell most heavily on the poorer classes, as wealthier men could legally provide substitutes, at prices varying with the locality and the year, on average about 2,000 francs in 1805 and 5,000 francs in 1813.

Although the penalties for conscription evasion and desertion were harsh, including abrogation of civil rights, sentences in prison or the galleys, imposition of heavy fines, and even the quartering of troops in the homes of recalcitrants, both conscription evasion and desertion were a serious problem throughout the entire period. The real crisis came with the military disasters of 1812–13.

The problem was not only the loss of manpower for the army but internally a large number of men outside the law who had to be dealt with by the police and the judicial system. It is impossible to provide an exact figure representing the total of conscription evaders and deserters from 1800 to 1815, but 500,000 does not seem unreasonable given the evidence of widespread opposition to Napoleon's conscription.

E. A. Arnold, Jr., "Some Observations on the French Opposition to Napoleonic Conscription, 1804-1806," *FHS* 4 (1966); M. Baldet, *La Vie quotidienne dans les armées de Napoléon* (Paris, 1964); R. Darquenne, *La Conscription dans le département de Jemappes, 1798–1813* (Mons, 1970); E. d'Hauterive, ed., *La Police secrète du premier Empire: bulletins quotidiens adressés par Fouché à l'Empereur, 1804–1810*, 5 vols. (Paris, 1908–64).

Eric A. Arnold, Jr.

Related entries: ARMY, FRENCH; CARNOT; JOURDAN.

CONSTANT (1778–1845), Napoleon's valet, 1800–14. Born Constant Wairy in the Austrian Netherlands (Belgium), he was the son of prince de Croï's maître d'hôtel. Constant served Eugène de Beauharnais in 1799 and then, briefly, Josephine, who sent him to Bonaparte (1800). For fourteen years, until the abdication at Fontainebleau (April 1814), Constant was Napoleon's valet de chambre, serving in the palace of the Tuileries and on campaign, indefatigable and faithful. Unfortunately his memoirs, which might tell so much of Napoleon's private life, were a publisher's venture, written by a team of professional writers.

Harold T. Parker

Related entry: NAPOLEON, DAILY ROUND.

CONSTANT DE REBECQUE, BENJAMIN (1767–1830), Swiss-born member of the opposition to Bonaparte in the Tribunate, later a political exile, who returned to author the Additional Act, which liberalized the Imperial Constitution of 1815. Constant converted to the moderate republican cause when he settled in France in 1795 with his well-known mistress, Mme. de Staël (their stormy liaison lasted from 1794 to 1811). She engineered his appointment to the Tribunate in 1799 and concurrent recognition of his questionable claims to French nationality. He loudly advocated giving the Tribunate real power, opposed the special courts of 1801 and other authoritarian measures, and was purged from the Tribunate in 1802.

In political eclipse, he went into exile during the late Consulate and Empire. In 1814 he strongly supported Bernadotte for the French throne but was forgiven by the returning Louis XVIII. In March 1815, after Napoleon's landing in France, he wrote a violent newspaper diatribe against the modern-day ''Attila'' or ''Genghis Khan.'' Yet three weeks later he joined the Council of State to help draft the Additional Act, called *la benjamine* by contemporaries.

During the Restoration, Constant achieved a considerable reputation as a novelist (*Adolphe*, 1816) and as a historical analyst of religion (*De la Religion*, 5 vols., 1824–31). He was also a prolific opposition journalist and had formidable oratorical talents as a liberal in the Chamber of Deputies (1819–22, 1824–30). He helped Lafayette advance the cause of Louis-Philippe during the Revolution of 1830. In his political essays, he stressed his consistent defense of liberty against despotism as well as against democracy, which he equated with tyranny of the majority.

Actes du Congrès Benjamin Constant (Geneva, 1968); P. Bastid, *Benjamin Constant et sa doctrine*, 2 vols. (Paris, 1966); B. Constant de Rebecque, *Oeuvres* (Paris, 1964); J. Cruickshank, *Benjamin Constant* (New York, 1974); G. Poulet, *Benjamin Constant par lui-même* (Paris, 1968).

Martin Staum

Related entries: CONSTITUTIONS; HUNDRED DAYS, THE; *IDEOLOGUES*; INSTITUT NATIONAL DES SCIENCES ET DES ARTS; LITERATURE; STAEL-HOLSTEIN.

CONSTITUTION OF 1791. See ESTATES GENERAL.

CONSTITUTIONS. The Consulate and Empire saw four constitutions: that of the Year VIII (22 Frimaire Year VIII; 13 December 1799), which established the Consular Republic; that of the Year X (14, 16 Thermidor Year X; 2 and 4 August 1802), which transformed the decennial Consulate into the Consulate for Life; that of the Year XII (28 Florial Year XIII; 18 May 1804), which created the Empire; and finally the ''Additional Act to the Constitutions of the Empire,'' promulgated during the Hundred Days, 22 April 1815.

The government of the Directory had been the first constitutional republican government (the Convention of 21 September 1792–26 October 1795 had provided only provisional ones.) It had functioned badly since 18 Fructidor Year V (4 September 1797). There had been successive coups since the separation of powers was so complete that any conflict among them was beyond resolving by legal means. Toward the end of 1797, a certain number of politicians—Charles-Maurice Talleyrand, the Abbé Emmanuel Sieyès, Benjamin Constant, General Napoleon Bonaparte—considered it essential to change the constitution. Drafts were prepared, all envisioning a strengthening of the executive power. However, it would have taken nine years to revise the constitution by legal procedures, and nothing was done.

In 1799, however, France was being attacked on its northern and eastern frontiers, its armies beaten in Italy and on the defensive in Holland, Switzerland, and Germany; in France, counterrevolution was again threatening. Sieyès, who became a director in June 1799, was looking for a sword capable of carrying through a coup d'état that would abolish the Constitution of 1795 and substitute a new one. He offered the task to General Moreau, who refused, and then to General Joubert, who was killed in Italy on 15 August. He was undecided whom next to turn to, when, on 9 October, Bonaparte returned from Egypt, having escaped capture by the English fleet. On 14 October, he was in Paris.

Sieyès and Bonaparte immediately completed plans for a coup de force on 18 and 19 Brumaire Year VIII (9 and 10 November 1799). The deputies of the legislative councils of the Directory were dispersed, and a consulate composed of Bonaparte, Sieyès, and Roger Ducos (another former director) was created. Two commissions, one composed of twenty-five deputies from the Council of Five Hundred, the other of twenty-five from the Council of Ancients, were formed to draft a new constitution. What was produced was the work of Sieyès, revised by Bonaparte. Sieyès had set forth certain principles: "Divide [power] to prevent despotism." "Confidence from below, strength from above." "A constitution ought to be short and obscure." Bonaparte insisted that the executive power, which was given to him, be very strong. The constitution was completed on 13 December 1799 and submitted to a referendum, of which the results were not proclaimed until 7 February 1800: 3,011,007 for and only 1,562 against. But without waiting for the results, the constitution had been put in effect on 25 December 1799, when the consuls presented it, declaring, "The Revolution is fixed on the principles on which it began, it is finished."

The Constitution of the Year VIII, as Sieyès had asked, was short: 95 articles (as against 377 in the Constitution of 1795). Unlike preceding constitutions, it had no bill of rights. Only the inviolability of homes and the liberty of the individual were guaranteed; there was no mention of general liberty, equality, or fraternity. The chief of state, called the first consul, named for ten years, received immense powers, both executive and legislative. Bonaparte received the office by name. The two other consuls (J.-J. Régis de Cambacérès and Charles-François Lebrun) had only a consultative voice. The first consul could initiate laws and name magistrates and members of the Council of State.

Universal suffrage, suppressed in 1795, was reestablished, but Sieyès had invented a complicated system to annul its effectiveness. Citizens were to be elected communal notables in number one-tenth that of the voters. The communal notables were to elect departmental notables, who in turn chose national notables. A Senate, composed of eighty members named for life and recruited by co-option, chose from the national lists the consuls (in theory) and the members of the legislative bodies, the Legislature (corps législatif) and Tribunate. The Tribunate was to discuss laws; the Legislature was to vote on them only; the latter was an "assembly of mutes." A Council of State, whose members were named by the first consul, was to draft new laws and judge administrative disputes. The Senate was charged with conserving the constitution, but, on the proposal of the consuls, it could modify it by *senatus consultum*. The judiciary power was vested in new judges, appointed but irremovable.

Bonaparte, provided with quasi-dictatorial powers, reestablished peace, domestic and foreign. The Tribunate and Senate judged that for his work he should positively be accorded a "testimony of National recognition." When consulted, Bonaparte let them know that he wanted the "consulate for life," if the people would support it. The question, presented in plebiscite, received 3,568,000 votes for and 8,374 against. Two *senatus consulta* of 2 and 4 August 1802 modified the constitution. The first consul had his income increased and was provided with a Privy Council. The system of lists of notables (Sieyès' concept) had proved impractical; electoral colleges were substituted in each district and department, elected by universal manhood suffrage, but from among the "most imposing" of the richest citizens. The colleges were to nominate two persons for each opening in the Tribunate or Legislature. At the same time, the Tribunate, which had displayed some mild opposition, was reduced from one hundred to fifty members. The Napoleonic dictatorship became stronger, but the new powers were not sufficient for Bonaparte.

When war with England began again, on 12 May 1803, royalist plots again became evident in France. Bonaparte was threatened with assassination. What would France do if he disappeared? The best means to discourage assassins appeared to be to transform the life consulate into a hereditary monarchy. The *senatus consultum* of 28 Floreal Year XII (18 May 1804) created for Napoleon the French Empire. Submitted to popular referendum, it received 3,572,000 votes for and 2,569 against. The *senatus consultum*, or Constitution of the Year XII, regulated succession to the throne, the total of the "civil list" or salary for the emperor (equal to that of Louis XVI in 1790), and the formation of a court. The powers of the chief of state were again increased. The Tribunate was retained but would be suppressed in 1807, removing the last obstacle to the will of the emperor. However, that constitution appeared to make a concession to French liberal aspirations in creating two senatorial commissions, one charged to safeguard individual liberty and another liberty of the press. In fact, these commissions were ineffectual. The perpetual wars made of the French Empire a veritable military dictatorship.

In 1814, after the disasters of Russia and Germany, the French were weary. The constitutional charter offered by Louis XVIII on his return to France seemed infinitely more liberal than the Napoleonic constitutions. Thus when Napoleon returned from the Isle of Elba (1 March 1815) and reestablished the Empire, it appeared impossible to put the unaltered constitutions back into effect. Napoleon commissioned the liberal writer Benjamin Constant to frame a new constitution, called the Additional Act to the Constitutions of the Empire, promulgated on 22 April 1815. Title VI of that document contained a sort of declaration of rights, guaranteeing equality before the law, of taxation, and eligibility for office, individual liberty, freedom of religion without restriction, liberty of the press, the abolition of the old nobility, of feudal rights, both seigneurial and of the tithe. The executive power was confided to the emperor but limited by the legislative power, which was divided between two chambers, a Senate with hereditary members and a Chamber of Representatives elected directly by electoral colleges composed according to the Constitution of the Year X. The regime was not altogether parliamentary since the ministers were named and removed by the emperor.

That constitution, like those before it, was submitted to referendum, but it drew only 1,305,000 votes for and 4,200 against. It was applied for only two months since the Empire collapsed after the defeat of Waterloo on 18 June 1815.

J. Godechot, *Les institutions de la France sous la Revolution et l'Empire*, 2d ed. (Paris, 1968), and *Les constitutions de la France depuis 1789*, 2d ed. (Paris, 1975).

Jacques Godechot

Related entries: BRUMAIRE, COUP OF 18, YEAR VIII; CADOUDAL; ENGHIEN; FOUCHE; LAW, CODES OF; MONTALIVET; POLICE, MINISTRY OF GENERAL; SIEYES.

CONSULATE, the government established by Napoleon in 1799 after the coup d'état of 18 Brumaire under the Constitution of the Year VIII. See CONSTITUTIONS.

CONTINENTAL BLOCKADE (or CONTINENTAL SYSTEM), a self-blockade of Europe that Napoleon tried to enforce (1806–14) against British commerce in an effort to bankrupt the Nation of Shopkeepers. This extreme form of economic isolation had doctrinal links with earlier protectionist theories (*blocus mercantiliste*). Its more immediate practical antecedents lay in the wartime prohibition (*blocus guerrier*) of British trade with France and its satellites during the National Convention, the Directory, the Consulate, and the early Empire. Its official proclamation came with the Berlin decrees of 21 November 1806. Britain and its possessions were declared in a state of blockade and communications with them forbidden. Seizure of British ships and goods was sanctioned as lawful prize. The formal pretext for such action was the British naval blockade of 16 May 1806; and when in January and November 1807 new orders in council intensified that blockade and also required neutral vessels to call at a British port and have their cargoes inspected, pay duties, and seek licenses for trade with enemy ports, Napoleon responded with his Milan decrees of 23 November and 17 December of the same year. These extended the terms of the Berlin decrees to all neutral ships that complied with the orders and in effect assimilated them to British shipping.

Since the French Empire lacked the naval power to enforce that policy at sea, the Continental Blockade was a misnomer (*blocus fictif*). It was in reality a self-blockade or boycott. In this form it was imposed on the subject states of the Empire during 1807 and officially adopted by some of its allies, notably Russia, following the Tilsit agreement of July. Napoleon's occupation of Portugal and Spain (1807–8) and of the Papal States (1809), his annexation of Holland (1810) and of the Hanse towns and Oldenburg (1810–11), and his Russian campaign (1812) were all aimed, partly at least, at strengthening the blockade. In 1810, however, Napoleon modified his original policy. The Trianon tariffs of 5 August and 17 September permitted the import of many contraband goods on payment of high duties. This measure considerably widened the range of the licenses trade, which was regularized by the Saint-Cloud decree of 3 July 1810. The Fontainebleau decree of 18 October 1810, however, tightened the ban on British-manufactured goods during the next two years. But the blockade was dependent throughout on French military dominance and fell apart as that power was eroded during 1813–14.

Generally historians have judged the Continental Blockade harshly. As a war machine it manifestly failed to force Britain to sue for peace, although it did cause discomfort when relatively effective customs surveillance coincided with a rupture in Anglo-American relations, particularly in 1810–12. It worsened the plight of the maritime ports of continental Europe and so indirectly boosted Britain's comparative naval and commercial strength. It encouraged smuggling, tempted many customs officers into corrupt practices, and helped to enrich wartime speculators and other opportunists, whom in turn it could as quickly ruin. Its applied principle of "France first" (*la France avant tout*) through one-sided tariffs and preferential trade treaties was ultimately self-defeating in some client states. Though not the direct cause of, it certainly exacerbated the general economic crisis of 1810–11. It prolonged the depression in many predominantly agricultural areas of subject Europe, which then reacted unfavorably on French export markets there, chiefly in 1813–14. However, given French naval eclipse, heavy colonial losses, and the cumulative momentum of an economy geared for war, the blockade was arguably the only practical way Napoleon could strike at Britain. Moreover, more recent research has shown that in some vassal states of the continental interior, industry and trade responded well when protected from British competition. The eastern (notably the Rhenish) and Belgian departments were probably the principal beneficiaries of the reorientation of trade routes toward mainland markets. The expansion was most noticeable in cottons, silkstuffs, woolens, the war industries, secondary metallurgy, and the wine trade, especially between 1807 and 1810. The final judgment on the blockade ought to take account of this important shift in the major growth points of the French economy away from the Atlantic littoral toward the mainland markets.

L. Bergeron, *Banquiers, négociants et manufacturiers parisiens du Directoire à l'Empire* (Paris, 1978); F. Crouzet, *L'Economie britannique et le Blocus continental (1806-1813)*, 2 vols. (Paris, 1958), and "Wars, Blockade, and Economic Change in Europe, 1792–1815," *Journal of Economic History* 24 (1964); G. J. Ellis, *Napoleon's Continental Blockade: The Case of Alsace* (Oxford, 1981); E. F. Heckscher, *The Continental System: An Economic Interpretation* (Oxford, 1922).

Geoffrey J. Ellis

Related entries: ECONOMY, FRENCH; GREAT BRITAIN; WARFARE, ECONOMIC.

CONVENTION (1792–95), elected by universal manhood suffrage to write a constitution for a French republic after the overthrow of Louis XVI on 10 August 1792. The Convention tried the king and sent him to the guillotine on 21 January 1793. It established as the new executive the Committee of Public Safety, initially dominated by Jacques Danton. France's foreign enemies had multiplied, however, after the king's execution. Further, a peasant rebellion had begun in the Vendée. The dominant faction in the Convention, styled the Mountain, expelled the moderates (Girondins) from the body in June 1793 in an effort to create a stronger government. This led to a revolt of the federal cities—Lyon, Bordeaux, Marseille, and Toulon. With France at war with all the major European powers (except Russia), backed by Great Britain and with two internal uprisings in progress, a war government was formed with a new Committee of Public Safety ultimately dominated by Maximilien Robespierre. France entered the period of the Terror (1793–94).

By centralization of power and ruthless execution of presumed enemies, the government of Terror managed to suppress the internal rebellions and turn the tide in the foreign war. The organizer of victory was Lazare Carnot, who instituted the *levée en masse* and purged the officer corps. He promoted to general many young officers who distinguished themselves, among them Napoleon Bonaparte, who became famous for his handling of the artillery at Toulon. The Terror government also had plans for social reform, a system of public education, and the establishment of the Great Schools, the Louvre museum and others. Robespierre, however, was not radical enough for the socialist members of his committee and was too radical for many others. And by July 1794, danger to France had been removed, and the Convention finally rebelled against the Terror. Robespierre went to the guillotine on 28 July 1794 (10 Thermidor). The following year, 1794–95, witnessed the so-called Thermidorian Reaction under which the machinery of the Terror was dismantled and the constitution for a conservative republic (Constitution of the Year III) was written. Before it could be put into effect, however, Paris rebelled against the Convention sitting in the Tuileries. With his famous "Whiff of Grapeshot" Napoleon on 5 October 1795 (13 Vendémiaire, Year IV) saved the Convention and allowed the constitution (approved by the vast majority of French voters) to go into effect. Under the ensuing government of the Directory (1795–99) Napoleon gained increasing influence and finally made himself master of the republic by the coup d'état of 18 Brumaire (9 November 1799).

J. Y. de Castelnau, *Histoire de la Terreur* (Paris, 1970); A. Mathiez, *The Thermidorian Reaction* (New York, 1931); R. R. Palmer, *Twelve Who Ruled* (Princeton, N.J., 1941); A. Patrick, *Men of the First French Republic: Political Alignments in the National Convention of 1792* (Baltimore, 1972); M. Reinhard, *Le Grand Carnot*, 2 vols. (Paris, 1950-52); M. J. Sydenham, *The Girondins* (London, 1961).

Related entries: BRUMAIRE, COUP OF 18 YEAR VIII; CARNOT; COALITIONS AGAINST FRANCE; CONSTITUTIONS; DIRECTORY; TERROR, THE; VENDEE, WAR IN THE; VENDEMIAIRE.

CORONATION OF NAPOLEON I (2 December 1804). See NAPOLEON I.

CORPS. See ARMY, FRENCH.

CORPS LEGISLATIF, a legislative body of the Consulate and Empire. See CONSTITUTIONS.

CORSAIR WAR (1800–14). ''Corsair'' is considered here to be the equivalent of ''privateer'': a privately owned vessel licensed by a recognized political entity, normally a state, to pursue warfare against the vessels of a declared enemy and also a person engaged in privateering, defined as belligerent action against enemy maritime commerce and supply lines. Today that aspect of conflict at sea is known as commerce raiding and is carried out exclusively by national naval forces.

During the Napoleonic phase of the Franco-British struggle for world predominancy, privateer warfare was governed by a voluminous and complex body of national and international agreements, laws, regulations, customs, and jurisprudence. Theoretically western powers observed generally accepted rules for proclaiming states of belligerency, of truce, and of peace, for licensing privateersmen and pursuing commerce raiding, for determining the nationality of vessels and crews, for judging the validity of prizes, and for exchanging prisoners, to mention only a few salient points. There was, however, no true consensus as to the rights and obligations of neutrals or as to what constituted contraband. Problems resulting from the American and French revolutions had been resolved in the first case by acceptance of the existence of a new maritime state and in the second by the restoration of French privateering regulations and prize law to principles compatible with *ancien régime* jurisprudence and with international agreements and customs. Within the context of Franco-American relations, one point remained ambiguous: that of the crew list (*rôle d'équipage*) as key proof of nationality.

From the rupture of the Peace of Amiens (1803) to Waterloo (1815), belligerent naval forces were strained to the breaking point by blockade and convoy duties, and commerce raiding was left largely to privateers. Proclaimed blockades became so theoretical as to be fictitious but sufficed to condemn prizes. As belligerent merchant shipping diminished, only neutral carriers could keep supply lines open. The neutrals suddenly found themselves at the heart of the struggle, wooed and harassed simultaneously by the two belligerents and their allies.

As initiative at sea belonged to Great Britain, the main theaters of privateering activity were in zones of vital importance to France: in the vicinity of its ports, particularly on the western coasts, on its major shipping lanes, and around its colonial possessions in the Atlantic and Indian oceans. French warships and privateers operated in British theaters, off coasts of Great Britain and its colonies. Approaching the possessions of either belligerent was dangerous for enemy and neutral shipping alike. The Baltic Sea was another highly contested area, with the control of Scandinavian and Baltic trade, especially in naval stores, at stake. As Spanish insurrectional forces and the British army gained control of Iberic ports, the waters around Spain and Portugal, particularly in the Bay of Biscay, became crucial privateering grounds for French raiders preying on ships carrying supplies to Iberic ports in enemy hands. The main objective of both France and Great Britain, however, was to control American shipping, each attempting to attract U.S. ships to its own ports and to capture those trading with the other. The United States was in fact the only neutral power whose maritime capacity, if thrown into the balance, was sufficient to tip the scales in favor of one or the other. Nowhere was the role of U.S. shipping more important than in the Caribbean where the survival of the French islands depended on U.S. commerce.

Traditional reasons for capturing merchant vessels (running blockades, carrying contraband goods, enemy ships and goods disguised under false colors and papers) were vastly extended by the belligerents: entire zones were declared under blockade without the physical presence of naval forces capable of enforcing it, definitions of contraband became all inclusive, the use of false flags and ship papers was so widespread that it was alleged by captors as either real or intended whether or not proof was found. Almost any merchant ship could be claimed to be sufficiently suspect to be carried into port as a prize. Not all were condemned by any means, but in the war of attrition being waged at sea the results were the same: import-export trade, not to speak of supply lines, were disrupted, and the goods detained on captured ships, even if later released, rarely reached their intended destination.

Neutrals—that is, northern European powers and the United States—resisted diplomatically and with legal and administrative countermeasures but were unable to impose their views. Step by step England extended control over the waters; by 1810 it dominated the Caribbean and the Baltic and tightened control of the coasts of the French Empire.

Both the land and the sea powers were in fact seriously overextended, and both soon were confronted with situations they could not control. Russia proved to be a more serious threat to the existence of the French Empire than the United States, at war with England in 1812, was to British supremacy at sea. France was finally defeated, but on land, and it took ground forces from virtually all of Europe, including Great Britain, to do it. The Anglo-American War of 1812, hardly glorious for either side, left the United States confirmed within its own vast boundaries and at sea. Napoleon's pro-neutral policy (French actions against neutral shipping were declared to be measures of exception for which claims for indemnity would be entertained after the return of peace) had finally borne fruit.

It is not to be concluded that France was ever completely sealed off from the sea and from vital supplies such as northern European naval stores. Naval construction continued in French naval shipyards, and the men of war Napoleon built equipped the French navy up to the age of steam. By the same token, French armed vessels, both public and private, remained at sea to the end, as is indicated by the number of American prizes they captured: some 600 between 1800 and 1813, as compared with 834 taken from 1797 to October 1800 during the quasi-war. French captures of British vessels were greatly superior in numbers, judging from the volume they represent today in French prize records. In other words, the French flag was not swept from the seas even though the British blockade did keep French squadrons and fleets bottled up in port. As a way of gauging the numerical importance of the U.S. merchant fleet of the time, while France captured some 1,450 U.S. ships, Great Britain captured many more, which, along with impressment of seamen, largely explains the War of 1812.

During the war years and the peace negotiations that followed, much was said of abuses and lawlessness in privateering, and the allegation of piracy was bandied about. Certainly the rules to which lip-service had previously been paid had been cast aside by all concerned, but it cannot be said that one side was more guilty of abuses than the other. Two troubled zones existed briefly, however, on the French side: the Caribbean during local rebellion, as in Saint Domingue (1800–1803), again during the final stage of siege (1808–10), and in some Spanish ports as French occupation forces gradually lost control and faced defeat. In both cases the fundamental reason was the same: the breakdown of governmental structure.

U. Bonnel, *La France, les Etats-Unis et la guerre de course (1797-1815)* (Paris, 1961), (in collaboration) *Sainte-Hélène, Terre d'exil* (Paris, 1971), "Histoire de la station navale de Santo-Domingo de 1803 à 1809," *Revue d'histoire économique et sociale* 40 (1962), "The Privateer as a Vector of Revolutionary Ideas (1775-1825)" *CRE* (1979), *Privateering and Piracy*, 1975 Symposium, San Francisco, International Commission for Maritime History (Paris, 1975), *The American Revolution and the Sea*, 1974 Symposium, National Maritime Museum, Greenwich (London, 1975); J. R. Garitee, *The Republic's Private Navy: The American Privateering Business as Practiced by Baltimore during the War of 1812* (Mystic Seaport, Conn., 1977).

Ulane Bonnel

Related entries: CONTINENTAL BLOCKADE; DIPLOMACY; FOREIGN POLICY; NAVY, BRITISH; NAVY, FRENCH; UNITED STATES; WARFARE, ECONOMIC.

CORSICA, island province of France (later a department) where Napoleon was born on 15 August 1769 in the capital, Ajaccio. Corsica lies about one hundred miles southeast of the southern coast of France in the Mediterranean. It had been owned by the Republic (city state) of Genoa between 1347 and 1768. In 1729 it revolted for independence, and between 1755 and 1768, under the leadership of Pasquale Paoli, virtually achieved it. In 1768 Louis XV of France, fearful that Britain would establish naval bases on the island, bought it from Genoa. French forces crushed the rebellion; Paoli fled to England; his followers, including Napoleon's father, Carlo, were offered amnesty, and most took it. See BONAPARTE; NAPOLEON I; PAOLI.

COULOMB, CHARLES-AUGUSTIN (1736–1806), major figure in the history of physics and engineering. Patronized by Napoleon, Coulomb worked in the fields of applied mechanics, electricity, and magnetism. He was born in Angoulême into a family that had been prominent in legal and administrative circles at Montpellier. He early showed an aptitude for mathematics and was admitted in February 1760 to the celebrated military engineering school at Mézières. Upon graduation in November 1761, he served as military engineer in the West Indies and at Cherbourg and Rochefort. By 1781 his scientific memoirs on magnetism, torsion, and friction won him election to the Royal Academy of Science. Thereafter, as a member of the Academy and then of its successor, the Institut, he devoted his life in Paris largely to research. In his scientific papers, he applied the Newtonian concepts of attraction and repulsion to mechanics, electricity, and magnetism. The careful, quantitative, experimental nature of his contribution is perpetuated in the scientific term *coulomb*, the unit of electric charge. Under Napoleon, from 1802 to 1806, he was also one of the hard-working inspectors general of public instruction who vigorously supervised the establishment of the *lycées*.

C. S. Gillmor, *Coulomb and the Evolution of Physics and Engineering in Eighteenth-Century France* (Princeton, N.J., 1971).

Harold T. Parker

Related entries: EDUCATION; SCIENCE; UNIVERSITY, IMPERIAL.

COUNCIL OF STATE. See ADMINISTRATION.

COUNCILS OF PRUD'HOMMES. See LABOR LEGISLATION.

COURT, IMPERIAL. See NOBILITY, IMPERIAL; SOCIETY.

COWLEY, HENRY WELLESLEY, FIRST BARON (1773–1847), minister plenipotentiary and envoy extraordinary to Spain, 1810–12, and ambassador to Spain, 1812–21. Appointed to the embassy in Spain by his brother, Marquess Wellesley, Henry Wellesley owed his position to more than mere familial ties. As a young man, Wellesley had served as a précis writer in the Foreign Office, as an attaché in Stockholm and the Hague, as secretary to Lord Wellesley during his governor-generalship in India, and as secretary to the treasury. Despite this preparation, his years in Spain proved difficult. During the Peninsular War (1808–13), Wellesley's primary goal was to help rebel Spain mobilize for an effective effort against Napoleon's armies, a task complicated by Spain's suspicions of British motives. The rebel Cortes, governing in the name of Ferdinand VII, was besieged in Cadiz, protected largely by the British navy. Until 1812, the French occupied all but the most remote areas of Spain. The Spanish remained prideful, all the same. Wellesley got no trade concessions for the British in the Spanish colonies but supported and advised the Spanish in the interest of Allied victory. The fact that the Spanish government survived these years was due in large part to the practical and decisive measures taken by Wellesley. During his embassy he advanced money to the Spanish when necessary, coordinated the provisioning and supplying of the Spanish military, and he helped Spain organize the nucleus of a reformed army.

After leaving Spain, Lord Cowley served England as ambassador to Austria from 1823 to 1831 and to France from 1841 to 1846.

G. Lovett, *Napoleon and the Birth of Modern Spain* (New York, 1965); C. W. C. Oman, *A History of the Peninsular War* (Oxford, 1903–30); H. Wellesley, *Diary and Correspondence of Henry Wellesley, 1st Lord Cowley* (London, 1930).

John K. Severn

Related entries: PENINSULAR WAR; SPAIN.

CRAONNE, BATTLE OF. See FRANCE, CAMPAIGN OF.

CRETET, EMMANUEL (1747–1809), comte de Champmol, director of the administration of bridges and highways (1799–1806), governor of the Bank of France (1806), minister of the interior (1807–1809). Born in Pont-de-Beauvoisin in Dauphiné, the son of a well-to-do merchant, Crétet built his own fortune by trading with America, which he visited seven times, and becoming head of a Paris fire insurance company. During the Revolution he substantially increased his fortune by the purchase of confiscated land, notably in the vicinity of Dijon, in the department of Côte d'Or. In 1795 the propertied voters of his neighborhood elected him member of the Council of Ancients, where he specialized in tax legislation, and specifically in pushing the enactment of a tax for the improvement of roads. Although elected in 1799 president of the council, he rallied along with many propertied associates to Bonaparte and to his promise of stable, efficient government. Bonaparte named him councillor of state, senator, and director of the administration of bridges and highways. Ignorant of engineering, Crétet yet won the esteem of the engineers and of Napoleon himself by his probity, attentiveness to business, intelligent administrative decisions, and persuasive tact. Besides promoting a strong public works program (Paris bridges, highways from Paris to Brest, to Boulogne, to Cherbourg, and over the Alpine passes of Mont-Cénis and Simplon to Italy, canals of Burgundy and Saint-Quentin), he insisted on the removal of illegal obstructions, such as old mills, from navigable streams, and assured the prompt payment of contractors. By the decree of 25 August 1804 he reorganized the bridges and highways administration and its *école* for greater efficiency (for example, the inspectors general of the engineering corps were to be named no longer by their colleagues but by the government).

After the scandalous banking crisis of 1805, Crétet was named governor of the Bank of France (25 April 1806), which he reorganized within a year. Napoleon then named him minister of interior (9 August 1807). A terminal illness forced his early retirement, however, before he could have much effect on the ministry's operations. Not a Talleyrand, a Fouché, or even a Cambacérès, he was yet a very able official who typified the *ralliement* of the propertied class to Napoleon and who helped him reorganize the central administration for honesty, efficiency, and stability.

A. Lorion, "Un grand commis du Consulat et de l'Empire: Emmanuel Crétet," *RIN* 114 (1970); M. Marion, *Histoire financière de la France depuis 1715*, Vol. 4: *1797–1818* (Paris, 1927); J. Petot, *Histoire de l'administration des ponts et chaussées 1599–1815* (Paris, 1958).

Harold T. Parker

Related entries: ADMINISTRATION; BANK OF FRANCE; BARBE-MARBOIS.

CUOCO, VINCENZO (1770–1823), Italian propagandist for unification. He was allowed to publish newspapers in the Bonaparte Kingdom of Italy and later in the Kingdom of Naples.

Related entries: ITALY, KINGDOM OF; NAPLES, KINGDOM OF.

CZARTORYSKI, name of prominent princely family of Poland. After Napoleon established the Duchy of Warsaw (1807), the head of the family, Adam Czartoryski (1734–1823), cooperated with the French. His son, Adam Jerzy (1770–1861), however, fled to Russia where he served the czar. The younger Adam Czartoryski became prominent in the Russian-sponsored Kingdom of Poland established in 1815.

Related entries: ALEXANDER I; RUSSIA; WARSAW, DUCHY OF.

CZECHS, THE. Except for the Battle of Slavkov (Austerlitz) in 1805 and the French occupation of southern Bohemia and Moravia in 1805–6 and 1809, the Czechs felt Napoleonic influences only indirectly. Napoleon had plans for a separate Czech state, independent or united with Saxony or Bavaria, but it never materialized. The heavy war costs and rampant inflation fell heavily on the peasantry, though Bohemian textile manufacturing temporarily benefited from the Continental System. The upper classes generally supported governmental surveillance, censorship, and counterrevolutionary propaganda. But Revolutionary tenets appealed strongly to the peasants, who expressed themselves openly, notably in the tragic "Helvetian Rebellion" of 1797, when peasant military deserters fought government troops in the Bohemian-Moravian highlands. Most important was the galvanizing effect of the Napoleonic era on the growth of Czech national consciousness in the following century, fueled especially by contacts with Russian troops and the pride of their fellow Slavs in Russian victories over Napoleonic armies.

J. Polišenský, *Napoleon a srdce Evropy* (Prague, 1971).

Joseph F. Zacek

Related entries: AUSTRIA; WARSAW, DUCHY OF.

D

DABROWSKI, JAN HENRYK (1755–1818), Polish and sometime French general; organizer of the Polish Legions in the French army. Dąbrowski served in the Saxon Guard and Polish cavalry and was a general in the ill-fated Polish uprising of 1794, of which he wrote a history, published in German in 1796.

Hoping ultimately to win aid for Polish independence, he took service in the French army and organized (1797) a Polish Legion, and later several, which fought in Italy and elsewhere. In 1806, Dąbrowski was commissioned by Napoleon to raise 40,000 Poles to fight alongside the French. This he did, and more, personally commanding troops in battle. He was greatly disappointed, therefore, when Prince Poniatowski, not he, was made minister of war of the new Duchy of Warsaw (1807). He became insubordinate and in effect was retired. From his estates he made contacts with radical, even republican, elements in both Poland and Germany.

When Austria attacked the French Empire in 1809, however, Dąbrowski thought Poland was in jeopardy and returned to service. He gave his full cooperation to Poniatowski, even assisting in army reforms. In 1812, he participated in the invasion of Russia and was wounded during the bloody crossing of the Berezina. In 1813, he fought for Napoleon at Leipzig.

Thereafter, however, the Russian czar's offer to create and protect a Polish kingdom seemed Poland's best hope. When Alexander I summoned Dąbrowski to Warsaw, he went and took service on the Military Committee of the Grand Duke Constantine, the Russian viceroy. He was made senator-palatine and general of the artillery, offices he held until his death.

Dąbrowski's direct contributions to Polish history were military, but his role in perpetuating Polish national consciousness and a Polish state is very great.

S. Askenazy, *Napoleon a Polska*, 3 vols. (Warsaw, 1918–19); L. Chodźko, *Histoire des légions polonaises en Italie*, 2 vols. (Paris, 1829); K. Kołączkowski, *Henryk Dąbrowski twórca legionów polskich we Włoszech 1755-1818* (Cracow, 1901); A. Skałkowski, *Jan Henryk Dąbrowski* (Cracow, 1904).

John Stanley

Related entries: ALEXANDER I; POLISH LEGIONS; VIENNA, CONGRESS OF; WARSAW, DUCHY OF.

DALBERG, KARL THEODOR VON (1744–1817), prince primate of the Confederation of the Rhine. The leading representative of the Catholic Enlightenment, Dalberg became administrator of the Bishopric of Erfurt in 1772, coadjutor of Mainz in 1787 and also of Constance in 1788, bishop of Constance in 1800, and archbishop-elector of Mainz in 1802. In 1803 Dalberg was the only German ecclesiastical prince to survive the secularization and was compensated with Aschaffenburg, Wetzlar, and Regensburg for the loss of his territories on the left bank of the Rhine.

In 1806 Napoleon added Frankfurt to Dalberg's lands and had him named prince primate of the Confederation of the Rhine. Dalberg had made friends with Bonaparte in the hope of fostering German unity and, with the pope's approval, establishing a German national church. But the Confederation of the Rhine, formed in 1806, broke up the Holy Roman Empire and did not contribute to either dream. And Dalberg's plan for converting the confederation into a federal state foundered.

In 1810, Napoleon created the Grand Duchy of Frankfurt, adding Fulda and Hanau to Dalberg's territories but detaching Regensburg, which went to Bavaria. Dalberg added grand duke to his other titles and began immediately to modernize the new state through French-style reforms. With Napoleon's defeat in Germany in 1813, however, Dalberg lost all his secular offices. Of all his dignities he retained only that of archbishop of Regensburg.

K.von Beaulieu-Marconnay, *Karl von Dalberg und seine Zeit* (1879); P. Darmstädter, *Das Grossherzogtum Frankfurt* (1901); A. Freyh, *Karl Theodor von Dalberg* (1978); W. Hertel, *Karl Theodor von Dalberg zwischen Reich und Rheinbund* (1952).

Eckhardt Treichel

Related entries: BEAUHARNAIS, E.; CONFEDERATION OF THE RHINE; FRANKFURT, GRAND DUCHY OF; GERMAN WAR OF LIBERATION.

DALMATIA. See ILLYRIAN PROVINCES.

DALMATIE, DUC DE. See SOULT.

DANDOLO, VINCENZO (1758-1819), Venetian Francophile who directed the civil government of Venetian Dalmatia (for General, later Marshal, Auguste Marmont) while it was part of the Kingdom of Italy (1805–9). For reasons that are obscure, he retired from the government when Dalmatia was integrated into the Illyrian Provinces in 1809. See ILLYRIAN PROVINCES.

DANZIG (GDANSK), FREE CITY OF (German: Freistadt Danzig; French: Ville Libre de Dantzig). By the Treaty of Tilsit, Gdansk, which had been under Polish rule as recently as 1793, was made a free city under the protection of Prussia and Saxony. The French maintained control, however, with a French-Polish garrison.

The territory of Gdansk extended two leagues beyond the city limits; thus it had some 60,000 inhabitants. The French governor was General J. Rapp for the city's entire existence, seconded by General Michał Grabowski. The free navigation of the Vistula was guaranteed for the Duchy of Warsaw, and Gdansk could not tax its ships or cargoes.

The major merchant families, supported by the French, dominated the city. Gdansk had no constitution despite Napoleon's promise of one. The civil governing bodies were an appointive Senate of twelve and a "Third Order" of sixteen (later twenty-three). Although both Tilsit and the Franco-Gdansk treaties of 1807 guaranteed the city its ancient laws, essentially the Chelm laws of 1346, the Code Napoléon became the law in 1809.

The pro-Prussian feelings of Gdansk's citizens were generally exaggerated by Prussian historians of the Wilhelmine period. The introduction of the Code Napoléon met with some resistance, but in general the city was peaceful throughout this period. Pastor A. F. Blech was a genuine opponent of the French occupation, as the books say, but had little following. The French Revolution had many sympathizers among Gdansk's merchants and the abolition of the city's and their privileges by the Prussians in 1793 had caused far more anger than anything the French did.

From January to December 1813 the city was under siege by a Russian army commanded by Prince Platov. The garrison surrendered only after almost a year of fighting, and Gdansk's own military detachment as well as a volunteer battalion were active in the defense. Gdansk's diplomatic representative in Paris appealed to Alexander I, Robert Castlereagh, and even Clemens von Metternich to prevent the return of Gdansk to Prussia. Nevertheless, the Vienna settlement gave Gdansk to the Hohenzollerns.

S. Askenazy, *Gdańsk a Polska* (Warsaw, 1923); A. F. Blech, *Geschichte der siebenjährigen Leiden Danzigs von 1807–1814* (Danzig, 1815); L. Bourelly, *Les sièges de Dantzig et l'occupation française (1807–1813)* (Paris, 1904); G. Köhler, *Geschichte der Festungen Danzig und Weichselmünde bis zum Jahre 1814*, 2 vols. (Breslau, 1893); J. Rapp, *Mémoires* (Brussels, 1823); E. Rozenkranz, *Napoleońskie Wolne Miasto Gdańsk* (Gdańsk, 1980).

John Stanley

Related entries: ALEXANDER I; FRIEDRICH AUGUST III; PRUSSIA, KINGDOM OF; SAXONY, KINGDOM OF; TILSIT, TREATIES OF; WARSAW, DUCHY OF.

DARU, PIERRE-ANTOINE-NOEL-BRUNO, COMTE (1767–1829). Daru, like Lazare Carnot, led a double life. He was the translator of Horace, a minor poet, and during the Restoration author of a history of Venice in seven volumes. But he is known to history as a military administrator who fed, clothed, paid, and otherwise supplied the Napoleonic armies. Napoleon thought him the ablest of his administrators: "Daru est bon à tout, il a du jugement, de l'esprit, une grande capacité de travail, une âme et un corps de fer." He was born in Montpellier, the son of Noël Daru, a barrister who first practiced law before the local parlement, then worked for the Company of the Indies, and finally in 1749 became chief of the bureau and in 1762 secretary general of the intendancy of Languedoc. The young Daru, between ages fifteen and seventeen, was employed for a time as a clerk in the bureau of the intendancy until in 1784 his father purchased for him the office of *commissaire provincial des guerres* in the Royal Army. Essentially Daru was in the quartermaster corps, responsible for tallying the number of effectives in his provincial contingent, providing their pay, and assuring their subsistence, clothing, transport, and lodging. During the 1780s and wars of the Revolution, Daru, a hard worker, rose in the ranks until in 1799 he was *ordonnateur en chef* (chief quartermaster) of the Army of Switzerland under André Masséna, responsible for food, clothing, transport, and hospitals. After tours of duty in the Ministry of War as chief of its first division (subsistence) during the Directory and its secretary general under Bonaparte, he was appointed to the Tribunate in 1802 and named councillor of state and intendant of the imperial household in 1805.

The wars of 1805, 1806, and 1807 propelled Daru into immense operations. On 30 August 1805 he was named *commissaire général* (intendant general) of the Grand Army that was about to invade southern Germany and Austria and charged with its supply. On 14 November 1805 Napoleon appointed him intendant general of the conquered territories (largely taken from Austria) and on 1 January 1806 commissioner charged with the execution of the Treaty of Pressburg. Again, in the war with Prussia, he was named on 19 October 1806 intendant general of the Grand Army and of the conquered territories, and on 13 and 17 July 1807 commissioner for the execution of the convention of Königsberg and the Treaties of Tilsit. As intendant general of the army, he was responsible for its food, clothing, transport, and hospitals; as intendant of conquered territories, he levied the contributions on the defeated countries that paid for the Grand Army's supplies and returned a surplus to Napoleon's treasury. Daru's voluminous thousand-page report of 15 January 1809 giving the receipts and expenses of his double activity from October 1806 to November 1808 shows how Napoleon used war to pay for war (La Barre de Nanteuil, p. 163; printer's errors corrected).

Contributions in money levied (francs) on the conquered country	513,744,410.15
Payments in kind	90,483,511.94
Total receipts	604,227,922.09
Expenses of the campaign	233,544,363.37
Supplies in magazine	11,465,028.16
Paid into the treasury	359,218,530.56

Under "expenses of the campaign" he had supplied the army with bread and often meat and had manufactured 1 million pairs of shoes and 300,000 shirts. With the Austrian war of 1809, he again was intendant general of the Grand

Army. When Hugues Maret became foreign secretary, Daru succeeded him on 17 April 1811 as minister secretary of state and in that capacity accompanied Napoleon during the invasion of Russia and aided the new intendant general of the Grand Army, Mathieu Dumas. On 20 November 1813 Napoleon appointed Daru minister of the administration of war, a post he also held during the Hundred Days. Sturdily independent, he opposed both the Austrian and Russian marriages (he wished Napoleon to marry a Frenchwoman), he warned against the invasion of Russia, and he favored acceptance of the Austrian peace terms in 1813; but once Napoleon decided, Daru just as sturdily obeyed.

H. de la Barre de Nanteuil, *Le comte Daru, ou l'administration militaire sous la Révolution et l'Empire* (Paris, 1966); M. Bergerot, ''Daru'' (dissertation, Sorbonne, 1979); S. d'Huart, *Les archives Daru* (Paris, 1962), ''Daru et le projet impérial de code militaire,'' *RIN* 85 (1963), and *Lettres, ordres et apostilles de Napoléon Ier, extraits des Archives Daru* (Paris, 1965); C. Lesage, *Napoleon Ier, créancier de la Prusse (1807-1814)* (Paris, 1924).

Harold T. Parker

Related entry: ADMINISTRATION, MILITARY.

DAUNOU, PIERRE-CLAUDE-FRANCOIS (1761–1840), legislator, *idéologue*, historian. An Oratorian priest and professor, he was defrocked in the Terror. A nonregicide *conventionnel*, he was imprisoned with the Girondins. Daunou was a prominent deputy of the Council of Five Hundred, member of the National Institute, which he helped found together with the central schools by the Law of 3 Brumaire Year IV (25 October 1795), and commissioner for organizing the Roman Republic. He disapproved of the coup of 18 Brumaire but made a draft of the Constitution of Year VIII, from which Napoleon excised many liberal provisions. Daunou thrice refused to become councillor of state but sat in the Tribunate until 1802 when he was purged for his opposition along with nineteen other *idéologues*. Napoleon, however, admired Daunou's integrity and appointed him director of the National Archives, which he reorganized. At Napoleon's request, he composed in 1809 his *Essai historique sur la puissance temporelle des papes*, which served the emperor in his conflict with Pius VII. Daunou remained a stalwart and outspoken liberal in the Bourbon and Orleanist regimes. He authored and edited scores of books and over four hundred articles on history, literature, and politics.

Emmet Kennedy

Related entry: IDEOLOGUES.

DAURE, JEAN-PAUL. See NAPLES, KINGDOM OF; NAPLES, KINGDOM OF: MINISTERS.

DAVID, JACQUES-LOUIS (1748–1825), first painter to the emperor. David's position allowed him to promote liberal ideals through his artistic activities. In the *Leonidas at Thermopylae* (1799–1814) he attempted to demonstrate the viability of these ideals, while in several portraits and in the *Coronation* (1807) and the *Distribution of the Eagles* (1810) (conceived as parts of a series depicting the new social orders), he purveyed an image of Napoleon as guarantor of the gains of the Revolution. With Napoleon's blessing, he ran private art classes and exhibited the *Sabines* (1799) commercially. He also expressed interest in establishing cooperative working relationships among artists, artisans, and manufacturers now freed from guild controls.

David's independent spirit placed strains on his relations with Napoleon and with his fellow artists. The emperor resisted his requests for larger commissions and real administrative authority. At the same time David fought artists' efforts to turn the Ecole des Beaux Arts and Salon into closed corporate bodies.

Historically this phase of David's career is significant. He set the style for later historical painting and raised the social and economic status of his profession to new heights. He identified the cluster of entrepreneurial attitudes, methods, working relationships, and institutions that many later artists would adopt in their stand against the establishment.

E. Delécluze, *Louis David* (Paris, 1855); M. Levin, "David, de Staël, and Fontanes," *Gazette des Beaux-arts* (January 1980); D. and G. Wildenstein, *Louis David, documents* (Paris, 1973).

Miriam R. Levin

Related entries: ARCHITECTURE; ART; CANOVA; DENON; GERARD, F.-P.-S.; GROS; GUERLIN; INSTITUT NATIONAL DES SCIENCES ET DES ARTS; ISABEY; LOUVRE; SCULPTURE; SYMBOLISM AND STYLE; VIGEE-LEBRUN.

DAVOUT, LOUIS-NICHOLAS (1770–1823), duc de Auerstädt, prince d'Eckmühl, marshal of the empire; probably Napoleon's most effective independent commander. Louis N. d'Avout was born of an old noble Burgundian family at Annoux in 1770. He was educated at the military school at Auxerre and the Royal Military School in Paris. He served in the king's army until 1791 when he was discharged for Revolutionary activities. The same year he joined a volunteer battalion, was elected lieutenant colonel, and served in the armies of northern France and the Rhine until the Peace of Campo Formio in 1797. In 1798, he met General Bonaparte and served under him in the Egyptian campaign. With the creation of the Empire in 1804, Davout was named among the original sixteen marshals of the empire. He commanded the Third Corps of the Grand Army in the campaign of 1805 and contributed to the victory of Austerlitz. On 14 October 1806, Davout's Third Corps won a brilliant victory over the bulk of the Prussian army at Auerstädt, while Napoleon destroyed the remainder of the Prussian force at Jena. In recognition of this victory, Davout was given the title of duc de Auerstädt in 1808.

Davout fought at Eylau in 1807 and then at Eckmühl and Wagram in 1809. He was named prince d'Eckmühl in 1810 and military governor of the Duchy of Warsaw (1810–11). When Napoleon invaded Russia in 1812, Davout commanded the First Corps of the Grand Army. He was seriously wounded at the Battle of Borodino and took part in the disastrous retreat from Moscow. In 1813, he held the lower Elbe with the Thirteenth Corps. After the defeat at Leipzig and the French retreat west of the Rhine, Davout was besieged in the fortified city of Hamburg for seven months. Following Napoleon's abdication in April 1814, Davout retired to his estate in the disfavor of the restored Bourbon king. With Napoleon's return to power in 1815, he was named minister of war and remained in Paris during the Waterloo campaign. After the second abdication, he was exiled to Louviers because of his defense of Marshal Michel Ney. Through the intercession of friends at court he was received by Louis XVIII in 1818 and subsequently had his marshal's baton restored and was named a peer of the realm. He died in Paris in 1823.

Archives de la Guerre, K[1]-K[100], "Donation Davout"; A.-L. de Blocqueville, *Le Maréchal Davout prince d'Eckmühl: raconté par les siens et par lui-même*, 4 vols. (Paris, 1887); L. N. Davout, *Correspondance du maréchal Davout prince d'Eckmühl: ses commandements, son ministère, 1801-1815*, ed. Charles de Mazade, 4 vols. (Paris, 1885); J. G. Gallaher, *The Iron Marshal: A Biography of Louis N. Davout* (Carbondale, Ill., 1976).

John Gallaher

Related entries: AUSTERLITZ, BATTLE OF; AUSTERLITZ CAMPAIGN; BORODINO, BATTLE OF; JENA-AUERSTÄDT, BATTLES OF; JENA-AUERSTÄDT-FRIEDLAND CAMPAIGN; MARSHALS OF THE EMPIRE; RUSSIAN CAMPAIGN; WAGRAM; WATERLOO CAMPAIGN.

DECRES, DENIS (1761–1820), admiral, minister of the navy from 2 October 1801 to April 1814 and during the Hundred Days. He entered the Royal Navy at the age of eighteen in April 1779. He fought valiantly in successive naval combats during the wars of the American Revolution and the French Revolution, including Bonaparte's Egyptian expedition, and rose to the grade of rear admiral by 1798. As minister (and vice-admiral, 1804) he was an excellent administrator, a worker who drove himself and his subordinates, but he was not liked. He organized the naval preparations for the invasion of England, though he did not believe in the feasibility of the project. After Trafalgar, as directed by Napoleon, he steadily rebuilt the French fleet until by 1813 the French had in commission over 80 ships of the line and 35 more under construction—at a time when Great Britain could muster only 102 such ships. Despite Decrès' strenuous efforts, however, the quality of the French fleet was probably inferior in design of ships (the French still followed the obsolescent model of the 1780s), in training and practice of crews, and in esprit de corps. He withdrew from public life after 1815.

E. Chevalier, *Histoire de la marine française sous le Consulat et l'Empire* (Paris, 1886); R. Glover, "The French Fleet, 1807–1814: Britain's Problem and Madison's Opportunity," *JMH* 39 (1967); P. Masson and J. Muracciole, *Napoléon et la marine*

(Paris, 1968); Napoléon I, *Correspondance de Napoléon avec le ministre de la marine depuis 1804 jusqu'à avril 1815*, 2 vols. (Paris, 1909).

Harold T. Parker

Related entries: NAVY, FRENCH; TRAFALGAR, BATTLE OF.

DEGO, BATTLE OF. See ITALIAN CAMPAIGN, FIRST.

DEJEAN, JEAN-FRANCOIS-AIME, COMTE (1749–1824), minister of war administration, 1802–10. An able engineering officer in the Royal Army and then during the Revolutionary wars, Dejean rose to become by 1795 inspector general of fortifications and a general of division. Bonaparte appointed him councillor of state, resident French minister at Genoa charged with reorganizing the Ligurian Republic, and then in 1802 head of the new war ministry of the administration of war, responsible for provisions, clothing, hospitals, and transport of the army. On 2 January 1810 he left office over a budgetary dispute with Napoleon, who was unwilling or unable to give army supply as much money as Dejean thought was needed. Napoleon continued to use him in positions of responsibility: inspector general of the engineers in Holland (1810), president of the military commission that judged the conspirator Claude Malet (1812), inspector general of engineers (1815), and grand chancellor of the Legion of Honor (1815).

Harold T. Parker

Related entry: ADMINISTRATION, MILITARY.

DELILLE, JACQUES (1738–1813). Probably the most noted French poet between 1780 and 1810, Delille was the natural son of a M. Monpanier, an *avocat*. His mother was a descendant of Chancellor Michel de l'Hospital. Recognized and supported by his father, he was educated at the Collège de Lisieux in Paris and became a teacher, first at Beauvais and Amiens and later at the Collège de la Marche in Paris.

He first received general acclaim in 1770 with his translation of Virgil's *Georgics*. Voltaire himself called for his election to the Académie française, and after an aborted election in 1772 (vetoed by Louis XVI ostensibly because of his youth but more likely because of academic internecine wars), he finally received a chair in 1774. He also became professor of Latin poetry at the Collège de France. In 1780 his reputation increased with the publication of his didactic and descriptive poem, *Les Jardins*.

In spite of his humble origins, he was lionized by high society and admitted to the "little" court of Marie Antoinette. The count d'Artois (later Charles X) conferred on him the benefice of the Abbey of St. Severin, which brought him 30,000 francs a year in rent and the title of abbé. In 1786 he accompanied the count de Choiseul-Gouffier on an embassy to Constantinople, where he lived for a year, sending back to France letters for publication. He also visited Greece.

At the Revolution, he lost his abbey and its income and his teaching post. During the Terror he was imprisoned, and it is said that he was saved from death by a mason who beseeched the committee ''de ne pas tuer tous les poètes'' because ''qu'il était même utile d'en conserver quelques-uns, ne serait ce que celébrer nos victoires.'' Released, Delille wrote a ''Dithyramb sur l'immortalité de l'âme'' for the Fete of the Supreme Being. But at the end of 1793 he emigrated, going to Switzerland, Germany, and, finally, England, where he translated Milton's *Paradise Lost* into French.

He returned to France in 1802 and resumed his position at the Collège de France, although now nearly blind and paralyzed. He also continued to write, publishing *L'Homme de champs* (1802), *La pitié* (1803), a translation of the *Aeneid* (1804), *L'imagination* (1806), *Poésies fugitives* (1807), *Les trois règnes de la nature* (1808), and *La conversation* (1812).

When Napoleon established a decennial prize for poetry, the literary jury, even though it included political enemies, awarded it to Delille for his *L'imagination*, partially inspired by his sojourn in Turkey, and his translation of *Paradise Lost*. But when Napoleon offered Delille other high distinctions, the poet, old and ill, declined them graciously, wishing only to live quietly in retirement.

His wife, Marie-Jeanne Vaudechamp, was an uneducated domestic who had been his concubine for many years before he received special dispensation to marry her. He called her his Antigone, but, to judge by contemporary anecdotes, she may have been more of a Xantippe. She is said to have kept her aging husband under lock and key and to have continually urged him to write: '' 'Il faut battre monnaie,' elle disait. 'Oui, ma chère,' lui repliquait le poête, 'mais quand on frappe trop souvent cette monnaie, elle passe pour fausse!' ''

Delille died in 1813, and his wife raised a monument to him in Père Lachaise cemetery in Paris. His complete works were published in 1824. His literary reputation declined rapidly after his death because of the advent of romanticism, although some critics have seen a touch of the Romantic in his sentimental nature poetry. However, the 1855 edition of the *Biographie universelle* still contained five pages on him and his work by the critic J.-B. Sansor de Pongerville, who mixed strong criticism with praise in assessing Delille's poetry. *La Grande Encyclopédie*, at the turn of the twentieth century, gave him only two columns and noted ''Son élégance un peu banale.'' The article observes further that his *Les jardins* was ''artificiel et froid'' and that although he was capable of ''happy, touching images,'' his tours de force were now only ''simple curiosities.'' A modern literary historian, Louis Cazamian, says his contemporary reputation was so high because ''he stood for learning as well as art'' and wrote of the gardens and landscapes so dear to the heart of the late eighteenth century. Another modern critic, Geoffrey Brereton, calls him ''a mild water-colorist'' whose ''indefatigable purring'' is the only poetic sound between André Chenier and Lamartine and de Vigny.

L.Audiat, *Un poète abbé, Jacques Delille* (Paris, 1902); G. Brereton, *A Short History of French Literature* (Baltimore, 1954); L. Cazamian, *A History of French Literature*

(Oxford, 1955); F. Delzangle, *Biographie et morceaux choisis d'écrivains d'Auvergne* (Aurillac, 1933); *La Grande Encyclopédie* (Paris, 1886–1902); *Mercure de France*, July 1938; V. Z. Ors, *Jacques Delille* (Paris, 1936); P. Robert, *Les poètes du XIX*[e] *siècle, période romantique* (Paris, 1899); G. Stenger, *La société française pendant le Consulat*, 4th series (Paris, 1903).

Nancy Nolte

Related entries: ACADEMIE FRANCAISE; INSTITUT NATIONAL DES SCIENCES ET DES ARTS; LITERATURE.

DEMOGRAPHY. See POPULATION.

DENMARK, ruled by Frederick VI (as regent until 1808); backed into the Wars of the Revolution by joining the League of Neutrality organized by Czar Paul I in 1800. As a result, the Danish fleet was destroyed at Copenhagen by the British. After the assassination of Paul I (1801), Frederick allied with Britain. However, in 1807, with the proclamation of Napoleon's Continental Blockade, the British again feared that Denmark would cooperate in closing the Baltic and again bombarded Copenhagen. In October 1807 Denmark allied with France but was never a very active ally. Nevertheless, after Napoleon's defeat in 1814, Frederick was forced to cede Norway to Sweden.

Related entries: ALEXANDER I; GERMAN WAR OF LIBERATION; PAUL I; VIENNA, CONGRESS OF.

DENON, DOMINIQUE-VIVANT (1747–1825), a courtier, artist, diplomat, traveler, and author who effected a revolution in art collecting between 1802 and 1815 as Napoleon's director-general of museums. Denon's family belonged to the *petite noblesse provinciale*. He was sent to Paris to study law but failed to apply himself, lured instead into the world of arts and letters. His handsome appearance and delightful personality, which made him a great success with women throughout his life, led to some actresses at the Comédie française encouraging him to write plays while he studied drawing under Noël Hallé. Deciding that he wanted to meet Louis XV, he frequented Versailles and got his wish. The monarch and Madame de Pompadour enjoyed his brilliant conversation and rewarded him with a position as caretaker of a royal collection of medals and engraved stones and the title of gentleman ordinary of the king's bedroom.

Denon next decided on a diplomatic career. In 1772 at age twenty-five, he was sent to St. Petersburg as secretary to Ambassador Charles-Maurice de Talleyrand for whom he handled correspondence with Versailles. When Louis XV died, Denon left Russia to join Count C. G. de Vergennes in Sweden and soon thereafter accompanied the newly appointed minister of foreign affairs back to Paris. Denon's travels continued when Vergennes sent him on a secret mission to the Helvetic Confederation. Denon's next post was as chargé d'affaires at Naples from 1778 until 1785. This fateful assignment enabled him to become an expert on the excavations at Pompeii and Herculaneum and made him much sought after by European enthusiasts. Denon used his leisure time to copy church paintings and established himself as a connoisseur of the Italian school. From Naples he went to Rome and became acquainted with Cardinal de Bernis, then French ambassador to the Vatican. But the death of Vergennes halted his diplomatic career.

By this time Denon wished to devote himself completely to art. He joined the Academy of Painting at Paris in 1787 as an "artist of diverse talents," but he had returned to Italy by the outbreak of the French Revolution and his property was listed for confiscation since he appeared to be a political *émigré*. In 1792 Denon courageously returned to Paris and was aided by the politically astute painter J.-L. David. His friend got him lodgings in the Louvre and a commission from the Convention to design Roman-style costumes suitable for the rejuvenated populace of the French Republic. Denon's knowledge also prepared him to serve on a committee that handled confiscated artworks. In order to repay David, Denon made an engraving of the pageant master's *Tennis Court Oath* and Jean-Baptiste Isabey's *Barère at the Tribune*. When the latter arranged for a showing of François Gérard's painting *Belisarius* (1795) in Denon's studio, Josephine de Beauharnais attended. She was charmed by Denon's manners and invited him to frequent her *salon* in the rue de la Victoire where eventually he met General Bonaparte, who also found him interesting.

The general was preparing for the Egyptian expedition in May 1798 when fifty-one-year-old Denon joined the 157 savants who embarked on the frigate *La Junon*. Denon actually accompanied General Louis Desaix to Upper Egypt and won everyone's admiration by surveying and drawing the pyramids, sphinxes and temples, even amid battles between the French soldiers and the Mamluks. The results of his dangerous and energetic labor were volumes of engravings and the beginning of the science of Egyptology.

After the Louvre began serving as the central depot for all the art treasures being sent to France, Denon suggested to the first consul that the art gallery be called the Musée Napoléon. On 19 November 1802 Denon was named director general of museums, and the Musée Napoléon was dedicated on the third anniversary of 18 Brumaire (9 November 1803). In addition to overseeing the Louvre, Denon was put in charge of minting medals, hiring painters, erecting monuments, and administering the Sèvres, Beauvais, and Gobelins factories.

Cecil Gould has discussed Napoleon's astonishing choice of Denon for this significant position. Initially the sculptor Antonio Canova probably turned down Napoleon's first offer. Denon certainly was not a great artist of David's stature either. Moreover, Denon had a reputation for interest in erotic art, and Napoleon was prudish about sex publicly. And then there was Denon's age. In any case, Denon's appointment as director general marks the beginning of a new stage in the acquisition system of the Louvre.

Thereafter, instead of delegating *commissaires*, the looting of artworks was led by Denon himself, who arrived on the heels of the victorious armies to select whatever he liked for the museums of France, imperial residences, and the Empress Josephine's collection. Between 1804 and 1809, Denon traveled to Italy, Germany, and Austria, to Spain, and again to Austria always for a dual purpose—to choose artworks and to make topographical drawings of battle sites for his projected book of drawings of the emperor's campaigns. He was successful everywhere except in Spain where he arrived only after Joseph had the power to save the best for himself and the Spanish procrastinated in sending their convoys of art treasures to Paris.

The architectural alterations of the Louvre by P.-F.-L. Fontaine and Charles Percier necessitated its closing from 1808 to 1810. After it reopened, an event that coincided with Napoleon's religious marriage to Marie-Louise with a procession through the Grande Galerie, Denon went on mission to Italy for the last time. But this time there was no war on, and Denon had to acquire masterpieces for the French museums by using all the diplomatic acumen he had acquired under the Old Regime. Denon left in August 1811 and returned from going as far as Rome in January 1812, taking Benjamin Zix along to make drawings. Denon's taste that guided his choices this time had advanced astonishingly since his earlier looting expeditions for he had come to appreciate early Italian art and regarded Cimabue, Giotto, and Masaccio as leading progressively to the age of Raphael. The resulting display readied to open at the Louvre on 25 July 1814 was Denon's best claim to fame as a museum director. However, Denon could not stop the dismantling of the collection following the fall of Napoleon. He spent the last decade of his life in retirement arranging his private collection and preparing publications. He was buried at Père Lachaise cemetery in 1825.

M. L. Blumer, "La Mission de Denon en Italie (1811)," *REN* 39 (1934); A de La Fizelière, *L'Oeuvre originale de Vivant-Denon* (Paris, 1872-73); A. France, *Notice historique sur V. Denon* (Paris, 1890); C. Gould, *Trophy of Conquest, The Musée Napoléon and the Creation of the Louvre* (London, 1965); P. Lelièvre, *Vivant Denon, directeur des beaux-arts de Napoléon* (Paris, 1942); A. de Pastoret, *Vivant Denon* (Paris, 1851).

June K. Burton

Related entries: ART; DAVID; EGYPTIAN CAMPAIGN; FONTAINE; GERARD, F.-P.-S.; ISABEY; LOUVRE; PERCIER.

DENUELLE DE LA PLAIGNE, ELEONORE. See LA PLAIGNE, LEON-CHARLES DE.

DEPARTMENTS. In 1790 France was divided into 83 governmental/administrative units called departments by the National Assembly which "abolished" the traditional provinces. In the course of the wars of the Revolution, the number grew; there were 98 by the time of the coup d'état of Brumaire (1799). These had been established in Belgium, the Rhineland, Savoy, and Swiss territory. Napoleon was responsible for raising the number to 130. Every new foreign territory taken directly under French government was divided into departments. The territories of the satellite kingdoms and lesser states under the rule of mem-

bers of Napoleon's family and also the duchies of Warsaw and Frankfurt and even the Illyrian Provinces were also remapped according to the French departmental system.
Related entries: ADMINISTRATION; EMPIRE, FRENCH; FOREIGN POLICY.

DESAIX DE VEYGOUX, LOUIS-CHARLES-ANTOINE (1768–1800), one of the best generals of the early Revolution. Though of noble birth, Desaix supported the Revolution, remained with the army, and was made general of brigade in 1793 and general of division in 1795. He was second in command (to Jean Moreau) of the Army of the Rhine and Moselle (1796–97) and has been credited with much of the army's success. Implicated with Moreau and Jean Reynier in the Pichegru (royalist) conspiracy of 1797, he was transferred to the Army of Italy and became a disciple of Napoleon. In 1798, with the Army of the Orient, he was given the task of pacifying Upper Egypt. With limited resources, he cleared the province of Mamluk armies and won the sobriquet ''Just Sultan'' from the natives. After Bonaparte's departure (August 1799) he served J.-B. Kléber briefly and then returned to France. In the Marengo campaign (1800) Desaix with his division was dispatched to block the presumed Austrian line of retreat. When Michael Melas' Austrians attacked Bonaparte unexpectedly at Marengo, Desaix heard the sound of the guns and hastened to the field of battle. His arrival enabled Bonaparte to take the offensive and turn defeat into victory. Desaix was killed as he led the final advance. His death cost Bonaparte one of his most brilliant officers.

A. Bonnal, *Histoire de Desaix* (Paris, 1881); F. De Mons, *Le général Desaix: étude critique* (Paris, 1852); A. Sauzet, *Desaix, le sultan-juste* (Paris, 1954).

Milton Finley

Related entries: EGYPTIAN CAMPAIGN; ITALIAN CAMPAIGN, SECOND; MARENGO, BATTLE OF; MELAS.

DESTUTT DE TRACY, ANTOINE-LOUIS-CLAUDE, COMTE (1754–1836), philosopher, senator, and a leader of the liberal opposition to Napoleon. He had been a court noble and colonel under Louis XVI and a member of the Constituent Assembly. His wealth consisted in hectares in the Allier. He conceived his comprehensive philosophy in prison in 1793–94 and in the National Institute after 1796, coining the word *ideology* to designate ''science of ideas'' and ''general grammar,'' logic, political economy, morality, and politics, ''the greatest of the arts.'' Because Napoleon disparaged ''ideology'' and *idéologues* after 1800, Tracy earned the epithet *Têtu* (''stubborn'') de Tracy, by adamantly defending the central schools as a member of the Council of Public Instruction (1799–1800) and by publishing his famous *Elémens d'idéologie* (4 vols., Paris, 1801–15). Jefferson published in English two of his works that contained critical allusions to the Empire. While Tracy pushed sensationalism to its materialist limits, he inadvertently spawned the spiritualist philosophy of Maine de Biran, his protégé. He was alien to the Christian revival and was regarded as the main spokesman of the Enlightenment after 1800. Although he was circumspect in his opposition, he was remotely compromised in the Malet conspiracies of 1808 and 1812, and on 2 April 1814, he proposed in the Senate the deposition of Napoleon.

E. Kennedy, *A Philosophe in the Age of Revolution: Destutt de Tracy and the Origins of Ideology* (Philadelphia, 1978); F. Rastier, *Ideologie et théorie des Signes: Analyse structurale des élements d'idéologie d'Antoine Louis Claude Destutt de Tracy* (The Hague, 1972).

Emmet Kennedy

Related entry: IDEOLOGUES.

DIPLOMACY. Napoleon entered the diplomatic game during the first Italian campaign, when he handled relations with the small Italian states and negotiated with Austria the Treaty of Campo Formio (1797). He remained immersed in diplomatic activity until his second abdication (1815). As first consul and emperor, he continued many of the structures and procedures of European and French diplomacy, but when it suited his desire for rationality, uniformity, efficiency, and power, he altered them.

He continued the foreign office in Paris with its minister of foreign affairs and its organization into six or seven divisions, each with a *chef*, *sous-chef*, and clerks. He continued in foreign capitals the French embassies, each with its hierarchy of ambassador or minister, secretary of legation, and clerks. However, while reserving his freedom to dispatch personal envoys as ambassadors in crisis situations, he supported professionalizing the bureaucracy of the foreign service. He ordered that, below the rank of minister of foreign affairs and ambassador, there be stability of employment, orderly, step-by-step promotion, and pensions on retirement. He also instituted training programs, first in 1800 through a system of apprenticeship (of *aspirants*, *élèves*) and then from 1806 through the appointment of *auditeurs* who had been schooled by attendance on the Council of State. Napoleon thus "created the best diplomatic service of the period and probably one of the best in the nineteenth century. . . the vast majority of whose members had been professionally trained or prepared for the positions they held" (Whitcomb).

The trained staff existed to execute the will of Napoleon, who was, in effect, his own minister of foreign affairs. Even Charles-Maurice de Talleyrand, no amateur at his post, had to submit to Napoleon daily reports of French ambassadors and other heads of mission; the emperor read them and often dictated the replies.

Napoleon continued the expansion of French territory inaugurated by the Convention and Directory. He continued as well the export of basic Revolutionary reforms through the direct incorporation of conquered territories into France or through the perpetuation of sister republics (converted under the Empire to satellite kingdoms). However, he continued the career of conquest immoderately until he finally mobilized an overpowering coalition against him. He did this despite the advice of his own diplomatic staff: of his ambassador to England in 1802–3, General Andréossy, who urged the cessation of Bonaparte's provocative aggressions in time of peace; of Talleyrand, who in 1805 counseled a moderate treaty of peace with Austria; of Armand de Caulaincourt and J.-A.-B. Law de Lauriston, ambassadors to Czar Alexander I, who steadily warned against an invasion of Russia; and of Caulaincourt again, in 1813–14, when he was minister of foreign affairs and pressed Napoleon to accept allied peace terms.

Historians have sought a theme, a goal, of Napoleon's diplomacy. Albert Sorel and R. B. Mowat found it in the defense of the Revolutionary conquest of France's natural frontiers, including the left bank of the Rhine, an acquisition that England could never accept. In their view, Napoleon's wars were all defensive. Other historians, such as Emile Bourgeois, have seen a beckoning Oriental vision—mastery of the Mediterranean, of Egypt, and of India. Still others, including Georges Lefebvre, find the clue to his diplomacy in the deeper springs of his personality and imagination: the *esprit de principauté* of which his mother spoke; the desire to be first in ever-enlarging circles of family, France, Europe, posterity; to leave a name as conqueror and builder of institutions.

E. Bourgeois, *Manuel historique de politique étrangère,* vol. 2: *Les révolutions, 1789–1830*, 6th ed. (Paris, 1920); A. Fugier, *La révolution française et l'empire napoléonien* (Paris, 1954); G. Lefebvre, *Napoléon*, 4th ed. (Paris, 1953); R. B. Mowat, *The Diplomacy of Napoleon* (London, 1924); S. T. Ross, *European Diplomatic History, 1789-1815: France against Europe* (Garden City, N.Y., 1969); A. Sorel, *L'Europe et la révolution française*, 8 vols. (Paris, 1885–1904); E. A. Whitcomb, *Napoleon's Diplomatic Service* (Durham, N.C., 1979).

Harold T. Parker

Related entries: CAULAINCOURT; CHAMPAGNY; FOREIGN POLICY; MARET; REINHARD; TALLEYRAND-PERIGORD.

DIRECTORY, the government of France between October 1795 and November 1799. Created by the Constitution of the Year III, the executive consisted of five directors, who were elected by the legislative branches and were jointly responsible for the conduct of affairs. Membership changed, for each year one man, chosen by lot, had to retire; Louis de LaRevellière-Lépeaux, Jean François Reubell, and Paul de Barras held office longest. The system, designed to prevent dictatorship, actually paved the way for it, for there was perpetual conflict between the legislative bodies and Directory, and among directors, which made the government weak.

Coming between the great days of the Revolution and those of the Consulate, the Directory has been so denigrated by historians that its name is almost synonymous with inefficiency and corruption. In fact only one director, Barras, was notoriously corrupt, and the directors generally did much to reorganize the Republic and to make it a major power in Europe. They had some success in reviving trade and agriculture, and their fiscal and administrative reforms provided the basis for the more far-reaching reconstruction later undertaken by

Bonaparte. Real recovery from the Revolution was nevertheless unattainable, for successive political crises prevented the growth of public confidence in the regime. Initially the directors had to crush conspiracies by the communist ''Gracchus'' Babeuf and by royalist extremists. Their success seems to have reinforced their resolve to perpetuate the narrowly defined republicanism of 1795. Twice, in 1797 and again in 1798, they annulled elections, proscribing all their opponents indiscriminately as extremists and thus depriving themselves of much potential support from both Right and Left. By 1799, when the abbé Emmanuel Sieyès became a director and began to plan a third coup to make central government much stronger, the executive had become as isolated as it was repressive. It had also forfeited all claim to constitutional legitimacy.

The directors' position was further compromised by their involvement in wars that they could not win but would not end. Two of the most permanent directors, LaRevellière-Lépeaux and Barras, favored republican conquests, the one for idealistic and the other for more material reasons; and the third, the Alsatian Reubell, believed that French power should extend to, but not beyond, the Rhine. During crises, however, policy was swayed by events in the field and by the interests of the generals, particularly Bonaparte. Sent in 1796 to command the Army of Italy, Bonaparte turned a sideshow into a major theater of war, annexing territory and practically forcing the Directory as well as Austria to accept at Campo Formio in 1797 a peace that so embroiled France in German affairs that further war was inevitable.

The formation of the Second Coalition against France in 1799 was also a consequence of both the French occupation of Switzerland and the Egyptian expedition in 1798, both of which were undertaken in part at Bonaparte's behest. The upshot was that in 1799 all that had been won was lost; the French system of satellite republics extending from Holland to southern Italy crumbled under the combined assault of Russian, Austrian, and British forces. Although these armies were defeated and an invasion of France prevented—before Bonaparte returned from Egypt on 9 October 1799—he nevertheless was seen as a savior, an invincible soldier and a peacemaker. It was thus not difficult for him to act with Sieyès to destroy the discredited Directory by the coup d'état of 18-19 Brumaire, Year VIII (9–10 November 1799).

C. H. Church, ''In Search of the Directory,'' in *French Government and Society, 1500–1850*, ed. J. F. Bosher (London, 1973); A. Goodwin, ''The French Executive Directory: A Revaluation,'' *History* 22 (1937); G. Lefebvre, *The Directory*, trans. R. Baldick (London, 1975); A. Soboul, *La Première République, 1792–1804* (Paris, 1968); M. J. Sydenham, *The First French Republic, 1792–1804* (London, 1974).

M. J. Sydenham

Related entries: BRUMAIRE, COUP OF 18, YEAR VIII; EGYPTIAN CAMPAIGN; FRUCTIDOR, COUP OF 18, YEAR V; ITALIAN CAMPAIGN, FIRST; NAPOLEON I; VENDEMIAIRE.

DISTRICT. See ADMINISTRATION.

DIVORCE. See LAW, CODES OF.

DIVORCE OF NAPOLEON. See JOSEPHINE.

DOS DE MAYO, violent popular uprising in Madrid on 2 May 1808. See PENINSULAR WAR.

DOUGLAS, WILLIAM (1769–1825), a Manchester wool manufacturer who moved to France in 1801. Douglas was a controversial figure in the first mechanization phase of the French woolens industry during the Consulate and Empire. Subsidized by the Ministry of Interior under Jean Chaptal and given an exclusive privilege to manufacture sets of woolens machines after the English model, Douglas was able to establish his factory by 1802 on the Ile des Cygnes in Paris. His first set was completed in the fall of 1803, and by 1810, according to his own account, 949 machines had been supplied to 100 enterprises throughout 38 departments. But by then Douglas had lost his exclusive privilege in France. A revealing patent rights battle in 1808 between Douglas and William Ternaux, the leading French woolens manufacturer, convinced the Ministry of Interior of the superiority of equivalent machines constructed as early as 1801 by William Cockerill, Douglas' main competitor at Liège. For French government officials, the Douglas affair was a lesson in the risks of monopoly granting as a modernization strategy.

C. Ballot, *L'introduction du machinisme dans l'industrie française* (Paris, 1923); L. Bergeron, "Douglas, Ternaux, Cockerill, aux origines de la mécanisation de l'industrie lainière en France," *RH* 247 (1972).

Richard J. Barker

Related entries: CONTINENTAL BLOCKADE; ECONOMY, FRENCH; WARFARE, ECONOMIC.

DRAMA. See THEATER.

DRESDEN, BATTLE OF. See GERMAN WAR OF LIBERATION.

DROUET, J. B. (1765–1844), comte d'Erlon, one of three corps commanders under Napoleon at Waterloo, later blamed, probably unjustly, by Napoleon for not fully employing his troops. Drouet enlisted as a private in the armies of the Revolution and rose to the rank of general of brigade (1799). Napoleon elevated him to major general in 1800. He served valiantly in the 1806–7 campaign and was gravely wounded at Friedland. Napoleon gave him the title comte d'Erlon and the cross of grand officer of the Legion of Honor. Thereafter he served without great distinction in Spain. In 1815 Napoleon, faced with a shortage of experienced commanders, gave him a corps for what became the Waterloo campaign. After Napoleon's fall, Drouet was forced to go into exile in Bavaria. He returned to France after the Revolution of 1830 and was restored to rank by

King Louis Philippe, who in 1843 made him a marshal of France. He left memoirs, *Notice sur la vie militaire du maréchal Drouet, comte d'Erlon, écrit par lui-même et publiée par sa famille* (Paris, 1844).
Related entries: FRIEDLAND, BATTLE OF; PENINSULAR WAR; WATERLOO CAMPAIGN.

DUCOS, ROGER (1747–1816), French politician from 1792 to 1815 who played an important role in bringing Bonaparte to power in 1799. He was born at Montfort (Landes) on 23 July 1747 and died near Ulm on 16 March 1816. A lawyer before the Revolution, Roger Ducos represented the department of Landes in the Convention and held an unassuming position in the Committee of Public Assistance. He voted for the death of King Louis XVI but afterward sat in the Convention alongside other men of the Plain who preferred obscurity to the dangers of the Terror.

Under the Directory, Ducos acquired a reputation as a staunch antiroyalist; as a member of the Council of Ancients, he associated himself with all the strong measures enacted against royalists and *émigrés*. Ducos was president of the Ancients during the coup d'état of Fructidor (September 1797), which denied to royalists their newly won seats in the legislative chambers. Ducos was reelected in 1798 to represent the Oratoire section of Paris in the Council of Ancients, but his election was nullified by the coup of Floréal (May 1798). Yet another coup in June 1799 (30 Prairial, Year VII) made Ducos a director—one of the five-man executive—replacing Merlin de Douai.

Ducos served as a director until the coup d'état of 18 Brumaire (9 November 1799), when he conspired with the abbé Sieyès, Charles-Maurice de Talleyrand, Joseph Fouché, and others—and of course Napoleon—to overthrow the Directory. On 19 Brumaire, Ducos, Sieyès, and Napoleon were named provisional consuls and authorized to write a new constitution. When the temporary consuls met at Luxembourg, the abbé Sieyès expected to dominate, but Ducos commented to Sieyès, "You can clearly see that it is the general who presides." By the Constitution of the Year VIII, Napoleon made himself first consul, and J. J. Régis de Cambacérès and Charles Lebrun second and third consuls. Ducos and Sieyès were to be senators.

Ducos had been an insignificant legislator under the Convention, an antiroyalist but not a rabid republican in the Council of Ancients, and a puppet of Sieyès as a director and temporary consul. Ducos as a senator was not a commanding figure either, though in 1804, in view of his past services, Bonaparte made him a count of the Empire and a member of the Legion of Honor. In 1815, during the Hundred Days, Ducos was appointed by Napoleon to the chamber of Representatives. The government of the second Restoration expelled him as a regicide. In March 1816, Ducos died of injuries after his carriage overturned near Ulm.

J. B. Morton, *Brumaire: The Rise of Bonaparte* (New York, 1976); A.Soboul, *Le Directoire et le Consulat* (Paris, 1967); A. Vandal, *L'avènement de Bonaparte*, 2 vols. (Paris, 1903–7).

Fred E. Hembree

Related entries: BRUMAIRE, COUP OF 18, YEAR VIII; FRUCTIDOR, COUP OF 18, YEAR V; SIEYES.

DUPONT DE L'ETANG, PIERRE, COUNT (1765–1840), French general best remembered for his disastrous defeat at Baylen (1808) in Spain. Dupont was one of the young noble officers who continued to serve in the armies of the Republic after the execution of Louis XVI. He rose to major general in the armies of the Directory. He served under Napoleon at Marengo (1800), Ulm (1805), Jena (1806), and Friedland (1807). Napoleon valued him highly and awarded him the grand cordon of the Legion of Honor. In 1808 he was dispatched to Spain and commanded a corps of 30,000 men that marched south from Madrid to subdue Andalusia. Unknown to the French, large regular and guerrilla forces had been assembled in the south. Dupont was surrounded and forced to surrender his entire command at Baylen on 22 July 1808. Most of his troops were imprisoned. He was repatriated, only to be disgraced by Napoleon.

Under the Restoration, he was rehabilitated immediately (1814) and named minister of war and peer of France by Louis XVIII. In 1815 he returned to serve in the Privy Council of the king. After 1815 he held various appointive and elective offices. He left no memoirs but was the author of various books, including a ten-part poem, *L'art de la guerre*.

M. Leproux, *Le général Dupont* (Paris, 1934); G. Pariset, "La capitulation de Baylen," *Journal des Savants* (1905); Lt. Col. Titeux, *Le général Dupont*, 3 vols. (Paris, 1903–04).

Related entry: PENINSULAR WAR.

DU PONT DE NEMOURS, PIERRE-SAMUEL (1739–1817), *paterfamilias* of the Du Ponts of Delaware. A latter-day *philosophe*, Du Pont de Nemours was a disciple of the physiocrat François Quesnay and a friend of Jacques Turgot, and he propagated laissez-faire ideas from 1765 to 1775. In the 1780s he served first Charles Gravier de Vergennes and then C. A. de Calonne, whom he helped prepare the reform program presented to the Assembly of Notables in 1787. During the Revolution he was an apostle of constitutional government and moderation. He was a member of the Constituent Assembly (1789–91) and was imprisoned during the Terror but emerged to serve in the Council of Ancients of the Directory (1795–97).

Disheartened by the coup d'état of 18 Fructidor (1797), he emigrated with his family to the United States (1799). There his son, Eleuthère Irénée, founded the gunpowder factory that became the ancestor of the modern Du Pont enterprises. Du Pont de Nemours returned to France in 1802, hoping to be named a senator and to be accorded the Legion of Honor, but Napoleon had no patience with a prolix, theoretical "driveler," to use his terminology. Nevertheless, during the Consulate and Empire, Du Pont de Nemours kept busy as a member of the Institut and a vice-president of the Society for the Encouragement of (French) National Industry. During the recession of 1810–11, as administrator of household relief in Paris, he supervised the daily distribution of food to over 100,000 indigents. Moving with his friend Charles-Maurice de Talleyrand into opposition to Napoleon's "tyranny," he was secretary-general of the provisional government that formally deposed Napoleon in 1814. On Napoleon's return from Elba, Du Pont de Nemours took ship for his son's home in Delaware, where he died in 1817.

R. F. Betts, "Du Pont de Nemours in Napoleonic France, 1802–1815," *FHS* 5 (1967); J. Dubuisson-Bertin, "Dupont de Nemours et Napoléon," *Recueil des Travaux et Documents de l'Institut Napoléon* (1946); A. Saricks, *Pierre Samuel Du Pont de Nemours* (Lawrence, Kansas, 1965).

Harold T. Parker

Related entries: DIRECTORY; FRUCTIDOR, COUP OF 18, YEAR V; INSTITUT NATIONAL DES SCIENCES ET DES ARTS; TALLEYRAND-PERIGORD.

DUROC, GERAUD-CHRISTOPHE-MICHEL (1772–1813), duc de Frioul, Napoleon's grand marshal of the palace. Son of a captain of the Royal French Army, Duroc entered the army in 1792, fought in the wars of the Revolution, served as one of Bonaparte's aides-de-camp during the Italian and Egyptian campaigns, and participated in the coup d'état of 18 Brumaire. In 1800 he was appointed governor and in 1804 grand marshal of the palace, a post that brought him into daily contact with Napoleon. Duroc managed the service of the palace economically, efficiently, and imperturbably. He was also dispatched on diplomatic missions to Berlin, Vienna, St. Petersburg, and Copenhagen. He was promoted to general of brigade (1800), general of division (1803), and made duke of Frioul (1808). Nevertheless, toward the end of the imperial regime, Duroc protested to Napoleon against his war policy and specifically against the invasion of Russia, but like the other intimate advisers Duroc obeyed the emperor loyally, if sometimes grimly. Duroc was wounded while escorting Napoleon at the Battle of Wurzen (in Saxony) on 22 May 1813 and died the next morning.

A. de Caulaincourt, *Mémoires du général de Caulaincourt*, ed. J. Hanoteau, 3 vols. (Paris, 1933); C.-F. de Méneval, *Mémoires*, ed. Baron N. J. de Méneval, 3 vols. (Paris, 1893–94; trans. New York, 1894); Mme. de Rémusat, *Mémoires (1802-1808)*, ed. P. de Rémusat, 3 vols. (Paris, 1880).

Harold T. Parker

Related entry: NAPOLEON, DAILY ROUND.

DUTCH REPUBLIC. See BATAVIAN REPUBLIC; HOLLAND, KINGDOM OF; NETHERLANDS entries.

E

EBLE, JEAN-BAPTISTE (1758–1812), French general, hero of Napoleon's crossing of the Berezina River in 1812. Son of a gunnery sergeant, Eblé enlisted in the artillery of the Royal Army and was made an officer shortly before the Revolution began. He rose rapidly in rank during the wars of the Revolution and was promoted to major general in 1793. He came to Napoleon's notice during the Austerlitz campaign and in 1808 was assigned as minister of war of Westphalia under King Jerome Bonaparte. During 1810–12 he served with distinction in Spain and Portugal. In 1812 he commanded the engineers of the Grand Army on the retreat from Moscow and made possible Napoleon's last brilliant victory at the Berezina by constructing and reconstructing bridges across the river that facilitated the escape of most of the surviving French forces in Russia. Eblé died as a result of debilitation from cold and exposure after reaching East Prussia.
Related entries: PENINSULAR WAR; PORTUGUESE CAMPAIGNS; RUSSIAN CAMPAIGN.

ECKMÜHL (Eggmühl), BATTLE OF. See WAGRAM CAMPAIGN.

ECKMÜHL, PRINCE D'. See DAVOUT.

ECOLE MILITAIRE, central military school of the Old Regime. Founded in 1751 by Louis XV, it was located in Paris, where the buildings may still be seen on the south bank of the Seine. Napoleon graduated from this school in 1785 and was commissioned a sublieutenant of artillery. It was replaced ultimately by Napoleon's military school at St. Cyr (1802).
Related entries: ARMY, FRENCH; EDUCATION; NAPOLEON I.

ECONOMY, FRENCH, 1800–15. Development shows a moderately positive balance sheet dominated, for both better and worse, by continuous military and economic war. The loss of overseas empire, the British blockade, and the Continental System destroyed the dynamic eighteenth-century growth of the ports as international trading entrepôts, as processors of colonial goods (sugar, tobacco, hides), and as centers directing the production and export of textiles and other products of their hinterlands. This long-run deindustrialization of the ports and especially the Atlantic coastal region was partly offset by the stimulus of vast continental markets opened by conquest and partially closed to the British, although French markets were also thereby exposed to competition from the future Belgium and the Rhineland, the most economically advanced of the annexed territories. Napoleon's grandiose plans to build a modern transport network of roads and canals that would turn the legal fact of a unified national market into an economic reality foundered for lack of funds. Even maintenance and repair were neglected except where military needs overrode budgetary considerations. Economic war with Britain also exacerbated the usual depressive effects of credit and subsistence crises on the business cycle. The bad years of 1798–1801, 1803, and 1805–7 culminated, after a brief but heady boom, in deep industrial (1810–11) and agricultural (1811–12) crises from which the imperial economy never fully recovered. More serious in the long run, Revolution and war cut France off from twenty-five years of rapid technological development in Great Britain. Imports of men, machines, and ideas almost ceased. Already lagging in 1789, France emerged in 1815 with a full-blown technological gap, which encouraged both industrialists and government to agree to continue by more peaceful and settled means the extreme protectionist policies of the Empire.

Technological lag was particularly critical in the iron industry, whose methods and geography remained preindustrial. Scattered blast furnaces still depended on charcoal rather than coke fuel, and the even more dispersed refineries continued to produce wrought iron on forges rather than by puddling and rolling, *la méthode anglaise*. The development of heavy industries based on coal fuel lay largely in the future, and the coal industry itself made only modest gains in output and mechanization. Textiles, overwhelmingly the most important industrial sector, saw the older (and larger) branches either decline (linen) or grow slowly (woolen, silk). Only in woolens was there the bare beginning of mechanization in centers like Elbeuf and Louviers. Philippe de Girard's linen-spinning machine and Joseph Jacquard's automatic silk loom, although invented by 1810, were of no immediate economic significance. Only cotton, the infant textile industry of the eighteenth century, underwent a partial technological revolution. Mule jennys and waterframes were rapidly replacing hand spinning after 1796, and the number of spindles quadrupled between 1806 and 1810. Still, Great Britain probably had five times as many spindles, power even in the larger spinning factories was as often supplied by horses as by waterwheels, and the use of the steam engine was rare. None of the other cotton processes had been mechanized (except printing), and one of the major effects of the growth of factory spinning in Alsace, Picardy, and Flanders, Normandy, and in and around Paris was the spread of domestic out-work into the countryside where agriculture did not provide sufficient labor for the peasantry. Moreover, the cotton boom was a hothouse plant nurtured on the absence of cheap British yarn and luxury Indian cotton cloths. Increasing shortages of raw material, bankruptcies after

1810, and the return of peace and British competition put this showpiece of French industry (along with the nascent machine-building and chemical industries, both closely tied to textiles) in a precarious position in 1815. Overall, while French industrial output grew moderately, Britain widened its lead quantitatively as well as qualitatively. On the other hand, while undergoing no broad-based industrial take-off, France (together with Belgium, Switzerland, and the Rhineland) widened its lead over the rest of the Continent. Some of the merchants who organized and financed the new industrial ventures perceived that the future lay with factories, machines, and inorganic sources of power, with emulating and overtaking Britain and following it down the path of industrial revolution.

In the longer run, they were aided by the Empire's reestablishment or modernization of institutional arrangements adumbrated under the Old Regime or the Revolution. The Napoleonic Code provided a modern system of property rights, economic freedom for the entrepreneur, and potentially useful array of modern forms of business organization. The Ecole Polytechnique and other high technical schools prepared the way for French engineering predominance on the Continent. A stable franc and the Bank of France contributed to the reconstitution of the Parisian *haute banque* (fortified by new recruits from Neufchatel, Basel, Frankfurt, and the provinces) and thereby greatly increased the power of Paris as the national economic capital for money, goods, and entrepreneurial talent. Even such ostensibly temporary measures as the first industrial exhibitions, subsidies for inventors and firms in difficulty, quasi-governmental advisory councils of bureaucrats and businessmen, and an exaggerated protectionism symbolized the imperial government's belief in economic progress, enhanced businessmen's sense of their worth, and stimulated a feeling of optimism about French economic development that outlived the Empire.

Annales des arts et manufactures (1800–15); L. Bergeron, *Banquiers, négociants et manufacturiers parisiens du Directoire à l'Empire* (Paris, 1978); L. Bergeron et al., "La France à l'époque napoléonienne," numero special, *RHMC* 17 (1970); F. Crouzet, "Wars, Blockade and Economic Change in Europe, 1792–1815," *Journal of Economic History* 24 (1964); P. Deyon et al., "Aux origines de la révolution industrielle: industrie rurale et fabriques," numéro special de la *Revue du Nord* 61 (1979); G. Ellis, *Napoleon's Continental Blockade: The Case of Alsace* (Oxford, 1981); R. Geiger, *The Anzin Coal Company, 1800–83: Big Business in the Early Stages of the French Industrial Revolution* (Newark, N.J., 1974):1981; O. Viennet, *Napoléon et l'industrie française: La crise de 1810–1811* (Paris, 1947).

Reed Geiger

Related entries: CONTINENTAL BLOCKADE; DOUGLAS; FULTON; LABOR LEGISLATION; NOTABLES; SCIENCE; SOCIETY; TERNAUX; WARFARE, ECONOMIC.

ECOUEN, CHATEAU OF. In 1807, the chateau of Ecouen, built for the *connétable* Anne de Montmorency (c. 1540) in the north of the Paris region, was transformed into the Maison Impériale Napoléon—the first government school for orphaned sisters, daughters, and nieces of members of the Legion of Honor.

Napoleon was skeptical about the value of intensive formal female education and thought that as most other girls' schools then operated, they destroyed the rare qualities with which nature had endowed women to enhance society. Therefore any new establishment ought to correct these pedagogical tendencies so that girls would be trained to be the better wives and mothers that France needed.

The first sign appearing in his correspondence that Napoleon had become interested in educating girls in regular institutions occurred in 1804 when he asked his ministers to see if they could develop a "reasonable" proposal. His "Exposé de la Situation de l'Empire" of 1806, which was meant for public consumption, boasted that three houses of education had been established for girls because that sex contributed so much to manners that their education had to be considered by the legislature in the interest of public morality. But in January the following year, he wrote from Warsaw that since he was too busy, the organization of Madame Campan's St.-Cyr and the other similar institutions would be provisional until he could decide what the permanent organization should be. Finally, in May 1807, the emperor wrote the long note on the direction of the school at Ecouen, which is usually treated by historians as the basis for his ideas about female education.

Among the various subjects with which Napoleon envisioned young ladies of modest circumstances being occupied, he gave priority to religion because he believed that the Gospel would equip them with the resignation, indulgence, and charitable manner useful to persons destined for their station in life. To ensure the girls' religiosity, Napoleon gave instructions for them to spend part of their time in prayer, attending Mass, and learning the catechism. In addition, they were supposed to learn the 3 Rs, some geography, history, and botany but only a smattering of factual physical and natural history—just enough to keep them from being crassly ignorant and superstitious. All of these activities were to take up only one-fourth of their day. Most of their time was to be spent making socks and shirts and doing embroidery or other sorts of handwork that a woman normally must do in the home. He wondered, too, if it would be possible to teach them a little cooking and enough nursing skill so that they could care for their families in sickness as in health. By this plan, Latin and foreign languages were taboo, dancing, which he considered necessary for their health, should be restricted to a lively kind, and only vocal music should be taught.

The actual curriculum of Ecouen did not strictly conform to the emperor's note. Nor did the first 300 girls who attended really come from families of modest means as he envisaged. Instead, the head mistress, Mme. Campan, followed the curriculum that she had used at her Saint-Germain *pension*, which included the study of foreign languages by the older pupils, as well as instrumental music. This is corroborated by a letter from young Nancy MacDonald to her father, the maréchal duc de Tarente, telling how she sometimes spent her day reading *Les leçons de littérature et de morale* by Noel, walking in the park, drawing, playing both piano and harp, embroidering, and having an English lesson. Moreover, Napoleon was familiar with the regimen at the school through his official visits. That he accepted the routine and curriculum indicates that he was not adamant or inflexible regarding the education offered by this state institution. During the Restoration Napoleon's detractors unfairly pointed out that Ecouen failed to produce the modest, sensitive young ladies that the emperor said he wanted—unfairly because it was assumed that his original directives had been closely adhered to and that those courses had been aimed at making girls merely camp followers or housewives rather than cosmopolitan women who could discuss philosophy, converse in a foreign language, or skillfully pluck the strings of a harp. Such was not the case although sole reliance on Napoleon's previous correspondence might suggest that conclusion, which was reached by anti-Bonapartists with prejudice and without full knowledge of the facts.

In 1813 Ecouen was in the direct line of Czar Alexander's army advancing toward Paris, but Mme. Campan obtained a safe conduct from General Dmitri Sacken in order to protect her charges. Later the czar himself paid a social visit to Ecouen. Since the chateau had been the property of the Condé family before the Revolution, Louis XVIII sent the girls to Saint-Denis and restored it to its former occupants. Ecouen became a state property in 1830 and was turned over to the Legion of Honor again in 1851.

M.S. Ratier, *De la condition et de l'influence des femmes sous l'Empire, et depuis la Restoration* (Paris, 1822); G. Reval, *Mme Campan, Assistante de Napoléon* (Paris, 1931); B. Scott, "Madame Campan," *History Today* 23 (October 1973).

June K. Burton

Related entries: CAMPAN; WOMEN; WOMEN, EDUCATION OF.

EDUCATION. In the schools of France, Napoleon's reforms had lasting effects. Napoleon devoted a great deal of personal attention to education, for he considered it to have propagandistic value. His main concern, however, was to train the future military and civic leaders of France. He paid little attention to the elementary schools and neglected education for women.

A law of 11 Floréal Year X (1 May 1802) completely reorganized primary and secondary education, under the Directory of Public Instruction, headed by a councillor of state, in the Ministry of the Interior. The main purpose of the law was to create a new form of secondary school, the lycée, because Bonaparte considered those in existence suspect. Each court of appeal area was to have at least one lycée, whose teachers and administrators Bonaparte chose. The government offered 6,400 scholarships to the lycées, 2,400 of them for sons of soldiers and officials; but the number of scholars never reached 6,400. At first the lycées were divided into Latin and mathematics sections, but starting in 1809 all students had the same curriculum. The baccalaureate examination, instituted in 1809, persists today as a prerequisite for admission to an institution of higher education.

For a number of reasons the lycées were not popular. Strict military discipline was imposed on the students. The minister of the interior regulated what subjects the lycées could teach and what books would be used. For a time they were considered irreligious. Above all there was the regimentation by the government.

In every area there was a high degree of centralized control. All secondary schools—besides the lycées, there were communal collèges and private schools—were under the control of the prefects. Even the private schools, which prospered, had to follow the mode of teaching of the communal secondary schools, each of which in October 1803 received an administrative council as a means of giving the government more voice in the selection of teachers.

The law of 1802 made no mention of private schools on the primary level, where education was the responsibility of the communes. Only by heavy reliance on the Brethren of the Christian Schools could the communes carry out their educational function.

Napoleon concerned himself with technical education and with a variety of special schools, such as in the fields of law and medicine. The Higher Normal School in Paris was excellent. The establishment of theological faculties was designed to inculcate Gallican teachings. A major change in higher education was substitution of two faculties, of letters and sciences, for the former faculty of arts.

Whatever its shortcomings, Napoleon's system of education did prevent the Catholic church from once again dominating education on a national scale. His attempt to keep the education system secular continued the Revolutionary tradition. And the lycées—next to the university Napoleon's most important educational creation—did train functionaries.

F.V.A. Aulard, *Napoléon Ier et le monopole universitaire* (Paris, 1911); J. Godechot, *Les institutions de la France sous la Révolution et l'Empire*, 2d ed. (Paris, 1968); R. B. Holtman, *The Napoleonic Revolution* (Baton Rouge, 1978).

Robert B. Holtman

Related entries: FONTANES; UNIVERSITY, IMPERIAL; WOMEN, EDUCATION OF.

EGYPTIAN CAMPAIGN (1798–1801). Conceived as a means to cut British trade routes to India and make Egypt a permanent French colony, it was militarily a failure, but Bonaparte manipulated it to increase his popularity at home. Numbering 38,000, the Army of the Orient departed Toulon on 19 May 1798 accompanied by scholars of the future Institute of Egypt. Admiral F. Paul Brueys commanded the fleet and some 400 transports, which took the army first to Malta and then to Egypt where it disembarked at Marabout with great difficulty 1–3 July 1798. Alexandria was taken by storm 2 July; the ensuing march on Cairo through the desert by part of the army (the rest went up the Nile by barge) caused many deaths among troops unprepared and ill equipped for the climate. Bonaparte decisively defeated the Mamluk army of Murad-Bey and Ibrahim-Bey at Embabeh (the Battle of the Pyramids) on 21 July. Jean-Louis Reynier's subsequent victory over Ibrahim at El-Hanka 6 August and L.-C.-A. Desaix's campaign against Murad in Upper Egypt temporarily ended organized resistance. Bonaparte organized a colonial administration while his institute set about its work.

Meanwhile, Lord Nelson destroyed Brueys' fleet in Aboukir Bay, and the Turkish declaration of war against France jeopardized Bonaparte's position. In February 1799 after crushing a revolt in Cairo, he launched an invasion of Palestine and Syria with 13,000 men to forestall a Turkish attack. He and Reynier took El Arish on 19 February; Jaffa fell 7 March, and Bonaparte gave the notorious order to massacre its Turkish garrison. On 18 April, Bonaparte and J.-B. Kléber routed the Turkish Army of Damascus at Mount Tabor, but British control of the sea and an outbreak of plague in the French army prevented the capture of the key fortress of Acre. Beginning on 20 May, Bonaparte retreated back into Egypt. On 25 July, he annihilated a Turkish invading force at Aboukir.

On 22 August, Bonaparte abandoned the army and slipped through the British blockade to return to France. General Kléber, to whom command fell, felt betrayed, and promptly agreed to evacuate Egypt by the Convention of El Arish. After the surrender by Kléber of several key fortresses, however, the British Admiral Keith repudiated the Convention, and Cairo was captured by a Turkish army. Kléber destroyed the main Turkish army at Heliopolis (20 March 1800) and recaptured Cairo; however, he was assassinated 14 June.

General J.-F. Menou, both incompetent and unpopular, took command of the French. He allowed a British army under General Sir Ralph Abercromby to land and on 21 March 1801 was badly defeated at Canopus. The French were demoralized, and Menou quarreled with his officers while the British and Turks isolated the French in Alexandria and Cairo. The Cairo garrison under Auguste Belliard surrendered 28 July 1801, and Menou surrendered Alexandria 2 September. As provided by the surrender, the French were transported home. While militarily insignificant for France, the Egyptian campaign prepared the way for the modernization of Egypt, and the work of the institute founded the science of Egyptology.

M. Barthrop, *Napoleon's Egyptian Campaigns, 1798–1799* (London, 1978); J. E. Gody, "Principaux témoins utiles de l'expédition d'Egypte," *RIN* 135 (1979); J. C. Herold, *Bonaparte in Egypt* (London, 1963); C. F. de la Jonquiere, *L'expédition d'Egypte*, 5 vols. (Paris, 1889–1902); D. Lacroix, *Bonaparte en Egypte* (Paris, 1898).

Milton Finley

Related entries: DIRECTORY; KLEBER; MAMLUKS; MENOU; NAPOLEON I; NAVY, FRENCH.

ELBA, first place of exile of Napoleon, 1814–15; island in Mediterranean between the west coast of Italy and Corsica. It was annexed to France in 1802 by Napoleon as first consul and ceded to Napoleon as his personal domain and place of exile by the Allies in April 1814. The area of the island is approximately 86 square miles, and when Napoleon arrived on 3 May 1814 it had a population of approximately 12,000 Italian-speaking people. He set to work with zest and created a court, government, army of 1,600, and a navy of five little ships. He redecorated palaces at five different locations. He poured money into improving mining, agriculture, and fishing. The population initially was hostile since Elba had been under military occupation since 1802, but it became friendly under the impetus of prosperity brought on by Napoleon's projects and the spending of curious foreign visitors. Napoleon, however, had failed to receive the 2 million francs per year that by treaty was supposed to be sent him by Louis XVIII, and he was forced to attenuate some of his schemes. Further, he had expected the Empress Marie-Louise and his son to join him, and the Allies would not allow it. The Mamluk Ali and his valet, Louis Marchand, recorded his growing anger. Napoleon's discontent plus news from France that Louis XVIII was extremely unpopular and growing more so, plus news from Vienna that the Allies were at odds with each other, induced Napoleon to sail from Elba on 1 March 1815—the famous "flight of the eagle." There ensued the Hundred Days and Waterloo campaign.

R. Christophe, *Napoléon, empereur de l'Ile d'Elbe* (Paris, 1959); G. Godlewski, *Trois cents jours d'exil: Napoléon à l'Ile d'Elbe* (Paris, 1961); N. Mackenzie, *Escape from Elba: The Fall and Flight of Napoleon, 1814–1815* (London, 1982); V. Gellini Ponce de Leon, *Napoleone I al Isola d'Elba,* 2d ed. (Florence, 1962); L.-E. Saint-Denis (called Ali), *Souvenirs du mameluck Ali sur l'empereur Napoléon* (Paris, 1926).

Related entries: ABDICATION, FIRST; HUNDRED DAYS, THE; NAPOLEON I; VIENNA, CONGRESS OF; WATERLOO CAMPAIGN.

ELCHINGEN, DUC DE. See NEY.

EMIGRES. The French Revolution caused the flight of a number of its enemies from France. There were several waves of emigration. Those who opposed any modification of absolute monarchy left France immediately after the fall of the Bastille, 14 July 1789. One was the count d'Artois, brother of Louis XVI. The first *émigrés* were few. A second wave departed after the attempted flight of Louis XVI on 20 June 1791. That time many noble officers, including those of infantry, cavalry, and the navy, went to foreign countries. They congregated notably in the German Rhineland, in the region of Koblenz, where they formed the Army of the Princes, and to the south, in Baden, where two armies were born, that of the prince de Condé and the Black Legion of the vicomte de Mirabeau-Tonneau, brother of the Revolutionary orator. These armies participated in the invasion of France in 1792, but after the Prussians were defeated at Valmy, the Army of the Princes was dissolved.

The *émigrés* dispersed, some going to England, there to join others who had come directly from Normandy and Brittany. Two new waves of emigration marked the year 1793. On the one hand, Girondins and federalists left France to escape reprisals of the Montagnards, and on the other hand numerous Alsatian peasants, compromised by collaboration with the Austrian army, followed it when it evacuated Alsace. There was still another wave under the Directory after the coup d'état of 18 Fructidor Year V (4 September 1797). The moderates, or *Clichyens*, felt threatened, and fled across the frontiers. All told, the list of *émigrés* in 1800, compiled after 1792, counted 145,000 names, but it was quite inexact. On the one hand, real *émigrés* had been omitted, deliberately or otherwise, and on the other, the list named individuals who had left their homes but had not left France. In fact, there were not over 100,000 *émigrés*, of whom 17 percent were nobles, as many bourgeois, 14 percent artisans, 20 percent peasants, and 25 percent clergy (7 percent were unidentified by class).

The Revolutionary assemblies had passed severe laws against the *émigrés*. The Constituent Assembly, on 22 December 1790, decreed that any *émigré* holding public office in France would lose it, together with his salary and other income, if he did not return within one month. After the attempted flight of the king, the Legislative Assembly, on 9 November 1791, ordered the *émigrés* to return to France within a month on pain of death. On 8 April 1792, several days before the war with Austria and Prussia began, the same assembly ordered the sequestration of *émigrés*' properties. The Convention, a year later, on 8 March 1793, ordered outright confiscation. They were to be sold like the properties of the church and were called "National Properties of Second Origin." *Emigrés* returning to France were subject to death after simply having their identity verified. Thus, after the defeat of an invading force of English and *émigrés* at Quiberon in July 1795, 748 *émigrés* were shot. The legislation relative to the *émigrés* was not modified until after the coup d'état of 18 Brumaire Year VIII, which put Bonaparte in power. Nevertheless, under the Directory, a certain number of individuals were struck off the general list under various pretexts, and returned to France.

Bonaparte, as first consul, said he wanted to "terminate the Revolution" and "reconcile all the French." His early actions contradicted that, however, obstructing the return of *émigrés* by stringent laws, thus keeping on the frontiers of France enemies prepared to fight against it. The Constitution of Year VIII stipulated in article 93, "The French Nation declares that in no case will she allow the return of Frenchmen, who, having abandoned their country since 14 July 1789 are not included in the exceptions made to laws against the émigrés." But by the Law of 12 Ventôse Year VIII (2 March 1800), these exceptions were multiplied. A decree of 28 Vendémiaire Year IX (20 October 1800) ordered many persons stricken from the list of *émigrés*, notably "peasants, day-laborers, workers, artisans," women and children under sixteen, and knights of Malta present on the island at the time of its capitulation to the French, 10 June 1798. In sum, there remained on this list only *émigrés* who had borne arms against France and those who had served the *émigré* French princes personally and accepted civil or military office under them. But Bonaparte wished to act yet again in favor of the *émigrés*. The *senatus consultum* of 6 Floréal Year X (26 April 1802) proclaimed almost general amnesty for them. Excluded were individuals who had been chiefs of groups armed against the Republic; those who held commissions in enemy armies; those who since 1792 had held positions in the households of the *émigré* princes; those who had been *agents* in the civil or foreign war; army and navy officers, representatives of the people who had been guilty of treason against the Republic; and archbishops and bishops, who, after the proclamation of the Concordat of 1801 with the pope, refused to resign.

All other *émigrés* were invited to return, preferably via Calais, Brussels, Mainz, Strasbourg, Geneva, Nice, Bayonne, Perpignan, or Bordeaux, where commissioners had been charged to receive their declarations of return and of fidelity to the government of the Consulate. The *émigrés* rushed to return. This was certainly the case with Chateaubriand. There remained abroad only those excepted from the amnesty, who appropriately could not return to France until after the restoration of Louis XVIII in 1814.

The returning *émigrés* recovered such of their property as had not been sold or bought back much from purchasers (often agents of nobles who had bought and held it). The nobility was therefore able to recover most of its holdings.

Emigration did not disappear, however, under the Consulate and Empire. Some *émigrés* who returned again left France; they could not support the new regime. Others left for political reasons, notably after the scandalous execution of the duke d'Enghien (21 March 1804) or in connection with police persecutions of dissidents. That was the case with Mme. de Staël. But the *émigrés* of the consular and imperial epoch were exceptions, and no punitive legislation was applied against them.

In a general sense, one can say that Bonaparte, by measures that he took between 1800 and 1802, practically put an end to political emigration. Different from the loyalists after the American Revolution, who could not go home, the French *émigrés* reentered their *patrie*.

Duc de Castries, *Les émigrés* (Paris, 1962); J. Godechot, *The Counter-Revolution, Doctrine and Action, 1789–1804* (New York, 1971); D. Greer, *The Incidence of Emigration during the French Revolution* (Cambridge, Mass., 1951); J. Vidalenc, *Les émigrés français, 1789–1825* (Association des publications de la Faculté des Lettres et Sciences humaines de l'Université de Caen, Caen, 1963).

Jacques Godechot

Related entries: ARTOIS; BRUMAIRE, COUP OF 18, YEAR VIII; CHURCH, ROMAN CATHOLIC; CONCORDAT OF 1801; CONSTITUTIONS; LOUIS XVIII; NOTABLES; SOCIETY.

EMPIRE, FRENCH. At its height, the Empire included (1812) 130 departments of France (originally 83 departments, 1789), including those formed of the former Kingdom of Holland (dissolved 1810), the Hanse cities of Bremen, Hamburg, and Lübeck (annexed 1810), Belgian, Swiss, German, Piedmontese, and Italian departments, annexed 1809 or before, and encompassing Rome. Technically part of France but ruled separately were the Illyrian Provinces of the Balkans, the Grand Duchy of Tuscany, the Grand Duchies of Berg and Frankfurt in Germany, and the Duchy of Warsaw. Ringing France were the remaining satellite kingdoms (ruled by Napoleon's relatives) of Italy, Naples, Spain, and Westphalia. In

addition there were the Confederation of the Rhine (Rheinbund)—all the German states except Prussia—and the Swiss Confederation, of which Napoleon was Protector.
Related entries: ARMY, FRENCH; DIPLOMACY; FOREIGN POLICY; NAPOLEON I.

EMPIRE, HOLY ROMAN, the some 350 German states (all of Germany) over which the Austrian Hapsburg emperor held suzerainty as Holy Roman Emperor. By legend the empire had originated with the crowning of Charlemagne in Rome on Christmas Day 800 by the pope. In the medieval period, the empire had extended to all or part of Germany and at times Switzerland, Italy, and Sicily. Napoleon crowned himself using the crown of Charlemagne on 2 December 1804, a deliberate affront to the Holy Roman Emperor. Then in 1805 he decisively defeated the Austrian emperor and in 1806 created the Confederation of the Rhine, which ultimately included all the German states except Prussia. Francis II, Holy Roman Emperor, abdicated on 6 August 1806 and assumed the title emperor of Austria as Francis I. This was the end of the thousand-year Reich. After Napoleon's defeat, the Holy Roman Empire was not restored.
Related entries: AUSTERLITZ CAMPAIGN; AUSTRIA; CONFEDERATION OF THE RHINE; FOREIGN POLICY; FRANZ II; PRESSBURG, TREATY OF.

ENGHIEN, LOUIS-ANTOINE DE BOURBON CONDE, DUC D' (1772–1804), last of the Condés, Bourbon First Princes of the Blood; executed by Napoleon. In 1803–4 Napoleon and his police minister, Joseph Fouché, made an end to royalist plotters in France. Of the leaders, Georges Cadoudal was executed, General J.-C. Pichegru died in prison, and General J.-V. Moreau (who was probably innocent) was exiled from France. Napoleon wished further to discourage the *émigrés* in Germany from any thought of attacking France and to deliver a forceful warning to the Bourbon pretender, Louis XVIII, and his court. He sent soldiers into Baden—altogether illegally—who seized the duc d'Enghien and returned him to Vincennes to be tried for treason. The duke was guiltless unless one considers that ten years earlier he had served in the *émigré* army of his grandfather. Nevertheless, a court-martial, formed at Vincennes, found him guilty, and he was executed by firing squad on 20 March 1804. The hereditary monarchs of Europe were deeply shocked, since the Condés had produced famous generals for generations and because the duke was remembered as young and handsome and known to be the last of his line, but Napoleon's act had the desired effect, at least temporarily. He was able to establish the Empire in peace.

At the time and in his last testament, Napoleon admitted responsibility for the duke's execution and proclaimed it necessary for the perpetuation of his government and the security of the French people. In the intervening years, however, aware that European aristocrats generally considered that he had committed an act of terror, he shifted responsibility to others when the subject arose—especially Talleyrand. It became a scandal and a *cause célèbre*.

J. P. Bertaud, *Bonaparte et le duc d'Enghien, le duel des deux Frances* (Paris, 1972); R. Bittard des Portes, *Histoire de l'Armée de Condé pendant la Révolution française (1791-1801)* (Geneva, 1975); J. Dontenville, "La catastrophe du duc d'Enghien," *REN* 24 (1924); B. Melchior-Bonnet, *Le duc d'Enghien* (Paris, 1961).

Related entries: CADOUDAL; CONDE, HOUSE OF; FOUCHE; POLICE, MINISTRY OF GENERAL; TALLEYRAND-PERIGORD.

ENGLAND. See GREAT BRITAIN.

ENGLAND, ATTEMPTED CONQUEST OF. Bonaparte's nemesis, like Hitler's later, was England (or properly Britain). The unconquered island gave aid to all Bonaparte's other enemies and served as a base for counterattack. In 1813 alone England shipped nearly 1 million muskets and 200 cannon, besides ammunition and money, to his continental opponents, and, on 14 October 1813, when Napoleon was still undefeated in Germany, British troops from Spain invaded France.

There were four stages in Bonaparte's confrontation with England. In the first he planned a direct invasion across the channel, a threat that reached its peak in August 1805. By then he had assembled enough landing craft to lift 167,000 troops; these vessels lay secure in four new harbors specially built to shelter them, at Ambleteuse, Wimereux, Boulogne, and Etaples; from these the whole flotilla could put to sea in six tides. Once at sea, each flight would need some twelve hours to complete its crossing, under Admiral Pierre de Villeneuve's protection. Bonaparte's intended landing beach was "somewhere between Deal and Margate"—presumably Pegwell Bay, a spot conveniently handy to three harbors, Margate, Broadstairs, and Ramsgate, of which none was defensible against an invader attacking from the landward side and all would be most useful for off-loading his field and siege artillery, ammunition wagons, engineers' stores, and other heavy equipment. This plan was thwarted, first by Villeneuve's failure to arrive, and second by the outbreak of war with Austria in late August. Given proper naval protection, Bonaparte's initial landing probably would have succeeded, but the end should have been a heavy defeat, since he could not resupply his troops in England once the Royal Navy had arrived in force and driven off his covering fleet.

The second stage runs from August 1805 to July 1807. Then, while the War of the Third Coalition prevented Bonaparte from doing anything, the English made his flotilla obsolete by completing their Martello towers and royal military canal, fortifications that rendered virtually impregnable all beaches within reach of landing craft sailing from France.

The third stage began with the Treaty of Tilsit in July 1807. The czar's submission there opened two new possibilities. One was Bonaparte's Continental

System, the other a scheme to overwhelm the Royal Navy with the united fleets of all Europe. But the latter hope was crippled when the British seized the Danish fleet in September 1807 and in November compelled the Portuguese to sail theirs to Brazil and then ruined in May 1808 when the Spanish revolt robbed Bonaparte of all Spain's ships and six of his own then in Spanish harbors.

The last stage, running from 1808 to the war's end, saw Bonaparte busy with his menacing, but never-completed, task of building a French fleet strong enough to defeat the English.

F. Beaucour, "Le Grand Projet Napoléonien d'expédition en Angleterre: Mythe ou Réalité," *CRE* (1982); E. Desbrière, *Projets et tentatives de debarquement aux Isles Britanniques, 1793–1805* (Paris, 1902); H. C. Deutsch, *The Genesis of Napoleonic Imperialism, 1800–1805* (Cambridge, Mass., 1938); R. Glover, *Britain at Bay: Defence against Bonaparte 1803–1814* (London, 1973); J. H. Rose, "Did Napoleon Intend to Invade England?" in *Pitt and Napoleon: Essays and Letters* (London, 1912).

Richard Glover

Related entries: DIPLOMACY; FOREIGN POLICY; GREAT BRITAIN; GREAT BRITAIN, DOMESTIC; NAVY, FRENCH.

ERFURT, INTERVIEW AT (18 September 1808), a conference between Napoleon and Alexander I of Russia at which the latter agreed to cooperate in keeping the peace in northern Europe while Napoleon shifted his forces to Spain to restore Joseph Bonaparte to the throne. The meeting was attended by four kings, including Jerome Bonaparte of Westphalia, thirty-odd German princes, and numerous members of the German, Austrian, and Russian nobility.

Related entries: PENINSULAR WAR.

ESSLING, BATTLE OF. See WAGRAM CAMPAIGN.

ESSLING, PRINCE D'. See MASSENA.

ESTATES GENERAL (Etats Généraux), the traditional parliament of France, called for the first time in one hundred seventy-five years by Louis XVI in May 1789 because of his government's acute financial problems. It comprised representatives of the three "estates"—clergy, nobles, and commoners or the Third—each house sitting and voting separately. The Third seized control of the body, however, with the help of some liberal clergy and nobles, and converted it into a National Assembly, which determined to give France a written constitution. Louis called troops to Paris, but the people responded by storming the Bastille, and he sent his soldiers away. Parisians protected the assembly with subsequent mass actions until it produced the Constitution of 1791, under which Louis XVI had limited executive power and laws were made by a legislative assembly elected on a regular basis. The experiment in constitutional monarchy lasted less than a year (September 1791–August 1792) before Louis was deposed by the mobs of Paris. There followed government under various republican systems and then under Napoleon's Consulate and Empire. See CONSTITUTIONS; CONVENTION; DIRECTORY.

EXCHANGE RATE. Napoleon was a hard-money man. He had a horror of going into debt (he borrowed as little as possible), and he abhorred paper money. The value of his franc coins in silver (or gold) equaled their face value, the Bank of France's *billets* of 500 francs, backed by commercial paper, were redeemable in metallic currency, and by 1812 Napoleon had stored 400 million francs in bullion in the cellar of the Tuileries. By 1810 the French franc on the exchange was the strongest currency in Europe, the standard by which other currencies were measured. At that time the lire (Kingdom of Italy) equaled 0.76 franc; the ducat (Naples), 4.45; the réal (Spain), 0.27; the florin (Holland), 2.17; the dollar (United States), 5.00; the pound sterling (Great Britain), 20.30. Meanwhile Britain was financing war expenses by borrowing (its debt doubled during the Revolutionary and Napoleonic period), by issuing paper money, and by going off the gold standard. By April 1811 the British pound bought only 17 to 18 francs. The hard-money franc was victor in the battle of exchange rates.

O. Connelly, *French Revolution/Napoleonic Era* (New York, 1979); M. Marion, *Histoire financière de la France depuis 1715*, vol. 4: *1799–1818: La fin de la Révolution, le Consulat et l'Empire, la libération du territoire* (Paris, 1927).

Harold T. Parker

Related entries: BANK OF FRANCE; CONTINENTAL BLOCKADE; ECONOMY, FRENCH; FINANCES; FRANC; WARFARE, ECONOMIC.

EXILES. See *EMIGRES*.

EYLAU, BATTLE OF. See JENA-AUERSTÄDT-FRIEDLAND CAMPAIGN.

F

FAIN, AGATHON-JEAN-FRANCOIS, BARON (1778–1837), Napoleon's secretary. A clerk of the military committee of the Convention at age sixteen, Fain was recruited by Paul Barras for the bureaucracy of the Directory. Under the Consulate he passed to the division of archives in the state secretariat under Hugues Maret. When in 1806 Napoleon's secretary, C.-F. Baron de Méneval, was overwhelmed by the burgeoning imperial correspondence, Fain, with the title of secretary archivist, was brought into Napoleon's private office to help. When Méneval's health failed in 1813, Fain succeeded him as Napoleon's secretary. Ever faithful, efficient, and unobtrusive, he served through the Hundred Days. His memoirs on Napoleon's work habits are among the most valuable we possess: *Mémoires du baron Fain, premier secrétaire du cabinet de l'Empereur* (Paris, 1908).

Harold T. Parker

Related entry: NAPOLEON, DAILY ROUND.

FASHION. See CLOTHING FASHION, MEN'S; CLOTHING FASHION, WOMEN'S.

FEDERAL CITIES, cities that revolted against the government of Terror in 1793. They were Lyon, Bordeaux, Marseille, and Toulon. It was as artillery commander of the French Republican army besieging Toulon that Napoleon Bonaparte first gained fame.
Related entries: CONVENTION; NAPOLEON I; TERROR, THE; TOULON, SIEGE OF.

FELTRE, DUC DE. See CLARKE.

FERDINAND IV. See NAPLES, KINGDOM OF.

FERDINAND VII DE BOURBON (1784–1833), prince of Asturias, 1789–1808; King of Spain, 1808, 1814–33; in exile, 1808–14. As crown prince Ferdinand became a devious leader of secret opposition to his father and mother,

King Charles IV and Queen Maria Luisa. He especially despised Manuel Godoy, the king's perennial first minister who had long been his mother's lover. He loathed his mother and had no respect for his father, a pleasant, innocuous, and occasionally insane monarch. Ferdinand became the hope of the liberals in Spain, largely because he opposed Godoy. In 1807 Ferdinand was caught plotting against the throne and betrayed all of his followers, who were imprisoned or exiled. The liberals nevertheless considered him their only hope.

In 1808, as Joachim Murat's French army approached Madrid, Ferdinand overthrew his father at Aranjuez and proclaimed himself Ferdinand VII. Napoleon called both Ferdinand and Charles IV to Bayonne where he forced them to abdicate. Ferdinand was sent into exile at Valençay. He lived there comfortably until 1813, refusing to cooperate with British secret agents, who had arranged his escape. Meanwhile Spanish rebels fought furiously for five years to return him to this throne. He gave them no encouragement and initially had sent his congratulations and good wishes to Joseph Bonaparte.

In December 1813 Napoleon set him free under an agreement by which Ferdinand would resume the throne of Spain. However, the Cortes of Cadiz would not accept him as a client of Napoleon. Thus Ferdinand reentered Spain only in 1814, after Napoleon's abdication. He proceeded to renounce the liberal constitution of 1812 and persecute the Spanish liberals. His tyranny promoted a revolution in 1820 during which he was forced to accept the 1812 constitution. As soon as he was freed, however, he again renounced it and returned to his old policies. After 1814 many of the liberals who had maintained the resistance against the French in the name of Ferdinand VII wished that they had supported Joseph Bonaparte.

J. Gomez Arteche y Moro, *Fernando VII en Valençay* (Madrid, 1880); M. Artola, *La España de Fernando VII* (Madrid, 1968); J. Chastenet, *Godoy, Master of Spain, 1792-1808* (London, 1953); Pedro Jordan de Urriey, *Memórias sobre la estancia de Don Fernando VII en Valençay . . .* (Zaragossa, 1893); G. H. Lovett, *Napoleon and the Birth of Modern Spain*, 2 vols. (New York, 1965); W. Ramirez, Marquis de Villa-Urrutia, *Fernando VII, rey constitucional* (Madrid, 1922).

Related entries: BAYONNE, "INTERVIEW" OF; PENINSULAR WAR; SPAIN, KINGDOM OF.

FESCH, JOSEPH (1783–1839), cardinal, half-brother of Napoleon's mother. Fesch entered the church under the Old Regime but happily conformed with the Civil Constitution and Oath prescribed by the Revolution. He nevertheless abandoned his robes for a few years to be an army supplier. In 1800, however, Napoleon as first consul brought him back into the church and had him named archbishop of Lyon and later cardinal (1803). In 1804 he was sent as ambassador to the Vatican, where he served ineptly. His letter to Pius VII demanding rather than requesting the pope's presence at Napoleon's coronation elicited a refusal. Napoleon had to write Pius personally to induce him to come to Paris, which the pope did. Fesch nevertheless assisted at the coronation and was afterward

made grand almoner of the Empire and provided with various other titles and incomes. After Napoleon's fall, Fesch retired to Rome where he indulged himself in the collection of art. After his death, most of his fabulous collection went to the village of Ajaccio, in Corsica, where he had been born.
Related entries: NAPOLEON I; PIUS VII.

FEZENSAC, RAYMOND-AYMERY-PHILIPPE-JOSEPH DE MONTESQUIOU, DUC DE (1784–1867), French soldier. Fezensac joined the French army in 1804 and rose rapidly from private to sous-lieutenant. He fought in the German campaigns of 1805–7 and was captured by the Russians in 1807. On his release he married the daughter of General Henri Clarke and spent several years on staff duty. A participant in the Russian campaign, he took command of the Fourth Infantry Regiment following the Battle of Borodino; he led it back on the retreat, recording that its numbers fell from 2,600 officers and men to 230. Fezensac did not serve during the Hundred Days but thereafter pursued a military and diplomatic career until 1848. He left extensive and valuable memoirs, notably of the 1812 campaign.

Duc de Fezensac, *Souvenirs militaires de 1804 á 1814* (Paris, 1863), and *The Russian Campaign, 1812*, trans. Lee Kennett (Athens, Ga., 1970).

Lee Kennett

Related entries: CLARKE; RUSSIAN CAMPAIGN; SOCIETY.

FICHTE, JOHANN GOTTLIEB (1761–1814), German philosopher. Fichte studied theology but, unable to obtain a pastorate, for many years earned his living as a private family tutor. Attracted to Immanuel Kant's philosophy, he wrote in 1792 *Essay toward a Critique of All Revelation*, which paved the way for his appointment in 1794 as professor of philosophy at Jena University. In 1799, however, he was unjustly accused of atheism and forced to leave. Thereafter he resided in Berlin and socialized with the leading German Romantics. He helped organize the new University of Berlin (founded in 1810) and became its first president but died in 1814 of typhoid fever.

Most of Fichte's attention was devoted to philosophy, but he also engaged in political polemics. The first of these (1793) supported the French Revolution; later ones, particularly *The Closed Trading State* (1800) and the *Doctrine of Law* (1812), sympathized with notions of state socialism. His focus became more direct after 1806 when he began to oppose Napoleon as the betrayer of the ideals of the French Revolution. In *Patriotism and Its Opposite* (1807), he championed a nation in arms. His *Addresses to the German Nation*, delivered on fourteen consecutive Sundays in the winter of 1807–8 at the Berlin Academy and subsequently published, has been regarded as his most significant contribution to the struggle against Napoleon. In the *Addresses* he renounced the cosmopolitanism of the Enlightenment and urged loyalty to the nation. In the nation, its people, and the national language, he saw reflected godhead and earthly eternity. He regarded the Germans alone as capable of realizing the freedom betrayed by the French and, through the instrument of national education, of fashioning the socialist state of the future.

The *Addresses* failed to influence immediate political events and contributed little to the destruction of Napoleon. Nevertheless, their long-range impact was great. Fichte looms large as one of the founders of the concept of a German nation state.

E. N. Anderson, *Nationalism and the Cultural Crisis in Prussia, 1806–1815* (1939); H. C. Engelbrecht, *Johann Gottlieb Fichte: A Study of His Political Writings with Special Reference to His Nationalism* (1933); J. Fichte, *Addresses to the German Nation* (1922); F. Meinecke, *Cosmopolitanism and the National State* (1970); G. H. Turnbull, *The Educational Theory of Fichte* (1926); N. Wallner, *Fichte als politischer Denker* (1926); M. Weber, *Fichtes Sozialismus und sein Verhältnis zur Marxschen Doktrin* (1925); B. Willms, *Die totale Freiheit. Fichtes politische Philosophie* (1967).

Peter W. Becker

Related entries: GERMAN WAR OF LIBERATION; JAHN; KLEIST; PRUSSIA, KINGDOM OF.

FILM, NAPOLEON IN. Relatively few films have been made that deal directly with the life of Napoleon Bonaparte. There are many where he is a minor character, such as the versions of *War and Peace*, or major but obscure, as in the Waterloo films. There are also those, especially old ones, where Napoleon acts as a deus ex machina to solve (usually) romantic problems, and, of course, the stock comic figure of the nut-house crazy who thinks he is Napoleon.

The one major attempt to do a life of Napoleon is the classic work of the French filmmaker, Abel Gance. Gance planned six films to cover the entire life through St. Helena. Because of money problems he completed only one, which carries Napoleon from military school through the Italian campaign of 1796–97. The original version, first shown at the Paris Opéra in 1927, ran over six hours. Gance was far ahead of his time. He used a triple screen, three separate images, and at the end one great fused image. In 1934 he reissued his masterpiece in shortened form, with stereophonic sound track added. For the film historian, this film is of great importance, but for the historian it is something of a joke. Gance brought the Napoleonic myth alive, though some critics thought his Bonaparte would inspire young fascists. The Bonaparte we see, played by Albert Dieudonné, is the embodiment of the "Will to Power."

Among the more successful "Napoleons" in film has been Herbert Lom (a Czech, whose real name was Herbert Charles Angelo Kuchacevich ze Schluderpacheru) who essayed the role several times, first in *The Young Mr. Pitt* (1942) and best in *War and Peace* (1956), directed by King Vidor. Vladimir Strzhelchik made an outstanding Napoleon in the Soviet *War and Peace* (1966, 1967) directed by Sergei Bondarchuk. Worst performance honors probably should go either to Marlon Brando in *Desirée* (1954), to Rod Steiger in *Waterloo* (1970), or to Kenneth Haigh in *Eagle in a Cage* (1971). The most enjoyable and authentic film on the period is probably *Madame Sans-Gêne* (1963), based on the 1893

Sardou play, which features almost true-life adventures of the young lieutenant Bonaparte, Sergeant (later Marshal) Lefebvre, and the laundress Catherine Hubscher, later duke and duchess of Danzig. Catherine was played by Sophia Loren; Napoleon by Julien Bertheau.

Some of the others who have attempted the role of Napoleon in film include: Charles Boyer in *Conquest* (1937) with Greta Garbo as Madame Walewska, Emil Drain in the Hollywood *Madame Sans-Gêne* (1925), George Campbell in *Monte Cristo* (1922), Slavko Vorkapitch in *Scaramouche* (1923), Paul Muni in Fox's *Seven Faces* (1929), Otto Matiesen in *Vanity Fair* (1923), William Humphrey in *Devil May Care* (1929), Max Barwyn in De Mille's *The Fighting Eagle* (1927), Pasquale Amato in *Glorious Betsy* [Patterson] (1928), Emile Drain in Sacha Guitry's *Les perles de la couronne* (1937), Rollo Lloyd in *Anthony Adverse* (1936), Sergei Mezhinsky in the Soviet *1812* (1944), Arnold Moss in *The Black Book* (1949), and Pierre Mondy in *Austerlitz* (1960).

A. Thépot and J. Tulard, *L'histoire de Napoléon au cinéma* (Lausanne, 1969); J. Tulard, *Le Mythe de Napoléon* (Paris, 1971).

Hugh Bonar

Related entries: AUSTERLITZ, BATTLE OF; BONAPARTE, ELIZABETH PATTERSON; LEFEBVRE; NAPOLEON I; RUSSIAN CAMPAIGN; WALEWSKA; WATERLOO CAMPAIGN.

FINANCES. Napoleon's chief financial problem was to find ever greater amounts of money for his government, his military forces, and, eventually, his empire. In 1799 he inherited from the Directory a desperate fiscal situation: taxes were not coming in; overdue bills for supplies and salaries of civil servants and soldiers were not being paid; government bonds were selling at 11.38 (par 100); and the government was forced to borrow at 5 percent per month. Bonaparte had no special competence in finance, but he recognized his ignorance of fiscal mechanisms and was willing to learn. He appointed officials from among civil servants trained largely under the Bourbon monarchy. The more notable ones were Michel Gaudin, minister of finances (in charge of collecting taxes); François de Barbé-Marbois, minister of the treasury (responsible for payments); and Nicolas Mollien, director of the sinking fund. In the early weeks of the Consulate, by catch-as-catch-can expedients, they and Bonaparte managed to get some money into the till. They then began to build fundamental financial structures.

They introduced a rigorous collection of direct taxes (real estate and personal property) by appointing a hierarchy of efficient collectors (*percepteurs* at the first level, a *receveur particulier* for each *arrondissement*, a *receveur général* for each *département*). Eventually these officials were required to pay the taxes into a Service Fund (*caisse de service*) as they received them. To ensure a fair assessment of real estate taxes, the Ministry of Finances initiated the preparation of a *cadastre*, a register of the ownership, quantity, and value of every parcel of land in France. Until the disasters of 1812–13 direct taxes were kept moderate and constant at about 250 million francs annually. To balance the budget, the government levied a variety of indirect taxes (customs duties, stamp and registry dues, excises on the sale of tobacco, liquor, and salt), which could be raised or lowered according to need. Expenses were rigorously monitored. A hierarchy of paymasters in the Ministry of the Treasury paid only those bills authorized by a law, a decree, or the warrant of a minister. An audit commission (*cour des comptes*) reviewed the bookkeeping accounts of collectors and paymasters. Included in expenses was interest on the old debt inherited from the Directory, which the Consulate in part assumed and in part repudiated. Interest was paid in coin in a new standard franc. A sinking fund (*caisse d'amortissement*) was established, chiefly to intervene on the *bourse* (stock market) and by purchase keep the price of government bonds high.

Napoleon strained to have a balanced budget and never to incur a large, standing indebtedness. The budget was presented annually to the Tribunate and legislative body for approval, but only after the budgetary year had begun, and it was often altered during the year. Ratification was sought in effect only for tax levies and not for expenses, which were not detailed. Still, the legislative bodies had a greater role than is generally thought.

In years of relative peace (1802 for the Consulate and 1810 for the Empire) the budget was balanced. In expensive war years, it was nearly balanced, until 1812, by quartering troops in foreign lands and by levying contributions on allies and defeated enemies. After Jena, for example, Prussia was assessed an indemnity of 311 million francs. The money and property acquired in this way were placed in a separate fund, the extraordinary domain, under separate administration. A balanced wartime budget thus depended on victory. War expenditures did not bear hard on the French until the defeats of 1812–13. Very early (1800) the Bank of France was set up, largely to assure French businessmen credit at a reasonable interest rate.

The fiscal result of these measures was a vigorous, durable fiscal administration. The French people were habituated to punctual discharge of their tax obligations. Even during the turbulent, disastrous years of 1814–15, they paid regularly, to the amazement of the prefects. The government debt had been kept moderate and could be assumed without great distress by the Restoration monarchy. The new franc de Germinal was stable and in 1811 commanded a better exchange rate than the pound sterling. The market price of government bonds rose from 11.38 (November 1799) to 93 (summer 1807), though it declined after the invasion of Portugal and Spain. A form of annual legislative review had been introduced into the budgetary process. A central bank had been brought into existence. If Napoleon did not understand the advantages of public credit in financing a war and peacetime projects, at least he knew its dangers. He tried to run a tight financial operation, and in the process he kept his own regime going and founded structures that endured.

Louis Bergeron, *France under Napoleon*, trans. R. R. Palmer (Princeton, 1981); J. F. Bosher, *French Finances 1770–1795* (Cambridge, 1970); M. Marion, *Histoire financière de la France depuis 1715*, vol. 4: *1799–1818: La fin de la Révolution, le Consulat et l'Empire, la libération du territoire* (Paris, 1927); R. Stourm, *Les finances du Consulat* (Paris, 1902); G. Thuillier, "Pour une histoire monétaire du XIXe siècle: la crise monétaire de l'automne 1810," *RHq* 237 (1967), "Pour une histoire monétaire de la France du XIXe siècle: la réforme de l'an XI," *RIN* 131 (1975), and "Les troubles monétaires en France de 1803 à 1808," *RIN* 133 (1977).

Harold T. Parker

Related entries: BANK OF FRANCE; BARBE-MARBOIS; CONTINENTAL BLOCKADE; ECONOMY, FRENCH; EXCHANGE RATE; FRANC; GAUDIN; MOLLIEN; WARFARE, ECONOMIC.

FIVE DAYS, BATTLES OF (February 1814), series of offensive actions directed by Napoleon in person at Champaubert (February 10), Montmirail (February 11), Château-Thierry (February 12), and Vauchamps (February 14). Taken together, these actions comprise the high point of Napoleon's inspired though unsuccessful defense of France in 1814.

After three days of fighting at Brienne-La Rothière (29 January–1 February), Prince Karl zu Schwarzenberg, with the principal allied force, advanced toward Paris generally via the Seine valley; Prince G. L. Blücher von Wahlstatt, with his Army of Silesia, went via the valley of the Marne. To contain Blücher, Napoleon assigned Marshal Jacques MacDonald with a very small force (not over 5,000 men). Blücher was anxious to arrive in Paris; MacDonald seemed no obstacle, and he considered that Napoleon would be securely held in the valley of the Seine by Schwarzenberg's greatly superior numbers. He also felt that the inferior roads in the region, plus poor weather conditions, would prevent rapid maneuver by the French. As a result of these assumptions, Blücher badly overextended his forces, and Napoleon was able to surprise him.

Striking northward, Napoleon overwhelmed a Russian corps at Champaubert on 10 February. Striking westward the following day, he defeated a combined Russian-Prussian force at Montmirail, driving the beaten elements northwest. On 12 February Napoleon pursued vigorously, driving the enemy across the Marne at Château-Thierry and capturing prisoners, guns, and baggage. The next day, as he rested his weary men, Napoleon learned that a Prussian force was pushing westward toward Montmirail. Hastily regrouping during the night, he concentrated against the new force (this time commanded by Blücher in person) and struck it at Vauchamps on 14 February. Blücher sustained heavy losses and withdrew toward Châlons. Napoleon prepared to return to the Seine valley to confront Schwarzenberg.

D. Chandler, *Campaigns of Napoleon* (New York, 1966); H. Houssaye, *1814* (Paris, 1888); J. Lawford, *Napoleon: The Last Campaigns, 1813-15* (London, 1977).

George Winton

Related entries: BLÜCHER VON WAHLSTATT; MACDONALD; SCHWARZENBERG.

FLORENCE, TREATY OF (18 March 1801), agreement forced on Naples by Napoleon. The Neapolitan Bourbons agreed to close their harbors to British and

Turkish ships. Naples also ceded Piombino and the island of Elba to France and accepted the placing of French troops in Otranto, Taranto, and Brindisi.
Related entry: FOREIGN POLICY.

FONTAINE, PIERRE-FRANCOIS-LEONARD (1762–1853), one of the pair of architects who provided unity for the Empire style by designing neoclassical interiors, grandiose yet intimate decorations, graceful furniture, elegant carpets, wallpaper, fabrics, porcelain, and metallic objects to complement the basic structure of additions and complete buildings. Born at Pontoise as the son of a stonework contractor, he attended the local collège before going to Paris in 1779 to become an architectural pupil of Antoine François Peyre, the king's building inspector. At Peyre's he met Charles Percier with whom he was formally associated in business from 1794 to 1814. In 1784, he won second prize in the *Prix de Rome* competition. Shortly after he went to Rome and earned his living by selling pen drawings and watercolors of the tourist attractions to foreigners. He returned to France in 1790, where by now his father had been ruined by the emigration of his wealthy clients. He lived at Montmartre and designed furniture for Georges Jacob, made wallpaper samples, and worked for the architect Claude Ledoux. Influenced by his trip to Italy, he used antique inspiration for his designs that manifested the vogue for the cult of antiquity that caught on at the beginning of the Revolution. While Fontaine traveled to England in 1792, he did not stay long. By the time he returned, Percier was already designing sets at the Opéra, and the two soon became successful designers for the minor arts and building construction. Among Fontaine's early achievements are the façade of Saint Joseph's Church of Montmartre, conversion of the former theater in the Tuileries into a meeting hall for the Convention, finishing the Panthéon, and with Alexandre Guy de Gisors arranging the ground floor of the Palais Bourbon for the Council of Five Hundred.

As Fontaine restored the hotel of Chauvelin on rue Chantelaine, he was noticed by a neighbor, Josephine de Beauharnais, who presented him to Bonaparte in November 1799. When Fontaine suggested that captured enemy flags should be placed in the Invalides, the first consul put him in charge of such a ceremony at a memorial service for George Washington held 9 February 1800. Since Fontaine became the official architect of the Consulate, he worked at Malmaison, where he designed the music room, council room, and library, the Chateau of Saint-Cloud, and the Musée des Monuments Françaises. On 6 February 1805 he and Percier became the architects of the Louvre and the Tuileries. The two also made decorations for public festivities beginning with the coronation and the distribution of the eagles and, eventually, the Austrian marriage. Later he furnished plans for a proposed palace for the king of Rome and the entire Grenelle quartier. In 1811 Fontaine was rewarded by the emperor by being named to the Legion of Honor as well as to the Institute (Beaux Arts), and in 1813, he officially became Napoleon's first architect.

During the Restoration, Fontaine functioned as court architect to Louis XVIII.

As architect for Louis Philippe during the reign of Charles X, he improved the Palais Royal and later became the July monarch's chief architect, in charge of the Louvre, Tuileries, and all royal buildings until the Revolution of 1848. During the Second Republic, he became president of the Council of Civil Buildings. Since Percier had died in 1838, Fontaine enjoyed a longer career of public service. Nevertheless, both of them influenced French architecture for more than half a century by spreading the Empire style.

E. Driault, *Napoléon architecte* (Paris, 1939); A. Gonzalez-Palacios, *The Empire Style* (New York, 1970); M. Fouché, *Percier et Fontaine* (Paris, 1907); F. Halévy, *Notice historique sur la vie et les travaux de M. Fontaine* (Paris, 1854); J. F. Vacquier and P. Marmottan, *Le Style Empire: Decorations extérieurs et intérieures, mobilier, bronzes* (Paris, 1914–30).

June K. Burton

Related entries: ARCHITECTURE; ART; CONVENTION; DENON; INSTITUT NATIONAL DES SCIENCES ET DES ARTS; JOSEPHINE; LOUVRE; MARIE-LOUISE VON HABSBURG; NAPOLEON II; PERCIER.

FONTAINEBLEAU, TREATY OF (27 October 1807), which allowed French troops to cross Spain to attack Portugal. It permitted a French reserve force at Bayonne, which was really intended to invade Spain. In return, by secret provisions, Spain's treacherous first minister, Manuel Godoy, was to have a kingdom in south Portugal, to be styled Lusitania.

Related entry: PENINSULAR WAR.

FONTAINEBLEAU, TREATY OF (6 April 1814), which gave Napoleon sovereignty over the island of Elba (contingent on his abdication). See ABDICATION, FIRST.

FONTANES, LOUIS DE (1757–1821), essayist and poet under the Old Regime. Fontanes was a spokesman for moderation throughout the Revolution. He went into hiding during the Terror (1793–94) and was exiled by the Directory, going to England, where he was converted to Roman Catholicism and to fanatical enmity toward eighteenth-century rational philosophy. On his return to France after 18 Brumaire, he became a favorite of Bonaparte's sister, Elisa Bacciochi, and moved in a conservative Catholic circle that included Chateaubriand. Fontanes was appointed to the legislative body in 1802 and was its president from 1804 to 1808.

In 1808 Fontanes was made grand master of the Imperial University, which represented a victory of the conservative Catholics over the progressive scientific group. This gave him supervision of the entire French school system. He sponsored in the lycées the restoration of the old-time curriculum whose base was Latin and Greek rather than science, and he added a year of formal philosophy. He introduced into the educational system many priests more devoted to the pope and the Bourbons than to Napoleon and appointed no lay teacher without the approval of the local bishop. Thus an opposition to the Empire was developed within the university. As the official orator of the legislative body of the Empire, it was easy for him to slip smoothly during the Restoration into being the official orator of the chamber of peers, eloquently apostrophizing Louis XVIII as he had Napoleon.

Harold T. Parker

Related entries: EDUCATION; UNIVERSITY, IMPERIAL.

FOREIGN POLICY. Napoleon Bonaparte began influencing the foreign policy of France while general of the Directory in Italy (1796–97). He not only defeated France's major enemy, Austria, and its Italian allies but gained political clout by sending millions in treasure to the government. Moreover, he sent General Pierre Augereau to Paris in 1797 to engineer the coup d'état of Fructidor, which conserved a moderate Directory. Thus he was allowed to make peace essentially as he chose. It has been speculated that the Treaty of Campo Formio with Austria forecast Napoleon's later interest in the East, particularly the provision ceding the Ionian Islands to France, since they can be seen as a stepping-stone into the Middle East and India. In 1798–99, the expedition to Egypt was conceived by Napoleon and Charles-Maurice de Talleyrand rather than by the government and diverted men and resources to the Middle East, which might have been used elsewhere, perhaps to invade Ireland.

Napoleon's full direction of foreign policy began in 1800 after he had created the Consulate. At first he seemed bent on consolidating certain modest conquests of the Revolution and establishing peace. He again defeated Austria and made peace at Lunéville (1801), then peace with Britain at Amiens (1802), and meanwhile secured a concordat with the pope (1801). He reorganized only the most solid of the sister republics of France: the Batavian (Dutch) Republic, the Helvetic (Swiss) Republic, the Ligurian (Genoan) Republic, and the Cisalpine (northern Italian) Republic. The Roman Republic was dissolved and its territory restored to the pope; the Parthenopean Republic similarly was returned to the Neapolitan Bourbons. Napoleon made a short-lived effort to restore the French empire in America, forcing Spain to retrocede Louisiana to France (1801) and preparing to use it as the bread basket of the French sugar-producing islands of the West Indies. This plan was exploded by the debacle of Haiti, where Napoleon's army perished of fever. He sold Louisiana to the United States for a pittance, hoping that it would be a source of trouble between the United States and his archenemy, Great Britain, which indeed it became in 1812.

During 1801–3, appearances to the contrary, Napoleon was preparing to extend the power of France in Europe. In 1802 he annexed to France Piedmont and Elba (just evacuated by the British); he kept garrisons in Naples, obstructed British trade with the Dutch, and incited Spain to attack Portugal, which was allied with Britain. But the British refused to give up Malta as agreed at Amiens and resumed war with France in the spring of 1803. Napoleon immediately occupied Hanover, which constituted a further interference in Germany where he had already forced a reorganization of the states under the provisions of the Treaty of Lunéville. In 1804 Napoleon created the Empire and in his coronation presented himself as the successor of Charlemagne, who was by tradition the first Holy Roman Emperor, a title held by Francis II of Austria. In 1805 Napoleon made himself king of Italy, a title going back to the Lombards, which also belonged to the Austrian Habsburgs. In 1805 Austria allied with Britain against France. Russia also joined since the new czar, Alexander I, felt his interests in the Balkans were threatened and resented Napoleon's earlier attempts to close the Baltic. There resulted the campaign of Austerlitz (1805), a triumph for Napoleon. At the same time, a British fleet under Lord Nelson destroyed the French and Spanish fleets at Trafalgar. This did not directly affect Napoleon's plans for Europe, but it is an indication that he had broader plans; he began building a new navy in Dutch, French, Italian, and other ports for an eventual challenge to the British, which was never made.

In 1806 Napoleon seems to have begun the implementation of a grand design that involved placing various European kingdoms under members of his family and bringing his allies under closer control. He had created the Kingdom of Italy (1805) under the Viceroy Eugène de Beauharnais, his stepson. In 1806 he conquered Naples and made Joseph, his elder brother, king. He dissolved the Dutch Republic and created the Kingdom of Holland, making Louis Bonaparte king. He had previously styled himself protector of the Swiss Confederation (1802) and in 1806 created the Confederation of the Rhine, which included virtually all of the German states (eventually all but Prussia). This indication of French power in Germany induced Francis II to abdicate as Holy Roman Emperor and assume the title Francis I, emperor of Austria. Napoleon's moves were challenged by Russia and Prussia, which were, however, defeated in the campaigns of Jena-Auerstädt-Friedland (1806–7).

At Tilsit (July 1807) he enlarged his system by adding the Kingdom of Westphalia in Germany under his brother Jerome and the Duchy of Warsaw, which he placed temporarily under King Augustus of Saxony. Warsaw, the Poles believed, was an earnest of intent to resurrect the Kingdom of Poland, which had disappeared in the partition of 1795. Napoleon further emphasized the European character of his system by creating the Continental Blockade by the Berlin decree (1806) and the Milan decree (1807). Prussia and Russia were forced to commit themselves to ban British goods from Europe, which had already been pledged by the rest of Napoleon's allies, whose territories covered the entire face of Europe.

At the end of 1807, Napoleon's empire was truly European in scope. The situation in the Iberian Peninsula bothered him, however. Spain, his ally, had furnished him unreliable troops, rotten ships, and no money. Further, the Spanish were trading with the British under the most transparent subterfuges. The regent of Portugal (the queen was insane) kept pledging to observe the Continental Blockade but in fact traded freely with the British. Moreover, the Spanish Bourbons seemed degenerate and ineffective. The king was at intervals insane; the queen was the mistress of the first minister; the crown prince plotted continually to overthrow his father. Thus Napoleon believed that the Spanish would welcome a change of dynasty, and he proceeded to replace the Spanish Bourbons with his progressive and kind-hearted brother, Joseph. With the connivance of Manuel Godoy, the Spanish first minister, the French invaded Portugal in 1807 and Spain in 1808. There ensued the Peninsular War. Nevertheless another kingdom was added to Napoleon's system—Spain under Joseph. Naples was given to Marshal Joachim Murat and Caroline Bonaparte.

In 1809 Austria again challenged and was again beaten at Wagram. By this time Napoleon had decided to perpetuate his dynasty and give it an element of legitimacy by taking a wife from one of the great dynasties of Europe. He divorced Josephine (1809) and married Marie-Louise of Austria (1810). He expected his new bride to give him a son for whom he selected the title of king of Rome. (Rome was to be the second city of the Empire.) The son, Napoleon-François-Charles-Joseph, was born in March 1811.

In 1810 Napoleon conceived a new grand design. He decided to dismantle the satellite kingdoms, governed by his relatives, and integrate their territories into France. Each state would be divided into departments, which ultimately would be governed from Paris, thus discouraging nationalistic tendencies. The departments, fully integrated into France, would have representation in the Senate and legislative bodies of the Empire. Thus a centralized European empire would evolve. In 1810 Napoleon took the first step toward implementing this design by forcing Louis Bonaparte to abdicate the throne of Holland and annexing Holland to France. He had already secured the agreement of Eugène, in Italy, to step down after twenty years. Murat in Naples and Jerome in Westphalia were subjected to the same harassment and public humiliation as Louis had been, seemingly with the object of forcing them to abdicate. In Spain Joseph was struck even more severe blows. He was reduced to governing the area of Madrid, and the rest of his kingdom was divided into military governments under marshals and generals.

At the end of 1810, however, Czar Alexander issued a *ukase* withdrawing from the Continental Blockade, thus throwing down the gauntlet to Napoleon. Napoleon, in the interest of mobilizing maximum force, effected reconciliation with the satellite kings. Since he lost in Russia, his grand design was never implemented. If he had won, however, he probably would have returned to it.

It is difficult to say that Napoleon had a policy during 1813–14, except one of expediency tempered by a paranoid suspicion of his enemies. He refused successive offers of the Allies that would have guaranteed him first France and parts of the Empire and then an expanded France—as late as October 1813, France, Belgium, and the Rhineland—in March 1814 with the boundaries of 1792. He was still rather gently treated after his abdication in 1814, though he was reduced to emperor of Elba.

On Napoleon's return to France for the Hundred Days, he professed satisfaction with the borders of France (those of 1792) and promised to govern peacefully as a constitutional monarch. It is doubtful if he could have lived up to his pledge, even if the Allies had believed him—which they did not. There ensued the Waterloo campaign in which Napoleon was defeated and again forced to abdicate.

On St. Helena, Napoleon stated that his grand design had been to create a "Europe of Free Peoples," by which he seems to have meant national kingdoms cooperating under a loose imperial system. Probably this was not his plan, but what he decided in retrospect he might realistically have achieved. Even this, however, would have meant that he would have organized a sort of European state.

Napoleon had schemes stretching beyond Europe, however. In 1807 he discussed with Alexander I the possibility of the division of the Ottoman Empire between France and Russia. Considering his behavior between 1807 and 1812, one must conclude that he had no intention of giving Alexander any part of the Turkish territory and probably meant to take it (and more) for himself. He had kept the Ottoman Empire at war with Russia between 1806 and 1812; he had managed to embroil the Persian Empire with Russia similarly between 1806 and 1810. By ceding Louisiana to the United States and by exploiting the differences between the British and Americans on the high seas, Napoleon managed to bring the United States to war with Britain in 1812 at the very time he was invading Russia. Moreover, using French and Dutch officials and officers, he held for as long as possible and exploited to the maximum colonies in Senegal, South Africa, Madagascar, Borneo, and Java. If Napoleon had been successful in Europe, he might well have begun the process of expanding his empire outward to other parts of the world. A fact supporting this is that as of 1812 he had almost overtaken the British in the construction of first-line warships, and experts estimate that by 1814 he would have had more ships of the line than Britain. Whether he could have found the crews is another question. That he was building a huge navy shows that his ambitions knew no bounds.

O. Connelly, *Napoleon's Satellite Kingdoms* (New York, 1965); A. Fugier, *La Révolution française et l'empire napoléonienne*, vol. 4 of *Histoire des relations internationales*, ed. P. Renouvin (Paris, 1954); R. Glover, "The French Fleet, 1807–1814," *JMH* 39 (1967); H. Kissinger, *A World Restored: Metternich, Castlereagh, and the Problems of the Peace, 1812–1822* (New York, 1957); S. Ross, *European Diplomatic History, 1789-1815* (Garden City, N.Y., 1969).

Related entries: ABDICATION, FIRST; ABDICATION, SECOND; AMIENS, TREATY OF; AUSTRIA; BRUMAIRE, COUP OF 18, YEAR VIII; CAMPO FORMIO, TREATY OF; CONCORDAT OF 1801; CONSTITUTIONS; DIPLOMACY; DIRECTORY; ELBA; EMPIRE, FRENCH; FONTAINEBLEAU (1807); FRANCE, CAMPAIGN OF; HUNDRED DAYS, THE; LUNEVILLE, TREATY OF; PRESSBURG, TREATY OF; RUSSIAN CAMPAIGN; ST. HELENA; SCHÖNBRUNN (1809); TILSIT, TREATIES OF; VIENNA, CONGRESS OF.

FORFAIT, PIERRE-ALEXANDRE-LAURENT (1752–1807), minister of the French navy from 22 November 1799 to 2 October 1801 (under the Consulate) and a leading naval engineer and architect. As a member of the naval committee of the Legislative Assembly, he had planned the construction and launching of five ships of the line on the Havre ways. As Bonaparte's minister of marine for twenty-three months, he started the reconstitution of the French fleet, organized the French coast into six maritime prefectures, built a channel flotilla of small boats for the projected invasion of England, deepened the port of Boulogne, and repulsed two attacks of Nelson on the flotilla and the port. When the backbiting and calumny of his colleagues compelled him to resign as minister, he continued to serve France and Napoleon as a councillor of state, inspector general of the channel flotilla, and maritime prefect, first at Havre and then at Genoa.

P. Masson and J. Muracciole, *Napoléon et la marine* (Paris, 1968).

Harold T. Parker

Related entries: ENGLAND, ATTEMPTED CONQUEST OF; NAVY, FRENCH.

FORJAZ, D. MIGUEL PEREIRA (1769–1827), count of Feira, secretary for foreign affairs, war, and marine in the Portuguese Regency Council, 1807–1820. Early in life, Forjaz chose a military career but demonstrated more competence for administration and staff work than field command. In November 1807, with a French army at the gates of Lisbon, the Portuguese royal family fled to Brazil aboard British warships. Forjaz, appointed secretary of the regency council in Lisbon, had to deal with the French conqueror, General Andoche Junot. He soon resigned his post, however, and devoted himself to organizing an anti-French insurgent army.

In July 1808, however, a British army forced the French to evacuate the country. The Regency Council was reestablished (September 1808) to cooperate with the British, and Forjaz was confirmed secretary of foreign affairs, war, and marine (navy). In that office he played a leading role in expanding and modernizing the Portuguese army, of which many units were Anglo-Portuguese.

Considered by the duke of Wellington to be the ablest man in Portugal, Forjaz was largely responsible for the valuable contributions of the Portuguese army to the Allied effort during the Peninsular War. Forjaz held a dominant position in the Regency until the liberal revolt of 1820 forced his withdrawal from public life.

J. Accursio das Neves, *Historia General da Invasao dos Francezes em Portugal*, 5 vols. (Lisbon, 1810–1811); C. Oman, *A History of the Peninsular War*, 6 vols. (Oxford, 1902–1930); S. J. da Luz Soriano, *Historia da Guerra Civil e do Estabelecimento da Governo Parlamentar em Portugal*, 15 vols. (Lisbon, 1866–1887).

Francisco A. de la Fuente

Related entries: ARMY, PORTUGUESE; PENINSULAR WAR; PORTUGAL; PORTUGUESE CAMPAIGNS; WELLINGTON.

FOUCHE, JOSEPH (1760–1820), duc d'Otrante, minister of general police. Born near Nantes on 27 May 1760, son of a merchant sea captain, Fouché was educated by the Oratory in his home town. Young Fouché showed an aptitude for mathematics and science, and he was encouraged—and decided after his father's death—to become a teacher. In 1781, he enrolled at the Oratorian College in Paris, and on completion of his studies a year later, he was sent to Niort, then to Saumur, and later to Paris and Arras.

At Arras, he joined the Academy of the Rosati, a politically liberal club, where he was associated with Maximilien Robespierre. Fouché lent money to the future terrorist to go to Versailles after he was elected to the Estates General of 1789.

Fouché was sent to Nantes in 1790. In 1792, he married (he was in orders but untonsured) and was elected to the National Convention, where he initially associated with the moderate Girondins. After the trial of Louis XVI, however, he opportunistically voted for the death of the king. As an Hébertist representative on mission, his position became more radical than that of Robespierre, whom he helped to bring down. But Fouché had not anticipated the conservative Thermidorian Reaction; he dropped from sight, to reemerge in 1797 and 1798 as a diplomatic agent for the Directory in the Netherlands and Italy.

On 20 July 1799 he became minister of general police, an office he proceeded to vitalize. Having assisted, if in a passive role, in the Brumaire coup (he neglected to inform the republican directors of the plot of Bonaparte and the abbé Sieyès), he was retained as minister of general police by Bonaparte. He served effectively, if not totally loyally, until 13 September 1802, when he was dismissed, and again from July 1804 to 29 May 1810, when he was fired for negotiating with the English.

Until 1814, he held a variety of minor posts, when, during the Hundred Days (1815) the emperor reinstated him at the Police Ministry. After Waterloo, he collaborated with the victorious Allies in restoring Louis XVIII, and he retained his post until 13 September 1815. He was then summarily exiled, as a regicide, first to Saxony and then to Trieste where, on 26 December 1820, he died.

As Napoleon's minister of general police, Fouché created the first modern political police. Using ideas, techniques, and personnel from the *ancien régime* and the Revolution, Fouché was an effective and feared policeman. His political opportunism, amply demonstrated, explains his effectiveness as well as his downfall and exile.

A. Arnold, Jr., *Fouché, Napoleon, and the General Police* (Washington, D.C., 1979); H. Buisson, *Fouché, duc d'Otrante* (Bienne, 1968); H. Cole, *Fouché, the Unprincipled Patriot* (London, 1971); L. Madelin, *Fouché*, 2d ed., 2 vols. (Paris, 1903); L. Madelin, ed., *Les mémoires de Fouché* (Paris, 1945).

Eric A. Arnold, Jr.

Related entries: HUNDRED DAYS, THE; POLICE, MINISTRY OF GENERAL.

FOURCROY, ANTOINE-FRANCOIS, COMTE DE (1755–1809), scientist, planner of the Imperial University. Born in Paris, son of an apothecary, Fourcroy was a scholarship pupil in the Faculty of Medicine of the University of Paris. He obtained his medical degree in 1780, but he never practiced. As a student he had already shown considerable aptitude for chemistry. In his research he applied chemical analysis to a large number of animal and vegetable substances and with his associate Nicolas-Louis Vauquelin isolated urea. As professor of general chemistry at the Jardin du Roi from 1784 and at its successor institution, the Museum d'Histoire Naturelle, he excelled at high-level popularization. A gifted lecturer, able to make abstruse subjects systematically clear and attractive, he held the attention of very large audiences for years. His textbook, *Philosophie chimique* (1792), was translated into eleven languages.

Drawn into public life with his election to the Convention, he wielded considerable influence on legislation regarding education from July 1793 until his death in 1809. He was thus one of the founders of the Ecole Polytechnique, the Ecole de Santé, and the Institut. Appointed by Bonaparte to the Conseil d'Etat, section of the interior, he drafted the fundamental law of 1802 that set up the hierarchy of primary schools, lycées and colleges, and advanced specialized schools. He then implemented the law as director general of public instruction. The decree of 1808 setting up the Imperial University was also his work.

G. Kersaint, *Antoine François de Fourcroy, sa vie et son oeuvre* (Paris, 1966); W. A. Smeaton, *Fourcroy, Chemist and Revolutionary* (London, 1962).

Harold T. Parker

Related entries: EDUCATION; INSTITUT NATIONAL DES SCIENCES ET DES ARTS; SCIENCE; UNIVERSITY, IMPERIAL.

FOX, CHARLES JAMES (1749–1806), Whig politician and statesman, proponent of peace with France. He was the second son of Henry Fox, first Baron Holland, and Lady Caroline Lennox, great granddaughter of Charles II. Educated at Eton and Hertford College, Oxford, he entered Parliament in 1768. He was the member of Parliament for Midhurst from 1768 to 1774, for Malmesbury from 1774 to 1780, and for Westminster from 1780 to 1784 and again from 1785 to 1806. Fox began as a Tory, an opponent of American claims, and served in Lord North's administration but left it in 1774. By 1778, under the tutelage of Edmund Burke, Fox was won over to Whig views on America and the major reform issues of slave emancipation and religious toleration. The determining experiences of his life came with the defeat of the Rockingham-Shelburne ministry in 1782 and the Fox-North coalition in 1783, by what Fox regarded as the criminal misuse of royal or executive power. He determined to attack the growth of executive power, with the result that George III kept him out of government until 1806. Meanwhile he made bold to praise initially the French Revolution and all but its most bloodthirsty proponents. On the death of Pitt (1806), Fox became foreign minister under Grenville and proposed peace to Napoleon. His death, the same year, ended what would probably have been a failed effort.

J. Cannon, *The Fox-North Coalition* (London, 1969); J. W. Derry, *Charles James Fox* (London, 1972); L. G. Mitchell, *Charles James Fox and the Disintegration of the Whig Party* (London, 1971).

Leslie G. Mitchell

Related entries: DIPLOMACY; FOREIGN POLICY; GREAT BRITAIN.

FOY, MAXIMILIEN-SEBASTIEN (1775–1825), French general. He first became prominent for his service under Jean Moreau in 1800. He marched with Andoche Junot during the conquest of Portugal (1807) and served in Spain, 1808–13. He rallied to Napoleon during the Hundred Days and was in the Battle of Waterloo. His history of the war in Spain is a well-accepted source: *Histoire de la guerre de la Péninsule*, 4 vols. (1827).

Related entries: PENINSULAR WAR; PORTUGAL; PORTUGUESE CAMPAIGNS; SPAIN, KINGDOM OF.

FRA DIAVOLO, nom de guerre of Michele Pezza, dashing Neapolitan guerrilla leader who often wore the robes of a friar. He gave the French army and Neapolitan police great trouble during the first year of the reign of Joseph Bonaparte (1806) in Naples but was captured in November 1806 and executed by firing squad. His capture resulted from the work of Christophe Saliceti, the minister of police, who probably had him executed before Joseph could intervene. The king admired Fra Diavolo's daring and flattered himself that if they could talk, he could win the guerrilla over to his side.

Related entries: NAPLES, KINGDOM OF; SALICETI.

FRANC. To end the anarchic miscellany of French coins, old and new, Bonaparte established by the Law of 7 Germinal Year XI (28 March 1803) the *franc de germinal*. A coin of one franc was to weigh five grams of silver, nine-tenths fine. New coins were struck in denominations of one-half, three-fourths, one, two, and five francs in silver and ten, twenty, and forty francs in gold. The ratio of gold to silver was 1 to 15.5. "For the first time in its history France was provided with a clearly defined 'real money' which coincided in value with its money of account" (Godechot). Newly minted, sound, and practical, it gradually replaced the old coins and became the strongest currency on the European continent. In 1811 it commanded a premium even against the British pound sterling. Indeed, the Law of 7 Germinal fixed the monetary standard of France for 123 years.

J. Godechot, *Les institutions de la France sous la Révolution et l'Empire*, 2d ed. (Paris, 1968); M. O. Piquet-Marchal, "Pourquoi la France a-t-elle choisi le bimetallisme en 1803?" *Revue historique de droit français et étranger* 51 (1973); G. Thuillier, "La crise monétaire de l'automne 1810," *RHq* 238 (1967), "Pour une histoire monétaire de la France du XIXe siècle: la reforme de l'an XI," *RIN* 131 (1975), and "Les troubles monétaires en France de 1803 à 1808," *RIN* 133 (1977).

Harold T. Parker

Related entries: EXCHANGE RATE; FINANCES.

FRANCE, CAMPAIGN OF (January–April 1814), defensive campaign, commonly regarded as one of Napoleon's most brilliant, which nevertheless resulted in his defeat and abdication. After his disastrous defeat at Leipzig in October 1813, Napoleon withdrew the remnants of his field army west of the Rhine, leaving very substantial garrisons in Germany, however, mostly in the Hamburg area, under Marshal Louis Nicolas Davout. In November 1813, the Allies offered peace on the basis of French natural boundaries: the Rhine, the Alps, and the Pyrenees. Napoleon saw this offer as a diplomatic maneuver to rob him of popular French support, and he rejected it. Although he later agreed to negotiate on this basis, the Allies had already decided to invade France.

Three allied armies comprised the invasion forces: one of some 60,000 under J. B. Bernadotte moving west through the Low Countries; one of some 75,000 under Prince G. L. Blücher von Wahlstatt moving up the Moselle valley into Lorraine; and one of around 210,000 under Prince Karl zu Schwarzenberg coming from Switzerland via the Belfort gap.

French forces to oppose the Allies in northern France were meager. In addition to the garrisons left in Germany, Prince Eugène had 50,000 men in northern Italy, and 100,000 were deployed in the south to meet Wellington's invasion from Spain. Except for one corps plus some cavalry from Spain, none of the outlying forces reinforced Napoleon in eastern France. His operations were conducted by the remnants of the Leipzig campaign, reinforced by half-trained conscripts and National Guardsmen, to a total of perhaps 120,000 men in all. Fully recognizing his numerical inferiority, Napoleon resolved to exploit his superior skill and leadership by striking the invading columns separately and playing on the Allies' mutual distrust.

He struck Blücher at Brienne (29 January) and La Rothière (30 January), with favorable results, but Schwarzenberg's leading elements made themselves felt on the third day (1 February), and Napoleon was obliged to withdraw in the face of overwhelming numbers.

The Allies pushed on toward Paris but by separate routes that diverged dangerously. Napoleon, who had selected a central axis of withdrawal, was thus positioned to strike first one enemy force, then the other. He did so with devastating effect.

Blücher, moving down the valley of the Marne, decided he could save time by moving from the north to the south bank of the river, which left his column exposed to French counterattack. Moving with disconcerting speed and resolution, Napoleon struck into Blücher's south flank by surprise. In the "Five Days," the overextended elements of Blücher's column were defeated successively and driven north of the Marne with heavy losses (Champaubert, Montmirail, Château-Thierry, Vauchamps; 10–14 February). Napoleon then left minimum forces to contain Blücher and moved rapidly south with the bulk of his army. At Montereau on 18 February, he attacked Schwarzenberg, who was greatly superior numerically but promptly withdrew forty miles.

But Blücher had by now regrouped and resumed his advance. Napoleon left

Marshal Jacques MacDonald to contain Schwarzenberg and moved northward with the bulk of his force. Blücher was driven northward and was defeated at the Craonne (7 March), but by now Bernadotte's force was coming within reach. Two of his corps reinforced Blücher, who determined to hold Laon. In a two-day battle (9–10 March), Napoleon was defeated and withdrew to Soissons.

While giving his exhausted troops a brief rest, Napoleon learned of an isolated Prussian corps to his east at Rheims. Marching boldly across Blücher's front, he attacked Rheims by surprise and drove out the Prussians with heavy loss. He next decided to move southward, hoping that the resultant threat to Schwarzenberg's communications would impel the Austrians to turn back. But at Arcis-sur-Aube on 20–21 March, he found himself greatly outnumbered and was repulsed. Schwarzenberg resumed his westward march, as Blücher had already done. At La Fère-Champenoise, Marshals Marmont and Mortier, attempting to carry out Napoleon's order to join him, were struck by Schwarzenberg on 25 March and driven toward Paris. Blücher and Schwarzenberg finally united in front of Paris on 28 March, leaving Napoleon with his main army far to the east in the general area of Vitry-St. Dizier. Threats to the Allied communications had not served to stop their advance. Napoleon hoped to reach Paris with his main army and rejuvenate the defense, but he was too late.

After a spirited defensive Battle of Paris, Marmont (with the express approval of Joseph Bonaparte, Napoleon's deputy) agreed to an armistice, and the city was surrendered to the Allies on 31 March. Napoleon halted at Fontainebleau. He was eager to continue the struggle, and no doubt many of his troops would have followed him. But his senior officers, including Ney, Lefebvre, and MacDonald, would not. On 6 April he abdicated in favor of his son. The Allies rejected this. On 11 April he abdicated unconditionally.

Despite its disastrous outcome, this campaign will always repay study as an example of what can be achieved against odds by leadership, tenacity, and tactical skill.

A.A.L. de Caulaincourt, *No Peace with Napoleon* (New York, 1936); T. A. Dodge, *Napoleon*, vol. 4 (New York, 1907); J. Lawford, *Napoleon: The Last Campaigns, 1813–15* (London, 1977); A.F.L.V. de Marmont, *Mémoires*, vol. 6 (Paris, 1857).

George Winton

Related entries: ABDICATION, FIRST; FIVE DAYS, BATTLES OF; PARIS, BATTLE OF.

FRANCIS I, of Austria. See FRANZ II.

FRANCIS II, Holy Roman Emperor. See FRANZ II.

FRANKFURT, GRAND DUCHY OF (1810–13), French satellite state in Germany created in 1810 for Eugène de Beauharnais. It was to compensate him (and his descendants) for the loss of income from the Kingdom of Italy, which after twenty years was to go to Napoleon's son or a second son (if there was one). The first grand duke, by the Treaty of Paris (1810), was Karl Theodor von Dalberg, prince primate of the Confederation of the Rhine. He had ruled since 1806 in the imperial cities of Regensburg, Wetzlar, and Frankfurt and the German lands of the Electorate of Mainz. In 1810 Dalberg lost Regensburg but gained the principalities of Hanau and Fulda (without their crown lands). Eugène was to succeed him as grand duke.

The grand duchy covered an area of approximately 97 square miles, had 300,000 inhabitants, and except for the enclave of Wetzlar was a contiguous territory. By the organizational charter of August 1810, the grand duchy was divided into four departments: Frankfurt, Hanau, Aschaffenburg, and Fulda. In the central government the ministers were Franz Joseph von Albini (interior, justice, police), Carl Theodor von Eberstein (foreign affairs, culture, military administration), and Leopold von Beust (finances; after December 1810 this function was assumed by Dalberg). The grand duke, his ministers, and seven state councillors formed the state council. It was the executive branch and, together with the estates, elected by the departmental colleges, also played a legislative role. The departments were under prefects, who were assisted by appointed councils. Each department was divided into districts and these in turn into municipalities or *mairies*. Local administration lay in the hands of a *maire* and his adjutants, and an elected municipal council. After January 1811 the Code Napoléon and the French penal code were in effect. Model emancipation edicts were issued (abolition of serfdom, equality for Jews), whose implementation, however, was tied to high redemption payments. Dalberg effected a drastic change in the political leadership on the intermediate and lower levels by replacing nobles with bourgeois officials. Privilege of birth was replaced by privilege of money and property. Dalberg's policies were modified according to French requirements for war, which also affected the limits of all reforms. After the Battle of Leipzig (October 1813), Dalberg handed the government over to the state council and fled to Konstanz. The Allies dissolved the grand duchy in rapid stages.

W. Bitz, "Die Grossherzogtümer Würzburg und Frankfurt. Ein Vergleich" (Diss., Würzburg, 1968); P. Darmstaedter, *Das Grossherzogtum Frankfurt. Ein Kulturbild aus der Rheinbundzeit* (Frankfurt, 1901); E. Fehrenbach, *Traditionelle Gesellschaft und revolutionäres Recht. Die Einführung des Code Napoleon in den Rheinbundstaaten* (Göttingen, 1974); R. Koch, *Grundlagen bürgerlicher Herrschaft. Verfassungs- und sozialgeschichtliche Studien zur bürgerlichen Gesellschaft in Frankfurt am Main, 1612–1866* (Frankfurt, 1981).

Rainer Koch

Related entries: BEAUHARNAIS, E.; CONFEDERATION OF THE RHINE; DALBERG; GERMAN WAR OF LIBERATION.

FRANZ I. See Franz II.

FRANZ II (later FRANZ I of Austria) (1768–1835), Holy Roman Emperor, 1792–1806; Austrian emperor, 1806–35. Shortly after the accession of Franz

(Francis) to the throne in 1792, France declared war on Austria. He thus became party to successive coalitions against France and against the ideas of revolution to preserve the status quo. Franz was indecisive, however, and incapable of translating his antirevolutionary way of thinking into a consistent foreign policy. He also failed to strengthen his own position through comprehensive internal reforms. As a consequence, the peace treaties from Campo Formio in 1797 to Schönbrunn in 1809 reduced the Habsburg monarchy to Hungary, Bohemia, Upper and Lower Austria, and Styria. When Napoleon proclaimed himself emperor of the French, Franz responded in 1804 by changing Austria into an empire. In 1806, after the creation of the Confederation of the Rhine, Franz declared the Holy Roman Empire dissolved in order to bar Napoleon from taking his place.

In 1809 Franz appointed Clemens von Metternich foreign minister, and Vienna thereafter cautiously jockeyed between France and Russia. For reasons of state, Franz had his daughter Marie-Louise marry Bonaparte. Only the Corsican's reverses in the Russian campaign (1812) persuaded the Austrians to assume a position of armed mediation and then (1813) join the Allies. After Napoleon's defeat, which appeared to Franz as a victory over the Revolution, the Congress of Vienna in 1814–15 restored the old borders of Austria and compensated it with Lombardy, Venetia, and Dalmatia for the loss of the Austrian Netherlands and territories on the Rhine. The Holy Roman Empire, however, was not restored.

For the rest of his reign, Franz supported Metternich's conservative policies. In the interest of preserving the existing political and social order, he favored a European balance of power. Seeing the status quo threatened in domestic affairs, he advocated the preventive suppression of liberal and national movements. At home, he promoted an absolutist welfare state that did not hesitate to employ police state methods in order to keep the people in tutelage.

K. O. von Aretin, *Heiliges Römisches Reich* (1967); W. C. Langsam, *Francis the Good* (1949); M. Rauschensteiner, *Franz und Erzherzog Carl* (1972); W. Tritsch, *Metternich und sein Monarch* (1952).

Eckhardt Treichel

Related entries: DIPLOMACY; FOREIGN POLICY; GERMAN WAR OF LIBERATION; LUNEVILLE, TREATY OF; MARIE-LOUISE VON HABSBURG; PRESSBURG, TREATY OF; RUSSIAN CAMPAIGN; SCHÖNBRUNN, TREATY OF (1809); VIENNA, CONGRESS OF.

FREDERICK I of Württemberg. See FRIEDRICH II.

FREDERICK II of Württemberg. See FRIEDRICH II.

FREDERICK AUGUSTUS I of Saxony. See FRIEDRICH AUGUST III.

FREDERICK AUGUSTUS III of Saxony. See FRIEDRICH AUGUST III.

FREDERICK WILLIAM II of Prussia. See FRIEDRICH WILHELM II.

FREDERICK WILLIAM III of Prussia. See FRIEDRICH WILHELM III.

FREEMASONS. Freemasonry had vague origins in medieval stonemasons' guilds, which supported charities. The modern lodges originated in Britain and spread to the Continent. National lodges of the eighteenth century promoted the ideals of the Enlightenment. That of France, of which the duke d'Orleans was grand master and Lafayette a member, was suspected of fomenting the Revolution but was destroyed by it. Napoleon revived the order in France. European Freemasons generally supported him. The most demonstrative were the Poles of the Duchy of Warsaw, whose arms bore the Napoleonic "N" and whose grand master was Count Stanislas Potocki, president of the council of ministries.

M. Bernardin, *Précis du Grand Orient de France* (Paris, 1909); J.-L. Q. Bodin, "La franc maçonnerie dans les armées de la Révolution et de l'Empire," *RIN* 136 (1981); A. Bouton, *Les francs-maçons manceaux et la Révolution française, 1741–1815* (Le Mans, 1958); M. Gaston-Martin, *Manuel d'histoire de la Franc-maçonnerie française* (Paris, 1929); A. Le Bihan, *Francs-maçons et Ateliers Parisiens de la Grande Loge de France au XVIII*[e] *siècle* (Paris, 1973); D. Ligou, *Dictionnaire universel de la Franc-Maçonnerie. Hommes illustres, pays, rites, symboles* (Paris, 1974), and *La Franc-Maçonnerie* (Paris, 1977).

Related entries: ITALY, KINGDOM OF; NAPLES, KINGDOM OF; SOCIETY; WARSAW, DUCHY OF.

FREIRE DE ANDRADE, GOMES (1757–1817), general, Portuguese commander of the Lusitanian Legion of the Napoleonic armies, 1808–14. Perhaps the most capable Portuguese military officer of his time, Freire began his career in the navy, where he distinguished himself in a naval attack on Algiers in 1784. After Freire transferred to the army, his search for adventure led him to the service of Catherine the Great in 1788. Returning to Portugal in 1793, he participated in the Roussillon campaign and the War of Oranges. In 1808, Freire entered French service and was named general and commander of the Lusitanian Legion. He was attached to Napoleon's general staff for the Russian campaign in which he served as military governor of Dsjisma, Lithuania, and then he accompanied the defeated French army during its retreat to Königsberg. In 1813, he served as military governor of Jena and then Dresden, where he surrendered to the Allies on 11 November 1813. In 1817 after his return to Portugal, Freire was falsely implicated in a liberal plot to eliminate British influence from the Portuguese army and government. As a result of his subsequent execution, Freire became, and remains, a martyr to the liberal cause in Portugal, as well as one of Portugal's most romantic and able military officers.

R. Arthur, *A Legiao Portugueza zo Servico de Napoleao, 1808–1813* (Lisbon, 1901); M. Barradas, *O General Gomes Freire* (Lisbon, 1892); R. Brandao, *1817* (Porto, 1917);

R. Cavalheiro, *Um Artigo de Barbosa Colen Sobre Gomes Freire de Andrade* (Lisbon, 1932); F. Gil, *A Infanteria Portuguesa na Guerra da Peninsula*, 2 vols. (Lisbon, 1913).

Francisco A. de la Fuente

Related entries: GERMAN WAR OF LIBERATION; PORTUGAL; RUSSIAN CAMPAIGN.

FRIEDLAND, BATTLE OF (14 June 1807), victory of the French army, led by Napoleon, over the Russian army, commanded by General Levin von Bennigsen. The defeat was so decisive that the czar made peace at Tilsit. The Grande Armée had wintered in Poland after defeating the Prussians in 1806. In June 1807 Napoleon sent his five army corps northward along the left bank of the Alle River in East Prussia in pursuit of the retreating Russian army on the right bank. He was seeking to reach the Russian base of Königsberg before the Russians (*manoeuvre sur les derrières*). On the evening of 13 June, an outpost of Jean Lannes' corps at Friedland on the left bank of the Alle made contact with the Russians on the right bank. During the night, Bennigsen, aiming to destroy Lannes' apparently isolated corps, moved his army of 60,000 across four frame bridges to the Friedland side and arranged it in a four-mile line parallel to the Alle with his back to the stream. While Lannes' corps pinned down the Russians, Napoleon marched in the Imperial Guard, Michel Ney's and Joseph Mortier's corps, and heavy cavalry, for a total French force of nearly 80,000. In the ensuing battle, which opened at 5:30 P.M., Mortier and Lannes kept the Russian center and right wing occupied while Ney's corps, supported by a powerful artillery onslaught and cavalry charges, hit the Russian left wing from the front and flank, pushed it into Friedland, and destroyed the frame bridges over the Alle, the only avenue of retreat. Mortier and Lannes then advanced against the Russian center and right in a slaughter that lasted until nightfall. The Russian casualties were estimated at 20,000, the French at 8,000.

D. Chandler, *The Campaigns of Napoleon* (London, 1966); O. von Lettow-Vorbeck, *Der Krieg von 1806 und 1807* (Berlin, 1896); H. T. Parker, *Three Napoleonic Battles* (Durham, N.C., 1983).

Harold T. Parker

Related entries: BENNIGSEN; JENA-AUERSTÄDT-FRIEDLAND CAMPAIGN; LANNES; TILSIT, TREATIES OF.

FRIEDLAND, CAMPAIGN OF. See JENA-AUERSTÄDT-FRIEDLAND CAMPAIGN.

FRIEDRICH II (later FRIEDRICH I) (1754–1816), duke, elector, then king (1797–1816) of Württemberg. Called "the last enlightened despot," he battled the Württemberg parliament from 1797 to 1806, when he abolished it, with the approval of Napoleon, who agreed it was an obstacle to reform (and revenue collection). He introduced a highly centralized administration modeled after that of France and granted religious toleration to all three Christian faiths (1806).

He was educated in Treptow/Rega by Johann Georg Schlosser, brother-in-law of the poet Goethe. He entered the Prussian army in 1774, but in 1782, after his sister married the future Czar Paul I of Russia, he entered Russian service and was governor of Finland, then of Kherson, and commanded a regiment in the Turkish War. He had two wives: Auguste of Brunswick (1764–88), mother of King William I and Katharina (married to Jerome Bonaparte), and Princess Charlotte of Great Britain, who was childless.

In 1803 he gained territory and the title of elector. In 1805 he allied with Napoleon against Austria and in 1806 became king Friedrich I of Württemberg, which was again enlarged. His possessions were further guaranteed by Napoleon in treaties of 1809 and 1810. After Napoleon's defeat at Leipzig, he joined the Allies (Fulda, 1813). At the Congress of Vienna, he was hostile to the idea of restoring his Parliament and on 15 March 1815 introduced a conservative constitution unilaterally. The battle for *das gute alte Recht* continued to 1819 when King William I negotiated the establishment of a more modern constitution.

W. Grube, *Der Stuttgarter Landtag 1457–1957* (Stuttgart, 1957); E. Hölzle, *Das alte Recht und die Revolution* (Munich and Berlin, 1931), and *Württemberg im Zeitalter Napoleons* (Stuttgart and Berlin, 1937); A. Pfister, *König Friedrich von Württemberg und seine Zeit* (Stuttgart, 1888).

Helen P. Liebel-Weckowicz

Related entries: AUSTERLITZ CAMPAIGN; CATHERINE OF WÜRTTEMBERG; CONFEDERATION OF THE RHINE; GERMAN WAR OF LIBERATION; JENA-AUERSTÄDT-FRIEDLAND CAMPAIGN.

FRIEDRICH AUGUST III (later FRIEDRICH AUGUST I) (1750–1827), elector of Saxony; after 1806 king by grace of Napoleon. Friedrich August (or Frederick Augustus) acceded to the throne as a boy in 1763 and in 1768, not yet eighteen, assumed the leadership of the state. Pedantic, orderly, and punctual, the elector remained throughout his life a conservative prince of the Old Regime. However, he earned the appellation "The Just" because of his demonstrated sense of personal responsibility for the welfare of his state and people. In his first decades, he devoted himself to the reconstruction of the country, impoverished and devastated by the Seven Years War.

After Napoleon defeated the Prussians in 1806, he succeeded, by the Treaty of Posen, in inducing Saxony to join the Confederation of the Rhine, and Friedrich August became king Friedrich August I of Saxony. He was also entrusted with governing the Duchy of Warsaw and became a loyal ally of the Corsican. In spite of the crushing defeat of the Grand Army in 1812, the king—though wavering—remained on the French side. Although his troops changed sides during the Battle of Leipzig (1813), the king was treated as a prisoner of war. The Congress of Vienna, despite the revived principle of legitimacy, gave almost half of his lands to other states. By obstinately defending Saxon claims, the king had earned the devotion of his people. During the remaining twelve years of his reign, Friedrich August devoted himself to the reconstruction of his state.

A. Bonnefons, *Un allié de Napoleon* (1902); H. Kretzschmar, "Das sächsische Königtum im 19. Jahrhundert," *Historische Zeitschrift* (1950); K. von Weber, "Zur Geschichte des sächsischen Hofes und Landes unter Friedrich August," *Archiv für sächsische Geschichte* 8 (1870).

Joachim Niemeyer

Related entries: CONFEDERATION OF THE RHINE; GERMAN WAR OF LIBERATION; JENA-AUERSTÄDT-FRIEDLAND CAMPAIGN; LEIPZIG, BATTLE OF; SAXONY, KINGDOM OF; VIENNA, CONGRESS OF; WARSAW, DUCHY OF.

FRIEDRICH WILHELM II (1744–97), king of Prussia, 1786–97. Long before Frederick the Great died, he had realized that he was without a successor to whom he could entrust the state with confidence. The king had no children; thus, his younger brother, August Wilhelm, was in line for the throne until he died in 1758, and then his son Friedrich Wilhelm (Frederick William). The king thought so little of the latter that he began preparing his younger brother Heinrich for the throne, but Heinrich died in 1767. Thus the most eminent of Prussia's kings was succeeded in 1786 by a man who had few of his characteristics. In his favor, however, were the earnest intention of performing his royal office with dignity, imposing stature, and considerable popularity. He was already divorced, and the heir, Friedrich Wilhelm III, had been born.

Friedrich Wilhelm II had no intention of fundamentally deviating from the policies of his predecessor. However, unpopular laws were nullified and favors dispensed by a king who wanted to be liked. Discipline gave way to license. Foreign policy remained in the experienced hands of Ewald Friedrich von Hertzberg, responsible for thirty years of peace since the Seven Years War. His plan for a Prussian-dominated north European alliance was ruined by the French Revolution, however, which gave Prussia no good alternative but to side with Austria. Friedrich Wilhelm's foreign policy, all the same, shifted as his advisers changed. He managed, however, to give Prussia its largest territorial size through the second and third Polish partitions (1793 and 1795). The king's civil service was enlightened but accomplished little. Unsuccessful in the campaigns of 1792–94 against France, Friedrich Wilhelm made peace at Basel in 1795, deserting the Holy Roman (Austrian) Emperor.

Domestically, legal and judicial reforms initiated by Frederick the Great were completed. The Prussian Law Code was the most advanced of its time and influenced similar attempts in France and Austria. Cultural life prospered in the arts and sciences, music, theater, and architecture. Yet Friedrich Wilhelm left to his son and successor no solid guidelines in domestic or foreign policy, making the state an easy target for Napoleon.

W. M. von Bissing, *Friedrich Wilhelm II. König von Preussen. Ein Lebensbild* (Berlin, 1967); I. Bussenius and W. Hubatsch, *Urkunden und Akten zur Geschichte der preussischen Verwaltung in Südpreussen und Neuostpreussen 1793–1806* (Frankfurt, 1961); W. Höhm, *Der Einfluss des Marquis von Lucchesini auf die preussische Politik 1787–*

1792 (diss., Kiel, 1925); W. Real, *Von Potsdam nach Basel 1786–1795* (Basel, 1958); G. Stanhope, *A Mystic on the Prussian Throne: Frederic William II* (1912); F. Valjavec, "Das Wöllnersche Religionsedikt in seiner geschichtlichen Bedeutung," *Historisches Jahrbuch* 72 (1953).

Walther Hubatsch

Related entries: FRIEDRICH WILHELM III; PRUSSIA.

FRIEDRICH WILHELM III (1770–1840), king of Prussia, 1797–1840, who steered Prussia through the Napoleonic years. During his first years, the king accomplished a number of partial reforms, especially the liberation of the peasants on the crown lands. In foreign policy he continued his father's neutrality and even in 1805, in spite of an alliance with Russia and Napoleon's provocations, shunned entry into the war. In 1806–07, with the support of his wife, Luise of Mecklenburg-Strelitz, he managed to save the monarchy despite the destruction of the army at Jena-Auerstädt, French occupation of Berlin, the monarchs' flight to East Prussia, and the coercive Peace of Tilsit. He lent his authority to the efforts of the reformers and, after 1810, to K. A. von Hardenberg's risky diplomatic balancing act between France and Russia, while mollifying Prussian patriots with exaggerated expectations. He helped guide the war of liberation without being affected by the pathos of the national German movement. His conservative inclinations and his emotional ties to the Russian czars motivated his early cooperation with Russia and compromise with Austria at the Congress of Vienna and his full cooperation in Clemens von Metternich's policies after 1815. His domestic policy after 1815 was characterized by ambivalence. He rejected a uniform constitution for the state and persecuted dissidents, but he maintained the most essential reforms, demanded a high degree of efficiency from his civil service, and (joining the *Zollverein*) pursued a progressive economic policy. In religion, it was at his initiative that the Reformed church and the Lutheran church combined in the Prussian Union.

A. S. Cohnfeld, *Ausführliche Lebens-und Regierungs-Geschichte Friedrich Wilhelms III, König von Preussen*, 3 vols. (Berlin, 1840–42); R. F. Eylert, *Character-Züge und historische Fragmente aus dem Leben des Königs von Preussen Friedrich Wilhelm III*, 3 vols. (Berlin, 1842–46); P. Haake, "König Friedrich Wilhelm III, Hardenberg und die preussische Verfassungsfrage," *Forschungen zur Brandenburgischen und Preussischen Geschichte* 26–33 (1913–1920); F. R. Paulig, *Friedrich Wilhelm III, König von Preussen* (Frankfurt/Oder, 1905).

Peter G. Thielen

Related entries: DIPLOMACY; FOREIGN POLICY; GERMAN WAR OF LIBERATION; GNEISENAU; HARDENBERG; JENA-AUERSTÄDT-FRIEDLAND CAMPAIGN; PRUSSIA; SCHARNHORST; STEIN; TILSIT, TREATIES OF; VIENNA, CONGRESS OF.

FRUCTIDOR, COUP OF 18, YEAR V. In 1797, while Bonaparte was extending his conquests in Italy, a major political crisis occurred in France. Elections eliminated the old Revolutionary majority in both Legislative Councils, so that the Directory was confronted by a combination of royalists and right-wing republicans. These men demanded the repeal of repressive legislation against priests and the relatives of *émigrés*. They condemned Bonaparte's conduct and called for peace, and they asserted that the directors were bound to govern in accordance with the will of parliament. The directors were at first divided, but once assured of the support of Bonaparte and other generals, three of them (Paul Barras, Jean Reubell, and Louis LaRevellière-Lépeaux) resolved to resort to force.

On 18 Fructidor Year V (4 September 1797) a military force commanded by General Pierre Augereau—who was Bonaparte's deputy and one he could renounce if necessary—occupied the Tuileries, making many arrests. Reassembled the next day under armed supervision, the purged councils decreed the deportation as royalists of sixty-five prominent men, including two directors—François de Barthélemy and Lazare Carnot. The recent elections were annulled, and the old repressive laws were reaffirmed and made still more stringent.

For some, this coup seemed the salvation of the Republic from a menacing royalist conspiracy, but many moderates saw it as the extinction of constitutional republicanism. Its other consequences are less controversial: desultory negotiations for peace with Britain were promptly abandoned, and on 18 October a conqueror's peace was imposed on Austria at Campo Formio.

A. Soboul, *La Première République, 1792–1804* (Paris, 1968); M. J. Sydenham, *The First French Republic, 1792–1804* (London, 1974).

M. J. Sydenham

Related entries: AUGEREAU; BARRAS; CAMPO FORMIO, TREATY OF; CARNOT; DIRECTORY; ITALIAN CAMPAIGN, FIRST; REUBELL.

FULTON, ROBERT (1765–1815), inventor who gave Napoleon the chance to have the first steam-powered fleet. He went to France in 1797 to patent a canal system he had devised in England. With the constant support of his countryman and mentor Joel Barlow, the occasional support of some French scientists, and less often the French government, Fulton developed a succession of naval warfare schemes to achieve freedom of the seas. He actually built a three-man submarine, which he tested in the English Channel during the summers of 1800 and 1801, though he was never able to close with a British warship. In 1803 Fulton and Robert Livingston built a steamboat and demonstrated it on the Seine. He then proposed that Bonaparte use a fleet of these craft to carry an invading army to England. By the time the first consul appreciated the significance of the scheme, however, Fulton had gone over to the enemy. He used his mines in English raids on Boulogne in 1804 and 1805. Fulton finally secured his fortune and his reputation with a steamboat enterprise in his native United States in 1804, but until his death he continued work on naval warfare, which he had first undertaken in France.

W. Hutcheon, Jr., *Robert Fulton: Pioneer of Undersea Warfare* (Annapolis, Md., 1981); A. Roland, *Underwater Warfare in the Age of Sail* (Bloomington, Ind., 1978).

Alexander Roland

Related entries: BERTHOLLET; MONGE; MONTALIVET; NAVY, FRENCH; SCIENCE.

FUSILIERS. See ARMY, FRENCH.

G

GAETA (Fr. Gaëte), Neapolitan coastal fortress that withstood the siege of French armies in 1806 (February–July) after the rest of Naples had been conquered and Joseph Bonaparte placed on the throne. Afterward it was garrisoned by French troops until 1813 when it was given over to Joachim Murat's Neapolitan army.
Related entry: NAPLES, KINGDOM OF.

GAETE, DUC DE. See GAUDIN.

GALLO, MARQUIS DE. See NAPLES, KINGDOM OF; NAPLES, KINGDOM OF: MINISTERS.

GAUDIN, MARTIN-MICHEL-CHARLES (1756–1844), duc de Gaëte, minister of finances, 1799–1814, 1815. In Bonaparte's system of fiscal administration, finances had two ministries, one of Finances and the other of the Treasury. Gaudin was minister of finances from 1799 to 1814 and during the Hundred Days and was responsible for the collection of taxes. The minister of the treasury (François de Barbé-Marbois and then Nicolas Mollien) was charged with the payment of expenses. Born at Saint-Denis, near Paris, the young Gaudin entered at age seventeen those bureaus of the Contrôle Générale that under the Bourbon monarchy handled the collection of direct taxes. During the first three Revolutionary assemblies (Constituent, Legislative, Convention) he was one of six commissioners of a central treasury board that reported to the legislature's Committee on Finances. He declined the invitation of the Directory government to serve as minister of finances but accepted that of Bonaparte (10 November 1799).

A prodigious worker—honest, methodical, and intelligent—Gaudin educated Bonaparte in the basic principles of a sound financial administration, recruited and supervised a hierarchy of able tax collectors, and initiated the preparation of a national *cadastre*, the official register of the quantity, value, and ownership of every parcel of land in France. The register could serve as the basis for a fair system of real estate taxes. Napoleon appreciated (Caulaincourt tells us) Gaudin's "clear ideas and severe probity" and in 1809 gave him the title duc de Gaëte.

After Napoleon's second abdication, Gaudin was elected to the Chamber of Deputies, where he offered wise financial advice, and then served as governor of the Bank of France from 1820 to 1834.

M.M.C. Gaudin, *Mémoires, souvenirs, opinions et écrits* (Paris, 1926); Marcel Marion, *Histoire financière de la France depuis 1715*, vol. 4: *1799–1818: La fin de la Révolution, le Consulat et l'Empire, la libération du térritoire* (Paris, 1927).

Harold T. Parker

Related entries: BANK OF FRANCE; BARBE-MARBOIS; ECONOMY, FRENCH; FINANCES; MINISTERS OF NAPOLEON; MOLLIEN.

GDANSK. See DANZIG.

GENDARMERIE. See POLICE, MINISTRY OF GENERAL.

GENOA, Ligurian Republic, one of the satellites or sister republics of Revolutionary France, established by an agreement between Napoleon Bonaparte and Genoese representatives at Mombello, a palace near Milan, on 5 and 6 June 1797, just before the conclusion of the first Italian campaign against the Austrians. This agreement put an end to the old aristocratic Republic of Genoa, but the popular uprising was largely in the hands of aristocrats and well-to-do merchants of the city. A provisional government, consisting of twenty-two members, excluding the most radical democratic elements among the revolutionaries, was formed to rule during the transition to the new republic and to draft the new constitution. The task of the provisional government was not easy. Representing a minority supported by the French, it faced a great deal of popular opposition and had to deal with a revolt of nobles and commoners from the countryside in September. The resulting document was a close copy of the French Constitution of the Year III. It was approved by a plebiscite on 2 December and went into effect at the beginning of January 1798.

The new constitution set up municipalities, many of which were taken over by more radical elements, divided the territory into departments, and established legislative assemblies, an upper house (senior) of thirty members and a lower house (juniors) of sixty members. There was a five-member Directory, and five ministers were dependent on the Directory. The position of the government was very difficult. A major source of disorder had been created by making all government positions elective. There were disputes among the councils and between them and the Directory, which was dependent on French forces for its survival and was criticized on all sides as being weak and ineffective. After the dishonorable termination of a French-inspired armed conflict with Piedmont in June 1798, a commission of inquiry led to the dismissal of many of the wisest members of the assemblies.

The continual strife and inability of the Directory to govern effectively led to a coup d'état by the French generals L. de Gouvion Saint Cyr and Radon de Belleville. The councils were suspended on 7 December 1799 and power entrusted to a commission. Its most influential member was Luigi Corvetto, who had been a member of the Directory and of the provisional government.

The following year the Austrians attacked. The republic was overrun and its defenders besieged in the city of Genoa. The French general André Masséna, sent by Napoleon to command what was left of the French army in Italy, lost two-thirds of his troops and retreated to Genoa. The city suffered terrible privation, and Masséna, lacking resources to continue fighting, capitulated on 5 June 1800.

The Austrian occupation was very brief. Napoleon, having crossed the Alps and recaptured Milan, defeated the Austrian army led by General Michael Melas at Marengo (between Milan and Genoa) on 14 June and demanded the evacuation of Genoa. On 24 June forces under Louis Suchet entered the city and reestablished French rule.

General Jean François Déjean, Napoleon's minister plenipotentiary, took control on 29 June. He presided over an assembly that drew up plans for a new constitution of the consular type. These plans were sent to Napoleon, who formulated the final version and also designated members for three colleges of scholars, landowners, and merchants. The republic was headed by a doge and a thirty-member Senate, divided into five administrative sections: justice, interior, finances, war and navy, and supreme magistrate. The last, composed of the doge, the presidents of the four other sections, and four senators elected by their colleagues, was to exercise the central power. The whole structure was complex and fragmentary, the power diffuse and undefined. The main reason for its ineffectiveness, however, was that it governed in appearance only. The real power was in the hands of the French representatives, first Déjean, and in 1802 Cristoforo Salicetti. French control was complete and oppressive. Déjean oversaw the republic's finances and was charged with raising money to finance French military operations. This was particularly burdensome since Genoese wealth depended primarily on commerce, which had been destroyed by the war. Genoese patriots who sought some real measure of autonomy were frustrated and disillusioned with the republic. The republican facade was no longer in Napoleon's best interest either and came to an end in 1805 when the territory was annexed to the French Empire.

G. Candeloro, *Storia dell'Italia moderna*, vol. 1 (Milan, 1956); R. Ciasca, *Relazioni diplomatische fra la Republica Ligure e la Cisalpina nel 1797–1798* (Genoa, 1935); A. Clavarino, *Annali della Rep. Ligure 1797–1805* (Genoa, 1852–53); "Ligure, Republica," *Enciclopedia Italiana di Scienze, Lettre ed Arti* (Rome, 1951) 21: 121; J. Marshall-Cornwall, *Marshal Masséna* (New York, 1965); Edward A. Whitcomb, *Napoleon's Diplomatic Service* (Durham, N.C., 1979).

William I. Miller

Related entries: CONSTITUTIONS; DIRECTORY; FOREIGN POLICY; ITALIAN CAMPAIGN, SECOND; MELAS; SALICETTI; SISTER REPUBLICS.

GENTZ, FRIEDRICH (1764–1832), German political publicist and adviser to Clemens von Metternich. Gentz grew up in Berlin, where his father was director of the royal mint, and received an excellent education, which culminated with studies under Immanuel Kant at Königsberg. In 1785 he joined the Prussian civil service but never rose higher than war counselor, in part because of his libertine life-style. At the same time, he became a champion of progress, justice, freedom, and equality and in 1789 hailed the French Revolution as bringing the world closer to these ideals.

When in 1792–93 the Republic turned to war and terror, however, Gentz grew disillusioned. When he read Edmund Burke's *Reflections on the Revolution in France*, he published it in German with his commentary. It earned him the attention of Europe and a reputation as the most gifted political writer in the German language. Later he also fiercely condemned Napoleon for his aggression even though he approved of his work in France. In countless articles, books, personal conversations, and letters and memoranda to the crowned heads, princes, and statesmen of Europe, Gentz argued that Napoleonic France must be defeated to restore the European balance of power and traditional national freedoms.

His adamant stance contradicted Prussia's neutral position (1795–1806). In 1802 he went to Vienna where he was made a privy counselor and assigned to mold German public opinion. Continually in debt, nevertheless, he augmented his income by freelance writing. England especially paid him well, but he never sold his soul; his principles and ideas remained the same as they had been for a decade.

Whenever Austria was at peace, Gentz became an embarrassment, particularly after 1809, and was sent into exile. During the final campaign against Napoleon, however, Gentz returned to the good graces of Vienna. He became Metternich's private adviser and acted as secretary to the Congress of Vienna. His pragmatism reinforced Metternich's perceptions and helped to translate them into policy. Gentz opposed France's reduction to a second-rate power and even favored Napoleon's retention on the throne. In this sense he had become a partisan of Austria's interests, but on a larger scale his ideas remained unchanged until his death. His apprehension of all revolutionary tendencies led him to oppose German nationalism and liberalism as endangering law and order and the federative European arrangements.

Only during the last fifteen years of his life did Gentz enjoy an active role in statecraft, but for the preceeding twenty years his pen had helped to mobilize Europe against the French Revolution and Napoleon.

G. Mann, *Secretary of Europe. The Life of Friedrich Gentz, Enemy of Napoleon* (1946); P. R. Reiff, *Friedrich Gentz: an Opponent of the French Revolution and Napoleon* (1912); P. R. Sweet, *Friedrich von Gentz, Defender of the Old Order* (1941).

Peter W. Becker

Related entries: AUSTERLITZ CAMPAIGN; AUSTRIA; FRANZ II; GERMAN WAR OF LIBERATION; METTERNICH; WAGRAM CAMPAIGN.

GEORGE, MADEMOISELLE (1787–1867). As a very young actress, this French tragedienne was one of Napoleon's mistresses. Daughter of an itinerant theater manager–orchestra conductor and a singer, she was born in Amiens as Marguerite-Joseph Weimer (or Weymer) and as a young girl acted in her parents' troupe. She was seen there by Mademoiselle Raucourt, a prominent member of the Comédie française, and taken by her to Paris as her protégée.

Mademoiselle George, who early in her career took her father's first name as her stage name, made her debut at fifteen, in 1802, as Clytemnestra in Racine's *Iphigenia in Aulis*. She was immediately successful and was quickly noticed by First Consul Napoleon, who by that time had had several actress mistresses, among them two other members of the Comédie, Mademoiselles Bourgoin and Duchesnois. Mademoiselle George, in her memoirs written many years later, claimed that Napoleon was her first lover, although his brother Lucien and Prince Sapieha had previously paid her attentions, and she always remained somewhat in awe of him. Even when their apparently warm and playful affair ended soon after the consul became emperor, she remained an ardent Bonapartist, daring to demonstrate this while in Russia in 1812 and in Paris after the Bourbon Restoration.

As a young woman, she was frank and generous, never seeking favors from her lovers. But she was also willful, capricious, and extravagant. To avoid debts, she suddenly departed the Comédie française in 1808 for Russia, where she hoped to marry a nobleman. The marriage did not take place, but she remained a popular actress there until her return to Paris in 1813, a fact attested to by Queen Louise of Prussia who attended one of her performances at Czar Alexander I's court and praised her naturalness.

Under pressure from Napoleon, she was readmitted to the Comédie française, but her now imperious temper and jealousy of other actresses caused the troupe to ask for her resignation in 1817. After touring the provinces and appearing in London, she returned to Paris in 1822 as star at the Odéon, an important secondary theater.

Throughout the 1830s, Mademoiselle George starred in Romantic dramas by Dumas and Hugo at both the Odéon and Porte-Saint-Martin under the direction of a prominent man of theater, Charles Harel, with whom she lived for many years. After his death in 1846, prosperity abandoned her. As she grew older, she became extremely fat and was nicknamed "the Whale." But she continued to act until she was sixty-two. The respect with which her ability was still held is evident from the fact that from 1849 until her death in 1867, she was adjunct member (as was only one other woman, Augustine Brohan, for a few years) of the otherwise all-male committee that supervised the dramatic declamation class at the Conservatoire. When she died poor in 1867, Napoleon III paid for her funeral.

G. Aretz, *Napoleon and His Women Friends* (Philadelphia, 1927); P. A. Chéramy, ed., *A Favorite of Napoleon. Being the Memoirs of Mademoiselle George* (New York,

1909); H. Fleischman, *Une maîtresse de Napoléon* (Paris, 1908); H. Lyonnet, *Histoire du théâtre, Mademoiselle George* (Paris, 1907); F. Masson, *Napoléon et les femmes* (Paris, 1897); E. Saunders, *Napoleon and Mademoiselle George* (London, 1958).

Nancy Nolte

Related entries: BONAPARTE, LUCIEN; NAPOLEON I; THEATER.

GERARD, ETIENNE (1773–1852), French general who participated in the great campaigns and rallied to Napoleon in 1815. During the Battle of Waterloo, he tried in vain to persuade Marshal Emmanuel Grouchy to march to the sound of the guns, which might have given Napoleon the victory. He was promoted to marshal by Louis Philippe.

Related entries: GROUCHY; WATERLOO CAMPAIGN.

GERARD, FRANCOIS-PASCAL-SIMON (1770–1837). This portraitist and history painter was born in Rome, on 4 May 1770, the son of a bureaucrat attached to the French embassy there and an Italian woman. Gérard early showed signs of artistic talent and was sent at the age of twelve to receive schooling in France at the Pension du Roy. In due course he was enrolled in the studios of Augustin Pajou, the sculptor Nicolas Brenet, and that of the most celebrated artist, Jacques-Louis David. Gérard was torn from his work by the onset of the French Revolution only weeks after having received a Second Prix de Rome. He enlisted in the Engineer Corps, but David saved his young protégé from active service by having him billeted in Paris.

After the death of his father, Gérard and his mother returned to Italy where he spent three years. Returning to Paris in 1792, he was plunged into the maelstrom of the Revolutionary tribunal. Displaying considerable foresight, Gérard never served on the tribunal in capital cases, pleading ill health. Always a political opportunist, he sought above all else to survive and to prosper. Gérard avoided the fate of Maximilien Robespierre by leaving the Jacobins six weeks before 9 Thermidor.

Gérard launched his artistic career with the appearance of his mythological, neoclassical work *Belisarius* in 1793. Some authorities consider him the best pupil whom David trained, and his early work is in much the same vein as that of his master. The same elegance, clean lines, and delicate colors are emphasized in his early work. Gérard assisted David on many paintings and probably did most of the actual painting of the celebrated *Assassination of Monsieur Le Pelletier* (1793).

Although Gérard always preferred neoclassical or historical paintings to portraits, it was in the field of portraiture that he made his mark. At the height of his career in 1800, Gérard painted Napoleon. Napoleon appreciated the talent of Gérard through a munificent pension of 40,000 francs per annum. Napoleon may have also appreciated the fact that Gérard resembled himself physically and was part Italian. During the period from 1800 to 1820, Gérard painted most of the other celebrated men and women of his day. In time Gérard's fame rivaled that of David, and he was honored increasingly as he grew older, with appointments to the Académie des Beaux Arts, to the Legion d'Honneur (1812), and with a peerage by Louis XVIII (1819).

Under the Bourbon Restoration, Gérard was officially first court painter, and his portraits of the *Coronation of Charles X* and Louis Philippe are well known. Increasingly, in the last years of his life, his style veered away from neoclassicism and became heavily influenced by romanticism.

The gifted painter's talent extended to being a brilliant conversationalist and the host of one of the most famous salons in Paris. The Gérard Salon was a place to see and to be seen. Yet his paintings were de rigueur in some measure due to the clever exertions of their creator who was his own best promotion agent. Nevertheless, François Gérard produced about 300 portraits showing nearly all of the celebrities of the era. Gérard was often at his best in portraying women. His portrait of Madame Récamier was preferred by the subject to that of David, which was too lifelike. Gérard's work at its height is his *Napoléon*, finished at the onset of the Consulate in 1800. His historical works such as *The Battle of Austerlitz* suffer from over precision and lack of spontaneity.

At the end of his life, suffering from high blood pressure and increasing debility, Gérard devoted little time to painting as infirmity gradually took its toll. Still the toast of Paris, he died suddenly 11 January 1837 in his sixty-seventh year, having made a significant contribution to the Empire style.

C. Ephrussi, "François Gérard: D'Après les lettres publiées par le Baron Gérard," *Gazette des Beaux Arts* 4 (1890) 5 (1891); Hubert Gérard, "L'Ossian de François Gérard et ses Variants" *Revue des Beaux Arts* 17 (1967); W. Kalnein, *Art and Architecture of the 18th Century in France* (Baltimore, 1972); James A. Leith, *The Idea of Art as Propaganda in France 1750–1799* (Toronto, 1972); C. Lenormant, *François Gérard: Peintre d'Histoire* (Paris, 1846); Jacques Letheve, *Daily Life of French Artists in the Nineteenth Century* (New York, 1972).

Francis Laurence Butvin

Related entries: ART; DAVID; DENON; GUERIN; ISABEY; RECAMIER.

GERMAN LITERATURE. With rare exceptions, almost all German intellectuals, imbued with the spirit of classical and cosmopolitan humanism, initially acclaimed the French Revolution. It found a sympathetic echo above all in those areas of Germany where the bourgeoisie had made the most progress in its quest for liberty. In many cases, though, sympathy with the French ideas was tempered by devotion to the local monarchs, many of whom, to be sure, had been putting into practice certain ideas of the Enlightenment, for which the French Revolution seemed to stand.

In Stuttgart, Georg Wilhelm Friedrich Hegel and Friedrich Hölderlin planted liberty trees, and Hegel in his youthful enthusiasm called for the destruction of old and the creation of new institutions. Friedrich Schiller, to whom the French Republic gave honorary citizenship, toyed with the idea of moving to France. Friedrich Gottlieb Klopstock rejoiced at having become a French citizen after the French occupation of Mainz. Christoph Martin Wieland, together with Friedrich Gentz, August Wilhelm von Schlegel, Friedrich Wilhelm Schelling, and others, reacted positively to the ideas of 1789. Johann Gottlieb Fichte admired the French social reforms and employed them as a foundation for his *Geschlossener Handelsstaat*.

A number of Germans temporarily resided in Paris in order to study the Revolution at close quarters. Among them were Wilhelm von Humboldt, the future founder of the University of Berlin, and world traveler and natural scientist Georg Forster. As a resident of Mainz, Forster was convinced that the Revolutionary accomplishments could be preserved only if the Rhineland became an integral part of France. In Paris, however, he was disillusioned by the excesses of the Terror. Another German Jacobin, the publicist Joseph Görres, underwent a similar transformation. As an indefatigable fighter against secular and ecclesiastical despotism, he at first favored the annexation of the Rhineland by France but grew increasingly skeptical and finally came to the conclusion that the Revolution was a failure.

Görres' change of mind was typical of that of other German intellectuals whose views had been fashioned divorced from the world of reality, of business, and of politics and whose dreams of individual freedom were shattered by the violence of the Revolution. The only one who did not change his positive attitude toward the Revolution was Immanuel Kant. He resolutely refused to be deterred by the shortcomings of the Revolutionaries and insisted on focusing on the permanent value of the changes, particularly those that enhanced human dignity.

One who remained true to his initial disdain was Johann Wolfgang von Goethe. Neither anti-Revolutionary nor hostile to the French, he abhorred violence and conflict. He became an admirer of Napoleon, who appointed him, together with Wieland and others, a knight of the Legion of Honor. Unlike most other German intellectuals, whose dreams of the universal nature of the French Revolution were destroyed with the arrival of French troops and Napoleon on German soil and who in response began to extol the virtues of German nationalism, Goethe remained true to his ideals of universal culture.

G. P. Gooch, *Germany and the French Revolution* (1927); H. Kohn, *The Mind of Germany* (1960); K. S. Pinson, *Modern Germany* (1966); E. Weis, *Der Durchbruch des Bürgertums, 1776–1847* (1978).

Peter W. Becker

Related entries: FICHTE; GENTZ; GOETHE; GRIMM; JAHN; KLEIST; KOTZEBUE; MÜLLER, A.; MÜLLER, J.; SCHILLER; SCHÖN; STEIN.

GERMAN TERRITORIES, NORTH COASTAL. Napoleon's acute interest in the north German coast began with the establishment of the Continental System or Blockade (1806) and the Peace of Tilsit (1807) after his victory over Prussia and Russia. To make the Continental System effective, control over the north German coast became vital. This objective was served by adding East Frisia to the satellite Kingdom of Holland (1807) and placing the northern part of Hanover under French military authorities. The Hanse cities of Lübeck, Hamburg, and Bremen remained officially sovereign but were occupied by French troops in 1806. Whereas so far they had profited from the close association with France, the constriction of their sea trade hit at the core of their existence. The French left Oldenburg, also occupied in 1806, relatively in peace since the duke was a relative of the Russian czar. As it became evident, however, that the Continental System had failed in its aim—to bankrupt England—Napoleon's suspicion grew that the Hanse cities and Oldenburg were too lax in enforcing it. In 1810, when the alliance with Russia, born in 1807 at Tilsit, began to break down, he no longer had to be considerate of Oldenburg, and Napoleon determined to tighten his control over north Germany. The Hanse cities bid for a special status but gained no concessions. In 1810, they were annexed to France together with northern Hanover, Oldenburg, Lauenburg, and other small territories. Disregarding all traditional borders, three departments were fashioned out of northern Germany: Upper Ems (capital at Osnabrück), Weser Estuary (Bremen), and Elbe Estuary (Hamburg). Hamburg was also the seat of the governing commission, headed by Marshal Louis Davout, which controlled the three Hanseatic departments.

The constitution, the administrative system, and the legal system of the French Empire were imposed without modification. This meant, among other things, separation of justice and administration, the abolition of feudalism and serfdom, freedom of trade, civil registration of births, deaths, and marriages, and a strictly organized budget and tax system. The Code Napoléon became law. Doubtless much of this constituted fundamental progress, though it could hardly be noticed under the martial conditions prevailing from 1811 to 1813. Moreover, unemployment resulting from the stagnation of trade and commerce, military conscription, war taxes and levies, and the ever-present police embittered the population. Thus not only in the rural areas but also in the Hanse cities, where initially people had been sympathetic, annexation to France was quickly seen as tyrannical foreign domination. It was not surprising that after the liberation in 1813–14, the French governmental structures—with few exceptions, such as the civil registry in Bremen—disappeared without a trace. Old conditions were restored even where, objectively speaking, this meant retrogression. The French period remained an episode.

H. Herfurth, *Die französische Fremdherrschaft und die Volksaufstände vom Frühjahr 1813 in Nordhannover* (1936); M. Hoffmann, *Geschichte der Freien und Hansestadt Lübeck* (1889); J. Mistler, "Hambourg sous l'occupation française," *Francia* 1 (1973); R. Patemann, "Die Beziehungen Bremens zu Frankreich bis zum Ende der französischen Herrschaft 1813," *Francia, Forschungen zur westeuropäischen Geschichte*, 1 (1973); G. Rüthnig, *Oldenburgische Geschichte*, vol. 2 (1911); A. C. Schwarting, *Die Verwaltungsorganisation Nordwestdeutschlands während der französischen Besatzungszeit 1811–13* (1936); K. H. Schwebel, *Bremen unter französischer Herrschaft 1810–1813* (1949);

J. Vidalenc, ''Les 'départements hanseatiques' et l'administration Napoléonienne,'' *Francia* 1 (1973); A. Wohlwill, *Neuere Geschichte der Freien und Hansestadt Hamburg, insbesondere von 1789–1815* (1914).

Reinhard Patemann

Related entries: CONTINENTAL BLOCKADE; DIPLOMACY; EMPIRE, FRENCH; FOREIGN POLICY; GERMAN WAR OF LIBERATION; NAPOLEON I.

GERMAN WAR OF LIBERATION (1813). Following the disaster in Russia in 1812, the advance of Russian troops into Prussia and the conclusion of a Russian-Prussian alliance (28 February 1813) forced the remnants of the Grande Armée, under Eugène de Beauharnais, to retire behind the Elbe-Saale river line. Meanwhile Napoleon, at Paris, raised a new army. From September 1812 to April 1813, 630,000 men were called up, and 540,000 responded, mostly conscripts and National Guardsmen. Their numbers appeared sufficient, but they were largely inexperienced levies, and the cavalry contingents were inadequately mounted and trained.

At the head of a French army of nearly 200,000, Napoleon crossed the Saale River on 28 April, defeated the Russo-Prussian army at the battles of Lützen (2 May) and Bautzen (20 May), and forced it to yield Leipzig, Dresden, and Breslau and to retire behind the Oder. French casualties had been large (20,000 at each battle), however, and French cavalry was badly needed for reconnoitering and the decisive battle charge. To give himself time to rebuild his army, Napoleon accepted the Austrian Clemens von Metternich's offer to mediate peace between the combatants during a prolonged armistice, which lasted from 4 June to 10 August. However, when Napoleon declined the proffered terms (that he relinquish all of his conquests outside Italy and France's natural frontiers), Austria joined England, Spain, Russia, Prussia, and Sweden against France.

The Grande Armée, concentrated in Saxony, now had to fight three armies: that of Jean Bernadotte, crown prince of Sweden, coming from the neighborhood of Berlin; that of G. L. Blücher von Wahlstatt from Breslau; and that of Karl zu Schwarzenberg from Bohemia. The allied generals adopted the strategy of not pressing an attack on the French army when Napoleon was present. (Napoleon thrashed Schwarzenberg at Dresden, 26–27 August.) When he was absent, they fell on his lieutenants in charge of isolated corps: Nicolas Oudinot at Gross-Beeren (23 August), Jacques Macdonald on the Katzbach (26 August), Dominique Vandamme at Kulm (29–30 August), and Michel Ney at Dennewitz (6 September). On 8 October Bavaria defected to the Allies. The three allied armies, numbering approximately 300,000, converged on Napoleon, with nearly 200,000, at Leipzig. There ensued the three-day Battle of the Nations (16–19 October), an Allied victory that compelled Napoleon to retire behind the Rhine. His army was reduced to 70,000 combatants and 40,000 stragglers. Except for a few besieged garrisons in Germany (Jean Rapp at Danzig, Louis Nicolas Davout at Hamburg), France was forced back of its former frontiers. Napoleon's Confederation of the Rhine was dissolved; a provisional government in Holland proclaimed the independence of the United Provinces (21 November 1813); French troops withdrew from Spain and by the Treaty of Valençay (8 December 1813) Napoleon returned Ferdinand VII to his throne. Joachim Murat, hoping to receive the crown of the Kingdom of Italy from Austria, defected from Napoleon, leaving Eugène to fight three foes—Murat himself, the Austrians, and the English.

W. Andreas, *Das Zeitalter Napoleons und die Erhebung der Völker* (Heidelberg, 1955); D. G. Chandler, *Campaigns of Napoleon* (New York, 1966); J.B.A. Charras, *Histoire de la guerre de 1813 en Allemagne* (Leipzig, 1866); E. d'Odeleben, *Relation de la campagne de 1813*, 2 vols. (Paris, 1817); J. G. Gallaher, *Iron Marshal: A Biography of Louis N. Davout* (Carbondale, Ill., 1976); D. Klang, "Bavaria and the War of Liberation, 1813–1814," *FHS* 4 (1965); F. L. Petre, *Napoleon's Last Campaign in Germany, 1813* (London, 1912).

Harold T. Parker

Related entries: AUSTRIA; BADEN; BAVARIA, KINGDOM OF; COALITIONS AGAINST FRANCE; FOREIGN POLICY; LEIPZIG, BATTLE OF; METTERNICH; PRUSSIA, KINGDOM OF; SAXONY, KINGDOM OF; WESTPHALIA, KINGDOM OF; WÜRTTEMBERG, KINGDOM OF.

GERMANY. See BADEN; BAVARIA, KINGDOM OF; BERG, GRAND DUCHY OF; CONFEDERATION OF THE RHINE; EMPIRE, HOLY ROMAN; FRANKFURT, GRAND DUCHY OF; GERMAN TERRITORIES, NORTH COASTAL; PRUSSIA, KINGDOM OF; SAXONY, KINGDOM OF; WESTPHALIA, KINGDOM OF; WÜRTTEMBERG, KINGDOM OF.

GIRONDINS. See CONVENTION; DIRECTORY; TERROR, THE.

GNEISENAU, AUGUST NEIDHARDT VON, COUNT (1760–1831), Prussian field marshal. Born and brought up in poverty until the age of nine, Gneisenau eventually studied at Erfurt University and began an adventurous life as a noble soldier-of-fortune, first in 1778 in the Austrian army and then in 1780 in Ansbach service. In 1782–83 he was in Canada as a lieutenant in an Ansbach regiment hired by the British. There he became acquainted with the concept of a people in arms and with the open skirmish. In 1786 he joined the Prussian service but for the next twenty years saw only garrison duty in Silesia. As a major in 1806 he fought at Jena and then successfully defended the city of Kolberg until after the Treaty of Tilsit in 1807. This brought Gneisenau's name to the attention of the public. He employed a new tactic, the forward defense based on sorties from the city.

In 1808, General Gerhard von Scharnhorst brought him into the Military Reorganization Commission, the Commission to Investigate the Events of the 1806–7 Campaign, and the Commission to Draft a New Drill Regulation. He was also made inspector of fortifications and commander of the corps of engineers.

In various memoranda he demanded the abolition of corporal punishment, the reorganization of the army based on the experience of Napoleonic warfare, abolition of caste privileges, appointment of officers according to merit, establishment of military academies, and new principles of recruitment and training. His were the basic principles of the reformers: to remove the barriers between the people and the army and to have the people participate in public life. The reactionaries viewed him and the other reformers as revolutionaries.

With the dismissal of Stein in 1808, Colonel von Gneisenau also resigned his commission and in a secret mission conducted talks with the British to explore the possibility of continued resistance to Napoleon. Another such mission in 1810 saw him in Austria, Russia, England, and Sweden. In 1811 he vainly urged war against the French. In 1813 he joined Scharnhorst's staff in G. L. Blücher's Silesian Army and after Scharnhorst's death succeeded him as chief of staff with responsibility for strategic operations. He also contributed to the plan of operations at Leipzig. Together with Blücher he recognized that only Napoleon's complete defeat would bring peace.

After the fall of Paris, Major General von Gneisenau was made a count, but his hopes of being given an independent command were destroyed by the suspicions of the king and the intrigues of the court party. Once again he was chief of staff to Blücher and as such totally responsible after the defeat at Ligny for the decision to move in the direction of Waterloo, enabling the British to assure Napoleon's defeat.

Gneisenau called for a peace of revenge against France, was disappointed by the results of the Congress of Vienna, and had no sympathy for Clemens von Metternich's European concept. In 1816 he retired from the service, finding his liberal and national views totally at variance with the government's policy of reaction. In 1825, on the tenth anniversary of Waterloo, he was promoted to field marshal.

While Gneisenau was without a doubt one of the major figures in the drive to reorganize the army and revitalize the state after 1806, it was his fate to remain in the second echelon, chief of staff but never commander. Yet there is also no doubt that without his drive, intelligence, and motivation, the future of the Prussian army would have been quite different.

H. Delbrück, *Gneisenau*, 2 vols. (1920); G. Heine, *Gneisenau* (1944); G. Ritter, *Gneisenau und die deutsche Freiheitsidee* (1932); H. Teske, "Gneisenau, Staatsbürger und Mensch," *Wehrwissenschaftliche Rundschau* (1960).

Peter W. Becker

Related entries: BLÜCHER VON WAHLSTATT; GERMAN WAR OF LIBERATION; JENA-AUERSTÄDT, BATTLES OF; PRUSSIA, KINGDOM OF; SCHARNHORST.

GODOY ALVAREZ DE FARIA, MANUEL (1767–1851), first minister of Charles IV of Spain, lover of the queen, Maria-Luisa; in 1807 also commandant of the armies and grand admiral of the navy. He was bitterly resented by the heir to the throne, the future Ferdinand VII. He was responsible for the original

alliance between Spain and France made in 1795. Because it had brought Spain nothing but misery and because his position would certainly be forfeit if Charles IV passed away, Godoy sold out to Napoleon in 1807. By the Treaty of Fontainebleau (29 October 1807), French troops were to be allowed to cross Spanish territory to invade Portugal and, in effect, to invade Spain masquerading as friendly forces. When Ferdinand VII overthrew his father in 1808, he clapped Godoy in prison but delivered him to Napoleon to gain the favor of the French emperor. Godoy went into exile in France with Charles IV and his queen, who were deposed, along with Ferdinand VII, during the interview at Bayonne with Napoleon. Godoy left memoirs published in French and English in 1836.
Related entries: BAYONNE, "INTERVIEW" OF; FONTAINEBLEAU, TREATY OF (1807); PENINSULAR WAR; SPAIN, KINGDOM OF.

GOETHE, JOHANN WOLFGANG VON (1749–1832), German poet, dramatist, writer, and eventual proponent of Napoleon. Considering his connection with the ducal court in Weimar, Goethe was a singularly apolitical person, especially during the first twenty-five years of his life. When he returned in 1788 from his famous two-year sojourn in Italy, he dropped most of his courtly duties. Though still in the pay of the duke, he regarded himself as a private man and tended to view German happenings from an aloof, European vantage point. His views of the early French Revolution were ambivalent, but he reacted with revulsion to the Reign of Terror. In 1792, Goethe accompanied Duke Carl August, whose troops marched with the duke of Brunswick's Prussian army in the invasion of France, which ended in defeat at Valmy. Goethe witnessed the victory of a peoples' army over Prussian regulars. By general agreement, he declared to his companions, "Here and today a new epoch of world history begins." He confirmed that only in his *Kampagne in Frankreich*, however, written much later.

Goethe's early reaction to Napoleon was characteristic. Until French troops entered Weimar, he seemed indifferent. In 1808 in Erfurt, Goethe was introduced to Napoleon, who, calling him Germany's foremost playwright, urged him to come to Paris to glorify the French Empire in dramas. Goethe gave evasive answers, and Napoleon abandoned the idea. During this interview, Napoleon is reputed to have said of Goethe, referring less, perhaps, to his work than imposing appearance: "*Voila un homme*!" The emperor had read *Werther* but little else of Goethe. He nevertheless caused Goethe to be awarded the Legion of Honor. Goethe's position at the Weimar court clearly called for tact and even deference; Napoleon could have dissolved the duchy with a stroke of his pen.

Even in 1813, however, when Napoleon's star appeared to have set, Goethe urged against journalistic forays against the emperor. He forbade his son (to no avail) to fight against the French in the German War of Liberation. He seems to have feared that Russia would replace France in Germany. The question as to whether Goethe admired Napoleon as a man or as a military genius is difficult to answer, but the preponderance of evidence indicates that there was much admiration, one genius for another.

J. Eckermann, *Conversations with Goethe* (London, 1971); R. Friedenthal, *Goethe: His Life and Times* (Cleveland, 1965); E. Staiger, *Goethe*, 3 vols. (Zurich, 1952–59); F. Strich, *Goethe and World Literature* (London, 1949); K. Vietor, *Goethe the Poet* (Cambridge, Mass., 1949).

James N. Hardin

Related entries: CARL AUGUST; FOREIGN POLICY; NAPOLEON I; SCHILLER.

GOGEL, IZAAC JAN ALEXANDER (1765–1821), Dutch statesman and financial expert; minister of finances of the Kingdom of Holland under Louis Bonaparte (1806–1813). Gogel had earlier been one of the patriot-republicans who had welcomed the French armies (1794) and helped to establish the Batavian Republic. He served as agent (minister) of finance under the Republic, including the authoritarian regime of Rutger Jan Schimmelpenninck, who was ousted in 1806 by Napoleon in favor of Louis Bonaparte, king of Holland, who continued Gogel in office as finance minister. Throughout, Gogel's aim was to create a system of national taxes, one that would make possible an effective centralized government. (Gogel considered the old federal republic—the United Provinces of the Netherlands—to be an anachronism.) William of Orange, on his return from exile (1813), received Gogel into the new government of the Kingdom of the Netherlands. The ideas of the aging financial expert agreed with his own concepts.

S. Schama, *Patriots and Liberators: Revolution in the Netherlands, 1780–1813* (New York, 1977); L.G.J. Verberne, *Gogel en Uniteit* (Nijmwegen, 1967); C.H.E. de Wit, *De Strijd Tussen Aristocratie en Democratie in Nederland, 1780–1848* (Heerlen, 1965).

Related entries: BATAVIAN REPUBLIC; HOLLAND, KINGDOM OF; HOLLAND, KINGDOM OF: MINISTERS.

GOHIER, LOUIS (1746–1830), one of five directors of the French government in 1799. He opposed the coup d'état of 18 Brumaire and afterward retired from politics. See BRUMAIRE, COUP OF 18, YEAR VIII.

GOURGAUD, GASPARD, BARON (1783–1852), general, with Napoleon on St. Helena. An artillery officer who entered the French army as second lieutenant in 1802, Gourgaud fought in every Napoleonic campaign and battle from Ulm to Waterloo and rose to be general aide-de-camp. On St. Helena, however, this frank, turbulent, and jealous warrior whose great days had been a gallop in action could abide neither the enforced idleness and boredom of secluded isolation nor the intense rivalries of his quarreling, intriguing companions, and he left in 1818. His record of his conversations with Napoleon, more naive than that of Las Cases, often catches "the accent and gesture of the master" whom he adored.

(Gaspard Gourgaud, *Journal de Saint-Hélène 1815–1818*, ed. O. Aubry, 2 vols. [Paris, 1947].)

Harold T. Parker

Related entries: BERTRAND; LAS CASES; MONTHOLON; ST. HELENA.

GOUVION SAINT CYR, LAURENT, MARQUIS DE (1764–1830), marshal of France. Son of a tanner, he was a painter and then an actor before the Revolution. He volunteered for the army in 1792, just as the great exodus of noble officers began, and by 1798 was a major general, serving mostly in the Rhineland.

Under Napoleon, he had secondary and foreign commands: service with the Army of the Kingdom of Italy (1805), Naples (1806–7), and Spain (1808–9). He left Spain without being properly relieved, and the emperor left him unemployed until 1811.

Gouvion fought bravely in Russia, however, and was made a marshal at the end of 1812. In 1813 he was left to defend Dresden and eventually had to capitulate. He did not rally to Napoleon in 1815 and was made a peer, marquis, and later minister of war and minister of marine by the restored Bourbons.

J.L.C. Gay de Vernon, *Gouvion Saint Cyr* (Paris, 1856); L. Gouvion Saint Cyr, *Mémoires pour servir a l'histoire militaire sous la Directoire, le Consulat et L'Empire*, 4 vols. (Paris, 1831).

Related entries: MARSHALS OF THE EMPIRE; PENINSULAR WAR.

GOYA Y LUCIENTES, FRANCISCO DE (1746–1828), court painter (1808–13) to King Joseph Bonaparte of Spain. One of the great painters in the history of Western culture, Goya was drawn into the whirlpool of Napoleon's activity by the French invasion of Spain in 1808. Born near Saragossa, he was first a tapestry designer and then a painter of charming village pastorals and a portraitist of the royal court. But from 1792 on, probably because a severe illness left him permanently deaf, his work took on somber hues. Sets of etchings, *Los Caprichos* (c. 1797) and *Los Proverbios* (1805), savagely satirized the foibles of a degraded society. In 1808 Napoleon forced the abdication of the Spanish Bourbons and made Joseph Bonaparte king of Spain. Before Joseph arrived in Madrid, the populace rose in insurrection (2 May 1808) against Joachim Murat's occupying French army and was ruthlessly put down, with executions running into the next day. Goya in two great paintings, *The Second of May* and *The Third of May*, caught in the one the wild fury of a rioting mob and in the other the wild individuality of the rioters facing the impassive disciplined anonymity of the French firing squad. These were not made public, however, until after Joseph's (and Napoleon's) fall.

Goya accepted the largesse of the Bonaparte king. In 1814, he brought out his dark etchings, *The Disasters of War*, to prove his patriotism to the returning Bourbon, Ferdinand VII. They record the vicious cruelties of guerrilla conflict, the horrors men and women of both sides inflict on each other. His painting

Colossos portrays a huge muscular male figure, War, striding across the country spreading panic, following its own stern, inexorable necessity. The emotions provoked by these works are anger, despair, and divine pity for the men and women of both camps. Goya was not a usual turncoat; he served whoever was in power in order to do his work.

B. L. Myers, *Goya* (Feltham, Middlesex, 1968).

Harold T. Parker

Related entries: BONAPARTE, JOSEPH; FERDINAND VII DE BOURBON; PENINSULAR WAR; SPAIN, KINGDOM OF.

GRAND ARMY. See ARMY, FRENCH.

GRASSINI, JOSEPHINA (1773–1850). Mme. Grassini, operatic prima donna patronized by Napoleon, was born in Varese, Lombardy, 8 April 1773, of humble parents. She first studied voice in Varese with Domenico Zucchinetti and then with Antonio Secchi in Milan. She progressed rapidly because of her natural beauty and the quality of her voice, which, although contralto, was capable of being light and responsive. Her debut was in Parma in 1789 in Guglielmi's *La Bella Pescatrice*, and she soon became the first singer in Italy, appearing triumphantly in all the major cities. After the Battle of Marengo in 1800, she sang in two concerts at La Scala given in honor of Napoleon. Although this was their second meeting, at the first Napoleon was still too enamored with Josephine to notice the singer. At this encounter, however, he was obviously attracted, so she chided him, saying that when she was in her "finest flush" of "beauty and talent" he ignored her and now she claimed that she was "no longer worthy of him." She was twenty-seven and on the threshold of a brilliant career.

The morning after one of the concerts, Marshal Alexandre Berthier came into Napoleon's room and found them smiling and having breakfast, and he was instructed to arrange transportation to Paris for Mme. Grassini. On 22 July 1800 she sang at the national festivities held at the Champ de Mars. Following tours of Germany and the Netherlands, she spent three seasons in London, where her greatest acclaim came as Proserpine in Winter's *Il Ratto di Proserpina*, in which the very popular Mrs. Villington sang Ceres. She returned to Paris in 1806 as the leading singer of the Empire, receiving the extraordinary salary of 36,000 francs, plus a 15,000 franc bonus.

The emperor's appreciation of music was not particularly keen, but his preference ran to Italian music and musicians. It was said that he could listen to Mme. Grassini by the hour. At the Tuileries she sang the title role of *Didone*, which Paër had written for her, Cherubini's *Pigmalione*, and she appeared at the Théâtre Italien as Horatia in *Gli Orazi* in November 1813. After Waterloo Grassini returned to Italy, teaching voice as her voice faded, and retiring in 1823. A portrait by Vigée-Lebrun depicts her in the Turkish dress which she wore in Winter's opera, *Zaira*.

A. Gavoty, *La Grassini* (Paris, 1947); E. Gara, "Giuseppina Grassini," *La Scala*, nos. 29–30, (Milan, 1952); R. Jeanne, "La chanteuse de l'empereur," *Les oeuvres libres*, n.s., no. 34 (1949); A. Pougin, *Une cantatrice "amie" de Napoléon; Giuseppina Grassini* (Paris, 1920); R. de Renais, *La cantarte del l'imperatore* (Rome, 1948); P. Scudo, "Josephina Grassini," *Revue des deux mondes*, January 1, 1852.

Rachel R. Schneider

Related entries: CHERUBINI; LE SUEUR; MEHUL; MUSIC; PROPAGANDA; THEATER.

GREAT BRITAIN, the most persistent enemy of Revolutionary France and of Napoleon. Britain and France were at war with each other for twenty-one years (1793–1814) with an intermission of fourteen months after the Peace of Amiens (March 1802) and in 1815 during the Hundred Days. They were locked both in a desperate struggle for survival and power and in an ideological conflict. For France, especially at first, it was in part a war to defend and then to spread liberty, equality, and Revolutionary reforms. For Britain, it became a war to prevent French acquisition of Belgium, to restore the balance of power on the European continent, and to check the spread of Jacobin principles.

During the Napoleonic period, the two countries were not unevenly matched. France had a larger population (28 million versus Britain's 12 million), resources mobilized by an efficient centralized administration, large armies organized and led by a military genius, and a people highly motivated by patriotism and pride in the *Grande Nation*. Britain had an impregnable island position, a powerful navy, a large merchant marine, growing industrial and financial resources, and a people proud of being free-born Britons and who could be easily aroused to fight a hereditary foe.

Britain applied against Napoleon the same policy that William Pitt the Elder had brilliantly used against France during the Seven Years War. Gaining naval superiority, it set up around imperial France a naval blockade that protected British commerce, disrupted French trade and industries dependent on foreign sources, and interdicted France's communications with colonies. Meanwhile the British swept up French, Dutch, and Danish colonial possessions and encouraged (and underwrote by subsidies) successive coalitions of continental powers against Napoleon. It also landed expeditionary forces on the Continent, at first unsuccessfully but in time triumphantly under the duke of Wellington on the Iberian Peninsula. From 1805 to 1807 Britain was joined by Austria, Russia, and Prussia, in 1808 by Portugal and the Spanish people, in 1809 by Austria again, and from 1812 to 1813 by Russia, Prussia, and Austria. Unable to invade England, Napoleon smashed the European alliances one after another (until 1812) and waged economic warfare using the Continental System.

According to François Crouzet and A. Gayer, among others, the major effect of the wars and Continental System was perceptibly to slow Britain's industrial growth, if temporarily. The Berlin Decrees prohibited all commerce with the British. At that time Europe took one-third of Britain's exports, chiefly manufactures. Napoleon calculated that exclusion from the European market would ruin British industries, throw its factory workers on the streets, and ruin its banks. If so, the British government might sue for peace. But events did not work out as planned. Napoleon could enforce the self-blockade of Europe only in brief intervals of peace: July 1807 to June 1808 and November 1810 to November 1812. During those years, British exports to Europe nearly ceased, its industrial production declined (5 percent in 1807–8, 25 percent in 1811), and the factory districts were in grave distress. However, Napoleon's invasion of Portugal and Spain opened the Iberian Peninsula and the markets of Central and South America, and his break with Russia in 1812 opened the markets of eastern Europe.

A second major effect of the wars in Britain was to suspend for nearly a generation effective agitation for the reform of Parliament. The British government was in the hands of the Tories, who in fact controlled the House of Commons nearly uninterruptedly from 1784 to 1830. From self-interest and philosophical conviction, they defended electoral arrangements that kept them in office, and they opposed giving the vote to the middle and lower classes. As late as 1792 there was an active reform movement demanding universal suffrage or at least the vote for taxpaying householders. But the mob violence of the French Revolution frightened the ruling classes and discredited even moderate reformers. Even in the popular mind, British reformers became fellow-traveling Jacobins. Even in a year (1812) of industrial depression, occasioned in part by the Continental System, when rioting workers smashed machinery, the rioters had no program for reform or overthrow of the political system.

Great Britain survived the prolonged ordeal with its fundamental institutions (Parliament, an independent judiciary, the common law, and jury trial) intact. Its naval, commercial, industrial, and financial supremacy in the Western world had been assured. Its influence in international diplomacy was second to none.

F. Crouzet, *L'économie britannique et le blocus continental (1806–1813)*, 2 vols. (Paris, 1958), "Remarques sur les origines des Ordres en Conseil de novembre 1807: Groupes de pression et politique de blocus," *RHq* 228 (1962), and "Bilan de l'économie britannique pendant les guerres de la révolution et l'empire," *RHq* 234 (1965); L. Dehio, *The Precarious Balance* (New York, 1962); C. Emsley, *British Society and the French Wars, 1793–1815* (Totowa, N.J., 1979); A. Gayer, W. Rostow, and A. Schwartz, *The Growth and Fluctuation of the British Economy, 1790–1850*, 2 vols. (London, 1953); S. T. Ross, *European Diplomatic History, 1789–1815* (Garden City, N.Y., 1969).

Harold T. Parker

Related entries: ARMY, BRITISH; CASTLEREAGH; CONTINENTAL BLOCKADE; ENGLAND, ATTEMPTED CONQUEST OF; GREAT BRITAIN, DOMESTIC; WARFARE, ECONOMIC.

GREAT BRITAIN, DOMESTIC. When Napoleon Bonaparte seized power in France in 1799, the people of the British isles were ending an unusually riotous decade. There had been an uprising in Ireland, a mutiny in the navy, and food riots and industrial strikes. George III had been booed in the streets of London, and William Pitt, who had headed the king's government since 1783, had seen the windows of his house smashed by a London crowd. There was economic distress created by bad harvests or the social dislocations of industrialization.

Most worrisome to the government, however, were the radical societies that had proliferated since the commencement of the French Revolution. The clubs, many of them led by artisans and laborers and linked by corresponding societies, were dedicated, as the Sheffield Society recorded, to "radical reform consistent with the Rights of Man." In the capital, the Society of the Friends of the People attracted middle-class proponents of parliamentary reform. Displaying more dangerous tendencies, from the perspective of the wealthy and landed interests, were the Society for Constitutional Information, which spoke the language of Tom Paine, and the London Corresponding Society, whose shoemaker secretary, Thomas Hardy, communicated with Revolutionary groups in France.

The hubbub of radical voices, particularly after the beginning of the war with France (1793), had helped to strengthen Pitt's hold on the government since sedition and treasonable practices seemed rife in the land. Notwithstanding the eloquent liberal voice of Charles James Fox, the Whig leader, Crown and Parliament, judges and justices of the peace cooperated with Pitt to restore order and patriotism. Repressive legislation was passed to restrain the radical press and prohibit seditious meetings; in 1794 Pitt got the writ of habeas corpus suspended. A broader definition of treason was framed to curb criticism of king, Parliament, and constitution. Radical leaders were arrested and tried for high treason. In Scotland they received harsh sentences of death or transportation. In England, however, the trials of Thomas Hardy, J. Horne Tooke, and John Thewall of the Society for Constitutional Information ended in their acquittals. Popular agitation in 1798 brought more repression. The Corresponding Society was outlawed; by 1799 the radicals were mute and dispirited. Nevertheless, the government delivered a blow against workers' associations with the Combination Acts (1799, 1800), stifling the trades union impulse. At the outset of the new century, Pitt seemed free to concentrate on destroying the French Republic.

There was unfinished business in Ireland, however. Pitt had promised to join Ireland with Britain, abolish the Dublin Parliament, and allow both Catholics and Protestants to vote in elections to the Westminster parliament. Prompted by Lords Castlereagh and Cornwallis, the Dublin Parliament was persuaded to end its own life, and the Act of Union (1801) proclaimed the United Kingdom of Great Britain and Ireland. On the crucial question of Catholic emancipation, however, Pitt was blocked by the ailing George III, who adamantly opposed the measure as a violation of the constitution. Pitt resigned on 14 March 1801, which enabled the new ministry of Henry Addington to make peace with France. In 1803, however, war with France resumed, and Pitt was recalled to preside over the conduct of the war until his death in January 1806. A Foxite ministry followed under the direction of Lord Grenville; the government abolished the slave trade but lost its greatest talent when Fox died in September. Successive administrations were headed by the duke of Portland (1807–09), Spencer Perceval (1809–

12), and Lord Liverpool (1812–27). The authority and prestige of the Crown diminished steadily because of the permanent disability of George III and the erotic adventures of the prince of Wales, who became regent in 1811.

Distracted by war and politics, British governments failed to comprehend that silent, inexorable forces generated a tumultuous population. Demographic growth was confirmed by the results of John Rickman's census in 1801. In the kingdom resided 15.8 million people (almost double the number in 1701). The landscape of the country was being transformed by industrial and urban growth, by canal, road, and bridge construction, and by the expansion of docks and shipping facilities. Technological advances in textiles and light-metal industries were creating new urban centers in the North and Midlands. The agricultural revolution continued in the countryside. Starvation was not uncommon, and most people, rural or urban, lived at a subsistence level.

Personal insecurity magnified all other fears, such as the threat of a French invasion. The commercial war with France brought inflation, high prices, and bankruptcies. War accelerated the process of mechanization, bitterly resisted by Luddite machine breakers. The incidence of violence rose alarmingly and reached even to the lobby of the House of Commons, where Spencer Perceval, the prime minister, was assassinated.

Despite war and popular misery, however, for reasons that are not clear, the death rate was falling and the birthrate remained high. An evangelical revival contributed to the enormous growth of Methodism and an increase in other nonconformist congregations. Literacy was advancing; education was accessible to more people. Women joined with men to promote ideas of liberty and equality, not least of all for themselves. Radicalism fostered political consciousness, and reformers persisted in their efforts. War strengthened the national resolve. Britain after Waterloo was a vibrant, resourceful nation.

J. L. Baxter and F. K. Donnelly, "The Revolutionary 'Underground' in the West Riding—Myth or Reality?" *Past and Present* 64 (1974); J. Bohstedt, "The Politics of Riot and Food Relief in England during the Industrial Revolution," *CRE* (1980); C. B. Cone, *The English Jacobins: Reformers in Late 18th Century England* (New York, 1968); A. Goodwin, *The Friends of Liberty: The English Democratic Movement in the Age of the French Revolution* (Cambridge, Mass., 1979); D. Rapp, "The Left-Wing Whigs: Whitbread, the Mountain and Reform, 1809–1815," *Journal of British Studies* 21 (1982); G. Rudé, *The Crowd in History, 1730–1848* (New York, 1964), and *Paris and London in the Eighteenth Century* (London, 1970); M. I. Thomis, *The Luddites: Machine Breaking in Regency England* (Newton Abbot, 1970).

Carolyn A. White

Related entries: FOX; GREAT BRITAIN; PITT, W.

GREAT BRITAIN AND SPAIN (1808–14). Britain initially supplied Spain with arms and material following the Spanish insurrection against Napoleon in the spring and summer of 1808 and signed a formal alliance with the rebel government in January 1809. At no time, however, did relations between the new allies proceed smoothly. Throughout the years of the Peninsular War (1808–

13), the Spanish complained that Britain was not providing Spain with adequate military support, supplies and money. In turn, the British charged the Spanish with corruption, neglect, inefficiency, and narrow-mindedness. The degree to which this animosity manifested itself depended on the military situation, but even in the best of times relations were tense. The British were particularly aggressive in their efforts to rectify what they considered deficiencies in the Spanish war effort, including a grossly ineffective quartermaster corps and a chaotic chain of command.

Britain meddled in Spain's domestic politics in an effort to influence the form and course of its government. Since King Ferdinand VII was in exile in France (a prisoner of Napoleon), the foreign secretary, Lord Wellesley, considered it imperative that a Cortes (national assembly) convene to give the junta government (replaced by a regency) a semblance of national backing. Yet once the Cortes convened, Lord Wellesley worked to prevent that body from becoming too liberal. He further encouraged the Spanish to undertake sweeping military reforms, for which he offered British officers to train and lead the army. For the most part, Spain resisted these efforts to intrude into what were considered purely Spanish matters.

The most difficult issue confronting the Allies during the war years was the future of the Spanish-American colonies. Revolts in present-day Mexico, Venezuela, Colombia, and Argentina created serious problems. The rebel Spanish government was anxious to subdue the rebellions. Since, until 1812, Napoleon's armies occupied most of Spain, however, the British resisted transporting Spanish troops to the colonies. Also, Spanish-American governments had unofficially opened trade with the British, though the British chose not to support the colonies and risk permanently alienating the Spanish. Britain adopted a middle course—mediating between the two parties—in an effort to defuse the issue at least until year's end. Spain rejected mediation, and the issue remained a persistent source of controversy. The alliance persisted amid suspicion and latent hostility for the duration of the war despite Wellington's key role in expelling the French from Spain.

G. Lovett, *Napoleon and the Birth of Modern Spain* (New York, 1965); W.F.P. Napier, *History of the War in the Peninsula* (London, 1828–40); C.W.C. Oman, *A History of the Peninsular War* (Oxford, 1903–30).

John K. Severn

Related entries: CONTINENTAL BLOCKADE; DIPLOMACY; FOREIGN POLICY; PENINSULAR WAR; WELLESLEY.

GREEKS AND NAPOLEON. Early in his career, Napoleon was acclaimed by Greek patriots as the liberator of subjugated peoples. In 1798, the distinguished classicist Adamantios Korais urged Greeks to support General Bonaparte's campaign in Egypt as a prelude to their own liberation. Bonaparte's alleged plans for peoples under Turkish rule were published by Constantinos Stamatis, who entered the French diplomatic service after Napoleon became emperor. Another

Greek in Napoleon's diplomatic service was Panayiotis Kodrikas, translator of Fontenelle into Greek and former secretary of the Ottoman embassy in Paris. In 1796–97, the Greek revolutionary and leader of the neohellenic Enlightenment, Rhigas Velestinlis, attempted, during Bonaparte's first Italian campaign (1796–97), to request support for a rising against the Turks in Greece timed to occur when Napoleon's armies reached the Adriatic.

In 1797–98, Bonaparte sent personal envoys to the Greeks, two French citizens of Greek origin, Dimo and Nicolo Stephanopoli, who went to Mani in the Peloponnesus to examine insurgent military capabilities. They reported that the prospect of French intervention was greeted with great enthusiasm by the Greeks. In 1798, a leading local notable, Gregorakis, "a Spartan from Mani," addressed a message to Napoleon expressing Greek readiness to make common cause with the French.

During the Egyptian campaign, Napoleon's army had a Greek unit under Colonel N. Papazoglou. In 1806, troops were redesignated to the *Chasseurs d'Orient* and assigned to the Illyrian Provinces.

The most direct impact of Napoleonic policies on the Greek world was felt in the seven Ionian islands, ceded by Venice to France by the Treaty of Campo Formio (1797). General Anselm Gentili installed a French government, which abolished aristocratic privileges, promoted Greek education, and prescribed the celebration of rites of liberty. Korais addressed his edition of Theophrastus to the "free Greeks of the Ionian Sea," urging them to embrace wholeheartedly the spirit of their French liberators. A local poet, Antonios Martelaos, composed a hymn to "celebrate France and General Bonaparte." An anthem by the "whole of Greece," composed by the republican patriot Christophe Perraivos, was dedicated to Bonaparte. French rule was terminated in 1799, however, and in 1800 the seven islands, under Russian protection, formed the Septinsular Republic.

The Treaty of Tilsit (1807) restored the Ionian islands to French imperial rule, which lasted in Corfu, under General François Donzelot, until 1814. (Britain occupied the other islands in 1809.) During the second period of French rule, the Ionian Academy was founded, and the *Regiment Albanais* was formed, comprising mostly refugee military chieftains from mainland Greece, who experienced for the first time the discipline and training of a modern army. The Congress of Vienna, however, assigned the Ionian islands to British protection, which lasted until 1864.

French agents remained active on the mainland throughout the Revolutionary and Napoleonic periods. From 1803 onward, there is positive evidence that French agents promised arms and support for revolution in the Peloponnesus. In 1806, François Pouqueville was appointed French consul at Jannina and worked to promote French influence in the domains of Ali pasha in northwestern Greece.

Conservative religious leaders, meanwhile, opposed French influence. In 1799, the ecumenical patriarchate addressed an encyclical to the Ionian islanders warning them against the spiritual dangers of French concepts. Bonaparte's campaign in Egypt, which threatened the integrity of the Ottoman Empire, precipitated the publication of a counterrevolutionary tract entitled *Paternal Instruction* (1798), ascribed to the Greek patriarch of Jerusalem. To this, Korais responded with the pamphlet *Fraternal Instruction*.

The autocratic evolution of Napoleon's rule eventually forced his liberal Greek supporters to denounce him as a dynast. These included Korais and the anonymous author of the radical republican treatise *Hellenic Nomarchy* (1806). Nevertheless, the activity of Napoleon's agents in Greece contributed to the revolutionary expectancy that prepared the War of Independence in which some former Napoleonic officers, like Fabvier and Maison, played important roles.

E. Legrand, ed., *Documents inédits concernant Rhigas Velestinlis et ses compagnons de martyre tirés des archives de Vienne en Autriche* (Paris, 1892); H. Pernot, ed., *Nos anciens à Corfou. Souvenirs de l'aide-major Lamare-Picquot (1807–1814)* (Paris, 1918); E. Rodocanachi, *Bonaparte et les îles Ioniennes* (Paris, 1899); C. Rodos, *Napoléon Ier et la Grèce* (Athens, 1921); J. Savant, "Napoléon et la libération de la Grèce," *L'Hellenisme contemporain*, vols. 4, 5, 6, 2d Series (1950, 1951, and 1952); D. and H. Stephanopoli, *Voyage en Grèce* (Paris, 1800).

Paschalis M. Kitromilides

Related entries: FOREIGN POLICY; ILLYRIAN PROVINCES; RUSSIA; RUSSIAN CAMPAIGN.

GREGOIRE, HENRI-BAPTISTE (1750–1831), ex-*conventionnel*, bishop of the Constitutional church, senator, member of the Institute, comte de l'Empire, abolitionist, member of the liberal opposition to Napoleon. The abbé Grégoire was the most accomplished leader of the so-called third party, which espoused both Christianity and the liberal principles of the Revolution. He tried unsuccessfully to obtain recognition from Napoleon for his Constitutional church in schism from Rome. Although he was somewhat suspect to both republicans and Catholics, he was elected president of the Corps Législatif in Year VIII and senator in Year X. He opposed the Concordat with Rome and Napoleon's divorce and voted against the establishment of the Empire and the reestablishment of noble titles. An avid proponent of toleration and equality, Grégoire strove to maintain his Constitutional church and effect black emancipation in Santo Domingo, but to no avail. He became involved in conspiracies against the emperor and supported his deposition in 1814.

A. Aulard, *Le christianisme et la Révolution française* (Paris, 1924); A. Mathiez, *La Révolution et l'église* (Paris, 1910); R. Neccles, *The Abbé Grégoire, 1787–1831: The Odyssey of an Egalitarian* (Westport, Conn., 1971).

Emmet Kennedy

Related entries: CHURCH, ROMAN CATHOLIC; HAITI; INSTITUT NATIONAL DES SCIENCES ET DES ARTS.

GRENADIERS. See ARMY, FRENCH.

GRIBEAUVAL, JEAN-BAPTISTE VACQUETTE DE, COUNT (1715–89), inspector of artillery for Louis XV and later Louis XVI. Gribeauval was responsible for designing the field artillery used by the armies of the Revolution and of Napoleon. His light, maneuverable, twelve-, eight-, six-, and 4-pound guns were, in effect, the tools of Napoleon's glory.
Related entry: ARMY, FRENCH.

GRIMM, JACOB LUDWIG CARL (1785–1863), served Jerome Bonaparte in Westphalia; philologist, famous, with his brother, for *Fairy Tales*. Born in Hesse-Kassel, Grimm studied under the jurist F. Karl von Savigny at Marburg and followed him to Paris in 1805. He returned to Kassel to be the court librarian (1808–13) of Napoleon's brother Jerome, king of Westphalia. After the collapse of Napoleon's empire, Grimm entered the diplomatic service of the restored elector of Hesse-Kassel to help recover German books and manuscripts confiscated by the French. He then resumed a scholarly career at the university at Göttingen (1817–37) and at the Academy of Sciences in Berlin (1841–63). His interest in medieval German literature led him into the history of the German language and to the publication of his massive historical *Deutsche Grammatik* (1819ff.). In 1852 he and his brother, Wilhelm, began work on an exhaustive German dictionary, which had to be completed by others. As a by-product of their interest in early German literature, the Grimm brothers published from 1812 to 1815 the first edition of the *Kinder- und Hausmärchen* (fairy tales) that in many translations became a household treasure throughout the Western world.

Harold T. Parker

Related entries: LITERATURE, GERMAN; WESTPHALIA, KINGDOM OF.

GROGNARDS, the "grumblers," proud sobriquet of the men of the Imperial Guard. The term was applied especially to the grenadiers. See ARMY, FRENCH.

GROS, ANTOINE-JEAN, BARON (1771-1835). Although Jacques-Louis David's favorite pupil was, like his master, a Napoleonic propagandist, he was undoubtedly more talented and his paintings more varied and original—so much so that his style has been termed romantic classicism. His father, an obscure miniaturist, had his sixteen-year-old son enter David's newly opened studio in 1787. When David judged that his protégé had outgrown what he had to offer him, he obtained a passport from the Convention that enabled Gros to visit Genoa, where he was able to study Rubens' paintings at length, enough to free him from David's ponderous style. At Genoa, the wife of a French diplomatic agent presented him to Madame Bonaparte, who was about to rejoin her husband. Gros accompanied Josephine to Milan where he was presented and given a position in the commander in chief of the Army of Italy's *état-major*. Gros soon began making portraits of people around him. Bonaparte was so flattered by Gros' painting of the Battle of Arcola, which occurred on 15 November 1796, that he promoted him to inspector of revenues, enabling the artist to follow the campaign, and also made him a member of the commission selecting art objects for the Louvre.

As Gros acquired experience, his talents developed, and his patronage grew. After he won first prize in the competition of 1801, Bonaparte expressed the desire that he paint for him exclusively. When *Bonaparte Visiting the Plague-Stricken Soldiers at Jaffa*, which was commissioned by the emperor, was unveiled in the Salon of 1804, it was well received by the public, artistic colleagues, and the hero. This, his most important painting, combines rich emotional coloring as in Rubens and the Italian baroque with the heart-felt pathos typical of Delacroix. Here Gros depicted Napoleon as a beneficent healer about to work saintly miracles. Immediately after the success of this colossal work, Gros started *The Battle of Aboukir*, which was equally successful at the Salon of 1806. When a competition was held in March 1807 on the subject *Napoléon Visiting the Battlefield at Eylau*, Gros won again with a painting that depicted Napoleon as a mild and magnanimous conqueror with exhausted features and sad eyes, wearing Oriental garb, seated high atop a white horse, and about to grant remission to the kneeling, penitent Lithuanian hussar.

Between the execution of his twenty-four, mostly colossal, paintings and six large decorative murals, Gros painted fifty-five portraits that show his originality and ability to execute works of varied style. His subjects were usually well known and colorful people, whom his imagination enhanced, such as the cavalry general Antoine de Lasalle, Jerome Bonaparte, the king of Westphalia, and Christine Boyer, Lucien Bonaparte's long-dead first wife (1812). The latter he depicted in that melancholy mood so typical of romanticism.

In 1812, Gros was commissioned to decorate the dome of the Pantheon; he did not complete it until 1824, after he had suitably exorcised the figures of Napoleon and the king of Rome. Gros adapted easily to the Restoration; his popularity continued at the Salon of 1817, where he showed *The King Leaving the Tuileries during the Night of 19–20 March*, a portrait of Louis XVIII, and *The Duchess of Angoulême Embarking on 25 July 1815*. When the colossal dome of the Pantheon was unveiled in November 1824, Charles X made him a baron as a manifestation of public acclaim.

Unfortunately for Gros, shifting popular taste began to reject the school of David, and at the Salon of 1835 his painting *Hercules and Diomède* was so ridiculed that he fell from favor with the monarchy. On 25 June, Gros left Paris during the night and went to the forest of Meudon where he drowned himself in four feet of water. That he had trained 432 artists in his studio, which was the continuation of David's, had not mattered as much to him as the loss of his ruler's favor.

J.-B. Delestre, *Gros, sa vie et ses ouvrages* (Paris, 1867); E. Garnier, *Funérailles de Baron Gros* (Paris, 1835); A. Gonzales-Palacios, *The French Empire Style* (London,

1966); A.-J. Gros, *Institut Royal de France Académie royale des beaux-arts, Funérailles de M. Denon* (Paris, 1825); J. Tripier Le Franc, *Histoire de la vie et de la mort du baron Gros* (Paris, 1880).

June K. Burton

Related entries: ART; DAVID; DENON; EGYPTIAN CAMPAIGN; INSTITUT NATIONAL DES SCIENCES ET DES ARTS; LOUVRE; SCULPTURE.

GROUCHY, EMMANUEL, MARQUIS DE (1766–1847), marshal of France; often blamed for Napoleon's defeat at Waterloo. Born in Paris to an old family of nobles of the sword, Grouchy was intended for the military from birth and entered the king's army at age fourteen. In 1789 he was an officer of *gardes-du-corps* at Versailles. In 1792 he served in the army of Lafayette and was promoted to brigadier general. He remained loyal to the Republic after the execution of Louis XVI, served in the Vendée, became a major general in 1795, and in 1796 was second in command to Louis Hoche of the (abortive) expedition to Ireland. In 1798, he served under Jean Moreau in Italy, and was captured at Lodi, unconscious and bleeding, after leading his corps in the hottest fighting and sustaining fourteen wounds. Released after a year, he served under Moreau at Hohenlinden, which ended the War of the Second Coalition. Distraught at the exile of Moreau for royalism, he nevertheless served Napoleon with vigor. His corps was the first to enter Berlin in 1806; at Friedland (1807) he commanded the cavalry and thus helped end the Fourth Coalition. In 1808 he served in Spain and in 1809 in the Wagram campaign. In the Battle of Wagram (5–6 July 1809), his cavalry put to flight that of the Austrian count Rosenberg. This so impressed Napoleon that he made Grouchy colonel general of *chasseurs*, which made him a grand officer of the Empire. During the Russian campaign, Grouchy commanded the cavalry of Prince Eugène at the Battle of Borodino. He fought in Germany in 1813 and in France until 7 March 1814, when he was gravely wounded at Craonne, and had to leave the army.

When General Grouchy rallied to Napoleon during the Hundred Days (1815), the emperor gave him a marshal's baton. He was the twenty-sixth and last marshal of the Empire. (Of the other 25, only Michel Ney, Nicolas Soult, and L. N. Davout were both willing and able to serve in the Waterloo campaign.) On 16 June 1815, at Ligny, Grouchy commanded Napoleon's right wing, and the Prussians, under Prince G. L. Blücher von Wahlstatt, went down in defeat. Next morning (17 June), Grouchy was sent in pursuit of the Prussian army, with orders to prevent its juncture with Wellington's Anglo-Dutch army. Napoleon and Marshal Ney pursued Wellington toward Brussels, and on 18 June, at 11:00 A.M., opened battle against him at Waterloo. Grouchy, meanwhile, had lost Blücher on 17 June, and on 18 June his advance guard had just encountered Prussian forces near Wavre—where, in fact, Blücher had reorganized and, leaving a screen against Grouchy, was marching for Waterloo, only nine miles away. Grouchy heard the sound of the guns in the all-day Battle of Waterloo but had no specific orders to march to reinforce Napoleon (since he still was unsure of the Prussians' location). Grouchy had 33,000 troops. Napoleon at Waterloo had 72,000 against Wellington's 68,000. Grouchy's appearance could have weighted the odds for Napoleon early in the day or evened them later, after Blücher reinforced Wellington. But Grouchy did not move and thus became—to Napoleon and the French—the villain of the day. Grouchy had followed orders (to his satisfaction; those dispatched by Napoleon in mid-afternoon were ambiguous).

His withdrawal of his corps—and the survivors of Waterloo—after Napoleon's defeat was a masterpiece, but to no avail. After Napoleon's abdication (22 June) he turned his troops over to Davout and emigrated to the United States. In 1821 however, he was allowed to return to France, where his property, and eventually his rank, were restored. Until his death, Grouchy battled in print against those who accused him of culpability in the defeat of Waterloo. As early as 1819 he wrote a refutation (published in Philadelphia and Paris) of accounts of the campaign by Gourgaud and others and continued to answer every account that appeared, even observations in memoirs. His chief detractor was General (later marshal) Etienne Gérard, who had served under him in 1815 and claimed to have begged him to "march to the guns." Their most violent exchange appeared in 1840 in the *Journal des débats*. Grouchy's own memoirs (assembled by his son and published in 1873–74) were also directed to clearing his name. The attempt was unsuccessful. Grouchy's role in the Waterloo campaign is still a subject of controversy among military historians.

Lord Chalfort, *Waterloo* (New York, 1980); D. Chandler, *Waterloo* (New York, 1980); L. Chardigny, *Les Maréchaux de Napoleon*, new ed. (Paris, 1980); R. P. Dunn-Pattison, *Napoleon's Marshals* (London, 1977); E. de Grouchy, *Mémoires*, 5 vols. (Paris, 1873–74); C. Hibbert, *Waterloo: Napoleon's Last Campaign* (New York, 1968).

Related entries: ABDICATION, SECOND; HUNDRED DAYS, THE; WATERLOO CAMPAIGN.

GUARD, IMPERIAL. See ARMY, FRENCH.

GUARD, NATIONAL, French national guard, composed of citizen-soldiers. The first unit was Paris militia formed after the fall of the Bastille in July 1789. The marquis de Lafayette was designated commander and gave it the name National Guard. Other cities in France followed the example of Paris and organized National Guard units, which were combined by *fédération*—or agreement among the cities. Thus the National Guardsmen of the Revolution were alternately called *fédérés*. The Paris National Guard was particularly troublesome during the events of Vendémiaire and had to be neutralized. Under the Directory the National Guard was reorganized to reduce its strength and to prevent its further political involvement. Napoleon, however, revived the National Guard and gradually increased its strength. In 1810 he organized its 90,000 members into cohorts, which thereafter were called to active duty, especially in coastal defense, in emergencies. Napoleon called up the guard in 1814 and again in 1815 for interior duty.

Ch. Comte, *Histoire de la garde national de Paris de sa fondation à 1827* (Paris, 1827); R. Dupuy, *Garde nationale et les débuts de la Révolution en Ille-et-Vilaine (1789–Mars 1793)* (Paris, 1972); L. Girard, *La garde nationale, 1814–1871* (Paris, 1964); A. Picq, *La legislation militaire de l'époque révolutionnaire* (Paris, 1931).
Related entry: ARMY, FRENCH.

GUERIN, PIERRE-NARCISSE (1774–1833). Guérin, a painter who was selected for honorable mention by the jury for the Decennial Prizes in 1810, primarily produced canvasses that resembled theatrical settings lacking animation. The usual explanation for the intellectual rather than inspired quality of his work is that an artistic career was imposed on him by his parents. He studied initially with the history painter, Nicolas-Guy-Antoine Brenet, who dismissed him for laziness, and later with J. B. Regnault, whose *Three Graces* (1799) is now in the Louvre and who was then, along with Jacques-Louis David and François André Vincent, at the head of the French school. Regnault inspired Guérin to do better, but the military draft temporarily halted his artistic career.

After the Committee of Public Safety gave him a leave, which was prolonged indefinitely, Guérin resumed painting and competed in the Prix de Rome, winning a second prize in 1796 and one of three first prizes in 1797. Because the *pensions* for Rome were not yet reestablished, he stayed in Paris and in the Salon of 1800 showed the painting that made him famous: *Marcus Sextus*. The subject was a man who, on returning home from exile in Rome, discovered that his wife had died during his absence and that his son was about to join her in death. This timely painting of grief appealed to a public that was increasingly sympathetic to the plight of the *émigrés* then returning to France. The painting was politically controversial, and advocates ignored its excessive theatricality while critics claimed that it was too unoriginal. Nevertheless, crowds gathered around the displayed painting for three months, and artists presented Guérin with laurel wreaths.

In 1802 Guérin exhibited *Phèdre accusant Hippolyte devant Thesée*, which had some beautiful, realistic detail in the faces, brighter colors than *Marcus Sextus*, and was equally acclaimed in spite of the fact that it more closely resembled a set for Racine's *Phèdre* at the Théâtre française than reality. In turn, he produced the *Sacrifice à Esculape, L'Empereur pardonnant aux révoltés du Caire, sur le place d'Aboukir* (Salon of 1808), *Andromaque* (1810), *Didon* (1813), and during the early Restoration, *Clytemnestre* (1817). The last and the *Cupid* were his best works, free of the coldness of his earlier style.

As the Restoration began, Guérin was established at the forefront of the French school, and in 1816 he was asked to direct the Ecole de Rome but refused due to ill health. Nevertheless, then at the height of his talents, he maintained his reputation for his teaching ability and having a jovial personality, as well as a good singing voice that delighted the high society with whom he mingled socially. In 1822 he accepted the twice-proffered directorship of the Ecole de Rome and died in Rome in 1833. The pupils whom his school encouraged extended his fame, among them Géricault, Eugène Delacroix, Ary Scheffer, Cogniet, and the engraver Henriquel-Dupont. He was buried in the Church of the Trinity of the Mountains beside Claude Lorrain. His successor at the Ecole de Rome was his friend Horace Vernet.

Besides his neoclassical works Guérin produced some interesting portraits, including those of the Vendéan leaders *Talmont* and *Henri de la Rochejacquelein*, the *Countess of Montesquiou and the King of Rome*, and *Stendahl*.

Artistically Guérin is still a controversial figure. Some critics who praise his perfect taste in layout, use of harmonious colors, and purity of contours place him at the head of the French school, while others tend to agree with Alvar Gonzales-Palacios who concludes that "a consummate technique and a rich repertory of exquisite stage props—antique-style beds with gilded bronze, leopard skins, purple hangings—do not suffice to make his paintings works of art even though they are handled with great intellectual sophistication."

E. Bénézit, *Dictionnaire critique et documentaire des peintres, sculpteurs, dessinateurs et graveurs*, vol. 4 (Paris, 1966); A. Gonzales-Palacios, *The French Empire Style* (London, 1970); P.-N. Guérin, *Funérailles de M. le Bon Regnault (14 novembre 1829)* (Paris, n.d.), and *Réflexions sur une des opérations distinctives du génie, morceau lu à la séance des quatre Académies, le 24 avril 1821* (Paris, 1821); A. C. Quatremère de Quincy, *Notice historique sur la vie et les ouvrages de M. Guérin* (Paris, 1833).

June K. Burton

Related entries: ART; DAVID; DENON; LOUVRE.

GUERRILLAS. The principal guerrilla activity during the Napoleonic period was in Spain, during the Peninsular War (1808–13). Bands turned out informally in 1808. More organized activity began in 1809, when the rebel government proclaimed all-out warfare against the French, designating guerrillas as soldiers under the rules of war and offering commissions as colonels and generals to chiefs of bands already in existence. At the same time, church officials issued a catechism that instructed the faithful that it was not only right to kill Frenchmen but a holy obligation.

During 1809–10 after the shattering defeat of the Spanish regular armies by the French, guerrilla activity died down. But, as French aggressiveness waned and Joseph was put on the defensive in 1811–12 by the duke of Wellington, guerrilla bands appeared in great strength all over Spain. Aragon and Valencia were an exception; there Marshal Louis Suchet had made operation very difficult. He had captured the handsome, dashing Xavier Mina, called "the Student," who was replaced by his uncle, Don Francisco Espoz y Mina, who, however, confined himself to Navarre. In Old Castile the most famous guerrilla chief was the priest Jéromino Merino; in New Castile the leader was Don Juan Martín Diez, "El Empecinado"; in Catalonia, Mílans del Bosch; in Leon "Capucino."

The guerrillas never risked open attack against sizable French forces but confined themselves to actions where they had the French outnumbered—sometimes by as much as fifty to one. They were extremely vicious, devising painful means of executing victims they could not hold for ransom. Some were not patriots but simply bandits. Nevertheless, their continual shadowy presence ruined the morale of the French, and their almost daily depredations led Frenchmen to overestimate their effectiveness. General Bigarré, for example, wrote that the guerrillas killed 100 Frenchmen a day, which, over a five-year period, would have meant a veritable army of almost 200,000—at least four times the number of French killed by any means (although French casualties—dead and wounded—approached 300,000 between 1808 and 1813).

The guerrillas did have military importance, however. First, they provided intelligence to the Allied armies. Second, they forced the French to maintain garrisons to protect convoys, which reduced the number of men available for combat. Finally (if occasionally), they cooperated effectively with Allied forces against the French.

The most spectacular of these attacks were carried out on outposts on the northern coast of Spain (1811) by Captain Sir Home Riggs Popham and the guerrilla chieftains El Pastor and Longa. Popham would dispatch British marines from his small fleet to land near a French fort while the guerrillas swarmed down from the mountains to attack from the land side. Since they always picked French forts separated from the flying squadrons that were supposed to protect them, the effectiveness of the raids was devastating. The most massive assemblage of guerrillas was for Wellington's Vitoria campaign, when the Spanish army reinforced its ranks with the guerrilla chiefs and their bands.

It seems certain that the guerrillas could not have won the Peninsular War by themselves or in cooperation with the Spanish armies, but both, with the assistance of the British, were able to defeat the French.

A secondary guerrilla area was Naples. The irregulars' activity began in 1806 after the entry of Joseph Bonaparte. The Neapolitan guerrillas were never very dangerous, however, because few of them were patriots or retained any loyalty for the exiled Bourbon dynasty. With some exceptions such as the famous Fra Diavolo (Michele Pezza), most of them were more bandits than guerrillas. Joseph's police, directed by Christophe Saliceti, and his very tough military, headed by André Masséna, quashed the guerrillas in northern Naples within months.

Nevertheless, when Joachim Murat took over in 1808, there were guerrillas operating in Calabria. No man to tolerate challenge to his authority, Murat assigned the shrewd and merciless General Charles Antoine Manhes to eradicate them. By the end of 1810 he had done so by blockading villages at night, shooting anyone who left after dark, and requiring that food and anything that could be used by the guerrillas be brought within the village walls at night. A few "Robin Hoods" held out, among them the swashbuckling Capobianco, who was, however, captured and shot at the end of 1811.

D. Alexander, *Rod of Iron: French Counterinsurgency Policy in Aragon during the Peninsular War* (Wilmington, Delaware, 1984); J. Gomez de Arteche y Moro, *Guerra de la independencia, historia militar de España de 1808 à 1814*, 14 vols. (Madrid, 1886–1903); O. Connelly, *The Gentle Bonaparte: A Biography of Joseph, Napoleon's Elder Brother* (New York, 1968); J. M. Iribarren, *Espoz y Mina: el Guerrillero* (Madrid, 1965);

G. H. Lovett, *Napoleon and the Birth of Modern Spain*, 2 vols. (New York, 1965); C. Oman, *A History of the Peninsular War*, 7 vols. (Oxford, 1902–1930); M. Pardo de Andrade, *Los Guerrilleros gallegos de 1809* (La Coruña, 1892); B. Perez-Galdos, *Juan Martin, El Empecinado* (Madrid, 1950).

Related entries: NAPLES, KINGDOM OF; PENINSULAR WAR; SPAIN, KINGDOM OF.

GUILLOTINE, instrument of execution designed during the early Revolution by Dr. Antoine Louis, a surgeon at the prison of Salpêtrière. It was Dr. Joseph Guillotin, however, who proposed to the National Assembly that it be used in official executions, and it came to be called after him. It was considered a more humane form of execution than hanging, beheading, or the firing squad (earlier used) because death was instantaneous and sure. The guillotine became notorious because of its frequent use under the Terror (1793–94). Nevertheless, it was in continuous use by French governments until the abolition of capital punishment in France in 1981.

Related entry: TERROR, THE.

H

HAITI, name of former French colony, Saint-Domingue, on the West Indies island of Hispaniola. The colony had seen war and internal chaos since 1791 and British occupation from 1793 to 1797. The Directory considered sending an expeditionary force there in 1798 to regain control, but war with England prohibited it. With the signing of the preliminary Peace of Amiens (1801), Napoleon reactivated the project and appointed his brother-in-law, General Charles V. E. Leclerc, to command the army.

The French force reached Le Cap François in February 1802, and by mid-month it held most of the southern province and the coastal towns. In May the black leader François Toussaint L'Ouverture capitulated after receiving guarantees of continued black freedom. That June, however, following Napoleon's instruction, Leclerc began a pacification program designed to resubjugate the blacks and restore the colonial trade system. Also in June, he received Napoleon's specific orders to restore slavery. Among other things, Leclerc ordered all cultivators to return to their original plantations. He also encouraged French merchants to return to the colony.

By August, insurgent resistance was increasing, and an epidemic of yellow fever was devastating the French army. When news of the restoration of slavery at Guadeloupe reached the island, black and mulatto leaders in the French force defected en masse, and the insurrection became general. By late October only the largest cities were still under French control. Leclerc died in early November, to be replaced by the vicomte de Rochambeau, who launched a counteroffensive. The arrival of new troops in April 1803 gave the expedition its greatest strength ever, and hope of success.

In May, however, England renewed its war on France. The French force in Haiti increasingly suffered from lack of supplies and reinforcements. The main body of troops surrendered to the English on 30 November. A small contingent at Santo Domingo (on the Spanish side of the island) held on until 1809. Meanwhile, on 1 January 1804 the independence of the Republic of Haiti was proclaimed.

R. R. Crout, "The Napoleonic *Exclusif*: Saint-Domingue and the Leclerc Expedition," *Proceedings of the French Colonial Historical Society* 1 (1976); S. T. McCloy, *The*

Negro in the French West Indies (Lexington, Ky., 1966); T. O. Ott, *The Haitian Revolution: 1789-1804* (Knoxville, 1973); University of Florida Libraries, Rochambeau Collection.

Robert R. Crout

Related entries: BONAPARTE, P.; COLONIES, FRENCH; DIPLOMACY; FOREIGN POLICY; LECLERC; TOUSSAINT L'OUVERTURE.

HAMBURG, SIEGE OF (2 December 1813–27 May 1814), remarkable for defense of Hamburg by Marshal Louis Davout, who held out for weeks after Napoleon abdicated in France. In the spring of 1813, Marshal Davout was placed in command of the Thirty-second Military Division and the Thirteenth Army Corps to hold the lower Elbe. After the defeat of Napoleon in October at Leipzig, Allied armies crossed the Rhine, and by early November Davout was totally cut off from France. With 40,000 troops he fell back into Hamburg, which he had fortified earlier in 1813. Napoleon ordered him to hold the city until relieved in the spring of 1814—relief that never arrived. Davout's defensive operations were so skillful as to make them an example to be studied for the next fifty years. The Allied forces, under the Russian General Levin Bennigsen, were twice the size of the French garrison but were repeatedly beaten back. Moreover, the principal Allied assaults—made in February 1814—resulted in heavy casualties among the attackers. Thus, on 15 April, after the abdication of Napoleon, Bennigsen opened negotiations with Davout and informed the marshal of Napoleon's abdication. Davout refused to surrender, however, even after the abdication was confirmed on 28 April, since he still had no orders or instructions from the new government in Paris. The siege continued. Then on 11 May General Maurice-Etienne Gérard arrived with orders to relieve Davout of his command and to negotiate the withdrawal of the French garrison. On 27 May 1814, seven weeks after Napoleon's abdication, the French army marched out of Hamburg with full military honors and returned to France.

J. G. Gallaher, *The Iron Marshal: A Biography of Louis N. Davout* (Carbondale, Ill., 1976); P. P. Holzhausen, *Davout in Hamburg: Ein Beitrag zur Geschichte der Jahre 1813–1814* (Mülheim, 1892); C. de Laville, "Mémoire sur le siège et la défense de Hambourg," in *Correspondance du maréchal Davout prince d'Eckmühl: ses commandements, son ministère, 1801–1815*, ed. C. de Mazade, 4 vols. (Paris, 1885).

John Gallaher

Related entries: ABDICATION, FIRST; DAVOUT; FRANCE, CAMPAIGN OF; GERMAN WAR OF LIBERATION.

HAMILTON, LADY EMMA LYON (c. 1761–1815), wife of Sir William Hamilton, the British envoy at Naples, and famous as the mistress of Admiral Lord Nelson. Emma Lyon, born about 1761 and baptized 12 May 1765, was the daughter of a blacksmith, Henry Lyon, who died shortly after her birth, leaving her and her mother in poverty. In 1781, calling herself Emma Hart, she was taken to London by the Honorable Charles Francis Greville to become his mistress. Greville had her educated and instructed in singing, dancing, and acting. She became famous for her attitudes, in which she portrayed historical characters. Greville introduced her to the painter George Romney, and she became a model for other painters, such as Reynolds, Lawrence, and Vigée-Lebrun. In 1786 Greville sent her to become the mistress of his uncle, Sir William Hamilton, British envoy to the Kingdom of Naples, in return for Hamilton's paying off Greville's debts. Hamilton and she were married in London on 6 September 1791, when she was about thirty and he was sixty-one. In Naples, Lady Hamilton became a close friend of Queen Maria-Carolina, daughter of the great Austrian Empress Maria-Theresa and sister of Marie Antoinette, and played a considerable role in the court of Naples.

Emma and Horatio Nelson first met in Naples in 1793 and became lovers five years later, after the victorious Battle of the Nile. In 1800 both Nelson and the Hamiltons were recalled to England and traveled through Europe together, attracting attention and often ridicule. Nelson returned to his wife, but after one month the Hamilton ménage à trois was reestablished. Emma Hamilton bore Nelson a daughter, Horatia Nelson (Thompson), in January 1801. Nelson had bought a country home, Merton Place, and after Lord Hamilton died, in 1803, she and Nelson lived there. When Nelson died in 1805 at the Battle of Trafalgar, he left Merton to her, together with annuities for her and their daughter, but gambling and extravagance exhausted what money she had. In 1813 she went to debtors' prison for a year. On her release she fled to Calais to escape her creditors and died there on 15 January 1815.

M. Hardwick, *Emma, Lady Hamilton* (New York, 1970); J. C. Jeaffreson, *Lady Hamilton and Lord Nelson* (London, 1814). *Letters of Lord Nelson to Lady Hamilton* (London, 1814); A. T. Mahan, *The Life of Nelson* (Boston, 1899); A. Morrison, ed., *The Hamilton and Nelson Papers* (privately published, 1893); Nelson-Hamilton manuscripts, National Maritime Museum at Greenwich, British Museum, and Nelson Museum at Monmouth; C. Oman, *Nelson* (New York, 1946); J. Russell, *Nelson and the Hamiltons* (New York, 1969); H. Tours, *Life and Letters of Emma Hamilton* (London, 1960); D. Walder, *Nelson* (New York, 1978); O. Warner, *Lord Nelson, a Guide to Reading* (London, 1955), *Lady Hamilton and Sir William* (London, 1963).

Rachel R. Schneider

Related entry: NELSON.

HARDENBERG, KARL AUGUST VON, PRINCE (1750–1822), Prussian state chancellor. Hardenberg was the son of a Hanoverian field marshal, studied law at Göttingen and Leipzig, and in 1770 entered the Hanoverian state service. In 1790, by Prussian favor, he became minister of the Margraviate of Ansbach-Bayreuth, and in 1791, as its regent, he supervised its transfer to Prussia. He immediately began comprehensive reforms, which became a model for similar reforms throughout Prussia and even influenced the French. Hardenberg was handsome and sophisticated. (He was married three times.) He suffered from increasing deafness after forty, however, which impeded his work and made him irritable and suspicious.

In 1795 he negotiated for Prussia the peace Treaty of Basel with France and got better terms than had been expected. By 1804, he was chief minister of the Prussian king; however, he was unable to prevent—by diplomacy—Napoleon's reach for central Europe. The ultimate step—military resistance—was taken too late. In 1806, supported only by Saxony, Prussia was soundly defeated. The Treaty of Tilsit (1807), which reduced Prussia to a rump state between the Rivers Elbe and Memel, seemed the result of Hardenberg's policy. He was replaced by Baron vom Stein.

The reforms of the state introduced by Stein in 1807 and 1808 were conceptually shared by Hardenberg. A memorandum he wrote in Riga proposed essentially the same measures, and many of Hardenberg's earlier collaborators in Franconia were associated with Stein. When Napoleon banned Stein from Prussian state service (late 1808), Hardenberg was called once more to head the state. The sexagenarian surely carried Stein's reforms as far as was possible at the time. He conducted domestic and foreign policies firmly and cautiously and had Stein—whom he secretly visited in exile—advise him. He worked for free trade and saw to the emancipation of the serfs and granting of full citizenship to Jews.

In three subsequent periods of that fast-moving time Hardenberg's masterful statecraft guided the fate of Prussia. He initiated the political struggle for liberation from Napoleon. He secured the restoration of Prussia as a great power at the Congress of Vienna. And he saw to it that Prussia's liberal reform policy was continued despite its membership in the Austrian-dominated German Confederation. The realization of elected councils at county and provincial levels, the revised regulation of municipalities, the reintroduction of a Council of State, and the procedures for forming standing committees and a United Diet became elements of Prussia's constitution and remained lasting factors of public political life. Hardenberg was surely the most important Prussian statesman of the nineteenth century before Bismarck.

F. Hartung, *Hardenberg und die preussische Verwaltung in Ansbach-Bayreuth von 1792–1806* (Tübingen, 1806); H. Haussherr, *Die Stunde Hardenbergs (1810–1812)*, 2d ed. (1965); W. Hubatsch, *Die Stein-Hardenbergschen Reformen* (1977); E. Klein, *Finanzpolitik und Reformgesetzgebung des preussischen Staatskanzlers Karl August von Hardenberg* (1965); L. von Ranke, *Denkwürdigkeiten des Staatskanzlers Fürsten von Hardenberg*, 5 vols. (Leipzig, 1877); P. Thielen, *Karl August von Hardenberg* (1967).

Walther Hubatsch

Related entries: FRIEDRICH WILHELM III; GNEISENAU; PRUSSIA, KINGDOM OF; SCHARNHORST; STEIN.

HELVETIC REPUBLIC. See SISTER REPUBLICS; SWITZERLAND.

HERALDRY. Four weeks after the announcement was made that Napoleon had become hereditary emperor (18 May 1804), the *Moniteur* stated that the eagle had been adopted for the state armorial bearing, replacing the Roman lictor's axe and fasces surmounted by the red Phrygian cap of the Republic and Consulate. The matter had been discussed at the first meeting of the Imperial Council, held at St. Cloud on 12 June 1804, after a preliminary discussion of the coronation arrangements. Emmanuel Crétet's study committee had recommended the historic national emblem of ancient Gaul, the cock, or the eagle, lion, and the elephant. After discussing the merits of these symbols as well as use of the fleur-de-lys, a swarm of bees, an oak tree, or an ear of corn, the council voted to use the sleeping lion because Napoleon refused to consider the cock. But overnight the emperor changed his mind, and when he signed the committee's report laid before him, he crossed out *lion* and replaced it with an eagle with extended wings. So the eagle of Charlemagne's empire was adopted, and Jean-Baptiste Isabey was ordered to produce it. The designer used a sketch he had made from an eagle taking wing sculptured on one of the tombs of the Visconti in the monastery of the Certosa of Pavia.

Besides being the symbol of the Empire at large, the eagle of the Roman legions was adopted as the battle-standard of the army and navy for world conquest by the emperor who had also crossed the Alps and was about to cross the English channel from Boulogne. Hence, the silken tricolor flag below each eight- by nine-inch eagle with wings inverted, head to the sinister, grasping thunderbolts, weighing three and a half pounds, and attached to an imperial blue staff, was secondary, merely an ornament for the eagle itself. For a while Napoleon also considered changing the national colors of the flags to his favorite color, Corsican green. In time, as the emperor Napoleon became known affectionately as "the eagle," the king of Rome was referred to as the "*Aiglon*" so that books today frequently make statements to the effect that Hitler reunited the eagle with the eaglet on 10 December 1940 on the centennial of Napoleon's remains being placed in the Invalides.

The golden bee *volant en arrière* was adopted by Napoleon as a badge and was used on his own coronation mantle. The emperor used an ermine-lined mantling of purple semé of golden bees; princes and grand dignitaries used a similar azure mantling. The mantling of dukes was plain and lined with vair. The pavilion around the armorial bearings of the Empire was also semé of these insects. Napoleon changed the fleur-de-lys on the chief in the coat of arms of the city of Paris to golden bees on a chief of gules. These insects appeared as decorative motifs on every type of furniture and interior decoration, including sheer window curtains that Josephine had hanging at Malmaison.

While controversy surrounds the meaning, Napoleon adopted the golden bee, believing that it had been the badge of Childeric, the father of Clovis. J. J. Regis de Cambacérès had urged the adoption of a swarm of bees as a national emblem because that represented a republic with a presiding chief. Moreover, the bee is attractive because it possesses a sting, as well as the ability to build combs and manufacture honey, thus typifying peaceful industry rather than offensive power.

Initials also were important symbols under the Empire. The distinctive capital *N* enclosed in a circle of laurel leaves was used on Napoleon's coronation cape (at the back of the collar), on the throne at Fontainebleau, as well as on palace exteriors, bridges, and other blocks of granite. The simplicity and proportions of the Napoleonic *N* were in keeping with the simplicity and clean lines of Empire-style designs and contrasted with the baroque *L* of the previous reigns. Similarly, the Roman-style initial *J* was used by the Empress Josephine.

The official round wax seal affixed to documents and correspondence is now displayed at the Musée de l'Histoire de France on the "premier étage" of the Hôtel Rohan de Soubise, rue des Archives. It contains an effigy of the enthroned emperor facing full front, wearing a Roman-style robe, with legs astride each of two steps, staves in both hands, against a heraldic mantle surmounted by a large imperial crown. The staff in his left hand is identifiable as the distinctive, carved ivory hand of justice of Napoleon with the first two fingers pointing up and the third and fourth fingers bent down. (The seal is now displayed at Fontainebleau). His simple golden crown adorned with cameos on the braces, supposedly copied from Charlemagne's, is displayed in the Salon of Apollo at the Louvre.

Other animal motifs popular during the Empire included Egyptian birds, griffins, dolphins, and centaurs. Empress Josephine was fond of the swan emblem, as her bedroom and state rooms at Malmaison prove. The swan was woven into red Savonnerie carpet, carved into the headboard of her bed, woven into firescreens and upholstery fabric, and worked into the wooden back sections of gondola chairs; contemporary paintings of Malmaison show both black and white swans swimming on the lake in the park as Josephine and her ladies are taking a *promenade en bateau*.

N. Apra, *Empire Style* (London, 1972); Arthur C. Fox-Davies, *The Complete Guide to Heraldry* (New York, 1950 and 1978), and *The Art of Heraldry* (London, 1904); Edward Fraser, *The War Drama of the Eagles* (New York, 1912).

June K. Burton

Related entries: ART; ARCHITECTURE; PROPAGANDA; SYMBOLISM AND STYLE.

HISTORY, WRITING OF. Napoleon's historical mindedness and his belief that history is factual science as well as propaganda, in addition to his preoccupation with military affairs and desire to patronize the arts, afforded historians opportunity to pursue their interests in archives, museums, and libraries. Under government patronage members of the Institut inventoried collections and edited important series of documents. Textbooks and narrative history were published frequently, sometimes commissioned by the emperor personally (notably for the lycées), and officially adopted so that a uniform version of history, especially modern French history, could be taught. Among those representative of the prodigious and disparate writers were the antiquarian creator of the Musée des Monuments français, M. A. Lenoir (1761–1839); Jean Lacretelle (1766–1855), author of the first narrative history of the Revolution; the advocate of history as science, P. N. Chantreau (1741–1808); the meticulous archival researcher, Pierre

Lemontey (1762–1826); and the prolific Antoine Serieys (1755–1819), whose historical catechisms were used for decades and make his influence inestimable.

Imperial historians advanced beyond the level of the previous century by being more critical of sources, writing more objectively, and documenting better. They wrote on many subjects, including the Bourbons and the French Revolution. Writers noted the causal relationship between the American and the French Revolutions; plot theorists identified responsible individuals, while others saw it stemming from the Renaissance or Reformation; spontaneity was considered too. This was a positive development in historiography.

J. K. Burton, *Napoleon and Clio* (Durham, N.C., 1979).

June K. Burton

Related entries: EDUCATION; LITERATURE; UNIVERSITY, IMPERIAL; WOMEN, EDUCATION OF.

HOFER, ANDREAS (1767–1810), Tyrolean patriot and guerrilla leader executed on order of Napoleon. A natural leader, Hofer at twenty-two was elected to represent his valley in the Tyrolean Assembly at Innsbruck. He made his living by innkeeping and trading in wine, grain, and horses, which gave him much contact with the people, who respected and liked him. In the wars of 1796 and 1805, Hofer led armed resistance against the French to protect both his beloved Tyrol and the house of Habsburg. In 1805 the Treaty of Pressburg transferred the Tyrol from Austria to Bavaria, an ally of Napoleon. The Tyrolean people, fervently loyal to the Habsburgs, were incensed, and the more so when Bavaria abrogated their autonomous constitution.

When Austria once again took up arms against Napoleon in 1809, the Tyrol, under the leadership of Hofer, rose to liberate itself from Bavaria and the French. Hofer won two battles against Bavarian and French troops (25 and 29 May and 13 August) and one against Saxon-Thuringian allies of France (4 and 5 August). The Tyrol celebrated its glorious liberation and elected Andreas Hofer regent. By the Treaty of Schönbrunn, however, defeated Austria again ceded the Tyrol to Bavaria. Encouraged by the false hope of assistance from Vienna, Hofer continued the war on his own. His forces were shattered, and he fled into hiding. According to contemporary sources, Hofer's whereabouts were betrayed by Joseph Raffl in return for the price the French had placed on Hofer's head. At Mantua Hofer was court-martialed, but the court was unable to reach a decision. The issue was resolved by Napoleon, who telegraphed the order to execute Hofer within twenty-four hours. Hofer was soon celebrated as a Tyrolean hero in songs, plays, and novels. In 1822 the Habsburg monarchy honored Hofer by interring his remains in the Hofkirche of Innsbruck.

A. Bethouart, *Andreas Hofer. Heros national historique du Tyrol* (Paris, 1977); K. Paulin, *Das Leben Andreas Hofers und der Tiroler Freiheitskampf 1809* (Innsbruck,

1970); L. Reiter, "Hätte Österreich den Sandwirt retten können?" in *Kulturnachrichten der Marktgemeinde Deutsch-Wagram*, vol. 17 (1976).

Siegfried Erich Kraus

Related entries: HORMAYR ZU HORTENBURG; JOHANN VON HABSBURG; SCHÖNBRUNN, TREATY OF; WAGRAM CAMPAIGN.

HOGENDORP, GIJSBERT KAREL VAN (1762–1834), Dutch politician who set the stage for the founding of the modern Kingdom of the Netherlands. He was the son of a member of the Rotterdam government, W. van Hogendorp, who was saved from bankruptcy in 1773 by the stadholder William V of Orange, who gave him a post in the Dutch East Indies. Moreover, the prince of Orange gave his wife an annual pension so that her two sons, Dirk and Gijsbert Karel, could attend the Prussian military academy in Berlin. In 1783–84 Gijsbert Karel was also able to visit America and England.

During the revolutionary movements of the 1780s, Hogendorp naturally took the Orangist side. In 1785, he became a courier between the English ambassador, Sir James Harris, the Orangists in the Hague, and the family of the stadholder, which had fled to Nijmegen. He helped organize the lower classes against the burgher free corps and in 1787 was dispatched to brief the duke of Brunswick, who commanded a Prussian army of intervention, about the country's internal situation. The Prussians restored the stadholder to power. Van Hogendorp hoped to become councillor pensionary of Holland but received the lesser post of pensionary of Rotterdam.

In 1795 the Batavian Revolution swept him from office. Thereafter, despite the reconciliation of the two branches of the aristocracy in 1801, he held no prominent office until 1813. (His brother, however, was briefly minister of war for King Louis Bonaparte.) With an eye to the future, he drafted a constitution for an independent Netherlands, in which, wrote the Dutch statesman-historian J. R. Thorbecke, "he had fixed his best eye on our old system, and the other one on England." After Napoleon lost the Battle of Leipzig in October 1813, Van Hogendorp boldly led a Dutch uprising and invited stadholder William VI to return to his country.

It looked as if the prince of Orange had become the client of Van Hogendorp. But William's personality and popular enthusiasm over his return allowed moderate groups to upset Van Hogendorp's plans. He did not get sovereignty divided between Orange and the States-General under his leadership; instead, the prince became King William I of the Netherlands. Van Hogendorp became vice-chairman of the Council of State, but after a year he resigned and spent his remaining years in the opposition.

H. van der Hoeven, *Gijsbert Karel van Hogendorp. Conservatief of Liberaal?* (Groningen, 1976); J. W. Schulte Nordholdt, "Gijsbert Karel van Hogendorp in Amerika, 1783–1784," in *Tijdschrift voor Geschiedenis* 4 (1975).

C.H.E. de Wit

Related entries: BONAPARTE, LOUIS; HOLLAND, KINGDOM OF; NETHERLANDS entries.

HOHENLINDEN, BATTLE OF (3 December 1800), victory of General Jean Moreau over the Austrian Archduke John. Although Napoleon had defeated the Austrians at Marengo, they refused to make peace until after Hohenlinden. The Treaty of Lunéville (9 February 1801) resulted. See ITALIAN CAMPAIGN, SECOND; LUNEVILLE; MARENGO; MOREAU.

HOHENLOHE-INGELFINGEN, FRIEDRICH LUDWIG VON, PRINCE (1746–1818), Prussian infantry general. At the age of fifteen, Hohenlohe was commissioned a captain in his father's Franconian infantry regiment. In 1766 he transferred as a major to the Prussian army and by 1786 was a brigadier general. In 1791 he was appointed governor of Breslau. During the War of the First Coalition, he distinguished himself as a corps commander at Weissenburg and Kaiserslautern (1794); he was promoted to general of the infantry in 1798.

The great test of Hohenlohe's career came on 14 October 1806, at Jena, where he commanded the Prussian-Saxon corps against the French main force under the direct command of Napoleon. He was inadequately informed about the enemy and ill advised by the confused Quartermaster General Rudolf von Massenbach. Control of his troops gradually slipped out of his hands, and despite his great personal bravery, he was decisively defeated. Meanwhile, the same day, the duke of Brunswick had been mortally wounded at Auerstädt. Hohenlohe assumed command over all Prussian troops, whom he intended to march to Stettin. Believing himself surrounded at Prenzlau, however, Hohenlohe surrendered to Joachim Murat on 28 October, and other Prussian field and fortress commanders followed his example.

He was never given another command. Until his death, Hohenlohe lived quietly on his estates in Silesia.

R. von Lilienstern, *Bericht eines Augenzeugen vom Feldzuge des Fürsten Hohenlohe* (1809); C. von Massenbach, *Historische Denkwürdigkeiten* (1809, reprint 1979); K. von Priesdorff, *Soldatisches Führertum*, vol. 2 (1937).

Joachim Niemeyer

Related entries: BRUNSWICK, C.; JENA-AUERSTÄDT-FRIEDLAND CAMPAIGN; PRUSSIA, KINGDOM OF.

HOLLAND, KINGDOM OF (1806–10), Napoleonic incarnation of the Dutch (Batavian) Republic. In May 1806 Emperor Napoleon removed his faithful servant Rutger Jan Schimmelpenninck (1761–1825) as councillor pensionary of the Batavian Commonwealth, which was restyled the Kingdom of Holland to be governed by his brother Louis. Napoleon expected his brother to govern as a loyal member of the Bonaparte dynasty and in the primary interest of France.

Louis, however, was determined to be his own master and tried to protect the Dutch against Napoleon's excessive demands. During his short reign, Louis introduced a new criminal code, stimulated agriculture, and established the Royal Academy of Sciences and the Royal Library. He was well liked by his subjects despite his extravagance, erratic and sometimes despotic behavior, and failure to restore economic prosperity. Out of concern for his subjects and a desire to be more independent, he resisted the emperor's demands for more troops and for stricter enforcement of the Continental System. Napoleon bombarded Louis with complaints and finally decided to remove his disobedient brother. The British invasion of Walcheren in 1809 probably hastened Napoleon's decision. In November Louis was called to Paris where he agreed to cede Dutch territory south of the Waal and Meuse rivers and to enforce the Continental System. He returned to Holland in April 1810 but found his powers usurped by French officials. He abdicated in July. Before he heard about the abdication, Napoleon had annexed Holland to his empire.

H. T. Colenbrander, *Schimmelpenninck en Koning Lodewijk* (Amsterdam, 1911); G. D. Homan, *Nederland in de Napoleonische tijd, 1795–1815* (Haarlem, 1978); S. Schama, *Patriots and Liberators. Revolution in the Netherlands, 1780–1813* (New York, 1977).

Gerlof D. Homan

Related entries: BONAPARTE, LOUIS; CONTINENTAL BLOCKADE; GOGEL; HOGENDORP; NETHERLANDS, RELIGION; NETHERLANDS, SOCIETY AND ECONOMY.

HOLLAND, KINGDOM OF: MINISTERS.

Finance	Gogel, Izaac	1806-9
	Appelius, J. H.	1809-10
War	Bonhomme, H. D.	1806
	Hogendorp, Dirk Van	1806-8
	Janssens, Jan W.	1808-9
	Cambier, Jacob-Jean	1809
	Krayenhoff, Cornelis	1809-10
Marine	Verhuel, Karel	1806-7
	Van der Heim, G. J.	1807-10
Interior	Gogel, Izaac (provisional)	1806
	Mollerus, Hendrik	1806-8
	Van Leyden van Westbarendrecht, F.	1808
	Twent Van Raaphorst, H.	1808-9
	Van der Capellan, Derk	1809-10
Foreign Affairs	Van der Goes, Maarten	1806-8
	Roëll, Willem F.	1808-10
	Mollerus, Hendrik (acting, in Roëll's absence, Nov.-Jan.)	1809-10
Justice and Police	Van Hof, J.D.R.	1806-7
	Cambier, J.-J. (interim)	1807-8
	Van Maanen, Cornelis	1808-9
	Hugenpoth, Alexander van	1809-10
Colonies	Van der Heim, G. J. (under Marine, 1807-10)	1806-7

Ecclesiastical Affairs (created in 1808)	Mollerus, Hendrik	1808-10
Watterstadt (created in 1809)	Twent Van Raaphorst, H.	1809-10
Minister Secretary of State (eliminated in 1808)	Roëll, Willem F.	1806-8

Related entry: HOLLAND, KINGDOM OF.

HOLY ROMAN EMPIRE. See EMPIRE, HOLY ROMAN.

HORMAYR ZU HORTENBURG, JOSEF, BARON (1781–1848), Austrian historian, patriot, and opponent of Napoleon. Hormayr began his career in the Austrian civil service in 1797 in Innsbruck and by 1809 had risen to be director of the archives and court counselor. In 1809 Archduke Johann charged him to plan and organize an uprising in the Tyrol against Bavaria (which held the state for Napoleon). Hormayer acquitted himself well, though he shamefully downplayed the accomplishments of Andreas Hofer. In 1813, he was prominent in the Alpine League, whose aim was the liberation from Napoleon's Empire of the Tyrol and adjacent states. Bavaria, however, had joined the Allies, and Clemens von Metternich had Hormayr arrested. It was a hard blow for a lifelong Austrian patriot, who lost no opportunity later to castigate Metternich. He was "rehabilitated" in 1816, nevertheless, and appointed court historian. In 1828 Hormayr moved to the Bavarian foreign service of King Ludwig I, and served as representative to Hanover and later Bremen. In 1846 he was recalled to Bavaria and until his death was the director of archives. During the Napoleonic period, Hormayr was important in promoting Austrian and Tyrolean patriotism. In the long run, his historical work was more important, including the editing of Austrian and Bavarian sources and the expansion and organization of Austrian and Bavarian archives. His journal, *Archiv*, allowed space for the national literatures of the Austrian monarchy and thus contributed to the growth of various nationalisms.

K. Adel, *Josef Freiherr von Hormayr und die vaterländische Romantik in Österreich* (1969); M. Bezdeka, *Biographie des Freiherrn von Hormayr* (1949); J. Hirn, "Zu Hormayrs Tätigkeit in Tirol 1809," *Historisches Jahrbuch der Görres-Gesellschaft* 30 (1909); A. Robert, *L'idée nationale autrichienne et les guerres de Napoléon. L'apostolat du baron de Hormayr et le salon de Caroline Pichler* (Paris, 1933).

Viktoria Strohbach

Related entries: HOFER; JOHANN VON HABSBURG; WAGRAM CAMPAIGN.

HOSPITALS. See MEDICINE.

HUNDRED DAYS, THE (20 March–22 June 1815), the period of Napoleon's attempted reestablishment of the Empire, dating from his entry into Paris to his second abdication; a term first used by G. J. Gaspard de Chabrol, prefect of the Seine, in welcoming Louis XVIII to Paris (8 July 1815). Learning of popular discontent with Bourbon rule and believing that the Congress of Vienna was on the verge of dissolution, Napoleon escaped from exile on Elba to restore the Empire. He entered Paris on the evening of 20 March and formed a government, naming to the principal posts L. N. Davout (war), Joseph Fouché (police), Lazare Carnot (interior), and Armand Caulaincourt (foreign affairs). Napoleon's choice of ministers made it obvious that his government was one of national defense. Although hoping for peace, the emperor was compelled to prepare for war.

The Allies disdained his pacifist statements and launched a decree of outlawry (13 March) against him. Austria, Prussia, Russia, and Great Britain renewed (28 March) the Treaty of Chaumont of the previous year. Napoleon still believed that either Austria or Russia might be detached from their allies but was speedily disillusioned. Although tempted by the possibility of a regency for Napoleon's son (the Austrian emperor's grandson), the Austrians remained loyal to the coalition. The Russians remained equally committed to the alliance. Not even the revelation of Bourbon duplicity in allying France with Great Britain and Austria (4 January 1815) over the Polish-Saxon question could shake the determination of Czar Alexander. War was Napoleon's only chance.

Successful warfare required both a strong army and political unity. In a brilliant display of energy, Napoleon revitalized the army that a year of Bourbon neglect had reduced to 50,000. Men on half-pay were recalled, and the conscription class of 1815, the *Marie-Louise* of 1814, was called up. By May Napoleon had an army of 300,000, which appeared to be more solid than any other since the campaign of 1809, although most of Napoleon's marshals had not returned. Among those absent was Alexandre Berthier, the emperor's long-time chief of staff, who would be sorely missed. Poor staff work surely contributed to the French defeat in the Waterloo campaign. Yet the emperor remained confident that a rapid movement into the Low Countries to shatter the armies of the Duke of Wellington and Prince G. L. Blücher von Wahlstatt—preferably separately—would produce victory.

Adequate military mobilization was achieved, but political unity was not. On his return to Paris, the emperor had been surprised and delighted at the violence of hostility toward the Bourbons and of anticlericalism (similarly expressing repugnance for the Old Regime). Napoleon hoped this enthusiasm would facilitate establishment of the authoritarian government of the Empire, unchanged. To his dismay, however, the emperor discovered that many of his partisans had become liberal constitutionalists, insisting that only a parliamentary government could rally a divided nation to the imperial cause.

In the interest of national unity, Napoleon agreed, granting liberty of the press (25 March) and entrusting to the liberal Benjamin Constant the task of drafting a constitution, called the Acte Additionnel aux Constitutions de l'Empire, which established on 23 April a parliamentary regime. The Acte Additionnel was approved by a vote of 1,532,450 to 4,800, but Napoleon's misgivings were confirmed by the large number of abstentions. Republicans were angered by the limited franchise and inclusion of a house of peers, liberals by the dictatorial powers remaining to the emperor, and the Bonapartists by the whole thing.

The defeat of the emperor at Waterloo on 18 June doomed the Empire. When Napoleon returned to Paris on 21 June, he was faced by an Assembly determined not to be dictated to and adroitly manipulated by Fouché and his agents. Voices were raised in support of the emperor, but after two days of debate, the Assembly demanded Napoleon's abdication, and got it (22 June). Fouché and Lafayette had convinced the assembly that it was in the interest of France. An Executive Commission sought to negotiate with the Allies, but to no avail. Napoleon, compelled to flee on 29 June to avoid capture, sought refuge in England but was sent into exile at St. Helena. Paris capitulated on 3 July, and on 8 July Louis XVIII returned, inaugurating the Second Restoration.

F. Bluche, *Le plébiscite des Cent-Jours* (Geneva, 1974); R. Cubberly, *The Role of Fouché during the Hundred Days* (Madison, 1969); R. Grand, *La Chouannerie de 1815* (Paris, 1966); E. Saunders, *The Hundred Days* (London, 1964).

Ray E. Cubberly

Related entries: CONSTITUTIONS; ELBA; FOUCHE; LAFAYETTE; LOUIS XVIII; TALLEYRAND-PERIGORD; VIENNA, CONGRESS OF; WATERLOO CAMPAIGN.

HUNGARY. During the years of peace between 1802 and 1805, Napoleon sent several observers to Hungary. Gérard Lacuée (1774–1805), who visited Hungary in the spring of 1802, reported that the Hungarian nobility was dissatisfied with Habsburg rule and might even be ready for an armed uprising. He recommended encouraging feudal resistance to the Habsburg government in Vienna and supporting "noble independence and peasant enslavement." Another observer, Adrien Lezay-Marnesia (1769–1814), advocated, after a brief visit to Hungary later in 1802, not the liquidation of the Habsburg Empire but gaining the support of the Magyar nobility by encouraging the transfer of the capital to Budapest (along with the emperor). He judged the Hungarian nobility, the only politically relevant force, to be loyal supporters of the dynasty but resentful of the subordinate position of the country, which was true. But events would show that the nobles trusted the Habsburgs more than the French.

The French observers did not realize that there was an antifeudal variant in Hungarian politics despite the elimination of the Jacobins of 1795. A small number of noble reformers and non-noble intellectuals survived in the underground and would have welcomed French (Napoleonic) assistance to their program of a bourgeois transformation of Hungary.

In 1805, when Napoleon's troops first entered Hungarian territory, friendly overtures were made by the Hungarian general Count Pálfy, to which the French replied by offering neutrality, but the only result was that Pálfy was dismissed by his emperor. On the advice of Charles-Maurice de Talleyrand (in his famous Strasbourg project), Napoleon had opted for the preservation of the Habsburg empire. The years 1806–9 witnessed a certain political polarization in Hungary. Napoleon's policies in the Duchy of Warsaw seemed to suggest that if Napoleon overthrew the Habsburgs, it would mean the end of noble privilege in Hungary.

In 1809, the overwhelming majority of the nobles rallied to the Habsburgs. The antifeudal reformers, in turn, hoped for the fall of the dynasty. For example, Gergely Berzeviczy (1763–1845), an enlightened nobleman, reformer, and economist, addressed a memorandum in French to Napoleon recommending the emancipation of serfs and the bourgeois transformation of Hungary. On 15 May 1809, after the capture of Vienna, Napoleon issued a manifesto to the Hungarians, calling on them to rise and establish their independence. No practical results were achieved, partly because Napoleon tried to appeal to the feudal nobles, and the general tone was not much changed by the minor corrections inserted into the Hungarian version, most likely by the poet János Batsányi (1763–1845) with the aid of his friend, Hugues-Bernard Maret (the later duc de Bassano), which hinted at the convocation of the Diet and possible constitutional reforms.

A French army marched into Hungary as far as Györ (Raab) where the assembled Hungarian noble insurrection (actually this was the last occasion when this medieval levy was mobilized) suffered ignominious defeat. In Napoleon's name, General Louis Narbonne made attempts to mobilize the dissatisfied elements in Hungary, but in vain. Thus Napoleon once again decided to spare the Habsburg monarchy as a future ally against Russia, and his troops left the country. Only Batsányi returned with Napoleon to Paris and served him as a publicist until 1814, when he was arrested by the Austrians. He was kept interned in Linz to the end of his life.

E. H. Balázs, ''Notes sur l'histoire du bonapartisme en Hongrie,'' *Nouvelles études hongroises* (1969–70); K. Kecskeméty, *Témoignages français sur la Hongrie à l'époque de Napoléon 1802–1809* (Brussels, 1960); D. Kosáry, *Napoléon et la Hongrie* (Budapest, 1979).

Domokos Kosáry

Related entries: AUSTERLITZ CAMPAIGN; AUSTRIA; FRANZ II; WAGRAM CAMPAIGN.

I

IDEOLOGUES, a term coined by Napoleon in 1800 to discredit the secular republican intellectuals who turned against his regime, some of whom—Emmanuel Sieyès, C. F. de Volney, and Georges Cabanis—had earlier supported Napoleon's coup assuming that he would preserve basic liberties. *Idéologue* derived from *idéologie*, a word coined by A.L.C. Destutt de Tracy in 1796 to denote a sensationalist "science of ideas" having broad application to the social sciences. Napoleon disparaged *idéologues* as metaphysicians or the "worst revolutionaries"; spiritualists and Christians like René de Chateaubriand attacked their materialism. An *idéologue* was one who analyzed ideas with a rational or philosophical method (Destutt de Tracy), a physiological one (Cabanis), or a geographical-anthropological one (Volney). But *idéologues* also frequented the salons of Mme. Helvétius and Mme. Condorcet, collaborated with the group's journal, the *Décade philosophique*, and were members of the National Institute's Class of Moral and Political Sciences (which Napoleon abolished in 1803). Joseph Garat, Pierre Daunou, Emmanuel Sieyès, Pierre-Louis Ginguené, Marie-Joseph Degérando, J. B. Say, and Victor Jacquemont were the other leading *idéologues*. Some of their names were compromised in the Moreau and Malet conspiracies, but lack of incriminating evidence protected them. They were not Revolutionaries but muffled, legal opponents who sought to temper the inflammatory liberties of 1789 through industrial labor, social hierarchy, and the leadership by the enlightened. They accepted appointments from Napoleon while awaiting the Empire's collapse. Their contributions to psychology, anthropology, medicine, education, liberal economics, and political science formed an essential link between the Enlightenment and positivism.

G. Gusdorf, *La conscience révolutionnaire, Les idéologues* (Paris, 1978); T. Kaiser, "Politics and Political Economy in the Thought of the Ideologues," *History of Political Economy* 12 (1980); E. Kennedy, *A Philosophe. . .Destutt de Tracy and the Origins of "Ideology"* (Philadelphia, 1978); S. Moravia, *Il pensiero degli Idéologues* (Florence, 1974), and *Il tramonto dell' illuminismo* (Bari, 1968); M. Staum, *Cabanis* (Princeton, 1980).

Emmet Kennedy

Related entries: CABANIS; DESTUTT DE TRACY; INSTITUT NATIONAL DES SCIENCES ET DES ARTS; LEGISLATORS; SIEYES; VOLNEY.

ILLYRIAN PROVINCES, a state, technically part of France, created by Napoleon on part of the territory of present-day Yugoslavia. In 1797, the Venetian Republic and its possessions on the northeastern Adriatic were ceded to Austria by the Treaty of Campo Formio. After Austerlitz (1805), Venetian lands, together with Austrian Istria and Dalmatia, were transferred by the Treaty of Pressburg to France. During 1806–9, they were nominally part of the Napoleonic Kingdom of Italy; Ragusa was added in 1808. Actual governance was by General (later Marshal) A.-F.-L. Marmont, who placed civil administration under *provédideur* Vincenzo Dandolo.

The administrative forms of Venetia and Austria, as well as their taxes, remained in force. Education and communication were improved. The provisions of the Civil Code (Code Napoléon) on family law, succession, and inheritance were introduced. The chief reform projects concerned the church and peasant land ownership. The number of bishoprics was reduced, convents were suppressed, church property confiscated, and the ecclesiastical tithe abolished. The Grimani law (1756), under which all peasant land was owned by the state, was repealed, and legal possession was transferred to the tenants; the state tithe became a land tax. To prevent exploitation of peasants by speculators, the law made alienation of peasant ownership almost impossible.

In 1809, the Illyrian Provinces were created from Istria (with Trieste and Fiume), Dalmatia, and parts of Carniola, Carinthia, and Croatia—all ceded or receded by Austria by the Treaty of Schönbrunn. (Italy kept Venetia.) The military District of Croatia was accorded a special regime, which preserved its traditional social order.

Laibach (Ljubljana) became the capital of Illyria, which was divided into ten intendancies (in 1811 were reduced to six). Dandolo withdrew in 1809; Marmont became the first governor and implemented the provisional organization of 25 December 1809, which centralized the government and effected uniformity in administrative and legislative practice. (He was succeeded by General Henri Bertrand in 1811 and Andoche Junot in 1813.) On 1 January 1812, the Civil Code was adopted in its entirety. By decree of 4 July 1810, the Croatian language was introduced in primary education. French taxes were imposed in 1810–13, and conscription was introduced in 1810. Forced labor was used to carry out a program of public works geared to strategic requirements.

On 15 April 1811, the feudal system was abolished, which ingratiated the regime to the peasants, but it turned the nobles to Austria. Peasant discontent soon emerged, however, over the abolition of customary rights and in the middle class because of the damage to export and transit trade (especially of Trieste) because of wars and the Continental System. Although the parish clergy, mostly Josephists, submitted to secular authority and remained neutral, the Catholic orders, especially the Franciscans, opposed French rule ferociously. The regime's major support therefore was found among radical francophile intellectuals.

By creating the first modern state and by establishing the first institution of higher learning on the territory of the south Slavs, the French stimulated national awareness. Charles Nodier, librarian in Ljubljana in 1813, contributed by his research to the cultural awakening of the provinces, and the Slovene poet B. Vodnik celebrated the regeneration of Illyria. The French interlude left a generally favorable imprint on local popular tradition. The Congress of Vienna returned the Illyrian Provinces to Austria, and between 1816 and 1849 they formed the Kingdom of Illyria under the Habsburg crown. Napoleon's Illyrian experiment laid the foundations of the literary and political movement of Illyrism, which nurtured resistance to the Habsburgs and contributed to the cultivation of Yugoslav national sentiment.

J. Kastelic et al., *Napoleonove Ilirske Province, 1809–1814* (Les Provinces Illyriennes de Napoleon) (Ljubljana, 1964); C. Nodier, *Souvenirs de la révolution et de l'Empire*, new ed. (Paris, 1872); P. Pisani, *La Dalmatie de 1797 à 1815* (Paris, 1893); M. Pivec-Stellé, *La vie économique des Provinces Illyriennes, 1809–1813* (Paris, 1930).

Paschalis M. Kitromilides

Related entries: AUSTERLITZ CAMPAIGN; BERTRAND; ITALY, KINGDOM OF; JUNOT, J.-A.; MARMONT, MARSHAL; PRESSBURG, TREATY OF; SCHÖNBRUNN, TREATY OF; WAGRAM CAMPAIGN.

IMPERIAL CATECHISM. See CATECHISM, IMPERIAL.

INDUSTRY. See ECONOMY, FRENCH.

"INFERNAL MACHINE" PLOT. See FOUCHE; NAPOLEON I; POLICE, MINISTRY OF GENERAL.

INSTITUT D'EGYPTE. See EGYPTIAN CAMPAIGN.

INSTITUT NATIONAL DES SCIENCES ET DES ARTS, the unified Revolutionary version of the *ancien régime* academies (abolished in 1793), which represented the cultural elite of France. Established by the Convention in October 1795, the Institute included the Class of Physical and Mathematical Sciences, the entirely new Class of Moral and Political Sciences, and the successor to the Académie française and to the two artistic academies, the Class of Literature and Fine Arts.

Bonaparte's ambivalent association with the Institute began with his election, largely as the hero of the Italian campaign, to a vacancy in the Mechanical Arts section of the First Class in December 1797. His early enthusiasm was evident in frequent appearances at Class and Institute sessions and in his creation in Cairo in 1798 of the Institute of Egypt. Institute members, including future opponents in the Second Class, played key roles in the Brumaire coup, and Bonaparte rewarded them with at least honorific, and sometimes genuinely powerful, positions in the political elite of the Consulate.

The first consul continued to favor the First Class, as, for example, in the endowment of an Institute prize in 1802 for research on electricity and galvanism.

He grew resentful, however, of the vocal minority in the Second Class, who were still anticlericals at the time of the Concordat and who, outside the Institute, criticized the special courts of 1801 and wished to preserve the central schools. Bonaparte's government abolished the Class of Moral and Political Sciences in January 1803 in part to rob these *idéologues* of a forum. Other motivations included administrative rationalization and the desire to appease partially proponents of a restored Académie française. Probably because the *idéologues* could not dominate the Institute, the government did not purge them from its ranks but merely removed potentially dangerous subject areas. The reform redistributed Second Class members to a new Second Class of French Language and Literature and a new, politically harmless, Third Class of History and Ancient Literature.

The government of the Empire retained interest in the Institute. It solicited reports on progress in the domain of each class since 1789 (completed in 1808). In 1811 the Ministry of the Interior sponsored the award of decennial prizes by Institute juries for outstanding works of the decade after Brumaire but cancelled the awards to show disapproval of some selections. Nevertheless, Napoleon kept the Institute alive, and it persists today.

L. Aucoc, *L'Institut: Lois, statuts, règlements* (Paris, 1889); R. Hahn, *The Anatomy of a Scientific Institution* (Berkeley, 1971); *Institut de France. Célébration du Deuxième Centenaire de la Naissance de Napoléon* (Paris, 1969); J. Simon, *Une Académie sous le Directoire* (Paris, 1885); M. S. Staum, "The Class of Moral and Political Sciences, 1795–1803," *FHS* 11 (1980).

Martin Staum

Related entries: ACADEMIE FRANCAISE; CHATEAUBRIAND; CONSTANT DE REBECQUE; DESTUTT DE TRACY; IDEOLOGUES; STAEL-HOLSTEIN; VOLNEY.

IRELAND. In the years of protracted struggle with Great Britain, Ireland was a missed strategic opportunity that France might have exploited. Napoleon told Las Cases at St. Helena, "If, instead of the expedition to Egypt, I had made that of Ireland. . . what would England have been today? and the continent? and the political world?" Bonaparte, however, did not seize the opportunity in 1798 when he might have. Prior to the Egyptian campaign, while he commanded the land-bound Army of England, he told Wolfe Tone and Edward Lewines, two emissaries from the separatist United Irish movement, "What more do you desire of the Irish? You see their movements already operate a powerful diversion."

The Society of United Irishmen by the late 1790s was a secret revolutionary army numbering perhaps 200,000 men and awaiting a French landing to free Ireland from British rule. It was founded in 1791 at Belfast and Dublin as a radical reform organization that sought to rise above Ireland's age-old religious divisions and join liberal members of the Anglo-Irish ruling class, republican dissenters and Presbyterians from Ulster, and the vast majority of Irish Catholics in a program for Catholic emancipation and reform of the Irish Parliament. The reform society was disbanded by the British when war began in 1793, went underground, and began preparing for an uprising. Best organized in heavily Presbyterian Ulster (Belfast), the United Irishmen had considerable success in recruiting new members in Leinster (Dublin) and, to a lesser degree, in Munster (Cork) and in the remote western province, Connaught (Galway to Sligo). The government counteracted the movement by infiltrating it with informers, arresting leaders, disarming whole districts of Ireland by force, and fanning into flame the embers of traditional Protestant-Catholic hatreds.

The French Directory was aware of Britain's weakness in Ireland and sought several times to take advantage of it by landing troops. It authorized General Lazare Hoche's Bantry Bay attempt, an expedition of 14,500 men on 40 ships that threatened the southwest Irish coast for three weeks in December 1796 and January 1797. Command blunders, bad weather, worse luck, and poor seamanship prevented success. In 1797 the Directory planned to embark 15,000 men aboard Dutch vessels for another attempt. The Dutch fleet was defeated by the British (Admiral Adam Duncan) in October, however, and the expedition foundered. In 1798 there was open rebellion in Ireland, mostly in the Catholic Wexford district, with some action in the Dublin and Belfast areas. France prepared five separate expeditions to assist, of which only one actually landed. General Jean Humbert's thousand-man army acquitted itself quite well in a two-week campaign in western Ireland (August–September 1798) but succumbed to a vastly superior force commanded by Lord Lieutenant Charles Cornwallis. The tiny and tardy French force had arrived when Britain's stern repression of the 1798 Irish rebellion was all but complete.

For Ireland the years 1800 through 1815 were a time of political impotence, bitter religious rivalries, and increasing social distress. The Irish Parliament was eliminated by the Act of Union in 1801. The ruling class of a half-million Anglo-Irish had traded legislative independence for greater security and 100 seats in the British Parliament. Catholic emancipation, which was to have accompanied union, was not enacted. The million dissenters or Presbyterians of Ulster welcomed closer ties with Britain, joined the antipapist Orange order in great numbers, and lost their attachment to separatist and republican ideas because they feared their numerous Catholic neighbors. Four and a half million Irish Catholic peasants sank lower in poverty on their tiny, potato-lot farms. A Malthusian time bomb was ticking as population increased; the explosion came with the great potato famine of 1846. The only bright spot for Ireland's majority was Catholic emancipation, which was won in the 1820s through Daniel O'Connell's Catholic Association Movement.

Napoleon promised to send aid to Ireland while the Army of England was in preparation at Boulogne in 1803–04. On the strength of this promise, Robert Emmet staged his abortive uprising in Dublin and became an Irish martyr. His brother, Thomas Addis Emmet, sent Napoleon yet another proposal for invasion in 1804 but soon despaired at the lack of French interest and left France to settle permanently in America. French archives contain about a dozen Irish invasion projects dated between 1799 and 1810. The last one, written by Humbert, the

1798 veteran, called for a force far greater than France could have sent against Ireland.

Napoleon's failure to attack Britain on its vulnerable western flank in Ireland has given historians and Irish patriots room for much hypothesizing. The reality is that England would never have permitted Napoleon to separate Ireland from it permanently. As Sir Edward Petrie has written, "The government of George III could no more have allowed Ireland to become the satellite of a Continental Power than those of Elizabeth I and William III had been able to do." Perhaps Napoleon did not exploit the Irish opportunity because he knew that too.

M. Elliot, *Partners in Revolution: The United Irishmen and France* (New Haven, 1982); E. Guillon, *La France et l'Irlande sous le Directoire* (Paris, 1888); R. Hayes, *The Last Invasion of Ireland* (Dublin, 1937); R. B. McDowell, *Ireland in the Age of Imperialism and Revolution* (Oxford, 1979); E. H. Stuart-Jones, *The Invasion that Failed: The French Expedition to Ireland 1796* (Oxford, 1950).

W. Ben Kennedy

Related entries: DIRECTORY; ENGLAND, ATTEMPTED CONQUEST OF; GREAT BRITAIN; PITT, W.

ISABEY, JEAN-BAPTISTE (1767–1855). The miniaturist Isabey, whose career began as Marie-Antoinette's "Little Court Painter," managed to remain in favor with every regime, culminating with Napoleon III's promoting him to the rank of commander of the Legion of Honor the year before his death. Born at Nancy in Franche-Comté, Isabey was the seventh but only second surviving child of a grocer. Much is made of the fact that he was born with a birthmark resembling a fleur-de-lys, thus marking him for royal service. He studied with J.B.C. Claudot and was befriended by the miniaturist François Dumont. During his first years in Paris, he painted buttons and snuffboxes until the father of a fellow art student introduced him to the marquis de Serent, who hired him to paint likenesses of the young dukes of Angoulême and de Berri on the lid of a snuffbox that Marie Antoinette wanted secretly painted as a gift for their mother. Subsequently he met the queen, who invited him to the Trianon. With Isabey's success now assured, Jacques-Louis David, whose works were of colossal size, accepted him into his studio, and his new apprentice was able to pay the master's fees from Marie Antoinette's commissions. Prior to the Revolution, Isabey painted Mme. de Staël and the painter Adèle Hall, daughter of then famous Adolphe Hall, the "Van Dyck of Miniature."

Being David's pupil helped to save Isabey from the guillotine, and he joined the Jacobin club to please him. Isabey's laundress introduced him to a publisher who commissioned him to illustrate biographies of 200 members of the Convention who afterward became his personal clients. After his marriage to Jeanne Laurice de Saliennes, he experimented with a new medium for miniature—*aquarelle*—in his own studio on rue Boissy d'Anglas near Place de la Révolution. Most miniaturists painted with *gouache* on ivory, leaving the flesh tints transparent, but this technique was too slow for the pace of the Revolutionary era.

By painting with watercolor on paper, Isabey could make faithful portraits rapidly enough to sell them at affordable prices.

The Directory was the happiest period of Isabey's life. He attended dinner parties at Paul Barras' and Louis Gohier's and attended get-togethers at Mme. Tallien's, Mme. de Staël's, and E. Louise Vigée-Lebrun's. Mme. Campan hired him to be drawing master at her Saint-Germain pension; so he met Hortense de Beauharnais and, through her, Eugène and Josephine.

After Josephine became Mme. Bonaparte, Isabey renovated Malmaison. He also supervised the coronation, designing Josephine's white dress with the lace *chéresque* and velvet train semé with golden bees. As Napoleon's painter of ceremonies, Isabey did seven sepia drawings of the event. For the emperor's second marriage, Isabey painted a diamond set medallion and a ring as gifts for the bride and accompanied Napoleon to Compiègne to record his first meeting with his proxy bride. Napoleon's last favor to Isabey was making him decorator of the Opéra.

Charles-Maurice de Talleyrand took Isabey, who had spent some time with the Metternichs on his previous trip to Vienna in 1811, along to the Congress of Vienna. The Bourbons, who had been his first patrons, patronized Isabey, but being bored by the dullness of their court, he associated with the frivolous set led by the duchess de Berri. After the police ransacked his studio searching for caricatures, he toured London and Italy, filling sketchbooks with buildings and ruins, often including himself in his drawings. Both Charles X and Louis-Philippe appointed him *peintre de cabinet particulier*, and his studio became as crowded again as it had been under the Directory with clients, writers, artists, musicians, and actresses.

The painter who had perfected the *aquarelle* technique for miniatures became one of the first French painters to experiment with lithography, a process invented by the German Alois Senefelder and introduced into France only in 1814. When Isabey was seventy-two years old, Daguerre perfected the discovery that sounded the death knell for miniature art. Isabey retired during the his last years, allowing himself time to enjoy the retrospective of a fascinating long life in which he made and witnessed the history of kings while art and culture were being irreversibly changed by the advancement of scientific technology.

M. de Basley-Callimaki, *J. B. Isabey, sa vie, son temps. . .Suivi du catalogue de l'oeuvre gravée par et après Isabey* (1909); H. Bouchot, *La miniature française, 1750–1825* (Paris, 1907); G. Hediard, *Les maîtres de la lithographie—Isabey* (Châteaudun, 1896); J.-B. Isabey, *Voyage en Italie. . .en 1822. . .trente dessins* (Paris, 1823); F. Masson, *Le livre du sacre de l'Empereur Napoléon* (Paris, 1908); M. W. Osmond, *Jean Baptiste Isabey, The Fortunate Painter, 1767–1855* (London, 1947); E. Taigny, *J.-B. Isabey, sa vie et ses oeuvres* (Paris, 1859), and *Mélanges, études littéraires et artistiques* (Paris, 1869).

June K. Burton

Related entries: ART; BEAUHARNAIS, E.; BEAUHARNAIS, H.; CAMPAN; DAVID; JOSEPHINE; SCULPTURE; STAEL-HOLSTEIN; TALLIEN; VIGEE-LEBRUN.

ISTRIE, DUC D'. See BESSIERES.

ITALIAN CAMPAIGN, FIRST (1796–97) in which Bonaparte first gained international fame. In March 1796, Napoleon Bonaparte, age twenty-six, took command of the Army of Italy. His orders were to attack Austrian and Piedmontese troops in Italy in order to prevent the Habsburgs from reinforcing their forces in Germany. The main French blow was to fall in southern Germany, with forces in Italy playing a supporting role. The French offensive in Germany was a failure, and the Austrians drove the republican forces back to the Rhine. While in Italy, Napoleon scored a series of outstanding victories.

With his small, ill-equipped army, Napoleon decided to wage a campaign of rapid movement coupled with sharp blows against isolated elements of the numerically superior enemy armies under Johann von Beaulieu. He struck alternately against the Austrians and Piedmontese (13–18 April 1796), separating the armies in the battles of Montenotte, Millesimo, Dego, and Ceva. He then turned his full force on the Piedmontese under General Michael von Colli, crushing them at Mondovi, and forcing King Victor Amadeus to sign an armistice and leave the war. He then turned on the Austrians again, outflanking them at Piacenza, defeating them at Lodi, pushing into the Po Valley, and seizing Milan. After detaching small forces to drive Tuscany and the Papal States out of the war, Napoleon moved east, where he surrounded a large Austrian force in Mantua.

The Austrians then sent a series of relief expeditions toward Mantua. Fortunately for the French, they were uncoordinated, and Napoleon was able to concentrate his forces and defeat them in detail. In August 1796, he demolished Dagobert von Wurmser's separated forces at Lonato and Castiglione, in September at Bassano and Vicenza, and then drove the remnants into Mantua, with their commander, Field Marshal Wurmser. In November Napoleon was defeated by Joseph Alvinczy at Caldiero but recovered to down the Austrians at Arcola (November 1796) and at Rivoli (January 1797). The Mantua garrison was forced to surrender, and Napoleon mounted an offensive on Vienna over the Alps. This effort, coupled with a successful French advance in Germany, compelled Austria (the Archduke Karl) to ask for an armistice (Leoben, 6 April 1797).

Napoleon dominated the armistice negotiations at Leoben and the subsequent peace talks at Campo Formio. The peace treaty in fact embodied more of Napoleon's intentions than it did those of the Directory. Although the peace was in fact little more than an armed truce, it, like the campaigns leading to it, greatly enhanced Napoleon's prestige. He became the Republic's most successful soldier-diplomat, thus setting the stage for his future adventures and ambitions.

D. Chandler, *The Campaigns of Napoleon* (New York, 1966); J. Colin, *Études sur la campagne de 1796–97 en Italie* (Paris, 1900); T. A. Dodge, *Napoleon*, 4 vols. (Boston, 1904); G. Fabry, *Histoire de l'armée d'Italie 1796–1797*, 3 vols. (Paris, 1900–01); W. Jackson, *Attack in the West, Napoleon's First Campaign Re-read Today* (London, 1953);

Ministère de la guerre État-major de l'armée: Archives historiques. Armée d'Italie campagnes de l'an IV et de l'an V: Mémoires historiques, no. 417.

Steven T. Ross

Related entries: ALVINCZI; ARCOLA, BATTLE OF; CAMPO FORMIO, TREATY OF; KARL VON HABSBURG, ARCHDUKE; WURMSER.

ITALIAN CAMPAIGN, SECOND (1800), not decisive militarily but vital to Napoleon's political survival. After the coup of November 1799 (Brumaire), Napoleon became the leading figure in the new government, the Consulate. To keep his position safe from a possible counter-coup and in order to retain the support of the war-weary French public, he had to conclude the War of the Second Coalition quickly and victoriously.

During the waning days of the Directory, French arms had already scored a number of important triumphs. Anglo-Russian forces had capitulated in Holland, and the French had driven Russian and Austrian forces out of Switzerland. Russia had quit the coalition, leaving only Austria with forces actively engaged against France. Napoleon's problem therefore was to defeat the Austrians while preventing any other general from gaining popular acclaim for the victory. Consequently he decided to launch the campaign of 1800 in Italy and assign French forces in Germany a subordinate role.

Napoleon concentrated a 60,000-man Army of Reserve at Dijon and ordered André Masséna to command the garrison at Genoa. Masséna was to attract the bulk of the Austrian forces in Italy to Liguria while Napoleon struck across the Alps into Lombardy, where he had operated so successfully four years earlier.

The Reserve Army began to move in April, and by 1 June Napoleon was once again in Milan. He ordered several divisions to cut the Austrian escape routes to the Tyrol and led the rest of his army into Piedmont to defeat the scattered Austrian forces. The Austrians, however, under General Michael Melas, had taken Genoa and gathered a 34,000-man force to face Napoleon. Failing to realize that the Austrians were preparing to fight, not flee, Napoleon continued to detach units to block potential escape routes. It was thus a much-reduced French army that encountered the Austrian army at Marengo on 14 June 1800.

In the ensuing battle, Bonaparte was nearly defeated. Fortunately for him, Louis -C.-A. Desaix's division, one he had detached from the main body, returned to the battlefield when its commander heard the sounds of battle, and in time to turn the tide of combat. The Austrians requested a truce, but peace talks failed and fighting resumed in Germany. The war went on until December 1800, when French forces under Jean Moreau won a decisive battle at Hohenlinden. Austria made peace in 1801.

Marengo did not end the war. It was, in fact, a near defeat for Napoleon; however, in his bulletin after the battle, Napoleon pictured it as a major victory, thereby bolstering his popularity at home.

D. Chandler, *The Campaigns of Napoleon* (New York, 1966); Captain de Cugnac, *Campagne de l'armée de Reserve en 1800* (Paris, 1901); T. A. Dodge, *Napoleon*, 4 vols. (New York, 1904).

Steven T. Ross

Related entries: DESAIX; LANNES; MELAS; MURAT, J.

ITALY, KINGDOM OF, originally the Cisalpine Republic, created (1796–97) during Bonaparte's first Italian campaign; renamed Republic of Italy (1801), with Bonaparte as president; converted to kingdom (1805). Napoleon, already emperor of the French, assumed the crown. He appointed as his viceroy Eugène de Beauharnais, Josephine's son, who married Princess Augusta of Bavaria (1806). Eugène ruled well and remained loyal to Napoleon to the end despite the emperor's divorce from his mother (1809).

The kingdom comprised the duchies of Milan and Modena, part of Piedmont, Ferrara, Bologna, Mantua, and the Romagna. In 1806, Venetia was added; in 1807, the papal states of Urbino, Macerata, Ancona, and Camerino; and in 1809, the southern Tyrol. The constitution was that of the Republic, with some modifications. It provided for a legislature elected, indirectly, by universal manhood suffrage. After 1805, however, an appointive senate was created to assume the legislative function. The constitution had a bill of rights and abolished feudalism. The law was the Code Napoléon, translated into Tuscan Italian. The kingdom was divided for administration into twenty-four departments under *prefetti* appointed by the viceroy. The courts were restructured on the French model.

At Napoleon's order, careers were made open to talent, so that Eugène employed in high office nobles of the Old Regime, new nobles created by Napoleon, and commoners (if overwhelmingly of the upper middle class). Eugène used the army as an instrument of social change, especially military schools. They were open to suitably educated young men of all the provinces who were forced to live, study, work, and march together—and to employ the Tuscan dialect of Italian, which was native to none of them. This social engineering did not prevent Eugène from developing an effective army. The Royal Guard had a fierce esprit de corps. Similarly the College of Auditors of the Council of State trained young men for civil office. Aristocrats more often went into judicial service and middle-class young men into the administration. Overall a new leadership element—civilian and military—was formed.

Eugène assembled an all-Italian ministry of exceptional talent, assisted heavily by Melzi d'Eril, former vice-president of the Italian Republic. Giuseppe Prina, minister of finance, performed the miracle of keeping the budget in balance until 1813. His taxes, moreover, were much lower than those in France. Giovanni Paradisi was the minister of waterways and roads. He not only improved communications within the kingdom but cooperated with French authorities on the completion of new roads over the Alps and to Trieste. He also refurbished the La Scala Opera in Milan and built arches and monuments that remain today. The minister of education, Giovanni Scopoli, brought all schools—from primary to the universities at Bologna, Pavia, and Padua—under central control. He provided salaries for scholars, evenhandedly making grants (for example, to the poet Vicenzo Monti and the scientist Alessandro Volta). He established a Royal Academy, a conservatory of music, and an academy of fine arts, which had among its members Antonio Canova, Europe's greatest sculptor. Freedom was missing from intellectual life, but there was little opposition to Eugène's government, even after the loss of 20,000 Italians in Russia in 1812.

Italy's economy suffered somewhat in the beginning because French tariffs made unprofitable the export of finished cloth. However, they made very profitable the exportation of raw silk and food, and Italians adjusted quickly. They converted to the manufacture of silks, which the French could not produce, and moved into wool and cotton cloth. At the same time Italians vastly expanded production of grain, fruit, and meat and even began growing cotton. This sort of enterprise, together with their quick mastery of smuggling to circumvent the Continental System, resulted in general prosperity.

The all-around solid character of Eugène's government, institutions, and economy meant that the viceroy had unusually broad support among his people. This accounts for the fact that Eugène was still fighting with his Italian army when he heard of Napoleon's abdication in 1814. If there had been an ounce of treason in Eugène's soul, he might well have bargained with the Allies and kept his kingdom, but he did not.

E. de Beauharnais, *Correspondance*, 10 vols., ed. A. du Casse (Paris, 1858–60); F. de Bernardy, *Eugène de Beauharnais 1781–1824* (Paris, 1973); O. Connelly, *Napoleon's Satellite Kingdoms* (New York, 1965); *L'Italie jacobine et napoléonienne*, special issue of *AHRF* 230 (1977); F. Melzi d'Eril, *I carteggi di Francesco Melzi d'Eril, Duca di Lodi*, ed. C. Zaghi, 6 vols. (Milan, 1958–1965); G. Natali, *L'Italia durante il regime Napoleonico* (Bologna, 1955); C. Oman, *Eugène de Beauharnais* (London, 1965); R. J. Rath, *The Fall of the Napoleonic Kingdom of Italy* (New York, 1941), and *The Provisional Austrian Regime in Lombardy-Venetia, 1814–1815* (Austin, 1969).

Related entries: BEAUHARNAIS, E.; CONTINENTAL BLOCKADE; ECONOMY, FRENCH; ITALY, KINGDOM OF: MINISTERS.

ITALY, KINGDOM OF: MINISTERS.

Justice	Spannocchi, Giovanni (interim)	1805
	Luosi, Giuseppe	1805–14
Interior	Felici, Daniele	1805–6
	Di Breme, Arborio, Marchese	1806–9
	Vaccari, Luigi	1809–14
War, Marine	Pino, Domenico	1805–6
	Caffarelli, François A.	1806–11
	Fontanelli, Achille (interim)	1811
	Veneri, Antonio (interim)	1811
	Biragio, Ambrogio	1811–14
Cults (Ecclesiastical Affairs)	Bovara, Giovanni	1805–14

Finance	Prina, Giuseppe	1805–14
Treasurer	Veneri, Antonio	1805–14
Foreign Affairs	(At Paris) Marescalchi, Ferdinando	1805–14
	(At Milan) Testi, Carlo	1805–14
	Aldini, Antonio (Sec. of State)	1805–14
Public Instruction	Moscati, Pietro	1805
	Scopoli, Giovanni	1805–14
Police	Guicciardini, Diego	1805–9
	Mosca, Francesco	1809–11
	Luini, Giacomo	1811–14
Roads and Waterways	Paradisi, Giovanni	1805–14

Related entry. ITALY, KINGDOM OF.

J

JACOBINS. The term *Jacobin* was first used in a political sense in early 1790 shortly after a Jacobin (Dominican) convent in Paris became the headquarters of a pro-Revolutionary club, the Society of Friends of the Constitution. Originally it denoted a member of this club or its sister societies in the departments. The first members, who included the marquis de Lafayette, were conservative compared to the leaders of 1791–92 and ultraconservative compared to those of 1793–94, who included, most prominently, Maximilien Robespierre. His Montagnards, the architects of the Terror, are considered the only true Jacobins by many historians.

Napoleon, as a young officer, helped organize Jacobin clubs in Corsica. He attended the opening sessions of Globo Patriottico of Ajaccio (January 1791) and enrolled in a club at Valence the following June. He also may be identified with the Montagnards. He wrote a pro-Montagnard pamphlet, *Le Souper de Beaucaire*, in July–August 1793. It was through the influence of the Corsican Jacobin, Joseph Saliceti, that he got command of the artillery at Toulon, where he first gained military fame. Whether Napoleon's Jacobinism was motivated by ambition is unclear. After witnessing the invasion of the Tuileries (1792), which finished Louis XVI, he reported to Joseph that the Jacobins were ''idiots.'' But his letters exude a Revolutionary spirit, and Robespierre's sister, who knew him in 1794, described him as a convinced Montagnard.

During the Directory and the Consulate, Jacobinism was synonymous with left-wing opposition (led by such future marshals as J. B. Jourdan and Jean Bernadotte). Most Jacobins merely wanted a more democratic republic, though a few favored the reintroduction of Terroristic measures. By this time Napoleon was indisputably anti-Jacobin. On learning while in Italy (1797) of the Babeuf affair, he remarked that he might have to ''save'' France from the Jacobins. The justification for the coup d'état of Brumaire (1799), which put Bonaparte in power, was a ''Jacobin conspiracy.'' After Brumaire, to consolidate his power, he played on moderate fears of a Jacobin takeover. The explosion of an ''infernal machine'' in the rue St.-Nicaise (24 December 1800) offered him an opportunity to crush the Left. Some 130 ''Jacobins'' were arrested; and although Joseph Fouché demonstrated their innocence, many were deported.

C. Brinton, *The Jacobins* (New York, 1930); M. L. Kennedy, *Jacobin Club of Marseilles* (1973) and *The Jacobin Clubs during the French Revolution: The First Years* (Princeton, 1981); F. Masson, *Napoléon dans sa jeunesse, 1769–1793* (Paris, 1909); I. Woloch, *Jacobin Legacy: The Democratic Movement under the Directory* (Princeton, 1970).

Michael L. Kennedy

Related entries: BRUMAIRE, COUP OF 18, YEAR VIII; DIRECTORY; FOUCHE; NAPOLEON I; POLICE, MINISTRY OF GENERAL.

JACOBINS, ITALIAN. The *Giacobini* were drawn from the ranks of professionals—doctors, lawyers, officials, professors, and liberal clerics; craftsmen, shopkeepers, and peasants were rare. Generally they had played no role in the governments of eighteenth-century enlightened rulers. Many Italian Jacobins (exiles) participated in the French Revolution, however, and some served in the republican armies. Maximilien Robespierre was their ideal and his government of Terror (Year II) the high point of the Revolution. The *Giacobini* wanted an independent, unified Italian republic created by a popular constitutional convention. They proposed the abolition of peasant dues and land redistribution and held that the state was obligated to provide for the needy. They advocated a secular state, the exclusion of the pope from power, and religious freedom.

Initially the *Giacobini* placed their faith in France, inviting invasion by French armies and promising mass insurrection against the princes in support. When Bonaparte actually drove into northern Italy, however, it was evident that they lacked popular support. The French gave support instead to moderate Italian republicans, who formed sister republics. The *Giacobini* went into opposition. Ultimately the French thought of them as anarchists, and their countrymen rejected them as tainted by association with the French. In fact, they were the first party of Italian unification.

D. Cantimori, *Utopisti e reformatori italiani* (Florence, 1943); R. DeFelice, *Italia Giacobina* (Naples, 1966); G. Vaccarino, *I patrioti ''anarchistes'' e l'idéa dell unita italiana (1796–1799)* (Turin, 1955).

Leonard Macaluso

Related entries: ITALIAN CAMPAIGN, FIRST; ITALY, KINGDOM OF; NAPLES, KINGDOM OF.

JACQUARD, JOSEPH-MARIE (1752–1834). Son of a Lyon silk weaver, Jacquard dedicated his life to the improvement of the silk loom. His work won him first prize at the Paris Industrial Exhibition of 1801 and in 1803 a post at the Paris Conservatoire des Arts et Métiers. An inspection of Jacques de Vaucanson's antique loom, deposited there, suggested to Jacquard various further improvements, which in 1805 resulted in the first automatic-pattern silk loom. Napoleon granted him an annual pension of 3,000 francs on condition that he secure the loom's adoption by the Lyon silk weavers. But fearing they would be put out of work by Jacquard's looms, they publicly burned them. The efficient new device was used elsewhere, however, and soon forced them to adopt it. By 1812 there were 11,000 Jacquard looms in France; by the time of the inventor's death, 30,000.

J. Schober, *Silk and the Silk Industry*, trans. R. Cuthill (London, 1930).

Harold T. Parker

Related entry: ECONOMY, FRENCH.

JAFFA, SIEGE OF. See EGYPTIAN CAMPAIGN.

JAHN, FRIEDRICH LUDWIG (1778–1852), gymnast and patriot, opponent of Napoleon and French domination. The son of a minister, Jahn studied theology, history, and German at various German universities and joined a Masonic student organization. In 1810 he and Friedrich Friesen founded the German League, forerunner of the *Burschenschaften*. The principal objectives of the league were the liberation of Germany from French domination and national unification. In 1811 Jahn opened the first of many gymnastics fields in Berlin, combining physical and patriotic training, which gained great popularity. Between 1813 and 1815 Jahn served in Adolf Lützow's Free Corps against the French. After the war, the Prussian authorities wished to see gymnastics incorporated into the general school curriculum. Jahn regarded "patriotic gymnastics" as essential to building a wider German nationalism, as his *Deutsches Volkstum* (1810) made clear. While gymnastics initially was designed as a preparation for the war of liberation, afterward it was intended to support the struggle for unity, liberty, and a liberal constitution. This was the particular purpose of the Jahn-inspired student movement, founded in 1815 at Jena. The bond between fraternities and gymnastics grew very close, and after 1816 they were increasingly drawn into the conflict with the reactionary authorities.

In 1819 the poet Alexander von Kotzebue was assassinated by a radical student gymnast, Karl Ludwig Sand. Gymnastics were provisionally banned and in 1820 outlawed permanently by the Carlsbad Decrees. Suspected of secret and treasonous connections, Jahn was arrested. He was not held for long but for twenty years was forbidden to live in a city with a high school or university. Only in 1840 did Friedrich Wilhelm IV lift restrictions on his political activity (and awarded him the Iron Cross, Second Class). In 1848 Jahn was elected as a delegate to the National Assembly.

Jahn's gymnastics, with its emphasis on national characteristics and patriotism, was clearly political. Thus after 1871 he was glorified as a champion of German national unity and after World War I was idealized and made a hero. After 1933 this image was perverted by the Nazis into one of the political soldier and precursor of National Socialism, a falsification to which Jahn's racist and nationalistic expressions unfortunately lent themselves.

C. Euler, *Friedrich Ludwig Jahns Leben und Wirken* (1881); F. Jahn, *Über die Beförderung des Patriotismus im Preussischen Reiche* (1800), *Bereicherung des Hochdeutschen Sprachschatzes* (1806), *Deutsches Volkstum* (1810), *Runenblätter* (1814), and

Deutsche Turnkunst (1816); E. Neuendorff, *Turnvater Jahn* (1928); *Stadion* (International Jahn Symposium, 1978); H. Ueberhorst, *Zurück zu Jahn?* (1969).

Horst Ueberhorst

Related entries: FICHTE; FRIEDRICH WILHELM III; GERMAN WAR OF LIBERATION; PRUSSIA, KINGDOM OF.

JENA-AUERSTÄDT, BATTLES OF (14 October 1806), decisive victories by Napoleon and Louis Davout over the Prussian army, which resulted in the collapse of Prussia. On 12 October 1806 the left wing of the French army came into contact with leading units of the Prussian army commanded by Prince F. L. von Hohenlohe. The French army, which was marching north between Saalfeld to Naumburg, turned west and began to converge on Jena. The Prussian force had been divided into three separate armies, commanded by the Prince von Hohenlohe, the duke of Brunswick (C.W.F., the elder), and General Ernst von Rüchel. The Prussians had decided not to fight in the vicinity of Jena-Weimar. Thus the principal Prussian army, commanded by Brunswick (although accompanied by King Frederick William III), was to march to the northeast toward Freiburg, while Hohenlohe guarded the flank and rear at Jena. Rüchel, with a small army of 15,000, supported Hohenlohe. Both were to follow Brunswick while keeping the French at bay.

During the night of 13–14 October, Napoleon began moving his army corps across the River Saale, through Jena, and onto the heights to the northwest. On the morning of 14 October 1806 the corps of Marshals J. Lannes, N. J. de Dieu Soult, M. Ney, and P. Augereau, together with the Guard and Joachim Murat's cavalry, attacked Hohenlohe on the plains between Jena and Apolda. Napoleon had 96,000 to Hohenlohe's 53,000 (including Rüchel's 15,000, who arrived too late to play a significant part in the battle), but fighting was fierce throughout the morning. By 3:00 P.M., however, the Prussian army was in full retreat. The victory was complete.

On the same morning, 14 October, Marshal Davout, commanding 26,000 men of the Third Corps, engaged Brunswick's army of twice its number at Auerstädt, eleven miles to the north. Davout, who had been at Naumburg on 13 October, was ordered to march southwest across the Saale at Kösen to Apolda and to take the Prussian army on its left flank. However, his leading division, commanded by General Charles Gudin, ran into Brunswick's leading division at Hassenhausen. For nearly two hours Gudin fought off two Prussian divisions plus General Blücher's cavalry. Davout, who was with Gudin, rushed forward the divisions of Generals Louis Friant and C.-A.-L. Alexis Morand. Brunswick was mortally wounded, and King Frederick William assumed command of the army. But not even the Prussian king was able to rally his men to stand firm against the French attack, despite his numerical advantage. Davout drove the Prussian army before him to the west and south, completing the work of Napoleon at Jena. The Prussian army ceased to function as a fighting force and fled as best it could.

K. von Clausewitz, *Notes sur la Prusse dans sa grande catastrophe: 1806*, trans. A. Niessel (Paris, 1903); L. N. Davout, *Opérations du 3e Corps, 1806–1807: Rapport du maréchal Davout duc d'Auerstädt*, ed. General L. Davout (Paris, 1896); General Service School, General Staff School, *The Jena Campaign: Source Book* (Fort Leavenworth, 1922); J. Thiry, *Iéna* (Paris, 1964).

John Gallaher

Related entries: ARMY, FRENCH; ARMY, PRUSSIAN; AUGEREAU; BRUNSWICK, C.; DAVOUT; HOHENLOHE-INGELFINGEN; MURAT, J.; NEY; SOULT.

JENA-AUERSTÄDT-FRIEDLAND CAMPAIGN (1806–7). This campaign against Prussia and Russia illustrates the major features of Napoleon's way of waging war. After the Austerlitz campaign and the Treaty of Pressburg, Napoleon did not return the Grande Armée (except for the Guard at Paris) to France but kept it cantoned in six corps along the Danube River valley in south Germany. When war between France and Prussia impended in September 1806, the Prussian army of 171,000, feebly mishandled, moved forward to the area of Erfurt-Weimar in central Germany. Swiftly and secretly, Napoleon concentrated his Guard and his six corps, totaling 180,000 men, on the Bamberg-Bayreuth line and moved them northward in three columns along the Austrian frontier over the twisting, rocky mountain roads of the Thuringian forest to get in the rear of the Prussian army and cut its lines of communications with Dresden, Leipzig, and Berlin (*manoeuvre sur les derrières*). Once the army was across the Thuringian highlands, Napoleon pivoted his army to the west in a squared battalion formation, threw his net of six corps over the retreating Prussian army, and defeated it in the double battle of Jena–Auerstädt on 14 October 1806. Joachim Murat's cavalry, strengthened by horse artillery and supported by infantry, remorselessly pursued the disintegrating, demoralized Prussian army, capturing fortified town after fortified town of the collapsing Prussian monarchy.

Napoleon entered Berlin on 25 October. However, the Prussian king, Frederick William IV, and his beauteous and courageous queen, Louise, had moved to Königsberg. Assured by Czar Alexander I of Russian support, they fought on. Napoleon's army wintered in Prussian Poland during a stalemate that was punctuated in February by a bloody battle against the Russians at Eylau. In the spring of 1807, after Danzig surrendered on 26 May, Napoleon resumed the offensive, this time against the Russian army, commanded by General Levin Bennigsen. Again Napoleon sent out his cavalry and army corps to operate on the enemy's rear. When the retreating Russian army was discovered at Friedland, Napoleon rapidly assembled the available French army corps and at the Battle of Friedland on 14 June inflicted on the Russian force such a severe defeat that Czar Alexander I sued for peace at Tilsit.

H. Camon, *La guerre Napoléonienne*, 4 vols. (Paris, 1907–11); D. Chandler, *The Campaigns of Napoleon* (New York, 1966); V. J. Esposito and J. R. Elting, *A Military*

History and Atlas of the Napoleonic Wars (New York, 1964); O. von Lettow-Vorbeck, *Der Krieg von 1806 und 1807*, 4 vols. (Berlin, 1896); S. J. Watson, *By Command of the Emperor: A Life of Marshal Berthier* (London, 1957).

Harold T. Parker

Related entries: ARMY, FRENCH; ARMY, PRUSSIAN; ARMY, RUSSIAN; BERNADOTTE; BRUNSWICK, C.; BRUNSWICK, F.; DAVOUT; DIPLOMACY; FOREIGN POLICY; HOHENLOHE-INGELFINGEN; LANNES; PRUSSIA, KINGDOM OF.

JEWS AND NAPOLEON. Napoleon proclaimed the civic emancipation of the Jews as his victorious armies entered the countries of Western and Central Europe and reputedly issued a manifesto in Palestine promising the Jews return to their country. In France, however, he ignored the Jews whom the Revolutionaries had emancipated 28 January 1790 and 27 September 1791. While free to practice their religion publicly, they, unlike the Protestants and Catholics, were denied state payment of their clergy. Lacking any official organization, they were left on their own to discipline their communities and resolve any contradictions between their political status and religious commitments. Alsatian French complaints that soon all their property would be mortgaged to the enemies of the church, rather than Jewish pleas to be included with the Protestants in the decree of 1802, finally prompted Napoleon to turn his attention to the Jews of France. Influenced by the liberal Revolutionaries in his Council of State and the pragmatics of post-Revolutionary consolidation, he convened the Assembly of Jewish Notables (1806) to redefine traditional Judaism and to establish an institutional body to transform the Jews into French citizens. This was followed (1807) by the Grand Sanhedrin of European rabbis.

To a degree, Napoleon reversed the process by which the Revolutionaries had emancipated the Jews. He questioned their loyalty and demanded doctrinal as well as concrete economic proofs of their worthiness for citizenship. His settlements united all the Jews of France in one centrally controlled organization (the consistories) and assured the French that all Jews viewed France as their country and the French as their brethren. They were proclaimed by the Assembly of Notables and sanctioned by the Grand Sanhedrin. However, they also relieved Alsatians of much of their indebtedness to Jewish moneylenders and the northeastern Jews of their economic freedom (enacted on 30 May 1806 and 17 March 1808).

Whatever his personal feelings, Napoleon saw little value in restricting the Jews indefinitely to an inferior status. He sought to achieve, as did many Jewish sympathizers during the Revolution, the economic, social, and political assimilation of French Jewry. Restricted economically and discriminated against socially and politically, however, the vast majority of the Jews remained in their rural communities and retained their traditional economic and religious practices. Napoleon elicited from the Jews a blueprint for their successful emergence as citizens, but the actual transformation only followed the Napoleonic era and accompanied the industrialization and urbanization of France.

R. Anchel, *Napoléon et les Juifs* (Paris, 1928); Archives départementales de la Gironde, Série I; Archives Nationales, F^{19}11005, AF^{IV}pl 2151, F^{19}11007; B. Blumenkranz, ed., *Le Grand Sanhédrin de Napoléon* (Paris, 1979); F. Malino, *The Sephardic Jews of Bordeaux: Assimilation and Emancipation in Revolutionary and Napoleonic France* (University, Ala., 1978); S. Schwarzfuchs, *Napoleon, the Jews and the Sanhedrin* (London, 1979).

Frances Malino

Related entries: CHURCH, ROMAN CATHOLIC; LAW, CODES OF; PROTESTANTS; SOCIETY.

JOHANN VON HABSBURG, ARCHDUKE (1782–1859). Austrian field marshal; thirteenth child of Leopold II, Holy Roman Emperor; brother of Emperor Franz II. In 1792 when he was ten, his brother decided on a military career for Johann (or John), who was more interested in the natural sciences and history. In 1800 Franz thrust on him the command of the Austrian army in Germany. Predictably he was defeated by the French under Jean Moreau at Hohenlinden, and Austria was forced to make peace. He was subsequently director of engineers and fortifications, director of the military engineering academy in Vienna, and head of the military academy at Wiener Neustadt. In 1805, he was charged with preparations for mountain war in Tyrol. In 1808 he was instrumental in establishing a national guard (*Landwehr*). In 1809 at the head of the Army of Inner Austria, he invaded Italy, defeated the viceroy, Eugène de Beauharnais, and advanced to Verona. Because of Napoleon's victories in Germany, however, Johann marched northward to reinforce the main army under Archduke Karl. He was overtaken by Eugène, however, defeated at Raab, and was prevented from joining Karl for the decisive Battle of Wagram. After 1815 he was not given prominent posts, though in 1836 he was made a field marshal. In 1848, he accepted the call of the Frankfurt National Assembly to be regent of the German Empire, a position he held until the assembly was dispersed in 1849.

Archduke Johann's importance lies in his quiet economic, cultural, and social achievements, especially in Styria. They ranged from the energetic promotion of agriculture, mining, trade, commerce, and industry to the establishment of communal enterprises and experimental institutes to care for the old and the sick. Countless important innovations, including the Semmering Railway, resulted from the initiative of the archduke. Always a popular figure, his marriage in 1828 to the commoner daughter of a postmaster magnified his appeal.

A. Schlossar, *Erzherzog Johann von Österreich* (1908); V. Theiss, *Erzherzog Johann, der steirische Prinz* (1950).

Brigitte Holl

Related entries: AUSTERLITZ CAMPAIGN; PIAVE, BATTLE ON THE; RAAB, BATTLE OF; WAGRAM CAMPAIGN; WAGRAM CAMPAIGN, ITALIAN PHASE.

JOHN VI (1767–1826), prince regent and king of Portugal (1792–1826). The second son of Queen Maria I and Dom Pedro III, Dom John (João) was married in 1785 to Carlotta Joaquina, daughter of Charles IV of Spain. Dom John became heir to the throne in 1788 on the untimely death of his elder brother, José, and prince regent in 1792 after his mother's insanity became permanent. Benevolent and good natured, John was always popular with his subjects. His slow-witted and indecisive nature made him a ruler unsuited for his turbulent time, although he had an innate talent for survival, which enabled him to retain the throne in a time of unparalleled political upheaval.

From the outbreak of the Anglo-French conflict, Portugal was placed in the position of having to choose between alliance or war with one or another of the combatants. Finally yielding to British pressure, John and his court embarked for Brazil on 27 November 1807, three days before the French entered Lisbon. Establishing his court at Rio de Janeiro, John quickly settled into the tranquil colonial life and displayed little interest in events in Portugal during the tumultuous period of the Peninsular War. He was crowned king in 1816 on the death of his mother and forced by the liberal revolt of 1820 to return to Portugal and accept a constitutional government.

M. Cheke, *Carlotta Joaquina* (London, 1947); J. M. Latino Coelho, *Historia Politica e Militar de Portugal desde os fins do seculo XVIII ate 1814*, 3 vols. (Lisbon, 1874–91); O. Lima, *D. João VI no Brasil* (Rio de Janeiro, 1908); S. J. da Luz Soriano, *Historia da Guerra Civil e do Estabelecimento do Governo Parlamentar em Portugal*, 15 vols. (Lisbon, 1866–87); L. Norton, *A Corte de Portugal no Brasil* (São Paulo, 1979); A. Pereira, *D. João VI Principe e Rei* (Lisbon, 1953); D. Peres, *Historia de Portugal*, 6 vols. (Barcelos, 1934).

Francisco A. de la Fuente

Related entries: BRAZIL; CONTINENTAL BLOCKADE; PORTUGAL; PORTUGUESE CAMPAIGNS.

JOMINI, ANTOINE-HENRY, BARON (1779–1869), Swiss soldier and military writer. Jomini began his military career in Switzerland, entering the French service in 1805. He was never completely at home in Napoleon's military circle, though his talents as staff officer were appreciated by the emperor. Jomini received the title of baron and rank of *général de brigade* but in 1813 found his further advancement blocked. Profiting from the truce of Parschwitz, he offered his sword to Czar Alexander I and entered Russian service. This defection was much criticized, but on St. Helena Napoleon ruled his conduct honorable and dismissed out of hand the story that Jomini had betrayed the French plans to the Allies. After Napoleon's downfall, Jomini continued for a time in the Russian service. He spent his last years in Paris.

Jomini is known chiefly for his thirty volumes of military writings. He was the partisan of a rational system of warfare in which victory was assured by the proper ordering of a number of calculable elements. It was in this conception that he placed the generalship of Napoleon, of which he was the chief interpreter for much of the nineteenth century.

J. Alger, *Antoine-Henri Jomini: a Bibliographical Survey* (West Point, 1975); F. Lecomte, *Le général Jomini, sa vie et ses écrits: esquisse biographique et stratégique* (Paris, 1860).

Lee Kennett

Related entries: ARMY, FRENCH; NAPOLEON I; TACTICS, NAPOLEONIC.

JOSEPHINE, EMPRESS (1763–1814). One of the great beauties of her day, she was born Marie-Joseph-Rose Tascher de la Pagerie in Martinique, the daughter of French parents of minor nobility. Married in Paris at age fifteen to the Vicomte Alexandre de Beauharnais, she produced a son Eugène (1781) and a daughter Hortense (1783). The vicomte, who was an army officer, diplomat, and man of affairs, traveled constantly, which perhaps encouraged his very young wife to misbehave—or appear to. The vicomte denied the paternity of his second child, and the two were legally separated.

In 1789 the vicomte favored the Revolution; he was a member of the Constituent Assembly (1789–91). He remained loyal to the Republic after the overthrow of the king and commanded the Army of the Rhine in 1793. He even served in the Convention and supported the Terror, but in 1794 he was accused of treason and arrested. Josephine was also arrested. The vicomte was sent to the guillotine, but Josephine escaped, gaining freedom by the influence of Jean Tallien and his wife, the former Thérèse Cabarrus.

During the reaction (1794–95) that followed the execution of Maximilien Robespierre, Mme. Tallien was the social leader of Paris, dubbed "Our Lady of Thermidor." Josephine was frequently at her salon. After the events of Vendémiaire (the "whiff of grapeshot"), General Bonaparte was also invited, and it is probably there that the two met. Napoleon had a more interesting version of their meeting, which he repeated at St. Helena. This was that after the events of Vendémiaire, he ordered Paris disarmed, and Eugène, then fourteen, came to his office to ask if he could retain his father's sword. Bonaparte was impressed with the boy and granted permission. The next day Josephine came to thank him, and they became friends. Napoleon and Josephine (at the time called Rose) met in the fall of 1795. They were married on 9 March 1796 over the objections of Napoleon's family, who considered Josephine a dissolute woman and were certain that at age thirty-two she was incapable of bearing children. Napoleon almost immediately departed to command the Army of Italy.

Josephine returned to the high life of Paris and refused for many months to go to Italy. She was at Mombello, though, to celebrate Napoleon's victories. They were then again separated when Napoleon led the expedition to Egypt (1798–99), and Josephine's infidelity was too public to be denied. Napoleon returned to Paris in 1799 determined to divorce her, but Hortense and Eugène brought about a reconciliation.

Thereafter Josephine committed herself to the marriage. When Napoleon was crowned emperor in 1804, he crowned Josephine empress. Prior to the ceremony, with the coaxing of Josephine, Napoleon had allowed Pope Pius VII to marry them in a religious ceremony. Josephine as empress performed her duties in impeccable style. Her daughter, Hortense, married Louis Bonaparte and became queen of Holland. Her son, Eugène, became viceroy of Italy. Nevertheless, in 1809, Napoleon decided to remarry in order to have a direct heir to perpetuate his dynasty, and he divorced Josephine. Their parting was tearful, however, and the settlement given Josephine very generous. It included the chateau of Malmaison and an annual income appropriate for an empress. Josephine lived at Malmaison until her death in 1814. Napoleon always had a warm spot in his heart for her. After Waterloo, en route to Rochefort, where he surrendered to the British, he visited Malmaison and walked with an expression of great melancholy through the chambers where Josephine had spent her last years.

B. Cartland, *Josephine, Empress of France* (New York, 1974); A. Castelot, *Joséphine* (Paris, 1977); H. Cole, *Josephine* (London, 1963); N. C. Epton, *Josephine: The Empress and Her Children* (London, 1975 & New York, 1976); A. Gavoty, *Les amoureux de l'impératrice Joséphine* (Paris, 1961).

Related entry: NAPOLEON I.

JOUBERTHON, ALEXANDRINE, wife of Lucien Bonaparte, Napoleon's brother. See BONAPARTE, LUCIEN.

JOURDAN, JEAN-BAPTISTE, COMTE (1762–1833), marshal of France. The son of a surgeon of Limoges, Jourdan enlisted at sixteen and fought as a sergeant in the American Revolution. With the onset of the French Revolution, he reentered the army as an officer via the National Guard of Limoges and by 1793 was a *général de division*. Wounded the same year by a cannonball, Jourdan retired. He returned in 1794, however, to become a national hero for his victory over the Austrians at Fleurus.

Thereafter his reputation declined as Bonaparte's rose. In 1796 he was elected to the Council of Five Hundred. In 1798 he authored the Jourdan-Delbrel Law, which spelled out the system of military conscription used by the Republic and Napoleon. In 1799, he took an active command against the armies of the Second Coalition but did poorly.

A staunch republican, Jourdan opposed the coup d'état of 18 Brumaire and was briefly imprisoned. Napoleon, who wanted the Republic's heroes around him, had Jourdan freed (in 1800) and made him inspector general of the infantry and the cavalry. In 1804, for the same reason, Napoleon made him one of the original marshals of France.

Jourdan was not given important assignments, however. He was chief of staff to King Joseph Bonaparte in Naples (1806–8) and followed the king to Spain. There he was given the blame for Joseph's defeats at Talavera (1809) and, more important, at Vitoria (1813), which brought down the kingdom.

Jourdan rallied to Napoleon during the Hundred Days (1815). Nevertheless, Louis XVIII restored his rank, and he served at Michel Ney's court-martial. In

1817 he was created a peer of France and in 1830 made governor of Les Invalides, a position he held until his death in 1833 at age seventy-one.

J.-B. Jourdan, *Mémoires militaires* (Paris, 1899); R. Valentin, *Le Maréchal Jourdan* (Paris, 1957).

Related entries: CONSCRIPTION; MARSHALS OF THE EMPIRE; NAPLES, KINGDOM OF; SPAIN, KINGDOM OF.

JUNOT, JEAN-ANDOCHE (1771–1813), general, duc d'Abrantès. A middle-class law student, Junot volunteered into the army in 1790 and was a sergeant at the siege of Toulon (1793). Made Bonaparte's secretary, his coolness under fire impressed the Corsican, who had him commissioned. Junot served Napoleon in Italy (1796–97) and in Egypt (1798–99) where Napoleon promoted him to *général de brigade*. On his return to France (1801), he became *général de division* and in 1805 was sent as ambassador to Portugal. He returned to fight under Napoleon at Austerlitz. In 1806 he was governor-general of Parma and Piacenza and in 1807 governor of Paris.

Late in 1807 he commanded the almost unopposed conquest of Portugal, for which he received the title duc d'Abrantès. He seemed in line for a marshal's baton. In August 1808, however, he was attacked and defeated by Sir Arthur Wellesley (later duke of Wellington) and agreed to evacuate Portugal, his army to be carried to France by the British navy. Napoleon never quite forgave him and never made him a marshal.

Junot fought in the Wagram campaign of 1809 and in 1810 marched on Portugal from Spain with André Masséna's ill-fated expedition. Despite valiant service and wounds, he could not regain his reputation. In Russia during 1812 it was the same. He returned a broken man.

In 1813, Napoleon made him governor of the Illyrian Provinces, where it soon became clear Junot was going insane. He was returned to his father's home, where he leaped from a window to his death.

M. Foy, *Histoire de la guerre de la péninsule sous Napoléon*, 4 vols. (Paris, 1827); J. Lasserre, *Junot* (Paris, 1947); A. Massèna, *Mémoires*, 7 vols. (Paris, 1849–50); A.-F.-L. Viesse de Marmont, *Mémoires*, 9 vols. (Paris, 1856–57).

Related entry: PENINSULAR WAR.

JUNOT, LAURE PERMON (1784–1838), duchesse d'Abrantès; leader of Napoleonic court society, memoirist and novelist during the Romantic era. Born Laure Permon and educated in her mother's popular Parisian salon during the Directory, she married Jean-Andoche Junot, Napoleon's aide-de-camp and commandant of Paris, in 1800. In 1805, she followed Junot to Portugal where he had been appointed ambassador, and she attempted to establish a court modeled on the Parisian style. After Junot's appointment as governor of Paris, she played a role in the fusion of the aristocracy of the Old Regime with the Napoleonic nobility. She noted that the protocol and etiquette of Napoleon's court began to resemble the traditional courts of Europe. While in 1807 Junot led a French invasion of Portugal, she became embroiled in court intrigue and a scandal allegedly involving Clemens von Metternich. In 1810, at her husband's request, she accompanied him to Spain where he led a corps of the French army of Portugal. Her capacity there was no longer sheltered by diplomatic immunities, and she traveled with the troops to the frontiers of Portugal as an eyewitness to the horrors of the Peninsular War. On her husband's death (1813) and Napoleon's abdication, she became a recluse until the 1830s when Honoré Balzac encouraged her to become a writer. In fewer than eight years, she wrote over three dozen volumes, including her popular, informative, and gossipy memoirs of the Napoleonic era.

J. Bertaut, *La duchesse d'Abrantès* (Paris, 1949); Bibliothèque Spoelberch de Lovenjoul, "Journal Intime," D633 bis; L. Junot, *Mémoires de Madame la duchesse d'Abrantès*, 18 vols. (Paris, 1831–35), and *Mémoires sur la Restauration*, 6 vols. (Paris, 1835–38); H. Malo, *Les années de bohème de la duchesse d'Abrantès* (Paris, 1927), and *La duchesse d'Abrantès au temps des amours* (Paris, 1927).

Susan P. Conner

Related entries: JUNOT, J.-A.; NOBILITY, IMPERIAL; PORTUGUESE CAMPAIGNS.

JUSTICE. See ABRIAL; CAMBACERES; LABOR LEGISLATION; LAW, CODES OF; MOLE; REGNIER; WOMEN.

K

KALISCH, TREATY OF (28 February 1813), alliance between Prussia and Russia following Napoleon's defeat in 1812. In return for fighting with Russia, Prussia was to regain as much territory as it had lost since 1806. See also FOREIGN POLICY; GERMAN WAR OF LIBERATION.

KARL FRIEDRICH (1728–1811), margrave, then grand duke of Baden (1738–1811). An enlightened despot, he was influenced by physiocratic ideas. He ruled without a parliament but was guided by a reformed, Francophile bureaucracy. Leading officials included J. J. Reinhard, J. G. Schlosser, N. F. Brauer, W. von Edelsheim, and S. von Reitzenstein. He abolished torture in 1767 and serfdom in 1783. His succession in Roman Catholic Baden-Baden (reunited in 1771) was eased by his well-known spirit of religious tolerance. Compensations for loss of left-bank territories (to France) gained him the elector's title in 1803; Napoleon made him a grand duke in 1806 when he joined the *Rheinbund*. He was married first to Caroline of Hesse-Darmstadt; they had three sons. His heir, however, was his grandson, Karl I (1786–1818), since his eldest son, Karl Ludwig, died prematurely. His second marriage was to Baroness Luise von Hochberg (Geyersberg) and was morganatic. The succession rights of this line were later recognized, however, and the eldest son reigned as Leopold I from 1830 to 1852.

C. W. von Drais, *Geschichte der Regierung...Carl Friedrich*, 2 vols. (Karlsruhe, 1816–18), and *Gemälde über Karl Friedrich*, 2 vols. (Mannheim, 1828–29); Karl Friedrich, *Politische Korrespondenz Karl Friedrich von Baden 1783–1806*, 6 vols. (Heidelberg, 1888–1900); H. Liebel, *Enlightened Bureaucracy vs. Enlightened Despotism in Baden, 1750–1792* (Philadelphia, 1965).

Helen P. Liebel-Weckowicz

Related entries: CONFEDERATION OF THE RHINE; FOREIGN POLICY.

KARL LUDWIG FRIEDRICH (1786–1818), grand duke of Baden (1811–18), who gave the state a constitution and a parliament. He was the grandson and successor of Karl Friedrich, whose son, Karl Ludwig, was killed in an accident in 1801. He married the Empress Josephine's cousin, Stéphanie Beauharnais, in 1806. Napoleon's financial contributions saved the state from bankruptcy. Karl commanded Baden's *Rheinbund* troops in 1807, was made co-regent with Karl Friedrich in 1809, and succeeded in 1811. His son having died in infancy, he negotiated recognition of the succession rights of Karl Friedrich's sons by his morganatic marriage to Luise von Hochberg. There was a popular story that an orphan, Caspar Hauser, was in reality Karl's son whom Luise von Hochberg had caused to disappear. He was succeeded by his uncle, Ludwig (1818–30) and then by Hochberg's eldest son, Leopold I (1830–52).

W. Andreas, *Geschichte der badischen Verwaltungsorganisation und Verfassung, 1802–1818* (Leipzig, 1913); R. Haas, *Stephanie Napoleon, Grossherzogin v. Baden* (Mannheim, 1978); R. Haebler, *Ein Staat wird aufgebaut 1789–1818* (Baden-Baden, 1948); F. Schnabel, *S. v. Reitzenstein* (Heidelberg, 1927).

Helen P. Liebel-Weckowicz

Related entries: CONFEDERATION OF THE RHINE; DIPLOMACY: FOREIGN POLICY; GERMAN WAR OF LIBERATION.

KARL VON HABSBURG, ARCHDUKE (1771–1847), Austrian field marshal; perhaps closest contemporary rival in military talent of Napoleon; brother of Franz II, Holy Roman Emperor. An epileptic and of very sensitive nature, his great desire was to be a soldier. He entered the Austrian army in 1790, and in 1792, his brother, the emperor, permitted him to participate in the war against France, destined to continue until 1797. Early on a strong animosity developed between him and the Austrian chancellor, Baron Franz von Thugut, which for years would affect his relationship with his brother Franz. Karl was a corps commander in 1794, when the Austrians lost the Netherlands. In 1796, Franz placed the whole Austrian army in Germany under his authority. He rapidly drove apart the French armies of Jean Moreau and Jean-Baptiste Jourdan and defeated each, in turn, at Würzburg and Amberg. The French were forced to give up the right bank of the Rhine, and Archduke Karl was acclaimed as the savior of Germany. The Viennese court nevertheless denied him any political role. He was ordered to Italy to revitalize the Austrian army in Italy, repeatedly bested by Napoleon, but it was too late. He was forced to conclude the armistice of Leoben. After the Peace of Campo Formio, he was named governor and captain general of Bohemia.

In 1799 Karl once again assumed command against the French in Germany and won victories over Jourdan at Ostrach and Stockach and André Masséna at Zürich. But interference from the Viennese court impelled him to resign his command in 1800. In December 1800, his eighteen-year-old brother Johann was defeated by Moreau at Hohenlinden, and Karl was again called to command but could negotiate only the armistice of Steyr. Austrian defeat meant Thugut's fall, however, and a turn in the fortunes of Karl.

In 1801 he was named field marshal, president of the Imperial War Council, and minister of war and navy. He attempted to strengthen Austria through a comprehensive military reform and an alliance with France. Adamant resistance by court and bureaucracy frustrated his initial reforms, though a few were realized, notably the abolition of lifelong military service. In 1805, he judged war with France foolhardy, and it cost him his offices. The unhappy course of the war confirmed the negative prognoses of Karl, however. He took command of Austrian forces in Italy and scored the only real military success of the war through his victory over Masséna at Caldiero.

Named commander in chief in 1806, Karl resumed his attempts to reform the army. His improvement of the drill manual was so impressive that parts of it were adopted by the Prussians. He published essays on military training, founded the magazine *Österreichische Militärische Zeitschrift* (1807), reorganized the general staff, created a military reserve, and, in conjunction with his brother Johann, a national guard.

In 1809, he still felt that he needed more time to remake the army; however, he reluctantly gave in to the pressure of the war party for a new war against Napoleon. But the anticipated German people's rising to aid Austria did not materialize, and Napoleon occupied Vienna. While at Aspern and Essling Karl inflicted defeat on Napoleon, the Corsican turned the tables at Wagram. Though beaten, Karl's army was intact, but he chose to accept an armistice and resigned from the army. In 1815 Karl became interim governor of Mainz, but in essence he devoted the rest of his life to his family and his military writings, one of which, *Grundsätze der Strategie* (1813), was widely acclaimed and translated into many languages. Thus, Karl's didactic efforts seemed to represent his major contributions. Nevertheless, he is now recognized as one of the two most skilled military opponents of Napoleon. The other is Wellington.

O. Criste, *Erzherzog Carl von Österreich*, 3 vols. (1912); M. Rauchensteiner, *Kaiser Franz und Erzherzog Carl. Dynastie und Heerwesen in Österreich 1796–1809* (1972); G. Rothenberg, *Napoleon's Great Adversaries: The Archduke Charles and the Austrian Army 1792-1814* (Bloomington, Ind., 1982).

Brigitte Holl

Related entries: ARMY, HABSBURG; AUSTERLITZ CAMPAIGN; ITALIAN CAMPAIGN, FIRST; WAGRAM, BATTLE OF; WAGRAM CAMPAIGN.

KELLERMANN, FRANCOIS-ETIENNE-CHRISTOPHE (1735–1820), duc de Valmy, marshal of France; "first hero of the French Republic" (at Valmy). Kellermann, of Alsatian gentry, entered the Royal French Army at fifteen as a cadet (1752), was commissioned in 1753, served in the Seven Years War, and by 1784 was a colonel.

In 1789 Kellermann welcomed the Revolution, and in 1792, after the overthrow of Louis XVI, he remained loyal to the Republic and was promoted to lieutenant general. At the Battle of Valmy (20 September 1792) he played a crucial role in turning back the invading Prussian army under the duke of Brunswick. It was touted as the victory that saved the Revolution in France.

In 1793 Kellermann commanded the Armies of the Alps and of Italy but was imprisoned for allegedly not pressing the siege of the city of Lyon (in revolt).

He was acquitted, however, and returned to his command, from which the Army of Italy was separated (1795). Bonaparte took it over in 1796, and Kellermann's importance in the field was much reduced. In September 1797 he retired from active duty.

Bonaparte, anxious to have the old hero grace his regime, made Kellermann a senator in 1799, although he had not supported the coup d'état of 18 Brumaire. In 1804 Napoleon appointed him marshal of the empire, though the title was honorary, and later duc de Valmy. In 1814 Kellermann offered his services to the Bourbons and was made a peer of France. He refused to rally to Napoleon during the Hundred Days.

M. Heim, *Le Nestor des armées françaises, Kellermann, duc de Valmy*, new ed. (Paris, 1949).

Jesse Scott

Related entries: ITALIAN CAMPAIGN, FIRST; MARSHALS OF THE EMPIRE.

KIEL, TREATY OF (14 January 1814). Denmark ceded Norway to Sweden in return for western Pomerania and Rügen. Britain returned to Denmark all territories it had seized, except Helgoland. See also FRANCE, CAMPAIGN OF; GERMAN WAR OF LIBERATION; VIENNA, CONGRESS OF.

KLEBER, JEAN-BAPTISTE (1753–1800), Revolutionary general who was given command in 1799 of the French army in Egypt when Napoleon left for France; he died in that post. An Alsatian, Kléber served in the Austrian army (1776–83), but back in France became enamored of Revolutionary ideas and joined the French National Guard in 1789. He distinguished himself in the Vendée in 1793 and became general of division in the Army of the Sambre and Meuse (1794–96). He was assigned to Bonaparte's Egyptian expedition (Army of the Orient) in 1798. During the invasion of Syria (1799), he held off 35,000 Turks at Mount Tabor with 2,000 men until help arrived. In August 1799, when Napoleon left for France, Kléber received sealed orders making him commander of the army. Kléber had disliked Bonaparte from the start and now felt that he had betrayed the army. He signed the Convention of El Arish with the Turks, promising to evacuate Egypt, but the British repudiated it and the war resumed. Kléber defeated the Turks at Heliopolis (20 March 1800) and crushed a revolt in Lower Egypt, only to be assassinated in Cairo by Muslim fanatics (14 June 1800).

A field general of determination and ability, Kléber was nevertheless a difficult and quarrelsome subordinate, as well as a dedicated republican. Had he lived, he probably would not have had a great future in Napoleon's armies.

C. Desprez, *Kléber et Marceau* (Paris, 1870); B. Ernouf, *Général Kléber* (Paris, 1870); J. Lucas-Dubreton, *Kléber, 1753–1800* (Paris, 1937); C. Pajol, *Kléber, sa vie et sa correspondance* (Paris, 1877).

Milton Finley

Related entries: ARMY, FRENCH; EGYPTIAN CAMPAIGN; NAPOLEON I.

KLEIST, HEINRICH VON (1777–1811), Prussian dramatist and German nationalist; opponent of Napoleon. After a brief military career in the family tradition, Kleist resigned his commission, having come completely under the influence of the humanitarian and moral ideals of the Enlightenment. He studied science and mathematics, read Rousseau, Fichte, and Kant, and in 1801 began to write. He predicted the fiasco of Jena-Auerstädt (1806) a year before when he urged the king to rally his people and set an example by "making his gold into iron." He was not really involved, however; in 1806 the poet in him triumphed over the patriot. In 1808, however, when Austria began planning a war of German liberation, he threw himself into the movement and wrote *Die Hermannsschlacht*, a play unlike all of his other works in that its sole purpose was to arouse his fellow Germans to action. The drama did not dwell on the past but the present, under French domination. He prefaced it with the words: "Woe, my fatherland! I, your poet, am forbidden to play the lyre in your glory as my heart commands." He could find no theater in Germany that would allow it to be performed, even free. Kleist then planned the patriotic weekly *Germania* (1809) as an open forum for writers to inspire the German people: "This journal is to be the first breath of German freedom." His own contributions were to be "Satirical Letters," "Textbook for French Journalism," "The Catechism of the Germans," and "What Is This War About?" The project came to naught after the Austrian defeat at Wagram. After a series of personal disappointments, Kleist committed suicide.

R. Loch, *Heinrich von Kleist* (Leipzig, 1978); H. Mayer, *Heinrich von Kleist: Der geschichtliche Augenblick* (Pfullingen, 1962); R. Michaelis, *Heinrich von Kleist* (Velber, 1965); H. Sembdner, ed., *Heinrich von Kleist: Sämtliche Werke und Briefe* (Munich, 1965); E. L. Stahl, *Heinrich von Kleist's Dramas* (Oxford, 1961).

Gerda Jordan

Related entries: FICHTE; FOREIGN POLICY; JAHN; WAGRAM CAMPAIGN.

KOTZEBUE, AUGUST (1761–1819), German monarchist, writer, and sometime Russian civil servant; opponent of French domination of Germany. He studied law in Jena and Duisburg and practiced in his home town of Weimar (1780) but was soon banished because of his political lampoons. He went to St. Petersburg, entered Russian service, and quickly advanced. In 1795 he retired to his estate in Estonia where he wrote plays and polemical essays. He was soon called to Vienna to be dramatist at the Burgtheater but quarreled with the actors and returned to Russia. He was immediately arrested on suspicion of treason and sent to Siberia but was pardoned as a known Russophile by Czar Paul I. After a short interlude as director of the German Theater in St. Petersburg, Kotzebue returned to Weimar, where he feuded passionately with Goethe and the Romantics. He meanwhile visited Paris several times and in 1803 met Napoleon who proved unimpressed with his writings.

As Napoleon extended his power into Germany, Kotzebue made vociferous attacks against him and the French in his satirical *Die Biene* (1807–10) and *Die*

Grille (1811–12). In recognition of his work, he was appointed Russian privy councillor and later consul general in Königsberg. He accompanied Czar Alexander I during the War of Liberation of 1813–14.

After 1817, he lived in Weimar and Mannheim and continued to write plays (200 in all), essays, and satires ridiculing the national and liberal ideas of the younger generation, waging war against freedom of the press and academic independence, and deriding the representatives of such democratic trends, particularly the *Burschenschaften* (students' associations). He also reported regularly to the czar on political and cultural affairs in Germany and was suspected of being a Russian agent. He was marked as a reactionary by the liberal German youth, and his books were burned at gatherings of the *Burschenschaften*. In 1819, he was stabbed to death by Karl Ludwig Sand, a fanatical revolutionary theology student. Ironically Kotzebue's death caused the issuance of the Carlsbad Decrees, which suppressed radical agitation, introduced severe censorship of the press, and placed the universities under close government supervision.

In his lifetime, Kotzebue was well known as a playwright (even more popular than Goethe) and infamous as a political figure. Today he is almost forgotten.

P. Brückner, "*. . .bewahre uns Gott in Deutschland vor irgendeiner Revolution!" Die Ermordung des Staatsrats v. Kotzebue durch den Studenten Sand* (Berlin, 1975); R. L. Kahn, "Kotzebue's Treatment of Social Problems," *Studies in Philology* 49 (1952); A. Kotzebue, *Theater*, 40 vols. (Vienna, 1840–41), *Prosaische Schriften*, 45 vols. (Vienna, 1842–43), *Schauspiele* (Frankfurt a.M., 1972), and *Erinnerungen aus Paris im Jahre 1804* (Berlin, 1804); F. Stock, *Kotzebue im literarischen Leben der Goethezeit. Polemik-Kritik-Publikum* (Düsseldorf, 1971); L. F. Thompson, *Kotzebue—A Survey of His Progress in France and England: Preceded by a Consideration of the Critical Attitude to Him in Germany* (Paris, 1928).

Margit Resch

Related entries: ALEXANDER I; FOREIGN POLICY; GOETHE; PAUL I; RUSSIA.

KOZIUTELSKI, JAN LEON HIPOLIT (1781–1821), colonel; leader of the charge of the Polish cavalry of the Imperial Guard at Somosierra, Spain (30 November 1808), perhaps the most celebrated action of Poles in Napoleon's service. A Polish patriot, young Koziutelski was prevented by his father from joining a Polish legion in the French Revolutionary army to fight the powers occupying his homeland. In 1803, however, he became a member of the Society of the Friends of the Fatherland and in 1807 volunteered into a Polish unit of Napoleon's army. Chief of squadron in the Polish light cavalry of the Imperial Guard, he was sent to Spain in 1808. His unit assisted in the capture and evacuation of Madrid and formed Napoleon's main army that marched to retake the city. On 30 November 1808, the army was stalled at the pass at Somosierra in the Guadarrama mountains. The pass was held by 13,000 Spaniards with four artillery batteries under the command of General Benito San Juan. Napoleon, counting on the valor and patriotism of his Polish troops, gave Koziutelski and his eighty-seven men orders to clear the pass. The Poles charged the cannon head on, twice. Koziutelski's horse was shot from under him after taking the first battery, but his squadron went on to open the way to Madrid, though forty-two men were killed. Koziutelski and his men, living and dead, were given the Cross of the Legion of Honor. Koziutelski also fought in the Battle of Wagram (1809) and in 1811 was made a baron of the empire. The same year he was awarded the highest Polish military decoration, the *Virtuti Militari* cross. During the Russian campaign of 1812, he was in the Battle of Borodino and with the emperor in Moscow. During the retreat at Horodnia, he saved Napoleon from a charge of Cossacks, and the emperor made him a colonel on the spot.

After returning to the Duchy of Warsaw, Koziutelski helped reorganize the Polish army. In 1813, he rejoined Napoleon and fought in the battles of Bautzen, Reichenbach (Dzieronów), Dresden, and Leipzig. He accompanied Napoleon across the Rhine, and in 1813, at Fountainebleau, he took part in the emperor's final military review. In 1814, Koziutelski joined the army of the Kingdom of Poland. He commanded the fourth corps of Uhlans and received the order of St. Anne (second class) from the Grand Duke Constantine, viceroy of the kingdom. He died in 1821.

Koziutelski's exploits, particularly the charge at Somosierra, became legend and still contribute to Polish patriotism.

M. Brandys, *Koziutelski i inni* (Warsaw, 1967); M. Pouzerewsky, *La charge de la cavalerie de Somo-Sierra (Espagne) le 30 Novembre 1808* (Paris, 1900); A. Rembowski, ed., *Zródło do historii pułku polskiej lekkiej gwardii Napoleon I.* (Warsaw, 1899).

John Stanley

Related entries: ARMY, FRENCH; BORODINO, BATTLE OF; FRANCE, CAMPAIGN OF; GERMAN WAR OF LIBERATION; PENINSULAR WAR; RUSSIAN CAMPAIGN; VIENNA, CONGRESS OF; WAGRAM, BATTLE OF; WAGRAM CAMPAIGN.

KULM, BATTLE OF (30 August 1813), victory of Prussians and Austrians over General Dominique Vandamme, ordered by Napoleon to pursue the Allies after the victory of Dresden.

KUTUZOV, MIKHAIL ILARIONOVICH, PRINCE (1745–1813), Russian field marshal, best known for his victory over Napoleon in 1812, despite his failure to win a major battle. Born at St. Petersburg the son of a lieutenant general who had served under Peter the Great, Kutuzov entered an engineering-artillery school as a cadet-private at the age of twelve. Highly intelligent, he became proficient in French, German, Polish, Swedish, English, and Turkish. Within two years he became a junior teacher in the entering class, teaching arithmetic and geometry. At age sixteen he was promoted to ensign and a year later had risen to captain.

He saw his first service in Colonel Alexander Suvorov's regiment at Astrakhan. Kutuzov was then assigned as aide to the military governor of Estonia at Reval.

At age twenty-five Major Kutuzov joined Count Rumyantsev's army in Bessarabia and engaged in the war against Turkey. Rumyantsev's prime concern was to ensure that his forces kept the upper hand by keeping his army in being. For this purpose he gave up territory if doing so promised him a better opportunity to deal with the enemy. It was from him that Kutuzov learned the valuable lesson, which he was to apply in 1812, that the objective was not the occupation of a geographical position but the destruction of enemy forces.

In 1773 Lieutenant Colonel Kutuzov was severely wounded when a bullet struck his head and destroyed his right eye. Search for medical treatment and recuperation took him to Prussia, Holland, England, and Austria. By 1776 he began to serve under Suvorov in the Crimea, where he spent the next ten years, becoming a brigadier general in 1782 and a major general in 1784. It was from Suvorov that he learned how to treat soldiers. Suvorov showed unusual concern for the welfare of his soldiers, and Kutuzov followed his example. In consequence he won the respect of his soldiers, whom he referred to, as did Blücher, as his "children."

In the Russo-Turkish War of 1787–91, he distinguished himself at Ochakov, when he was again severely wounded, and was promoted to lieutenant general. After his recovery he was active in the Polish campaign, for which he was rewarded with an estate with 2,667 serfs.

Between 1793 and 1801 Kutuzov was successively ambassador to Turkey, governor general of Finland, ambassador to Prussia, governor-general of Lithuania, and military governor of St. Petersburg. These were positions in which he displayed his intense shrewdness, charm, and diplomacy but also led him to refuse to take a firm stand with respect to the plot against Czar Paul. Consequently he earned Czar Alexander's distrust and was sent into virtual exile.

With the formation of the Third Coalition (1805) Alexander was compelled to recall this aggressive, resourceful, and intelligent military leader. Kutuzov was to head a Russian army to act jointly with the Austrians. Napoleon's severe defeat of the Austrian General Karl Mack at Ulm (20 October 1805) forced the Russians to retreat, but Kutuzov, after defeating the French at Dürrenstein, preserved his army intact. He proposed withdrawing all the way to Russia, there to await reinforcements, but Alexander took command and insisted on a battle. He got one at Austerlitz (2 December 1805), where the Russo-Austrian army was decisively beaten by Napoleon.

Alexander placed the blame for Austerlitz on Kutuzov and assigned him to the minor posts of military governor of Kiev in 1806 and military governor of Lithuania in 1809. In 1811 Alexander sent him to Moldavia to prosecute the war against Turkey, a war that had been simmering for longer than four years. Kutuzov inflicted major defeats on the Turks and within less than a year helped induce them to sign the Treaty of Bucharest. The peace freed Russia from having to worry about the Turks while war clouds gathered in the west. Kutuzov was made a count.

In June 1812 Napoleon invaded Russia with superior forces. The Russians retreated and in August, after the loss of Smolensk, public opinion compelled Alexander to appoint Kutuzov in place of Barclay de Tolly. Kutuzov decided to give battle at Borodino but was compelled to continue the retreat, giving up Moscow in the process.

Avoiding another pitched battle, Kutuzov waited until Napoleon gave orders to retreat. Only then did he begin to harry the French. For his successful disruption of the French retreat at Smolensk, he received the title of prince of Smolensk. He inflicted additional heavy casualties on the French at Viazma, Krasnoe, and, above all, at the crossing of the Berezina River.

In the spring of 1813 the Allies began their advance into Prussia, with the main Russian army under Kutuzov's leadership. His health, however, having been precarious for decades, took a turn for the worse, and in April he died at Bunzlau in Silesia.

For a long time Kutuzov was criticized for being lethargic and unwilling to give battle. Only gradually was it recognized that, as in the Turkish war, Kutuzov could act quickly and decisively when this was advisable but that in 1812 the Russians had no choice but to adopt a Fabian delaying strategy. Napoleon's assessment of Kutuzov as the ''sly old Fox of the North'' was probably closest to the truth.

M. Bragin, *Kutuzov* (1970); D. Chandler, *The Campaigns of Napoleon* (New York, 1966); C. von Clausewitz, *Campaign of 1812 in Russia* (London, 1843); C. Duffy, *Borodino and the War of 1812* (London, 1972); R. Parkinson, *The Fox of the North: The Life of Kutuzov, General of War and Peace* (New York, 1976); L. O. Rakovskii, *Kutuzov* (1971).

Peter W. Becker

Related entries: AUSTERLITZ, BATTLE OF; AUSTERLITZ CAMPAIGN; BORODINO, BATTLE OF; RUSSIAN CAMPAIGN.

L

LABOR LEGISLATION. Labor legislation in the Napoleonic period synthesized two antagonistic trends: laissez-faire capitalism and government regulation. The French Revolution had taken its greatest steps in the direction of a liberal economy with the destruction of all forms of privilege on 4 August 1789 and the abolition of the guild system by the D'Allard Law of 2 March 1791. Under Napoleon, there were frequent calls by some tradesmen and government officials, particularly the police, for a return to a modified corporate economy. The proponents of laissez-faire were influential enough to block such schemes, but even they shared in the widespread and powerful sentiment that workers' indiscipline had increased since 1789. Consequently, in labor relations, there was gradual movement back to more control. Regnault de Saint-Jean-d'Angély clarified the government's position when he remarked before the Corps Legislatif on 1 April 1803, "Liberty was once too restricted; since then, license has been unchecked." He promised that the government would strike a balance between the "overly rigorous regulation" of the Old Regime and the "anarchy" of Revolutionary days.

The cornerstone of the Revolution's labor policy was the Le Chapelier Law (14–17 June 1791), which outlawed all trade associations and banned collective action by employers or workers. It was based on the premise that collective action of any kind was prejudicial to individual rights and therefore violated the constitution. It also reflected a fear that trade associations might tend to resurrect the guild system. It was a specific reaction to labor unrest in Paris that spring. The Le Chapelier Law remained on the books until 1884.

Under Napoleon, its strictures on labor were reiterated with even more force in the Law of 22 Germinal Year XI (12 April 1803). This law banned employers' combinations (*coalitions*) when these acted "unjustly or abusively" to lower wages and workers' combinations that challenged established wages or hours of work. The penalty for a worker who violated the law was three months in prison. Articles 414 through 416 of the Penal Code (1810) retained most of the wording of the Law of 22 Germinal but increased the penalty to two to five years in prison for the leader of a strike. Workers' mutual aid societies, also technically illegal, were officially tolerated and even encouraged, but all attempts by wage earners to organize and press collective demands met with swift repression. Employers encountered fewer obstacles to the pursuit of their common interests. They were rarely prosecuted for combination, and, indeed, the government even authorized them to form permanent trade associations (*syndicats*) in Paris.

Arbitration was preferred to repression in labor disputes which did not involve strikes. By the Law of 22 Germinal, the police were to deal with labor disputes in Paris and the municipal authorities with those elsewhere. These were not usually the most suitable courts for specialized problems. Napoleon therefore replaced them with Conseils de Prud'hommes, one of his most enduring achievements. The government created these councils for the specific purpose of judging and conciliating disputes between employers and employees and enforcing industrial laws and regulations. Composed of an equal number of manufacturers and "licensed workers," elected by their peers, the councils were not quite the democratic bodies that some historians represent them to be. Licensed workers were not ordinary wage earners but master artisans who took out an annual trade license (*patente*). Even so, the councils served their purpose well. The Lyon silk industry was granted the first council on 15 March 1806, and by 1815 there were councils operating in thirty-one cities, although Paris did not get one until 1844.

Article 12 of the Law of 22 Germinal and the subsequent Decree of 9 Frimaire Year XII (1 December 1803) required a passbook (*livret*) on all wage earners in workshops, factories, or construction yards. It did not apply to agricultural laborers, domestic servants, and some categories of unskilled workers. Women, too, were apparently exempt, with the exception of female silk workers in Lyon after 1812. The guilds had administered a similar system of passbooks in the eighteenth century. Now it was the municipal or police authorities who issued the passbooks, which had to be carried by a worker whenever he traveled in France. He surrendered the passbook to his employer during a period of employment. No employer could hire a worker whose passbook was not in order and lacked certification by his previous employer that all his obligations had been fulfilled. The passbook had a dual purpose: to ensure government supervision of the labor force and to guarantee a worker's good conduct. Workers resented the system, which was abolished only in 1890. There is much evidence, however, that many workers as well as employers ignored the regulations.

Many unskilled workers, such as porters, water carriers, and chimney sweeps, though not required to have a passbook, were subject to local police regulations, which required them to register with the authorities and to wear special numbered badges while on the job. The Imperial Decree of 3 October 1810 also compelled domestic servants in Paris—a special case because of the great number in that city—to register with the police, who issued them certificates. However, the resistance of employers, who feared registered servants might be police spies, made the decree unenforceable. Employment agencies set up by the Paris police in 1804 and subsequently by mayors in many other cities were a further means of controlling labor. The overall assumption was that the worker was not to be trusted. Napoleonic labor legislation, supplemented by police regulations, severely restricted his freedom, to the advantage of his employer and the state.

G. Bourgin, "Contribution à l'histoire du placement et du livret en France," *Revue politique et parlementaire* 71 (1912); C. P. Higby and C. B. Willis, "Industry and Labor under Napoleon," *AHR* 53 (1947–48); M. D. Sibalis, "The Workers of Napoleonic Paris, 1800–1815" (Ph.D. dissertation, Concordia University, 1979).

Michael D. Sibalis

Related entries: ECONOMY, FRENCH; LAW, CODES OF; SOCIETY; WOMEN.

LACHAPELLE, MARIE-LOUISE DUGES (1769–1822). Mme. or *Veuve* Lachapelle was the preeminent midwifery practitioner and teacher in France for a quarter century. Her mother, Marie Jonet, had been initially *sage-femme jurée* at the Châtelet Hospital, but in 1775 she became midwife in chief at the Hôtel Dieu of Paris. Since Lachapelle actually lived with her mother on the premises amid pregnant women lying in, she acquired her skills early. She reputedly performed her first solo complicated delivery when only twelve. She was widowed at age twenty-six, three years after her marriage to a resident surgeon at Hospital St. Louis; therefore she remained childless herself and continued to practice beside her mother. In 1795 Lachapelle was officially named associate chief midwife at the Hôtel Dieu, which could train only a half-dozen midwives at a time.

In response to public demand, the National Convention decreed on 25 Messidor Year III (13 July 1795) the creation of a separate successor maternity hospital at Val-de-Grâce; Lachapelle was appointed director of clinical instruction conjointly with the most experienced obstetrical professor of the day, Jean-Louis Baudelocque. During the first year after Napoleon's minister Jean-Antoine Chaptal reorganized the school as La Maternité, on 11 Messidor Year X (30 June 1802), fifty-four pupils were recruited to attend the two-year course. By 1813, 194 women were enrolled under Lachapelle's direction. After graduating, her pupils returned to their native locales to practice or teach in the departmental hospitals for indigent and unwed mothers.

At La Maternité, Lachapelle gave three daily, two-hour lessons while the professor lectured twice weekly on the theory of childbirth. In addition, the head midwife developed the professor's lessons in her *conférences*, putting them into her own words to make them more meaningful to her pupils who came from all over the Empire. Her pupils were divided into attending or service groups, each of which assisted patients in labor while Lachapelle supervised. If cases became too complicated, she took over while the students observed. In the rare instance when forceps were advised, the professor was called unless speed was too critical; then the head midwife applied the forceps. Each pupil wrote reports about the deliveries she assisted, and Lachapelle corrected these before giving them to Baudelocque or, after his death, to professor Antoine Dubois, his successor.

Lachapelle wrote many articles recording her observations and furnished statistics for the Conseil d'administration des hospices. Under her direction, La Maternité became famous throughout Europe for training many distinguished pupils both theoretically and clinically as it carried out Napoleon's plans to improve female and infant mortality. Her most famous pupil was Marie Boivin, author of *Mémorial de l'art des accouchemens*, which consisted of notes she herself made as a student and teaching assistant of Lachapelle at La Maternité. That the University of Marburg sent Boivin a diploma of doctor of medicine is a testimony to the ability of these women to develop skills equal to that of their male counterparts who practiced obstetrics.

Annuaire medico-chirurgical, vol. 1 (1819); A. Buck, *The Dawn of Modern Medicine* (New Haven, 1920); J. G. Cross, *Sketches of the Medical Schools of Paris* (London, 1815); P. Delaunay, *La Maternité de Paris* (Paris, 1909); M.-L. Lachapelle, *Pratique des accouchemens, ou Mémoires et Observations choisies sur les points les plus importants de l'art*, ed. A. Dugès (Paris, 1821–25); H. Tucker, *Elements of the Principles and Practices of Midwifery* (Philadelphia, 1848).

June K. Burton

Related entries: MEDICINE; WOMEN; WOMEN, EDUCATION OF.

LACUEE, JEAN-GERARD (1752–1841), comte de Cessac; minister of war administration, 1810–13. A specialist in military administration, according to Napoleon his ablest administrator after Pierre Daru, Lacuée always showed an intelligent awareness of the broader social and political context in which he was operating and the courage to contradict those in authority. He was an infantry captain in the Royal Army of the Old Regime. During the Revolution, as consultant to the military committee of the Constituent Assembly and then as member of the Legislative Assembly and reporter of its military committee, he was influential in securing legislation for the reorganization of the French army. After the suspension of Louis XVI on 10 August 1792, he was briefly minister of war and then organized the Army of the Pyrenees to repel a Spanish invasion. Napoleon appointed Lacuée president of the war section of the Council of State, where from 1800 to 1805 he drafted legislation dealing with conscription. When within the War Ministry Napoleon combined the conscription bureau with the committee of reviewers (which policed the payrolls), he made Lacuée director general (1806–10) and corresponded with him directly.

Lacuée had the good sense to retain the diligent chief of the conscription bureau, Antoine-Auden Hargenvilliers; together they tuned the conscription procedure until to the next director general, Mathieu Dumas, it seemed to run of itself. Appointed minister of the administration of war on 3 January 1810, Lacuée undertook the gigantic task of organizing the supply of the 650,000-man army for the invasion of Russia and, after that army's destruction, the supply of the new forces Napoleon raised for the campaign of 1813.

Reputed to be a yes-man, Lacuée is revealed by his correspondence with Napoleon to be a courageous administrator who spoke up when he disagreed with the emperor. He argued over the details of the enforcement of conscription, opposed the Austrian marriage and the invasion of Russia, and left office in November 1813 when he could not countenance Napoleon's continuation of the war.

W. S. Moody, "The Introduction of Military Conscription in Napoleonic Europe, 1798–1812" (Ph.D. dissertation, Duke University, 1971).

Harold T. Parker

Related entries: ADMINISTRATION, MILITARY; DARU.

LAFAYETTE, MARIE-JOSEPH-PAUL-YVES-ROCH-GILBERT DU MOTIER (1757–1834), figure in the American and French Revolutions; declined office under Napoleon until elected deputy during the Hundred Days. After service in America (1777–81) Lafayette became active in the cause of constitutional monarchy in France. In the Estates General he was a leader among liberal nobles. In the National Assembly he presented the first draft of the Declaration of the Rights of Man. After the fall of the Bastille (14 July 1789), he was named commander of the Paris National Guard. In 1790 he renounced his title and never used it again. As an exponent of law and order while the constitution was being written, he soon lost popularity, however, with both aristocrats and radicals. When the Constitution of 1791 was approved, Lafayette retired to his farm in Auvergne but was recalled to serve as a general in the army. After Louis XVI was overthrown in August 1792, he fled into the Austrian Netherlands (Belgium), was captured by Austrians, and was held a prisoner at Olmütz for five years.

Released from prison by the Treaty of Campo Formio in 1797, he was allowed to return to France only in 1800 after Napoleon came to power. Bonaparte hoped Lafayette would support him, but it was not to be. He voted against the life consulship, refused the ambassadorship to the United States, and refused membership in the Senate and in the Legion of Honor. Nevertheless he was left alone on his farm. His complaint about Napoleon's regime was that it lacked a free constitution and civil liberties.

During the Hundred Days, under the revised constitution, he was elected a member of the Chamber of Deputies. After Waterloo, however, he led the Chamber to demand Napoleon's abdication. At Helena, Napoleon called Lafayette "a simpleton" for not supporting him after Waterloo and a weakling infected with "English ideas," by which he meant constitutionalism.

During the rest of his life, Lafayette opposed the policies of the Restoration. He supported democratic revolutions in Europe and elsewhere. He is praised and condemned for his repeated refusal to attempt to become a popular military dictator and for his lifelong effort to imitate Washington in a country where such a model seemed inappropriate.

P. Chanson, *La Fayette et Napoléon* (Paris, 1958); R. de la Croix, duc de Castries, *La Fayette* (Paris, 1974); L. Gottschalk, *Lafayette*, 5 vols. (Chicago, 1935–69); L. Gottschalk and M. Maddox, *Lafayette in the French Revolution: From the October Days through the Federation* (Chicago, 1973); S. Idzerda, "Character as Destiny: A New Look at Lafayette's Career,'' *La France et l'Esprit de '76* (Clermont, 1977), and ''When and Why Lafayette Became a Revolutionary,'' *Bourgeois, Sans-Culottes and Other Frenchmen* (Waterloo, Ont., 1981).

Stanley Idzerda

Related entries: ABDICATION, SECOND; DIPLOMACY; *EMIGRES*; FOREIGN POLICY; HUNDRED DAYS, THE; UNITED STATES.

LAFFITTE, JACQUES (1767–1844), banker; governor of the Bank of France under Napoleon. A native of Bayonne, son of a carpenter, Laffitte came to Paris in 1788 seeking work. Hired as a clerk by the Swiss banker Jean-Frédéric de Perregaux, he learned quickly and by 1806 was a partner in Perregaux, Laffitte, and Company, by then one of the largest private banks in Paris, with a declared capitalization of 2 million francs. In 1809 Napoleon appointed Laffitte a regent of the Bank of France, and the provisional government on 25 April 1814 named him the bank's governor. During 1814 and 1815, he made loans to the bankrupt royal and municipal authorities. As a deputy of Paris in the legislature of the Restoration, Laffitte worked for a true constitutional monarchy, which brought him into opposition to the ultraroyalist Bourbon ministries. With Charles-Maurice de Talleyrand and Thiers he helped engineer the overthrow of Charles X in July 1830 and his replacement by Louis Philippe. But as the new Orleanist regime became increasingly conservative, Laffitte, again a deputy, moved into the liberal opposition.

J.M.S. Allison, *Thiers and the French Monarchy* (Boston and New York, 1926); L. Bergeron, *Banquiers, négociants et manufacturiers parisiens du Directoire à l'Empire* (Paris, 1978).

Harold T. Parker

Related entries: BANK OF FRANCE; ECONOMY, FRENCH.

LA FOREST, ANTOINE-RENE-CHARLES MATHURIN, COMTE DE (1768–1833), of minor nobility. A career officer in the consular service, La Forest was brought into the diplomatic service under the Consulate. He helped negotiate the Treaty of Lunéville (1801), served in Munich (1803–5), and participated in the negotiations with Prussia of 1805. His great role was as Napoleon's ambassador to Spain (1808–13), an assignment he began after thirty years of service. From Madrid he kept Napoleon informed of the most minute happenings, as well as the general situation. At the same time he gave King Joseph friendly advice, which, however, always carefully conformed with the emperor's policies. His *Correspondance* is a valuable source for the history of the Napoleonic Kingdom of Spain.

A.-R.-C. Mathurin, Comte de La Forest, *Correspondance du Comte de La Forest, ambassadeur de France en Espagne 1808–1813*, 7 vols., ed. A. du Casse (Paris, 1905–13).

Related entries: BONAPARTE, JOSEPH; DIPLOMACY; PENINSULAR WAR; SPAIN, KINGDOM OF.

LAGRANGE, JOSEPH-LOUIS, COUNT (1736–1813), one of the great mathematicians of the eighteenth century. Lagrange was born in Turin, the member of a family that originally had been French. His great-grandfather, a cavalry captain with the French army, had taken service with Charles Emmanuel II, duke of Savoy; his grandfather and father served as treasurer of the Office of Public Works and Fortifications of Turin. Lagrange spent the first thirty years of his life in his native Turin (1736–66) before moving to Berlin (1766–87) and then to Paris (1787–1813). During the first two periods he made discoveries in calculus and its application to mechanics and celestial mechanics and in the theory of numbers. During his Paris period, he summarized his mathematical conceptions in the *Mécanique analytique* (1788; rev. ed., 1811, 1816). During the Revolution he chaired the commission of scientists entrusted with the task of standardizing weights and measures on a rational basis. From 1795 he was a member of the Bureau of Longitudes, which directed the observatories of France, and taught analysis at the Ecole Polytechnique. Napoleon appointed him a senator, grand officer of the Legion of Honor, and count of the Empire. "The last great mathematician of the eighteenth century, he opened up magnificently the route to the abstract mathematics of the nineteenth century" (Itard).

R. Dugas, *Histoire de la mécanique* (Neuchatel-Paris, 1950); R. Taton et al., *Histoire générale des sciences*, vol. 2: *La science moderne*, and vol. 3: *La science contemporaine* (Paris, 1958–61).

Harold T. Parker

Related entries: INSTITUT NATIONAL DES SCIENCES ET DES ARTS; SCIENCE.

LAMARCK, JEAN-BAPTISTE-PIERRE-ANTOINE DE MONET DE (1744–1829), a significant contributor to botany, invertebrate zoology, and paleontology, and developer of a comprehensive theory of evolution. Lamarck was born in Bazentin-le-Petit (Picardy), the son of a semi-impoverished noble army officer. On the death of his father in 1759, the young Lamarck enrolled in the French army during the Seven Years War. During five years of peaceful garrison duty (1763–68) in French forts along the Mediterranean and France's eastern border, he began to botanize. Moving to Paris he studied medicine for four years and became interested in meteorology, chemistry, and shell collection. The publication of his *Flore française* (1779), which classified all known French plants, won him the recognition of French scientists and election to the Royal Academy of Sciences. As a member of the Royal Academy and later the Institut, he was first of all a botanist who systematically identified and classified French plants. As professor and research associate of the Muséum d'Histoire Naturelle from 1793, he was a zoologist who identified the invertebrates, living and fossil. But while capable of doing excellent detailed work, he was always seeking a total view of nature. Down to 1799 he believed in the fixity of species. But the problem of fossil forms of shells, those that were extinct and those with living analogues, led him to assert in 1800 the mutability of species. A geologist who believed in eons of time and a meteorologist aware of changing climate, he explained evolution in terms of changing environmental conditions. In meeting new demands presented by environmental changes, animals and plants developed new responses that strengthened certain parts and organs through use. Gradually new organs were formed and passed on to descendants. These views were most extensively presented in his *Philosophie Zoologique* (1809). He was decidedly a precursor of Charles Darwin.

R. W. Burkhardt, Jr., "The Inspiration of Lamarck's Belief in Evolution," *Journal of the History of Biology* 3 (1970); C. C. Gillispie, "The Formation of Lamarck's Evolutionary Theory," in *Archives internationales d'histoire des sciences* 9 (1956).

Harold T. Parker

Related entries: EDUCATION; INSTITUT NATIONAL DES SCIENCES ET DES ARTS; MEDICINE; SCIENCE.

LANDSHUT, BATTLE OF. See WAGRAM CAMPAIGN.

LANNES, JEAN (1769–1809), duc de Montebello, marshal of France. Handsome, hot tempered, and impetuous, he typified the élan of the Grande Armée. Few other men excelled Lannes in courage on the battlefield; he probably received more wounds than any other soldier or officer in the army. For Napoleon, his bravery excused an habitual tendency to violence. Bonaparte valued him as a friend and officer and was clearly much stricken by his death from wounds in 1809. Of the working class, Lannes was apprenticed as a youth to a dyer, but in 1792, at age twenty-three, he entered the army as a volunteer. For two years he served in the Pyrenees, was wounded, commissioned, and promoted several times but was mustered out in 1795. He returned to serve Bonaparte in Italy in 1796–97 and distinguished himself at Bassano, Arcola (three wounds in three days), and Rivoli. Napoleon had him made *général de brigade*.

In 1798–99 Lannes was with Bonaparte in Egypt and Syria and sustained wounds at Jaffa and Aboukir. He returned to France with Napoleon and assisted in the coup d'état of 18 Brumaire. In 1800 Lannes was made inspector general of the Consular Guard, distinguished himself again in Italy, was promoted to *général de division*, and was given a *sabre d'honneur* for his bravery at Marengo.

In 1804 Napoleon made Lannes one of the original marshals of the Empire. In 1805 he fought at Ulm and Austerlitz and received the grand cordon of the Legion of Honor. In 1806 he defeated the Prussian elements at Saalfeld to arrive early at Jena, where he commanded the center of Napoleon's army. He bested a Russian force at Pultusk in December 1806 but received a wound from which it took months to recover. In June 1807, however, he set the stage for Napoleon's climactic victory at Friedland. He was made duc de Montebello (where he had won a battle in 1800).

Dispatched to Spain (1808), he defeated General Francisco Xavier de Castaños at Tudela, commanded the siege of Saragossa in December, and negotiated its surrender in February 1809. In 1809 also he fought in Germany at Abensberg,

Landshut, Eggmühl, Regensburg, and finally Aspern-Essling. On 21 May 1809, Lannes and André Masséna led Napoleon's ill-fated first attempt to cross the Danube below Vienna. Trapped on the far bank by overwhelming Austrian forces, he valiantly held Essling while the French withdrew on 22 May. In mid-afternoon a cannonball smashed both of Lannes' legs; he died nine days later. The emperor and the army mourned.

C.L.M. Lannes, *Le Maréchal Lannes*, par son petit-fils (Tours, 1900); R. Périn, *Vie militaire de J. Lannes* (Paris, 1809).

Related entry: MARSHALS OF THE EMPIRE.

LAON, BATTLE OF. See FRANCE, CAMPAIGN OF.

LAPLACE, PIERRE-SIMON (1749–1827), perhaps the most influential scientist of his generation, a mathematician of genius who worked in the fields of celestial mechanics, probability, and physics. He was born in Beaumont-en-Auge (Normandy), the son of a prosperous small farmer who engaged in the cider business and was syndic of the parish. After seven years as a day student in the local Benedictine *collège*, the young Laplace, age seventeen, matriculated at the University of Caen. He so impressed his mathematics professors that within two years they sent him on to Paris and to Jean Le Rond d'Alembert, who secured him the post of professor of mathematics at the Ecole Militaire. After a few years, his outstanding mathematical memoirs won him election to the Royal Academy of Sciences in 1773. His major works were *Mécanique céleste*, 5 vols. (1799–1825), which described the solar system and its probable origins, and *Théorie analytique des probabilités* (1812). Each major work was paralleled by a volume of elegant popularization: the *Exposition du système du monde* (1796), in which he advanced his nebular hypothesis on the origin of the solar system, and *Essai philosophique sur les probabilités* (1814).

During the French Revolution he was drawn into public life. He played a central role in the preparation of the metric system, dominated the physical science section of the Institut, and helped organize the new Ecole Polytechnique. Under the Empire he and the chemist Claude-Louis Berthollet gathered around them a brilliant group of young French scientists who called themselves the Société d'Arcueil. Napoleon made Laplace minister of the interior in November 1799 but relieved him after six weeks and thereafter used him as an ornament to the imperial regime. He appointed Laplace in 1803 chancellor of the Senate with an annual income of 72,000 francs, named him to the Legion of Honor in 1805, and the following year ennobled him with the title of count.

M. P. Crosland, *The Society of Arcueil: A View of French Science at the Time of Napoleon I* (Cambridge, Mass., 1967); R. Hahn, *Laplace as a Newtonian Scientist* (Los Angeles, 1967).

Harold T. Parker

Related entries: BERTHOLLET; INSTITUT NATIONAL DES SCIENCES ET DES ARTS; SCIENCE.

LA PLAIGNE, LEON-CHARLES DE (1806–81), called "le comte Léon." He was one of two illegitimate sons acknowledged by Napoleon in his will (the other was Count Florian Alexandre Walewski). Born 13 December 1806 in Paris, he died 15 April 1881. His mother, Eléonore Denuelle de La Plaigne, was a reader to the Empress Josephine.

Some observers, contemporary and recent, have doubted that Léon was Napoleon's son and have asserted that Napoleon shared those doubts when he found that Eléonore had also been the mistress of his brother-in-law, Joachim Murat. Napoleon's actions do not bear out these claims, however. Before Léon's birth, his mother was settled in a house and given an income. At the birth, two officials—Jacques Aymé, treasurer of the Legion of Honor, and Guillaume Andral, the physician to Les Invalides—were witnesses. Napoleon almost immediately settled an income of 30,000 francs on the child. Léon was entrusted to the same nurse who had cared for Napoleon's nephew, Achille Murat, and later he was educated at the Hix School in Paris along with the sons of high officials.

Although Napoleon apparently did not resume his affair with Léon's mother after their son's birth and perhaps never even saw her again, he frequently had young Léon brought to him and gave him many gifts. In Napoleon's tumultuous last years of rule, he still thought of the boy and saw to it that he was financially well off. During the Hundred Days he increased Léon's income by 12,000 francs and after Waterloo gave him canal shares worth 100,000 francs. Napoleon also bequeathed Léon a large sum of money with which to buy an estate, a sum Léon did not receive for many years.

At one time, Napoleon expressed the hope that his son would become a magistrate, but while Léon did become litigious it was only as a persistent seeker of funds from Bonaparte relatives and from his mother. An inveterate gambler who piled up huge debts—at one time he asked relatives to pay a debt of 800,000 francs—he eventually went to debtor's prison at Clichy for two years (1838–40).

In 1840, in London, he sought help from his cousin Louis-Napoleon, who refused to see him. Léon challenged him to a duel, which was, however, prevented by the police. In spite of this incident, Louis-Napoleon, when he became the Emperor Napoleon III, paid Léon's legacy (about 250,000 francs), gave him a pension of 6,000 francs, and had the Civil List pay his gambling debts from time to time.

From 1854, Léon lived with a seamstress, Françoise Jonet, whom he married in 1862, and by whom he had four children. After the fall of the Second Empire, Léon and his family lived in England, presumably still supported by the Bonapartes. (Another story has it that he emigrated to the United States and married a cook.) He returned to France in 1875, finally settling in Pontoise, where he lived—and died—in destitution.

Léon's mother, Louise-Catherine-Eléonore Denuelle de La Plaigne (1787–1868) had only a fleeting affair with the emperor. In fact, it seems to have been instigated by Napoleon's family to embarrass Josephine, and to have meant little to either participant. The affair was important, however, in proving to Napoleon that he could father a child, a capability he had not previously demonstrated, and which made feasible his divorce and remarriage.

The affair was not Eléonore's first fleeting relationship. Like many other socially ambitious parents, hers, of uncertain means and shadowy background, sent their daughter to Madame Campan's school in St. Germain-en-Laye, fashionable because Josephine placed several young female relatives there. One of Eléonore's classmates was Anunziata Bonaparte, later Caroline Murat.

When Eléonore had finished her schooling without having contracted a suitable marriage, her mother took a theatre box where the young girl was displayed. She was seen, wooed and won by a "Captain" Revel, who was revealed, after only two months of marriage, to be merely a sergeant and a forger. He was sent to jail, and Eléonore, through Madame Campan and Caroline Murat, became a reader for the Empress, and was propelled into the affair with Napoleon.

Almost immediately becoming pregnant, Eléonore got a divorce from Revel. But, as noted above, after the birth of her son, Napoleon apparently never saw her again although he gave her an income of 22,000 francs a year when she married, in 1808, Lieutenant Pierre-Philippe Augier, with whom she lived in Spain for a time, and who died during the Russian campaign. She married again in 1814, this time to Count Carl de Luxbourg, a major in the service of the King of Bavaria.

Her first husband, Revel, reappeared after the fall of Napoleon, publishing scurrilous pamphlets about his ex-wife's affair, and seeking money from her, as did Léon, more than once. Eléonore held on to her money and her marriage amidst these storms from her past, and lived with Luxbourg in Germany and elsewhere for 26 years, finally returning to Paris when Luxbourg became Baden's envoy to France.

G. Aretz, *Napoleon and His Women Friends* (Philadelphia, 1927); T. Aronson, *The Golden Bees. The Story of the Bonapartes* (Greenwich, Conn., 1964); M. Billard, *Un fils de Napoléon Ier* (Paris, 1909); Breton, *Napoleon and His Ladies* (New York, 1965); R. F. Delderfield, *Napoleon in Love* (Boston, 1959); Funck-Bretano, "L'Aigle et l'aiglon," *Le Grande Revue* (Paris, 15 March 1904); F. Masson, *Napoléon et les Femmes* (Paris, 1897); C. Nauroy, "Les Enfants des Napoléon Ier, le Comte Léon et le Comte Walewski," in *Les Sécrets de Bonaparte* (Paris, 1899); C. de Rémusat, *Mémoires* (Paris, 1885); J. F. Revel, "Souvenirs," *Nouvelle Revue Retrospective*, 2d Series (Paris, 1903).

Nancy Nolte

Related entries: JOSEPHINE; NAPOLEON I.

LA ROTHIERE, BATTLE OF. See FRANCE, CAMPAIGN OF.

LARREY, DOMINIQUE-JEAN, BARON (1766–1842), French surgeon, known for his contributions to military medicine during the Republican and Napoleonic eras. Born at Baudéan on 8 July 1766, he later began his medical studies at Toulouse, where his uncle was surgeon in chief of the city's hospital.

In 1787, he went to Paris and secured the post of surgeon-major aboard the frigate *La Vigilante* on an expedition to North America. His diligence in providing medical care for the sick was such that only one man died during the voyage. Returning to Paris, he received the position of second resident surgeon at Les Invalides.

In 1792, while attached as surgeon-aide-major to the Rhineland Army, he became appalled at the slowness with which the wounded were transported to often remote field hospitals. As a result, he organized a system of mobile field hospitals, using light carts drawn by horses to move the wounded from the battlefield, which provided the surgeons with the means of following the armies in order to avoid delays in treating the wounded. This system made him famous. He was promoted to chief surgeon of the army, received a reward from l'Académie de Chirurgie, and in 1796 was named professor of the recently created school of military medicine at Val-de-Grâce in Paris. He was called on by Napoleon to organize his ambulances for the Italian campaign, and after its victory, he took charge of the military hospitals there and halted an epidemic that was ravaging Venetian Friuli, for which he received the Ordre de la Couronne de Fer.

Larrey was also present at the Egyptian campaign, where his devotion to rescuing the wounded was outstanding. Risking his own life, he helped to move the wounded to the hospitals during the heaviest fighting. For example, at the Battle of Aboukir, he performed life-saving surgery on the battlefield on General Jean-Urbain Fugières, who had been shot in the shoulder, before moving him to the hospital. Larrey also supervised the care given to and the nourishment and hygiene of all those who stayed in the field hospital, which the soldiers nicknamed *La Providence*. From the Egyptian campaign onward, Larrey assisted all of the major military campaigns of the era.

On his return to France in 1802, Larrey was named surgeon in chief of the hospital of the Guard of the consuls; in 1804, officer of the Legion of Honor; and in 1805, inspector general of the Office of Health of the Army. He served as surgeon in chief of the Guard in Napoleon's military campaigns. His most distinguished efforts were at the Battle of Eylau (18 February 1807), where his efforts in moving the wounded in the extremely cold weather earned him the cross of commander of the Legion of Honor; the Battle of Wagram (5–6 July 1809), where he was created baron, with a revenue of 5,000 francs; and the Russian campaign, where his observation on the effects of cold on the wounded led to his further research and publication of the topic in his *Mémoires de chirurgie militaire et campagnes*. He was recognized as a valuable asset to the army and was awarded a pension of 5,000 francs. In 1812, he was named by special decree as chief surgeon of the Grand Armée for the Russian campaign. He was also present at Waterloo, where he was taken prisoner after having been wounded. During the Restoration, he was named surgeon in chief of the Royal Guard; in 1820, member of l'Académie de Médecine; and in 1829, member of l'Institut. He died in Paris on 1 August 1842.

"Le vertueux Larrey," as Napoleon called him in his testament, is one of the glories of military medicine, in his courageous attempts to ameliorate the suffering of the wounded in battle, his skill in performing amputations, and in his scholarly works on military medicine.

P. Huard, *Sciences, médicine, pharmacie de la Revolution à l'Empire 1789–1815* (Paris, 1970); D. Vess, *Medical Revolution in France, 1789–1796* (Gainesville, 1974); O. Wangensteen et al., "Wound Management of Ambroise Paré and Dominique Larrey, Great French Military Surgeons of the 16th and 19th centuries," *Bulletin of the History of Medicine*, 46 (1972).

Dawn L. Corley

Related entries: MEDICINE; SCIENCE.

LAS CASES, EMMANUEL, COMTE DE (1766–1842), with Napoleon on St. Helena. *Mémorial de Sainte-Hélène* (1823) became a prime source of the Napoleonic legend. Before the Revolution, Las Cases was, ironically, a marquis, seigneur of several villages, and lieutenant in the Royal Navy. One of the first to emigrate in 1789, he served in the *émigré* army of the prince de Condé before returning to France after 18 Brumaire. In 1810 Napoleon was recruiting members of the old nobility to give the court of Marie-Louise a more aristocratic tone. He attached Las Cases to his person as chamberlain. Either from loyalty or because he saw in the fallen emperor good copy for a best-seller, Las Cases volunteered to accompany Napoleon into exile. For eighteen months, until he was expelled from St. Helena by the British governor, Sir Hudson Lowe, he daily took notes on his conversations with Napoleon and published them shortly after Napoleon's death. Las Cases had considerable journalistic talent, and his report reads well. However, he had a cause, Bonapartism, and he connived with the emperor to present him as a martyr for democracy and peace.

Emmanuel Las Cases, *Le mémorial de Saint-Hélène*, ed. M. Dunan, 2 vols. (Paris, 1951).

Harold T. Parker

Related entries: BERTRAND; GOURGAUD; MONTHOLON; ST. HELENA.

LAW, CODES OF. Napoleon considered these his greatest contribution. The *cahiers* of 1789 demanded uniform laws, and the French Revolutionaries had been interested in replacing the approximately four hundred codes used in France (roughly divided into Roman law in the south and common law in the north). But they had made little progress, except for preparing the way by sweeping away old legislation. Bonaparte's desire for uniformity led him to push the project. He appointed a commission of four to prepare a civil code, and he presided over more than half of the sessions devoted by the section of the Council of State to considering the commission's draft.

The Civil Code (also known as the Code Napoléon), promulgated in 1804, was more important than the Code of Civil Procedure (1806), the Commercial Code (1807), the Criminal Code and Code of Criminal Procedure (1808), the

Penal Code (1810), and the Rural Code (this last never went into effect). It has been adopted, or has influenced the codes of law, in all other European countries and those under European influence or control. The Code Napoléon is divided into three sections: persons, property, and the acquisition of property. The property aspects are significant because they provide for a division of estates; indeed, landed property was the kind most in evidence in the code, which tended to sanctify property. (In varying degrees all of the codes were conservative or reactionary.) The section on persons is important for the mastery it gives to the head of the household and the inferior status accorded women. Its overriding importance, however, lies in the civil rights it enumerates and its guarantee of equality in the eyes of the law.

J. Godechot, *Les Institutions de la France sous la Révolution et l'Empire*, 2d ed. (Paris, 1968); R. B. Holtman, *The Napoleonic Revolution* (Baton Rouge, La., 1978); B. Schwarz, ed., *The Code Napoleon and the Common Law World* (New York, 1956).

Robert B. Holtman

Related entries: CONSTITUTIONS; ECONOMY, FRENCH; LABOR LEGISLATION; SOCIETY; WOMEN.

LEBRUN, CHARLES-FRANCOIS (1739–1824), duc de Plaisance, third consul (1799), archtreasurer of the Empire. Born in Saint-Sauveur Landelin, Normandy, Lebrun was a top-level civil servant under the Old Regime. After the overthrow of the king, he remained loyal to the Republic but was imprisoned during the Terror. A member of the Council of Ancients of the Directory, he was considered all but counterrevolutionary. After the coup d'état of Brumaire, First Consul Napoleon chose him as third consul, undoubtedly to balance the executive branch, since the second consul was Jean-Jacques Cambacérès, an ex-Terrorist. (The two were opposites personally as well; Lebrun was spartan in habit and dress, Cambacérès a fat gourmet.) When the Empire was created, Napoleon named Lebrun archtreasurer. He had few specific duties but did contribute to the reorganization of justice (the province of Cambacérès, as archchancellor) and finances (the province of Charles Gaudin and Nicolas Mollien). After the forced abdication of Louis Bonaparte of the throne of Holland (1810), Napoleon sent Lebrun to reorganize the kingdom into French-style departments and prepare it for integration into the French Empire proper. Among Lebrun's first acts were to introduce the Code Napoléon and conscription, both of which Louis had rejected as "un-Dutch." Lebrun returned to serve Napoleon during the Hundred Days (1815). Louis XVIII, on his restoration, banished Lebrun from the House of Peers, and he lived out his life in political obscurity.

Related entries: CAMBACERES; CONSTITUTIONS; FINANCES; GAUDIN; HOLLAND, KINGDOM OF; LAW, CODES OF.

LE CHAPELIER LAW. See LABOR LEGISLATION.

LECLERC, CHARLES-VICTOR-EMMANUEL (1772–1802), general, brother-in-law of Napoleon. Leclerc entered the army as a volunteer in 1791 and quickly rose through the ranks. He distinguished himself at Toulon, where Napoleon gave him the honor of carrying news of the victory to Paris. He followed Napoleon to Italy (1796), where Napoleon recommended his promotion to *général de brigade*. In 1797 he married Pauline Bonaparte. Leclerc was named *général de division* in August 1799. On Napoleon's return from Egypt, Leclerc joined him and commanded the grenadiers that expelled the Council of Five Hundred in the coup of Brumaire. He served as a commander in the Army of the Rhine under Jean Moreau. In 1801 he commanded a successful expedition against Portugal, and in October Napoleon named him commander of an expedition to regain control of Saint-Domingue (Haiti). After an initially successful three-month campaign, Leclerc's force was ravaged by disease. In September 1802, general insurrection broke out, and during the ensuing conflict Leclerc succumbed to yellow fever.

R. R. Crout, "The Leclerc Instruction" (Master's thesis, University of Georgia, 1969); P. Roussier, *Lettres du General Leclerc* (Paris, 1937).

Robert R. Crout

Related entries: BONAPARTE, P.; BRUMAIRE, COUP OF 18, YEAR VIII; HAITI; ITALIAN CAMPAIGN, FIRST; TOULON, SIEGE OF.

LEFEBVRE, FRANCOIS-JOSEPH (1755–1820), duc de Danzig, marshal of France; the most proletarian of the marshals whose wife, an ex-laundress, was called "Madame sans gêne." Lefebvre was the son of an Alsatian miller. He enlisted in the Royal Gardes françaises in 1773 and in 1788 was a sergeant. In 1791 he was wounded while protecting the royal family.

Under the Republic his experience got him rapid promotion from captain (1792) to brigadier general (1793) to major general (1794). Between 1794 and 1799 he served in the Rhineland and Germany—thus never under Bonaparte. Nevertheless he gained great respect for the future emperor.

In November 1799, he threw his support—very important because of his rapport with the troops—to Napoleon in the coup d'état of 18 Brumaire. Bonaparte made him a senator (1800) and an original marshal of the Empire (1804).

Lefebvre fought in the Jena-Auerstädt campaign (1806) and commanded the siege of Danzig (1807). Napoleon created him a duke and took him to Spain (1808–9), where he contributed to the emperor's unbroken string of victories. In 1809 he commanded a corps in the Wagram campaign (though in the Tyrol). In 1812 he fought in Russia, in 1813 in Germany, and in 1814 in France, driving the Old Guard to new glory at Champagne, Champaubert, and Montmirail.

In April 1814, however, Lefebvre, with great reluctance, was one of the marshals who forced Napoleon to abdicate. He nevertheless rallied to Napoleon during the Hundred Days and was destituted under the Second Restoration. He was restored to his rank and honors only in 1819, a year before his death.

A. Fleury, *Soldats ambassadeurs sous le Directoire an IV–an VII*, 2 vols. (Paris, 1906); J. Wirth, *Le maréchal Lefebvre* (Paris, 1904).

Jesse Scott

Related entry: MARSHALS OF THE EMPIRE.

LEGEND, NAPOLEONIC. "Living he lost the world, dead he conquers it." That admirable formulation of Chateaubriand gives a resumé of the Napoleonic legend. Napoleon is the first of the modern myths. Contrary to what was for so long written, the Napoleonic legend was not born at St. Helena; it was forged during the first Italian campaign in newspapers created by Bonaparte with an eye to propaganda: *Le Courrier de l'armée d'Italie, La France vue de l'armée d'Italie*. There one reads: "Bonaparte flies like lightning and strikes like a thunderbolt. He is everywhere and sees everything." It was the same in Egypt. On the eve of Brumaire, Bonaparte was the most celebrated of all the generals.

Under the Empire, Bonapartist propaganda increased in volume. The press continued to exalt the master of Europe. The bulletins of the Grand Army—distributed all over the country as printed broadsides or placards, commented on from the pulpit by priests, declaimed in theaters by actors, analyzed by professors in the lycées—prolonged the reverberations of his victories. The effect of the bulletins was amplified by prints, medals, and paintings. The coronation painting of Jacques-Louis David springs to mind.

Religion was called into the service of Napoleon's cult with the introduction of the imperial catechism. The resulting gigantic conditioning of souls, above all those of children, explains the blossoming of the legend after 1823.

In 1814, however, another legend had developed: the "black legend," that of the ogre, spread by the pamphlets of Benjamin Constant (*De l'esprit de conquête et de l'usurpation*) and of Chateaubriand (*De Buonaparte et des Bourbons*), at the time of the restoration of Louis XVIII. The ephemeral return of Napoleon in 1815 changed nothing. Waterloo left behind the remembrance of disaster.

But the Restoration caused many to regret the loss of Napoleon: workers who were victims of the miseries attending the Industrial Revolution, officers retired on half pay, peasants alarmed by the return of the former proprietors of the national properties, officials without posts. Then came the clap of thunder, in 1823, of the *Mémorial de Sainte-Hélène*. Though described dispassionately by Emmanuel de Las Cases, the martyrdom of Napoleon on his rock stirred public opinion. The Romantics were in raptures for past glory; Victor Hugo and Alexandre Dumas remembered that they were sons of Napoleon's generals; Stendhal that he had been an auditor to the Council of State. Honoré Balzac noted: "What Napoleon began with the sword, I finish with the pen." The ballads of Béranger, the imagery of Epinal of J.-C. Pellerin, popularized the themes of the legend.

The Second Empire should have dealt a death blow to the legend. But Napoleon had been, at Jena, the victor over Prussia—the Prussia that had humiliated France at Sedan. He became the champion of the "revenge" movement, "the professor of energy'' toward whom turned, at the same time, Maurice Barrès and the popular novel. Later, it would be the cinema of Abel Gance and Sacha Guitry. Even today the tomb of Napoleon at the Invalides is the most visited monument in Paris.

F. Bluche, *Le Bonapartisme* (Paris, 1980); R. B. Holtman, *Napoleonic Propaganda* (Baton Rouge, 1950); J. Lucas-Dubreton, *Le culte de Napoléon* (Paris, 1959); J. Tulard, *Le mythe de Napoléon* (Paris, 1971).

Jean Tulard

Related entries: ARCHITECTURE; PRESS; PROPAGANDA; SCULPTURE; ST. HELENA.

LEGION OF HONOR. See NOBILITY, IMPERIAL.

LEGISLATORS (1800–15). Statistics on the legislators show how society developed under Napoleon. Slightly over 700 men served in the Corps Législatif (1800–14) and 628 sat in the Chamber of Representatives of the Hundred Days (1815). Electoral laws were written, rewritten, and sometimes ignored, so there was no regular turnover of legislators. The deputies were selected by the Senate, at large from 1800 to 1802 and thereafter from lists of elected candidates, which Napoleon annotated first. Nepotism and personality played a part in the selections, but such factors were generally less important than the role a person had played in society. The deputies had little power, but, as Napoleon wished, they represented the regime to the people.

In the beginning the deputies were men of the Revolution; 90 percent had served in a Revolutionary legislature and over 70 percent had held a government post. Two-thirds were solidly bourgeois and only 5 percent were *propriétaires* (landholders). Although these men had helped put General Bonaparte in power, few would ever become creatures of the emperor. Just one-quarter would hold a government position during his reign.

In 1803, when the first elections of candidates took place, the new legislators at the Palais Bourbon numbered fewer office-holders from the Revolution and more who were ready to serve the new regime. Former Revolutionary legislators now numbered only 60 percent, while over half the legislators eventually would accept a position and 20 percent a title from the emperor.

Movement away from the Revolution was more dramatic under the Empire, as Napoleon worked for a social amalgam. The average age of the legislators increased, and solidly bourgeois types dropped below a quarter by 1811–13, whereas *propriétaires* rose to 29 percent. Former holders of Revolutionary posts fell below one-half; former officials of the Old Regime climbed to 30 percent; 10 percent had an Old Regime title. Offices and honors cemented the amalgam of old and new society; over three-quarters of the legislators held office under the Empire, one-third won the Legion of Honor, and one-third became imperial nobles. Under the Empire Napoleon turned to his type of man: a man of maturity with service to the state, a pedigree, and strong ties to the land.

During the Hundred Days, however, the voters provided Napoleon with a new type of deputy. Half of the deputies were solidly bourgeois, while only 2 percent had Old Regime titles. Those holding office during the Revolution were three times more prevalent than those holding office under the Old Regime. Of the experienced legislators, 6 percent had begun their legislative careers in the elections of 1792 (the first of the Republic), more than in any other election. Despite this return to the men of the Revolution, dedication to Napoleon was still evident. Twenty-two percent had imperial titles, and over half accepted a government post. The legislators' changing characteristics over time represent well the evolution of the regime.

Archives Nationales, CC28-49, C1164A1; T. Beck, *French Legislators, 1800–1834* (Berkeley, 1974); F. Bluche, *Le plébiscite des Cent-Jours* (Geneva, 1974); I. Collins, *Napoleon and His Parliaments, 1800–1815* (London, 1979); A. Robert and G. Cougny, *Dictionnaire des parlementaires français*, 5 vols. (Paris, 1889–91); A. Gobert, *L'opposition des assemblées pendant le Consulat* (Paris, 1925).

Thomas Beck

Related entries: CONSTITUTIONS; HUNDRED DAYS, THE; NOTABLES.

LEIPZIG, BATTLE OF (16–19 October 1813), the Battle of the Nations. Napoleon with nearly 200,000 men was brought to bay at Leipzig by three converging allied armies: the Army of Bohemia (Karl zu Schwarzenberg, 203,000), from the south; the Army of Silesia (G. L. Blücher von Wahlstatt, 54,000), from the northwest; and the Army of the North (Jean Bernadotte, 85,000), behind Blücher. Napoleon's plan of battle was to mass 120,000 troops to envelop the right wing of the Army of Bohemia to the south, while containing the Army of Silesia in the north. On 16 October the French attack in the south went well, but Blücher's Army of Silesia, in the north, pinned down the French corps of Louis Marmont and Henri Bertrand that were needed to win a decisive victory. On 17–18 October, with the arrival of the Army of the North, the initiative passed to the Allies. The Allied superiority of numbers actually engaged (312,000 against 200,000 French) started to tell, as the French began to retire within the city. Napoleon, perceiving his position to be untenable, ordered a phased withdrawal, which was marred only at the end when an anonymous French corporal prematurely blew up the bridge over which the French army was retreating, thus trapping the French rear guard of 30,000, which was forced to surrender. The casualities were heavy on both sides: the Allies lost probably 54,000 killed and wounded; the French 38,000, plus the 30,000 taken prisoner.

Harold T. Parker

Related entries: BERNADOTTE; BLÜCHER VON WAHLSTATT; GERMAN WAR OF LIBERATION; PONIATOWSKI; SCHWARZENBERG.

LEOBEN, PRELIMINARY PEACE OF (18 April 1797), made in connection with an armistice between the Archduke Charles of Austria and Napoleon. Austria confirmed French possession of Belgium. A tentative agreement was made for

the disposition of Venetian territories and the Papal States of Romagna, Bologna, and Ferrara. Austria recognized the Cisalpine Republic. Definitive peace was to be made by a later congress (which met in October 1797 at Campo Formio).
Related entry: CAMPO FORMIO, TREATY OF.

LE SUEUR, JEAN-FRANCOIS (1760–1837), popular French composer of opera and sacred music during the Revolution, the Empire, and the Restoration. Le Sueur was born 15 February 1760 of Picardy peasants at Drucat-Plessiel near Abbeville. His early musical talent led his family to send him to choir schools in Abbeville and Amiens for instruction. In 1776, he began a ten-year period as choirmaster at Dijon, Le Mans, Tours, and finally at Notre Dame in Paris. He was twice dismissed from Notre Dame for introducing opera singers and large orchestras as accompaniment to the Mass, treating it as a theatrical production. He turned from religious music to writing odes, chants, and hymns for the massive open-air Revolutionary festivals and made his debut as an operatic composer in 1793 with *La Caverne*. Two other operas, *Paul et Virginie* (1794) and *Télémaque* (1796), were successfully performed before his greatest triumph, *Ossian ou les Bardes*, in 1804. Begun in the 1700s, it found a ready audience in Napoleon, who was especially fond of the poetry of Ossian. Le Sueur dedicated the opera to the emperor when he was appointed director of the Tuileries chapel in 1804.

From 1818 until his death, he was a professor of composition at the Paris Conservatoire. Among his pupils were Hector Berlioz, Charles Gounod, Ambroise Thomas, Ernest Guiraud, and twelve of the Prix de Rome winners between 1822 and 1839. Under the Restoration he was co-director of the Tuileries chapel until it was closed in 1830.

For Le Sueur music was intended to express nature and human emotions; without extramusical ideas, music loses its meaning or purpose. He believed that the traditional rules governing rhythm, harmony, and melody should be subservient to imitating nature or expressing a literary text. He was therefore most interested in vocal works, operas, and oratorios. As with most other French composers in the Napoleonic sphere, he was not affected by Romanticism and remained unmoved by the musical revolution in Germany. His religious music is noteworthy for its simplicity in harmony, form, and style yet is powerful due to his skill in handling melody and suiting the music to its intended purpose. His Christmas oratorio, composed in 1786, used themes in a manner suggesting Berlioz' *idée fixe* or Wagner's leitmotivs. Le Sueur died in Paris on 6 October 1837.

T. Fleischmann, *Napoléon et la Musique* (Brussels, 1965); M. M. Herman, *The Sacred Music of Jean-François Le Sueur: A Musical and Biographical Source Study* (Ph.D. diss., University of Michigan, 1964), and "The Turbulent Career of Jean-François Le Sueur, maître de chapelle," *Recherches sur la Musique Française Classique*, 9 (1969);

F. Lamy, *Jean-François Le Sueur (1760–1837)* (Paris, 1912); O. Saloman, "The Orchestra in Le Sueur's Musical Aesthetics," *Musical Quarterly*, 60 (1974).

Rachel R. Schneider

Related entries: CHERUBINI; GRASSINI; MEHUL; MUSIC; PROPAGANDA; THEATER.

LIGNY, BATTLE OF. See WATERLOO CAMPAIGN.

LIGURIAN REPUBLIC (GENOA), established in 1797, during Napoleon's first Italian campaign, by Genoan republicans with the support of Bonaparte. Besieged and finally taken by the Austrians in 1799–1800, Genoa was in economic collapse when Napoleon won the victory at Marengo that ended his second Italian campaign. In 1801, Antoine Saliceti installed a new government under a constitution rewritten in Paris. Bonaparte appointed the first doge (chief executive). After the creation of the Empire, the republic was an anachronism and had not served France well or even established a customs union with the Kingdom of Italy. In 1805 the republic was annexed to France and divided into the departments of Genoa, Montenotte, and Apennins.

G. Assereto, *La Repubblica Ligure, 1797–1799* (Turin, 1975); G. Bigoni, *La caduta della repubblica di Genova nel 1797* (Genova, 1897); G. Carbone, *Compendio della storia ligure. . .al 1814*, 2 vols. (Genova, 1836–37); A. Clavarino, *Annali della repubblica ligure dal 1797 a tutto il 1805*, 5 vols. (Genova, 1852); A. Fugier, *Napoléon et l'Italie* (Paris, 1947); G. Martini, *Storia della restorazione della repubblica di Genova, l'anno 1814. . .Con documenti inediti* (Asti, 1858); P. Nurra, *Genova nel Risorgimento* (Milan, 1948); G. B. Serra, *Memorie per la Storia di Genova degli ultimi anni del secolo XVIII al fino anno 1814* (Genoa, 1930); C. Varesse, *Storia della Repubblica di Genova dall origini al 1814* (Genoa, 1830); C. Zaghi, *Napoleone e l'Italia* (Napoli, 1966).

Leonard Macaluso

Related entries: EMPIRE, FRENCH; ITALIAN CAMPAIGN, FIRST; ITALIAN CAMPAIGN, SECOND.

LITERATURE. Several features of French literature and philosophy continued eighteenth-century trends. The providential interpretation of history was always deep in the mentality of many Frenchmen, and the conservative Joseph de Maistre used it to explain the French Revolution, in his view "a vomit of evil." During the Revolution a new group of *philosophes*, known as *idéologues* and including such a figure as Antoine Destutt de Tracy, succeeded the real *philosophes*. The *idéologues* gave to the main theses of the encyclopedists an extremely rationalistic interpretation. And then under Napoleon there was the versifier Jacques Delille who translated Virgil and wrote poetry in elegant classical verse.

The literature that endured, however, was created by three powerful egos: Napoleon, Mme. de Staël, and François Chateaubriand. They broke with the classical regularities of prose and poetry and especially dared to ask, "What about me?"

Napoleon too was a writer during the early years of the nineteenth century.

His proclamations were succinct and imperious, effective when read to the troops or when posted on public buildings. He read widely and even during military campaigns insisted on having the new publications sent to him from Paris. His two rivals for fame were Mme. de Staël and Chateaubriand.

Mme. de Staël published in 1800 an ambitious book, strongly influenced by Jean-Jacques Rousseau: *De la littérature considérée dans ses rapports avec les institutions sociales*. She attempted to prove that literature and social institutions are allied and change and develop together. Napoleon exiled her in 1803, depriving her of Paris and the conversations that only Paris provided.

More than any other single writer, Chateaubriand inaugurated and defined the great Romantic spell in French literature. Napoleon, the *parvenu* who became emperor, needed poets to immortalize him and develop his legend, but Chateaubriand was a legitimate noble who needed only himself, and he deliberately described himself in pose after pose that created the type of romantic hero: the lonely Breton boy who fell in love with the sea and the wind and the birds in the turrets of his feudal castle; the handsome French officer in the New World; the civilized European in the virgin forests of America; and, later, the writer who was world famous, representing his country and defending the traditional religion of his country. His apology, *Le génie du christianisme*, argues for the truth of Christianity by demonstrating its achievements in art, learning, and social action. Its publication on 15 April 1802 was synchronized with the concordat made legal by the First Consul Bonaparte on 14 April.

J. Charpentier, *Napoléon et les hommes des lettres de son temps* (Paris, 1935); H. J. Christopher, *Mistress to An Age; A Life of Madame de Staël* (Indianapolis, 1958); H. Guillemin, *Madame de Staël, Benjamin Constant, et Napoléon* (Paris, 1959), and *Madame de Staël et Napoléon* (Bienne, Switzerland, 1966); C. A. Sainte-Beuve, *Chateaubriand et son groupe littéraire sous l'Empire* (Paris, 1861).

Wallace Fowlie

Related entries: CHATEAUBRIAND; *IDEOLOGUES*; MAISTRE; STAEL-HOLSTEIN.

LITERATURE, GERMAN. See GERMAN LITERATURE.

LITHUANIA, GRAND DUCHY OF, under Napoleonic provisional government during the 1812 campaign. The Grande Armée captured Vilnius (Vilna), capital of Lithuania, on 26 June 1812. The Poles hoped that Lithuania would be combined with the Duchy of Warsaw to form a Kingdom of Poland. Napoleon, however, created a separate administration, headed, nevertheless, by seven Poles, among them Alexander Sapieha, from a prominent magnate family. The Baron Louis Bignon was the imperial commissioner in Vilnius; General Dirk van Hogendorp, a Dutchman, was military governor; and General Antoine de Jomini was commander of Vilnius itself.

The provisional government administered the *gubernias* of Białystok, Vilnius, Grodno, and Minsk, each under a French *intendant* with three Polish advisers.

(Vitebsk and Mahileŭ *gubernias* were also under French-Polish administration but were not subordinated to Vilnius.)

The provisional government essentially requisitioned supplies and recruited men. The French had depended for support on the Polish nobility in the region and generally got it. The peasantry, mostly Belorussians and many Uniate by religion, welcomed the invaders as well, initially. But the French soon alienated the peasants. When some in Minsk *gubernia* rebelled against their landlords, military courts-martial had the ringleaders shot. Napoleon's proclamation freeing the serfs, composed in October 1812, was never issued. Meanwhile Napoleon's wavering inclined some of the Polish nobility to support the czar. All this became academic, however, when Vilnius was recaptured on 10 December 1812 by the Russians.

Napoleon's ultimate plans for Lithuania undoubtedly depended on the outcome of the war, as did the proclamation of the Kingdom of Poland. He did not care to dispose of the former or proclaim the latter so long as either might serve to alienate his present allies, Austria and Prussia, or complicate making peace with Russia.

Academiia BSSR, Minsk, Instytut historyi, *Istoriia Belorusskoi SSR*, I (Minsk, 1961); B. Dundulis, *Napoléon et la Lithuania en 1812* (Paris, 1940); D. van Hogendorp, *Mémoires* (La Haye, 1887); J. Iwaszkiewicz, *Litwa w roku 1812* (Warsaw, 1912); V. Krasnianskii, *Minski Departament Velikago Kniazhestva Litovskogo 1812* (St. Petersburg, 1902); P. Rahác, *Karotki ahliad historyi Belarusi* (Cleveland, 1968); E. Tarle, *Napoleon's Invasion of Russia 1812* (New York, 1942).

John Stanley

Related entries: BIGNON; FOREIGN POLICY; HOGENDORP; JOMINI; RUSSIAN CAMPAIGN.

"LITTLE CORPORAL." See NAPOLEON I.

***LIVRET*.** See LABOR LEGISLATION.

LODI, BATTLE OF (10 May 1796), battle between the Army of Italy commanded by Napoleon Bonaparte and the Austrian army under General Jean Beaulieu. To outmaneuver the Austrian army defending Lombardy, Napoleon crossed the Po at Piacenza (neutral territory) and advanced to Lodi, defended by Austrian General Karl Sebottendorf with a rear guard of 8,500 men and 14 cannon. Lodi was seized, and the Austrians retreated across the 170-yard wooden bridge over the Adda River. While French cavalry crossed the Adda at the Mozanica ford to divert the Austrians, Generals André Masséna and Jean Cervoni seized the bridge, driving the Austrians before them. The Austrians lost 2,000 men and 14 cannon; French casualties reached 1,000. As a result of the battle, the French occupied western Lombardy and the capital of Milan.

F. Bouvier, *Bonaparte en Italie, 1796* (Paris, 1899); R. G. Burton, *Napoleon's Campaigns in Italy 1796–1797 and 1800* (London and New York, 1912); G. J. Fabry, *Histoire de l'armée d'Italie, 1796–1797* (Paris, 1900–01); G. Ferrero, *Adventure: Bonaparte en Italie (1796–1797)* (Paris, 1936); W.G.F. Jackson, *Attack in the West: Napoleon's First Campaign Re-read Today* (London, 1953).

Donald D. Horward

Related entries: ITALIAN CAMPAIGN, FIRST; MASSENA.

LONATO, BATTLE OF. See ITALIAN CAMPAIGN, FIRST.

LOUIS XVI (1754–93), King of France (1774–92). Louis XVI, his government in deep financial trouble, called the Estates General in 1789. Out of this assembly grew the French Revolution, during which, eventually, the Paris crowds unseated Louis (10 August 1792) and the French people elected a national Convention which tried him for treason and sent him to the guillotine (21 January 1793). His connection with Napoleon is ironic. It was Louis XVI who paid for the Corsican's military education at Brienne and the Ecole Militaire. Louis' queen, Marie-Antoinette, also went to the guillotine. His son, "Louis XVII," died in prison (1795) at age ten. Thus his brother acceded to the throne—by grace of the Allies—in 1814 (and again in 1815) as Louis XVIII. See CONVENTION; DIRECTORY; LOUIS XVIII; NAPOLEON; TERROR, THE.

LOUIS XVIII (1755–1824), Bourbon pretender in exile to the French throne, 1795–1814; previous title, comte de Provence; restored by the Allies in 1814 and again in 1815. Before the Revolution, Provence courted popularity by advocating limited reform, uncomprehending of possible consequences. His bureau in the Assembly of Notables (1788) was the only one that approved double representation for the Third Estate in the Estates General. Between May 1789 and June 1791 the count gave lip-service to the Revolution but maintained a low profile. He then fled France, however, and he soon voiced his true convictions. He called his brother, Louis XVI, a captive of the Revolution and attacked Revolutionary leaders in violent and provocative terms, which made matters worse for Louis XVI and Marie Antoinette.

As titular leader of the *émigrés*, Provence, after the execution of Louis XVI in 1793, proclaimed himself regent for the eight-year-old dauphin (Louis XVII, a prisoner in the Temple in Paris). When the boy died in June 1795, Provence assumed the title of Louis XVIII. In exile he (and his brother, the comte d'Artois) kept busy with military projects, conspiracies, proclamations, and circular letters, all directed to the restoration of the Bourbon monarchy. (Provence had no part in the assassination plots, however.)

In September 1800 Bonaparte rejected Provence's suggestion that he serve France by restoring the Bourbons. Later (February 1803) a representative of Bonaparte, promising indemnities and other rewards, attempted to convince Provence that the Bourbons should renounce their claims to the French throne. The count praised the first consul's valor, military talents, and some acts of his administration but refused to give up his birthright.

When Napoleon took the title of emperor in May 1804, Provence dispatched a circular letter to European capitals protesting this "usurpation." In October Provence met with Artois and other *émigré* princes in Kalmar, Sweden, where they drafted a "counter-offer" to the French, promising general amnesty and guaranteeing titles to confiscated properties. It came to nothing. In October 1807 Provence went to England where he lived out most of the remaining years of exile at Hartwell, some forty miles from London.

Through an intermediary, Napoleon offered Provence a pension of 1.2 million francs (plus an equal sum for his family) and up to 10 million francs to pay his debts if he would emigrate to the United States. He refused. When Spain rebelled against the emperor, Provence, as head of the House of Bourbon, offered to serve as regent for the Spanish king, held captive by the French. The English vetoed this arrangement. When news came of Napoleon's setbacks in Russia and elsewhere, Provence refused to join the English in celebrating French defeats. He asked Alexander I of Russia to treat with kindness French soldiers taken prisoner during the French invasion of Russia (1812). In January 1814, from Hartwell, Provence addressed a proclamation to the French people in which he declared that he recognized and sanctioned institutions that were legitimate conquests of the Revolution. This statement prepared the way for his restoration and the Charter of 1814, which, along with the Concordat of 1801 and the Napoleonic codes, incorporated much of the Revolutionary legacy. Restored a second time after Napoleon's defeat at Waterloo, Louis XVIII served as king until his death in 1824.

Archives du Ministère des Affaires Etrangères, *Fonds Bourbon*, France, vols. 588–647; Archives Nationales, *Pièces relatives á l'émigration*, 34AP–3A12; V. Beach, *Charles X of France: His Life and Times* (Boulder, Colo., 1971); Duc de Castries, *Les hommes de l'émigration, 1789–1814* (Paris, 1979); G. de Diesbach, *Histoire de l'émigration* (Paris, 1975); Public Record Office, *Papiers de Calonne*; J. Turquan and J. d'Auriac, *Monsieur Comte de Provence* (Paris, 1928).

Vincent Beach

Related entries: ABDICATION, FIRST; ELBA; *EMIGRES*; HUNDRED DAYS, THE; PARIS, FIRST TREATY OF; PARIS, SECOND TREATY OF.

LOUIS, LOUIS-DOMINIQUE, BARON (1755–1837), a subordinate fiscal official during the Empire and minister of finances during the early years of the Restoration and the July monarchy. Baron Louis maintained in the face of Napoleon, the ultraroyalists, and capitalists a consistent financial policy: he established government credit "by paying its debts, even its stupidities." His career illustrates the rise of new men during the Empire. Born at Toul, a younger son in a large family, he became an abbé during the Old Regime and a protégé of Charles-Maurice de Talleyrand. Forced to emigrate to England during the Terror, he assiduously studied its mechanisms of public credit, then the soundest in the world. After Napoleon came to power in 1799, his success in ordering the accounts of the War Ministry and of the Legion of Honor caught the attention of Nicolas-François Mollien, who appointed him administrator of the newly established Service Fund. The influence of Talleyrand secured Louis's appointment as finance minister during the First Restoration and the Second. In the confused, chaotic fiscal situation of 1814 and 1815, Louis, drawing on his English experience, made grim, unpopular decisions that set policies, traditions, and structures for French public finance: a new government assumes the debts of prior regimes; the governmental budget of both income and expenses is annually approved in advance by the legislature; indirect (sales) taxes are continued; valid bills are paid when presented; a sound public credit, thus stabilized, is cherished. He reaffirmed these traditions as minister of finance in Casimir Perier's ministry after July 1830.

M. Marion, *Histoire financière de la France depuis 1715*, vol. 4: *1799–1818: La fin de la Révolution, le Consulat et l'Empire, la libération du territoire* (Paris, 1927).

Harold T. Parker

Related entries: FINANCES; MOLLIEN; PERIER; SOCIETY; TALLEYRAND-PERIGORD; TREASURY.

LOUISE OF MECKLENBURG (1776–1810), queen of Prussia. This most lovable member of the Hohenzollern royal family was known for her sunny disposition, beauty, devotion, and nationalism, all of which earned her the undying respect of her people and the attention of numerous historians, artists, and writers. Daughter of Duke Charles of Mecklenburg-Strelitz and Frederica-Caroline of Hesse-Darmstadt, she was born in Hanover, a state she later was determined to keep from French control. She and her younger sister Frederica were betrothed to the two sons of Frederick William II of Prussia. At seventeen, Louise married the shy and unenthusiastic future Frederick William III (24 December 1793) at Berlin. At the reception following, the rather wild young bride scandalized her new mother-in-law by introducing the waltz to the Prussian court. But instead of the customary illumination of the city, the crown prince ordered that the money be used to aid war widows and orphans, a foreshadowing of the misery and events to come.

Louise's father-in-law died 15 November 1797, leaving the young couple a heritage of enormous debt and an inept cabinet. Living in economical simplicity, they both read the insipid literature popular at the time. While Louise still displayed little interest in politics, she did read Schiller, who became her favorite, as well as Jean Paul Richter, Herder, Gibbon, and Goethe. Gradually her husband deputed various official duties to her as they traveled around the kingdom. She had her sixth child in 1801, the year when Czar Alexander I's sister visited the Prussian court and, as an intimate of the queen, first told her about the czar whom she initially met in June 1802. The meeting between Frederick William and the Russian ruler was the most exciting event in Louise's life up to that time. Afterward Louise, who was then twenty-six and by all accounts a gorgeous woman with a melodious voice to match her great blue eyes and ash blonde hair, wrote vividly about breakfasting, serving tea, and dancing with Alexander, a "noble human being" whose strength she admired and dislike for etiquette she shared.

Louise's fascination with the czar became a pivotal element in Prussian diplomacy during the next three years. As her personality ripened, she discovered the incapacity of some of her husband's ministers and herself became the center of political activities of the war party that opposed Prussian neutrality. After Louise's second meeting with Alexander in October 1805, she became further convinced that Napoleon, whose troops had advanced to occupy Prussian territory, should be stopped. After signing the treaty between Russia, Austria, and Prussia, Frederick William, Louise, and Alexander visited the tomb of Frederick the Great where the czar kissed the sarcophagus and pledged eternal friendship with Prussia.

Although Louise now favored war with France, she was not able immediately to influence her husband, who through Haugwitz on 15 December, conditionally signed the Schönbrunn treaty with France whereby in exchange for disarming, Prussia was permitted to incorporate Hanover. But alleging that the treaty was signed too late, Napoleon rejected it and forced new terms on Prussia on 15 February 1806, making Prussia an ally against England. Thereafter Louise continued to disagree with her husband's policy and secretly directed Hardenberg to negotiate with Russia. The queen and the war party continued to be unable to comprehend how easy it might be for the French army, after Austerlitz, to defeat a Prussian army that had not fought since 1796. While at Pyrmont taking a cure, she also secretly intrigued with Baron vom Stein about the need for reform of the Prussian cabinet. Frederick William finally relented and mobilized for war on 7 August 1806, with a declaration of war following on 17 September. Louise continued to believe in the czar's steadfastness as her husband took the field. She went along to entertain, driving in a closed carriage amid the advancing army, between baggage and cannon. Wherever she appeared, soldiers cheered her presence and cursed Napoleon. Finally, just before Jena, she was forced to return to Berlin to avoid capture, but before she arrived, a bulletin came informing her that Napoleon had become the arbiter of the fate of Prussia. After the fall of Berlin, Stettin, and Magdeburg, Frederick William had to accept Napoleon's terms while the *Moniteur* and army bulletins blamed his wife for causing an unnecessary war. On 27 October, in bulletin 19, Napoleon bared Louise's liaison with Czar Alexander I. But her indecisive husband decided to break the truce in order to keep faith with Russia.

After the fall of Danzig in 1807, Napoleon set up his headquarters at Tilsit, and the czar's policy became less hostile toward France at their famous meeting on a raft in the Niemen River. Because negotiations with Napoleon were so difficult, the czar and the Prussian cabinet decided to ask the usually affable queen to mediate. For her country, she overcame her reluctance to meet "this devilish being, sprung from the mire," (Napoleon) whom Frederick William also found so repulsive. In the end, she made the sacrifice willingly, much to Charles-Maurice de Talleyrand's displeasure. She was not invited to Tilsit until

5 July. She went to her husband's house the next day in full dress—a white crêpe de chine dress, pearl diadem, and necklace—and Napoleon arrived on a white Arabian to visit her. During the interview, which her countrymen hoped would be their salvation, she impressed Napoleon by her intellect and beauty, although he did not change his policy—Jerome was to become king of Westphalia. In retrospect, at Tilsit Napoleon missed his opportunity to ally with or neutralize Prussia so that it would not rise up against him as it did in 1813. Louise was devastated by her failure to save Prussia from the indemnity Napoleon exacted for the war, for which she assumed responsibility.

During the last two years of her short life, she shared the suffering of her people, gave birth to the last of her ten children, and continued to be involved in politics. While the couple visited St. Petersburg in January 1809 and were treated royally, she lost her illusions about the czar's character when he seemed determined to fight Austria. Finally, Napoleon demanded their presence in Berlin and refused requests to decrease the Prussian indemnity. When Napoleon threatened to take Silesia if the debt was not paid, Louise interfered again. As a result Prince Wittgenstein presented his plan to create a state bank to fund the national debt by 25,000 citizens' contributions. Her last great political act was to draw up a memorial that showed her grasp of politics.

The heroic queen died at age thirty-four. Although an autopsy indicated damaged lungs and a heart defect, it was popularly said that Napoleon and Alexander had made her die of sorrow. Her tomb at Charlottenburg, with a recumbent statue by Christian Daniel Rauch, became a place of pilgrimage. The hope for German nationality that she inspired was realized when her son William, after defeating Napoleon III, was proclaimed emperor of a Prussian-led German empire in the Hall of Mirrors at Versailles in 1871.

As Constance Wright noted in the prologue to her 1969 biography, no historiographical consensus about Queen Louise was established by contemporaries. Napoleon and the French envisioned her as a war-mongering siren, a Helen of Troy with Russian sympathies; whereas Germans saw her through Goethe's eyes as a martyr, a Joan of Arc figure, the embodiment of the nation's hope "in shape a woman, but in daring, man." In any case, Louise developed from a pleasure-loving young princess to queenly stature through the adversity of the Napoleonic wars. She asserted herself more than her less able spouse and summoned K. von Hardenberg, G. von Scharnhorst, H. vom Stein, and other reformers around her who were able to resurrect Prussia after her death. Napoleon had not been altogether wrong when he had called her "the only man in Prussia."

G. Aretz, *Queen Louise of Prussia, 1776–1810* (New York, 1929); P. Bailleu, *Königin Luise* (Berlin, 1908 and 1926); F. M. Kircheisen, *Die Königin Luise in der Geschichte und Literatur* (Jena, 1906); A. Kluckhorn, *Louise, Queen of Prussia* (Cambridge, 1881); C. Wright, *Louise, Queen of Prussia, a Biography* (London, 1969).

June K. Burton and John Stine

Related entries: FRIEDRICH WILHELM III; HARDENBERG; PRUSSIA, KINGDOM OF; SCHARNHORST; STEIN.

LOUISIANA. See COLONIES, FRENCH; UNITED STATES.

LOUIS-PHILIPPE. See ORLEANS.

LOUVRE (Musée Napoléon). The museum was officially opened in the former Louvre palace on 23 Thermidor Year II (10 August 1793). The credit for opening the Louvre as a museum really belongs to the Girondin minister of interior, Jean Roland. Since the closing of the first public gallery, which was situated in the Luxembourg Palace, plans to move the museum elsewhere had been abortive until he moved speedily to open it for the first anniversary of the fall of the monarchy. Roland's efforts were opposed by his rival but subordinate, Alexandre Lenoir, who was in charge of the *dêpot* for art treasures at the abandoned monastery of the Petits Augustins that would become the Musée des Monuments français (1 September 1795). Further opposition came from the painter Jacques-Louis David and the art dealer Jean-Baptiste-Pierre Le Brun. Nevertheless, the museum opened on schedule, and its first catalog listed 537 paintings confiscated from the crown and the church. Lesser acquisitions from the defunct Academy of Painting and confiscations from *émigrés* were added shortly, but it was the addition of the trophies of conquest from the next two decades of Revolutionary and imperial warfare that transformed the Louvre for a short while into the world's finest collection of Old Masters ever assembled.

The Belgian campaign of 1794 set the style for the subsequent looting of works of art, something for which Roman legions had set a precedent in antiquity. Although several committees became involved in the planning so that conflicting policies emerged, responsibility for the policy that materialized—expert official looting—rests with the Commission Temporaire des Arts of the Committee of Public Instruction and its members C.-F. Lebrun, F.-L.-J. Baron, Alexandre Besson, and H. B. Grégoire, who had an interest in Hellenistic and Roman sculpture. The Temporary Commission appointed the painter Jean-Baptiste Wicar (18 July 1794) to enter the war zone and bring back valuable paintings; however, unknowingly, the chemist Louis Bernard Guyton de Morveau, the representative on mission with the headquarters staff at Brussels, appointed two army officers (the painter Luc Barbier and one Léger) to carry out the same task, which they did expertly, ruthlessly, and swiftly. They dispatched their first shipment from Antwerp by barge two weeks after the French armies arrived, bringing the central panel of Rubens' colossal *Descent from the Cross*, then one of the most famous pictures in the world. These first four paintings arrived in Paris 15 September and initially were displayed, as new arrivals were thereafter, in the Salon carré four days later so that a "free people" could enjoy the spoils of war, the glory of the Flemish school.

The confiscatory procedures for the first Italian campaign repeated those used in Belgium, with the exception being that the field commander now was General Bonaparte (appointed 3 March 1796) whose interest in Italy's only remaining assets was not aesthetic but symbolic in his mind of the transfer of world power from Rome to Paris. Bonaparte demanded the surrender of paintings as a clause in a peace treaty on his own initiative and for the first time, on 9 May 1796, in the armistice signed with the duke of Parma at Piacenza. He asked the Directory to send artists to help him select the best. After telling him to appoint his own choices, the directors decided to make the appointments themselves, but meanwhile, at Milan Bonaparte appointed Jacques-Pierre Tinet (19 May) as his agent. The Paris appointees who joined Tinet on 9 June included the botanist André Thouin, the mathematician Gaspard Monge, the chemist C.-L. Berthollet, the painters J. B. Wicar, Antoine Gros, and Jean Barthélemy, and the sculptor J. G. Moitte.

The expert official looters followed in the wake of the French armies fighting their war eastward across northern Italy and zeroed in on the collections of Parma, Modena, Milan, Bologna, and Cento. Some treaties listed precise numbers of art confiscations: Parma and Modena, twenty pictures each; at Bologna the pope's representative agreed to 100 pictures, busts, vases, or statues from Rome plus 500 manuscripts; Venice in May 1797 handed over 20 pictures and 600 manuscripts. After the commissars left, further removals sometimes occurred, such as the Horses of St. Mark's in Venice, which ended up on Fontaine and Percier's Arc de Triomphe du Carrousel. Moreover, collections that were spared in the first Italian campaign were not exempt in 1799 during the War of the Second Coalition. Unfortunately, from an artistic point of view, first-rate antique statuary was then scarce in the Lombardy plain except for Florence, which was still at peace with France, so the looters had to be content mainly with paintings. Yet like their contemporaries, they were still so unappreciative of fifteenth-century Italian painting that they overlooked some of the finest works (Tiepolo's, for example). Another factor was that Bonaparte decided on quantities for inclusion in treaties without taking into consideration what was available or knowing its quality so that figures were sometimes adjusted after the experts arrived for consultation. At any rate, they were required to make difficult decisions, but their morals allowed them to steal crucifixes and relics whether from altars of churches or private collections. Pursuant to the selection process, the artworks were carefully packed, so well that although some Etruscan vases from the Vatican were smashed, the most important Italian treasures survived the journey they began in Rome in September 1796. They arrived in stages beginning in November 1796, with the second convoy arriving in July 1797. The climactic one from Rome arrived 15 July 1798 and was celebrated on 27–29 July, the anniversary of 9 Thermidor, with a Roman-style triumphal parade through the streets of the capital to the Champs de Mars that included the Horses of St. Mark's, live ostriches, camels, vultures, and a military band.

While Dufourney and his small staff tried to solve the Louvre's current problems—restoration of damaged works, storage space, arrangement of displays, and how to distribute the additional paintings that kept arriving from the satellites as well as from Versailles among other national museums—Bonaparte was already on his way to Egypt with a group of savants that included the future director general of the Louvre, Dominique Vivant Denon (1747–1825). There Denon captivated Napoleon by ignoring the dangerous fighting going on around him as he surveyed and drew the tombs of the pharaohs.

When Napoleon changed the Louvre into the Musée Napoléon in July 1803 and placed Denon in charge, a new era for the museum began. Instead of sending out *commissaires*, the looting of artworks for the collections was conducted by the director general personally, and his choices expressed his own tastes. In the ensuing years he was found everywhere racing behind the shock troops, always close to the front lines. After Jena (14 October 1806) Denon went through the art centers of north Germany, reaping a harvest of notable Rembrandts, Rubenses, Titians, and Poussins. Only his travels to Spain resulted in failure when he left after a brief stay during the winter of 1808–9 to prepare for the resumption of war in the East European theater. He appeared in Vienna with General Pierre Daru in June 1809 for his third and penultimate effort while construction at the Musée Napoléon required that the Grand Galerie be closed for eighteen months. After its reopening for the wedding procession of Napoleon and Archduchess Marie-Louise (2 April 1810), Denon embarked on a collecting mission to Italy, the one that made the Musée Napoléon remarkably modern due to the richness of its collection of early Italian painting. This time, however, Denon had to negotiate with diplomatic style to get what he wanted from the region of Italy, which now belonged either to the Kingdoms of Italy and Naples or was organized as departments of France.

In the relatively brief span from 1810 to 1815, the Musée Napoléon was at its best, for Denon had not only increased the size of the collections but widened the museum's scope, as may be readily seen by comparing the catalogs for the exhibit opened on 25 July 1814 with earlier ones. Yet for the very reason that the Musée Napoléon was superlative, it had to be destroyed for political reasons. The movement for restitution came gradually, and the French resisted doggedly, possibly due to the prevailing sentiment that the artworks had been purchased with French blood and therefore were rightfully theirs. But the Allies became less accommodating after the Hundred Days, and when Denon continued to defy their orders, the Prussian army entered the Louvre and seized their own paintings, as well as those of their smaller German allies. Next, British officers arrived on behalf of the king of the Netherlands. The pope sent the sculptor Canova, who with the help of British diplomat William Richard Hamilton succeeded in obtaining agreement from Austria, Prussia, and England for restitution to the Vatican. As a final humiliation, the Horses of St. Mark's and the lion atop the Invalides were taken down, with the latter falling and breaking into twenty pieces in the process. In about three months the achievements of twenty years were undone, although what remained was far from inconsiderable. Ironically Denon's last and major improvement in the collection resulting from his diplomatic ventures in Italy rather than plunder was retained, and there were still enough Old Masters for the Louvre to continue to serve its educational function of training young artists and to stimulate the creation of rival national museums.

C. Aulanier, *Histoire du palais et du musée du Louvre* (Paris, 1947); F. Boyer, "Comment fut decidée en 1815 la restitution par la France des oeuvres d'art de la Belgique," *BSBN* 5 (1965), and "Le Retour en 1815 des oeuvres d'art enlevées en Lombardice, en Venetie et à Modene," *Revue des Etudes Italiennes* 16 (1970); C. Gould, *Trophy of Conquest. The Musée Napoléon and the Creation of the Louvre* (London, 1965); Louis Hautecoeur, *Histoire des Collections au Musée de Louvre* (Paris, 1930); D. M. Quynn, "The Art Confiscations of the Napoleonic Wars," *AHR* 50 (1945).

June K. Burton

Related entries: ARCHITECTURE; ART; CANOVA; DENON; FONTAINE; PERCIER.

LOW COUNTRIES. See BATAVIAN REPUBLIC; BELGIUM; HOLLAND, KINGDOM OF; SISTER REPUBLICS.

LOWE, SIR HUDSON (1769–1844), British general; governor of St. Helena during the exile of Napoleon. Lowe was born 28 July 1769 at Galway, Ireland, the son of an army surgeon. He entered the service before his twelfth birthday as an ensign in the East Devon Militia. Six years later he joined his father's regiment, the Fiftieth, then stationed at Gibraltar. After the war began with France in 1793, Lowe, then a captain, was active in the siege of Corsica. In 1799 at Minorca, he organized a corps, the Corsican Rangers, composed of royalist *émigrés*, whom he successfully commanded against the French in Egypt in 1800–1801. In 1803, as a lieutenant colonel, he reorganized the Royal Corsican Ranger Battalion for the defense of Capri. In October 1808, Joachim Murat attacked the island, and Lowe, lacking sufficient naval support and having only 1,362 men to oppose more than 3,000 French, was forced to withdraw. During 1809, however, Lowe and his Corsicans achieved victories in the Ionian Islands expeditions. In January 1813, he was sent to Russia to organize, under British command, a legion of German deserters from the Grande Armée. During the campaign of 1813–14, he participated in thirteen major battles and was praised by G. L. Blücher von Wahlstatt and A. von Gneisenau for his conduct. His military record resulted in his being knighted, promoted to major general, and decorated by the courts of Prussia and Russia. After Napoleon's escape from Elba, Lowe was named quartermaster of the army of the Prince of Orange (1814–15) and then commander of the British troops at Genoa.

In August 1815, Lowe was informed of his appointment as the new governor of St. Helena. Napoleon reached St. Helena ahead of him on 17 October 1815. For the first two months Napoleon lived in a garden pavilion at The Briars, the residence of William Balcombe, and had complete freedom of St. Helena. His only military guard was an orderly officer. In December 1815, he moved to Longwood, which had been remodeled to house his entourage. Its location was on a plateau 1,700 feet above sea level, five miles from the nearest port, and within sight of the army camp of Deadwood. Napoleon was permitted to ride for twelve miles without escort, and his own household issued visitors' passes.

All of this changed when General Sir Hudson Lowe arrived on 14 April 1816 with new regulations from Lord Bathurst, Britain's colonial secretary. Henceforth no item could be delivered to Napoleon that used any title or emblem of sovereignty; Napoleon would be addressed as General Bonaparte; all correspondence and visitors' passes would be handled by the governor; further limits were placed on where he could ride without surveillance; his presence at Longwood had to be confirmed twice a day; and the annual expenditure for the entire Longwood household was set at 8,000 pounds. Lowe's background, together with the new regulations, precluded any cordiality between the two men.

As the former commander of the Corsican Rangers, Lowe's appointment seemed tactless, if not insulting, to Napoleon. The punctilious manner in which Lowe enforced the rules led to charges of extreme severity. A campaign of what Lowe considered calumny was begun against the "jailer" by the Longwood contingent, including Napoleon's personal physician, the British naval surgeon, Dr. Barry O'Meara. Napoleon became a recluse, staying in his private apartments and threatening to shoot anyone who forced entry to verify his presence. He blamed his declining health on the riding restrictions. In August and again in December, to protest the stringent budget, he had the imperial eagles sawed off some of his silverware to destroy its souvenir value and then had it cut up, smashed, and publicly sold by the pound. Stories of pettiness and even cruelty reached Europe and England, until public opinion forced Bathurst to order Lowe to relax some of the restrictions. Napoleon's allowance was increased to 12,000 pounds. Lowe would not ease security, however, fearing most an escape from St. Helena against his record. In 1818, the Congress of Aix-le-Chapelle tacitly approved Lowe's work by reaffirming the conditions of exile.

Following the death of Napoleon in May 1821, Lowe returned to England, where he was thanked by George IV, but public opinion again rose up against him with the publication of *Napoleon in Exile, A Voice from Saint Helena*, written by Dr. O'Meara. Lowe intended to prosecute the doctor but, inexplicably, never did. From 1825 to 1830 he was military commander in Ceylon and was governor during 1830–31. In 1831 he returned to England and spent his last years trying to vindicate his actions on Saint Helena. He died impoverished on 10 January 1844 in London. Whether justly or not, it is as Napoleon predicted: Lowe is remembered only for his conduct toward Napoleon on Saint Helena.

W. Forsyth, *History of the Captivity of Napoleon at St. Helena* (London, 1853); R. Korngold, *The Last Years of Napoleon* (London, 1960); R. Markham, *Napoleon* (New York, 1963); G. Martineau, *Napoleon's St. Helena* (London, 1968); Barry O'Meara, *Napoleon in Exile* (London, 1822); A. P. Primrose, Earl of Rosebery, *Napoleon, the Last Phase* (London, 1900); R. C. Seaton, *Napoleon's Captivity in relation to Sir Hudson Lowe* (London, 1903).

Rachel R. Schneider

Related entry: ST. HELENA.

LUBIENSKI, FELIKS FRANCISZEK (1758–1848), Francophile; reforming minister of justice in the Duchy of Warsaw. As a young man he briefly studied law in Italy, then returned to Poland, and took service with Prince Michał Czartoryski. In 1806, before Prussia went to war with France, he worked with Prince Antoni Radziwiłł on a project to resurrect the Kingdom of Poland under the Hohenzollerns. After Napoleon defeated the Prussians at Jena, however, Łubieński cooperated with the French. In 1807 he was named director of the Justice Division of the Governing Commission (the Polish provisional government) and shortly after minister of justice in the new Duchy of Warsaw. He quickly gained the favor of King Frederick Augustus of Saxony, named duke of Warsaw by Napoleon, and the duchy's secretary of state in Dresden, Stanisław Breza.

It was Łubieński who pushed the Code Napoléon through the Council of State (1808) and who created a judicial system of civil and criminal courts based on the French model. He induced the *Sejm* of 1809 to accept the French Commercial Code (but had to withdraw the Criminal Code). The School of Law, which he organized in 1808 to educate lawyers in the new French legal system, became the School of Law and Administrative Sciences in 1811 (and in turn one of the cornerstones of the University of Warsaw founded in 1816). Łubieński was also the father of the December decree of 1807, which abolished serfdom (if only nominally).

Though personally devout, Łubieński fought a noisy battle with Primate Ignacy Raczynski over the introduction of civil marriage, divorce, and lay keeping of vital statistics. This and his defense of French institutions generally made him unpopular. Frederick Augustus wanted to, but could not, appoint him president of the Council of State in 1811. Among Łubieński's lasting monuments, however, were the National Archives in Warsaw, a government printing office, and the first public library in Poland. He was a founding member of the Credit Society (*Towarzystwo Kredytowe*) and an advocate of state sponsorship of the development of industry.

After 1809, Łubieński slowly lost influence with the king and was replaced as favorite by Tadeusz Matuszewicz. In 1813, Łubieński remained loyal to Napoleon and refused to participate in discussions with the Russians. In 1814, he refused service under Czar Alexander I and was frozen out of government permanently. Łubieński spent his declining years on his estate at Guzów, absorbed with introducing new agricultural methods.

W. Chomętowski, ed., *Pamiętnik Feliksa hr.* Łubieńskiego (Warsaw, 1876); H. Grynwaser, "Kodeks Napoleon w Polsce," *Pisma* 1 (Wrocław, 1951); B. Leśnodorski, "Elementy feudalne i burżuazyjne w ustroju i prawie Księstwa Warszawskiego," *Czasopismo prawno-historyczne* 3 (1951); T. Mencel, *Feliks* Łubieński minister sprawiedliwości *Księstwa Warszawskiego* (Warsaw, 1952), and "L'introduction du Code Napoléon dans le Duché de Varsovie (1808)," *C.P.-H.* 2 (149); S. Posner, ed., "Ostatni raport Łubieńskiego,'' *Gazeta Sądowa Warszawska*, R. 36 (1908); W. Sobociński, *Historia ustroju i prawa Księstwa Warszawskiego* (Torun, 1964); *Sześcioletnia korespondencja władz duchownych z rządem świeckim Księstwa Warszawskiego* (Warsaw, 1816).

John Stanley

Related entries: FRIEDRICH AUGUST III; RACZYNSKI; VIENNA, CONGRESS OF; WARSAW, DUCHY OF.

LUCCA, REPUBLIC OF, Napoleonic principality (1805–14) under Elisa Bonaparte Bacciochi. Until 1799, Bonaparte and other French officials in Italy left the Republic of Lucca undisturbed in return for contributions. In 1799, however, General Jean Sérurier imposed a government patterned on the French Directory, which was soon dismantled by the Austrians but restored by the French in 1800, after Marengo. In the fall of 1801, Bonaparte sent A. Christophe Saliceti to impose a new constitution, under which the Lucchese retained their independence until 1805, when on the advice of Saliceti, the Senate asked Napoleon to make Lucca an independent principality ruled by a member of his family. Napoleon agreed and granted the state to his sister, Elisa, and her husband, Felice Bacciochi. Elisa actually ruled, and well. Lucca netted prosperity and legal, administrative, and educational reform.

A. Mancini, *Storia di Lucca* (Florence, 1950); P. Marmottan, *Bonaparte et la Republique de Lucques* (Paris, 1896); C. Massei, *Storia Civile di Lucca dal 1796 al anno 1848* (Lucca, 1878); A. Mazzarosa, *Storia di Lucca dalle origini al 1814* (Lucca, 1833).

Leonard Macaluso

Related entries: BONAPARTE, ELISA; SALICETI; TUSCANY, GRAND DUCHY OF.

LUISE. See LOUISE OF MECKLENBURG.

LUNEVILLE, TREATY OF (9 February 1801), which made peace between Austria and France. Austria reaffirmed all cessions made in the Treaty of Campo Formio (17 October 1797). Austria also put the Grand Duchy of Tuscany at the disposition of France. Rulers who lost territory on the left (west) bank of the Rhine were to be compensated in Germany. These dispositions were made by the *Reichsdeputationshauptschluss* of 1803. Napoleon reorganized Tuscany as the Kingdom of Etruria, which he traded to Spain for Louisiana by the Treaty of Fontainebleau (1801).

Jesse Scott

Related entry: FOREIGN POLICY.

LÜTZEN, BATTLE OF. See GERMAN WAR OF LIBERATION.

LYCEES. See EDUCATION.

M

MACDONALD, JACQUES-ETIENNE-JOSEPH-ALEXANDRE (1765–1840), duc de Tarente, marshal of France. A descendant of a Scottish supporter of James II of England who settled in France (1688), he entered the Royal Army as an officer (1784) and rose to general (1794) in the wars of the Revolution. In 1799 he supported the coup d'état of 18 Brumaire and in 1800 aided Jean Moreau in the victory of Hohenlinden. Afterward he became known as an admirer of Moreau, Napoleon's sole rival for military reputation. In 1804, Macdonald alienated Bonaparte by publicly defending Moreau, charged with treason and exiled. Napoleon exiled Macdonald to Naples and then to the Kingdom of Italy. They were reconciled, however, in 1809, when Macdonald brilliantly seconded Eugène on the Piave and at Raab and became the hero of the Battle of Wagram. Napoleon made him a marshal and duc de Tarente. He fought in Russia (1812) and Germany (1813), escaping at Leipzig only by swimming the Elster River. He fought only in minor actions during the campaign of France and in March 1814 joined Michel Ney and other marshals in demanding Napoleon's abdication. During the Hundred Days he declined to serve Bonaparte. Under the Restoration he retained his rank, was made a peer of France, and served as minister of state and grand chancellor of the Legion of Honor.

J.-E.-J.-A. Macdonald, *Souvenirs* (Paris, 1892), and *Recollections of Marshal Macdonald,* 2 vols., trans. L. Simeon (London, 1892).

Related entries: ABDICATION, FIRST; BRUMAIRE, COUP OF 18, YEAR VIII; PIAVE, BATTLE ON; RAAB, BATTLE OF; WAGRAM, BATTLE OF.

MACK VON LEIBERICH, KARL, BARON (1752–1828); Austrian general remembered for the surrender of Ulm (1805). Mack entered the Austrian army in 1770; he served in the War of the Bavarian Succession and then as a lieutenant on the general staff, where he became the protégé of Field Marshal Peter Lacy. In the war with Turkey (1788–89) he was aide-de-camp to the emperor. After the capture of Belgrade, he was decorated and given the title of baron and for a time was military tutor to Archduke Karl. During the War of the First Coalition against France, he was a brigadier general and chief of staff to Prince Josias von Coburg in the Netherlands, where he helped negotiate the defection of

Charles Dumouriez but resigned in 1794 when his operations plans failed. In 1797 he was reactivated as major general and made chief of the general staff. In 1798 he was sent to command the Neapolitan army but won no victories and was captured by the French. (He escaped in 1800.)

In 1805 Mack was called from retirement and made chief of staff of the army, through the influence of Foreign Minister Count Ludwig Cobenzl and behind the back of Archduke Karl. At Ulm his advance army was trapped by Napoleon, and he surrendered with 27,000 men (20 October 1805). Repatriated, he was put before a court-martial, which sentenced him to the forfeiture of rank and medals and a two-year imprisonment. Only in 1819 did the emperor restore his rank and honors.

O. Regele, "Karl Freiherr von Mack und Johann Ludwig Graf Cobenzl. Ihre Rolle im Kriegsjahr 1805," *Mitteilungen des Österreichischen Staatsarchivs* 21 (1968); E. W. Sheppard, "Little Known Commanders of the Past. Karl Mack 1752–1828," *Army Quarterly and Defence Journal* 92 (1966).

Brigitte Holl

Related entries: ARMY, HABSBURG; AUSTERLITZ CAMPAIGN; COBENZL.

MADAME MERE, Napoleon's mother. See BONAPARTE.

MAGHELLA, ANTONIO (1766–1850), minister of police of Naples under Joachim Murat. Born in Varese, Republic of Genoa, Maghella studied law briefly and entered politics. Aligned with the oligarchy, he did not cooperate in the French-sponsored revolution of 1797 but by 1799 was a member of the Consiglio dei Giuniori of the Ligurian Republic. In 1800 Bonaparte appointed him minister of police in the Commissione Governitiva. Maghella suppressed brigandage and brought order to the Republic. Under the 1802 constitution, he was a senator, president of the Magistracy of Police, and later president of the Magistracy of War and the Navy. In 1805, he supported Bonaparte's annexation of Genoa to France and continued to hold high office. In 1808, Marshal Joachim Murat succeeded Joseph Bonaparte as king of Naples and made Maghella prefect of police for the city of Naples and a member of the Council of State. In June 1809, Murat appointed him interim minister of police during Saliceti's absence.

As prefect of police and later minister of police, he instituted rigorous surveillance of the secret societies and sought to shape the Carbonari to Murat's advantage. He was loyal to Murat and Naples and ultimately was an advocate of Italian unity. When Napoleon heard that he had urged Murat to withhold Neapolitan troops from the Russian campaign and to remain in his kingdom, the emperor called Maghella to Paris (March 1812). In December 1813 Napoleon allowed Maghella to return to Naples. He immediately advised Murat to ally with Austria and England, which he did. It saved Naples for Murat and Caroline in 1814. In 1815, however, Murat attacked the Austrians in northern Italy while Maghella maintained order in Naples. Murat's campaign—advertised as a war to unite Italy—failed dismally. In May 1815, Murat fled to France, but Maghella stayed at his post in Naples. On 22 May 1815, he presented himself to Leopold of Bourbon and surrendered his charge. Maghella had expected to be treated honorably but was imprisoned at Mantua and then at Fenestrelle in the Piedmont. He was released on the condition that he retire to Varese, where he lived until his death in April 1850.

A. Maghella, *Compendio Storico* and *Autobiografia* (n.d.); A. Valente, *Gioacchino Murat e l'Italia meridionale* (Turin, 1961); M. H. Weil, "Antonio Maghella" in *Studi Storici in onore de Antonio Manno* (Turin, 1912).

Leonard Macaluso

Related entries: HUNDRED DAYS, THE; MURAT, J.; NAPLES, KINGDOM OF; NAPLES, KINGDOM OF: MINISTERS.

MAINE DE BIRAN, PIERRE-FRANCOIS-MARIE GONTHIER (1766–1824), philosopher, deputy in the Corps Législatif (1810–14), subprefect of the Dordogne (1806–11), moderate royalist. Biran is the philosopher of the Empire who has best endured the test of time. His works were hailed by the National Institute, the Academy of Berlin, and the Academy of Copenhagen. He has been called the "reformer of empiricism" because he was fully imbued with the sensationalism of the *idéologues* yet went beyond them by insisting on a distinction between active and passive faculties. He launched the nineteenth-century spiritualist philosophy of Royer Collard, Victor Cousin, and Bergson by positing a "hyperorganic," self-established through the effort of the will. His most important works were *Influence de l'habitude sur la faculté de penser* (1803), *Sur la décomposition de la pensée* (1805), and *Sur l'apperception immédiate* (1807).

Emmet Kennedy

Related entries: EDUCATION; INSTITUT NATIONAL DES SCIENCES ET DES ARTS; LEGISLATORS.

MAISTRE, JOSEPH DE (1754–1821), leading conservative polemicist. He was born at Chambéry as a subject of the king of Sardinia. Forced by the advance of the French army to emigrate in 1792 to Switzerland, he published his first anti-Revolutionary tract, *Considérations sur la France*. In 1802 he was appointed by King Victor Emmanuel Sardinian minister plenipotentiary to Russia. At St. Petersburg between 1802 and 1817, he prepared his ablest works: *Essai sur le principe générateur des constitutions politiques* (1814), *Du pape* (1817), and *Les soirées de Saint-Pétersbourg*. A devout Roman Catholic, De Maistre saw God in everything. For him the French Revolution was "radically bad," "a pure impurity," and the bloodbath of the Napoleonic wars was not much better. They were to be explained as expiation for the sins of the eighteenth century, the arrogant application of reason to human affairs by the *philosophes*, the composition by proud Revolutionaries of a logical written constitution, and the corruption of the Roman Catholic clergy and the falling away of the faithful.

For De Maistre the national soul, and hence the divine voice, is to be found in the laws that a people develop over time. A wise lawgiver, such as Solon or Lycurgus, affirms these in institutions, but to begin *de novo* is impiety and folly. Once this torrent of evil is past, however, a better day will dawn. The infallibility of the pope will be recognized, and the Bourbon absolute monarchy, which harmonized with the divine will and the French national soul, will be restored.

M. Lombard, *Joseph de Maistre* (Boston, 1796).

Harold T. Parker

Related entries: *EMIGRES*; LITERATURE.

MAITLAND, FREDERICK LEWIS (1777-1839), captain. See ABDICATION, SECOND.

MALACHOWSKI, STANISLAW H. NALECZ (1736–1809), president of the Council of Ministers and (later) the Senate of the Duchy of Warsaw. He had been marshal of the great *Sejm* (Diet) of 1788–92, which tried to reform Poland to prevent its partition among Russia, Austria, and Prussia—and failed. Sometime exile and prisoner of Austria, he readily agreed (1806) to use his influence in the French interest. In 1807, Napoleon made him president of the Governing Commission (provisional government) of Poland, and he was shortly president of the Council of Ministers in the Duchy of Warsaw. Unfortunately, Małachowski clashed with Feliks Łubieński, champion of French-inspired reforms, and resigned. The duke (King Frederick Augustus of Saxony), out of respect for his age and patriotism, made him president of the Senate. He died in office in 1809.

B. Leśnodorski, *Dzieło Sejmu Czteroletniego* (Wrocław, 1951); E. Machalski, *Stanisław Małachowski* (Poznan, 1936); S. Małachowski, *Żywot i Pamiętniki* (Cracow, 1853); K. Koźmian, *Pamiętniki*, 3 vols. (Wrocław, 1973).

John Stanley

Related entries: FRIEDRICH AUGUST III; WARSAW, DUCHY OF.

MALET, CLAUDE-FRANCOIS DE (1754–1812), general, head of the Malet Conspiracy of 1812, news of which persuaded Napoleon to leave the retreating Grande Armée (in Russia) and hurry back to Paris. Born in Dôle of minor nobility, Malet served from age seventeen to twenty-one in the Grey Muscateers of the Bourbons—all noble household troops, colorful but anachronistic. He then lived on his estates until elected captain in the National Guard of Dôle in 1789, which led him into war service in 1792. He lost his commission briefly in 1793 but professed ardent republicanism and was reinstated. By 1799 he was a brigadier general but thereafter had no promotions, and his ineptitude and loudly voiced aversion to Napoleon got him cashiered in 1807. He immediately tried to organize a plot against the emperor, which landed him in prison, where he tried to hatch more conspiracies, but as time went on, his jailers did not take him seriously. Finally in 1810 he was transferred to a mental institution in Paris.

There he recruited followers (an abbé, two generals, and others) and made ready to overthrow the government. On 23 October 1812 he emerged in splendid uniform, appeared before the prefect of the Seine, Count Nicolas Frochot, and convinced him that Napoleon was dead in Russia and that a new republican government had been formed. He also bluffed most of the garrison commanders in Paris into obedience. The prefect of Paris police and the minister of police, General Savary, were imprisoned. Success made Malet's behavior more bizarre, however, and when he shot dead a general who asked for his credentials, he was seized and imprisoned. Embarrassed generals and police then released General Savary, who had Malet's followers rounded up. Seventeen of the conspirators, including Malet, were tried during the night and shot the next day.

When the news reached Napoleon in Russia, however, he reacted violently. If a maniac's plot could go so far, what if more talented politicians attempted a coup? It had long been a nagging fear of his while on campaign that such as Charles-Maurice de Talleyrand and Joseph Fouché would seize the government in Paris. He had just gotten the remnants of his army across the Berezina River and felt that Joachim Murat could lead the retreat while he attended to more important matters in Paris. On 5 December, at Smorgoni, Napoleon left the army, and on 19 December 1812, he was back in Paris. It is possible that he would have lost his throne earlier than 1814 if he had not returned, and his remaining with the Grande Armée surely would have done no good.

G. Artom, *Napoleon Is Dead in Russia: The Extraordinary Story of One of History's Strangest Conspiracies* (New York, 1970); B. Melchior-Bonnet, *La conspiration du général Malet* (Paris, 1963); A.-J.-M.-R. Savary, *Mémoires. . .pour servir a l'histoire de l'empereur Napoléon,* 8 vols. (Paris, 1828).

Related entries: RUSSIAN CAMPAIGN; SAVARY.

MALOUET, PIERRE-VICTOR, BARON (1740–1814), naval intendant under the *ancien régime*, member of the National Assembly 1789–91, holder of major government posts under the Empire, and first minister of the navy in the Restoration. Throughout his career, he was a prolific writer and commentator on government policies, naval and colonial administration, and political issues.

Educated by Oratorians at Juilly, he entered government service at eighteen. A succession of appointments followed, including commissioner and director of the colony of Saint-Domingue. Named naval intendant at Toulon in 1781, he served there until just prior to the meeting of the Estates General of 1789 to which he was elected by his native Riom (Auvergne). A close friend of Jacques Necker and personally devoted to the royal family, Malouet was politically aligned with the Anglophile right-center of Jean Mounier and T.-G. Lally-Tollendal. As the Revolution progressed, Malouet was identified with the extreme right; barely escaping arrest, he emigrated to England in September 1792. Returning to France during the Consulate, he was appointed in 1803 commissioner general of the navy at Antwerp and ultimately naval prefect of that port. For his services, he was made baron of the empire and chevalier of the Legion of Honor and appointed *conseiller d'état* (1810). His outspoken opinions and suspected royalist sympathies brought his exile to Touraine in 1812. The provisional government appointed Malouet minister of the navy in April 1814. He was confirmed in that post by Louis XVIII in May but died shortly after in September.

Carl Ludwig Lokke Manuscripts, Manuscript Department, Duke University Library; P. V. Malouet, *Collection de mémoires et correspondances officielles sur l'administration des colonies*, 5 vols. (Paris, 1802), *Collection des opinions de M. Malouet, député à l'Assemblée nationale*, 2 vols. (Paris, 1791), *Considérations historiques sur l'empire de la mer, chez les anciens et les modernes* (Antwerp, 1816), and *Mémoires de Malouet*, ed. Baron Malouet, 2 vols. (Paris, 1874); J. C. White, "L'Hôpital Maritime De Toulon (1782-1787)," *Annales du Midi* 83 (1971), and "Pierre Victor Malouet: Administrator and Legislator (1749-1792)" (dissertation, Duke University, 1964).

John Charles White

Related entries: MINISTERS OF NAPOLEON; NAVY, FRENCH.

MALOYAROSLAVETS, BATTLE OF. See RUSSIAN CAMPAIGN.

MAMLUKS, a generic term for slave soldiers of Muslim rulers. More specifically, it designates a series of warriors who held power in Egypt from 1250 until the early nineteenth century. Muslim rulers traditionally had acquired non-Muslim boys and given them excellent military training coupled with a basic Islamic education, culminating in their conversion. Such men often constituted the core of the army. Since Muslims could not legally enslave other Muslims, the children of the Mamluks (or Mameluks) were ineligible to become Mamluks themselves. This condition underscored the elite nature of the Mamluk forces.

In 1250, Mamluks of the Ayyubid dynasty, which then controlled Egypt, seized power from the ruling family, charging that it had been lax in dealing with Crusader challenges. The new rulers continued to train Mamluks, and leadership passed from one generation of soldiers to another until the Ottomans toppled this Mamluk dynasty in 1517.

Many Mamluks served in the Ottoman provincial government of Egypt, still maintaining their own forces. When Istanbul began to lose the ability to assert effective control over distant provinces, the Mamluks again became Egypt's de facto rulers. Thus, it was a Mamluk army that confronted Napoleon's forces during the Egyptian campaign (1798–1801). The Mamluks had a strong military heritage but had not kept pace with advances in military technology and proved no match for the French, who inflicted a severe defeat on them at the Battle of the Pyramids (1798).

Nevertheless, Napoleon was impressed by these warriors and recruited some of them for the Imperial Guard. Their Oriental attire and reputation for ferocity made them valuable shock troops despite their small numbers. In the Madrid uprising of 1808, a Mamluk contingent turned on rebel snipers, viciously murdering not only them but many innocent civilians. Perhaps the best known Mamluk in French service was Roustan, long the personal bodyguard of the emperor.

D. Ayalon, "L'Esclavage du Mamelouk," Oriental Notes and Studies, *The Israel Oriental Society, no. 1* (Jerusalem, 1951), and *Gunpowder and Firearms in the Mamluk*

Kingdom (London, 1956); al-Jabarti, Abd al-Rahman ibn Hassan, trans. Chefik Mansour et al., *Merveilles Biographiques et Historiques ou Chronique du Cheikh Abd-el-Rahman El-Djabarti* (Cairo, 1888-1896); S. J. Shaw, *Ottoman Egypt in the Age of the French Revolution* (Cambridge, 1964).

Kenneth J. Perkins

Related entries: ARMY, FRENCH; EGYPTIAN CAMPAIGN; ROUSTAN RAZA.

MANTUA. See ITALIAN CAMPAIGN, FIRST.

MARBOT, JEAN-BAPTISTE-ANTOINE-MARCELLIN, BARON DE (1782–1854). Son of one French general and younger brother of another, Marbot volunteered for military service in 1799 at age seventeen. He fought in the second Italian campaign and then as aide-de-camp, successively, of Pierre Augereau, Jean Lannes, and André Masséna, participated in every major campaign from Austerlitz to Waterloo, reaching the permanent rank of colonel. During the Restoration he became attached to the Orléans branch of the Bourbons. He undertook the military education of the duke of Chartres, who became duke of Orléans after the Revolution of 1830, and in the 1830s participated in the African campaigns, attaining in 1838 the rank of lieutenant general. Retired after the February revolution of 1848, he wrote his memoirs of the Napoleonic era, borrowing from accounts already in print (for example, Agathon Fain, Paul Thiébault, Adolphe Thiers) and filling in with tales of his own exploits. His reliability has been questioned; yet on the battles of Friedland and Waterloo, which I have studied, his narrative coincides or dovetails nearly perfectly with what is known from other sources.

J.-B.-A.-Marcellin, *Mémoires du général baron de Marbot*, 3 vols. (Paris, 1981; ed. R. Lacour-Gayet, Paris, 1966); H. T. Parker, *Three Napoleonic Battles* (Durham, N.C., 1944, 1983).

Harold T. Parker

Related entry: ARMY, FRENCH.

MARCHAND, LOUIS-JOSEPH (1791–1876). Marchand entered the domestic service of Napoleon in 1811, became his *valet de chambre* after the first abdication in April 1814, and accompanied him first to Elba and then to St. Helena. There he took his turn writing under Napoleon's dictation. The *Précis des guerres de Jules César* was dictated entirely to Marchand. On his deathbed, Napoleon named Marchand one of the three executors of his will and conferred on him the title of count. Marchand's memoirs concerning Elba, the Hundred Days, and St. Helena are most valuable but remained unpublished until after World War II.

L. Marchand, *Mémoires de Marchand, premier valet de chambre et exécuteur testamentaire de l'Empereur*, ed. J. Bourguignon, 2 vols. (Paris, 1952, 1955).

Harold T. Parker

Related entry: ST. HELENA.

MARENGO, BATTLE OF. See ITALIAN CAMPAIGN, SECOND.

MARET, HUGUES-BERNARD (1763–1839), duc de Bassano. As secretary-general to the government of the Consulate and as secretary of state under the Empire, Maret was in charge of Napoleon's personal working cabinet. Except for Charles-Maurice de Talleyrand, who as minister of foreign affairs insisted on conferring with Napoleon directly, the ministers regularly submitted their dossiers of documents requiring decisions to Napoleon through Maret. After Napoleon dictated the decisions, Maret returned the folders to the ministers, usually the same day. In the evening he selected those documents and stories that were to be published in the next day's *Moniteur*, the official newspaper, and thus ''orchestrated the press'' [Church]. Maret was smooth, diligent, discreet, and well organized, devoted to Napoleon and to his job. His tenure was interrupted only by his appointment of 17 April 1811 as minister of foreign affairs, when Napoleon needed someone he could trust to develop the diplomacy of a new anti-Russian policy. After two and a half years, Maret returned to his secretariat (November 1813) for the concluding months of the regime and the Hundred Days. It seems that he used his daily association with Napoleon to moderate the tone of his decisions, to influence appointments, and after 1812 to speak in behalf of peace.

C. H. Church, *Revolution and Red Tape: The French Ministerial Bureaucracy 1770-1850* (Oxford, 1981); A. A. Ernouf, *Maret, duc de Bassano* (Paris, 1878); J. Savant, *Les ministres de Napoléon* (Paris, 1959).

Harold T. Parker

Related entries: ADMINISTRATION; DIPLOMACY; FOREIGN POLICY.

MARIA-LUISA (1751-1819), queen of Spain. She was deposed by Napoleon in 1808, along with her husband, Charles IV. See CHARLES IV; SPAIN, KINGDOM OF.

MARIE-CAROLINE (1752–1814), Bourbon queen of Naples-Sicily driven (with her husband, Ferdinand IV) from the throne of Naples (1806) by Napoleon and replaced by Joseph Bonaparte. She was the daughter of the famed Austrian empress, Maria Theresa, and the sister of the ill-fated Marie Antoinette of France. See NAPLES, KINGDOM OF.

MARIE-LOUISE VON HABSBURG (1791–1847), Napoleon's second empress (1810–14). Napoleon's power appeared greater than ever in 1810, but his empire remained insecure because his marriage to the Empress Josephine had produced no son to inherit the vast domain. Before his divorce (December 1809), Napoleon had decided on a dynastic marriage, and negotiations began with Russia, but Czar Alexander was weary of his alliance with France and refused to offer his sister, the fourteen-year-old Archduchess Anna, to the forty-year-old French emperor. Napoleon turned next to Austria, where Emperor Francis

I, represented by Clemens von Metternich, contracted a marriage to his eighteen-year-old daughter, the Archduchess Marie-Louise. Although the two countries had been bitter enemies since the Revolution and the vivid memory of the execution of Marie Antoinette, the last Habsburg archduchess to reign in France, remained implanted in Austrian minds, Francis I and Metternich hoped that the marriage alliance would secure the Austrian empire. Napoleon trusted that the union would provide political stability and peace in Europe and ultimately an heir to perpetuate the Bonaparte dynasty in France.

Young Marie-Louise had been raised in an atmosphere of anti-French sentiment but obeyed her father's wish that she be betrothed to Napoleon. The pleasant-looking, fair-skinned, blonde-haired woman, with blue slanting cat eyes and small hands and feet, was married to Napoleon by proxy in the Vienna church of St. Augustine on 11 March 1810. The following day, the imperial bride embarked on her lengthy journey to France by carriage, accompanied by Queen Caroline Murat. Napoleon, eager to meet his new empress, intercepted the royal procession at Compiègne. The emperor of France immediately became enchanted by the freshness and youthfulness of his Austrian bride. Since Napoleon fully realized the animosity and fear that Marie-Louise might feel with regard to living in France with her country's most detested enemy, he made every conceivable effort to welcome her. Marie-Louise was continually showered with exquisite gifts, love letters, and items of personal interest that Napoleon had specifically requested from Austria. She soon adapted to the imperial French life-style and grew genuinely fond of the emperor. The religious marriage took place on April 2 in the Louvre.

Although the French people were extremely loyal to Josephine, they quickly accepted Marie-Louise, especially after it was disclosed that the new empress was carrying the possible heir to Napoleon's crown and possessions. Marie-Louise experienced a difficult delivery, and the doctor claimed that it would be impossible to deliver the child without the use of forceps. Indeed it seemed improbable that the lives of both mother and child could be saved. The young empress was terrified that her life would be sacrificed for that of the child, but the emperor ordered the doctors, "Do your utmost to save the mother. Do exactly what you would do if you were attending an ordinary citizen's wife." The population of Paris anxiously awaited information of the event. Tradition dictated that a salute of a 101 guns would announce the arrival of a boy, while only 21 shots signaled the birth of a girl. On 20 March 1811, the crowds of Paris went wild on the firing of the twenty-second shot, commencing numerous festivals to celebrate the arrival of Napoleon's long-desired, legitimate son. Both mother and child survived the delivery. The new heir was given the name Napoleon-Francis-Joseph-Charles and received the title king of Rome.

Napoleon was called to war with the 1812 campaign, and for the next two years he saw very little of Marie-Louise or his son. On 30 March 1813, the emperor appointed her to act as regent, with Joseph Bonaparte as lieutenant general of the realm during his absence in the field. The following year the empress and her son were forced to flee Paris, venturing first to Rambouillet and then to Blois, where she received the disastrous news of her husband's abdication. As Napoleon was being sent to his exile at Elba, Marie-Louise and the king of Rome were taken into her father's protection. Marie-Louise's personal aide was Count Adam Albert von Neipperg, the charming, swashbuckling general who would later win over the heart of the former empress. Francis I and Metternich intercepted all of Napoleon's letters ordering Marie-Louise to join him on Elba, thereby giving her no choice of obeying her husband. Besides, Marie-Louise fell under the influence of Neipperg and soon became his mistress and later the mother of several children by him. During the Hundred Days she remained in Austria and manifested no desire for the success of Napoleon in France. The Allies granted the ex-Empress Marie-Louise sovereignty over the duchies of Parma, Piacenza, and Guastalla. She promised her father, meanwhile, that she never again would write to Napoleon and would leave his son in Vienna to be raised as an Austrian prince with the title of duke of Reichstadt. In Parma, Marie-Louise and Neipperg were well respected by their subjects, and the Italian states prospered with the construction of hospitals, bridges, roads, and theaters. A civil code was promulgated in 1820, and a new penal code abolished many odious customs and punishments and allowed publicity in public trials. Napoleon always cherished the fond memories of his Austrian wife and attributed her misconduct with Neipperg to the influence of Francis I.

On Napoleon's death in 1821, Marie-Louise was married to Neipperg morganatically for seven years. She rarely visited her son by Napoleon in Vienna, who was a virtual prisoner of the city. Called simply Francis Charles, the boy was denied all influences of French culture and instead was educated to become Austrian. Marie-Louise was present at his untimely death in 1833, and public interest in her sharply declined thereafter. After Neipperg's death, Marie-Louise entered into another morganatic union in 1834 with Count Charles René de Bombelles. She died on 18 December 1847 in Vienna.

Some historians attribute Napoleon's downfall to his second marriage. Surely he sincerely believed that the union would bring France a long-term ally in the Austrian emperor, whose grandson would one day rule the French empire. In this he was disappointed. Moreover, Marie-Louise is often portrayed by historians as the avenger of Marie-Antoinette's death and as a traitor to Napoleon, abandoning the emperor and her son for her own security within the Austrian empire. This picture seems to be false. Her letters in 1814 indicate that she wanted to do Napoleon's will—or, secondarily, that of her father. Her father gained custody of her, and in her world, daughters obeyed.

J. Bertaut, *Marie-Louise, femme de Napoléon Ier, 1791-1847* (Paris, 1952); R. Bessard, *La vie privée de Marie Louise* (Paris, 1953); Marie-Louise, Empress, *My Dearest Louise: Marie-Louise and Napoleon, 1813-1814*, ed. C. F. Palmstierna, trans. E. M. Wildinson (London, 1958); F. Masson, *Marie Louise, Impératrice de France* (Paris, 1910); E. M.

Oddie, *Marie Louise, Empress of France, Duchess of Parma* (New York, 1931); A. Stoeckl, *Four Years an Empress: Marie Louise, Second Wife of Napoleon* (London, 1962); P. Turnbull, *Napoleon's Second Empress* (London, 1971).

Linda J. Nelson

Related entries: ABDICATION, FIRST; AUSTRIA; FOREIGN POLICY; FRANZ II; JOSEPHINE; METTERNICH.

MARMONT, AUGUSTE-FREDERIC-LOUIS VIESSE DE (1774–1852), duc de Raguse, marshal of France. Of minor nobility, Marmont entered the artillery school at Châlons as a sublieutenant at seventeen. He served at Toulon, where Bonaparte first observed him, was Napoleon's aide-de-camp during the first Italian campaign (1796–97), and served him as a general in Egypt (1798–99) and at Marengo (1800). He was bitter over not being among the first marshals (1804) but fought valiantly at Ulm (1805). In 1806 he was made governor of Dalmatia, to which he added Ragusa (which he seized from the Russians in 1807), and was dubbed duc de Raguse in 1808. After Wagram (1809) he was finally given a marshal's baton. In 1811 Marmont was sent to command the Army of Portugal. Wellington drove him into Spain, however, and defeated him at Salamanca (1812), where a cannonball shattered his arm. He was carried from the field unconscious and took a year to recover, but he fought in Germany in 1813.

In 1814 Marmont surrendered Paris—prematurely, in Napoleon's judgment. The emperor branded him a traitor. He lived under the shadow of that accusation, echoed by a legion of Bonapartist memoirists, for the rest of his life. He was made a peer by Louis XVIII and kept his rank. In 1830 he tried to save Charles X and then went into exile. His posthumously published *Mémoires* (1856–57), written in Venice, protested that he had always acted in the best interest of France. He devoted much space to defending his actions in 1814.

L.-V. de Marmont, *The Spirit of Military Institutions* (Westport, Conn., 1974), and *Mémoires du Maréchal Marmont, duc de Raguse, de 1792 à 1841*, 9 vols. (Paris, 1856–57); P. Saint-Marc, *Le Maréchal Marmont* (Paris, 1957).

Related entries: ABDICATION, FIRST; ILLYRIAN PROVINCES; PARIS, BATTLE OF; PENINSULAR WAR.

MARSHALS OF THE EMPIRE, officers of the highest military rank; Napoleon appointed twenty-six in all. With the creation of the Empire in 1804, he named eighteen who were either heroes of the Republic or men who had served him outstandingly during the early campaigns. Four of these—F.E.C. Kellermann, François Lefebvre, D. de Pérignon, and J.M.P. Sérurier—were named honorary marshals, though Lefebvre later saw combat duty. The others were Alexandre Berthier, Joachim Murat, J. de Moncey, J.-E. Jourdan, André Masséna, Pierre Augereau, Jean Bernadotte, Nicolas Soult, G. Brune, Jean Lannes, Joseph Mortier, Michel Ney, Nicolas Davout, and J.-B. Bessières. In 1807

Claude Victor was added to the list, and in 1809 after the victory at Wagram, Jacques Macdonald, the official hero of the battle, was named marshal, together with Louis Marmont and Nicolas Oudinot. In 1811 Louis Suchet was given the baton for his services in Spain, and in 1812 Laurent Gouvion-Saint-Cyr was named marshal during the Russian campaign. In 1813 the Polish prince, Joseph Poniatowski, was given his baton for services in Russia, the only foreigner to become a marshal. The last marshal, Emmanuel Grouchy, was appointed in 1815 and served in the Waterloo campaign, but not well. Of the twenty-six, ten were, like Napoleon, nobles of the Old Regime. Of the others only three were of peasant or working-class background: Lefèbvre, Murat, and Augereau.

M. E. Béchu, *Napoléon et la trahison des maréchaux, 1814* (Paris, 1970); L. Chardigny, *Les Maréchaux de Napoléon* (Paris, 1980); R. F. Delderfield, *The March of the Twenty-Six: The Story of Napoleon's Marshals* (London, 1962); R. P. Dunn-Pattison, *Napoleon's Marshals* (London, 1977); R. W. Phipps, *The Armies of the First French Republic and the Rise of the Marshals of Napoleon I...* (London, 1926–39).

Related entries: See under names of individual marshals.

MASONS. See FREEMASONS.

MASSENA, ANDRE (1758–1817), duc de Rivoli, prince d'Essling, marshal of France. Masséna was born near Nice on 6 May 1758. At seventeen he joined the Royal Italian regiment and was promoted to highest noncommissioned rank after fourteen years of service. Unable to advance further due to his humble origins, he resigned but reenlisted in the National Guard when the Revolution began. He was promoted through the ranks to general of brigade in the French Army of Italy after service in Italy and at Toulon (December 1793). In March 1796, Napoleon took command of the army and appointed Masséna to command the advance guard. He played a decisive role in the first Italian campaign and was dubbed *l'enfant chéri de la victoire* by Napoleon. In December 1798 he was given command of the Army of Helvetia (Switzerland), probably the most important assignment of his career. He collected some 80,000 men to face an equal number of Austrians and Russians in the vicinity of Zürich. In the Battle of Zürich (25–28 September 1799) he destroyed the Austro-Russian forces and then turned on a Russian relief army and defeated it decisively. This was undoubtedly Masséna's most brilliant victory. It saved France from imminent invasion and had a major impact on the dissolution of the Second Coalition.

With the return of Napoleon from Egypt and the coup d'état of 18 Brumaire, Masséna was appointed to command the Army of Italy, blockaded at Genoa. Masséna held the city for almost three months, evacuating with the honors of war only when his army was starving. Masséna's defense, however, had forced the Austrians to divide their forces and allowed time for Napoleon to cross the Alps and win a victory at Marengo (14 June 1800). The ordeal had impaired Masséna's health; he returned home to Reuil, where he remained for five years. He became a member of the Legislative Corps where he voted against Napoleon's life consulate. Nevertheless, Napoleon named him a marshal of France in May 1804. He commanded the Army of Italy in 1805, a corps in the Army of Naples in 1806, and a corps of the Grand Army in Poland (1807).

Masséna's corps formed the right wing of the French army in the Austrian campaign of 1809. He fought at the bloody Battle of Aspern-Essling (21–22 May) and again at Wagram (6 July). For his effort Napoleon made him the prince d'Essling. In April 1810 he was given command of the Army of Portugal and ordered to drive the Anglo-Portuguese army into the sea. After successfully besieging Ciudad Rodrigo (10 July) and Almeida (27 August), Masséna invaded Portugal. He fought the duke of Wellington at Bussaco (27 September 1810) and, although defeated, pursued Wellington to within twenty miles of Lisbon, only to be halted by the lines of Torres Vedras. Without reinforcements and supplies, Masséna was forced to retreat after three months to the Spanish frontier, closely pursued by Wellington, where he made one last unsuccessful attack at Fuentes de Onoro (3–5 May). He was relieved of command and recalled to France in disgrace. Broken in health and blamed for defeat by Napoleon, Masséna never again commanded an army in the field. During the Restoration he was made a peer by Louis XVIII, but when Napoleon returned to France in March 1815, he acknowledged Napoleon's government.

After the Bourbons returned to France, he was disgraced and retired to Nice where he died on 4 April 1817. Masséna was one of the most distinguished French generals of his day (Napoleon would probably have said his best marshal, as late as 1809). His brilliant victories in Italy, Switzerland, and Austria rank him among the greatest soldiers of France.

L.-C.-O.-D. de Beauregard, *Le maréchal Masséna, duc de Rivoli, prince d'Essling, enfant de Nice. Résumé de sa vie* (Nice, 1902); E. Gachot, *Histoire militaire de Masséna: 1809, Napoléon en Allemagne* (Paris, 1913), *Histoire militaire de Masséna. La troisième campagne d'Italie (1805–1806) guerre de l'an XIV—expédition de Naples—le vrai Fra Diavolo—lettres inédites des princes Eugène et Joseph Napoléon* (Paris, 1911), and *Histoire militaire de Masséna. Le siège de Gênes (1800)* (Paris, 1908); L. Hennequin, *Zurich. Masséna en Suisse, messidor an VII-brumaire an VIII (juillet-octobre 1799)* (Paris, 1911); D. D. Horward, *The Battle of Bussaco: Masséna vs. Wellington* (Tallahassee, 1965); J. B. Koch, ed., *Mémoires de Masséna rediges d'après les documents qu'il a laisses*, 7 vols. (Paris, 1848–50); J. H. Marshall-Cornwall, *Marshal Massena* (London, 1965).

Donald D. Horward

Related entries: ITALIAN CAMPAIGN, FIRST; ITALIAN CAMPAIGN, SECOND; ITALY, KINGDOM OF; LEGISLATORS; MARSHALS OF THE EMPIRE; NAPLES, KINGDOM OF; PORTUGUESE CAMPAIGNS; WAGRAM, BATTLE OF; WAGRAM CAMPAIGN.

MATUSZEWICZ, TADEUSZ WIKTORYN H. LABEDZ (c. 1765–1819), minister of the treasury in the Duchy of Warsaw. Noble intellectual and patriot, he was in the Supreme National Council during the Kosciuszko uprising (1794). After its failure, he busied himself with translating Horace and Virgil into Polish and was one of the founders of the Society of the Friends of Science (Towarzystwo Przyjaciół Nauk) in Warsaw.

During the Galician campaign of 1809 (in support of Napoleon), Prince Józef Poniatowski appointed him to the Central Council and afterward the Provisional Government of Galicia. He was a member of the Polish deputation sent to Napoleon in Vienna and was present at the peace negotiations with Austria. Partly because of his ties to two of the most powerful Polish magnate families, the Czartoryskis and the Zamoyskis, he was appointed to the Council of State in January 1810 and made minister of the treasury in October 1811. As minister he upheld the economic interests of the duchy in the face of Saxon pressures and quickly became one of the most important members of the government, rivaling Feliks Łubieński.

In June 1812, Matuszewicz' great skill as an orator proved useful to Napoleon in the extraordinary *Sejm*, which seemed to pave the way for the resurrection of the Kingdom of Poland. It was he who influenced the head of the Czartoryski family to come over to the French cause.

When the Russian campaign turned out badly, however, he was able to use his ties to Adam Czartoryski (in Russia) to establish contact with Czar Alexander I. In 1815 he was on the committee that prepared the constitution of the Russian-sponsored Kingdom of Poland and became the director of the Governing Commission of Income and the Treasury, a post he held until 1817. He was a senator until his death in 1819.

L. Dembowski, *Moje wspomnienia*, 2 vols. (St. Petersburg, 1898); J. Falkowski, *Obrazy z życia kilku ostatnich pokoleń w Polsce* (Poznan, 1877); B. Grochulska, *Handel zagraniczny Księstwa Warszawskiego* (Warsaw, 1967); K. Krzoś, *Z księciem Józefem w Galicji w 1809 r.* (Warsaw, 1967); K. Koźmian, *Pamiętniki*, 3 vols. (Wrocław, 1972); J. U. Niemcewicz, *Pamiętniki czasów moich* (Warsaw, 1957).

John Stanley

Related entries: RUSSIAN CAMPAIGN; SCHÖNBRUNN, TREATY OF (1809); VIENNA, CONGRESS OF; WAGRAM CAMPAIGN; WARSAW, DUCHY OF.

MAX I JOSEPH (1756–1825), first king of Bavaria; ally of Napoleon. Max was the second son of the younger brother of Duke Christian IV of Pfalz-Zweibrücken, an independent collateral line of the house of Wittelsbach. His father, Count Palatine Friedrich Michael, was a field marshal in the army of the Holy Roman Empire. Max Joseph, not raised as a prince, became colonel of the French foreign regiment Royal Alsace. Until the Revolution he led the life of a cavalier of the Old Regime. However, he spoke better French than German, was grounded in the concepts of the Enlightenment, and was a Freemason.

In 1795 Max became duke of Zweibrücken after the sudden death of his brother August II. The duchy was already occupied by the armies of the French Revolution, however, and Max Joseph and his family lived as refugees at Mannheim and Ansbach. Inasmuch as Elector Karl Theodor of Bavaria had no legitimate children, Max Joseph was also the heir to the Electorate of Palatinate-Bavaria. As early as 1796, he and his adviser, Maximilian von Montgelas, were planning for reforms in Bavaria. In 1799 he became elector of Bavaria as Max IV Joseph and after allying with Napoleon in 1805 (and until 1813) became King Max I in 1806. Between 1799 and 1813, the Bavarian state was modernized by Montgelas following the French example. Additions of territory between 1806 and 1816 gave Bavaria its current configuration. In 1818 Max I was one of the first German princes to grant a constitution in which he renounced some of his prerogatives in favor of a two-chamber parliament.

A. von Bayern, *Max I. Joseph von Bayern* (Munich, 1957). H. Glaser, ed., *Krone und Verfassung. König Max I. Joseph und der neue Staat* (Munich, 1980); E. Weis, *Montgelas* (Munich, 1971), and "Die Begründung des modernen bayerischen Staates unter König Max I. (1799–1825)," in M. Spindler, ed., *Handbuch der bayerischen Geschichte*, vol. IV 1 (Munich, 1979).

Eberhard Weis

Related entries: BAVARIA, KINGDOM OF; CONFEDERATION OF THE RHINE; MONTGELAS.

MEDICINE. A key period in French medical history, the Napoleonic era saw the reorganization of the profession, a renewed commitment to public health, and the formative years of the French clinical school. The Consulate adopted a major law on medical education and practice, 19 Ventôse Year XI (10 March 1803), and a law on pharmacy, 21 Germinal Year XI (11 April 1803), which strictly controlled the distribution of remedies. The Ventôse law (which was to remain in effect until 1892) provided the first uniform licensing system for all of French medicine, ending the medical anarchy that had prevailed after the Revolution destroyed the old corporate monopolies. The corporations would not be restored, but henceforth official approbation was required for medical practice, and unauthorized practitioners would be criminally prosecuted.

The new profession had two tiers. Doctors of medicine and surgery would train at the new medical schools created in 1794 to fill the gap left by the abolition of the old faculties. (The schools became faculties with the creation of the Imperial University in 1808.) They could practice all the branches of their art anywhere in France. *Officiers de santé* would receive a more practical training, a shorter program in a medical school or an apprenticeship at a hospital or under the supervision of a physician. Starting in 1806, the government designated certain teaching hospitals as secondary schools of medicine. Health officers normally would be examined by a special departmental *jury médical* and would be licensed to practice only in that department; they could not perform major surgery except under the supervision of a doctor.

The medical profession under Napoleon, while expensive to enter (doctoral training cost at least 1,000 francs), was not especially profitable or prestigious. The average physician could not expect to earn more than 2,000 francs a year from his practice; many practitioners relied on another source of income, such as land or even (for *officiers de santé*) a trade. Few physicians ranked among the notables, although the state made extensive use of those few, and a handful, such as Antoine-François Fourcroy (1755–1809) and Jean-Antoine Chaptal (1756–1832), occupied high positions.

In the field of political hygiene, physicians continued to produce medical topographies in the tradition of the old Société Royal de Médecine. The Conseil de Salubrité de la Seine, created by the prefect Antoine Dubois in 1802, provided a model for subsequent departmental health councils in the provinces. In the Bas-Rhin, the prefect Adrien de Lezay-Marnésia established a system of cantonal physicians, on the model of the German *Physikus*, but his example was not widely imitated. Vaccination, the most prominent public health project, began soon after Edward Jenner's publication of his work on cowpox in 1798; in 1800, François de La Rochefoucauld-Liancourt set up a central vaccination committee at the Paris Medical School, and in 1804 the Minister of the Interior ordered the creation of vaccination societies at the departmental level.

For the majority of physicians, medical theory remained eclectic and therapeutics more pragmatic than systematic; neo-Hippocratic doctrines and eighteenth-century schools such as Montpellier vitalism and Brownism retained their influence. In the capital, however, the leaders of the discipline systematically developed physical examination and autopsy as the bases for clinical medicine. Major contributions came from Philippe Pinel (1745–1826), Marie-François-Xavier Bichat (1771–1802), and François-Joseph-Victor Broussais (1772–1838). Pinel, in his *Nosographie philosophique* (1798), emphasized the classification of signs and symptoms associated with various disease categories, including "essential fevers," which occupied a third of the work. Pinel's student M.-F.-X. Bichat pioneered in the field of pathological anatomy, studying body tissues (rather than organs) as the sites of disease. Broussais, a student of both Pinel and Bichat, argued that the pathologist must look for local lesions; equating fever with the inflammation caused by local irritation, he rejected Pinel's notion of essential fevers. The leading clinician was Jean-Nicolas Corvisart (1775–1821), physician to the Emperor, who translated Auenbrugger's *Inventum Novum* on auscultation and helped popularize the use of this technique.

E. H. Ackerknecht, *Medicine at the Paris Hospital, 1794-1848* (Baltimore, 1967); M. E. Antoine and J. Waquet, "La médecine civile à l'époque napoléonienne," *RIN* 132 (1976); M. Foucault, *The Birth of the Clinic* (New York, 1973); P. Huard, *Sciences, médecine, pharmacie: de la Révolution à l'Empire* (Paris, 1970); J. Léonard, *Les médecins de l'Ouest au XIX*[e] siècle (Paris, 1978); "Les médecins dans la société," *Annales E. S. C.* 32 (1977); M. Ramsey, "Medical Power and Popular Medicine: Illegal Healers in 19th-Century France," *Journal of Social History* 10 (1977); D. Weiner, "Public Health under Napoleon," *Clio Medica* 9 (1974).

Matthew Ramsey

Related entries: LACHAPELLE; LARREY; POPULATION; PUBLIC WELFARE; WOMEN; WOMEN, EDUCATION OF.

MEDINA DEL RIO SECO, BATTLE OF. See PENINSULAR WAR.

MEHUL, ETIENNE-NICHOLAS (1763–1817), French composer who influenced the development of French *opéra comique* and the symphony. Méhul was born 22 June 1763 at Givet, Ardennes, in northeastern France. After early training as an organist, he went to Paris in 1778 or 1779. He studied with the composer Jean-Frédéric Edelmann who influenced his operatic and keyboard compositions. In 1782 he presented a cantata based on a Rousseau ode at the Concert Spirituel, and, after a favorable reception, he turned to dramatic music. Within a thirty-five-year period, 1787–1822, he wrote forty operas, most of which were presented at the Opéra-Comique. *Euphronsine*, in 1790, was his first performed work and remained in the repertory for over forty years.

Méhul had not been part of the Revolutionary festivals until after 8 November 1793, when the National Convention created an Institut National de Musique, with François Joseph Gossec as director and Méhul and Jean-François Le Sueur part of the faculty. That same month Méhul's *Hymne à la Raison* was sung at the former church of Saint Roch. In 1794, his most popular Revolutionary song, *Chant du départ*, with words by M. J. Chenier, was publicly performed. Although not used during the First Empire, the piece reappeared in the revolutions of 1830, 1848, and 1870. On commission he wrote *Horatius Cocles* (1794) using the neoclassical setting preferred by the republicans, and in 1800 Napoleon asked him for a composition to commemorate the fall of the Bastille and celebrate the victory at Marengo. The work, *Chant national du 14 juillet 1800*, was performed at the Invalides using two full-sized choruses and orchestras, plus soloists. Such massive scope was also being used by Le Sueur and Luigi Cherubini and became a characteristic of Berlioz.

Joseph was Méhul's most famous, and last important, *opéra comique*. His operas had emphasized the orchestra's role, with his overtures often being the most popular part, so he produced two symphonies, which, with *Joseph*, are considered his finest creations. Many of the effects he developed were later used by Berlioz, Schubert, Weber, and Beethoven. He exploited the individual tone of instruments, experimented with new modulations and the use of dissonance, and strove to make the orchestra an integral part of the operatic drama. Méhul was the recipient of many honors: an annual pension by the Comédie Italienne in 1794; appointment as one of five inspectors when the Paris Conservatoire was founded; and election to the Institut de France and as one of the first members of the Legion of Honor. He died of tuberculosis in Paris 18 October 1817.

R. Brancour, *Méhul* (Paris, 1912); David Charlton, "Orchestration and Orchestral Practice in Paris, 1789–1810" (dissertation, University of Cambridge, 1973); B. Deane, "The French Operatic Overture from Grétry to Berlioz," *Proceedings of the Royal Musical Association* 99 (1972–73); E. J. Dent, *The Rise of Romantic Opera*, ed. W. Dean (Cambridge, 1976); A. Pougin, "Notice sur Méhul par Cherubini," *Rivista musicale italiana* 16 (1909), and *Méhul* (Paris, 1889); P. A. Vieillard, *Méhul, sa vie et ses oeuvres* (Paris, 1859).

Rachel R. Schneider

Related entries: CHERUBINI; GRASSINI; LE SUEUR; MUSIC; PROPAGANDA; THEATER.

MELAS, MICHAEL FRIEDRICH BENEDIKT (1729?–1806?), knight and baron, Austrian general, opponent of Napoleon at Marengo (1800). Melas probably entered the army at sixteen; he served as adjutant to Field Marshal Leopold von Daun during the Seven Years War. In the War of the First Coalition (1792–97), Melas distinguished himself and in 1796 was severely wounded in the attempts to relieve Mantua. With the formation of the Second Coalition, he was promoted to general of cavalry and entrusted with the command of all Austrian troops. In 1799 he won victories over the French at Cassano and Novi Ligure. He found cooperation with the Russian general Alexander Suvorov difficult, however, and was soon at odds with Foreign Minister Franz Thugut. Even to get winter quarters for his men, he had to force the hand of the emperor by offering his resignation.

In 1800 Melas prepared to invade southern France and force peace. Napoleon, however, thwarted the plan by unexpectedly crossing the Great St. Bernard pass and deploying forces in northern Italy. Melas reversed the course of his army, actually surprised Napoleon at Marengo (14 June 1800), and left the field after apparently winning the battle. At dusk, however, L.-C.-A. Desaix reinforced Napoleon, who counterattacked and won the day. Napoleon's luck began twelve years of triumphs for him and ended Melas' active career. The seventy-year-old veteran was appointed commanding general of Inner Austria and later Bohemia. In 1803 he retired. Among his souvenirs was a saber given him by Napoleon "as a token of the special respect with which I was filled by your brave army on the battle field of Marengo."

V. Mökesch, *General Michael Freiherr von Melas* (Vienna, 1900); J. Thiry, *Marengo* (Paris, 1949).

Siegfried Erich Kraus

Related entries: ARMY, HABSBURG; ITALIAN CAMPAIGN, SECOND.

MELZI D'ERIL. See ITALY, KINGDOM OF; ITALY, KINGDOM OF: MINISTERS.

MENEVAL, CLAUDE-FRANCOIS, BARON DE (1778–1850), secretary to Joseph Bonaparte during the negotiations that preceded the Treaty of Lunéville, the Concordat, and the Peace of Amiens. Méneval served as secretary to Napoleon from 1802 to 1813. When his health failed in 1813, he was placed "in convalescence," to use a phrase of Napoleon, as secretary to Marie-Louise. His voluminous memoirs—*Mémoires pour servir à l'histoire de Napoléon Ier depuis 1802 jusqu'à 1815*—are still of value to historians.

Harold T. Parker

Related entry: NAPOLEON, DAILY ROUND.

MENOU, JACQUES-FRANCOIS (1750–1810), political general and favorite of Napoleon. Elected to the National Assembly in 1789, he was named general of division in 1792. In command of the Convention's troops on the eve of the coup of 13 Vendémiaire, he was removed for incompetence and would have faced a court-martial had Bonaparte not intervened on his behalf. Thereafter Menou supported Bonaparte with servile devotion. He served Napoleon in Egypt as general of division and was wounded in the storming of Alexandria (2 July 1798). Following Bonaparte's departure (August 1799) and Jean-Baptiste Kléber's assassination (June 1800), he took command of the army. That he had become a Muslim decreased his popularity with the troops, who referred to him as "Abdallah." Defeated by the British at Canopus, 21 March 1801, he surrendered Alexandria, 2 September. Bonaparte employed him on his return to France but never again gave him a military command. Named tribune in 1802, Menou subsequently served in several administrative posts including governor-general of Tuscany (1808–09) and governor-general of Venice (1809–10).

E. Reynier, *De l' Egypte après la bataille d'Héliopolis* (Paris, 1802); G. Rigault, *Le général abdallah Menou et la dernière phase d'Expédition d'Egypte* (Paris, 1911); M. Vertray, *L'Armée française en Egypte* (Paris, 1882).

Milton Finley

Related entries: EGYPTIAN CAMPAIGN; TUSCANY, GRAND DUCHY OF.

METTERNICH, CLEMENS FÜRST VON (1773–1859), Austrian diplomat, foreign minister (1809–11), chancellor (1811–48); enemy of Napoleon though architect of Franco-Austrian alliance and Napoleon's Austrian marriage. Metternich led the Habsburg monarchy to victory over Napoleon and consolidated its central position as the dominant power in Germany and Italy and the fulcrum of the continental balance of power.

Born in Koblenz on 15 May 1773, he came from a family of imperial counts, high nobility who held their estates directly from the Holy Roman Emperor and exercised governing powers over subjects. As a student at Strasbourg and Mainz, he experienced the violence of the early French Revolution, which launched him on a lifelong search for order, repose, and rational principles. Driven from their estate at Winneburg by invading French armies, the Metternichs moved in 1794 to Vienna, where Clemens married Eleonore von Kaunitz, who opened to him the doors of Austrian, as opposed to German, imperial society. He represented the counts of Westphalia at the abortive peace congress of Rastatt, missing a meeting with Napoleon there by only a few days. He then joined the Austrian service, becoming successively envoy to Dresden (1801), to Berlin (1803), and finally ambassador to Paris (1806). In Paris he developed an admiration for Napoleon's efficient administrative system even while his optimistic and inflammatory reports to Vienna encouraged warlike sentiment and military preparations that resulted in the disastrous war of 1809.

Despite his part in bringing on the war, Metternich negotiated the peace treaty of Schönbrunn and succeeded Count Johann Philipp von Stadion as foreign minister (1809). He then realistically, if unheroically, pursued a French alliance, his crowning achievement being the marriage of Emperor Francis's daughter, Marie-Louise, to Napoleon. Although his prediction of French victory in Russia in 1812 proved wrong, he displayed great flexibility and ingenuity in extricating Austria from its commitments and undertaking an armed mediation designed to draw Napoleon out of Central Europe without allowing the Russians in. Even after Napoleon refused and Austria declared war, Metternich continued negotiations to preserve a Bonapartist France and its German allies as counterweights to Russia and Prussia. Napoleon himself he could not save, but by concessions to Great Britain and Prussia he prevailed in Germany and in the Peace of Paris (30 May 1814) managed to keep France reasonably strong under the Bourbons but with many Napoleonic institutions intact.

Although opposed to Napoleon personally (he would have sent him to America), Metternich at the Congress of Vienna (1814–15) succeeded in preserving most of Napoleon's client states in Germany and uniting them, together with Prussia, into a loose defensive league, the German Confederation, under Austrian presidency. In Italy he supported Joachim Murat until the latter joined Napoleon during the Hundred Days. For Austria Metternich recovered the Tyrol and Salzburg from Bavaria, the Illyrian Provinces that Napoleon had annexed to France, and Lombardy and Venetia in Italy.

By these arrangements, which favored existing states, he established a stable balance of power but disappointed many liberal and national aspirations. Deservedly or not, Metternich over the years became increasingly the symbol of reaction and was finally driven from office by the revolutions of 1848. ''I was a rock of order,'' he insisted shortly before he died on 11 June 1859.

M. Botzenhart, *Metternichs Pariser Botschafterzeit* (Münster, 1967); E. Kraehe, *Metternich's German Policy*, Vol.1: *The Contest with Napoleon 1799–1814* (Princeton, N.J., 1963); P. R. Rohden, *Die klassische Diplomatie von Kaunitz bis Metternich* (Leipzig, 1939); H. R. von Srbik, *Metternich, der Staatsmann und der Mensch*, 3 vols. (Munich, 1925–54).

Enno Kraehe

Related entries: DIPLOMACY; FOREIGN POLICY; GERMAN WAR OF LIBERATION; MARIE-LOUISE VON HABSBURG; RUSSIAN CAMPAIGN; VIENNA, CONGRESS OF; WAGRAM CAMPAIGN.

MILAN DECREES. See CONTINENTAL BLOCKADE; WARFARE, ECONOMIC.

MILLESIMO, BATTLE OF. See ITALIAN CAMPAIGN, FIRST.

MINISTERS OF NAPOLEON (1799–1814 and 1815).

State Secretary	Hugues Bernard Maret	1799–1811
	Pierre Daru	1811–13
	Maret	1813–14 and 1815
Foreign Affairs	Charles-Frédéric Reinhard	1799
	C.-M. de Talleyrand-Périgord	1799–1807

	J.-B. Nompère de Champagny	1807–11
	Hugues Bernard Maret	1811–13
	A.-A. de Caulaincourt	1813–14
	Caulaincourt	1815
War	Alexandre Berthier	1799–1800
	Lazare Carnot	1800
	Alexandre Berthier	1800–1806
	Henri Clarke	1807–14
	Louis Nicolas Davout	1815
Navy and Colonies	Pierre-A.-L. Forfait	1799–1801
	Denis Decrès	1801–14 and 1815
Police	Joseph Fouché	1799–1802
	[Ministry combined with Justice 1802–1804]	
	Joseph Fouché	1804–10
	René Savary	1810–14
	Joseph Fouché	1815
Finance	Charles Gaudin	1799–1814 and 1815
Treasury	François Barbé-Marbois	1801–5
	François-Nicolas Mollien	1806–14 and 1815
Interior	Pierre Simon Laplace	1799
	Lucien Bonaparte	1799–1800
	Jean-Antoine Chaptal	1800–1804
	J.-B. Nompère de Champagny	1804–7
	Emmanuel Crétet	1807–9
	J.-P. Bachasson de Montalivet	1809–14
	Lazare Carnot	1815
Justice	J.-J. Régis de Cambacérès	1799
	André Joseph Abrial	1799–1802
	Claude-Ambroise Régnier	1802–13
	Louis-Mathieu Molé	1813
	J.-J. Régis de Cambacérès	1813–14 and 1815
Ecclesiastical Affairs	Joseph-M.-E. Portalis	1804–7
	F.-J.-J. Bigot de Préameneu	1807–14 and 1815

Related entries: ADMINISTRATION; names of individual ministers.

MIOLLIS, SEXTIUS-ALEXANDRE-FRANCOIS (1759–1828), general, one of the French administrators who during the Revolution and under Napoleon specialized in the management of conquered peoples. He entered the royal army in 1778 as a cadet officer and soon after received a severe, disfiguring wound at the siege of Yorktown. After participating in the campaigns of the army of southeastern France and of Italy from 1792 to 1797, he started his career as a civil-military administrator in February 1797, when Bonaparte appointed him governor of the recently captured fortress of Mantua. In the performance of similar civil-administrative duties, he passed to Lucca (1798), Leghorn (1799), Genoa and Tuscany (1800), Mantua and Verona (1801), Holland (1805), Venice (1806), and Rome (1808–14). Loyal to the Republic even during the life Consulate and to the emperor even during the Restoration, devoted to France and to the interests of the peoples he was governing, he was an austere public servant who could be counted on to carry out orders efficiently and with the utmost probity.

H. Auréas, *Un général de Napoléon: Miollis* (Paris, 1961).

Harold T. Parker

Related entries: ADMINISTRATION; ITALIAN CAMPAIGN, FIRST.

MIOT, ANDRE-FRANCOIS (1762–1841), comte de Melito. Intelligent, amiable, articulate, and observant, Miot was a useful administrator during the Revolution and Empire, as well as a companion and friend of Napoleon's older brother Joseph. Miot entered the War Ministry of the Bourbon monarchy as a boy and rose to be a chief of a division before transferring in 1793 to the Ministry of Foreign Affairs. He volunteered to be minister plenipotentiary to Tuscany (1795), where he met Bonaparte, and then to Piedmont (1797). After 18 Brumaire, Bonaparte appointed him to the tribunate and Council of State (1800–1806). He also governed Corsica for eighteen months (1801–2) after it was recovered by France. In 1806 he accompanied Joseph Bonaparte to Naples. There Miot founded and organized a Ministry of Interior, which the next king, Joachim Murat (1808–15) and later the restored Bourbons continued. In 1808 Miot followed Joseph to his second kingdom, Spain, where for six years he was Joseph's confidant, counselor, and intendant of the royal household. After Napoleon's final abdication (1815), Miot retired to private life and wrote his memoirs. Although the conversations with Joseph and Napoleon that he records sometimes seem too prescient—too affected by knowledge of what came after—the memoirs are a fundamental source for the Napoleonic era.

O. Connelly, *Napoleon's Satellite Kingdoms* (New York, 1965); C. Durand, *Etudes sur le Conseil d'Etat napoléonien* (Paris, 1949); A. F. Miot de Melito, *Mémoires du comte Miot de Melito*, 3 vols. (Paris, 1873).

Harold T. Parker

Related entries: BONAPARTE, JOSEPH; NAPLES, KINGDOM OF; SPAIN, KINGDOM OF.

MOLE, LOUIS-MATHIEU (1781–1855), minister of Justice, 1813–14. Molé, member of a distinguished family of *parlementaires*, had a meteoric career in the Napoleonic government. Auditor at the Council of State in 1806, his report on the Alsatian Jews attracted the favorable attention of Napoleon, who appointed him *maître des requêtes*, then prefect of the department of the Côte d'Or (1807), director of bridges and highways (1809), and minister of justice (*grand juge*) in 1813. Molé may have been pushed ahead too rapidly for the efficiency of the administration. As prefect, his haughtiness amused and alienated his experienced subordinates. As director of bridges and highways, he succeeded two able administrators, Emmanuel Crétet and Jean-Pierre de Montalivet, who had gained the esteem of the specialist engineers. But the harsh tone and distant and disdainful attitude of Molé ruined the relationship. His own work was not always satisfactory. On one occasion Montalivet, as minister of interior, had to return eight out of seventeen of his reports for redoing. As *grand juge* he lacked the special knowledge the position required. Yet Molé remained one of the emperor's favorites. Napoleon needed someone to talk to, and Molé knew how to listen with self-controlled courtesy to the confidences of the older man. Molé's early apprenticeship under Napoleon doubtless prepared him for a distinguished career in later regimes.

Marquis de Noailles, *Le comte Molé (1781-1855)* (Paris, 1922); L. M. Molé, *Souvenirs d'un témoin de la Révolution et de l'Empire (1791–1803)* (Geneva, 1943); J. Petot, *Histoire de l'administration des ponts et chaussées 1599–1815* (Paris, 1958); J. Savant, *Les préfets de Napoléon* (Paris, 1958).

Harold T. Parker

Related entries: ABRIAL; ADMINISTRATION; CAMBACERES; LABOR LEGISLATION; LAW, CODES OF; MINISTERS OF NAPOLEON; REGNIER; WOMEN.

MOLLIEN, NICOLAS-FRANCOIS, COMTE (1758–1850), minister of the treasury from 1806 until 1814 and during the Hundred Days. He was one of the three leading fiscal administrators Bonaparte recruited from the bureaus of the Old Regime, Martin Gaudin and François de Barbé-Marbois being the other two. Son of a merchant of Rouen, the young Mollien served from 1775 to 1781 as clerk in the General Farms, a well-run outfit that paid the royal government for the lucrative chore of collecting the indirect taxes. Then from 1781 to 1790 he worked as a chief clerk in that bureau of the *Contrôle Générale* which supervised the General Farms. He won the attention of Controller General Charles-Alexandre de Calonne by recommending that from 1786 the General Farms pay each year an additional 14 million *livres* and by pushing the adoption of A. L. de Lavoisier's proposal to enclose Paris with a wall that would check smuggling and evasion of the city tolls.

Mollien's experience in the fiscal bureaus of the Old Regime taught him two great lessons: the value of double-entry bookkeeping and the folly of allowing tax collectors to retain funds for any length of time. When in 1800 Bonaparte appointed him director of the Sinking Fund (*caisse d'amortissement*), Mollien introduced double-entry bookkeeping. On becoming minister (1806) he extended its use throughout the treasury. As minister he also insisted that tax collectors pay taxes into a treasury Service Fund immediately on their receipt, so that the monies were at once available. Mollien could be counted on always to have his accounts in perfect order, and for this Napoleon was grateful.

In fiscal policy Mollien often showed less flexibility and imagination than Napoleon. In his overcautious refusal to support Napoleon in his plan to found branches of the Bank of France in every French business city and thus facilitate the extension of commercial credit and industrial expansion, Mollien kept the bank to its restrained role of being essentially the bank of Paris. Mollien also vigorously objected to Napoleon's extending loans of nearly 18 million francs to businesses on the verge of bankruptcy during the depression of 1810–11, a policy that has become commonplace in the twentieth century. He also urged Napoleon to deposit in the French treasury the tribute levied on conquered regions. Instead Napoleon placed it in a special fund, "the extraordinary domain," to be used imaginatively in support of his grandiose imperial structures. More on track, Mollien objected to Napoleon's standard operating procedure of balancing his budget by not paying army and navy contractors on time and in full. When Mollien and his assistant, Baron Louis, sought to pay punctually and fully, Napoleon exclaimed that they were ruining him. They replied that on the contrary, his shyster tactics were damaging his credit.

After Napoleon's second abdication, Mollien declined the invitation of later French governments to serve as minister of finances. Instead he served France by entering the Chamber of Peers in 1819 and during the Restoration and the reign of Louis Philippe offering sage financial counsel. Napoleon III had the name of Mollien inscribed on one of the pavillions of the Louvre opposite that named after Turgot.

N. F. Mollien, *Mémoires d'un ministre du trésor public*, 3 vols. (Paris, 1898); Napoleon, *Lettres au comte Mollien du 16 mars 1803 au 9 juin 1815* (n.p., 1959).

Harold T. Parker

Related entries: ADMINISTRATION; BANK OF FRANCE; FINANCES; MINISTERS OF NAPOLEON.

MONCEY, BON ADRIEN JEANNOT DE (1754–1842), duc de Conegliano, marshal of France. Of the bourgeoisie, son of an advocate, he left school at age fifteen (1769) over his father's objection and served in the Royal Army off and on until the Revolution, which he welcomed. He returned to the army as a captain in 1791 and became a major general (1794) after distinguishing himself in the Pyrenees. In 1797, however, he was accused of royalism, and his career seemed finished.

Napoleon recalled Moncey in 1800 and gave him command in Switzerland and then in the reconquest of Italy. In 1804 he was made one of the original marshals of the empire and in 1808 duc de Conegliano. Moncey fought in Spain during 1808–9, but his performance disappointed Napoleon. Afterward he had command only of reserves. In 1814 his last command was the Parisian National

Guard; he acquitted himself well against the Allies at Clichy but was forced to surrender after Auguste Marmont went over to the enemy.

Moncey rallied to Napoleon during the Hundred Days, and after Waterloo the Bourbons imprisoned him because he refused to head Marshal Michel Ney's court-martial. Louis XVIII restored Moncey's rank and honors in 1816, however.

C. A. G. D. de Gillevoisin, *Le maréchal Moncey* (Paris, 1902).

Related entries: MARSHALS OF THE EMPIRE; PENINSULAR WAR.

MONDOVI, BATTLE OF. See ITALIAN CAMPAIGN, FIRST.

MONEY. See EXCHANGE RATE; FRANC.

MONGE, GASPARD (1746–1818), comte de Péluse; mathematician, scientist, founder of the Ecole Polytechnique. Monge worked in theoretical and applied science and in administration and education, all with equal genius. He created descriptive geometry, renewed analytic and infinitesimal geometry, and worked in physics, chemistry, and the theory of machines. He was born in Beaune (Burgundy), the eldest son of Jacques Monge, a merchant. A brilliant student at the local Oratorian college and at the Collège de la Trinité in Lyon (as a student he was even in charge of the course on physics), the young Monge attracted the attention of an army officer who recruited him for the staff of the Royal School of Engineering at Mézières. He was a distinguished professor of mathematics and physics at Mézières from 1769 to 1784, a member of the Royal Academy of Sciences from 1780, inspector of French naval schools from 1784 to 1792, minister of the navy for eight months after 10 August 1792, and then with other scientists participated in the wartime crash program for the manufacture of arms and ammunition.

Meanwhile he conceived of a central school in Paris for engineers that would maintain a fructifying balance of pure and applied science. With Antoine Fourcroy he brought the school into existence as the Ecole Polytechnique, and he taught there and served intermittently as its director, always fighting to maintain its standing as a foremost school of science, as well as a first-rate engineering school.

As member of a commission sent by the Directory in 1796 to northern and central Italy to select paintings, sculptures, and rare manuscripts for transport to Paris, he became an acquaintance and soon a friend of Bonaparte. With other savants he accompanied the Egyptian expedition and was president of the Institut of Egypt. After 18 Brumaire Bonaparte made him a senator and later showered on him other gifts and honors: grand officer of the Legion of Honor in 1804, president of the Senate in 1806, and comte de Péluse in 1808. Through all this activity, Monge continued his teaching at the Ecole Polytechnique to 1809, his preparation of scientific articles and treatises, and his interest in the practical applications of science to technology and industry. In 1801 he and other scientists founded the Society for the Encouragement of National Industry to promote technological advance in industry through the application of scientific discoveries.

P.-V. Aubry, *Monge, le savant ami de Napoléon: 1746–1818* (Paris, 1954); L. de Launay, *Monge, fondateur de l'Ecole Polytechnique* (Paris, 1933); R. Taton, *L'oeuvre scientifique de Gaspard Monge* (Paris, 1951).

Harold T. Parker

Related entries: EDUCATION; INSTITUT NATIONAL DES SCIENCES ET DES ARTS; SCIENCE.

MONTALIVET, JEAN-PIERRE BACHASSON, COMTE DE (1766–1823), minister of interior 1809–14. Montalivet was born at Neukirch, near Sarreguemines. A member of a family of noble lineage, he expected to follow his father's career as an army officer and enrolled at age thirteen in the Hussar regiment of Nassau. He soon transferred to the study of the law and became a distinguished councillor of the parlement of Grenoble. Partisan in 1789 of the liberal principles of constitutional government, he deplored the movement of the Revolution toward extremism. Once the storm had abated, he served from 1795 as an effective mayor of Valence, a post he wished to retain. In 1789, however, he had met in his mother's salon in Valence the young Lieutenant Bonaparte. When the latter became first consul, he appointed Montalivet prefect of the department of the Manche (12 April 1801), then prefect of Seine-et-Oise (31 March 1804), before advancing him to be successor of Emmanuel Crétet as director of bridges and highways (1806) and minister of the interior (1809).

During the Hundred Days Montalivet served as intendant general of the crown. As minister of the interior for four and a half years, he made his will reinforce that of Napoleon, whom he admired. He participated in the program to improve the quality of the prefects through careful selection and prior training. He supervised an extensive public works effort (construction of canals, roads, and bridges; ports of Cherbourg, Antwerp, and Ostend; at Paris, arches of triumph, the Bourse, quais, markets, slaughterhouses). He lent his authority to stop-gap measures of relief during the depression of 1810–11. He kept up a gigantic correspondence with prefects, subprefects, and mayors that the centralized administration required. And in his comprehensive reports to the Legislative Body on the state of the Empire in 1809 and in 1813, he used the multiple statistics his subordinates sent up. Yet he remained skeptical of the effectiveness of the administrative effort. In a low mood he wrote, "In general the prefects only report what they want to, as they want to. What I see most clearly is that we know nothing of what is going on."

L. Bergeron, *France under Napoleon*, trans. R. R. Palmer (Princeton, N.J., 1981); B. DesGrey, "Montalivet et la statistique au temps de l'Empire," *RIN* 108 (1968); H. Nomine and J. Rohr, "Le comte de l'Empire Jean-Pierre Bachasson de Montalivet (1766-1823), ministre de l'intérieur de Napoleon," *Cahier Sarregueminois* 7 (1969); J.-C.

Perrot, *L'Age d'or de la statistique régionale française (an IV–1804)* (Paris, 1977); J. Petot, *Histoire de l'administration des ponts et chaussees* (Paris, 1958).

Harold T. Parker

Related entries: ADMINISTRATION; ARCHITECTURE; CRETET; STATISTICS.

MONTEBELLO, DUC DE. See LANNES.

MONTENOTTE, BATTLE OF. See ITALIAN CAMPAIGN, FIRST.

MONTEREAU, BATTLE OF. See FRANCE, CAMPAIGN OF.

MONTGELAS, MAXIMILIAN VON, COUNT (1759–1838), first minister of Max I of Bavaria, Francophile, reformer, and architect of the alliance with Napoleonic France. Born at Munich, the son of a Bavarian general and diplomat of Savoyard ancestry, Montgelas studied in Nancy and Strasbourg, where he was influenced by the French Enlightenment. In 1785 he resigned as court counselor in the Bavarian civil service after discovering that his membership in the secret society of the Illuminati blocked his advancement. He entered the service of the duke of Zweibrücken, only to be dismissed in 1793 as a suspected Jacobin. He in fact agreed with the fundamental ideas of the French Revolution but repudiated the Terror engineered by the Jacobins of 1793–94.

In 1796 he presented to Duke Max Joseph his program for the future reforms of Bavaria. When Max Joseph became elector of Bavaria in 1799, he made Montgelas his foreign minister and later also minister of the interior and, for a time, minister of finances. From 1799 until his fall in 1817, Montgelas dominated the policies of the Electorate (after 1806, Kingdom) of Bavaria. He played a key role in Bavaria's alliance with France in 1805, in Bavaria's membership in the Confederation of the Rhine, and in the territorial expansion of the state between 1803 and 1816.

On the other hand, in cooperation with the Württemberg government, he prevented Napoleon from changing the Confederation of the Rhine into a federal state with a common constitution. The sovereignty of Bavaria was one of his guiding principles; another was the introduction of the reforms of the French Revolution and of the French Empire through a "revolution from above." Under his guidance Bavaria was thoroughly modernized.

H. Glaser, ed., *Krone und Verfassung. König Max I. Joseph und der neue Staat* (Munich, 1980); E. Weis, *Montgelas 1759–1799. Zwischen Revolution und Reform* (Munich, 1971), and "Die Begründung des modernen bayerischen Staates unter König Max I. (1799–1825)," in M. Spindler, ed., *Handbuch der bayerischen Geschichte*, vol. 4 (Munich, 1979).

Eberhard Weis

Related entries: BAVARIA, KINGDOM OF; CONFEDERATION OF THE RHINE; MAX I JOSEPH.

MONTHOLON, CHARLES-TRISTAN, COMTE DE (1783-1853), general, with Napoleon on St. Helena. A cavalry officer who saw little or no action in the wars of the Empire, Montholon was attached to Josephine as chamberlain after 1809 and sent on diplomatic missions. He returned to the Royal Army in 1814 but in 1815 volunteered to accompany Napoleon to St. Helena. In the infighting among Napoleon's four companions in exile, Montholon the social climber won out. The British deported Emmanuel Las Cases in November 1816; Gaspard Gourgaud left in January 1818; Henri Bertrand could offer no real competition. Toward the end it was Montholon, the courtier of palace antechambers, who was taking down Napoleon's conversations, in the last agony caring for his personal needs, and after his death closing his eyes. Montholon's memoirs, written in 1846 when memory to a degree had distorted reminiscence, still have value for the critical historian: *Récits de la captivité de l'Empereur Napoléon à Sainte-Hélène*, 2 vols. (Paris, 1847).

Harold T. Parker

Related entries: BERTRAND; GOURGAUD; LAS CASES; ST. HELENA.

MONTMIRAIL, BATTLE OF. See FRANCE, CAMPAIGN OF.

MOREAU, JEAN-VICTOR (1763–1813), general. Moreau, son of a lawyer and a law student at Rennes before the Revolution, left school to join the National Guard in 1789, saw active duty, and was rapidly promoted. In 1793 he was made *général de division*—before Captain Bonaparte, at Toulon, was vaulted to *général de brigade*.

In 1795 Moreau commanded the Army of the North, in 1796 the Army of the Rhine and the Moselle. In December 1800, he defeated the Austrians at Hohenlinden, driving them to make peace, which they had refused after Bonaparte's victory at Marengo (14 June 1800).

Moreau thus became Napoleon's rival for reputation, a fact not lost on the first consul. In 1804 Moreau was implicated in a royalist plot, probably unjustly. He was not executed but exiled. Moreau lived in the United States from 1804 to 1813, when he returned to Europe to accept a commission from Czar Alexander. He was mortally wounded at Dresden (August 1813), reportedly by fire from the artillery of the Imperial Guard.

E. Lambin, *Moreau* (Paris, 1869); J. Phillippart, *Memoirs of General Moreau* (Philadelphia, 1816); E. Picard, *Bonaparte et Moreau* (Paris, 1905).

Jesse Scott

Related entries: CADOUDAL; FOUCHE; POLICE, MINISTRY OF GENERAL.

MORTIER, ADOLPHE-EDOUARD-CASIMIR-JOSEPH (1768–1835), duc de Trévise, marshal of France. Of the bourgeoisie, son of a cloth merchant, he was educated at the college of Douai. He entered the army via the National Guard of Dunkirk (1789) and was a general by 1799. He had never served with

Bonaparte but had distinguished himself at Jemappes (1792), Fleurus (1795), and in Switzerland (1799).

He supported the coup d'état of 18 Brumaire, and Bonaparte made him colonel general of the Consular Guard, sent him to conquer Hanover (1803), and created him one of the original marshals (1804). He fought at Austerlitz (1805), Friedland (1807), and in Spain (1808–11). During the Russian campaign of 1812 he commanded the Young Guard at Borodino and was governor of Moscow. In 1813–14 he was in every major battle. Commanding a corps in Paris in March 1814, he was forced to give up after Auguste Marmont surrendered to the Allies.

Mortier supported Napoleon during the Hundred Days but because of illness was not in the Waterloo campaign. Nevertheless, he was destituted by Louis XVIII (1816), and his rank was not restored until after the Revolution of 1830. Under Louis Philippe he was ambassador to Russia and briefly minister of war (1834). He was killed by a bomb during a National Guard parade in 1835.

F. Despréaux, *Le maréchal Mortier*, 3 vols. (Paris, 1913–20); L. Moreel, *Le maréchal Mortier* (Paris, 1957).

Jesse Scott

Related entries: FRANCE, CAMPAIGN OF; MARSHALS OF THE EMPIRE.

MOSCOVA, PRINCE DE LA. See NEY.

MOSCOW, BATTLE OF. See BORODINO, BATTLE OF; RUSSIAN CAMPAIGN.

MOSCOW, BURNING OF. See RUSSIAN CAMPAIGN.

MÜLLER, ADAM HEINRICH, RITTER VON NITTERSDORFF (1779–1829), Prussian writer and political economist, literary opponent of Napoleon. Müller is considered a political Romanticist—that is, an opponent of eighteenth-century absolutism, as well as nineteenth-century liberalism. His writings include treatises on art, economics, law, history, and theology. Müller contributed to pan-German nationalism and anti-French, anti-Napoleonic sentiment through his writings and speeches. With Heinrich von Kleist, he founded the review *Phoebus* in Dresden and helped organize the Christian German Roundtable in Berlin. He found his spiritual home in Austria, however, since his ideal state was a modern German (Holy Roman) empire, reinforced by German nationalism. In it he hoped that the landed nobility (the female element) and the productive bourgeoisie (the male element) would work in harmony. To achieve this, he believed that the spirit of the feudal system had to be reawakened. It is not surprising that after Napoleon's fall, Müller entered the Austrian civil service and worked for his dream within Clemens von Metternich's system. He was ennobled for his service.

H. Kohn, *Prelude to the Nation States* (New York, 1967); A. Müller, *Die Elemente der Staatskunst* (Vienna, 1922).

Gerda Jordan

Related entries: GERMAN WAR OF LIBERATION; KLEIST; PRUSSIA, KINGDOM OF.

MÜLLER, JOHANNES VON (1752–1809), Swiss-German historian and statesman, called the "Swiss Tacitus." Long before the Napoleonic era, Müller was a respected member of the republic of scholars. His historical writings, particularly *Geschichten der Schweizerischen Eidgenossenschaft* and *Bücher Allgemeiner Geschichte besonders der europäischen Menschheit*, brought him into close contact with Herder, Schiller, Goethe, and other prominent German intellectuals. At the princely courts of Mainz, Vienna, and Berlin, Müller served in high state offices.

After the defeat of Prussia by France, Müller, in conversations with Napoleon, was converted from opponent to ardent admirer. In 1807, Müller was on the delegation of Germans called to Paris to write (actually only approve) Napoleon's constitution for the Kingdom of Westphalia. King Jerome shortly appointed him director of public instruction, a post he held until his death. He gave great attention to the universities, especially Göttingen, his alma mater.

K. Schib, *Johannes von Müller 1752–1809* (1967).

Helmut Berding

Related entries: NAPOLEON I; WESTPHALIA, KINGDOM OF.

MURAT, CAROLINE BONAPARTE. See BONAPARTE, CAROLINE.

MURAT, JOACHIM (1767–1815), grand duke of Berg and Cleves, king of Naples, marshal of France, the "First Horseman of Europe." Murat was the son of a Gascon innkeeper and one of twelve children. He was educated at the collège de Cahors and, although expected to enter the church, joined the cavalry in 1787 and in two years was a sergeant major. He was discharged (1789) for insubordination but was enlisted in the King's Constitutional Guard (1791) and was commissioned sous-lieutenant in the cavalry in 1792. He saw service on the Rhine and became an ardent Jacobin. By 1795, however, his taste for radical politics had faded, and in October 1795 it was Major Murat who brought the cannon with which Bonaparte delivered the "whiff of grapeshot." Thereafter his destiny was attached to Napoleon's. He was promoted to general of brigade during the first Italian campaign (1796) and to *général de division* (1799) on his return with Bonaparte from Egypt, having won glory, especially in the second Battle of Aboukir. He supported Napoleon during the coup of 18 Brumaire.

In 1800 he became head of the Consular Guard and married Napoleon's sister, Caroline Bonaparte. The same year he fought at Marengo and was awarded a saber of honor for his services. From 1800 to 1804 Murat served in Italy. In

1804 he was made governor of Paris and marshal of the empire; in 1805 grand admiral, prince, and *grand-aigle* of the Legion of Honor.

Murat, although criticized by Napoleon for his impetuous behavior, fought valiantly at Austerlitz (1805). In 1806 the emperor made him grand duke of Berg. He served at Jena-Auerstädt (1806), defeated G. L. Blücher at Lübeck (1806), conducted the siege of Königsberg (1806), and preserved his dash during the brutal Battle of Eylau (1807). Murat was the only marshal with Napoleon during the peacemaking at Tilsit.

In 1808 Murat served in Spain and was made king of Naples the same year, replacing Joseph Bonaparte. In 1809 he attempted to capture Sicily but failed—he thought because Napoleon denied him support. In 1812 the French emperor had to coerce Murat to join the Grande Armée, but he commanded the cavalry with his usual bravery at Smolensk and Borodino and was the first to enter Moscow. During the retreat he was given command of the army when Napoleon left for Paris (5 December 1812). He led it to Posen where, however, he left the command to Eugène (17 January 1813) and departed, without authority, for Naples. Although he returned and fought in the French army at Dresden and Leipzig, the latter defeat confirmed his conviction that Napoleon was doomed. In 1814 Murat and Caroline saved their kingdom by joining the Allies. In 1815, however, when Napoleon returned from Elba, Murat attacked the Austrians in northern Italy. (His conscience bothered him, but he had also lost confidence that the powers at Vienna would confirm his throne and hoped to unite all of Italy under his rule.) He was defeated and fled to France, where he offered his services to Napoleon for what became the Waterloo campaign. Napoleon did not even answer his letter.

Murat then organized a small expedition and attempted to recapture Naples, where the Bourbon rulers had been restored. He was captured at Pizzo, tried by court-martial, and shot (13 October 1815).

P. Colletta, *Sur la catastrophe de l'ex-roi de Naples, Joachim Murat. Extraits des mémoires du general Colletta. Traduction par Leonard Gallois* (Paris, 1823); J. Dubreton, *Murat* (Paris, 1944); M. Dupont, *Murat* (Paris, 1934); D.-C. Francechetti, *Mémoires sur les événements qui ont precedé la mort de Joachim Ier roi des Deux Siciles* (Paris, 1826), and *Supplément aux mémoires sur les événements qui ont précédé la mort de Joachim Ier, roi de Naples* (Paris, 1829); C. Galvani, *Mémoires sur les événements qui ont précédé la mort de Joachim-Napoléon, roi des Deux-Siciles* (Paris, 1843); J. P. Garnier, *Murat* (Paris, 1959); J. N. Murat, *Correspondance de Joachim Murat (1791–1808)*, preface by H. Houssaye (Turin, 1899), and *Lettres et documents pour servir à l'histoire de Joachim Murat, 1767–1815*, 8 vols. (Paris, 1908-1914).

Jesse Scott

Related entries: HUNDRED DAYS, THE; NAPLES, KINGDOM OF; VENDEMIAIRE.

MUSIC. The first known musical allusion to Napoleon's exploits was the *Hymne sur la prise de Toulon* (1792), words by Marie-Joseph Chénier and music by Charles Catel (1773–1830), a student of Joseph Gossec, the leading composer for the fêtes of the Revolution. Songs in several languages eventually referred to Napoleon.

After securing power, Napoleon ended the yearly cycle of Revolutionary fêtes in 1800. Thereafter, only 14 July and 22 September were observed. An imperial style of music developed to enhance Napoleon's image as heir to three traditions: the military and courtly pomp of monarchy, the liturgy of the church, and the civic cult sponsored by the Revolution. All three obeyed classical aesthetic theory, which posited the inculcation of ideology superior to the pleasures of music.

Napoleon's control of civic ceremonies was evident in the *Chant national* of 14 July 1800, which replaced references to the capture of the Bastille with praise for the new Caesar. In 1804 the republican *Marseillaise* was replaced by the *Veillons au salut de l'Empire*, composed in 1792, when "empire" denoted only France. The proclamation of an empire implied a hierarchical civic liturgy, which Napoleon supplied by turning the restored Catholic church, the most common source of music for the populace, to political use. The victories of the Grand Armée, his coronation, its anniversaries, and the birth of the king of Rome were celebrated with Te Deums and Masses for which music was commissioned from composers, such as Jean-François Le Sueur (1760–1837), who had served the church, the stage, and the Republic. The same composers would serve Napoleon's successors. Le Sueur later claimed that the music he employed for the coronation of Charles X had been composed for the coronation of Napoleon in order to blend the communitarian dicta of Jean-Jacques Rousseau, the enthusiasm of the Revolution, and traditions of the church with martial music "suited to the installation of any Christian prince anywhere."

The imperial style anticipated several aspects of nineteenth-century music. Restoration of the Catholic church following the Concordat was consonant with the Romantic interest in reviving traditions, including the medieval, as sources of nationhood anterior to the state. Massive choral and instrumental ensembles represented peoples assembled or on the march. Grandiosity, encouraged by the outdoor Revolutionary fêtes, and martial music, encouraged by the ever-increasing armies, fostered the development of band music. While the demand for loud or outdoor music was increasing, new techniques of constructing and playing wind instruments expanded their capabilities. An expanding interest in choral music was consonant with both the religious revival and attempts to achieve mass involvement. French compositions in martial style for men's chorus were influential. For example, the "Hunters Chorus" in Carl-Maria von Weber's (1786–1826) opera *Der Freischütz*, whose existence implied German cultural independence, seems to be patterned on Etienne Nicolas Méhul's (1763–1817) *Chant pour le retour de la Grande Armée*.

Personally Napoleon claimed a love of the fine arts, especially music, which he pronounced useful for enhancing public moral instruction. His actual preference ran less to the declamatory style favored by French neoclassical theory than to the entertainments by Italian operatic composers, such as his chapel master, Giovanni Paisiello (1740–1816), "whose music does not take my mind off important things."

Napoleon's career inspired extensive musical responses. Ludwig von Beethoven (1770–1827), originally dedicated his Heroic (Third) Symphony to Napoleon, who seemed a liberator and then, after the proclamation of the Empire, substituted "to the memory of a great man." Beethoven's stormy musical style is often said to epitomize the upheavals of the time. The romantic apotheosis of the artist as creator, hero, and rebel probably represented in part a transferral to the arts of ideals once attributed to the champions of the Revolution.

After Napoleon's death, his metamorphosis from Caesar to simple soldier of the Revolution was sometimes expressed musically. For the tenth anniversary of Napoleon's death, Hector Berlioz (1803–69) composed the *Cantate du 5 mai* (1831) whose text evoked sympathy for the soldier-prisoner of St. Helena. Other compositions, such as Robert Schumann's (1810–56) "The Two Grenadiers," which included musical quotations from the *Marseillaise*, were more ambivalent.

Berlioz, who was a pupil of Le Sueur, is renowned as a musical field marshal guiding vast orchestras, bands, and choruses supported by batteries of winds and percussion. His brilliant orchestral technique influenced the Russian national school of composers. Petr Ilich Tschaikowsky (1840–93) later employed it in his *1812 Overture*, which, though anti-Napoleonic, owed something to the imperial style.

For the funeral of Napoleon in 1840, music was commissioned from the popular opera composers Daniel François Auber (1782–1871), Eli Halévy (1799–1862), and Adolphe Adam (1803–56). Conspicuously absent was Berlioz, whose music was probably best capable of revivifying the fervor once associated with the spread of Revolutionary ideals. His *Requiem* and *Te Deum* remain the outstanding musical monuments directly inspired by the musical practices of the Revolutionary and Napoleonic eras.

C. L. Donakowski, *A Muse for the Masses: Ritual and Music in an Age of Democratic Revolution* (Chicago, 1977); L. Dufrane, *Gossec: Sa vie et ses oeuvres* (Paris, 1927); J. Mongredien, "La musique du sacre de Napoléon ler," *Revue de Musicologie* (1967); K. Nef, "Die Passionsoratorien J.-F. Lesueurs," *Mélanges de musicologie offerts à M. Lionel de La Laurencie* (Paris, 1933).

Conrad L. Donakowski

Related entries: ART; CHERUBINI; GRASSINI; LEGEND, NAPOLEONIC; LE SUEUR; MEHUL; PROPAGANDA; THEATER.

N

NAPLES, KINGDOM OF. Joseph Bonaparte, king, 1806–8; Joachim Murat and Caroline Bonaparte, king and queen, 1808–15. Naples was conquered in 1806 after Naples-Sicily had joined the Allies (1805) against France. The Neapolitan Bourbons fled to Sicily where they were protected by the British navy. Joseph got the support of nobles and bourgeoisie who had not fled. The king left military matters to Marshal André Masséna and, later, Marshal Jean-Baptiste Jourdan and devoted himself to reform. He assembled a ministry including such Frenchmen as André Miot de Melito and Pierre Louis Roederer and Neapolitans such as Michelangelo Cianciulli. Joseph abolished feudal rights (personal and juridical privileges) without compensation to owners and feudal dues with compensation to owners by the government as their money value was assessed. At the same time he made available for purchase royal lands valued at some 800 million francs and some confiscated monastic lands. He also brought in French experts to instruct farmers in the growing of cotton, sugar cane, and sugar beets. By 1809, Naples could supply 40 percent of the cotton needed by the empire and sugar to replace that kept out by the Continental System. Joseph delayed issuing a constitution until just before his departure; however, he installed French-style administrations in the existing provinces and decreed the right of male taxpayers to vote for lists of candidates from which he chose local officials. Cianciulli, meanwhile, instituted French-style courts and began preparing the judiciary to convert to the Code Napoléon. Roederer consolidated all of the Neapolitan banks into one and reworked the revenue system. By 1808 he had paid half the national debt by liquidating confiscated properties. Miot was in charge of administrative reform, public works, welfare, and education. The school system was considerably improved. Some 1,500 public schools were operating by 1808, and new faculty had been recruited for the university at Salerno. Joseph had also founded an art museum and, more important for the future, gave protection to the ruins at Pompeii, which for years had been looted for profit.

In 1808 Joseph was transferred to Spain, and Marshal Murat and his wife, Caroline Bonaparte, assumed the throne. Murat refused to accept Joseph's constitution (which he had promulgated in parting) and promised a new and more liberal one (which was never written). He retained Joseph's basic governmental-administrative organization, however. His principal ministers were Jean-Paul Daure (Police), Agar de Mosbourg (Finance), Giuseppe Zurlo (Interior), and Francesco Ricciardi (Justice). Murat's right-hand man became Antonio Maghella, police prefect of the capital (Naples) and Italian nationalist. Under Murat, Zurlo carried through the abolition of feudalism begun by Joseph but neglected public education. He and Agar continued the economic-financial policies of Joseph, with increasing success after 1810 when licenses alleviated many of the inconveniences of the Continental System. Murat's obsession, however, was to become independent of Napoleon. To this end he began building an army, which by 1812 numbered 80,000. As his forces grew, he became increasingly nationalistic. Caroline supported him because she (perhaps more than Murat) wanted a crown that their eldest son would inherit. At the same time, however, she tattled on Murat to Napoleon so as to be safe if her husband's plans failed.

Murat commanded Napoleon's cavalry during the Russian campaign of 1812 and assumed command of the remnants of the army when Napoleon left for Paris during the great retreat. However, he had lost faith in Napoleon's ability to survive as emperor, and his mind turned increasingly to saving his kingdom. In January 1813, at Posen he abruptly gave command to Eugène de Beauharnais and returned to Naples. In December 1814, to save his kingdom, he went over to the Allies. In 1815, however, when Napoleon returned from Elba, Murat attacked the Austrians in Northern Italy, by which he hoped at once to salve his conscience and unite all of Italy under his rule. Instead he lost both his kingdom and his life. Naples was returned to Bourbon rule.

U. Caldora, *Calabria napoleonica (1806–1815)* (Naples, 1960); O. Connelly, *Napoleon's Satellite Kingdoms* (New York, 1965); A. Fugier, *Napoléon et l'Italie* (Paris, 1947); J. Rambaud, *Naples sous Joseph Bonaparte 1806–1808* (Paris, 1911); A. Valente, *Gioacchino Murat e l'Italia meridionale* (Turzin, 1941); M. H. Weil, *Joachim Murat, roi de Naples*, 5 vols. (Paris, 1909–10); C. Zaghi, *Napoleone e l'Italia* (Milan, 1966).

Related entries: AUSTERLITZ CAMPAIGN; BONAPARTE, CAROLINE; BONAPARTE, JOSEPH; DIPLOMACY; ITALY, KINGDOM OF; MURAT, J.; RUSSIAN CAMPAIGN.

NAPLES, KINGDOM OF: MINISTERS.

Under Joseph Bonaparte (1806–8)

Finance	A. Christophe Saliceti	1806 (interim)
	Prince di Bisignano	1806 (February–November)
	Pierre Louis Roederer	1806–8
War	André François Miot (de Melito)	1806 (interim)
	General Mathieu Dumas	1806 (March-July)
	General Jacques Philippe d'Arcambal	1806 (interim)
	A. Christophe Saliceti	1806 July–1807 April

Police	A. Christophe Saliceti	1806–7 April
War and Police (War and Police formally combined April 1807	A. Christophe Saliceti	1807 April-1808
Marine	Prince di Pignatelli-Cerchiara	1806–8
Justice	Michelangelo Cianciulli	1806–8
Interior	Miot de Melito	1806–8
Foreign affairs	Marquis di Gallo	1806–8
Secretary of state	Ferri-Pisani (de Anastacio)	1806–8
Ecclesiastical affairs (ministry abolished November 1806)	Duke di Cassano-Serra	1806 (February-November)
Royal household (ministry abolished April 1807)	Duke di Campochiaro	1806–7 April

Under Joachim Murat (1808–15)

Finance	Pignatelli-Cerchiara	1808
	Agar de Mosbourg	1808–15
War and Marine	Jean Reynier	1808
	Marshal Pérignon	1808–14
	Michel Carascosa	1815
Police	A. Christophe Saliceti	1808–9
	Jean Daure	1809–11
	Antonio Maghella (Break in service 1812)	1811–15
Justice	Giuseppe Zurlo	1808
	Francesco Ricciardi	1808–15
Interior	Luigi Capecelano	1808
	Giuseppe Zurlo (Break in service 1812)	1808–15
Foreign Affairs	Marquis de Gallo	1808–15

NAPOLEON I (1769–1821), emperor of the French. Napoleon Bonaparte (originally Napoleone Buonaparte) was born 15 August 1769 in Ajaccio, Corsica, acquired by France from Genoa in 1768, the second of eight children of Carlo (Charles) Buonaparte and Letizia Ramolino Buonaparte. Of minor nobility, Napoleon was educated for the army at the expense of Louis XVI at Brienne (which he entered at age nine) and the Ecole Militaire, from which he emerged a sublieutenant of artillery in 1785, at age sixteen. After the Revolution began, he was elected a lieutenant colonel (1791) in the Corsican National Guard but came into conflict with Pascal Paoli (1793) and fled to France with his family. Returning to his regular army grade of captain, he was assigned to the army besieging Toulon, in revolt against the Republic and aided by a British fleet.

The artillery commander was wounded, and A. Christophe Saliceti, a fellow Corsican, got Bonaparte the position. His guns drove out the enemy fleet, and he was promoted to general of brigade at age twenty-four. In 1795, he saved the Convention with his "whiff of grapeshot."

In 1796 he married Josephine de Beauharnais, a widow with two children. Almost simultaneously he took command of the French Army of Italy. During 1796–97 he repeatedly defeated larger Austrian armies and forced all of France's continental enemies to make peace. He founded the Cisalpine (Italian) Republic as well and sent millions in treasure to Paris. Only Britain remained at war. To strike at its trade, he seized Egypt (1798), but Admiral Horatio Nelson destroyed his fleet, leaving him stranded. He turned to restructuring Egyptian government and law, and the French scholars with him created Egyptology. In 1799 he failed to capture Syria but crushed a Turkish invasion force at Aboukir. Meanwhile Austria, Russia, and lesser powers allied with Britain. Bonaparte, convinced that he must "save France," left his army and returned to Paris, where he overthrew the Directory (coup d'état of 18–19 Brumaire). Under the new Constitution of the Year VIII, all male adults could vote, but Bonaparte ruled. Nevertheless, the voters approved overwhelmingly. They similarly voted for amendments in 1802 (Year X) making Bonaparte consul for life and in 1804 (Year XII) making him emperor. In 1800, his victory over the Austrians at Marengo assured his power. He negotiated general peace in Europe, including the Concordat of 1801 with the pope. Bonaparte invited all political exiles back to France—Jacobins and royalists—except for the royal family and a few others. Careers were "open to talent." Bonaparte then initiated reforms (continued under the Empire) that left a permanent mark on French institutions.

Napoleon's aggressive behavior again brought war, however. His plans for Haiti and Louisiana failed, but in Europe he annexed Elba and Piedmont to France, became president of the Italian Republic, and interfered with British trade. In 1803 Britain resumed hostilities. In 1804 Napoleon nevertheless created the Empire, using at his coronation the crown and sword of Charlemagne, whom he claimed to succeed. This affronted the Holy Roman emperor, Franz (Francis) II of Austria, by tradition successor of the great king of the Franks. At the same time, Bonaparte put troops into Hanover (German duchy of the English king) and threatened both Austria and Russia by assuming (1805) the crown of Italy (the former republic). Russia and Austria allied against France. Napoleon turned his Grande Armée against the Austro-Russian forces, winning the war in a blitzkrieg culminating at Austerlitz. In 1806 Napoleon expanded the Kingdom of Italy (viceroy, Eugène de Beauharnais) and made his elder brother Joseph king of Naples and brother Louis king of Holland. He made himself protector of the Confederation of the Rhine (most of the German states).

Prussia allied with Russia to oppose all this. Napoleon defeated the Prussians at Jena-Auerstädt (1806) and the Russians at Friedland. By the treaties of Tilsit (July 1807) there were added to the empire the Kingdom of Westphalia, under Napoleon's brother Jerome, the Duchy of Warsaw, and lesser states. Russia and

Prussia joined the Continental Blockade, created by Napoleon (November 1806) to seal Europe against British goods. In 1807 Napoleon occupied Portugal. In 1808, he deposed the Spanish Bourbons and made Joseph Bonaparte king of Spain. (Naples went to Marshal Murat and his wife, Caroline Bonaparte.) Spain rebelled, but Napoleon appeared briefly (November 1808-February 1809) and left believing that Spain was subdued. The Peninsular War, however, continued for five years, with the British backing Spanish armies and guerrillas. The cost to France was enormous in blood and money, and it badly weakened the empire. In 1809 Napoleon beat the Austrians again at Wagram. The Treaty of Schönbrunn created the Illyrian Provinces. Napoleon seized the Papal States and divided them between France and the Kingdom of Italy.

In December 1809 he divorced Josephine and in March 1810 married the Archduchess Marie-Louise, eighteen, daughter of the Austrian emperor. With his dynasty thus allied with the oldest ruling house in Europe, he expected his son (born in 1811) to be accepted readily by established monarchs. (It was not to be.) In 1810 he expanded the empire by the annexation of Bremen, Lübeck, and parts of north Germany, and the Kingdom of Holland (after forcing the abdication of Louis Bonaparte).

Probably Holland's demise was Napoleon's first move toward the dissolution of all the satellite kingdoms (Italy, Naples, Holland, Spain, Westphalia) in favor of a centralized European state. If so, the ground had been prepared in the kingdoms and lesser states. In all the Code Napoléon was (or was to be) the common law. Each state had a constitution (though none was fully observed), providing for universal manhood suffrage, a parliament, and guaranteeing a bill of rights. Napoleonic administrative and judicial systems had been established or were planned. Schools were under centralized administration, and higher education was open to talent. All the states had an academy or institute for the promotion of the arts and sciences and provided incomes for eminent scholars, especially scientists. Not until some years after Napoleon's fall did commoners fully appreciate the benefits Napoleon had given them. They had been too blinded by taxes, levies, and military conscription. In 1812 Napoleon set out to punish Russia, which had left the Continental System (*ukase* of 31 December 1810 of Czar Alexander I). The campaign ended in the bloody retreat from Moscow in the ice and snow and the loss of 400,000 men. All Europe united against him. Defeated at Leipzig (October 1813), he withdrew from Germany. During the first three months of 1814, he fought the most brilliant campaign of his career, but the odds were impossible, and his war-weary marshals finally forced him to capitulate. He abdicated (6 April 1814) and was exiled to Elba. The empress and his son were turned over to her father, the emperor of Austria. He would never see either of them again. The Allies placed Louis XVIII on the throne.

Napoleon became restless on Elba, and news of Louis XVIII's unpopularity and the disputes of the Allies at Vienna encouraged him to seize power again. In March 1815, he escaped from Elba, reached France, and marched for Paris. Amid amazing scenes, he won over troops sent to capture him. Marshal Michel

Ney, who had promised the king to "bring Bonaparte back in an iron cage," fell into his arms. In Paris Napoleon was received by cheering crowds. To appease French politicians and (he hoped) to impress the Allies, he issued a more democratic constitution. With surprising speed, he rebuilt the Grande Armée while asking peace of the Allies. They outlawed him, and he decided to strike first—into Belgium. The campaign ended in the Battle of Waterloo in 18 June 1815. Napoleon returned to Paris, where crowds formed to shout for him to fight again. The politicians, however, withdrew their support, led by the marquis de Lafayette and Joseph Fouché. On 22 June, Napoleon abdicated in favor of his son. Lucien Bonaparte induced the Chamber of Peers to proclaim Napoleon II. But Napoleon's enemies got the decision reversed. Napoleon fled to Rochefort, where he surrendered to Captain Sir Frederick Maitland of the British battleship *Bellerophon*. He was exiled to St. Helena, in the south Atlantic. There he died on 5 May 1821 of stomach cancer.

During his exile, he gave his version of the history of his time (and much else) by dictation or in conversation with Emmanuel de Las Cases, Generals Gaspard Gourgaud, Charles de Montholon, and Henri Bertrand, the Irish physician Barry O'Meara, and others, who published accounts and memoirs. Surely he did much to create the Napoleonic legend at St. Helena. However, it was grounded in deeds and publicized while he was in power by the leading artists and writers of Europe—and by the long-remembered spectacles he staged—the inauguration of the Legion of Honor, the coronation, the marriage to Marie-Louise—and the splendor of the Guard on parade in every part of Europe. He was aware of his legacy to France. At St. Helena he said, "I am so identified with [French] institutions that I am inseparable from them." He had, he said, preserved the Revolution in France and offered its benefits to Europe. "The Imperial Guard always marched to the Marseillaise." His "Grand Design," he said, was to found a European "Federation of Free Peoples." He also broadcast his alleged mistreatment and effectively sold the world the image of the promethean eagle chained to a rock. In 1840, at the request of King Louis Philippe, happily honored by the British, his remains were returned to France and entombed with great ceremony in the Invalides. Thousands still visit the tomb every year.

Napoleon's influence is evident in France today. Monuments he ordered dot Paris. The basic law is still the Code Napoléon; the structures of administrative and judicial systems are still Napoleonic. Education is under national control, and the baccalaureate examination still determines who shall have higher education. The effects of his work outside France are detectable in the institutions and laws of almost every other European country.

There is truth in Napoleon's immodest claim, "I am not a man; I am a historical personage." He drove himself accordingly. "Power is my mistress," he said. His life was work centered, his tastes crude (simple food, workers' wine, cheap snuff), his amusements few. He could be hypnotically charming, however, when he wanted to be. He had intense loyalties especially to his family and old associates. Some, like Charles-Maurice de Talleyrand, were spared well-deserved punishment and repaid him by helping bring him down. He was sometimes a tyrant and positively an authoritarian—a Rousseauist, convinced that he ruled for the people—and who scorned their (or their representatives') advice, except as given in broad mandate. He must be listed among the great enlightened monarchs of all time, but he is best remembered as a military commander.

O. Connelly, *Napoleon's Satellite Kingdoms* (New York, 1965–1969), and *French Revolution/Napoleonic Era* (New York, 1979); J. Godechot, *Les institutions de la France sous la Révolution et l'Empire* (Paris, 1968); J. Mistler, ed., *Napoléon*, 2 vols. (Paris, 1969); J. Tulard, *Napoléon: Ou le mythe du sauveur* (Paris, 1977).

Related entries: ARMY, FRENCH; BONAPARTE; CAMPAIGNS; EDUCATION; FOREIGN POLICY; JOSEPHINE; LAW CODES; MARIE-LOUISE VON HABSBURG; NAPOLEON I, DAILY ROUND.

NAPOLEON I, DAILY ROUND. Napoleon, like Philip II of Spain, Louis XIV, and Frederick the Great, was a working executive. Like them he arranged his daily round (schedule) for the achievement of maximum administrative effectiveness.

As emperor he lived on the second floor of the palace of the Tuileries in rooms facing the garden that were arranged for work, convenience, and unobtrusive security. Viewed from the garden, the rooms, left to right, were: his *cabinet de toilette* or dressing room; his bedroom (with a staircase to the empress' bedroom below); the map room with a large table on which a map could be fully unrolled; his inner office where he worked in seclusion with his private secretary; an outer office where he met with ministers and other officials; and two outer antechambers for the aides-de-camp and pages of the day.

Generally Napoleon rose at 2 A.M. after a first sleep of four to five hours. In a plain dressing gown of dimity in summer and flannel in winter and with a white bandanna around his head, he walked from his bedroom through the map room into his private office. There he worked silently for two or three hours on administrative papers and problems. The Mamluk Roustan slept on a mattress outside the bedroom door, a deputy valet was close by at all times, and one of the two guards of the office's archives kept a vigil over the files in an alcove off the map room. An aide-de-camp was always on guard in the apartment's antechamber. At about 5 A.M. Napoleon went back to bed for a second sleep.

At 7 A.M. the emperor rose again. Constant (Wairy), the first valet de chambre, dressed him in the uniform of a colonel of Guard Cavalry, while he received his master of the wardrobe (M. de Rémusat or after 1811 M. de Turenne d'Aynac), his personal physicians (Jean Corvisart and A. U. Yvan), and often the grand marshal of the palace, G.-C.-Michel Duroc. After a simple breakfast, consumed in ten minutes, he went into his private office. By 8 A.M. he was down to work.

In the center of the office was a large table at which he rarely sat except to sign letters. On the table were booklets of accounts updated each month: reports of the exact state of his army down to the company level, of his navy down to the least warship, of foreign armies, and of the exact state of his finances. There was also a list of the day's prices of wheat in several cities throughout the Empire. At the corner of the fireplace was a settee; touching it was a small table on which were placed that day's incoming letters and reports. In the embrasure of the office's single window sat his private secretary (Méneval or Fain). Napoleon, on the settee, rapidly read through the incoming reports and letters. Those requiring no action he dropped to the floor; those for immediate action he placed in one pile; those needing further thought or research went in another. Returning to the action pile, Napoleon, pacing up and down, dictated replies smoothly and rapidly, leaving to the secretary the problem of keeping up.

Precisely at 9 A.M. Napoleon interrupted the dictation to hold his *lever* in his outer office. He gave audience first to his palace staff, to whom he issued orders, and then to the *grandes entrées* of members of the imperial family, officers of the crown, chief-of-staff Alexandre Berthier, cabinet ministers, senators, deputies, generals, and other high officials who had been invited. Napoleon spoke very briefly to each one, and unless an official had something urgent to present (in which case he was asked to stay over), the emperor was usually back at his dictation and annotation of ministerial reports by 9:30 A.M. By noon he had given his secretary enough letters to write to keep him busy through the rest of the day.

After a luncheon of never more than fifteen minutes with the empress and often an artist or savant, the afternoon was generally devoted to meetings with commissions and committees, the Conseil d'Etat, the Conseil des Ministres, and special councils of administration. These conferences were usually over by 5 P.M. when Napoleon met with his secretary of state, Hugues Maret, his chief of staff for civil administration. A disciplined expediter, Maret guided the traffic of administrative correspondence. At 5 P.M. he brought for Napoleon's signature the letters that had been prepared during the day. Napoleon was then free for a few moments to chat in the empress' quarters with Josephine (or later Marie-Louise) and ladies-in-waiting.

At 6 P.M. there was dinner with the empress (never more than twenty minutes) and a few moments of conversation or perhaps a game of cards. Then Napoleon, more often than not, retired to his private office for further administrative work, retiring about 10 P.M.

Sunday had a more open schedule, with public attendance at Mass, public review of a contingent of the Guard, and a public court dinner with the Bonaparte and Beauharnais relatives. But for six days a week, during the fifteen years from 1799 to 1814, Napoleon worked (while in Paris) fifteen hours a day at his self-assumed task of founding and organizing an empire.

A.-J.-F. Fain, *Mémoires* (Paris, 1908); F. Masson, *Napoléon chez lui: la journée de l'empereur aux Tuileries* (Paris, 1894); C.-F. de Méneval, *Mémoires*, 3 vols. (Paris, 1893–1894), translated as *Memoirs Illustrating the History of Napoleon I from 1802 to 1815* (New York, 1894); Madame de Rémusat, *Mémoires 1802–1808*, 3 vols. (Paris, 1879–80).

Harold T. Parker

Related entries: ADMINISTRATION; ADMINISTRATION, MILITARY; BERTHIER, A.; CAMBACERES; CONSTANT; DUROC; FAIN; FINANCES; JOSEPHINE; LEBRUN; MARET; MARIE-LOUISE VON HABSBURG; MENEVAL; REMUSAT; ROUSTAN, RAZA; TALLEYRAND-PERIGORD.

NAPOLEON II (1811–32), Napoléon François Charles Joseph, son of Napoleon I and his second empress, Marie-Louise of Austria, originally titled the king of Rome. Napoleon tried unsuccessfully to abdicate in his favor in 1814 and again in 1815. In 1814, however, the little prince, just turned three, was taken into custody by his grandfather, the Austrian emperor, and taken to Vienna, where he was reared as the duke von Reichstadt. When he matured, he was tall, handsome, charming, bright, and fully aware of his heritage. The young prince, if "dropped into France," as Clemens von Metternich sometimes threatened, would surely have been a problem for either the Bourbons or Louis Philippe. The propaganda of the Bonapartist movement, which eventually swept Napoleon III to power in 1848, had made the plight of the "Eaglet"—a "prisoner" in Vienna—well known in the years after Napoleon's death (1821) at St. Helena. Small pictures of him were to be found in many homes, especially of the peasantry. However, Napoleon II died at twenty-one, of tuberculosis, a Habsburg curse, after overexerting himself on maneuvers with the Austrian army.

At St. Helena, Napoleon had spent much of the last weeks of his life dictating advice and instructions to him, in the full expectation that he would one day rule France. It was not to be. Thus the ex-emperor's letters, which presented Bonapartism in the ideal, merely contributed to the Napoleonic legend. Similarly, the premature death of the prince made Napoleon's "martyrdom" seem more poignant.

O. Aubry, *L'Aiglon* (Paris, 1941); M. de Chambrun, *Le Roi de Rome* (Paris, 1941); A. Castelot, *L'Aiglon: Napoléon II* (Paris, 1959), trans. as *The King of Rome* (New York, 1960).

Related entries: ABDICATION, FIRST; ABDICATION, SECOND; BONAPARTE; LEGEND, NAPOLEONIC; MARIE-LOUISE VON HABSBURG; NAPOLEON I; ST. HELENA.

NAPOLEON III. See BONAPARTE.

NATIONAL GUARD. See GUARD, NATIONAL.

NAVY, BRITISH. The English navy (or Royal Navy) had gained dominance on the high seas during the eighteenth century. Its power, relative to that of France (the second power) can be gauged by numbers of ships of the line (fifty guns or over). As of 1789 the British had in commission 124 versus 70 for France. Moreover, the British were an island people who had become dependent on commerce for their prosperity. For 300 years, since the time of Henry VIII, they had been expanding their navy and honing their skills of seamanship to protect the trade routes and their colonies.

While the legendary figures on the French side in the Napoleonic period were army commanders, those on the British side—Wellington excepted—were admirals, preeminently Horatio Nelson. The British retained superiority on the sea throughout the Napoleonic period, and never doubted the fact. As Admiral St. Vincent said when Napoleon threatened invasion of England, "Buonaparte may cross the Channel, but it will not be by sea." This superiority was reasserted in the Battle of the Nile (1798) where Nelson destroyed one-sixth of France's ships of the line with no losses to himself. It was certified at Trafalgar (1805) where Nelson, though he lost his own life, crippled the French and Spanish fleets for good, sinking twenty-two ships, again with no losses to the British.

When Napoleon took over in France (1799), the ratio between British battleships in commission and French was slightly better than in 1789, with 104 for the British and 65 for the French. Hardly any of the British had been sunk but rather taken out of commission as obsolete or unneeded. The French were building more vigorously and had partially repaired the losses suffered in the Battle of the Nile. The ratio was again tipped radically in favor of the British by the Battle of Trafalgar.

Napoleon did not accept Trafalgar as decisive, however. He determined to build ships in every port. His goal was to have 150 ships of the line by 1814, which, if the goal had been achieved, would have given him almost a 50 percent advantage over the British, who in 1812 had only 107 ships in commission. For the figures on Napoleon's navy, see NAVY, FRENCH.

G. Bennett, *The Battle of Trafalgar* (New York, 1977); A. Bryant, *Nelson* (London, 1970); W. Clowes, ed., *The Royal Navy: A History from the Earliest Times to the Present*, 7 vols. (London, 1897–1903); C. Lloyd, *The Navy and the Nation* (London, 1954); C. Lloyd, *The Nile Campaign* (New York, 1973); A. T. Mahan, *The Life of Nelson*, 2d ed. (Boston, 1899); G. J. Marcus, *A Naval History of England*, 2 vols. (London, 1971); C. Oman, *Nelson* (London, 1947); O. Warner, *The Battle of the Nile* (London, 1960).

Related entries: CONTINENTAL BLOCKADE; ENGLAND, ATTEMPTED CONQUEST OF; NAVY, FRENCH; NELSON; NILE, BATTLE OF; WAR, ECONOMIC.

NAVY, FRENCH, under Napoleon. Sea power was of more concern to Napoleon than generally realized. As first consul (1799), Bonaparte inherited only the relics of Louis XVI's once-great fleet, now shorn of its highly trained officer corps and weakened by losses due to the British occupation of Toulon (1793) and defeats at "the Glorious First of June" (1794) and the Nile (1798). It was to suffer further losses, including, ultimately, all eighteen ships engaged at Trafalgar (21 October 1805), besides those incurred in C.-U.-Jacques-Bertrand de Leissègue's defeat off San Domingo (1806) and Admiral James Gambier's victory at Basque Roads (1800). But from 1803 to 1813, Bonaparte could treat virtually as his own the Dutch fleet and from 1804 to 1808 the Spanish fleet.

Bonaparte's ability in managing France's navy is often underrated. His orders to commanders seem by no means so unrealistically inflexible as supposed. He improved training and discipline and relied much on his professional minister of marine, Admiral Denis Decrès. He appreciated Nelson's maxim, "Only numbers can annihilate," and declared he could not safely make peace with England until he had 150 ships of the line (fifty guns or more), a near 50 percent superiority. To achieve that superiority, he ordered the entire seafaring population of his Empire to provide crews and assembled timber supplies at major dockyards, such as at Texel, Antwerp, Cherbourg (which he created), Brest, L'Orient, Rochefort, Toulon, Genoa, Naples, and Venice. And he worked hard, increasing his fleet from thirty-four battleships in French and Dutch ports in 1807 to over 80 ready for sea and 35 building in 1813 (while England commissioned only 102). Napoleon's fall ended a most impressive and, for Britain, ominous, rebirth of French seapower.

E. P. Brenton, *The Naval History of Great Britain*, 2 vols. (London, 1823–25); E. Chevalier, *Histoire de la marine française sous le Consulat et l'Empire* (Paris, 1886); J. Corbett, *Campaign of Trafalgar*, new ed. (London, 1919); R. Glover, "The French Fleet, 1807–1814: Britain's Problem and Madison's Opportunity," *JMH 39* (1967); E. J. de la Gravière, *Guerres maritimes sous la République et l'Empire*, 2 vols. (n.d., Paris); W. James, *A Naval History of Great Britain*, 6 vols., 3d ed. (London, 1837); E. H. Jenkins, *A History of the French Navy from the Beginning to the Present Day* (London, 1973); A. T. Mahan, *The Influence of Sea Power upon the French Revolution & Empire, 1793-1812* (numerous editions).

Richard Glover

Related entries: DECRES; ENGLAND, ATTEMPTED CONQUEST OF; MINISTERS OF NAPOLEON; NELSON; NILE, BATTLE OF; TRAFALGAR, BATTLE OF.

NEIPPERG, ADAM ALBERT VON, COUNT (1775–1829), Austrian major general, second husband of the ex-Empress Marie-Louise. Neipperg entered Austrian military service at the age of sixteen, fought against the French in the Netherlands during 1792–94, was taken prisoner, released, and in 1797 served in the Tyrol. During the War of the Second Coalition (1799–1801), Neipperg, as a major, distinguished himself in Italy, and was mediator in the negotiations at Turin, Milan, and Paris. During the 1809 war he was Archduke Ferdinand's adjutant general and was not in the major battles against Napoleon. In 1811 he became envoy in Stockholm. In 1813 he fought in the Battle of Leipzig and was promoted to major general. In 1815 he commanded a corps against Joachim Murat in Italy and occupied Naples. At the Congress of Vienna, Neipperg represented Napoleon's wife, the ex-Empress Marie-Louise, who became duchess of Parma and Piacenza. She subsequently appointed him commander in chief of her army and foreign minister and married him in 1821 after the death of Napoleon.

Brigitte Holl

Related entries: ABDICATION, FIRST; BONAPARTE, CAROLINE; MARIE LOUISE VON HABSBURG; MURAT, J.; NAPLES, KINGDOM OF.

NELSON, LORD HORATIO (1758–1805), celebrated English admiral, victor of the Battle of the Nile (Aboukir) and of Trafalgar, where he was killed. Nelson was born at Burnham Thorpe, Norfolk, England, 22 September 1758, one of eleven children of the village rector. After the death of his mother, Nelson went to sea in 1770 with a maternal uncle, Captain Maurice Suckling. He became an officer in the Royal Navy in 1777 and sailed for the West Indies, taking part in the American Revolution. From 1784 to 1787, he commanded a frigate, again in the West Indies, where shipowners and merchants criticized him for enforcing the largely ignored Navigation Act against American ships. He fell in love with Frances Nisbet, the young widow of a doctor. They were married on 12 March 1787 and returned to England to await another command.

After war broke out with France in 1793, he was given a sixty-four-gun ship and in May set sail for the Mediterranean. On 25 August Nelson was sent to Naples to convey Neapolitan reinforcements to Toulon. It was then that he made the acquaintance of the English minister to Naples, Sir William Hamilton, and Lady Hamilton. After Napoleon had retaken Toulon, Nelson became part of Admiral Samuel Hood's attempt to seize Corsica as an operations base. At Calvi a cannon shot struck a battery near him, blasting sand and gravel at him and blinding his right eye. He was victorious at the Battle of Cape St. Vincent on 14 February 1797 by successfully executing a brilliant, but unorthodox, tactical maneuver, for which he was knighted. In July 1797 in the Battle of Santa Cruz at the Canary Island of Tenerife, a piece of grapeshot shattered his right elbow. The arm was amputated in a hasty and badly performed operation in near darkness. He was sent home to recuperate, but in extreme pain because a nerve had been bound up in a suture. His wife nursed him for nine months before he was fit to return to duty in the Mediterranean.

His assignment was to block Napoleon's expedition, in preparation at Toulon, but on arriving there he found that the French fleet had already sailed. Nelson believed it was bound for either Sicily or Egypt, and, learning that it had bypassed Sicily, he made for Alexandria. The Egyptian harbor was empty so he sailed to Sicily to resupply. Returning to Alexandria, he found Aboukir Bay crowded with immobilized French ships, which were easy prey for the British, who attacked them individually. In the great Battle of the Nile (1 August 1798), victory was never in doubt; it began at sunset, and by dawn the French were destroyed. Nelson had received a severe wound on his forehead during the battle.

When the British fleet put into Naples for repairs, Nelson and Lady Hamilton again encountered each other. She nursed his wound, gave him the attention a great naval hero deserved, and flattery, which he thoroughly enjoyed. Nelson came completely under her influence and also became embroiled in the politics of the Kingdom of Naples. The British admiralty became impatient with his lingering in Naples and Sicily and then enraged when he accepted the dukedom of Bronte in Sicily from King Ferdinand. He was ordered home at about the same time that the Hamiltons were recalled, so they traveled together through Europe to England. Nelson was very much the popular hero, although shunned and ridiculed by British society. He returned to his wife but after a month of unpleasant arguments left her and rejoined the Hamiltons. Emma Hamilton gave birth to his daughter, Horatia Nelson (Thompson), in 1801, before he departed on his next assignment as second in command at the Battle of Copenhagen. The Treaty of Amiens in 1802 gave him a respite from duty and some time at Merton Place, the country home Emma had prepared for him.

As Napoleon's preparations for renewing the war became obvious, Nelson was given the task of again blockading Toulon to prevent a rendezvous between the French fleets at Toulon and Brest or, later, the French and Spanish fleets. When Admiral Pierre-Charles de Villeneuve broke out of Toulon, Nelson pursued the French to the West Indies and back to Europe, not setting foot on land for two years. He finally put in at Gibraltar, laid plans for the blockade of Cadiz, and on 19 August 1805 went home to Merton Place for twenty-five days. There he planned for a confrontation with the combined French and Spanish fleets. He returned to duty on 15 September, and, on his forty-seventh birthday, he dined with his "Band of Brothers," his fifteen captains, in his flagship, and outlined his plan. It was new, singular, and simple, according to Nelson. It surely had the Nelson touch. He had abandoned the orthodox, rigid tactics of in-line fighting: he intended to bear down on the Franco-Spanish fleet in two columns, one led by him and one by Admiral Cuthbert Collingwood. This would destroy the enemies' in-line formation, allowing their ships to be assaulted one at a time. On 19 October Villeneuve's Franco-Spanish fleet began to leave the harbor. The next day they were all at sea, and, as Nelson anticipated, the combined forces proceeded toward the Mediterranean. His ships took command of the Straits and on 21 October sighted the enemy fleet off Cape Trafalgar. Villeneuve's maneuvers afforded Nelson the opportunity to fall in behind the enemy as he had planned. The light winds died away to almost nothing, and progress was very slow. During the lull Nelson went to his cabin and wrote a codicil to his will, leaving Lady Hamilton and his daughter as a legacy to his king and country and asking that they be provided for, but no such action was ever taken by England.

As the enemy came closer, Nelson hoisted his famous signal, "England expects that every man will do his duty." The battle went according to plan, with Collingwood attacking the rear and Nelson preventing other ships from coming to the defense. Nelson's ship, the *Victory*, came under intense fire passing through the enemy's center and under the stern of Villeneuve's flagship. Nelson was pacing the quarter-deck when he was struck in the left shoulder by a musket ball, which passed through his lungs and spine and lodged in the muscles of his back. In his remaining three hours he continued to give the commands from below decks. When told that fifteen enemy ships had been taken, he said, "That is well; but I bargained for twenty." He died at half-past four on 21 October

1805, with his last words: "Now I am satisfied. I have done my duty." With the Battle of Trafalgar French sea-power was destroyed and the supremacy of the British Navy was established.

G. Bennett, *Nelson, the Commander* (London, 1972); C. Lloyd, *The Nile Campaign: Nelson and Napoleon in Egypt* (New York, 1973); J. Russell, *Nelson and the Hamiltons* (New York, 1969); D. Walder, *Nelson* (New York, 1978); O. Warner, *A Portrait of Lord Nelson* (London, 1958), *Battle of the Nile* (London, 1960), and *Lady Hamilton and Sir William* (London, 1963).

Rachel R. Schneider

Related entries: HAMILTON; NAVY, BRITISH; NILE, BATTLE OF; TRAFALGAR, BATTLE OF.

NETHERLANDS, POLITICAL PARTIES. Before the Batavian Revolution (1795) the northern Netherlands had been a confederation of seven provinces (Gelderland, Holland, Utrecht, Zeeland, Overijssel, Friesland, and Groningen), each a confederation of local units. Government was an oligarchy. Since the middle of the eighteenth century the princes of Orange, as stadholders, had extensive rights of patronage, and those whom they named to local governments were called "Orangist regents" (*regents* in Dutch usage meant members of governing bodies). Just as the Whigs in England came into conflict with George III and his Tories, so the non-Orangist Patriot regents sought to acquire political power with the assistance of the burghers. This alliance, born of necessity, paralleled a historical pattern, which can also be seen in England, France, and the southern Netherlands. The middle groups aimed at putting an end to both the oligarchical form of government and the confederative form of the state, which had become interwoven.

A revolution began around 1785, which R. R. Palmer believes illustrates the Western character of the French Revolution because it preceded the conflagration in France. An Anglo-Prussian intervention of 1787, led by the duke of Brunswick, put an end to this movement, but power was returned to the Patriot regents and burghers by the arrival of French troops in 1795.

As of 1795 we can no longer speak of a struggle between Orangists and Patriots. The word *Patriot* has historical meaning only in the context of its time. The Patriots as such never existed; there were, instead, Patriots old style who were regents in opposition and Patriots new style like the patriots of the American War of Independence. This explains why, after the Orangists were driven from office in 1795, the fundamental conflict within the Patriot alliance came to light.

The burghers came to power by the coup d'état of 1798, and they wrote a modern constitution establishing a unitary state. The two wings of the aristocracy, as the Dutch called the regent class, were reconciled at this time out of fear of the democratic forces. They recaptured political power in 1801 with the help of Napoleon and kept it until 1848 (although they called themselves conservatives). The osmosis that took place elsewhere in western Europe between the aristocrats and the burghers who moved up in the social scale, giving rise to the group of notables, did not occur in the Netherlands.

O. Connelly, *Napoleon's Satellite Kingdoms* (New York, 1965); I. L. Leeb, *The Ideological Origins of the Batavian Revolution: History and Politics in the Dutch Republic, 1747–1800* (The Hague, 1973); R. R. Palmer, *The Age of the Democratic Revolution: A Political History of Europe and America, 1760–1800*, 2 vols. (Princeton, N.J., 1959–64), and "Much in Little: The Dutch Revolution of 1795," *JMH* 26 (1954); S. Schama, *Patriots and Liberators: Revolution in the Netherlands, 1780–1813* (New York, 1977); C. H. E. de Wit, *De Strijd tussen Aristocratie en Democratie in Nederland, 1780-1848*, 3d ed. (Oirsbeek, 1980).

C. H. E, de Wit

Related entries: HOLLAND, KINGDOM OF.

NETHERLANDS, RELIGION. In the Republic of the United Netherlands, the Calvinist Reformed church had been a privileged but not a state church. Only its members could hold public office, but practical tolerance was greater in Erasmus' native land than anywhere else in Europe. At the end of the eighteenth century, the population of 2,205,000 was 55.47 percent Calvinist, 38.1 percent Catholic, 2.8 percent Lutheran, 1.79 percent Jewish, 1.41 percent Mennonite, and smaller fractions of others. The Dutch Enlightenment had not possessed any anti-Christian characteristics; for it the wonders of nature proved God's revelation just as the Bible did. It was among enlightened, or modern, Calvinists that the democratic reform movement of the Patriots had found its greatest support. Not surprisingly, they greeted the Batavian Revolution of 1795 with fervent approval.

Religious equality was decreed on 5 August 1796, when the National Assembly decided that no privileged or ruling church would be permitted. There was hesitation about the position of the Jews, who were divided into two groups: the Portugese Sephardim and the German Ashkenazim, who were more proletarian. A large majority was hostile to emancipation, fearing that assimilation would bring with it the loss of faith. Only a small group of German Jews who, with other democrats, had formed the society Felix Libertate, spoke in favor.

Perhaps under French pressure, the National Assembly nevertheless decided, on 2 September 1796, to extend equality of rights to the Jews. Public offices were opened to Catholics and Jews. They were expelled from them, however, after the reaction in 1801. Religious emancipation as such was not called into question, although the political authorities attempted to renew the control on the Calvinist Reformed church, especially during the Napoleonic period. Under King Louis Napoleon, who in general promoted religious equality, the Department of Religious Affairs prepared a draft law on supervision of the church (1809).

O. J. de Jong. *Nederlandse Kerkgeschiedenis* (Nijkerk, 1972); J. Michman, "Gotische Torens op een Corintisch Gebouw, de doorvoering van de emancipatie van de Joden in

Nederland,'' *Tijdschrift voor Geschiedenis* 87 (1974), 89 (1976); J. Michman, ed., *Studies on the History of Dutch Jewry* (Jerusalem, 1975); A. G. Weiler *et al.*, *Geschiedenis van de Kerk in Nederland* (Utrecht-Antwerp, 1962).

C. H. E. de Wit

Related entries: BATAVIAN REPUBLIC; BONAPARTE, LOUIS; HOLLAND, KINGDOM OF.

NETHERLANDS, SOCIETY AND ECONOMY. The highest social group in the Republic of the United Netherlands comprised the governing clans of the regents (members of the governing bodies) who were either nobles or urban patricians. Social historians now explain the wealth of the families, especially in the eighteenth century, more by the political offices they held than by their gains from trade and shipping. The overwhelming majority of these families were urban patricians, since nobles were numerous only in Utrecht, Gelderland, and Overijssel. In Holland, which had half of the Netherlands' population, the number of families was about 400 in the eighteenth century.

The second group—the middle classes—was quite weak, except for a few successful individuals, notably manufacturers and farmers in Friesland and Groningen. Burghers who held minor government offices were clients of the local oligarchy. Others were under mercantilist control by city governments, which forced them to join guilds or secure *octrois* (permission to engage in business). The decline of trade and shipping in the eighteenth century was only relative. Industry, however, operated mainly by burghers, fell back in absolute terms. The manufacturers could not compete with their English competitors because the governing class scorned manufacturing and allowed local units to levy import duties on raw materials and heavy taxes. The burghers reacted to this decline by calling into life the economic Patriot movement. The economic situation became one of the preconditions for revolution in the 1780s.

The third group, called the lower orders (*de smalle gemeente*) by the Dutch, included wage workers—employed or unemployed—and paupers. The workers were not viewed as a class. Their situation was much like that in the rest of Western Europe. A skilled worker earned about 300 guilders (about $130 in 1789 U.S. dollars) a year in Holland in the mid-eighteenth century, of which he paid 15 percent in indirect taxes and 20 percent for rent. In the second half of the century, prices rose about 70 percent, but wages remained the same.

Those who were unable to support themselves because of sickness, age, unemployment, or other reasons were fairly well taken care of by church or public charities. Structural unemployment plagued the maritime provinces, and the number of paupers continued to increase. There was talk of pauperism as a disease that made men fly to drink and undermined their physical strength. The Enlightenment made burghers understand, however, that unemployment was not the result of moral decline and drunkenness, as the aristocrats often declared, but that the contrary was true. In the period of the French-sponsored Republic (1795–1806), social-economic reform stood high in the program of the democrats.

Under the Batavian Republic (1795–1806) and Napoleonic rule (1806–13), Dutch harbors were blockaded by the English. There was no sudden fall into economic disaster, however, as has often been asserted. The new rulers of the country inherited a stagnant economy and a public debt amounting to almost 800 million guilders. In proportion to the population, this was five times higher than the notorious French royal debt that prompted the convocation of the Estates General in 1789.

According to Izaac Gogel, minister of finances and financial expert, the Netherlands remained the greatest staple market of the world until 1809 when the Continental System was really brought into force. It also functioned as a financial center. The United States purchased the Louisiana Territory from Napoleon in 1803 with money borrowed from the Dutch firm of Hope & Co. and the London house of Baring. It used to be common to look at Dutch history through the eyes of Holland, which gave a one-sided picture. The situation was bad in the maritime provinces, despite large-scale smuggling. Recent historians have shown, however, that at the same time agriculture, in which 50 percent of the population was employed, prospered, unaffected or helped by the blockade.

The Batavian Republic abolished the *Stände* (estates), formerly the sole possessors of political power. It began the improvement of the infrastructure, established workhouses for the unemployed, and created a national welfare law to make charity more effective and fairer. After 1801, however, the reforms came to a halt or were gradually undone. One can hardly speak of any social mobility; there was only sporadic intermarriage between the aristocracy and the burghers. The former ruling families even objected to Grand Pensionary R. J. Schimmelpenninck, who headed the Republic in 1805-6, because he was only a burgher, even though he was doing his best to promote their interests.

The middle groups fell far behind, as was noted by the astute German visitor B. G. Niebuhr who feared that in the long run only rich and poor would remain in the Netherlands, as in the Roman Empire of antiquity. The situation of the lower classes in the maritime provinces became catastrophic after 1808, and prices rose sharply after the country was incorporated into France in 1810. In 1811, 10.7 percent of the population was dependent upon charity, so that the municipal and religious poorhouses had to go to the national government to beg for money. Although Napoleon promoted social equality, there was almost no change in social stratification or the demographic situation in this period.

I. J. Brugmans, *Paardenkracht en Mensenmacht, sociaal-economische geschiedenis van Nederland, 1795-1940* ('s-Gravenhage, 1976); Marten G. Buist, *At Spes non Fracta, Hope & Co. 1770-1815* ('s-Gravenhage, 1974); B. G. Niebuhr, *Nachgelassene Schriften nichtphilologischen Inhalts* (Hamburg, 1842); Simon Schama, "Municipal Government and the Burden of the Poor in South Holland during the Napoleonic Wars," in *Britain and the Netherlands*, VI, edited by A. C. Duke and C. A. Tamse (The Hague, 1980).

C. H. E. de Wit

Related entries: BATAVIAN REPUBLIC; BONAPARTE, LOUIS; GOGEL, ISAAC; HOLLAND, KINGDOM OF.

NEUCHATEL, PRINCE DE. See BERTHIER, A.

NEUTRALS, LEAGUE OF. See PAUL I; RUSSIA, KINGDOM OF.

NEWSPAPERS. See LITERATURE; PRESS; PROPAGANDA.

NEY, MICHEL (1769–1815), prince of Moscow, duc d'Elchingen, marshal of France, "The Bravest of the Brave." The red-haired Ney was born the son of a cooper at Sarrelouis in 1769. He enlisted in the army in 1787, rose to sergeant major, and was commissioned (1792) after the overthrow of the king and founding of the Republic. He was promoted to *général de brigade* in 1796 and to *général de division* in 1799, in both cases for service on the Rhine frontier.

In late 1799 and 1800 Ney served in Switzerland and under Jean Moreau in his drive down the Danube against the Austrians, and distinguished himself at Hohenlinden (December 1800). In 1802–3 he served in Switzerland as minister plenipotentiary (and de facto commander of French troops). In 1804 Napoleon named him a marshal of the empire. In 1805 his corps played the major role in trapping the Austrian army of Karl Mack at Ulm. (His victory at Elchingen earned him his ducal title in 1808.) In 1806 he was at Jena and in 1807 at Eylau, Güttstadt, and at Friedland. In 1808 he was dispatched to Spain where he served until 1811, taking part in André Masséna's disastrous invasion of Portugal in 1810. He was recalled to Paris in 1811 for insubordination.

In 1812, however, he became the greatest hero of the Russian campaign and as commander of the rear guard during much of the retreat made legend. He was honored in 1813 with the title prince of Moscow. In 1813 Ney fought at Weissenfels, Lützen, Bautzen, Dennewitz, and Leipzig.

In 1814, however, Ney joined the other marshals who demanded that Napoleon give up and abdicate. This earned him the favor of Louis XVIII, who made him a peer. In 1815, however, he betrayed the Bourbons, joined Napoleon, and fought with insane bravery at Waterloo. When he returned to France, Ney was arrested, tried, and condemned to death in Paris by a court of peers. On 7 December 1815, two days after his arrest, Ney gave the order to shoot to his firing squad.

J. Dubreton, *Le maréchal Ney* (Paris, 1941); L. Garros, *Ney* (Paris, 1955); J. B. Morton, *Marshal Ney* (London, 1958); M.-L.-F. Ney, *Mémoires...publiés par son famille*, 2 vols. (Paris, 1883); H. Welschinger, *Le Maréchal Ney* (Paris, 1915).

Jesse Scott

Related entries: ABDICATION, FIRST; AUSTERLITZ CAMPAIGN; FRANCE, CAMPAIGN OF; HUNDRED DAYS, THE; PENINSULAR WAR; RUSSIAN CAMPAIGN; WATERLOO CAMPAIGN.

NILE, BATTLE OF (1 August 1798), destruction of Napoleon's fleet by Admiral Horatio Nelson. One result of Spain's declaration of war on Great Britain in 1796 and its own naval mutinies in 1797 was that Britain withdrew its fleet from the Mediterranean. This gave Bonaparte his chance to invade Egypt, where his troops landed on 1–2 July 1798. The commander of his naval escort, Admiral F. P. Brueys, then had three options: to withdraw to Corfu—but that seemed too distant; to enter Alexandria harbor—but that proved too shallow; or to prepare to defend himself at anchor in Aboukir Bay—and this he chose.

Meanwhile, some useful victories (St. Vincent, over the Spaniards; Camperdown, over the Dutch) and the end of the mutinies had strengthened the British, who knew of Bonaparte's sailing. Accordingly Admiral Lord St. Vincent, commanding off Cadiz, sent a squadron under Horatio Nelson back into the Mediterranean. On 1 August Nelson found Brueys' ships in Aboukir Bay, anchored in line, backs to the shore, and many of their portside guns shifted to the starboard, or seaward, side. But Nelson's observations convinced him that the water at the north end of Brueys' line was just deep enough for a ship to get inside it and enable him to pit two ships to one against the anchored French. It was risky, but it was done; the result was the virtual destruction of French seapower in the Mediterranean, only two of Brueys' thirteen ships managing to cut loose and escape to Toulon.

A. T. Mahan, *The Influence of Sea Power on the French Revolution and Empire* (Boston, 1894); C. Oman, *Nelson* (London, 1947); O. Warner, *The Battle of the Nile* (London, 1960).

Richard Glover

Related entries: EGYPTIAN CAMPAIGN; NAVY, FRENCH.

NOBILITY, IMPERIAL. Step by step, with perfect timing, Napoleon moved toward the creation of a new nobility, to bring the most influential individuals in his empire into dependence on him and to establish a durable institutional "pillar of granite" to sustain the imperial regime. The first major step in the revival of class distinctions abolished by the Revolution was the creation of the Legion of Honor (19 May 1802). Membership was a lifetime dignity for individuals judged to be of eminent merit and achievement but was accorded largely to military men. (In 1814 there were only 1,500 civilians among 32,000 members.)

The second major step was the organization of an imperial court by the *senatus-consultum* of 18 May 1804. The law provided for six grand dignitaries of the Empire (grand elector, constable, arch-chancellor of the Empire, arch-treasurer, grand admiral, and arch-chancellor of state) and ten grand civil officers of the imperial household (such as grand marshal of the palace, grand chamberlain, grand master of horse, and grand master of ceremonies). Military conquests permitted in 1806–7 a third major step, the creation of hereditary fiefs in conquered territories with appropriate incomes derived from confiscated land in Italy, Naples, Holland, the German states, and the Grand Duchy of Warsaw. They were granted to marshals and generals deemed to have rendered great service *à la patrie et à notre couronne*.

The decrees of 1 March 1808, the fourth step, generalized what had been accomplished. They established a hierarchy of princes, dukes, counts, barons, and chevaliers. To pass their titles to heirs the nobles had to bequeath substantial annual incomes: dukes, 200,000 francs; counts, 30,000; barons, 15,000; chevaliers, 3,000. One became a noble by one of two routes: by service in office (grand dignitaries of the Empire were princes; their eldest sons were dukes; cabinet ministers, senators, councillors of state, and archbishops were counts; mayors of large towns and bishops were barons; members of the Legion of Honor, chevaliers), or by letters patent from Napoleon. "From 1808 to 1814 there were 3,600 personal titles conferred by letters-patent, for 1,600 chevaliers, 1,090 barons, and 388 counts.... There were only 200 heads of family with heritable titles, 37 counts, 131 barons, plus the dukes and princes" (Bergeron).

Napoleon was essentially creating a nobility, which he hoped would be imbued with the values of honor and glory of the aristocratic French army officer corps in which he had been reared. But he was not restoring under another guise the nobility of the Old Regime. In size his corps of princes, dukes, counts, barons, and chevaliers was only one-seventh as large as the nobility of 1789. They enjoyed no legal privileges; the first principle of Napoleon's Civil Code, that "every Frenchman shall enjoy the same civil rights," held for them as for everyone else. They were not deeply rooted in the past or sustained by any profound philosophy of aristocratic origin and function. Yet Napoleon, in thoughtful moments, felt he was working with time and destiny: "I am of the race that builds empires." In time he expected his imperial nobility to promote a fusion of elites (old nobility, non-noble large landowners, top army officers, top administrators) into a single elite bound to him and to his dynasty.

If Napoleon had had time, a lifetime of rule, the policy might have worked as he envisioned. But even before the great defeats of 1812, 1813, and 1814, there is evidence that the situation was not evolving as he intended. Several causes of disaffection and disruption were operating. For Frenchmen the great charm of the Consulate and early Empire had been the promise of a stable constitutional government at peace with the world and the animating slogan of careers open to talent. As late as March 1808 Cambacérès in communicating to the Senate the statute that created a hierarchy of noble titles could still declare: "La carrière reste toujours à vertus et aux talents utiles; les avantages qu'elle accorde au mérite éprouvé ne nuiront point au mérite inconnu; ils seront, au contraire, autant de sujets d'espérance sur lesquels se dirigera une juste et louable émulation." However, as the Napoleonic epic unrolled, Napoleon's despotism increased, the wars enlarged in magnitude, and the chances of an ambitious young man of the lower and middle classes being rewarded by a noble title diminished. The top posts in the army were already occupied; the opportunity to make a quick fortune in confiscated lands was past. In addition, Napoleon himself in 1810 erected barriers to acquiring the noble title of *chevalier d'Empire* by becoming a member of the Legion of Honor. With the Austrian marriage in 1810, he increasingly appointed members of the old nobility to positions at court and recruited their sons as officers in elite guards of honor. The net effect of these measures was, on the one hand, to alienate both the seasoned veterans of the army and members of the bourgeoisie who saw careers closed to them and, on the other hand, to antagonize the older aristocrats who resented the drafting of their sons into dangerous military service. As the Empire crashed in defeat, the notables, both bourgeois and aristocrat, angry with each other and with the emperor, showed little zeal in coming to his aid. They allowed, indeed they often facilitated, the overthrow of the "fourth dynasty" they were supposed to support.

L. Bergeron, *France under Napoleon*, trans. R. R. Palmer (Princeton, 1981), and *La noblesse de l'Empire* (Paris, 1980); J. diCorcia, "Nobles, Commoners, and the French Revolution" (manuscript); P. Durye, "Les chevaliers dans la noblesse impériale," *RHMC* 17 (1970); M. Senkowska-Gluck, "Les donataires de Napoléon," *RHMC* 17 (1970); J. Tulard, "Problèmes sociaux de la France impériale," *RHMC* 17 (1970); and *Napoléon et la noblesse d'Empire* (Paris, 1979).

Harold T. Parker

Related entries: EMIGRES; NOTABLES; SOCIETY.

NOBILITY OF THE OLD REGIME. See SOCIETY.

NOTABLES, essentially the governing elite of the Empire. The term *notable* is an ambiguous one, having had a long history before Napoleon I ordered his administrators to compile lists of notables in 1802. The emperor's instructions prescribed that the prefects find those men of wealth, notoriety, and local influence who were reliable opinion leaders in their departments and potential recruits for the imperial administration. By 1810 these lists of notables had been perfected to include detailed information on the wealth, functions, and careers of some 100,000 men from the 130 departments of the Empire from Paris to Turin, from Bordeaux to Koblenz.

This was a much larger group than those notables later defined by the amount of taxes they paid to the governments of the Restoration and the July Monarchy—the *censitaires* of François Guizot. Therefore, the 100,000 notables cannot be identified exactly with the governing class of the First Empire. Nevertheless, it was from these lists that Napoleon drew his elite, his *class dirigeante*. In the process of selection, career promotion, and public service, the *grands notables* developed their own values and ideology, which gave them a sense of identity and cohesion apart from (though not necessarily opposed to) family, connection, or ancestry. Chosen largely from among landowners and professional men, the Napoleonic notability came to represent a new social amalgam of old and new landlords, of nobles and non-nobles, bound together by the functions and habits of a growing civil service.

As the nineteenth century advanced, the notables saw themselves as a service elite, the *capacités*, whose wealth (usually landed) and education, self-discipline and professionalism, made them peculiarly fit to rule and lead. It can be argued that this social amalgam, labeled *notables* and largely created by Napoleon, ruled France for the better part of a century after Waterloo.

L. Bergeron, *L'épisode napoléonien* (Paris, 1972); L. Bergeron et G. Chaussinand-Nogaret, *Les Masses de granit: cent mille notables du Premier Empire* (Paris, 1979); L. Bergeron, G. Chaussinand-Nogaret, and R. Forster, "Les notables du Grand Empire de 1810," *Annales, E.S.C.* (1971); C. Charles et al., eds., *Prosopographie des élites françaises, XVIe-XXe siecles. Guide de Recherche* (Paris, 1980).

Robert Forster

Related entries: ADMINISTRATION; ECONOMY, FRENCH; *EMIGRES*; NOBILITY, IMPERIAL; SOCIETY.

O

O'FARRILL, GONZALO. See SPAIN, KINGDOM OF; SPAIN, KINGDOM OF: MINISTERS.

OPERA. See MUSIC.

OPORTO, BATTLE OF. See PENINSULAR WAR.

ORANGE, HOUSE OF, RESTORATION (1813). Stadholders in the provinces of the old Dutch republic, the princes of Orange had not possessed any sovereign power, but William VI became King William I in 1813. Under the old regime, the real power of the princes of Orange had rested on their military achievements, their connection with the Calvinist Reformed church, and through it with the common people. When factions in the towns and the Estates clashed, one party inevitably claimed the stadholder as its leader. As a result, during the Batavian Revolution of 1795, when the opposition regents and burghers triumphed with the help of the French, William V was compelled to flee to England.

The period after 1795 had major, positive significance for the house of Orange because the hereditary prince, the later King William I, adopted modern notions about the state and government and because the Netherlands became a modern unitary state. In 1788 England and Prussia had guaranteed the Dutch *ancien regime* and the hereditary stadholdership. Prussia let this guarantee fall, however, when it made peace with France in 1795, and England recognized the Batavian Republic in the Peace of Amiens (1801). Under the influence of his son, the hereditary prince, William V accepted from the hands of Napoleon the principality of Fulda in Germany as compensation for his lost position in the Netherlands.

It appeared that the Netherlands and the house of Orange were to go separate ways for all time. William V went to rule his hereditary lands in Nassau, and his son took over Fulda, a Napoleonic satellite state. There he became an enlightened *Landesvater*.

In 1806 William V died, and his son considered himself to be hereditary stadholder William VI. He joined (1806) the Prussians and Russians against Napoleon, but his allies were defeated, and he lost all his territories. England became the sole remaining life preserver to which the Orangists could cling. Although the relations between England and William VI were difficult, the hereditary prince was in England in 1812, after the French debacle in Russia, hoping to recoup his fortunes.

His wait was short. England recognized him as hereditary stadholder. Then, in the fall of 1813, Napoleon was defeated at Leipzig, and a rebellion against the French broke out in the Netherlands under the leadership of Gijsbert Karel van Hogendorp. William VI returned to the Netherlands, landing at Scheveningen on 30 November, amid great enthusiasm, though his future position had not been settled.

In exile William VI had realized that a dynasty that was committed to one party remained weak and that foreign guarantees in the end would not be worth much. Having enjoyed ruling as prince in Fulda, he hoped to do the same in the Netherlands, where the government had already been centralized. However, most ''aristocrats''—the urban patricians and nobles who had dominated the old Republic—demanded a return to the old forms. Since they had regained their political power in 1801 and formed a solid bloc, William VI had to take them seriously. Van Hogendorp, the leader of the provisional government, desired a return not to the old confederation but to medieval forms, where sovereignty was divided between the ruling prince and the *Stände* (Estates).

Differences suddenly became irrelevant, however, after William VI paid a visit to the liberated capital city of Amsterdam on 1 December 1813. Events took an unexpected turn. The commissioners sent to Amsterdam by Van Hogendorp made contact with the principal burghers of the city and, on the initiative of J. M. Kemper, in the palace on the Dam, they offered the royal power to William VI in the name of the Dutch people. Understandably, in view of the political uncertainties, he hesitated but finally accepted the crown. The monarchy now guaranteed the unity of the state, and during his reign King William I sought to bring about a reconciliation between the aristocracy and the burghers.

J. A. Bornewasser, ''Konig Willem I,'' in *Nassau en Oranje*, ed. C. A. Tamse (Alphen aan de Rijn, 1979).

C. H. E. de Wit

Related entries: EMPIRE, FRENCH; HOLLAND, KINGDOM OF; LEBRUN; NETHERLANDS entries.

ORGANIC ARTICLES. See CONCORDAT OF 1801.

ORLEANS, LOUIS-PHILIPPE, DUC D' (1773–1850), duc de Chartres until 1793, prince of the blood, lieutenant general in the French Revolutionary army, *émigré*, and king of the French (1830–48). Eldest son of Louis-Philippe-Joseph, duc d'Orléans, Louis-Philippe received an intensive, enlightened education under his father's mistress, the remarkable comtesse de Genlis. Influenced by his father and the comtesse, he became an enthusiastic supporter of the Revolution and joined the Paris Jacobin club in 1790.

In the War of the First Coalition, Louis-Philippe performed well under fire and was promoted to general on 11 September 1792; he served at Valmy (20 September) and Jemmapes (6 November). But the Revolution was moving to the left, and the rank and wealth of the Orléans family made it suspect, despite its contributions to the Revolution. After the execution of Louis XVI, Louis-Philippe's enthusiasm for the Revolution waned, and on 5 April 1793 he defected to the Austrians with General Charles Dumouriez. His desertion caused the arrest of all Bourbons still in France and was a significant factor in turning the Convention against his father, the duc d'Orléans ("Philippe Egalité"), who was executed on 6 November 1793.

Louis-Philippe taught school in Switzerland, traveled widely in northern Europe, and spent several years in the United States before reaching England. Long since cured of Jacobinism, Orléans was reconciled with the comte d'Artois and by letter made his formal submission to the comte de Provence (later Louis XVIII). The English granted him an annual subsidy of 4,800 pounds but were suspicious of the former Jacobin and forbade him to visit the Continent.

Louis-Philippe helped make arrangements for the comte de Provence to reside in England, and in 1809 he married Marie-Amélie, daughter of Ferdinand IV, king of the Two Sicilies. He wanted action, however, and in 1809 tried to secure a command in the Austrian army through Clemens von Metternich, and in 1810 to serve in the Spanish army fighting Napoleon's forces in the peninsula. (The Spanish approved; the British would not.) He remained idle. After Napoleon's abdication, Alexander I of Russia included Orléans (along with Bernadotte and Eugène) on his list of possibilities for the kingship of France, but the other Allied leaders forced the selection of the comte de Provence. One of Louis XVIII's first acts as king was to restore Louis-Philippe's rank of lieutenant general in the army and to return the Palais Royal and the Park Monceau to the Orléans family. The duke fled to England when Napoleon returned in March 1815 and was Joseph Fouché's candidate for the kingship, but the duke of Wellington successfully argued for the second restoration of Louis XVIII. The Indemnity Law of 1825 compensated the Orléans family for its confiscated properties, and when Charles X abdicated in 1830, the two chambers invited Orléans to replace him as Louis-Philippe I.

M. Castillon du Perron, *Louis Philippe et la Révolution française*, 2 vols. (Paris, 1963); T. E. B. Howarth, *Citizen King, The Life of Louis-Philippe* (1961); Louis-Philippe, *Memoirs of Louis Philippe, 1773-1793* (1973, 1977).

Vincent Beach

Related entries: ARTOIS; *EMIGRES*; LOUIS XVIII.

OUDINOT, NICOLAS-CHARLES (1767–1847), duc de Reggio, marshal of France. Of the working class, the son of a brewer, he enlisted in the Royal Army in 1784 and began a military career that lasted four decades during which he sustained twenty-two wounds, incredible for a senior commander. After the Revolution began (1789), Oudinot became a captain and by 1799 was a major general. He served as chief of staff to André Masséna in 1800, facilitating Napoleon's victory at Marengo. He participated in the campaigns of Austerlitz (1805) and Jena-Auerstädt-Friedland (1806–7). His performance at Friedland earned him the title of count. In 1809 he distinguished himself at Wagram and afterward was made a marshal of the empire (1809) and duke of Reggio (1810). In 1810, under instructions from Napoleon, Oudinot put Holland under such tight military occupation that Louis Bonaparte abdicated.

In 1812 Oudinot fought in Russia but was wounded at the Berezina and forced to return to France. In 1813, however, he was with Napoleon in Germany and in 1814 in the Campaign of France. He became increasingly convinced, however, that victory was impossible. In March 1814, at Fontainebleau, he was one of the marshals who forced Napoleon to abdicate. He remained loyal to the Bourbons during the Hundred Days, became a member of the Privy Council, fought in Spain in 1823, and ended his career as governor of the Invalides.

J. Nollet-Fabert, *Histoire de Nicolas Charles Oudinot* (Bar-le-Duc, 1850); M. C. E. J. Oudinot, *Le maréchal Oudinot*, 6th ed. (Paris, 1894).

Jesse Scott

Related entries: ARMY, FRENCH; MARSHALS OF THE EMPIRE.

OUVRARD, GABRIEL-JULIEN (1770–1846), most notorious banker of the Napoleonic period. A bold, intriguing financier who was distrusted, despised, but utilized by the Directory, Napoleon, and later French governments, Ouvrard came to Paris from Nantes. In 1797 he won contracts to provision both the French navy and the Spanish fleet stationed at Brest. The first made him 15 million francs, but the second was paid in worthless paper. Overextended and unable to meet his obligations, Ouvrard was imprisoned in 1800. But Bonaparte, short of cash to buy grain to feed Paris, released the financial wizard in 1802 to secure funds for him. In 1804, with Napoleon's initial support, Ouvrard concocted a scheme to bring Mexican bullion through the British blockade to Spain on British ships, a complicated transaction that would profit rebel Spain, the French treasury, the private banks of Hope-Labouchère and Baring in Holland and Britain, the East India Company, U.S. merchants, and, not least, Ouvrard. However, implementation took too long, the Bank of France had to suspend certain specie payments, commercial credit in France contracted, and a current business recession was aggravated. The French minister of the treasury, François Barbé-Marbois, was dismissed. Ouvrard again was bankrupt but recovered. In 1810, he served as Joseph Fouché's go-between in a treasonable attempt to negotiate peace with England. Napoleon dismissed Fouché and put Ouvrard in prison until October 1813. Never daunted, Ouvrard in 1814 secured the contract to provision the Allied armies occupying France. He continued to prosper under the Restoration.

L. Bergeron, *Banquiers, négociants et manufacturiers parisiens du Directoire à l'Empire* (Paris, 1978); M. G. Buist, *At Spes non Fracta: Hope & Co., 1770–1815* (The

Hague, 1974); M. Marion, *Histoire financière de la France depuis 1715*, vol. 4: *1797–1818: La fin de la Révolution, le Consulat et l'Empire, la libération du territoire* (Paris, 1927).

Harold T. Parker

Related entries: BANK OF FRANCE; BARBE-MARBOIS; ECONOMY, FRENCH.

P

PAINTING. See ART; DAVID; DENON; GERARD; F.-P.-S. GROS; ISABEY; LOUVRE; VIGEE-LEBRUN.

PALAFOX Y MELZI, JOSE REBOLLEDO DE (1776–1847), duke of Saragossa (Zaragoza), hero of the sieges of Saragossa. Scion of a noble Spanish family of Saragossa founded by an Irish adventurer, Palafox was a professional soldier. In 1808, conscious of the sad state of Spanish military preparation, he concentrated Aragonese forces in Saragossa and could not be budged. Although the French marched on to Madrid and installed Joseph Bonaparte on the throne, Saragossa held out and was a source of Spanish pride—the more when Joseph withdrew his forces behind the Ebro (August 1808), leaving Saragossa free. When Napoleon came to Spain to command a greatly enlarged army in November 1808, Palafox again withdrew into Saragossa, which was put under siege (December 1808) and held doggedly again, though Napoleon took Madrid and restored Joseph. It took the French, under Marshals Jean Lannes and Jeannot de Moncey, until 21 February (after Napoleon had returned to France) to reduce the city. In the process they had to fight both soldiers and civilians and demolish every defensible wall and structure in the city. At least 54,000 Spanish died in the fighting or of disease, reducing the population of Saragossa to perhaps 15,000. Palafox was carried from the rubble, delirious from fever, and sent to prison in France. He had sacrificed a proud city and would fight no more in that war. Nevertheless, he represented Spanish courage and became the most celebrated hero of the Spanish "War of Independence."
Related entry: PENINSULAR WAR.

PAOLI, PASCAL-PHILIPPE-ANTOINE (1725–1807), leader of Corsican independence movement (1755–1769), governor for French (1790); delivered Corsica to the British (1793). Paoli's father, Giacinto, was descended from the Caporali and chief of the clan that had led the struggle for Corsican independence for 700 years. In 1739, Giacinto had fled to Naples, taking young Paoli with him. At Naples he attended the university and became a Freemason. Meanwhile, he joined a regiment of Corsican exiles. In 1755 his brother summoned him to return to Corsica, in revolt against Genoa. The Grand Council of the island gave him command of Corsican forces, and he soon became governor. He established suffrage, promoted economic regeneration, and gained a European reputation as an enlightened ruler.

In 1768, Genoa ceded Corsica to France. Paoli led the island's heroic defense against overwhelming odds. He was defeated in 1769 at Ponte Nuovo and fled to England. Most of his followers, including Napoleon's father, Carlo Buonaparte, accepted the French king's amnesty. Paoli remained a legend in Corsica, however, and was Napoleon's boyhood hero. In 1789, from London, Paoli voiced approval of the constitutional monarchy established by the Revolution. On the motion of A. Christophe Saliceti, the National Assembly (30 November 1789) invited Paoli to return to Corsica. In March 1790, he appeared before the National Assembly; the marquis de Lafayette presented him to the king. Corsica welcomed him as a hero. Although Paoli was sixty-five and ill, Louis XVI made him royal governor of Corsica, and the Corsicans made him head of the department and the National Guard. When the Republic was established and the king executed, his loyalty came in doubt. It was challenged in Corsica by Napoleon (lieutenant colonel of the National Guard) and Lucien Bonaparte, Jacobins and Francophiles. Paoli in 1793 declared Corsica independent and secured British protection. The Bonapartes were forced to flee to France. In 1795 Paoli, now seventy, turned Corsica over to an English viceroy and returned to London, where he died on 5 February 1807.

M. Bartoli, *Histoire de Pascal Paoli* (Bastia, 1891); J. Boswell, *An Account of Corsica, the Journal of a Tour in That Island and Memoirs of Pascal Paoli* (London, 1768); L. Cristiani, *Pascal Paoli* (Ajaccio, 1954).

Leonard Macaluso

Related entries: BONAPARTE; BONAPARTE, LUCIEN; NAPOLEON I.

PAPACY. See PIUS VI; PIUS VII.

PARADISI, GIOVANNI. See ITALY, KINGDOM OF; ITALY, KINGDOM OF: MINISTERS.

PARIS. As capital of the Grand Empire, Paris was transformed demographically, architecturally, and administratively. Its population, which had diminished during the Revolution, rose to 546,856 inhabitants in 1801, 580,609 in 1807 (a reliable figure), 622,636 in 1811, and 713,966 in 1817, an increase of almost 170,000 people.

Paris, like the west of France, was gently treated as to military conscription (only one Parisian per hundred died in battle under Napoleon). At the same time, in a city with a perpetually unhealthy environment, the mortality rate remained high (suicide was common). To sum up the period 1801–5, there were 111,926 deaths and 106,219 births. Deaths exceeded births by 5,707. For the period

1806–14, there were 181,071 deaths and 176,501 births. Deaths exceeded births by 4,570.

The increase in population is explained by immigration: businessmen, bureaucrats, workers. Paris appealed to many seasonal workers (such as masons and stonecutters), of whom many established themselves permanently in the capital. Thus the population was renewed.

If the city changed little, it was enhanced by new monuments that Napoleon expected to inscribe upon the landscape the memory of his victories: the Vendôme column, topped by a statue of the emperor by Antoine-Denis Chaudet, was dedicated on 15 August 1810, the Arc de Triomphe du Carrousel was finished in 1808; as to that of l'Etoile, begun in 1806, it was completed only under the July Monarchy. New bridges were constructed, bearing the names of victories: Austerlitz, Jena. The same applied to the quais along the Seine. New streets were cut in, like the route to the arcades, baptized the rue de Rivoli.

But it is in the administration that the most important changes can be observed. Paris lost its autonomy. The city had no municipal council; the council of the department assumed its functions. It had no single mayor but twelve mayors, one per district, all without real power and named by the national government. Authority was held by two prefects, also named by the government and jealous of each other. The prefect of the Seine was charged with general municipal administration, the prefect of Police with the problems of security and provisioning.

Henceforth Paris, seat of the French government, was solely in that government's hands. Neither in 1814, nor in 1815, did Paris play a political role comparable to that it had held between 1789 and 1795. The city disappeared from the political scene until 1830.

M.-L. Biver, *Le Paris de Napoléon* (Paris, 1963); L. de Laborie, *Paris sous Napoléon*, 8 vols. (Paris, 1905-11); J. Tulard, *Nouvelle histoire de Paris: Le Consulat et l'Empire* (Paris, 1970).

Jean Tulard

Related entries: ARCHITECTURE; ADMINISTRATION; NAPOLEON I; POPULATION.

PARIS, BATTLE OF (30 March 1814), culminating action of the Campaign of France. The resulting surrender of the city, coupled with the war weariness of many Frenchmen, accelerated the rebellion of Napoleon's marshals and the emperor's abdication. After his check at Arcis-sur-Aube on 20–21 March, Napoleon determined to assemble all available forces and attack Allied communications leading back toward the Rhine. This, he reasoned, would force the Allies to pull back. This was possibly a viable strategy, provided Paris held out. But on 22 March Cossacks had captured French couriers whose dispatches revealed Napoleon's plans and also indicated that opinion in Paris increasingly was defeatist. The Allies decided to ignore the threat to their communications and move on Paris. In the process, they encountered Louis Marmont's and Joseph Mortier's corps at La Fère Champenoise (25 March) and drove them westward, with heavy loss. Early on 30 March the two marshals disposed their remaining forces on the heights north of Paris. The initial line ran from the Seine near St. Ouen to Vincennes, with Mortier on the left and Marmont on the right. Between them they had something over 20,000 men. King Joseph Bonaparte, Napoleon's lieutenant, had sent the empress, the king of Rome (Napoleon's son, age three), the treasure, and the archives toward Tours the day before. He remained on the hill of Montmartre in overall command. The Allies, with forces five or six times more numerous than the defenders, attacked successfully all day. King Joseph left about noon after authorizing the two marshals to sign a capitulation if they found it necessary. Toward the close of the day, Marmont asked for an armistice: the city to be given up the next day and the French troops to be free to move toward Fontainebleau. Such an agreement was signed during the night, and on 31 March the Allies entered the city. The Campaign of France was over. Napoleon, who had been rushing his army to the rescue, was dissatisfied with the resistance offered by Marmont and Mortier. But considering the odds, it seems to have been a respectable fight, surely more creditable than the defense of Vienna in 1805 or the defense of Berlin in 1806.

George Winton

Related entries: ABDICATION, FIRST; BONAPARTE, JOSEPH; FRANCE, CAMPAIGN OF; MARMONT; MORTIER.

PARIS, FIRST TREATY OF (30 May 1814). To strengthen the restored Bourbon king, the Allies agreed to give France the borders of 1792. These included territory that had not been French in 1789: Avignon and the Comtat Venaissin and parts of the Rhineland, Belgium, and Savoy. Britain returned all French colonies except Tobago, Saint Lucia, and Mauritius. The parties agreed to the Congress of Vienna for a general European settlement.

Related entry: VIENNA, CONGRESS OF.

PARIS, SECOND PEACE OF (20 November 1815). Made following the Hundred Days and second restoration of Louis XVIII, it was more severe than the first peace (1814). France was reduced to the boundaries of 1790, which meant those of 1789 plus only the papal territories of Venaissin and Avignon. France was to support, for five years, Allied troops that garrisoned seventeen fortresses on the north and east frontiers and pay reparations of 700 million francs.

Related entries: HUNDRED DAYS, THE; VIENNA, CONGRESS OF.

PARMENTIER, ANTOINE-AUGUSTIN (1737–1813), pharmacist, chemist, and nutritionist. A Paris pharmacist, he was attached to the French army during the Seven Years War and in 1774 was made pharmacist at the Invalides. Parmentier used his chemical knowledge to demonstrate the nutrient value of the potato and increased its consumption by the French by his propaganda. During the Revolution and under the Consulate, he improved the salt provisions and hard tack of the French navy and the bread of the army. As member from 1801 of the Council of Hospitals of Paris, he drafted a pharmacopoeia for their use and made their cheap soup more palatable. When under the Empire the British blockade reduced the sugar supply, he proclaimed the advantages of a syrup derived from grapes. Always outgoing, ingenious, and dedicated to the service of humanity, rising at three o'clock each morning to start his beneficent daily round, Parmentier was something of a lay saint.

Harold T. Parker

PARTHENOPEAN REPUBLIC. See SISTER REPUBLICS.

PAUL I (1754–1801) Czar of Russia, son of Peter III of Russia (1761–62) and Catherine of Anhalt-Zerbst, who became Catherine II (the Great) of Russia (1762–96). Catherine played a role in the assassination of Peter. Paul was given a substantial, progressive education under Nikita Ivanovich Panin (1718–83), who was *oberhofmeister* of the grand prince's household and Catherine's principal adviser in foreign affairs until about 1780. Panin favored a quasi-constitutional government, which Catherine refused, and Paul became the hope of the Panin reform party at court. Consequently, Catherine isolated Paul from affairs of state and quite possibly was, at the time of her death, taking steps to exclude him from succeeding to the throne.

At his accession, Paul openly rejected most of his mother's policies. He ignored the emancipation of the Russian nobility (1762, confirmed 1785) from state service requirements. In foreign affairs, he proclaimed that his reign, unlike his mother's, would be one of peace, but he reckoned without the French Revolution. In the Second Coalition (1798) he worked primarily for balance in the European state system. He forsook the coalition at the end of 1799 because he was convinced that his Austrian ally was as dangerous to the traditional order in Italy and Germany as was France. He had also adopted the neutrals' view of English hegemony on the seas. His flirting with Bonaparte in the spring of 1801 influenced the Austrians to sacrifice too much at Lunéville (9 February 1801), and his League of Armed Neutrality (December 1800) threatened to cut off Great Britain from essential supplies of naval stores and grain in the Baltic. The Battle of Copenhagen (2 April 1801) broke the blockade, but Britain, dispirited, was soon engaged in negotiations that led to Amiens. Paul's simultaneous negotiations with Bonaparte were not productive, though his untimely death obscured the matter.

Paul was assassinated for reasons still not thoroughly understood. Surely his fastidious despotism weighed very heavily on the Russian nobility. To them, he seemed to have reversed previous policy and, abandoning good sense, to have embraced the cause of Bonaparte. The conspirators said he was mad, citing his behavior during his last months (the sudden expulsion of friendly diplomats, talk of settling the wars of Europe by a personal duel among sovereigns and prime ministers). Perhaps he was more rational than he seemed, however—or than they wanted the public to believe.

M. V. Klochkov, *Ocherki pravitel'stvennoi deiatel'nosti vremeni Pavla I*[go] (Petrograd, 1916); H. Ragsdale, *Détente in the Napoleonic Era* (Lawrence, Kansas, 1980); H. Ragsdale, ed., *Paul I: A Reassessment of His Life and Reign* (Pittsburgh, 1979); N. E. Saul, *Russia and the Mediterranean, 1797–1807* (Chicago, 1970); N. K. Schilder, *Imperator Pavel I* (St. Petersburg, 1901); E. S. Shumigorskii, *Imperator Pavel I* (St. Petersburg, 1907); A. M. Stanislavskaia, *Russko-angliiskie otnosheniia i problemy Sredizemnomor'ia, 1798-1807* (Moscow, 1962).

Hugh Ragsdale

Related entries: ALEXANDER I; DIPLOMACY; FOREIGN POLICY; RUSSIA, KINGDOM OF.

PEASANTS. See SOCIETY.

PELET, JEAN-JACQUES (1777–1858), general, baron of the empire. Born and educated in Toulouse, he enlisted in the army in 1799. Because of his technical education, he was assigned to the topographic section of the Army of Italy where he served until 1805, when he joined Marshal André Masséna's staff. He saw action in Italy (1805), Naples (1806), and Poland (1807) under Masséna, and he played a vital role in the French victory at Wagram by capturing the Isle de Moulin (2 July 1809). In 1810 he became Masséna's first aide-de-camp and chief tactician during the invasion of Portugal. Returning to France in 1811, he was assigned to the army staff during the invasion of Russia, but he was soon transferred to Marshal Louis Davout's corps. Following his efforts in the Battle of Smolensk and Borodino, Pelet was given command of the 48th Regiment, which he commanded in the retreat from Russia. Cut off and under attack by a Russian army at Smolensk, he joined Marshal Michel Ney and planned the escape of the rear guard at Shirokorenyay. Pelet served with distinction in the Saxon campaign (1813) and survived the major battles of the 1814 campaign in France. He commanded the Young Guard at Waterloo, so the Bourbons held him suspect.

Pelet turned to intellectual pursuits and published a four-volume memoir concerning the 1809 campaign. In 1830 Pelet was appointed director of the Depôt de la guerre and director of the Ecole d'Etat-major, where he worked until his retirement. Pelet proved to be a highly competent line and staff officer, a dedicated scholar, and an effective diplomat during his public career, and he was one of the founders of France's military archives.

D. D. Horward, ed. and trans., *The French Campaign in Portugal, 1810-1811: An Account by Jean Jacques Pelet* (Minneapolis, 1973), and "En campagne avec le général Pelet de Portugal à Russie," *Bulletin de la Société Littéraire et Historique de la Brie* 39 (1983); J. J. Pelet, *Mémoires sur la guerre de 1809*, 4 vols. (Paris, 1824–26).

Donald D. Horward

Related entries: ARMY, FRENCH; MASSENA; PORTUGUESE CAMPAIGNS; RUSSIAN CAMPAIGN; WATERLOO CAMPAIGN.

PENINSULAR WAR (1807–13), war in the Iberian Peninsula provoked by French invasion ordered by Napoleon; referred to by the Spanish as the War of Independence (Guerra de la Independencia) and by the French as the War of Spain (Guerre d'Espagne). It was a war that the French never won and which sapped their resources and morale. At St. Helena, Napoleon said, "It was that miserable Spanish affair. . .which killed me."

After the Treaties of Tilsit (1807), which settled affairs in northern Europe, Napoleon turned his attention to Iberia. Portugal was violating the Continental System and was a de facto ally of Britain; Napoleon meant to conquer it. Spain was allied to France, but Napoleon felt the Spanish Bourbons had served him very poorly and had determined to put Joseph, his elder brother, on the throne. His plans were facilitated by the Treaty of Fontainebleau (21 October 1807), negotiated for Spain by the treacherous Manuel Godoy. Jean-Andoche Junot in November 1807 led an army across Spain into Portugal almost unopposed. The British navy took the Portuguese royal family to Brazil. Napoleon next sent troops into Spain, ultimately commanded by Marshal Joachim Murat, who, as an ally of the Spanish king, marched, with scant resistance, to Madrid.

Napoleon meanwhile ordered a Spanish national Junta to meet at Bayonne to approve a constitution for Spain. Shortly before, the Spanish crown prince had overthrown his father, Charles IV, and declared himself Ferdinand VII of Spain. Both kings appealed to Napoleon for help, and he responded by calling both kings and all possible heirs to the throne to Bayonne for talks. The departure of the kings was followed by an uprising in Madrid, which was viciously suppressed by Murat on 2 May (Dos de Mayo). On 10 May 1808 the Bourbon kings abdicated. Napoleon had already called his brother Joseph, king of Naples, to Bayonne. The Junta of Bayonne declared him king under the new constitution.

Joseph was crowned at Burgos on 7 July and proceeded to Madrid as king of Spain and commander of French armies. On his arrival (20 July) he was faced with a crisis. The advance corps of his army were out of contact with him. Marshal B.-A. Jeannot de Moncey's corps soon appeared, having marched post-haste from Valencia to escape the threat of rebel armies. Then came the news that Pierre Dupont's corps had been captured at Baylen (19 July). Joseph ordered a retreat that did not end until he had crossed the Ebro. Meanwhile, in Portugal, a British army under Sir Arthur Wellesley (later the duke of Wellington) had landed and defeated Junot at Vimiero. By the Capitulation of Cintra, the French army was evacuated to France by the British navy.

Napoleon determined to go to Spain and settle the matter himself. He raced to Erfurt (October 1808) where Czar Alexander I promised neutrality. He then marched units of the Grand Armée to Spain. By November 1808 Napoleon had 300,000 men poised behind the Ebro. He arrived on 6 November at Vitoria and, detaching armies to his east and west, marched on Madrid. On 30 November he was impeded briefly by a force under Benito San Juan at the pass of Somo Sierra in the Guadarrama Mountains, but a charge of the Polish cavalry of the Imperial Guard cleared the way to Madrid. Napoleon began reorganizing the country for Joseph, using sometimes brutal methods to restore order. Only Saragossa, which stood under French siege until February 1809, bolstered Spanish pride. The commander, José Palafox, became a hero celebrated to this day.

Just before Christmas, however, Napoleon heard that Sir John Moore with a British army of only 30,000 had blundered into his rear echelons. He hastily restored Joseph to the throne and marched northward to crush "les Anglais," crossing the Guadarramas in a blizzard. Moore, however, made for Coruña, and Napoleon had news from Paris that Austria was mobilizing. On 16 January 1809, Napoleon made Joseph commander of the French army in Spain and departed for Paris. Marshal Nicolas Soult pursued Moore to Coruña, where the British and French fought to a draw that enabled Moore's force to escape on British battleships, though Moore was killed. Soult moved into Portugal, only to be surprised by Wellington at Oporto and driven out.

Wellington moved south, linked up with a Spanish army under Cuesta and marched on Madrid. Joseph and Marshal Jourdan, his chief of staff, conceived a plan that might have trapped the future British hero, but it was poorly executed; Napoleon's marshals had no respect for the king as a commander. The upshot was that Joseph met Wellington at Talavera (27–29 July 1809) and fought an indecisive battle that could have been a victory except that the corps of Soult, Mortier, and Michel Ney did not arrive. As it was, Wellington marched away to establish a base at Lisbon behind the lines of Torres Vedras. The French could never dislodge him, and he eventually emerged to take control of Portugal and attack the French in Spain.

In 1810, however, Joseph, with Soult, his chief of staff, marched south and conquered Andalusia, except for Cadiz, where the Spanish rebel government took refuge, protected by the British navy. Meanwhile Marshal Suchet conquered Aragon and Valencia so that, in effect, all of Spain was French by 1811. Napoleon, however, was dissatisfied with Joseph and relieved him of command of French forces except in the Madrid area. He remained king, but Napoleon's marshals ruled various parts of Spain. For many months, they were opposed by guerrilla bands operating out of the mountains. Napoleon meanwhile had conquered Austria at Wagram (1809), divorced Josephine, and married Marie-Louise of Austria (March 1810).

The French emperor knew that the main threat in the peninsula was from Wellington at Lisbon, with—as Napoleon put it—"30,000 miserable English." He dispatched Marshal Masséna with a seemingly overwhelming force of 60,000 men to eradicate Wellington. In September 1810, Masséna scored a victory at Bussaco and drove Wellington behind the lines of Torres Vedras. The French army, suffering from lack of food and supplies, battered in vain at the fortifications from October 1810 until March 1811. Masséna was then forced to retreat into Spain. In May 1811 Napoleon replaced him with Marshal Marmont. Marmont, however, found himself unable to push into Portugal. In January 1812 Wellington took Ciudad Rodrigo and in April Badajoz; he was poised to drive into Spain.

Meanwhile, Napoleon, departing for Russia (March 1812), again made Joseph commander of French forces in Spain. He did not consider Joseph a soldier but felt he could trust him and that the Russian campaign would be short. Joseph, who was not bereft of military talent, had seen his military reputation totally sullied by Napoleon himself, however, and was even less able to command than in 1809. His appointment was a mistake.

As Napoleon marched into Russia, Wellington invaded Spain and attacked Marmont. The marshal called on Joseph, at Madrid, for help, but the king responded too slowly, and Marmont was defeated at Salamanca on 22 July 1812. Wellington marched on to Madrid, and Joseph, his army encumbered by the members of his court and their families, fled to Valencia. Marshal Soult was forced to evacuate Andalusia. At Valencia Joseph and Soult combined forces and in November retook Madrid, but Wellington, untroubled, went into winter quarters at Ciudad Rodrigo.

Napoleon, on his return from Russia, devoted himself primarily to organizing a new army to fight in Germany (1813). He left 250,000 troops in Spain, however, and ordered Joseph to move north, establish headquarters at Valladolid, and place his armies between Wellington and the French border. Joseph moved with great reluctance because abandoning Madrid meant sacrificing his Spanish followers to the guerrillas. He did not evacuate Madrid until mid-March, and in June his army was scattered between Valladolid and Bayonne. Wellington, meanwhile, had been made generalissimo of Allied Forces in the Peninsula, a title that earlier the Spanish had been too proud to concede.

On 4 June Wellington appeared northwest of Valladolid with 95,000 British, Portuguese, and Spanish troops, accompanied by hordes of guerrillas. He had outflanked Joseph's positions on the Duero River and threatened his communications with France. Joseph ordered his armies to concentrate on Badajoz, and then at Vitoria, where he managed to assemble 70,000 troops. But Joseph and Marshal Jourdan did a poor job of deploying the troops for battle. They were attacked by Wellington on 21 June 1813, and the army was shattered.

Wellington's victory at Vitoria signaled the death of the Bonaparte kingdom of Spain. Napoleon dispatched Marshal Soult to take command of Joseph's army and ordered the king to retire to France. Soult fought a delaying action in the western Pyrenees but steadily lost ground. Suchet was forced to evacuate eastern Spain. In October 1813 Wellington invaded southern France.

Thus ended the Peninsular War. It had cost France perhaps 300,000 casualties, 3 billion francs in gold, and untold sums in material. The great hero of the conflict was the duke of Wellington, who had arrived in Portugal as a mere knight and had been elevated in the nobility with every victory from baron to viscount to duke. For Spain, the immediate result (once Napoleon abdicated in April 1814) was the restoration of Ferdinand VII as king of Spain. The rejoicing of the Spanish was short-lived. Ferdinand proved one of the most vicious tyrants Spain had seen since medieval times. He began by dispersing the Cortes of

Cadiz, renouncing the constitution of 1812, and persecuting the liberals who had supported him throughout the conflict with the French.

J. Gomez de Arteche y Moro, *Guerra de la Independencia*, 14 vols. (New York, 1978); M. Artola, *Los origines de la España Contemporanea*, 2 vols. (Madrid, 1959); J. R. Aymes, *Guerre d'Independance Espagnole (1808-1814)* (Paris, 1973); R. Glover, *Peninsular preparation: the Reform of the British Army, 1795-1809* (London, 1963); H. Lachouque, *Napoleon's War in Spain, 1807-1814* (London, 1982); Sir C. W. C. Oman, *A History of the Peninsular War*, 7 vols. (London, 1902-1930); J. Tranie and J. C. Carmigniani, *Napoleon's War in Spain* (London, 1980).

Related entries: BAYLEN, BATTLE OF; BUSSACO, BATTLE OF; DUPONT DE L'ETANG; GUERRILLAS; JOURDAN; JUNOT, J.-A.; MARMONT; MASSENA; MONCEY; MORTIER; NEY; PORTUGUESE CAMPAIGNS; SOULT; SUCHET; TORRES VEDRAS, LINES OF; VITORIA, BATTLE OF; WELLINGTON.

PERCIER, CHARLES (1764–1838), architect, designer, engraver, and professor of architecture. Percier was born in Paris, the son of the bridge tender at the Tuileries drawbridge. He studied with the painter J.-L.-F. Lagrenée and Antoine François Peyre, in whose studio he first met Pierre François Fontaine, with whom he collaborated as a team from 1794 to 1814. He left Peyre the Younger's studio to design for J.-F. Chalgrin and Pierre Paris and, finally, for Alexandre Guy de Gisors. Before the Revolution he obtained a second grand prize (1783) and the First Grand Prize of Rome in architecture (1786), the latter for building plans to house the combined academies. After the Revolution, he went to Rome on a government scholarship and again met Fontaine. He sent a study of Trajan's column back to Paris for publication. After returning home, Percier earned his living by designing furniture and decorations in the new antique style.

In 1794 the team of Percier and Fontaine was hired as set decorators at the Paris Opera, replacing Pierre Paris. Percier also assisted his other teacher, Guy de Gisors, in the work for locating the National Convention in the Tuileries.

Jacques-Louis David presented Percier and Fontaine to Josephine de Beauharnais, who influenced her husband, General Bonaparte, to use them first as architects for the renovation of Malmaison, which was supervised by Jean-Baptiste Isabey. From there they went on to direct projects at the Louvre and the Tuileries between 1802 and 1812, the Arc de Triomphe du Carrousel, the fountain of Desaix, place Dauphine, the Expiatory Chapel, expansions at the chateaux of Saint-Cloud, Versailles, Compiègne, Fontainebleau, the Elysée Palace, and imperial residences in far-flung cities of the Empire, notably Venice, Rome, Brussels, Mainz, Antwerp, and Strasbourg. As recompense Napoleon named them to the Legion of Honor and Institut de France.

In addition to Percier's architectural work during the Napoleonic era, some of his smaller designs are extant. One example is a pair of gondola-style arm chairs executed by the *ébenist* Georges Jacob, which have back pieces terminating in gracefully carved swans and are upholstered in white *gros de tours* patterned with golden stars and a central medallion enclosing two addorsed swans. Ordered by Josephine for the chateau of Saint-Cloud, she had them moved to Malmaison, where they now are.

From 1814 to his death in 1838, Percier devoted himself primarily to teaching architecture. The essential basis for the school of Percier was ability in the art of design and love and respect for antiquity. During the July Monarchy, Percier became architect of the king along with his former associate Fontaine; however, he publicly opposed the erection of works of fortification in the Tuileries garden, although it was his duty to direct their construction.

Although it is difficult to distinguish between the contributions of two men who worked so closely over such a long period, it is indisputable that Fontaine and Percier provided the unity of inspiration for the Empire style by going beyond merely designing the shell of public buildings and residences to complete the interior decoration with designs for furniture, carpets, silverware, fabric, china, and wallpaper. Without these two single figures, there would have been no Empire style. Students recognized this and came from France and abroad to study informally in Percier's workshop—among others Jean-Jacques Huve, Louis Visconti, Achilles Leclerc, Martin-Pierre Gauthier, Auguste-Nicolas Caristie and Hyppolyte Lebas. Those who could not come in person to study learned about the Empire style from their published pattern books, a continuing tradition.

E. Bénézit, *Dictionnaire des peintres, sculpteurs, dessinateurs et graveurs* (Paris, 1966); E. Driault, *Napoléon architecte* (Paris, 1939); M. Fouché, *Percier et Fontaine* (Paris, 1907); A. Gonzales-Palacios, *The Empire Style* (New York, 1970); J.-F. Vacquier et P. Marmottan, *Le Style Empire* (Paris, 1914-1930).

June K. Burton

Related entries: ARCHITECTURE; ART; DENON; FONTAINE; LOUVRE.

PERIER. Among the new French families coming to the fore during the Revolution, Napoleonic Empire, and Restoration, the Perier family was especially notable for its rapid rise in commerce, banking, and diverse industrial enterprises. Claude Perier (1742–1801), the founder of the family fortune, began in the linen trade and merchant-banking in Dauphiné before the Revolution. He invested 1,024,000 francs in 1780 to purchase the chateau of Vizille, near Grenoble, which he converted for the manufacture of printed cottons. In 1794–95, Claude associated with financiers and political leaders in Paris to become an owner and director of the largest coal mining firm in northern France, the Anzin Company. He joined these same *manieurs d'argent* in 1796 to organize the Caisse des Comptes Courants, a discount bank. He was one of the early supporters of the coup d'état of 18 Brumaire and in 1799–1800 one of the founders and first regents of the Bank of France.

Claude Perier's enormous legacy of 5.8 million francs was shared by his eight sons and two daughters. His two best-known sons, Scipion (1776–1821) and Casimir (1777–1832), founded a bank in Paris in 1801 and became leading directors of the Anzin Company. The eldest son, Augustin (1773–1833), associated with his younger brother, Alphonse (1782–1866), to manage and expand the family operations at Grenoble and Vizille. A fifth son, Alexander (1774–1846), went into cotton spinning at Anilly, near Montargis, where his father had acquired properties in 1790. Camille Perier (1781–1844) and the two youngest brothers, Amédée (1785–1851) and Joseph (1786–1868), became auditors in the Council of State in Paris and entered prefectoral careers. The two Perier daughters, Josephine (1770–1850) and Hélène (1779–1851), married into the Napoleonic high administration. The Perier bourgeois dynasty of the Empire endured and expanded into politics after 1815. Casimir Perier was premier and minister of interior of France in 1831–32.

R. J. Barker, "Casimir Perier (1777–1832) and William Ternaux (1763–1833): Two French Capitalists" (Ph.D. dissertation, Duke University, 1958); P. Barral, *Les Perier dans l'Isère au XIXe siècle, d'après leur correspondance familiale* (Paris, 1964); E. Choulet, *La famille Casimir Perier* (Grenoble, 1894); F. Vermale, *Le père de Casimir Perier, 1743-1801* (Grenoble, 1935).

Richard J. Barker

Related entries: ADMINISTRATION; ECONOMY, FRENCH; NOTABLES.

PERIGNON, DOMINIQUE, MARQUIS DE (1754–1818), marshal of France. Of the nobility, he was an officer in the Royal Army for a few years in the 1780s but retired early. In 1789 he supported the Revolution, took a commission in the National Guard, and was elected to the Legislative Assembly (1791). In 1792, when France desperately needed officers, he returned to active service against Spain. In the Pyrenees fighting, he became a hero, was promoted to major general (1794), and was made commander of the army in Spain (1794–95). After Spain made peace, he returned to civilian life, was elected to the Council of Five Hundred, and served as ambassador to Spain (1795–97).

In 1798 with France again in danger, Pérignon took service in Italy but was wounded and taken prisoner at Novio. By the time he was released, France was dominated by Napoleon, who made him a senator (1802) and one of the original marshals (1804). His title was honorary, however, and he served in largely administrative posts under the Empire between 1806 and 1813 in Naples.

From 1813 Pérignon supported the Bourbon Restoration. Louis XVIII made him a chevalier de Saint-Louis and peer of France in 1814. He did not rally to Napoleon during the Hundred Days.

Jesse Scott

Related entry: MARSHALS OF THE EMPIRE.

PIAVE, BATTLE ON THE (8 May 1809), victory of the French under Eugène de Beauharnais over the Austrians commanded by Archduke John, also referred to as the Battle of Conegliano. The Austrian army crossed over to the east bank of the Piave on 6 May. The pursuing French army under Eugène closed up on the west bank that night. The Austrian forces totaled 30,000; the French forces totaled 48,000. After making a reconnaissance on 7 May, Eugène determined to cross the Piave at two of three fords in the area and then attack and destroy the Austrian army. The battle began at dawn on 8 May. On the right, Paul Grenier's corps, consisting of three cavalry and two infantry divisions, crossed against light resistance at the San Nichiol ford. In the center, a light division under Joseph Dessaix made a crossing at Priula. On the left, Jean Serras' infantry division feinted at the Narvase ford.

Dessaix's crossing was contested, but he was reinforced by cavalry, and at 10:30 A.M., French horsemen charged and routed the opposing cavalry. The Austrians thereafter merely deployed their infantry to seal off the French lodgement. Archduke John planned to hold off the French until nightfall and then withdraw. The French were having troubles of their own. The waters of the Piave rose throughout the day, and by 3:30 P.M. it was impossible to bring over any more troops; however, 30,000 French troops were across, and they would do the job. Grenier, on the right, with two cavalry divisions and one infantry division, attacked the enemy brigade holding the Austrian left. The Austrian center totaling four infantry brigades was attacked by Jacques Macdonald's corps of two and one-quarter infantry divisions. The three Austrian brigades to the east were attacked by Dessaix's infantry division and a light cavalry divison. The Austrian line crumbled under the impact. The French pursued until nightfall. Austrian casualties totaled 7,000; French losses totaled 2,000.

Robert Epstein

Related entries: BEAUHARNAIS, E.; JOHANN VON HABSBURG; MACDONALD; WAGRAM CAMPAIGN; WAGRAM CAMPAIGN, ITALIAN PHASE.

PITT, JOHN. See CHATHAM; WALCHEREN, INVASION OF.

PITT, WILLIAM (1759–1806), prime minister of Great Britain, 1784–1801 and 1804-6; bitter enemy of Napoleon (and the Revolution before him). Second son of William Pitt, first earl of Chatham, he was educated at Pembroke College, Cambridge, and became a member of Parliament in 1781. He began as a firm adherent to his father's politics, favoring independence for the colonies, the abolition of slavery and the slave trade, concessions to Ireland, and religious toleration. Above all he wanted economical reform of government and administration, including the reduction of patronage and thereby the executive power. In short, his origins were Whig. In 1782, at twenty-three, Pitt was appointed chancellor of the Exchequer and in 1783 first lord of the treasury, the youngest man ever to hold either post. As prime minister (1784–89), he concentrated on reform of the government, and after the onset of the French Revolution in 1789, he abandoned advocacy of social and political change. Indeed, after war broke out with France on 1 February 1793, Pitt became a protagonist in an ideological war against French ideas. As "the pilot who weathered the storm," Pitt financed the European coalitions against France and instigated emergency legislation in

England. He pressed for Catholic emancipation in Ireland to discourage the Irish from siding with the French. When the king declined to concede this point, Pitt resigned on 14 March 1801, making possible the Peace of Amiens with Napoleon. He returned to office in 1804, however, and encouraged the Third Coalition against France. Shortly after hearing of Napoleon's victory at Austerlitz, he died (13 January 1806). He was interred with public ceremony in Westminster Abbey.

D. Barnes, *George III and William Pitt, 1783–1806*, Reprint (New York, 1965); J. E. D. Binney, *British Public Finance and Administration 1774–92* (Oxford, 1958); J. Ehrman, *The Younger Pitt* (London, 1969); Pitt MSS, Public Record Office, London.

Leslie Mitchell

Related entries: AMIENS, TREATY OF; DIPLOMACY; ENGLAND, ATTEMPTED CONQUEST OF; FOREIGN POLICY; GREAT BRITAIN.

PIUS VI (1717–99), pope. Gianangelo Braschi, a cultivated Italian aristocrat, was elevated to pope in 1775. His papacy (1775–99) witnessed the anticlerical reforms of Joseph II, the French Revolution, and the advent of Napoleon. Pius VI did not immediately condemn the Revolution of 1789 and the confiscation of church property because he did not want to jeopardize the position of Louis XVI and possibly provoke an even more extreme reaction against the church in France. Furthermore, he recognized the threat (soon carried out) to Avignon and the Comtat Venaissin, papal lands within France.

Not until March 1791, after the Civil Constitution of the Clergy and oath for clerics were harshly enforced, did the pope declare the Revolution anathema. The pontiff's ability to influence events was minimal, but the schism in the clergy—half "patriotic," half refusing the oath to the government—defied solution by successive Revolutionary governments.

Early in 1797 Napoleon invaded papal territory in Italy, and by the Treaty of Tolentino (February 1797), the pope ceded Bologna, Ferrara, and the Romagna to the Cisalpine Republic, sponsored by France. In December 1797, the French General Léonard Duphot, in league with republican patriots in Rome, was assassinated. In reprisal, the French occupied Rome (February 1798), a republic was established, and Pius VI took refuge in a monastery near Florence. When French troops invaded Tuscany, Pius VI was arrested and was moved successively to Bologna, Modena, Turin, Grenoble, and eventually to Valence where, despairing of the future of his church and a prisoner of the French, he died in August 1799.

E. E. Y. Hales, *Revolution and Papacy, 1769–1846* (Notre Dame, Ind., 1960); H. Jedin and J. Dolan, eds., *History of the Church*, vol. VII: *The Church between Revolution and Restoration* (New York, 1981). P. de LaGorce, *Histoire religieuse de la Révolution française*, 4 vols. (Paris, 1912–23); A. Latreille, *L'église catholique et la Révolution française*, vol.1: *Le Pontificat de Pie VI et la Crise française (1775–1799)* (Paris, 1946); C. Ledré, *L'église de France sous la Révolution* (Paris, 1949); J. Leflon, *La crise révolutionnaire, 1789–1846*, vol. 20 of A. Flîche and V. Martin, *Histoire de l'église depuis les origines jusqu' à nos jours* (Paris, 1949); J. McManners, *The French Revolution and the Church* (London, 1969).

Thomas F. Sheppard

Related entries: CISALPINE REPUBLIC; CHURCH, ROMAN CATHOLIC; ITALIAN CAMPAIGN, FIRST; TOLENTINO, BATTLE OF.

PIUS VII (1740–1823), pope. On being named pope in 1800, Pius VII (Barnaba Chiaramonti) was faced with all the problems that had troubled Pius VI. In June 1800, Napoleon, fresh from his victory at Marengo, opened negotiations with the papacy. Napoleon had domestic political reasons for seeking an accommodation: the schism in the French clergy and the clerical-royalist revolt in the Vendée. Peace with the Vatican could solve both. The pope wanted to resume firm possession of the Papal States, as well as improve his influence in France. Negotiations were concluded in 1801 and announced in France on Easter Day, 1802. Simultaneously the government made public the Organic Articles, which made church activities subject to police regulation (giving the false impression that they were part of the concordat). This and the coronation of Napoleon as the new Charlemagne (December 1804) set an uneasy tone for relations between Napoleon and Pius. While in Paris for the coronation, Pius VII remarried Napoleon and Josephine, (joined in 1796 only in a civil ceremony) but was not allowed to crown Napoleon. French-Vatican relations began to deteriorate in 1805; French troops occupied Rome in 1808 and in 1809 the Papal States, which were divided between France and the Kingdom of Italy. Pius VII excommunicated Napoleon (1809); the emperor, in turn, had Pius VII imprisoned at Savona (in palatial style) until 1812 and then at Fontainebleau. As Napoleon's fortunes crumbled, he sought a new concordat with the pope, but Pius VII refused. Pius was finally released in 1814 and returned to a triumphal welcome in Rome in May 1814 within days of Napoleon's arrival at Elba. Napoleon's cynical treatment of Pius VII and the pontiff's humiliation while in exile undoubtedly helped to raise the pope's standing with vast numbers of French Catholics. Elder statesman of the church as well as a martyr at the hands of Napoleon, Pius VII saw the church in France return to a position of respect and dignity—if not privilege—under the Bourbon Restoration.

E. E. Y. Hales, *The Emperor and the Pope* (Garden City, N.Y., 1961); H. Jedin and J. Dolan, eds., *History of the Church*, Vol. VII: *The Church between Revolution and Restoration* (New York, 1981). J. Leflon, *La crise révolutionnaire, 1789–1846*; vol. 20 of A. Fliche and V. Martin, *Histoire de l'église depuis les origines jusqu' à nos jours* (Paris, 1949); A. Latreille, *L'église catholique et la Révolution française*, vol. 2: *L'ère Napoléonienne et la crise Européenne (1800–1815)* (Paris, 1950); C. S. Phillips, *The Church in France, 1789–1848: A Study in Revival* (New York, 1966).

Thomas F. Sheppard

Related entries: CHURCH, ROMAN CATHOLIC; CONCORDAT OF 1801; ITALIAN CAMPAIGN, SECOND; NAPOLEON I.

POLAND. See WARSAW, DUCHY OF.

POLICE, MINISTRY OF GENERAL, Europe's first modern political police. Established by the Directory on 2 January 1796, the Ministry of General Police was not effective until the summer of 1799, when Joseph Fouché became minister. There had been a rapid turnover of ministers, and no consistent policy had been developed.

Fouché changed all this, although Napoleon abolished his ministry in 1802 and did not restore him for twenty-one months. The Law of 10 July 1804, however, gave the Ministry of General Police definitive organization. It established four regional counselors of state for police affairs and gave some authority to the police minister over departmental prefects. Through the six offices of the ministry (*sureté*, secretariat, censorship, prisons, food supplies and prices, and finances), and a superior system (for the time) of obtaining, storing, and retrieving information, Fouché could make his will felt throughout the Empire. Yet for all of this, and certainly in contrast to the political police of modern dictatorships, neither Fouché nor the men subject to his authority were cruel, vicious, or even excessively arbitrary. All of this changed under the direction of Fouché's more heavy-handed successor, General Anne-Jean Savary, who became minister on 31 May 1810.

Since he considered Savary totally trustworthy, Napoleon no longer applied certain safeguards erected to limit the power of Fouché. For example, Napoleon had given virtual independence to the national gendarmerie under Marshal Adrien de Moncey. Similarly, Louis Dubois, prefect of police for Paris, had been charged to spy on Fouché and report directly to the emperor. Savary probably used his authority more brutally than Fouché would have, though he was more loyal. For all this, the Ministry of General Police, which was abolished in 1816, played a vital part in maintaining Napoleon's authority and security in France.

E. A. Arnold, Jr., *Fouché, Napoleon, and the General Police* (Washington, D.C., 1979); A. Aulard, ed., *Paris sous le Consulat: Recueil des documents pour l'histoire de l'ésprit public à Paris*, 4 vols. (Paris, 1903–09), and *Paris sous le premier Empire: Recueil des documents pour l'histoire de l'ésprit public à Paris*, 3 vols. (Paris, 1912–14); E. d'Hauterive, *Napoléon et sa police* (Paris, 1943); L. Madelin, "La Police genérale de l'Empire," *Revue des deux Mondes* 60 (1940); Napoleon I, *Correspondance de Napoléon I*[er], 32 vols. (Paris, 1859–69).

Eric A. Arnold, Jr.

Related entries: FOUCHE; LAW, CODES OF; MINISTERS OF NAPOLEON; MONCEY; SAVARY.

POLISH LEGIONS, of the Army of the French Republic. The first was created in 1797 in Milan by General Jan Dąbrowski, a refugee of the Polish revolution of 1794, and a second in 1798. The legions were divided into half-brigades (regiments) of about 3,700 men each. They served the republic in Italy—the Cisalpine Republic, Rome, and against the Austrians in 1799–1800. Napoleon sent two half-brigades to Haiti, where all but a few hundred died of fever or in battle.

In 1801, the remaining units were integrated into the French army. Reinforced by recruits from Poland (after 1807 the Duchy of Warsaw), the Poles served Napoleon in every campaign. Those of the Imperial Guard especially distinguished themselves. The men of the legions kept alive the spirit of Polish national independence. The hymn of the Polish Legions, the *Mazurek Dąbrowski*, later became the Polish national anthem

S. Askenazy, *Napoleon a Polska*, 3 vols. (Warsaw, 1918–19); L. Chodźko, *Histoire des légions polonaises en Italie*, 2 vols. (Paris, 1829); W. Kozłowski, "Kościuszko et les légions polonaises en France (1798–1801)," *RHq* 119, 120 (1915); M. Kukiel, *Dzieje oręża polskiego w epoce napoleońskiej 1795-1815* (Poznan, 1912); J. Pachoński, *Legiony Polskie, Prawda i legenda 1794-1807* (Warsaw, 1969–79); A. Skałkowski, *Polacy w San Domingo 1802-1809* (Poznan, 1921), and *Les Polonais en Egypte 1798–1801* (Cracow, 1910).

John Stanley

Related entries: ARMY, FRENCH; PONIATOWSKI; WARSAW, DUCHY OF.

PONIATOWSKI, JOZEF, PRINCE (1763–1813), minister of war and general in the Army of the Duchy of Warsaw; marshal of France. Poniatowski did his first military service in the Austrian army. He was then commissioned a major general in the Polish army by his uncle, King Stanislas Augustus of Poland. However, the king was unable to prevent the partition of Poland among Russia, Austria, and Prussia (completed in 1795). Meanwhile, Józef Poniatowski had sided with Kósciuszko in the national rising (1794), which was crushed by Russia, and fled the country. He was soon allowed to return, however, and lived in Warsaw at his palace. After the destruction of the Prussian armies by Napoleon at Jena and Auerstädt, Poniatowski took charge of Warsaw until the French entered, when he was named to the governing commission of Poland. He also headed one of three Polish divisions that joined the French during the campaign of 1806–07. After Tilsit (1807), he was made minister of war in the Duchy of Warsaw. Poniatowski perpetuated in the Polish army the traditions of the Polish Legions in French service, maintaining French-style military regulations, and attempting to create a truly national army in the French mode.

During Napoleon's Austrian campaign of 1809, Poniatowski commanded the Polish army against twice his number of Austrians (Battle of Raszyn). He lost and was forced by the Austrians to abandon Warsaw but made the brilliant decision to invade Galicia. This cut Austrian lines of communication, forced them to evacuate Warsaw, and liberated Galicia, ceded to the duchy after Wagram (1809).

In the Russian campaign of 1812, Poniatowski headed the Fifth Corps with Josef Zajączek, Jan Dąbrowski, and other celebrated Polish generals under his command. After the disastrous retreat from Moscow, Poniatowski returned to

Warsaw and created another army of 13,000. But assailed by Russian armies and abandoned by the Austrians (Napoleon's reluctant allies), he was forced to leave Poland. Encouraged by Louis Bignon, the French ambassador, however, Poniatowski rejoined French forces in Saxony. On 16 October 1813, the first day of the Battle of Leipzig, Poniatowski was made a marshal of France by Napoleon, the only foreigner ever so honored. On 18 October, the last day of the battle, with half of his army dead or seriously wounded, Poniatowski covered Napoleon's withdrawal with suicidal bravery. Then the marshal, already twice wounded, attempted to cross the Elster River on his horse. Shot while crossing, Poniatowski fell into the water and died. In 1816 his remains were returned to Poland and interred with full honors at the cathedral on the Wawel in Cracow, next to Jan Sobieski and Tadeusz Kościuszko.

S. Askenazy, *Książę Józef Poniatowski 1763–1813* (Warsaw, 1922); Z. Denter, *Ksiąze Józef Poniatowski a sprawa polska na przełomie VXIII i XIX w.* (Warsaw, 1928); J. Poniatowski, *Korespondencya księcia...z Francyą*, 5 vols. (Poznan, 1921–29); *Rys historyczny kampanii odbytej w roku 1809...* (Warsaw, 1869); A. Skałkowski, *Ksiąze Józef* (Bytom, 1913); R. Sołtyk, *Relation des operations de l'armée aux ordres du prince Joseph Poniatowski* (Paris, 1841).

John Stanley

Related entries: GERMAN WAR OF LIBERATION; JENA-AUERSTÄDT-FRIEDLAND CAMPAIGN; LEIPZIG, BATTLE OF; RUSSIAN CAMPAIGN; WAGRAM CAMPAIGN; WARSAW, DUCHY OF.

PONTECORVO, PRINCE DE. See BERNADOTTE.

POPULATION. The population of France increased during the era of the French Revolution and Napoleon, from about 27 million in 1791 to 28 million under the Directory, 29 million in 1806, and 30 million in 1816. It thus seemed to continue the trends of the second half of the eighteenth century. Yet during the period of the Revolution and Napoleon, the rate of growth slowed. To be sure, from 1789 to 1815 the number of marriages increased more rapidly than did the total population. Several factors favored nuptiality: legislation lowering "the age before which parental consent was necessary, authorizing divorce, and laicizing marriage by making it a civil contract" (Bergeron) and conscription that exempted husbands. However, the birthrate declined from about 39 per 1,000 in the 1780s to 33 at the end of the Empire. The level of 1 million births annually during the last decade of the Old Regime was apparently maintained during the first decade of the Revolution. But during the years 1799 through 1804, the number of births dropped to 900,000 per year.

Historical demographers have advanced several reasons to explain this drop: the conscription of all young men into the Revolutionary armies, where they gained knowledge of contraceptive practices and diffused it; after the exhilaration of the Revolutionary years a mood of prudence, calculation, and security seeking set in; Revolutionary and Napoleonic legislation providing for the nearly equal division of inherited property among children led prudent parents to reduce the size of their families. The decline in the birthrate, however, was more than balanced by a declining death rate, which fell from 32 per 1,000 to 27 between the end of the Old Regime to the last years of the Empire. Again, historical demographers have suggested explanations: the disappearance of the great plagues; better-trained midwives; the introduction in 1799 of the smallpox vaccination; the absence of famine-producing food crises that had severe demographic consequences (the impact of the crop losses of 1811 was relatively moderate and to a degree minimized by the imperial administration's massive import of grain from abroad). The effect of these factors overbalanced the death or disappearance of some 900,000 war casualties between 1800 and 1815. The net result of these demographic phenomena (increase in marriages, decline in birthrate, decline in death rate) was continued growth of the French population at a slower rate.

L. Bergeron, *France under Napoleon*, trans. R. R. Palmer (Princeton, 1981); J. Dupaquier, "Problèmes démographiques de la France napoléonienne," in *La France à l'époque napoléonienne: actes du colloque Napoléon, RHMC* 17 (1970); M. Reinhard, *Etude de la population pendant la Révolution et l'Empire* (Paris, 1961), and *Premier Supplément* (Paris, 1963); M. Reinhard and A. Armengaud, *Histoire générale de la population mondiale* (Paris, 1961).

Harold T. Parker

Related entries: CASUALTIES; CONSCRIPTION; ECONOMY, FRENCH; SOCIETY.

PORTALIS, JEAN-ETIENNE-MARIE, COMTE (1745–1807), minister of ecclesiastical affairs, 1804-7. Born in Bausset (Var), Portalis was the son of a notary, a legal officer who in eighteenth-century France authenticated important documents. The young Portalis studied at the Oratorian collèges of Toulon and Marseilles and read for the law at Aix. Practicing before the parlement of Aix, he became one of the most distinguished lawyers of Provence, learned, eloquent, and often entrusted with provincial administrative duties. During the Revolution he deliberately withdrew from public life and moved to Paris. Elected to the Council of Ancients in 1795, he belonged, with his friends François de Barbé-Marbois and Charles François Lebrun, to the moderates and was forced by the coup d'état of 18 Fructidor to flee to Switzerland and later Holstein.

Bonaparte had use for such an able jurist and administrator. After 18 Brumaire Portalis was a member of the commission that drafted the Civil Code. There he helped reconcile the views of the partisans of the customary law, such as François-Denis Tronchet, with those of the supporters of the written Roman law, such as Félix Bigot de Préameneu and Jacques de Malleville. Pious as well as learned and a believer in the Gallican tradition of the French Catholic church, Portalis participated in the negotiation of the concordat between Napoleon and Pope Pius VII and helped prepare the Organic Articles. On 7 October 1801 Bonaparte appointed him councillor of state charged with the administration of ecclesiastical affairs and supervision of the implementation of the concordat. Portalis was now responsible for preparing drafts of laws, decrees, and regulations dealing with religious organizations, nominating clergymen of the different churches, examining papal bulls and briefs before their publication in France, and conducting all correspondence within France regarding these subjects. After building a bureaucratic department with a secretariat general, division and bureau chiefs, and clerks to discharge these duties, he was appointed in 1804 minister of ecclesiastical affairs, a post he held until his death in 1807. His persuasive powers as administrator went far toward reconciling the demand of Napoleon that the Roman Catholic church be subject to his will with the restoration of the normal life of Catholic worshippers. As Napoleon became increasingly domineering, this task of mediation became increasingly difficult, and Portalis had to accept measures, such as the preparation of the catechism, that he could not in conscience approve. Nevertheless, his reconciling effort served France and Napoleon well.

A. Latreille, *L'église catholique et la Révolution française*, vol. 2: *L'ère napoléonienne et la crise européenne (1800–1815)* (Paris, 1970); P. F. Pinaud, "L'administration des cultes de 1800 à 1815," *RIN* 132 (1976); P. Sagnac, *La législation civile de la Révolution française (1787–1804)* (Paris, 1898).

Harold T. Parker

Related entries: BIGOT DE PREAMENEU; CONCORDAT OF 1801; LAW, CODES OF.

PORTUGAL. Staunchly pro-British, Portugal ignored Napoleon's Continental Blockade (System) and was invaded by a French army in 1807; the royal family fled to Brazil. The Portuguese, however, provided the duke of Wellington with a base and troops and thus played a decisive part in the Allied victory in the Peninsular War.

Napoleon always regarded Portugal as a British satellite. Consequently Prince Regent Dom João was forced into the War of Oranges in 1801 with France and Spain. Following meager resistance and the Treaty of Madrid ending the war, Portugal became a diplomatic battleground among Spain, France, and Britain. Portugal attempted to maintain its neutrality, but the pressure of the French plenipotentiary, Jean Lannes, forced Portugal to promise lucrative trading concessions and subsidies to France. However, in 1807 the Portuguese refused to fulfill all of the terms of the Continental System against Britain. Napoleon reacted by signing the Treaty of Fontainebleau with Spain for the invasion and partition of Portugal. French and Spanish armies invaded Portugal in November 1807 hoping to capture the prince regent and his fleet. Prince João responded by sailing to Brazil after establishing a regency to administer the country.

General Andoche Junot, commanding the French, occupied Lisbon and central Portugal while Spanish armies seized the Algarve and Entre Minho and Douro in the north. The Portuguese military establishment was dismantled; fortresses and military establishments were seized by the French; the population was disarmed; high-ranking civilian and military officials unsympathetic to the French were removed; the regency was dissolved; and Junot assumed complete power.

Following the Spanish uprising in May 1808, Portuguese nationalists revolted against French rule in Porto. They began organizing an army and appealed to Britain for aid in regaining their independence. Soon a fleet commanded by Sir Charles Cotton, an army commanded by Sir Arthur Wellesley, along with financial and military resources, began to pour into Portugal. Junot was defeated at Vimeiro and forced to evacuate Portugal according to the terms of the Convention of Cintra. A British army remained in Portugal, and the regency was reestablished with some changes in membership.

Prince João, in Brazil, retained final authority, but the regency exercised considerable latitude in formulating and implementing policy to resist further French aggression. With an ever-increasing subsidy provided by the British government, a British commander in chief, William Carr Beresford, and British officers, the Portuguese army was reorganized and reequipped. A British plenipotentiary was sent to represent British interests to the regency, and in 1810 Charles Stuart was appointed ambassador to Portugal. Ultimately he secured a seat on the regency, and, in concert with Dom Miguel Pereira Forjaz, minister of war and secretary of the regency, he was able to implement the policies of Sir Arthur Wellesley, Viscount Wellington, supreme commander of the armies. Despite determined resistance from a minority of the regency, especially the principal, Gonzalo de Sousa, and the patriarch, Antonio de Castro, the legal, administrative, financial, political, and even social structures of Portugal were modified at Wellington's prompting to provide adequate resources to carry on the war against the French. The scorched-earth policy was introduced, guerrilla warfare was ordered, the lines of Torres Vedras were constructed to protect Lisbon, and the Portuguese army was all but incorporated into Wellington's British army. The results of these efforts turned back Napoleon's most ambitious efforts to subdue Portugal in 1810–11. These cooperative efforts continued through 1813 until the French were driven out of the peninsula. In the struggle, no other nation experienced more devastation or contributed more of its resources proportionally to the defeat of Napoleon than did Portugal. The Portuguese sacrificed their lives, property, national resources, and even their freedom of action temporarily to preserve their country and ultimately maintain their independence.

V. J. Cesar, *Breve estudo sobre a invasao Franco-Hespanhola do 1807 em Portugal e operacoes realizadas ate a convencao de Cintra-Rolica e Vimeiro; Invaso Francesa de 1809; D'Almeida as Linhas de Torres Vedras e das Linhas de Torres Vedras a Ruentes d'Onoro (1810–1811)*, 3 vols. (Lisbon, 1903–10). M. Cheke, *Carlota Joaquina*, (London, 1947); J. C. F. Gil, *A infantaria Portuguesa na Guerra da Peninsula*, 2 vols. (Lisbon, 1912–13); A. Halliday, *Observations on the Present State of the Portuguese Army, as Organized by Lieutenant-General Sir William Carr Beresford* (London, 1811); J. M. Latino Coelho, *Historia Politica e Militar de Portugal desde os fins do seculo XVIII ate 1814*, 3 vols. (Lisbon, 1874–91); O. Lima, *D. João VI no Brasil* (Rio de Janeiro, 1908); S. J. da Luz Soriano, *Historia da Guerra Civil e do Estabelecimento do Governo Par-*

lamentar em Portugal, 15 vols. (Lisbon, 1866–87); A. Pereira, *D. João VI Principe e Rei*, 4 vols. (Lisbon, 1953); D. Peres, *Historia de Portugal*, 6 vols. (Barcelos, 1934).

Donald D. Horward

Related entries: ARMY, PORTUGUESE; BERESFORD; BUSSACO, BATTLE OF; FORJAZ; JOHN VI; MARMONT; MASSENA; PENINSULAR WAR; TORRES VEDRAS, LINES OF; WELLINGTON.

PORTUGUESE CAMPAIGNS (1807–11). Napoleon ordered the first invasion of Portugal to force the Portuguese ruler, Prince Regent João, to join the Continental System and declare war on its traditional ally, England. While the Portuguese procrastinated, the Treaty of Fontainebleau (27 October 1807) was signed calling for the conquest and partition of Portugal by France and Spain. Hence, a French army of 25,000 men under the command of General Andoche Junot crossed the Portuguese frontier (19 November), supported by Spanish armies, which marched into the Algarve and Douro regions. Junot occupied Lisbon (30 November) without bloodshed. Prince João had sailed for Brazil.

Junot dismantled the military establishment and appointed pro-French officials. Meanwhile, rebellious Portuguese sent a delegation to London requesting aid, and in August 1808, Sir Arthur Wellesley landed a force of 17,000 men at Mondego Bay. Junot concentrated part of his army north of Lisbon to confront the advancing British, who were joined by 5,000 Portuguese troops. At Vimeiro, Wellesley decisively defeated Junot, forcing him to retreat toward Lisbon after suffering 1,800 casualties. With a demoralized army amid a hostile population, Junot judged he could fight no more and surrendered, on terms, to the British. By the Convention of Cintra (30 August 1808), the British navy transported Junot's army back to France, freeing Portugal from French domination. Sir John Moore took control with British forces.

Napoleon, however, sent new forces into the peninsula. On 17 January 1809, Sir John Moore's army had to be evacuated from Coruña. Napoleon meanwhile had personally put down a Spanish rebellion. He ordered Marshal Nicolas Soult, with some 20,000 troops, to begin a second invasion of Portugal. Soult defeated a large army of irregulars at Porto (30 March 1809) and halted there to await the advance of Marshal Claude Victor, marching from Spain to cooperate for the attack on Lisbon. However, Victor, fully occupied with Spanish insurrectionaries, was unable to invade Portugal, so Soult remained in Porto.

The British took full advantage of this insurrection in the peninsula. Wellesley was sent back to Portugal with orders to expel the French. With an army of 23,000 men, supported by a force of 15,000 Portuguese, he marched to Porto, surprised Soult, forced him to abandon the city, and drove the French across the Santa Catalina Mountains, inflicting almost 5,000 casualties on them.

With Portugal as the base of operations for the British army in the peninsula and a symbol of resistance to French domination, Napoleon instructed Marshal André Masséna (April 1810) to invade Portugal for the third time with an army of 65,000 men to drive the British into the sea. After successfully besieging the frontier fortresses of Ciudad Rodrigo and Almeida (28 August), Masséna invaded Portugal (15 September) and advanced to Bussaco where he met Wellesley's Anglo-Portuguese army of 60,000 men in the only major battle (27 September) of the campaign. Although Masséna was unable to drive Wellesley's forces off the Serra de Bussaco, he turned the position by the Boialvo road and forced him to retreat toward Lisbon. At Villafranca, nineteen miles from Lisbon, Masséna was confronted by the formidable lines of Torres Vedras. Unable to breach the reinforced lines, he appealed unsuccessfully to Napoleon for men, supplies, and siege guns. After 108 days before the lines, Masséna began his withdrawal (5 March 1811), pursued by Wellesley's army. Despite several brilliant rear-guard actions of Marshal Michel Ney and a last desperate battle at Fuentes de Onoro to retain a foothold in Portugal, Masséna retired to Spain, ending Napoleon's third and last major effort to invade Portugal.

The French failures can be attributed to a combination of factors, including the determined resistance of the Portuguese citizens who resorted to guerrilla warfare; the unfavorable topographic features of the country; the inability of Napoleon to comprehend adequately the nature of the war; the lack of adequate communications, supplies, and manpower as a result of Portugal's isolated location; and the support of the British government in providing supplies, an army, subsidies, and leadership to the Portuguese, who proved to be extraordinarily effective in resisting the French. The failure of the third invasion became the turning point in the Peninsular War and consequently a major factor in the collapse of the Napoleonic Empire.

J. W. Fortescue, *A History of the British Army*, 20 vols. (London, 1910–30); D. D. Horward, ed. and trans., *The French Campaign in Portugal, 1810–1811: An Account by Jean Jacques Pelet* (Minneapolis, 1973); C. W. Oman, *A History of the Peninsular War*, 7 vols. (Oxford, 1902–30); J. Weller, *Wellington in the Peninsula* (London, 1962).

Donald D. Horward

Related entries: BUSSACO, BATTLE OF; JUNOT, J.-A.; MASSENA; MARMONT; PELET; PENINSULAR WAR; WELLINGTON.

POTOCKI, STANISLAW KOSTKA (1752–1821), president of the Council of State and director of the Office of Education in the Duchy of Warsaw. Member of an important magnate family, he took part in the four-year *Sejm* (Diet) of 1788–92 and in the war with Russia (1792) commanded the artillery. In 1795, he settled at Wilanów, outside Warsaw, and helped found the Society of the Friends of Science. In 1806, when the French entered Warsaw, Potocki was appointed to the provisional Governing Commission; after the creation of the Duchy of Warsaw, he was a senator and, after 1809, president of the Council of State.

He was also director of the Office of Education where he continued the work of the pre-1795 Committee of National Education, laying the foundation for a modern Polish school system. He continued this work after the fall of the duchy (1815) in the Russian-sponsored Kingdom of Poland in which he was minister of religion and education (1815–20). He is considered the father of the University of Warsaw (1816).

J. Bystron, *Literaci i grafomani z czasów Królestwa Kongresowego 1815-31* (Lwów, 1938); W. Gorczyki, *Oświata publiczna w Księstwie Warszawskiem i organizacja władz i funduszów* (Lwów, 1921); E. Kipa, "Stanisław Kostka Potocki jako minister wyznań religijnych." *Studia i szkice historyczne* (Warsaw, 1959); H. Konic, *Kartka z dziejów oświaty w Polsce* (Cracow, 1895); E. Podgórska, *Szkolnictwo elementarne Księstwa Warszawskiego i Królestwa Kongresowego 1807–1831* (Warsaw, 1960); S. Potocki, *Pochwały, mowy i rozprawy*, 2 vols. (Warsaw, 1815).

John Stanley

Related entry: WARSAW, DUCHY OF.

PRADT, DOMINIQUE-GEORGES-FREDERIC DE RIOM DE PROLHIAC DE FOURT DE (1759–1837), imperial chaplain, archbishop of Malines, French ambassador to the Duchy of Warsaw. Pradt was a noble of the Old Regime, a priest (1783), a doctor of theology (Sorbonne, 1785), and vicar of the diocese of Rouen. He was elected a deputy to the Estates General of 1789, opposed the Revolution, and emigrated in 1791. After the coup of 18 Brumaire, he returned to France. Napoleon, after his coronation, made Pradt imperial chaplain, baron of the empire, and bishop of Poitiers. In 1808, Pradt was charged with delivering the Spanish royal family to Bayonne where they abdicated, making room for King Joseph Bonaparte. As a reward, Pradt was made archbishop of Malines.

In 1812, Pradt was made the first ambassador to the Duchy of Warsaw, a rank appropriate to a Kingdom of Poland, which the Poles hoped would be proclaimed. To add to speculation, an Extraordinary *Sejm* (Diet) was called, but Pradt cut it short. His arrogant manners and contempt for the Poles made him numerous enemies; he was disliked by virtually all Polish statesmen, as well as Louis Bignon, the former French resident, and finally the emperor himself. After the retreat from Moscow, Napoleon dismissed him. In 1815, Pradt published a justificatory *Histoire de l'ambassade dans le grand-duché de Varsovie en 1812*.

Under the Bourbon restoration, Pradt was named grand chancellor of the Legion of Honor (1814), but dissatisfaction with this appointment forced his resignation. Thereafter he went into retirement. Elected to the Chamber of Deputies in 1827, he appeared only once and resigned in 1828. He died in Paris in 1837.

A. Caulaincourt, *Mémoires*, vol. 2 (Paris, 1946); E. Dousset, *L'abbé de Pradt* (Paris, 1959); M. Handelsman, ed., *Instrukcy i depesze Rezydentów Francuskich w Warszawie 1807–1813*, 2 vols. (Cracow, 1914); M. Handelsman *Dyplomaci napoleońscy w Warszawie* (Warsaw, 1914).

John Stanley

Related entries: DIPLOMACY; FOREIGN POLICY; RUSSIAN CAMPAIGN; SPAIN, KINGDOM OF; WARSAW, DUCHY OF.

PRESS. Napoleon achieved greater success in controlling political periodicals than any previous French regime. Bonaparte had recognized the power of newspapers during the Revolution and after 1796 founded several to publicize his military exploits. As first consul he took forceful steps to quash journalistic criticism and to ensure praise, concentrating on the Paris political papers. On 17 January 1800 he suppressed sixty of seventy-three and forbade any new ones. Both the police and a special office designed to regulate the press monitored the remnants of the medium, encouraging loyalty and disciplined obedience. The government, under the Consulate and Empire, foisted its own appointees as editors on various newspapers and imposed prior censorship.

These measures, reinforced by others, did not sufficiently fetter the press for Napoleon, who increasingly worried about innuendo, the precise tone of praise, unintended inferences, and minor indiscretions. Consequently, in 1811, he eliminated all but four Paris journals: the *Moniteur*, *Journal de l'Empire*, *Gazette de France* and *Journal de Paris*. Although occasional articles disappointed or angered the emperor, he refrained from other major changes. Meanwhile, however, Napoleon applied similar sorts of pressure to provincial newspapers and to foreign publications in areas under his control.

Despite Napoleon's manipulation of the political press, other types of publishing thrived. Literary and technical publications, located mostly in Paris, concentrated narrowly on their specialties, and survived, though with diminished vitality. The provincial press actually experienced a great expansion. Napoleon required that various legal actions be publicly recorded, which provided revenues to support new newspapers—some in departments that had had none at all. Prefects wishing to bolster their own and their area's prestige gave further impetus to new publications. These publications contained biased political news, which diminished their local character, but they at least laid foundations for more genuine provincial papers. Thus, the proliferation of the provincial press, regardless of its political vapidity, provided one area of important growth in a profession generally constricted or decimated.

C. Bellanger, *Histoire générale de la presse française* (Paris, 1969); A. Cabanis, *La presse sous le Consulat et l'Empire (1799–1814)* (Paris, 1975); E. Hatin, *Histoire de la presse en France* (Paris, 1861); R. Holtman, *Napoleonic Propaganda* (Baton Rouge, 1950); A. Périvier, *Napoléon journaliste* (Paris, 1918); G. le Poittevin, *La liberté de la presse depuis la Révolution, 1789–1815* (Paris, 1901); C. Van Schoor, *La presse sous le Consulat et sous l'Empire* (Brussels, 1899); H. Welschinger, *La censure sous le premier Empire* (Paris, 1882).

Jack R. Censer

Related entries: CONSTITUTIONS; *IDEOLOGUES*; LEGEND, NAPOLEONIC; POLICE, MINISTRY OF GENERAL; PROPAGANDA.

PRESSBURG, TREATY OF (26 December 1805), between France and Austria. It recognized French possession of Piedmont, Parma, and Piacenza. Austria lost to Italy Venice, Istria (except Trieste), and Dalmatia (gained at Campo

Formio, 1797). Austria recognized Napoleon as king of Italy and ceded to Bavaria—ally of France—the Tyrol, Vorarlberg, the bishoprics of Brixen and Trent, Burgau, Eichstädt, Passau, Lindau, and Augsburg. What remained of the western possessions of the Habsburgs went to other allies of France—Württemberg (made a kingdom), and Baden (elevated to grand duchy).

Jesse Scott

Related entry: FOREIGN POLICY.

PRINA, GIUSEPPE. See ITALY, KINGDOM OF; ITALY, KINGDOM OF: MINISTERS.

PROPAGANDA. Attention to public opinion became significantly more important in the French Revolutionary–Napoleonic period because of the façade of mass participation in the government and because of the army's being composed of citizen-soldiers. While continuing censorship and suppression of undesired items and hostile or useless media, Napoleon stressed the positive side of propaganda to shape public opinion. This was an important innovation. Other contributions attributable to him include orders of the day to bolster morale in the army and bulletins to inform the public of military developments. He personally took an active part in drafting and overseeing the distribution of the latter. He was the first sovereign to speak directly and frequently to his subjects and to try to control opinion in satellite areas. His final major propaganda contribution was the systematic use of the organs of government. He made propaganda a necessary tool of politics and statesmanship.

Napoleon's main propaganda interest lay in the military and diplomatic areas. His propaganda was greatly influenced by his being at war all but fourteen months of the time he was in power. Therefore he castigated the enemy (especially Great Britain, his most persistent opponent) and strove to build up the morale of his own side while weakening that of the enemy.

The newspaper served as his main instrument. The *Moniteur universel* became an official paper for political affairs; various government officials, especially the respective ministers, wrote its articles. Other lesser political papers might be favored with subsidies and news handouts. In every area under Napoleon's control there was an official or semiofficial newspaper to present the Napoleonic viewpoint, and he also founded a monopolistic religious paper. After 1807 the departmental papers had to copy the *Moniteur*.

Napoleon utilized all possible media. The theater, festivals, and church services were useful especially because the illiterate lower classes could be influenced by them. Napoleon frequently suggested the topic to be dealt with. He put much store in pamphlets, but he considered handbills and posters to be of little value.

A great deal of the propaganda centered on Napoleon. He employed musicians and artists to celebrate outstanding events in his career, but he was concerned mainly with history when he put them and writers on his payroll.

One of Napoleon's favorite propaganda tools was the "big lie," especially for military affairs. He also paid a great deal of attention to the timing of propaganda items. Napoleon had rumors circulated, in part to influence opinion and in part to determine the state of public opinion.

On the negative, or censorship and repression, side, Napoleon limited the number of theaters, placed the important ones of Paris under a superintendent of spectacles, and had a theater censorship. He eventually limited the number of political papers to four in Paris and one in each department. The Ministry of Police, through its Press Bureau, especially controlled the press, ultimately directing all French papers. A preventive censorship system was built up.

Assessing the effectiveness of Napoleon's propaganda is difficult. A master at manipulating the soldiers, he did not successfully adapt his appeal to the lower classes. He thought the *Moniteur* very effective. His enemies would not have attacked his propaganda if they had not been concerned about its value. Propaganda is most effective during a time of emotional tension, such as the Napoleonic period. Napoleon's could have been more effective than it was if he had been willing to delegate authority and had more clearly defined the propaganda role of each branch of government. But in the long run, it is events that determine the success of propaganda, and they finally turned against Napoleon. Appraisal of his propaganda must be based on the fact that even as his activities grew out of developments in the French Revolution, modern dictators rely on an extension of the groundwork he laid.

A. Cabanis, *La presse sous le Consulat et l'Empire* (Paris, 1975); R. B. Holtman, *Napoleonic Propaganda* (Baton Rouge, La., 1950); A. Périvier, *Napoléon journaliste* (Paris, 1918); H. Welschinger, *La censure sous le premier Empire* (Paris, 1889).

Robert B. Holtman

Related entries: ARCHITECTURE; ART; CHURCH, ROMAN CATHOLIC; EDUCATION; MUSIC; PRESS; SCULPTURE; THEATER; WOMEN, EDUCATION OF.

PROTESTANTS. France's Calvinists (about 480,000) and Lutherans (about 200,000) were legally free but spiritually spent at the end of the Revolutionary decade. In October, having negotiated the Concordat of 1801 with Pius VII, Bonaparte commissioned the minister of ecclesiastical affairs, J. E. M. Portalis, to work out a parallel arrangement with the Protestants. Following consultations between Portalis and a number of Protestant notables (Pastor P. H. Marron, the ex-Girondin Pierre-Antoine Rabaut-Dupuis, and J. U. Metzger), Organic Articles for the Protestants were promulgated on 18 Germinal Year X (8 April 1802). The Calvinist community was thereby divided into congregations of 6,000 souls, often geographically scattered, each to be governed by a pastor in collaboration with elders chosen from among the substantial taxpayers. Lutheran churches were to be supervised by directories, a majority of whose members were named by the first consul. The civil government reserved the right of veto over the appointment of new pastors and over alterations in church doctrine. Two years later, Protestant pastors were salaried by the state. This regulatory legislation, welcomed by Protestant officials at the time, helped generate a Calvinist spiritual revival (*Le Réveil*) during the Restoration. Protestants came to play a key role in the public life of Napoleonic France as bankers, generals, scientists, and senators.

B. C. Poland, *French Protestantism and the French Revolution* (Paris, 1957); D. Robert, *Les églises réformées en France 1800–1830* (Paris, 1961).

Geoffrey Adams

Related entries: CONCORDAT OF 1801; CHURCH, ROMAN CATHOLIC; PIUS VII.

PROVENCE, LOUIS-STANISLAS-XAVIER, COMTE DE. See LOUIS XVIII.

PRUSSIA, KINGDOM OF (1786–1815). Frederick the Great bequeathed to his successor, his nephew Frederick William II (1786-97), the most modern state in Europe. The state's strength lay neither in its size nor in its agrarian economy but in its army, whose upkeep absorbed almost two-thirds of Prussia's revenues. Yet so well had Frederick managed the resources of the state that it was free of debt and had a full treasury. Because Frederick had shown that his army could contend with those of France, Austria, and Russia, Prussia had to be treated as a great power.

Internally, Frederick, one of the chief exponents of enlightened despotism, had begun to codify the law, making it independent of princely whim, abolishing torture, and creating an independent judiciary. He had decreed religious toleration and freedom of the press. Elementary education was compulsory, and Prussia boasted an honest and efficient civil service. Though more than 75 percent of the population still derived its living from the land, he had promoted industry under the principles of mercantilism and laid the foundation for a thriving mining industry in Silesia. Prussia's one great drawback was its rigid class system. Insurmountable barriers separated the nobility, middle class, and peasantry from each other. Many of the peasants lived in hereditary subjection to their landlords.

Frederick William II continued the absolutism of his uncle but was quite different from him. Sensuous and hedonistic, he enjoyed many mistresses and concubines. He was also a mystic and a Rosicrucian, two of whom became his chief advisers. In their struggle against the rationalism of the Enlightenment, they violated the principles of freedom of religion and freedom of the press. Immanuel Kant was compelled to refrain from writing about religion, and in edict after edict the king attempted to impose on his subjects his own obscurantist brand of Christianity.

On the positive side, Frederick William reformed the oppressive method of tax collecting, lowered customs duties in order to help trade, and expanded the system of roads and canals. He broadened the membership of the Prussian Academy of Sciences, increased the budget for schools and universities, and encouraged the arts and music, especially that of Mozart and Gluck.

In foreign policy the king at first pursued the anti-Austrian policy inherited from Frederick II, but the king's antipathy toward the French Revolution and his sympathy for monarchical solidarity induced closer relations with Austria, the declaration of Pillnitz, and participation (1792–95) in the First Coalition. The campaign in France was not very successful, however, and seriously depleted the Prussian treasury.

In 1795 Frederick William made peace at Basel. More concerned with getting a share of Poland (under partition among Austria, Russia, and Prussia) than war with France, he gave up the left bank of the Rhine for a sphere of influence in northern Germany. He was then free to bargain with Russia and Austria and obtained the Polish provinces of Posen and Warsaw. Thus Prussia attained its largest extension with a population of 8.7 million people. To be sure, 2.5 million of them were Poles, but in the age of dynastic politics this was of no concern. The arrangement with France made eminent sense in 1795, gave Prussia a decade of neutrality, and allowed the state to benefit greatly from the distribution of the former ecclesiastical territories parceled out by the *Reichsdeputationshauptschluss*, which remapped Germany in 1803.

Conditions changed eventually, however, and the next king, Frederick William III (1797-1840), could not maintain Prussia's neutrality in the face of Napoleon's expansionism. Frederick William III was Prussia's citizen king, modest, honest, hardworking, and well meaning but intellectually inadequate and insufficiently resolute. His feeble attempts at reform were blocked by the nobility.

Frederick William sanctioned real reforms only after the disastrous defeat at Jena and Auerstädt (1806) and the humiliating Peace of Tilsit (1807). Prussia was forced to surrender half of its territory, including all lands west of the Elbe, and Polish acquisitions of 1793 and 1795. Napoleon also demanded an enormous war indemnity, and until it was paid Prussia had to sustain a French occupation force of 150,000 men.

Prussia was saved from further territorial losses by Czar Alexander I, whom Napoleon made an ally at Tilsit. He preferred to have a buffer state between Russia and the French Empire. Prussia succeeded in regenerating itself with the reforms of the able ministers Karl vom Stein and K. A. von Hardenberg. The system of governing through personal advisers to the king was replaced by functional ministries. Serfdom was abolished, the legal distinctions between classes were removed, including the restrictions on land ownership, freedom of trade was decreed, the educational system was rejuvenated, and municipalities were granted autonomy. In the military sphere, the reforms of Gerhard von Scharnhorst, A. N. von Gneisenau, and H. L. von Boyen created a modern army capable of facing the French. Careers were opened to talent, promotions were based on merit, corporal punishment was abolished, conscription was introduced, and the limit of 42,000 men placed on the army by Napoleon was circumvented through quick rotation.

Frederick William's hesitant nature served him well when he resisted the exhortations of reformers to rise against Napoleon in 1809. The fate of Austria demonstrated that to do so would have been premature. In fact, only Napoleon's misfortunes in Russia (1812) and the fortuitous positioning of the Prussian contingent on the flanks of the main army enabled General J. Yorck von Wartenburg to conclude the convention of Tauroggen, which led to an alliance with Russia and later Austria (1813) against the French. In the subsequent campaigns against Napoleon, especially in the battles of Leipzig and Waterloo, the Prussian army proved the value of the reforms. Prussia's role was acknowledged at the Congress of Vienna, when in addition to what had been Prussian territory in 1807, Prussia acquired parts of Saxony, Westphalia, and the left bank of the Rhine. It did not regain the Polish territories of the second and third partitions, which meant that with only 250,000 Poles among its people, Prussia was well prepared for the nationalism of the nineteenth century. Unfortunately, Frederick William's very success at restoring Prussia also put an effective end to his willingness to promote internal social and political reforms.

O. Büsch and W. Neugebauer, eds., *Moderne Preussische Geschichte 1648–1947*, 3 vols. (1981); S. Haffner, *The Rise and Fall of Prussia* (1980); H. W. Koch, *A History of Prussia* (1978); G. Ritter, *The Sword and the Scepter. The Problem of Militarism in Germany*, 4 vols. (1969–73); H. J. Schoeps, *Preussen. Geschichte eines Staates* (1966).

Peter W. Becker

Related entries: BOYEN; FOREIGN RELATIONS; FRIEDRICH WILHELM II; FRIEDRICH WILHELM III; GNEISENAU; HARDENBERG; JENA-AUERSTÄDT-FRIEDLAND CAMPAIGN; RUSSIAN CAMPAIGN; SCHARNHORST; STEIN.

PUBLIC WELFARE. No comprehensive law or general system of public assistance to aid helpless children, the sick, and the elderly poor was enacted during the Empire. Humanitarian impulses had motivated the Convention to organize a welfare system for the purpose of alleviating the misery of poverty and eliminating begging and vagrancy, but by the time of the Directory, such altruism had largely disappeared. This change in philosophy coupled with the financial problems inherent in strict enforcement caused the generous laws of the Convention to be repealed. Instead, the guiding administrative philosophy of the Consulate and Empire aimed at reestablishing order and centralizing state services. In achieving this, the prefects played a remarkable role, whether executing Napoleon's orders transmitted through competent ministers of the interior or using their own initiative with ministerial sanction. Only the fine organization of the ministerial bureaus, which are detailed in the annual imperial *Almanachs*, kept this system functioning properly. On a national basis, then, the most important pieces of imperial legislation were the decree of 5 July 1808, establishing departmental *dépôts de mendicité*, and the decree of 19 January 1811, regulating aid to dependent children under age thirteen who were abandoned or orphaned.

One form of public assistance was exercised on an out-patient basis at home. Bureaus of *bienfaisance* of the Directory were centralized under a commission whose members were selected according to a decree of 7 Germinal Year XIII

(28 March 1805). These offices, which the prefects supervised, distributed the meager resources from the poor boxes in churches. Nuns usually helped to dispense this domiciliary aid in the form of money, food, clothing, and medicine. In some areas the bureaus of *bienfaisance* set up soup kitchens. But these fulfilled only such a small part of the needs of the poor that official committees of *bienfaisance* were also created in 1812 to replace them.

The most effective form of welfare was provided by institutions. The decree of 7 Germinal Year XIII also applied to staffing *commissions des hospices*, designed to oversee the departmental *dépôts de mendicité*, which were created after 1808 and which existed in addition to workshops of charity. All beggars were ordered to go to the poorhouses since alms were made illegal in the Empire. Those failing to submit voluntarily were supposed to be arrested and taken there, although this part of the penal code of 1810 never became fully operational. Special hospitals existed in Paris such as: Laënnec (for incurably ill women), Hôpital du Midi (for venereal diseases), Enfants Malades, Hospice La Rochefoucauld (for elderly men and women), and La Maternité (for unwed mothers, indigent pregnant women, and foundlings in the nursery section). In general, the hospital commissions fared better than under the Directory despite some inept members because the hospices were more adequately funded (*arrêt* of 23 February 1801) since some of their pre-Revolutionary wealth was restored by the government.

In their haste to reorder health care, imperial administrators resorted to the expedient of reconstituting institutions of the Old Regime that had proved their viability and usefulness. In addition, the government again permitted the existence of private and religious charitable foundations. Hospital congregations of nuns, for example, were reformed at the beginning of the Consulate and replaced staffs of lay nurses. Besides operating their own houses, private charities were expected to fund public welfare. One of these that was nationalized was the Society of Maternal Charity, under Empress Marie-Louise's protection after 1810, which gave needy married mothers lying-in expenses, layettes, and food for themselves while they nursed their babies. The Société philanthropique also revived, distributing goods and encouraging mutual aid societies. The Society for the Relief and Freeing of Prisoners was one of many local welfare societies that collected money.

Another interesting feature of Napoleon's decree of 19 January 1811, and one that also harkens back to pre-Revolutionary times, was the creation of the *tours* in government foundling hospitals. These revolving wooden cylinders permitted the deposit of infants for abandonment anonymously so as to prevent abortion and infanticide by mothers and midwives. Two hundred sixty-nine of these were installed, and the babies who were deposited usually were transported to mercenary nurses in the countryside by *meneurs* hired by the government. When orphans reached twelve years of age, they were expected to earn their own living and were removed from the welfare rolls. During the Third Republic, there was intense debate regarding the merits of reviving Napoleon's *tours* that were in harmony with the ideals of St. Vincent de Paul.

M. du Camp, *Paris, ses organes, ses fonctions et sa vie* (Paris, 1875), and *Paris bienfaisant* (Paris, 1888); J. Godechot, *Les institutions de la France sous la Révolution et l'Empire* (Paris, 1968); A. Husson, *Etude sur les hôpitaux* (Paris, 1862); J. Imbert, *Le droit hospitalier de la Révolution et de l'Empire* (Paris, 1954); L. Lalemand, *De l'assistance des classes rurales au XIX*[e] *siècle* (Paris, 1889), *Histoire de la Charité* (Paris, 1910–12), *Histoire des enfants abandonnés et délaissés* (Paris, 1885), and *La Révolution et les pauvres* (Paris, 1898); B. Mahieu et al., *Saint Vincent de Paul et l'hôpital* (Paris, 1960); A. Monnier, *Histoire d'assistance dans les temps anciens et modernes* (Paris, 1856).

June K. Burton

Related entries: LACHAPELLE; MEDICINE; WOMEN; WOMEN, EDUCATION OF.

PYRAMIDS, BATTLE OF. See EGYPTIAN CAMPAIGN.

Q

QUATRE-BRAS, BATTLE OF. See WATERLOO CAMPAIGN.

R

RAAB, BATTLE OF (14 June 1809), victory of Eugène de Beauharnais over Archduke John, which contributed to Napoleon's victory at Wagram. After joining with Napoleon's army at Bruck, Eugène was ordered to take his forces eastward. Napoleon wanted to clear his strategic right in preparation for an offensive north of the Danube. Eugène's mission was to neutralize Austrian forces in Hungary commanded by Archduke John. The French advance began on 5 June, and after several clashes with Austrian rear guards Eugène caught up with John on 14 June 1809 near the town of Raab, near the confluence of the Raab and Danube rivers.

John's force of 30,000 consisted of both regulars and newly raised Austrian and Hungarian levies. Because of the high percentage of new recruits, John declined offensive operations, and he took up a strong position south of the town. His right rested on the Raab river, his left on the Pancza marsh, and his center on a plateau where John positioned three infantry divisions. Two infantry divisions held the approaches to the plateau, while a third division was in reserve. John's left, extending from the plateau to the marsh, was held by a cavalry division, and his right, extending from the plateau to the Raab River, was also held by a cavalry division. An additional infantry division held an entrenched camp between the Raab and Rabnitz rivers and so was isolated from the battle.

Eugène's army totaled 33,000. His right flank consisted of Emmanuel Grouchy's cavalry corps of two divisions; his center of Paul Grenier's corps; his left of the corps of Louis Baraguey d'Hilliers. The army's reserve comprised infantry and cavalry divisions plus the Italian Royal Guard.

Eugène attacked at noon. Grouchy's cavalry corps drove off the Austrian horsemen covering John's left. Grenier's corps, supported by an infantry division from Baraguey's corps, frontally assaulted the infantry on the plateau. John committed his reserve division, which temporarily drove back the French, but Eugène sent forward a reserve infantry division, which turned the tide. Meanwhile, Baraguey's corps engaged the cavalry holding the Austrian right. John ordered a retreat northeastward toward the town of Komorn. An Austrian rear guard managed to hold off the French pursuit until nightfall. The Austrians suffered 6,000 casualties; the French lost 2,500. John eventually crossed to the north bank of the Danube at Komorn but did not reinforce the Archduke Charles at Wagram, whereas Eugène did reinforce Napoleon, who won the battle (5–6 July 1809).

Robert Epstein

Related entries: WAGRAM CAMPAIGN; WAGRAM CAMPAIGN, ITALIAN PHASE.

RACZYNSKI, IGNACY (1741–1823), primate of Poland, archbishop of Gniezno and Warsaw, opponent of Napoleonic secularization in the Duchy of Warsaw. Of a princely family, Raczyński attended a Jesuit school in Bydgoszcz, entered the Jesuit order (1760), studied at the Jesuit academy in Milan, and returned to Poland to become canon in Brodnica. He became bishop of Poznan in 1793 and in 1805 archbishop of Gniezno and primate of Poland. In 1807 Raczyński's diocese was included in the new Duchy of Warsaw. The constitution made Roman Catholicism the state religion but mandated toleration of other faiths. Moreover, secularization was a tenet of the new regime. Throughout the duchy's existence, Raczyński opposed the government and in practice largely prevented the civil registration of births and deaths and acceptance of civil marriage and divorce. He also maintained a strong church voice in education and even defied the Code Napoléon by supporting religious courts in much of their previous authority. In all this he had the tacit support of King Frederick Augustus of Saxony, who ruled the duchy for Napoleon. After French rule ended, he continued as archbishop of Gniezno until 1819.

J. Perkowski, *Krótki rys życia Ignacego Raczyńskiego*, (Lwów, 1844); M. Lehmann, *Preussen und die katholische Kirche seit 1640*, VII (Leipzig, 1894); I. Raczyński, *Sześcioletnia Korespondencya władzy duchownych z rządem świetckim księstwa warszawskiego* (Warsaw, 1816).

John Stanley

Related entries: FRIEDRICH AUGUST III; WARSAW, DUCHY OF.

RAGUSA, DUC DE. See MARMONT.

RAGUSA, REPUBLIC OF. See ILLYRIAN PROVINCES.

RASZYN, BATTLE OF (19 April 1809), first test of the army of the Duchy of Warsaw led by Prince Poniatowski against the Austrians under the leadership of the Archduke Ferdinand d'Este. At Raszyn 12,000 Poles held against an Austrian army of 25,000 for a day and retired in good order. This action forced the Austrians to continue to fight in Poland, which took pressure off Napoleon's army in the Wagram campaign of 1809.

J. Chelmiński and A. Malibran, *L'armée du Duché de Varsovie* (Paris, 1913); B. Gembarzewski, *Wojsko polskie, Księstwo Warszawskie 1807–1814* (Warsaw, 1912); B.

Pawlowski, *Historia wojny polsko-austriackiej 1809 roku* (Warsaw, 1935); G. Zych, *Armia Księstwa Warszawskiego 1807–1812* (Warsaw, 1961).

John Stanley

Related entries: WAGRAM CAMPAIGN; WARSAW, DUCHY OF.

RECAMIER, JEANNE-FRANCOISE-JULIE-ADELAIDE (1777–1849), celebrated for her beauty, charm, and conversation in the literary and political circles of the early nineteenth century. Mme. Récamier was born in Lyon on 4 December 1777 and died in Paris 11 May 1849. She was educated at Villefranche and Lyon at the convent of la Déserte. Her father, a banker of Lyon, moved to Paris in 1784. From 1792 she lived in Paris, where at her father's receptions on the rue des Saints-Pères she was admired for her beauty, modesty, and accomplishments. In 1793, at age fifteen, of her own free will she married Jacques Récamier, a rich forty-two-year-old banker. She felt only respect for him and he, in turn, writes Amélie Lenormant, considered her "like a child whose beauty charmed his eyes and flattered his vanity."

From the early days of the Consulate to almost the end of the July Monarchy, her salon in Paris was a meeting place for fashionable political and literary figures. Among the *habitués* were Mme. Germaine de Staël, C. A. Sainte-Beuve, Benjamin Constant, and René de Chateaubriand, to whom she devoted her later years. Mme. de Staël describes her enthusiastically in *Corinne*: her face was more candid than her heart, affectionate without passion; her decency and innocence contrasted with the corrupt and often cynical bourgeoisie; and she had a talent for delicately discouraging the passions that she provoked without rebuffing them. During the Consulate, she drew an increasingly larger group of admirers, including Adrien and Mathieu de Montmorency, Lucien Bonaparte, former royalists, and those hostile to the first consul, such as Jean Bernadotte and J.-Victor Moreau. While she did not actively take part in the political world, she was personally for the Bourbons. Her friendship with Mme. de Staël displeased Napoleon and by declining in 1803 to become a lady attendant on the Empress Josephine she further offended him.

In 1805 her husband's bankruptcy forced her to accept Mme. de Staël's hospitality at Coppet, where she met Prince August of Prussia, nephew of Frederick II. While she seemingly returned his affection, she refrained from urging a divorce, determined to devote herself only to friendship. A similar fate befell the young Ampère.

During the last years of the Empire, exiled from Paris by Napoleon, she returned for some time to her husband's family in Lyon where she acquired a new admirer, Balanche, and went to Rome where she met Antonio Canova, and to Naples where she was received by King Joachim Murat and Queen Caroline. At this time, the disasters of the Empire forced Napoleon's sister and brother-in-law to negotiate with the Bourbons. She advised them to stay faithful to France, but it is not clear whether she meant the France of Louis XVIII or the France of Napoleon. After the first abdication in 1814, Mme. Récamier asked

Benjamin Constant to write a statement to the Congress of Vienna claiming Murat's rights to the Kingdom of Naples.

During the first years of the Restoration, she lost most of the rest of her fortune and was obliged to occupy modest apartments in the Abbaye-aux-Bois, an old Paris convent. After the death of Mme. de Staël in 1817, in spite of warnings by his friends, Chateaubriand came to occupy the first place in her salon, if not in her heart. Suffering from his imperious temper, she fled to Rome in 1824; however, she returned to find solace with him in her old age surrounded by a large circle of admirers and friends. Widowed since 1830, she declined to marry Chateaubriand when his wife died in 1846. Blind, suffering from an attack of cholera, she died a few months after him.

Mme. Récamier's beauty often inspired the artists of her time. Besides the famous portrait by Jacques-Louis David (Louvre), there is a portrait by François Gérard (the prefecture of the Seine), a bronze medallion by David d'Angers, and others; she was the model for the bust of Beatriz by Canova.

P. Deschanel, *Figures de femmes. . .Mme. Récamier* (Paris, 1880); A. Lenormant, ed., *Lettres de Benjamin Constant à Mme. Récamier, 1807-1830* (Paris, 1882), *Mme. Récamier, les amis de sa jeunesse et sa correspondance intime* (Pais, 1872), and *Souvenirs et Correspondance tirés des papiers de Mme. Récamier* (Paris, 1859); M. Levaillant, *Chateaubriand, Mme. Récamier et les Mémoires d'outre tombe* (Paris, 1936), and *Une Amitié amoureuse, Mme. de Staël et Mme. Récamier* (Paris, 1956); M. Trouncer, *Mme. Récamier* (London, 1949); H. Williams, *Madame Récamier and Her Friends* (London, 1901).

Yolita Kavaliunas

Related entries: CANOVA; GERARD, F.-P.-S.; DAVID; STAEL-HOLSTEIN.

REGENSBURG, BATTLE OF. See WAGRAM CAMPAIGN.

REGGIO, DUC DE. See OUDINOT.

REGNAUD DE SAINT-JEAN-D'ANGELY, MICHEL, COMTE (1762–1819), member of Napoleon's Council of State and president of its section on the interior. Born at Saint-Fargeau (Yonne), son of the president of its bailliage, he was a distinguished student at the collège of Plessis in Paris and in that city read for the law. The family's financial difficulties, however, forced him to take a post in the navy at Rochefort. Elected to the Estates General, he belonged to the moderate constitutional center of the Constituent Assembly and later wrote for the *Journal of Paris*. Forced underground during the Terror, he emerged to become administrator of the hospitals of the Army of Italy (1796), where he and Bonaparte became acquainted. He accompanied the expedition to Egypt, but illness forced him to stop at Malta. After 18 Brumaire Napoleon appointed him in 1799 member of the Council of State, two years later president of its section of the interior, and with the coming of the Empire *procureur* of the imperial high court, as well as secretary to the imperial family.

Considered equal in ability to C.-M. de Talleyrand and Joseph Fouché, Regnaud was the complete statesman. He excelled in rapidly perceiving the essentials of a problem under discussion and proposing a rational solution. He could phrase propositions and supporting arguments gracefully (he was accounted the finest orator of the Napoleonic age). The emperor valued him highly and used him often to present his decisions persuasively. Thus, once Napoleon had decided to divorce Josephine, Regnaud wrote both Napoleon's and Josephine's parting speeches. The gracious sentences in Napoleon's speech, "She has embellished fifteen years of my life. The memory of them will remain always engraved in my heart," were Regnaud's.

Since the archives of the Council of State were destroyed in the fire that consumed the Tuileries in 1871, it has been difficult for historians to describe Regnaud's incessant administrative activity adequately. Nevertheless he was at the center of power for over fourteen years. As member of the special Council of Administration of the Interior, composed of the minister of the interior, Regnaud as president of the Council of State's section of the interior, two or three other experts, and Napoleon himself, Regnaud participated in a weekly review of the ongoing operation of the ministry. As one minister of the interior succeeded another (J.-A. Chaptal, J.-B. de Champagny, Emmanuel Crétet, J.-P.-B. de Montalivet), Regnaud, who was always there, came to know more about the ministry's activity than any incoming administrator and could maintain a watchful check on its work. From the Council of Administration of the Interior, from the minister of interior, and from Napoleon himself would emerge requests for new imperial laws, decrees, and regulations or for interpretations of old ones. Regnaud took these requests to his fellow councillors on his section of the interior of the Council of State. The section would draft the requested legislation or interpretation, submit it to Napoleon for revision, and then in print bring the revision before the full Council of State for discussion. It was not unknown for a draft to pass through six, seven, or even nine printings before winning final approval of the council and Napoleon. If a law was needed, Regnaud defended the draft to the Legislative Body and Tribunate. As president of the council's section of interior, Regnaud also personally reviewed the annual budget of each of the territorial departments into which France was divided and of each of the several thousand towns whose annual revenue exceeded 10,000 francs. In the full Council of State, which usually met two to three times weekly, he discussed all the other affairs that came before it and came to be considered its most eminent and influential member. Throughout the Consulate and Empire, Regnaud was an indefatigable worker, a tactful spokesman for intelligent, moderate governmental operation, one who helped to make Napoleon's administrative system function.

J. Bourdon, *Napoléon au Conseil d'Etat* (Paris, 1963); Cambacérès, *Lettres inédites à Napoleon*, ed. Jean Tulard (Paris, 1973); C. Durand, *Etudes sur le Conseil d'Etat napoléonien* (Paris, 1949), and *Le fonctionnement du Conseil d'Etat napoléonien* (Gap, 1954).

Harold T. Parker

Related entries: ADMINISTRATION; CONSTITUTIONS; MINISTERS OF NAPOLEON.

REGNIER, CLAUDE (1736–1814), duc de Massa, minister of justice, 1802–13. Born at Blamont (Meurthe), Régnier became under the Old Regime a distinguished member of the bar at Nancy. In 1789 he was elected a deputy of the Third Estate to the Estates General. As a member of the Constituent Assembly, he spoke on legal questions; thus, he persuaded the Assembly not to install juries in civil cases and not to send appeal judges on circuit. After disappearing from public life during the tumultuous years of the Legislative Assembly and Convention, he emerged to assume a prominent role as member for four years and eventually as president of the Council of Ancients of the Directory. However, believing the Directory to be incompetent, he actively participated in the coup d'état of 18 Brumaire (he was the deputy who presented to the Council of Ancients the decree transferring the next day's meeting of the two legislative houses to Saint-Cloud). Bonaparte appointed him member of the Council of State, where he became one of the drafters of the Civil Code. He was appointed head of the joint Ministry of Justice and Police on 14 September 1802 but returned the Ministry of Police to Fouché on 10 July 1804. He served as minister of justice under the watchful eye of Second Consul and then Arch-Chancellor Cambacérès until 19 November 1813. Régnier with his chief clerks conducted the routine of correspondence of the ministry. However, nominations of judges and recommendations for their promotion were for the most part obtained through the instrumentality of Cambacérès. Year after year, in collaboration with Cambacérès, Regnier prepared his nomination lists of judges for Napoleon, who then referred his recommendations to Cambacérès for comment and counsel, which was usually followed.

Perhaps Régnier's most important independent service to Napoleon and to France was to serve for seven years from 11 June 1806 as president of the commission of claims (*des affaires contentieuses*) of the Council of State. That council's chief function was to prepare laws, decrees, and regulations for Napoleon's approval and submission to the Tribunate and Legislative Body. However, it also had the secondary but important function of hearing citizens who accused an administrative officer or agency (a cabinet minister, a prefect, a subprefect, a council of the prefecture, a council of the arrondissement, or a tax court) of exceeding the limits of their legal authority and of acting arbitrarily or simply ignorantly and incorrectly. Such cases required establishing the facts of the situation and applying the administrative law that had set up the office or agency. The councillors of the five sections of the Council of State (legislation, interior, finances, war, and the navy) for the most part were poorly equipped to handle cases of that nature and in any case were too busy with their other tasks to do justice to a citizen's often legitimate complaint. So Napoleon established within the Council of State this claims commission composed of six *maîtres des requêtes* and six *auditeurs*, presided over by Régnier as minister of justice and grand judge. Decisions of the commission were by majority vote of Régnier and the six *maîtres des requêtes*. Régnier, even Napoleon's enemies agree, insisted on a high standard of legal scholarship and meticulous research into the circumstances and law of each case. He set a tradition of impartial rendering of justice to citizens who felt they had a grievance against the powerful centralized administration. This judicial tradition was followed in post-Napoleonic regimes when deciding such cases became the Council of State's chief function. For these services, Régnier was accorded in 1809 the title of duc de Massa. On retirement as minister of justice in 1813, he received the title of minister of state and the office of president of the Legislative Body. He died a few months after Napoleon's first abdication.

J. Bourdon, *La législation du Consulat et de l'Empire*, vol. 1: *La réforme judiciaire de l'an VIII* (Rodez, 1942); Cambacérès, *Lettres inédites à Napoleon 1802–1814*, ed. Jean Tulard, 2 vols. (Paris, 1973); C. Durand, *Le fonctionnement du Conseil d'état Napoléonien* (Gap, 1954).

Harold T. Parker

Related entries: ADMINISTRATION; CAMBACERES; MINISTERS OF NAPOLEON.

REICHSDEPUTATIONSHAUPTSCHLUSS (1803), "recess" or decision of a deputation of the Diet of the Holy Roman Empire—heavily influenced by France—remapping Germany, as agreed in the Treaty of Lunéville (1801). See AUSTRIA; DIPLOMACY; LUNEVILLE, TREATY OF.

REINHARD, KARL FRIEDRICH VON (1761–1837), German-born French diplomat. Born in Schorndorf, Württemberg, he was educated in Germany, studying theology, philosophy, languages, and poetry at the University of Tübingen. In 1787 he went to Bordeaux to visit and in 1791 was invited to Paris to give a speech on recent German literature. While in Paris he was caught up in the enthusiasm of the French Revolution and entered the French diplomatic service, serving under Louis XVI. While in the Foreign Office, he became friends with both Roger Ducos and the abbé Sieyès, both of whom were of help to him in later years. In 1792, Reinhard was appointed secretary of the French embassy in London, but he was expelled from England in 1793 after the beheading of Louis XVI. He continued in the diplomatic service, however, and served the Republic in many capacities, primarily representing the government in Naples. Reinhard survived the turmoil of the Terror and continued to serve the Directory, and in 1799 he became the minister for foreign affairs for France. During the period of the Directory, on 12 October 1796, he married Christine Reimarus in Neumühlen.

When Napoleon assumed power in France, Reinhard was sent, in 1800, to Switzerland where he assumed the duties of French ambassador. In 1802 he went to Hamburg to represent French interests in northern Germany. He remained in the German area during most of the first decade of the 1800s, serving the emperor in many different capacities. The longest service was as ambassador to the court of Napoleon's youngest brother, King Jerome. The emperor had heard rumors of his brother's problems and inability as king of Westphalia and wanted

Reinhard to keep an eye on him and report everything to Napoleon himself. This Reinhard did. From his reports we see Jerome as a king who at least could make decisions but one who did not always rule wisely or in the best interests of the Empire.

Reinhard left Westphalia along with Jerome in 1813 and retreated to Paris where he stayed until after Napoleon was defeated. He then stayed on but was not treated well by the ultras in the court of Louis XVIII. With the return of Napoleon, Reinhard moved to Brussels, refusing to work again for the former emperor. After Waterloo, Reinhard tried to move to his estates on the Rhine but was detained by German authorities and kept under close surveillance. However, Louis XVIII needed experienced diplomats, and again Reinhard was in the French diplomatic service. He served both Louis XVIII and Charles X as ambassador at the Bundestag in Frankfurt.

In the early 1820s, his wife died after a long period of nervous strain. Soon, at age sixty-two, Reinhard remarried, this time to the best friend of his daughter Sophie, a young woman named Virginie Freiin von Wimpfen. His friends noticed a distinct change in him at this time; he was more approachable, more amenable than ever before, and he seemed to be entirely wrapped up in his new life with his young wife. He traveled extensively with her in the late 1820s, and then from 1830 to 1832 served Louis Philippe as French ambassador in Dresden. His son served as his secretary at this time, and later he too entered the French diplomatic service. Reinhard became friends with many notables in Europe during his long career as a professional French diplomat. One of his good friends was Goethe, with whom he carried on a long and voluminous correspondence for many years. In fact, he was the godfather of one of Goethe's grandchildren. In addition he corresponded with Jacob Grimm, F. von Schlegel, J. von Müller, Hans von Gagern, Mme. de Staël, F. von Schelling, F. von Schiller, and latterly, François Guizot. He was noted for his justice and his noble character and served his adopted country well in the reigns of four kings, one emperor, and the years of the French First Republic. He was elevated to the rank of baron in 1809, to count in 1815, and to a peer of the French realm in 1832. Because of his many moves during his career, he said at one time that he felt like a man without a country, but these feelings did not deter him from fulfilling his many duties. He died in Paris on Christmas Day 1837, and Charles-Maurice de Talleyrand read the eulogy at his funeral. His wife Virginie survived him for fifty more years, dying in 1887.

Allgemeine Deutsche Biographie (Leipzig, 1889); O. Connelly, *Napoleon's Satellite Kingdoms* (New York, 1965), and *French Revolution: Napoleonic Era* (New York, 1971); K. F. Reinhard, *Briefwechsel zwischen Goethe und Reinhard in den Jahren 1807 bis 1832* (Stuttgart, 1859), and *Karl Friedrich Reinhard's Briefe an Ch. de Villers* (Hamburg, 1883); P. W. Sergeant, *Jerome Bonaparte: The Burlesque Napoleon* (New York, 1906); E. A. Whitcomb, *Napoleon's Diplomatic Service* (Durham, N.C., 1979).

David C. Riede

Related entries: DIPLOMACY; WESTPHALIA, KINGDOM OF.

RELIGION. See CHURCH, ROMAN CATHOLIC; CONCORDAT OF 1801; JEWS; PIUS VI; PIUS VII; PROTESTANTS.

REMUSAT, AUGUSTIN-LAURENT, COMTE DE (1762-1823) and **CLAIRE-ELISABETH GRAVIER DE VERGENNES, COMTESSE DE** (1780-1821), aristocratic husband and wife recruited by Napoleon as part of his policy of rallying members of the French aristocracy to his government and of giving a monarchical etiquette and aristocratic tone to his court. Rémusat was appointed prefect of the palace charged with the etiquette of the court and the administration of the Paris theaters. In 1804, under the Empire, he was named first chamberlain and master of the wardrobe. His wife became lady in waiting (*dame du Palais*) to Josephine.

The Rémusats had responded happily to the first consul's call. Their fortune had been destroyed by the Revolution, and they genuinely admired Bonaparte as the hero who was bringing, it seemed, order, sound constitutional government, and peace to tormented France. They served Napoleon willingly, and Claire became one of his confidants. But the execution of the duke d'Enghien (1804) horrified and repelled them. Afterward the increasing despotism of the imperial regime and the wars and conquests alienated them, and they drifted into the opposition headed by Charles-Maurice de Talleyrand. At the same time Napoleon had attracted to his court such great families as the Montmorencys and the Rochefoucaulds and had less use for such as the Rémusats. In 1810 he allowed Claire to accompany the divorced Josephine into seclusion at Malmaison, and in 1811 he replaced Rémusat as master of the wardrobe with a Turenne. During the Restoration, Rémusat was made prefect of Haute-Garonne (Toulouse) and Lille. Claire wrote her memoirs of life at Napoleon's court (1802–8) and praised Napoleon's opposition, particularly Talleyrand.

Madame de Rémusat, *Mémoires, 1802-1808*, ed. P. de Rémusat, 3 vols. (Paris, 1879-80).

Harold T. Parker

Related entry: NAPOLEON, DAILY ROUND.

REPUBLICS, "SISTER." See SISTER REPUBLICS.

RESTORATION, FIRST. See ABDICATION, FIRST.

RESTORATION, SECOND. See ABDICATION, SECOND.

REUBELL, JEAN-FRANCOIS (1747–1807), French revolutionary and director. Reubell was born in Colmar where he became a prominent lawyer and member of the local Conseil Souverain. He was elected to the Estates General and played a fairly important role in the National Constituent Assembly. In 1792 he was elected to the National Convention where he sided with the more moderate elements. He played an important role in the Thermidorian Convention and was elected a director in October 1795.

As a director, he assumed the direction of foreign affairs. He approved of the first Italian campaign and Bonaparte's appointment as commanding general, though he was unhappy over the terms of the Treaty of Campo Formio because they did not recognize Prussia's interests. Reubell strongly opposed Napoleon's Egyptian expedition. He retired in May 1799 and was a member of the Council of Five Hundred at the time of the coup d'état of 18–19 Brumaire. Subsequently he withdrew from public life, but financial difficulties tempted him to seek public office. First Consul Bonaparte was eager to secure Reubell's support and to take advantage of the former director's administrative skills. The two men had at least three meetings, but Reubell refused to ask for a position although he might have become a senator if he had so requested. Bonaparte also refused to assist Reubell in denying the rumors about his alleged wealth. Reubell died a poor man in Colmar. The emperor did grant his widow a pension and at Saint Helena praised Reubell's honesty and ability.

G. D. Homan, *Jean-François Reubell, French Revolutionary, Patriot and Director* (The Hague, 1971).

Gerlof D. Homan

Related entries: BRUMAIRE, COUP OF 18, YEAR VIII; EGYPTIAN CAMPAIGN; ITALIAN CAMPAIGN, FIRST; NAPOLEON I.

REYNIER, JEAN-LOUIS-EBENEZER (1771–1814), talented Swiss-born French general whose mercurial temperament and outspokenness probably prevented his being made a marshal. Of Huguenot background, Reynier entered the French army as a private (1792) and rose to general of brigade in 1794 and general of division in 1796. Chief of staff to Jean Moreau in the Army of the Rhine and Moselle (1796–97), he failed to reveal information concerning Jean-Charles Pichegru's treason (1797) and was dismissed. However, he was restored to duty with Bonaparte's Egyptian expedition in 1798. His victory over the Turks at El Arish, 15 February 1798, won him recognition, but after Bonaparte's departure, he quarreled with General Jacques-François Menou and was sent back to France (1801). There he published a book highly critical of the Egyptian expedition and in 1802 was exiled by Napoleon. He was restored to command in the Army of Italy (1804) and participated in the invasion of Naples, where he lost the Battle of Maida to Sir John Stuart but crushed the subsequent Calabrian revolt in 1806–7. He was minister of war in Naples until 1809. Napoleon called him to the Grande Armée in 1809 for the Wagram campaign. He served in Spain in 1810 and with the Army of Portugal (1810–11); he quarreled with André Masséna during the Portuguese campaign but performed well under difficult circumstances. In 1812 he commanded the Seventh (Saxon) Corps of the Grande Armée, which operated in the Ukraine, and was victorious at Gorodeczna (12 August) and Volkovisk (16 November). During the 1813 campaign, he continually warned Napoleon of the growing disaffection of the Empire's allied troops.

He commanded Saxons at Grossbeeren and Dennewitz and was captured at Leipzig (18 October 1813), when the Saxons changed sides. The czar offered him a command in the Russian army, but he refused and was exchanged. He died of exhaustion in 1814. Napoleon valued Reynier highly but was put off by his cold, aloof personality, his outspoken republicanism, and his penchant for quarreling with superiors.

M. Finley, "The Career of Count Jean Reynier, 1792–1814" (Ph.D. dissertation, Florida State University, Tallahassee, 1972); E. Reynier, *De l'Egypte après la bataille d'Heliopolis* (Paris, 1802).

Milton Finley

Related entries: EGYPTIAN CAMPAIGN; GERMAN WAR OF LIBERATION; LEIPZIG, BATTLE OF; MENOU, J.-F.; NAPLES, KINGDOM OF; PORTUGUESE CAMPAIGNS; RUSSIAN CAMPAIGN; WAGRAM CAMPAIGN.

RICHARD, FRANCOIS (known as Richard-Lenoir) (1765–1839), manufacturer. Born in Calvados in 1765, the son of a farmer, Richard entered trade as an apprentice at twelve. He accumulated a large fortune dealing in textiles in the 1780s. In 1796, he formed a profitable partnership with Lenoir-Dufresne to speculate in *biens-nationaux* (national properties, mostly confiscated from the church). The two men also dealt in contraband English textiles and then began to spin and weave cotton themselves with English-designed machinery. Richard bought out his partner in 1806 and, on the latter's death shortly afterward, added Lenoir to his own name.

Richard became one of the most important manufacturers of the Napoleonic period. He served the government in the Paris Chamber of Commerce, on the Conseil Général des Manufactures, and as commander of the Parisian National Guard. By 1812 he controlled 10 percent of the French cotton industry and employed 15,000 workers—1,000 of them in Paris, the rest scattered in towns and villages throughout northwestern France. His showpiece was a large factory established in a former convent on the rue de Charonne in Paris, which he bought with a state subsidy in 1801. Hard hit by the depression of 1810–11, Richard's survival thereafter was increasingly dependent on state loans, amounting to 1.5 million francs by 1814. The First Restoration dealt him a blow with the suppression of duties on English textiles (22 April 1814), and Richard never recovered, despite a subsequent return to a national protectionist policy. His Bonapartist sympathies were well known, and he was spied on by the royal police, who feared his influence over so many workers in the Faubourg Saint-Antoine.

Financial difficulties forced Richard to sell off his properties gradually, and by 1837 he was completely impoverished. His friends rescued him with a national subscription campaign, which brought in a few thousand francs. He died 19 October 1839. Despite his personal failure, which exemplifies the economic difficulties faced by French manufacturers at that time, he stands out as one of the founders of the modern French textile industry.

C. Ballot, *L'introduction du machinisme dans l'industrie française* (Paris, 1923); L. Bergeron, *Banquiers, négociants et manufacturiers parisiens du Directoire à l'Empire* (Paris, 1978); F. Richard, *Mémoires de M. Richard-Lenoir* (Paris, 1837).

Michael D. Sibalis

Related entries: ECONOMY, FRENCH; NOTABLES; SOCIETY.

RIED, TREATY OF (3 October 1813). Bavaria agreed to withdraw from the Confederation of the Rhine and join the alliance against France. It was guaranteed its territory as of the date of the treaty. See also FOREIGN POLICY; GERMAN WAR OF LIBERATION.

RIVOLI, BATTLE OF. See ITALIAN CAMPAIGN, FIRST.

ROBESPIERRE, MAXIMILIEN. See CONVENTION; TERROR, THE.

ROEDERER, PIERRE-LOUIS (1754–1835), political theoretician, journalist, politician, and top-level administrator under Napoleon. Born in Metz to a father prominent in judicial circles, Roederer became a councillor in the parlement of Metz and an industrialist and spokesman for the industrial interests of northeastern France, and he was elected to the Estates General of 1789 (soon the National Assembly) where he spearheaded the radical proposals of the Tax Committee. In 1791 he was elected *procureur-général-syndic* of the department of Paris. Disturbed by the increasing disorders that led to the fall of the monarchy, he developed an elaborate liberal socioeconomic theory to bring stability and rational government to France. During the Terror he went into seclusion but emerged in Thermidor to become editor of the *Journal de Paris* (1795), a member of the Institut, and an *idéologue*. He became disenchanted with the Directory, however, and favored a new government with a strong executive; thus he joined the conspiracy of 18 Brumaire. He collaborated with the abbé Sieyès in 1799 to draft a new constitution (of the Year VIII in finished form). To the original version he contributed the idea of the *grand électeur*, which Bonaparte eliminated, and the concept of having the central government select office-holders from local and national lists of nominees, which was adopted.

During the Consulate, Bonaparte often confided in Roederer, who dined frequently with the first consul and later recorded a number of their conversations for posterity. Roederer defended the actions of the Consulate before his old friends the *idéologues*, who were becoming disenchanted with Bonaparte, and became one of the early promoters of the establishment of a hereditary regime in order to provide political stability for France. Bonaparte appointed Roederer president of the Section of the Interior of the Council of State and director general of public instruction. In the latter capacity, he developed a highly ambitious scheme of public instruction, which called for the elimination of the *écoles centrales* in seventeen major cities and their replacement by lycées with a curriculum that emphasized the study of the classical languages and French, history, mathematics, physics, and chemistry, and the duties of the citizen. This detailed plan, opposed by the minister of interior, Jean Chaptal, was never implemented. Roederer's disagreement with Chaptal as well as his quarrels with Joseph Fouché, whom he had apparently distrusted since the Terror, led in 1802 to his dismissal from the Council of State and from the position of director general of public instruction and to his subsequent appointment to the Senate. Fouché was simultaneously removed from the Ministry of Police (if temporarily) and made a senator.

From 1806 to 1808 Roederer served King Joseph Bonaparte as minister of finance in Naples, where he reformed taxation along lines similar to those he had advocated in the Tax Committee of the Constituent Assembly. A tax-collecting bureaucracy was established and tax farming eliminated. A direct tax on land and industrial property was created to replace the myriad direct taxes from the Old Regime. The government monopolies on salt and tobacco were temporarily ended but replaced when revenues declined too drastically. Indirect taxes were simplified but not eliminated. He also established a single national bank and began liquidating the public debt. Roederer's basic financial reforms remained in place even after the return of the Bourbon rulers.

During 1810–13, he was the administrator of the Grand Duchy of Berg and, in 1813–14, imperial commissioner in Strasbourg. During the Hundred Days, he was imperial commissioner in troubled southeastern France. He retired from public office in 1815 but remained intellectually active by writing histories, dramas, and his memoirs.

J. Burton, *Napoleon and Clio: Historical Writing, Teaching, and Thinking during the First Empire* (Durham, N.C., 1979); A. Cabanis, ''Un Idéologue Bonapartiste: Roederer,'' *RIN* 133 (1977); O. Connelly, *Napoleon's Satellite Kingdoms* (New York, 1965); K. Margerison, *P.-L. Roederer: Political Thought and Practice during the French Revolution* (Philadelphia, 1983), and ''P.-L. Roederer: The Industrial Capitalist as Revolutionary,'' *Eighteenth Century Studies* (1978); J. Popkin, ''The Newspaper Press in French Political Thought,'' *Studies in Eighteenth Century Culture* (1981); P.-L. Roederer, *Oeuvres*, 8 vols. (Paris, 1853–59).

Kenneth Margerison

Related entries: BERG, GRAND DUCHY OF; CONSTITUTIONS; EDUCATION; HUNDRED DAYS, THE; NAPLES, KINGDOM OF.

ROELL, W. F. See HOLLAND, KINGDOM OF; HOLLAND, KINGDOM OF: MINISTERS.

ROMAN REPUBLIC. See SISTER REPUBLICS.

ROME, KING OF. See NAPOLEON II.

ROMERO, D. MANUEL. See SPAIN, KINGDOM OF; SPAIN, KINGDOM OF: MINISTERS.

ROUSTAN RAZA (1780–1845), Napoleon's famed Mamluk bodyguard; also known as Roustam Raza. Born in Tiflis, kidnapped at an early age and sold into slavery, Roustan was recruited into the famed Mamluks of Egypt and in 1799 given by the sheik of Cairo to Bonaparte to serve as his bodyguard. Bonaparte took him back to France. At the palace of the Tuileries, Roustan slept on a mattress outside Napoleon's bedroom. He accompanied Napoleon on campaign as his personal gun bearer and slept at the entrance to his tent. His appearance in turbaned oriental costume was always a signal that Napoleon was near. After the first abdication (April 1814), he refused to follow Napoleon to Elba, and during the Hundred Days he was imprisoned at Vincennes. Under the July Monarchy, Louis Philippe gave him the postmastership of Dourdan, where he passed the remainder of his days. His memoirs are filled with interesting anecdotes.

R. Raza, *Souvenirs de Roustam, mameluck de Napoléon*, ed. P. Cottin (Paris, 1911).

Harold T. Parker

Related entries: MAMLUKS; NAPOLEON, DAILY ROUND.

ROVIGO, DUC DE. See SAVARY.

RUSSIA. Before the French Revolution, Russia was characterized by an undiscriminating kind of Westernization and a style of monarchy known even in the eighteenth century as the police state. Catherine II (1762–96) had promised progressive reform, but the Pugachev revolt of 1773–74 had given her pause, and the French Revolution frightened her into near hysteria. The closing years of her reign saw a conservative reaction, the exile of Alexander Radishchev to Siberia, and the persecution of Nicholas Novikov and the Freemasons.

Paul I (1796–1801) attempted to implement sufficient reform to immunize Russia against "Western corruption and madness." His law on succession (1797) abolished the law of Peter I (1722) (which had produced much instability by allowing the sovereign to choose his successor) and established male succession by primogeniture. He ignored the privileged position granted the nobility in 1785, required mandatory service to the state, and made nobles subject to corporal punishment and taxation. He responded to complaints of enlisted men against officers. In general, he was popular among the common people and very unpopular among the nobility. His foreign policy, like his domestic policy, was unlike his mother's. It developed in three phases. In 1796–98 he sought peace during the wars of the Revolution by offering his services as mediator. In 1799, disappointed in the expansionist French Directory, he joined the Second Coalition against France. In 1800–1801, disillusioned with his allies, especially Austria, he made overtures to the new consular government of France, hoping it would be more moderate than its predecessor. Bonaparte advertised his relationship with Russia as an alliance, which it was not, and thus spoiled the chance for cooperation between the two powers. Both Paul's foreign and his domestic policy alienated the governing class, and he was assassinated (23 March 1801).

Alexander I (1801–25), like his father, was in revolt against his predecessor.

He reconfirmed Catherine's Charter of the Nobility, restored in full the 1775 Law on the (noble) Administration of the Provinces, and temporarily abolished the political police. Actually, however, Alexander's political attitudes were ambivalent. He was eager not to alienate the nobility, and yet he feared the consequences of allowing it too much independence. Fundamental reform was considered during the period 1801–5, between the Second and Third Coalitions, when planning was dominated by an unofficial committee of Alexander's young and liberal aristocratic friends, and came to naught. It was taken up again between Tilsit and Napoleon's invasion, 1804–12. Planning was by the brilliant but low-born Count Michael Speransky. He was one of the best political minds of the age, but he was wrongly suspected of radical French sentiments. The nobles forced his dismissal before the beginning of the hostilities in 1812.

In foreign policy, Alexander initially moved to establish good relations with both France and Britain. The Franco-Russian treaty of October 1801 left Italy at French disposal but stipulated Russian participation in the rearrangement of the Germanies, which led to the Imperial Recess of 1803 and the dissolution of the Holy Roman Empire in 1806. In the meantime, Alexander, whose foreign policy views were much influenced by personal sentiments, was offended by Napoleon's assumption of an imperial crown (18 May 1804) and by the execution of the duc d'Enghien (21 March 1804). He joined the Third Coalition. He was outraged when Austria made peace (1805) and allied with Prussia (1806) to fight on but was beaten and made peace at Tilsit (1807). Soviet research has shown that Alexander accepted the Treaties of Tilsit reluctantly and skeptically as the best bargain that he could make in a bad situation. The alliance was extremely unpopular among the Russian gentry, and it did not long hold Alexander's loyalty. He did nothing to help Napoleon against the Austrians in 1809. After 1812, of course, he was at the heart of the coalition against France.

L. G. Beskrovnyi, *Otechestvennaia voina 1812 goda* (Moscow, 1962); A. McConnell, *Tsar Alexander I* (New York, 1970); M. Raeff, *Michael Speransky* (The Hague, 1957); H. Ragsdale, *Détente in the Napoleonic Era* (Lawrence, Kan., 1980); H. Ragsdale, ed., *Paul I: A Reassessment of His Life and Reign* (Pittsburgh, 1979); N. K. Schilder, *Imperator Aleksandr I*, 4 vols. (St. Petersburg, 1904); E. S. Shumigorskii, *Imperator Pavel I* (St. Petersburg, 1907); A. Trachevskii, ed., *Diplomaticheskiia snosheniia Rossii s Frantsiei v epokhu Napoleona I*, 4 vols. (St. Petersburg, 1809–93); P. A. Zhilin, *Gibel' napoleonovskoi armii v Rossii*, 2d ed. (Moscow, 1974); M. F. Zlotnikov, *Kontinental'naia blokada i Rossiia* (Moscow and Leningrad, 1966).

Hugh Ragsdale

Related entries: ALEXANDER I; CONTINENTAL BLOCKADE; PAUL I; RUSSIAN CAMPAIGN; TILSIT, TREATIES OF.

RUSSIAN CAMPAIGN. The origins of this decisive event probably lie in the dissatisfaction of both Napoleon and Alexander I with the results of the Tilsit agreement. There was undoubtedly a personal antagonism between the two men and beyond that deep and irreconcilable differences in political and economic policy. Both men seem to have realized by 1811 that war alone could resolve their differences. Contrary to the common notion, Napoleon did not embark on the campaign without much preparation and intensive planning. The initial invasion force was assembled from all over Europe, with Frenchmen a clear minority. When Napoleon crossed the Niemen into Russia on 24 June 1812, his hope was to entrap and destroy the Russian armies quickly, but they succeeded in retreating to Smolensk, where the French followed them in hopes of a decisive battle. But the Russians evacuated Smolensk and withdrew farther east. Napoleon spurned the warning of some of his advisers, still hoping for the decisive battle. Finally, on 7 September 1812 the Russian army under General Mikhail Kutuzov turned to bar the road to Moscow at Borodino. This battle, one of the bloodiest of the Napoleonic wars, ended with a French victory.

The Grande Armée now advanced to Moscow and occupied the city but found little advantage there. The city was heavily damaged by a fire whose origin is still disputed; contrary to Napoleon's expectations, Czar Alexander did not sue for peace and indeed spurned all overtures. In October the Grande Armée began its withdrawal. Checked at the Battle of Maloyaroslavets (24 October 1812), the emperor and his troops had to retreat over the same desolated land they had crossed earlier. The retreating army was increasingly harassed by Russian light troops; a hopelessly overburdened supply system and severe weather completed the army's destruction. At Krasnoye (16–17 November 1812) Ney's corps sacrificed itself, allowing the rest of the army to break out of a threatened encirclement. In a final catastrophe, the remnants of the Grande Armée were compelled to cross the Berezina under heavy fire and Russian assaults on both sides of the river. The Russian army, exhausted from the pursuit, stopped its attacks at the Niemen. By the time Napoleon left the army for Paris (8 December 1812), the Grande Armée numbered about 10,000. In his celebrated twenty-ninth bulletin (3 December 1812), the emperor presented to the French people a version of the campaign that minimized the disaster and assured the public that the emperor's health had never been better. But the French defeat in Russia had enormous repercussions. In January 1813 Prussia defected; within a few months most of the Napoleonic satellites followed suit, bringing the Empire toppling down.

A.A.L. de Caulaincourt, *With Napoleon in Russia* (New York, 1935); P. P. de Segur, *Napoleon's Russian Campaign* (Boston, 1958); E. Tarlé, *Napoleon's Invasion of Russia, 1812* (New York, 1942).

Lee Kennett

Related entries: ALEXANDER I; ARMY, FRENCH; ARMY, RUSSIAN; CONTINENTAL BLOCKADE; DIPLOMACY; FOREIGN POLICY; RUSSIA; WARFARE, ECONOMIC.

S

SACILE, BATTLE OF (16 April 1809), a victory of the Austrian army of inner Austria, commanded by Archduke John, over the French Army of Italy, commanded by Prince Eugène de Beauharnais. The French forces consisted of 34,000 infantry divided into five divisions and 1,950 cavalry grouped in a light cavalry division. The Austrian army, consisting of the Eighth and Ninth Corps, totaled 35,000 infantry and 4,000 cavalry.

After the Austrian invasion of Italy, Eugène's forces evacuated the eastern portion of Venetia, falling back toward their reinforcements. Eugène was reluctant to give up any more territory to the Austrians, and so he offered battle with only half of his army. Eugène had hoped that he would be joined by an additional infantry and cavalry division during the day, which would give him numerical parity, if not superiority, against his opponent. In this he would be mistaken.

Eugène planned to attack the Austrian left with three infantry divisions while his other two infantry divisions and lone cavalry division protected his center and left. The ground over which the French attacked was broken, which impeded the superior Austrian cavalry but also favored the Austrian defenders. The three attacking divisions on Eugène's right became heavily engaged against the Austrian Eighth Corps. Archduke John then sent his fresh Ninth Corps to attack and roll up Eugène's weaker left flank. Without the arrival of the reinforcements, the French left was overwhelmed, and the entire army was forced to retreat. The French suffered 3,000 killed and wounded, 3,500 captured, and lost fifteen guns. Austrian losses totaled 4,000.

Robert Epstein

Related entries: WAGRAM CAMPAIGN; WAGRAM CAMPAIGN, ITALIAN PHASE.

SAINTE ILDEFONSO, TREATY OF (1 October 1800). Spain ceded Louisiana to France in exchange for the Kingdom of Etruria (Tuscany) in Italy. See also COLONIES, FRENCH.

ST. HELENA, final place of exile of Napoleon. After his second abdication (22 June 1815), Napoleon traveled from Paris to Rochefort, intending to take ship to the United States, but he decided not to try to run the British naval blockade. Thus he went on board the British warship *Bellerophon* (15 July) and asked for refuge in England. The British government did not wish such a seductive, intriguing personality in their land and shipped him as a prisoner to St. Helena, a tiny island in the south Atlantic. Until his death on 5 May 1821, Napoleon's trials on St. Helena were many: the monotony of life on the rock; the petty tyrannies of a fearful, suspicious jailer, Sir Hudson Lowe; the jealousies and rending quarrels of the French companions in exile (''If I had known what it would be like, I would have brought nothing but servants''); the bitter memories of past glories and might-have-beens, of the ''fine Empire'' that he had kicked away (''Do you not think that when I wake in the night I don't have bad moments, when I recall what I was and what I am now?''); and the onset of disease, possibly hepatitis, gastric ulcers, and surely cancer of the stomach, treated in the end with debilitating remedies by incompetent physicians, including a Corsican, Francesco Antommarchi, sent by his mother. Yet he so managed his publicity as to gain his last victory. He dictated his memoirs and encouraged his followers to record and publish his conversations. In them he fabricated a legendary account of his life: that he was a martyr and that he was a martyr for democracy. He had always intended, he said, to introduce constitutional government in France, when his son was mature, and he had always wanted peace. But the unyielding enmity of England had interrupted the execution of his pacific, beneficent designs. The account was plausible enough to be believed by many Europeans and Americans, as well as Frenchmen. Further, the glories of the Napoleonic epic eventually entered the folklore of the entire Western world.

O. Aubrey, *Saint Helena*, trans. A. Livingston (London, 1936); J. Duhamel, *Les cinquante jours de Waterloo à Plymouth* (Paris, 1963); P. Ganière, *Napoléon à Sainte-Hélène* (Paris, 1957), and *La lutte contre Hudson Lowe* (Paris, 1960); R. Korngold, *The Last Years of Napoleon: His Captivity at St. Helena* (New York, 1959); G. Martineau, *Napoleon's Last Journey* (London, 1976), and *Napoleon's Saint Helena* (New York, 1969); F. Masson, *Napoleon at Saint Helena* (Oxford, 1949); M. J. Thornton, *Napoleon after Waterloo: England and the Saint Helena Decision* (Stanford, Calif., 1968).

Harold T. Parker

Related entries: ANTOMMARCHI; BERTRAND; GOURGAUD; LEGEND, NAPOLEONIC; LOWE; MONTHOLON; NAPOLEON I.

ST. PETERSBURG, TREATY OF (April 1812), alliance between Russia and Sweden against France. Sweden was promised Norway (then part of Denmark) to oppose the coming French attack on Russia. See also FOREIGN POLICY; RUSSIAN CAMPAIGN.

SALAMANCA, BATTLE OF. See PENINSULAR WAR.

SALICETI, ANTOINE-CHRISTOPHE (1757–1809), Corsican-French Revolutionary, Terrorist, patron of the young Napoleon, later serving him in civil posts. Son of a non-noble proprietor of Saliceto di Rostino, Saliceti received the doctorat *in utruque jure* from the University of Pisa in 1783. During the 1780s he was a magistrate deputy to the Corsican Estates and *avocat* before the (French) Royal Council at Bastia. In 1789 he was elected deputy of the Corsican Third Estate to the Estates General at Versailles. There he secured Corsica's annexation as a department, pardon for Corsican patriots who had opposed the French in 1769, and a decree allowing Paoli to return from England. Corsicans hailed Saliceti as the "island's second liberator," and the *Consulta* of 1790 elected him *procureur général syndic in absentia*. Meanwhile, however, national service and affiliation with the Jacobin club began to erode his provincial loyalties. Nevertheless, in 1792 Saliceti was elected to the French Convention. In Paris Saliceti joined the Montagnards and voted for the execution of the king without appeal. As representative on mission with the army at Toulon (1793), he got his fellow Corsican, Bonaparte, appointed artillery commander. Napoleon's performance got him promoted to brigadier general, and his star began to rise. Saliceti also became notorious while supervising executions after the city's capture.

Under the Directory, he remained a Jacobin at heart. As supplier to Napoleon's Army of Italy in 1796, he helped organize what became the Cisalpine Republic. During 1797–99 he served in the Council of Five Hundred in Paris and was active in the Club du Manège and the Club de Rue du Bac. During the coup d'état of 18 Brumaire, he rallied Jacobins to Bonaparte (if only because he saw no alternative). Bonaparte repaid him by striking his name from a list of persons marked for exile. Subsequently Saliceti served Napoleon on missions to Corsica and Elba, imposed constitutions on Lucca and Genoa, and in 1805 orchestrated the Ligurian Republic's annexation to the Empire. In February 1806, Napoleon sent Saliceti to be minister of police for his brother Joseph, new king of Naples. He swiftly developed a terroristic system, which struck down opponents of the regime (and of which Joseph was largely unaware). Saliceti became minister of war in May 1807 and increased his influence by cultivating support among the Neapolitans. In 1808, Saliceti's power and reputation for intrigue seemed a threat to Joachim Murat, who replaced Joseph. Murat curtailed Saliceti's activities as minister of police and deprived him of the Ministry of War. Saliceti left to plead his cause before Napoleon but was sent back to assist in the seizure of the Papal States and the arrest of Pius VII. Saliceti died in Naples on 23 December 1809, producing rumors that Antonio Maghella (his successor as minister of police) had poisoned him. An autopsy ordered by Napoleon showed the belief to be false.

J. Godechot, *Les Commissaires aux armées sous le Directoire*, 2 vols. (Paris, 1941); L. Macaluso, "The Political Lives of Antoine Christophe Saliceti, 1789-1809" (Ph.D. dissertation, University of Kentucky, Lexington, 1972); J. Rambaud, *Naples sous Joseph Bonaparte, 1806–1808* (Paris, 1911).

Leonard Macaluso

Related entries: BRUMAIRE, COUP OF 18, YEAR VIII; NAPLES, KINGDOM OF; NAPOLEON I; TOULON, SIEGE OF.

SANHEDRIN, GRAND. See JEWS.

SANTO DOMINGO. See HAITI.

SARAGOSSA, SIEGES OF. See PENINSULAR WAR.

SAVARY, ANNE-JEAN-MARIE-RENE (1774–1833), duc de Rovigo, minister of police. Born at Marcq (Ardennes), the third son of a cavalry officer who was major of the chateau of Sedan, Savary in 1790 enrolled in the cavalry of the Royal Army as a volunteer. During the wars of the Revolution, he served first under Adam-Philippe de Custine, then Jean Pichegru and Jean Moreau before becoming aide-de-camp of L.-C.-A. Desaix and finally, with Desaix's death at Marengo, of Bonaparte himself. Savary belonged to Napoleon's "department of dirty tricks." Napoleon, counting on his blind, unconditional obedience and his moral insensitivity, used him on nasty missions: for example, to take charge of the execution of the duc d'Enghien at Vincennes, to dupe the Spanish prince Ferdinand VII and lead him into Napoleon's trap at Bayonne, and in 1810 to head the Ministry of Police after Joseph Fouché's dismissal.

For these and other services, Savary was liberally rewarded. He was made general of brigade (1803), general of division (1805), and duke of Rovigo (1808), and he received many extra gratifications. However, Savary's maladroitness as minister of police contributed to the latter-day unpopularity of Napoleon's regime. Fouché's operations as minister always had qualities of subtlety, finesse, and even fun. Savary was obtuse, heavy-handed, brutal, and (a cardinal sin for a policeman) sometimes ridiculous, and he brought discredit on the ministry. He became the laughing stock of Paris in 1812 when the Malet conspirators arrested him in bed and imprisoned him for a few hours. Yet Napoleon retained him as minister and during the Hundred Days appointed him first inspector general of the gendarmerie. A devoted follower, Savary tried to accompany Napoleon to St. Helena but was arrested on board the *Bellerophon* by the English and conducted to Malta. His memoirs, written to exculpate him from "calumny," are among the most inaccurate of the period.

B. Melchior-Bonnet, *Un policier dans l'ombre de Napoléon: Savary, duc de Rovigo* (Paris, 1962); A.-J.-M.-R. Savary, *Mémoires du duc de Rovigo*, ed. D. Lacroix, 5 vols. (Paris, 1900); J. Tulard, "L'affaire Malet," in J. Mistler, ed., *Napoléon et l'Empire*, vol. 2 (Paris, 1968).

Harold T. Parker

Related entries: DIPLOMACY; ITALIAN CAMPAIGN, SECOND; PENINSULAR WAR; POLICE, MINISTRY OF GENERAL.

SAXONY, KINGDOM OF. Its German and central European location lent Saxony great strategic importance in the age of Napoleon. In 1792 Electoral Saxony had mobilized for war against France and ultimately sent 10,000 men to fight beside the Prussians and Austrians. Prussia took a neutral stance in 1795, however, and in 1796 Saxony withdrew its contingent from the war. Neither the Prussian nor the Saxon army profited, however, from the bloody lessons of war against a revolutionary army. In 1806 still allied with Prussia, Saxony sent 20,000 men to the aid of the Prussians against France. It was crushed at Jena, along with the army of Prince Hohenlohe.

Elector Friedrich August shortly concluded the Treaty of Posen (11 December 1806) with Napoleon, which assured the territorial integrity of Saxony and made the elector a king. In return, Saxony allied with France and joined the Confederation of the Rhine. In 1807 Napoleon placed under the Saxon king the new Duchy of Warsaw (composed of the Polish possessions of Prussia). He had deliberately created a kingdom to rival Prussia, which he reduced to a pre-1740 size. He had transferred to Saxony Prussian Cottbus County, made Danzig a joint protectorate of Saxony and France, and gave Saxony access to roads in Silesia for military purposes.

Saxon forces fought beside the French in 1807, largely in the investment of Danzig. The alliance with Napoleon in 1809 catapulted Saxony into the war against Austria, and a Saxon corps of 19,000 men suffered heavy casualties at Wagram. In 1810, serious reform of the Saxon army was undertaken. The infantry finally dropped line tactics and adopted the more mobile French column. In 1812 a Saxon corps of 20,000 men marched into Russia with the Grand Armée; it was used by the commander of the Eighth Corps, Count Jean Reynier, to protect the flank of the right wing and to safeguard important lines of communication. Of these 20,000, only 2,500 returned home. In December 1812 King Friedrich August, still loyal to Napoleon, ordered the deployment of the troops still remaining in Saxony, which soon became a theater of war. By August 1813 when Austria joined the Allies, the Saxon army had grown to 15,000 and fought on with the French. At Dennewitz in September 1813, the Saxons suffered severe casualties. In the meantime, the attitude of the Saxon army had grown increasingly anti-French, and during the Battle of Leipzig large numbers deserted to the Allies.

Saxony was placed under a Russian governor, and Friedrich August was taken prisoner. Despite the total exhaustion and depletion of the kingdom, a new army was raised and employed by the Allies, largely in Flanders. After lengthy negotiations at Vienna, Saxony, contrary to the wishes of Prussia, was not completely ceded to Prussia but was reduced to less than half of its former size.

T. Flathe, *Neuere Geschichte Sachsens von 1806–1866* (1873); W. Hahlweg, "Die Grundzüge der Verfassung des Sächsischen Geheimen Kabinetts 1763–1831," *Zeitschrift für die gesamte Staatswissenschaft* 103 (1943); W. Kohlschmidt, *Die sächsische Frage auf dem Wiener Kongress und die sächsische Diplomatie dieser Zeit* (1930); R. Kötschke and H. Kretzschmar, *Sächsische Geschichte* (1977); O. Schuster and F. A. Francke, *Geschichte der sächsischen Armee* (1885).

Joachim Niemeyer

Related entries: ARMY, PRUSSIAN; FRIEDRICH AUGUST III; JENA-AUERSTÄDT-FRIEDLAND CAMPAIGN; LEIPZIG, BATTLE OF; TILSIT, TREATIES OF; WARSAW, DUCHY OF.

SCHARNHORST, GERHARD JOHANN DAVID VON (1755–1813), Prussian general and reformer. The first fifty years of Scharnhorst's life were unexceptional. Born into the family of a Hanoverian tenant farmer, he was commissioned into the Hanoverian army, became an instructor at the artillery school, wrote manuals for artillery officers, and founded a military journal, which he published until 1805.

He saw action in 1793 against the French in Belgium, where in 1794 he led the garrison of Menin, which broke through superior investing forces, and was promoted to major.

As early as 1797 Prussia attempted to gain his services by offering to triple his salary, and in 1801 he transferred his allegiance. Commissioned a colonel of artillery, he also evaluated military installations, supervised the cadet schools in Berlin, and lectured at the military academy, where Carl von Clausewitz was one of his students. In 1805 he assisted the Prussian commander in chief, the duke of Brunswick, in occupying Hanover.

In 1806 he became Brunswick's chief of staff. After the battle of Auerstädt (where the duke was fatally wounded), he accompanied G. L. von Blücher to Lübeck and ultimately made his way to East Prussia. The defeat of the combined Russian and Prussian armies at Friedland and the Peace of Tilsit signaled the nadir of Prussia's fortunes but also Colonel Scharnhorst's rise to historical prominence.

For some time, Scharnhorst, now a brigadier general, had been questioning the antiquated forms of eighteenth-century warfare. When he was appointed to the Prussian Military Reorganization Commission, he was able to give body to his ideas. They were guided by the new concept of the French republican armies. Assisted by August von Gneisenau, Hermann von Boyen, Karl vom Stein, and others, Scharnhorst proposed to augment the small, long-service, professional army with one of conscription. Legally, caste was replaced by merit in the selection and promotion of officers, the army organization was modernized, corporal punishment was abolished, and new tactics were introduced that allowed for greater speed and flexibility. Above all, Scharnhorst's *Krümper* system (rotating men in and out of the regular ranks) allowed the Prussian army to build up its reserves far beyond the limit of 42,000 men imposed by Napoleon. It was designed not merely to compensate for numerical deficiency but also to lay the foundation for what Scharnhorst had recognized as the crucial new element in warfare: the mass army.

Prussia's new national army was put to the test in the final struggle against Napoleon. Scharnhorst, serving as Blücher's chief of staff, was severely wounded and died less than two months later. His concept of the nation in arms survived him, as did the knowledge that the outcome of wars no longer depended on weapons alone. In the future, psychological and moral strength, nourished by political and social ideas, would be decisive.

C. von Clausewitz, *Über das Leben und den Charakter des Generals von Scharnhorst* (1832); S. Fiedler, *Scharnhorst* (1963); R. Höhn, *Scharnhorsts Vermächtnis* (1972); F. Hossbach, *Scharnhorst* (1955); M. Lehmann, *Scharnhorst*, 2 vols. (1886–87); R. Stadelmann, *Scharnhorst* (1952).

Peter W. Becker

Related entries: BOYEN; GNEISENAU; PRUSSIA, KINGDOM OF; STEIN.

SCHILL, FERDINAND BAPTISTA VON (1779–1809), Prussian major and free corps commander, posthumously idolized as a romantic hero of German unification. Schill developed a particular talent for partisan warfare after the Battle of Auerstädt (1806), where he was wounded. He reached Kolberg and with the fortress commander's approval carried out sorties against the French, of which the skirmish at Gülzow made him suddenly famous. The king awarded him the *Pour le mérite* medal and commissioned him to form and lead his own free corps. It was not always successful, but it became a symbol of the Prussian patriotic resistance along with the defense of Kolberg by August von Gneisenau and Joachim Nettelbeck. The king had Schill (then twenty-nine) take the lead with his regiment in the festive entry of the army into Berlin (1808) after the French withdrawal. The crowds cheered a popular hero who had already awakened the hopes of German reformers.

When Austria proclaimed a war of German liberation in 1809, Schill had agreed to inspire a popular uprising in northern Germany. Gerhard Scharnhorst warned Schill not to act hastily since Prussia was neutral. But Schill marched from Berlin with his regiment, ignored orders to return, and from Dessau directed a proclamation to the Germans, urging them to shake off the French yoke by force of arms. Although he quickly saw that there would be no German uprising and that the Austrians were in retreat, his officers begged him to fight on, and he did. Constantly attacked, Schill's corps made its way through Westphalia and Mecklenburg to Swedish Stralsund. There he intended to hold out until the arrival of English ships. But the French sent three times his numbers of Danish and Dutch troops against him, and he stood no chance. The city was stormed, and Schill and many of his followers were killed. His head was taken to King Jerome, who had put a prize on it. On orders by Napoleon, eleven of his officers were shot at Wesel and fourteen of his soldiers at Brandenburg. Of the rest, some escaped, but the majority were sent to the galleys.

Strictly as a military leader, Schill does not rate well; he had a tendency to depend too much on boldness and to underestimate his opponents. It was the same devil-may-care attitude, however, combined with his youth and good looks, that made him a symbolic hero of the War of Liberation of 1813 and of the later German unification movement.

C. Binder von Krieglstein, *Ferdinand von Schill. Ein Lebensbild* (1909); H. Bock, *Schill. Rebellenzug 1809* (1969); W. Janke, *Das Königlich Preussische v. Schillsche Freikorps. . .Eine heereskundliche Betrachtung* (1938).

Reinhard Stumpf

Related entries: ARMY, PRUSSIAN; JENA-AUERSTÄDT-FRIEDLAND CAMPAIGN; PRUSSIA, KINGDOM OF; WAGRAM CAMPAIGN; WESTPHALIA, KINGDOM OF.

SCHILLER, FRIEDRICH (1759–1805), German dramatist, poet, philosopher, and historian. In his early plays, Schiller championed bourgeois liberalism. The French National Assembly voted him an honorary citizenship (1792) because of his supposed support, but his reaction to the Revolution was not enthusiastic. He came to terms with events in France through theoretical writings on aesthetics dealing with the nature of beauty, the role of art in education, freedom, and political ideals (especially *Über die ästhetische Erziehung des Menschen*, 1794). Two well-known poems present man's historical development, culminating in a negative view of the French situation and a hope for future peace ("Der Spaziergang," 1795; "Das Lied von der Glocke," 1800). His drama *Wilhelm Tell* (1804) stresses that government must guarantee the individual's freedom and security. The individual was most important to Schiller; he objected that the French Revolution made individuals as subservient to the new society as they had been in the old. Contemporaries report that Schiller neither liked nor trusted Napoleon; direct statements from him are lacking, but the title figure in the late drama fragment *Demetrius* is often seen as a literary reference to him.

L. A. Willoughby, "Schiller on Man's Education to Freedom through Knowledge," *Germanic Review* 29 (1954); B. von Wiese, "Schiller und die französische Revolution," in his *Der Mensch in der Dichtung* (Düsseldorf, 1958).

Cora Lee Nollendorfs

Related entries: CARL AUGUST; GOETHE.

SCHIMMELPENNINCK, RUTGER JAN (1761–1825), grand pensionary (chief executive) of the Batavian Republic, as reorganized by Napoleon. He was removed in favor of Louis Bonaparte (1806), who became king of the newly created Kingdom of Holland (1806). See HOLLAND, KINGDOM OF.

SCHÖN, THEODOR VON (1773–1856), Prussian official and reformer, collaborator of the Baron vom Stein. While studying law and political science at Königsberg, Schön became an adherent of Immanuel Kant and while visiting England was impressed with the doctrines of Adam Smith and the English political and economic systems. He joined the Prussian civil service in 1793 and was soon in the circle of reformers around Karl Hardenberg. In 1807 he collaborated with Stein and helped shape the legislation on municipal autonomy and the emancipation of the peasants. In 1808, when Stein was dismissed, Schön drafted his political testament. As governor of East and West Prussia (after 1824), he was instrumental in the restoration of the war-damaged provinces. Because he favored a uniform constitution for the entire state, he was retired in 1842. In 1848 he presided over the Prussian National Assembly and until his death remained a chief proponent of Prussian liberalism.

H. J. Belke, *Die preussische Regierung zu Königsberg 1808–1850* (1976); M. Gray, "Theodor von Schön and the Prussian Reforms" (Ph.D. dissertation, University of Wisconsin, 1971); H. Rothfels, *Theodor von Schön, Friedrich Wilhelm III. und die Revolution von 1848* (1937).

Peter G. Thielen

Related entries: PRUSSIA, KINGDOM OF; STEIN.

SCHÖNBRUNN, TREATY OF (15 December 1805), between France and Prussia; not to be confused with the more famous treaty of 1809 with Austria. In return for Hanover, Prussia agreed to cede Cleves, Ansbach, and Neufchâtel to France. See also FOREIGN POLICY.

SCHÖNBRUNN, TREATY OF (14 October 1809), between France and Austria, following Napoleon's victory at Wagram and the British withdrawal from Walcheren. Austria ceded Salzburg, Berchtesgaden, and other Alpine territories to Bavaria, West Galicia to the Duchy of Warsaw, the Southern Tyrol to Italy, and the Tarnopol section of East Galicia to Russia. France received all Austrian territory beyond the Save River, which included Villach, Istria, Hungarian Dalmatia, and Ragusa. These areas, with the Ionian Islands (ceded to France in 1797, lost to Russia but regained in 1807), became the Illyrian Provinces, in theory part of France but ruled separately. Austria joined the Continental System.
Related entries: FOREIGN POLICY; WAGRAM, BATTLE OF; WALCHEREN, INVASION OF.

SCHOOLS. See EDUCATION.

SCHWARZENBERG, KARL PHILIPP ZU, PRINCE (1771–1820), Austrian field marshal, chief commander against Napoleon in 1813–14. Schwarzenberg entered the Austrian army at sixteen, fought in the Turkish war of 1788–89, and fought against France in the Austrian Netherlands in 1792–94. By 1800 he was a major general and fought under Archduke Johann at Hohenlinden. In 1805 he was vice-president of the Imperial War Council and, in a year of disasters for Austria, won a victory at Jungingen, near Ulm. In 1809 he went to St. Petersburg to try to prevent the czar from declaring for Napoleon but failed. He was Austrian cavalry commander at the Battle of Wagram and afterward was promoted to general of the cavalry, awarded the Golden Fleece, and appointed ambassador to Paris. In 1812, at Napoleon's request, he commanded the Austrian corps, which joined the French against Russia but did not commit his troops deeply, so that they escaped the catastrophic fate of the Grand Armée. Promoted to field marshal in 1812, he vainly attempted in 1813 to mediate a peace between Russia and France. When Austria joined the Allies (August 1813), he assumed charge of the main army (Bohemian Army). The Allied monarchs appointed Schwarzenberg commander in chief, a task that his diplomatic and military talents allowed him to execute brilliantly, especially at the Battle of Leipzig. Schwarzenberg planned the winter campaign against France in 1814 that ended with the entry of the Allies into Paris. In the same year, Schwarzenberg was appointed president of the Imperial War Council and after Napoleon's return from Elba commanded the hastily formed Allied army on the Upper Rhine, which, however, did not see action.

K. Schwarzenberg, *Feldmarschall Fürst Schwarzenberg* (1964).

Brigitte Holl

Related entries: ARMY, HABSBURG; FRANCE, CAMPAIGN OF; GERMAN WAR OF LIBERATION; RUSSIAN CAMPAIGN; WAGRAM, BATTLE OF; WAGRAM CAMPAIGN.

SCIENCE. The fifty years from 1775 to 1825 was one of the most brilliant periods in French science. A galaxy of genius and talent—Pierre Laplace, Joseph Lagrange, Gaspard Monge, and Joseph Fourier in mathematics, Antoine de Lavoisier, Claude Berthollet, Jean Chaptal, Antoine de Fourcroy, Louis Guyton, and Joseph Gay-Lussac in chemistry, Charles Coulomb, Lazare Carnot, and Etienne Malus in physics, and Jean de Lamarck, Georges Cuvier, and Etienne Geoffrey St.-Hilaire in biology—made Paris for the moment the scientific capital of the Western world. Older themes and trends in Newtonian science were continued and completed, and new routes of investigation for the nineteenth century to develop were opened up. What was the relation of Napoleon and the institutions he sponsored to this scientific achievement?

The historical record speaks with two voices. Positively, Napoleon was a genuine patron of science. He continued from earlier regimes those higher schools and research institutes that salaried eminent French scientists, brought them together, and disseminated their publications: the Collège de France; the Ecole Polytechnique, a first-rate school of engineering and science where Monge and Lagrange gave courses on mathematics and Berthollet, Chaptal, Fourcroy, Guyton, and Gay-Lussac shared the teaching of chemistry; the Bureau des Longitudes, whose salaried members under the supervision of Laplace directed the observatories of France and met weekly as a scientific society; the Muséum d'Histoire Naturelle, where Fourcroy and Lamarck, among others, were salaried researchers; and the Institut de France, where weekly meetings of the First Class (mathematics and natural science) apparently revived the glories of the old Royal Academy of Science.

General Bonaparte was flattered by his election to the Institut in 1797. In his letter of acceptance, he said the right thing: "True victories, the only ones which leave no regret, are those made over ignorance. The most honorable occupation and the most useful to nations is to contribute to the extension of human ideas." Berthollet and Monge were among his friends, and he took them and a large corps of learned men with him to Egypt, where they established the Institut d'Egypte. As first consul and emperor he appointed Berthollet, Chaptal, Fourcroy, Lagrange, Laplace, and Monge to the Senate. Their stipends as senators enabled Berthollet to build a private physical and chemical laboratory and with Laplace to support the influential scientific Society of Arcueil.

But in everything Napoleon did, there increasingly intruded the desire for personal power. He patronized scientists, but he insisted on obedience and limited freedom of inquiry more than had the Bourbon kings. He interfered in the affairs of the Institut. More seriously, over the protests of Berthollet, Fourcroy, and Monge, he militarized the Ecole Polytechnique. He stripped it of most of its research budget, reduced the number of courses in pure science, and directed its curriculum to the practical preparation of military engineers. Thus perhaps the foremost school of science in the world lost its long-term purpose of advancing pure science. To be sure, scientific research continued under Napoleon, but there was a danger that under the new imperial educational system, bright young men would not be recruited and properly trained as scientists, and French science ultimately would suffer.

M. Crosland, *The Society of Arcueil: A View of French Science at the Time of Napoleon I* (Cambridge, Mass., 1967); R. Hahn, *The Anatomy of a Scientific Institution: The Paris Academy of Sciences, 1666–1803* (Berkeley, Calif., 1971); René Taton et al., *Histoire générale des sciences*, 3 vols. (Paris, 1958–61); L. Pearce Williams, "Science, Education, and Napoleon I," *Isis* 47 (1956).

Harold T. Parker

Related entries: BERTHOLLET; CARNOT; CHAPTAL; COULOMB; EDUCATION; EGYPTIAN CAMPAIGN; FOURCROY; INSTITUT NATIONAL DES SCIENCES ET DES ARTS; LAGRANGE; LAMARCK; LAPLACE; MEDICINE; MONGE.

SCOPOLI, GIOVANNI. See ITALY, KINGDOM OF; ITALY, KINGDOM OF: MINISTERS.

SCULPTURE. In the Napoleonic era (1800–14), sculpture was international and neoclassical in style, with major centers of production in Paris and Rome. Although this classical revival drew inspiration from all phases of Greco-Roman antiquity, the style was highly original and diverse and marks the origin of modern sculpture. The early phase developed after 1750, faded by the 1830s, and became the symbol of the Napoleonic taste. Napoleon's favorite sculptor, the Italian Antonio Canova, served as the leading practitioner of the style. Other neoclassical sculptors were figures of various nationalities: Joseph-Charles Marin, Simon-Louis Boizot, Antoine-Denis Chaudet, Joseph Chinard, John Flaxman, Bertel Thorwaldsen, Gottfried Schadow, Johan Tobias Sergel, Christian-Daniel Rauch, Asmus-Jakob Carstens, Richard Westmacott, and John Gibson. Although Napoleon's aversion for public sculptures of himself is well known, many statues and busts of him were done, and he even sat for Canova. His strongest support, however, was for general sculptural production. Neoclassical sculpture held a political and serious place in Napoleonic culture. Artists and the public alike recognized that due to rapidly changing government situations, public sculpture, unlike painting, was often destroyed. Canova revived Roman production techniques, allowing for sculptors to produce plaster sculpture to be displayed in both the studio and later in the salon. In this way sculptors could afford to produce plasters at small expense, and destruction and changing political fortunes were not significant.

Arts Council of Great Britain, *The Age of Neoclassicism* (London, 1972); H. Honour, *Neoclassicism* (Harmondsworth, 1968); G. Hubert, *La sculpture dans l'Italie napoléonienne* (Paris, 1964), and *Les sculpteurs italiens en France* (Paris, 1964); S. Lami, *Dictionnaire des sculpteurs de l'école française au dix-neuvième siècle.*

Jean Henry

Related entries: ARCHITECTURE; ART; CANOVA; LOUVRE; PROPAGANDA; SYMBOLISM AND STYLE.

SEGUR, PHILIPPE-PAUL, COMTE (1780–1873), general famous for his history of the Russian campaign of 1812, *Histoire de Napoléon et la Grande Armée de 1812* (Paris, 1824), which has been translated into every major language. Of a family of nobles of the Old Regime, he was born in Paris, where his father was a diplomat under Louis XVI. The elder count Ségur survived the Revolution in France and in 1799 rallied to Napoleon, who made him grand master of ceremonies in the imperial court and a senator. The emperor made the younger Ségur an aide-de-camp and advanced him rapidly, promoting him to general in 1812. He was with Napoleon almost constantly in Russia and reported the campaign from that vantage point. He did not spare the emperor, however, and may have slanted his treatment against him to please the Bourbons, who had returned to rule France. Ségur also left *Mémoires* (8 vols., 1873), of which the Russian epic is part.

Related entry: RUSSIAN CAMPAIGN.

SENATE. See CONSTITUTIONS.

SERBS AND NAPOLEON. Disillusioned with Russian support, the Serbs ultimately pinned their hopes for independence on the French (Napoleon), but in vain. Napoleon was hostile to the Serbian revolt of 1804 against Turkey because of the traditional ties of the Serbs with Austria and (especially) Russia, his most powerful continental enemies. The combined attack of Russian and Montenegrin forces against French troops in Cattaro in 1805 confirmed Napoleon's suspicions. Furthermore, he feared the potential repercussions of the Serbian national movement in French-occupied Dalmatia. Accordingly, Horace Sebastiani, Napoleon's ambassador to the Sublime Porte, was told to urge the suppression of the Serbian revolt. In the same spirit, Napoleon wrote to Sultan Selim III on 20 June 1806. Napoleon discussed the future of Serbia inconclusively with the czar at Tilsit. On the outbreak of the Russo-Turkish war of 1808–12, the Serbs under Karageorge (George Petrović) rallied to the Russians, but the czar failed to defend them against the Turkish onslaught in the spring of 1809 and provoked the Serbs to a dramatic change of international orientation.

By a resolution of 16 August 1809, the Serbian National Assembly appealed for Napoleon's protection and offered all fortresses of the country to French garrisons. On the same date, Karageorge, the independence leader, addressed a personal message to Napoleon, inviting him to take Serbia under his wing. Captain Rado Vucinić, an Austrian Serb, was charged with the transmission of these messages to the French authorities. This mission took him first to Bucharest and then to Vienna where Napoleon had been holding court since his victory at Wagram in July 1809. In October 1809 Vucinić met with J.-B. de Champagny, the French foreign minister, who conveyed the emperor's interest, without, however, undertaking any concrete commitments. Napoleon's friendly relations with Austria and the Ottoman Porte precluded a French intervention in Serbia. Realizing this, Vucinić declared the Serbs' willingness to submit to Turkish sovereignty, if Napoleon would mediate an agreement giving them domestic autonomy.

In January 1810, the Serbian appeal was renewed, and Vucinić was appointed plenipotentiary to France. He crossed into the Illyrian Provinces and renewed his contacts at Trieste and Laibach. Receiving no definite answer, he departed for Paris, where he was kept in suspense from May 1810 onward. In desperation, Karageorge invited Austria to occupy Belgrade in the spring of 1810, but Napoleon, fearing a renewed Austro-Turkish conflict, prevented any action. With Napoleon's invasion of Russia imminent, Russia made peace with the Ottoman Empire, and the Russo-Turkish treaty of Bucharest (1812) granted autonomy to Serbia. However, Russia's war with Napoleon (1812) allowed the Turks to subdue the Serbs violently. Thus, in 1813, the first Serbian revolution collapsed. Karageorge took refuge in Russia while his plenipotentiary remained in Paris until 1814.

A. Boppe, *Documents inédits sur les relations de la Serbie avec Napoléon I* (Belgrade, 1888); M. Gavrilović, *Ispisi iz Pariskih Arhiva* (Belgrade, 1904); G. Yakchitch, *L'Europe et la résurrection de la Serbie (1804–1834)* (Paris, 1917).

Paschalis M. Kitromilides

Related entries: DIPLOMACY; FOREIGN POLICY; RUSSIA; TILSIT, TREATIES OF.

SERRA, GIAN CARLO (1760–1813), French diplomat, born in Genoa. A member of the first government of the French-sponsored Ligurian Republic, he was its ambassador to Paris and later to Madrid. When it was incorporated into the Empire, he became Napoleon's representative in Spain and then in the Duchy of Warsaw. There Serra became an ally of the Polish Jacobins, battled the duchy's government constantly, and tried to discredit it to Paris.

In 1809, when the Austrians invaded the duchy, he attempted to force the government to surrender power in Warsaw to the Jacobins. Warsaw fell, however, and both he and the government fled. He returned to Warsaw after the war

(July 1809), but the bitterness existing between himself and the government persisted. He was replaced by Louis Bignon in 1810 and killed during the siege of Dresden in 1813.

M. Handelsman, *Dyplomaci napoleonscy w Warszawie* (Warsaw, 1914); P. Nurra, *La coalizione europea contro la repubblica di Genova* (Genoa, 1933).

John Stanley

Related entries: DIPLOMACY; FOREIGN POLICY; PONIATOWSKI; WAGRAM CAMPAIGN; WARSAW, DUCHY OF.

SERURIER, JEAN-MATHIEU-PHILIBERT, COUNT (1742–1819), marshal of France. Of minor nobility, Sérurier entered the Royal Army as a cadet in 1755 and, as a career officer, reached the rank of colonel shortly after the Revolution began (1791). He continued to serve the Republic after the execution of Louis XVI (1793) and was a major general in 1795. He served Bonaparte in the first Italian campaign (1796–97) but thereafter was given civil posts. He supported the coup d'état of 18 Brumaire. Napoleon made him a senator (1800), governor of the Invalides, and an honorary marshal (1804). He rallied to Napoleon in 1815 and lost his rank and position, which were restored only when he was dying in 1819.

L. Tuetey, *Sérurier* (Paris, 1899).

Jesse Scott

Related entries: ITALIAN CAMPAIGN, FIRST; MARSHALS OF THE EMPIRE.

SIEYES, EMMANUEL-JOSEPH (1748–1836), abbé who served in successive governments of the French Revolution and Napoleonic era and played an important role in the early stages of the Revolution. He participated in the drafting of the Constitution of 1791, the Constitution of the Year III (1795), and the Constitution of the Year VIII (1799), and he initiated the coup d'état of 18 Brumaire, which brought Napoleon to power in 1799.

Sieyès was born on 3 May 1748 in Fréjus, the son of a successful notary *(contrôleur des actes)*. Sieyès studied for an ecclesiastical career at the Sorbonne, where he spent much of his time reading the metaphysical writings of the Enlightenment, especially those of John Locke, Etienne Condillac, and Charles Bonnet. When King Louis XVI in July 1788 agreed to summon the Estates General, Sieyès was chancellor of the diocese of Chartres, but not being of noble birth, he held little hope of advancing further. During the public controversy over the organization of the Estates General, Sieyès attacked the ancient privileges of the nobility and clergy in his *Essai sur les privilèges* (November 1788). His celebrated pamphlet, *Qu'est-ce que c'est le tiers-état?* (January 1789), placed Sieyès at the head of the publicists who promoted the cause of the Third Estate and popular sovereignty.

As a representative of the Third Estate to the Estates General that met on 5 May 1789, the abbé Sieyès was a key figure among those who persuaded the delegates to proclaim themselves on 17 June a National Assembly with power to legislate for the French people. In the debate of September 1789, Sieyès supported a unicameral legislature and no veto for the king. Sieyès signed with misgivings the Civil Constitution of the Clergy in 1790, and he sought to limit suffrage in the Constitution of 1791 by authoring property qualification provisions for passive and active citizens. Sieyès founded the exclusive Société de '89 and he and his fellow liberal monarchists (the Marquis de Lafayette, Jean-Sylvain Bailly, Antoine Barnave, Honoré de Mirabeau) also helped organize the Society of Friends of the Constitution. This early Jacobin club grew more and more radical as the Revolution began to take on a more republican tint, inspiring Sieyès and other heroes of 1789 to form a new, more moderate club in 1791, the Feuillants.

Sieyès was elected in 1792 to the National Convention where he took his place in the center, or the Plain, waiting for the Jacobin stage of the Revolution to expend itself. Speaking later of the Terror, Sieyès proudly stated, "J'ai vécu" ("I survived"). Upon the fall of Robespierre, Sieyès reasserted himself. He served for six months on the Committee of Public Safety, advocating an expansionist foreign policy. Sieyès and J.-F. Reubell negotiated the Treaty of the Hague (1795) with the Batavian Republic. Sieyès took the lead in drawing up the liberal yet bourgeois Constitution of the Year III (22 August 1795). Under this constitution Sieyès served on the Council of Five Hundred, and with the coup of Prairial (June 1799) the moderate Sieyès became a director along with the antiroyalist Roger Ducos and the Jacobins Jean-François-Auguste Moulin and Louis Gohier.

The Jacobins now controlled the legislative councils, which in turn controlled the Directory. Not happy with this state of affairs and ever fearful of a return of the Terror, Sieyès determined that yet another coup d'état was necessary in order to revise the constitution and strengthen the executive branch against the forces of the left. Sieyès persuaded the councils to abolish the Jacobin club, and he managed to get his friends Joseph Fouché and General François Lefebvre appointed minister of police and commander of the Army of the Interior, respectively. Sieyès envisioned a ceremonial head of government, a grand elector with a military background, to be manipulated by himself and one other civilian executive. Finding collaboration from many important quarters, Sieyès successfully organized the coup d'état of 18 Brumaire (9 November 1799), though he erred in his choice of Napoleon Bonaparte.

Sieyès on 19 Brumaire (10 November 1799) assumed his duties as a temporary consul with Ducos and Bonaparte. Napoleon, however, quickly altered Sieyès' draft of the Constitution of the Year VIII to make himself supreme ruler of France, and Sieyès was relegated to the Senate. Sieyès survived, characteristically, under the Consulate and Empire. He was influential in the Senate, was named a grand officer of the Legion of Honor (1804), and after 1808 held the distinction of count of the Empire. During the Hundred Days he served as a member of the Chamber of Representatives. After the second restoration of the

Bourbons in 1815, he was banished as a regicide. The aging Sieyès lived in Brussels until the overthrow of Charles X in July 1830, when he returned to Paris. Sieyès died in Paris on 20 June 1836.

J. H. Clapham, *The Abbé Sieyès: An Essay in the Politics of the French Revolution* (London, 1912); A. Desjardins, *Sieyès et le jury en matière civile* (Aix, 1869); J. Godechot, *Les constitutions de la France* (Paris, 1970); A. Stern, " Sieyès et la constitution de 1795," *La Révolution française* 39 (1900); G. G. Van Deusen, *Sieyès: His Life and His Nationalism* (New York, 1932); I. Woloch, *Jacobin Legacy: The Democratic Movement under the Directory* (Princeton, 1970); R. Zapperi, "Sieyès et l'abolition de la Féodalité," *AHRF* 44 (1972).

Fred E. Hembree

Related entries: BRUMAIRE, COUP OF 18, YEAR VIII; CONSTITUTIONS; DIRECTORY.

SIMEON, JOSEPH-JEROME. See WESTPHALIA, KINGDOM OF; WESTPHALIA, KINGDOM OF: MINISTERS.

SISTER REPUBLICS, created before Napoleon became French head of state by native liberals, dissidents, and Francophiles under the sponsorship of French Republican armies of conquest. They were: the Batavian Republic (Holland, 1795), the Cisalpine, later Italian, Republic (1797), the Ligurian Republic (Genoa, 1797), the Helvetic Republic (Switzerland, 1798), the Roman Republic (Rome, 1798), and the Parthenopean Republic (Naples, 1799). Napoleon as first consul eliminated the Roman and Parthenopean (by restoring the Papal States and Naples) and converted the Helvetic into the Swiss Confederation (1803). As emperor he converted the Italian Republic into a kingdom (1805), annexed the Ligurian Republic to France (1805), reconquered the Kingdom of Naples (1806), and converted the Batavian Republic into the Kingdom of Holland (1806).

E. Chapuisat, *La Suisse et la Révolution française* (Geneva, 1945); B. Croce, *La rivoluzione napoletana* (Bari, 1911); V. E. Giuntella, *La giacobina repubblica romano (1798–1799)* (Rome, 1950); J. Godechot, *La grande nation; l'expansion révolutionnaire de la France dans le monde de 1789 à 1799*, 2 vols. (Paris, 1956); G. D. Homan, *Nederland in de Napoleonische Tijd, 1795–1815* (Haarle, 1978); R. R. Palmer, *The Age of Democratic Revolution*, 2 vols. (Princeton, 1959–64); P. Villani, "Le royaume de Naples pendant la domination française (1806–1815)," *AHRF* 44 (1972).

Related entries: CISALPINE REPUBLIC; EMPIRE, FRENCH; HOLLAND, KINGDOM OF; ITALY, KINGDOM OF; LIGURIAN REPUBLIC; NAPLES, KINGDOM OF; SWITZERLAND.

SMOLENSK, BATTLE OF. See RUSSIAN CAMPAIGN.

SOCIETA POPOLARE DI MILANO, the "Jacobins" of Milan. When the Austrian government in Lombardy collapsed, Carlo Salvador formed the Società degli Amici della Libertà e Uguaglianza (Friends of Liberty and Equality) to propagandize for an Italian republic and conduct surveillance of the nobility.

Bonaparte sanctioned the 200-member club on 14 May 1796, but he closed it after uprisings in Milan and elsewhere proved it was dominated by *Giacobini* (Jacobins). These Republicans admired the government of the Terror and were too radical for the French Directory. Nevertheless, the club, publicly professing moderate republicanism, reopened in 1796 as the Accademia della Letteratura e d'Istruzione Pubblica (Academy of Literature and Public Instruction) but was disbanded after it fomented a demonstration for Lombard independence. Bonaparte reopened the club again in 1797 as a society of public instruction and picked the first twenty members. All the same, the *Giacobini* soon dominated the membership, and it was closed after five months. In 1798 the Cisalpine Republic sponsored a Circolo Costituzionale in Milan and each provincial capital, but they served merely to organize the radical republicans and were abolished within the year.

Nevertheless the club in Milan persisted underground. Its members advocated a unitary, independent republic for Italy, social reform, aid for the destitute, and religious freedom. It was later instrumental in forming the Lombard Legion. The principal leaders were Carlo Salvador, Gaetano Porro, and Matteo Galdi.

Archivio di Stato di Milano, Studi, p.a. cart. 18; F. Becattini, *Storia del memorabile triennale governo francese e sedicente cisalpino nella Lombardia* (Milano, 1799–1800); B. Peroni, "La Società Popolare di Milano: 1796–1799," in *Nuova Rivista Storica* (1951).

Leonard Macaluso

Related entries: CISALPINE REPUBLIC; ITALIAN CAMPAIGN, FIRST; ITALY, KINGDOM OF; JACOBINS, ITALIAN.

SOCIETY. John B. Wolf once opined that an *émigré* noble returning to France in 1814, after twenty-odd years of exile, would have been agreeably surprised to notice how little seemed changed. The peasants were still following the simple seasonal routines of agriculture with the same simple implements. In the towns and cities, the small workshop with a master craftsman working with two or three skilled artisan-employees still predominated. Although there were a few large-scale factories, as in the manufacture of glass, paper, and iron, these were scarcely more numerous in 1814 than in 1789. The changes associated with machine industrialization had not yet begun to affect French economy or society decisively.

Yet if the *émigré* thought that nothing important had happened during his absence, he would have been deceived. Profound changes had occurred, chiefly stemming from a redefinition of property. Under the Old Regime, there had been four types of property: absolute private property, the command of land and buildings that legal ownership gives; private property whose use was regulated in theory for the public good, as in the property a guildmaster used in the fabrication of articles for sale; property in public functions, as in the venal offices of judge in the parlement (high court) of Paris; and, overlapping with these, quasi-property in hereditary privileges, prerogatives, and distinctions. Revolutionary legislation, chiefly of the Constituent Assembly, abolished the last three types of property, leaving only the first to be defined in Napoleon's Civil Code: "Property is the right of enjoying the disposing of things in the most absolute manner, provided they are not used in a way prohibited by the laws or statutes." The code also enshrined another great principle of Revolutionary lawmaking: equality before the law. Book I, title I, chapter I of the Civil Code read: "Every Frenchman shall enjoy the same civil rights." These redefinitions changed the legal rules by which individuals operated and altered their relations with each other.

During the Napoleonic period, the peasants (farmers) still constituted the bulk of the French population. The Revolution had freed them from seigneurial dues, seigneurial justice, the tithe, and payment of a disproportionate amount of direct taxes, and Bonaparte maintained these gains. However, peasant income and wealth varied. There were large proprietors who had perhaps profited from the sale of noble and church land and a range of others below from those who owned or leased enough land to maintain a family in comfort to lesser owners who still needed to sharecrop and work by the day to keep alive, down to propertyless day laborers. Most French peasants belonged to the last two groups. Nevertheless, with the release from the onerous burdens of the Old Regime and with the years of prosperity under Napoleon (except 1810–11), French peasants were eating better and dressing better than ever before.

In the cities, the abolition of guilds had given every artisan the legal opportunity to have his own workshop. The abolition of guilds had also altered the relationship between master and journeyman from one of legal privilege versus obligation to the free bargaining of economic agents in the marketplace. With war and conscription draining young men to the army and thus reducing the supply of workers, unemployment was low except during the depression of 1810–11, and wages rose faster than prices. The attitude of the Napoleonic government toward the urban worker was ambivalent: fearful and *policier* and yet at times benevolent. It required the *livret*, a pass that each worker carried from employer to employer, and it required that on arrival at a new town he deposit the *livret* at police headquarters, thus placing the worker immediately under police surveillance. The government also maintained the Revolutionary prohibition of organizations both of employers and workers (12 April 1803). Yet when the workers, as under the Old Regime, formed fraternal societies (*confréries*) and *compagnonnages*, the government often looked the other way. It recognized that they gave the workers a severe moral code and a psychological security that promoted public order. In addition, the government authorized municipalities to set up employment bureaus and created labor courts (*conseils de prud'hommes*) to mediate disputes between employers and workers.

Above the world of manual labor were the *bourgeoisie* and the old and new nobility. At its lower levels, the bourgeoisie included the shopkeepers, lesser officials, and, in the countryside, to stretch a term, the larger peasant proprietors. At the middle and upper levels, the bourgeoisie embraced those who had accumulated modest to great fortunes as wholesale merchants, industrial capitalists (a very few), bankers and speculators, high government officials, civil and military, lawyers and physicians, and non-noble large landed proprietors. For the most part, the rich commercial, industrial, and banking families built their initial fortunes under the Old Regime, enlarged them during the Revolution by the purchase of confiscated land and by speculation, and affirmed them under Napoleon, although there were, as always, the *nouveaux riches*. The vicissitudes of the Revolutionary years had taught them to diversify their holdings. Merchants served as bankers, invested in industrial enterprises, and purchased government bonds; banks placed funds in industry and commerce, and all bought land—for income, security, and social prestige. Non-noble landed proprietors in turn invested in commercial and industrial projects and government securities.

The Revolution had initiated the decline of the old noble families, but they still held on. Revolutionary laws had deprived them of their titles, their privileges, and, if they emigrated, their property; however, many nobles had not emigrated and retained their land. Under Napoleon, many of those who had left France returned and received the unsold parcels of their estates or were able to repurchase plots that had been sold. Through retention or reconstitution of estates, the wealthiest noble families were often once again among the richest and most influential people in the French countryside. Some lived secluded in their chateaux; others actively participated in political life as mayors, members of the local electoral colleges, prefects, high army officers, and cabinet ministers. Those noble families who rallied to the Napoleonic regime and the families of the new nobility and *haute bourgeoisie* intermarried to form a new elite.

Napoleon's social policy evolved over the years as he responded to the necessities and opportunities of the hour. It is difficult to say how far ahead he was looking at any moment, but always he was working toward the consolidation of his power through the building of durable institutions.

He tried to capture for himself, his dynasty, and his regime existing social structures of influence and also the new structures created by himself. When he became first consul in 1799, France, after years of revolution, was an atomized society of individuals. To be sure, private property and the familiar routines of farm, village, and workshop continued. But the administration was decentralized, the Catholic church was in schism, guilds no longer existed, and the division of society into legally privileged and nonprivileged estates belonged to the past. Individuals were legally equal and to a degree free of control by a central authority.

An army of hierarchic ranks nevertheless existed, and so did conscription. Bonaparte won over most of the leading generals, captivated the rank-and-file soldiers, and controlled the machinery of conscription. He affirmed his hold on the generals by creating (14 May 1804) the rank of marshal and by richly endowing each marshal. Of the first eighteen marshals, three were nobles during the Old Regime (A. Berthier, L.-N. Davout, and F.-E.-C. Kellermann), four were of the lower classes (P. Augereau, F. Lefebvre, J. Murat, and M. Ney), and the rest were drawn "from diverse sectors of the bourgeoisie" (Bergeron). A new elite was being forged in action on campaign and in battle.

Bonaparte created a hierarchic, centralized administration, from cabinet ministers through prefects to subprefects and mayors, and set up a new system of courts. Under the slogans of careers open to talent and service in the honor and glory of France, he recruited able men for the administration and judiciary. They were drawn from former administrators, members of Revolutionary assemblies, and nobles of the sword and the robe. Here too a new socioeconomic professional elite was in formation.

By the constitution of the life Consulate (3 August 1802), Bonaparte sought to connect the influential and propertied men of each department to his regime. The constitution provided that resident male citizens of each canton would choose members of electoral colleges for the arrondissement and for the department. The electoral college of the department was to be selected from those 600 persons who paid the most taxes. These 600 notables included, as it turned out, noble and non-noble landed proprietors, businessmen, and lawyers. The departmental electoral colleges, another new elite fused in action, each nominated two candidates for a Senate seat. The Senate, and in effect Bonaparte, then made a final choice.

To fuse the new social elites in a common hierarchical order under his control, Napoleon created a new imperial nobility. By Jean Tulard's calculation, they were recruited for the most part from top army officers, top administrators, and large landowners; 22.5 percent were from the old nobility, 58 percent from the bourgeoisie, and 19.5 percent from the popular classes (largely through the army). Owing their distinctions to Napoleon, dependent on him for further favors, and won to the values of emulation, honor, and glory, they would in time form a new elite that would affirm the imperial regime. Or so Napoleon dreamed.

L. Bergeron, *France under Napoleon*, trans. R. R. Palmer (Princeton, 1981); L. Bergeron and G. Chassinand-Nogaret, *Les Masses de granit* (Paris, 1979); E. Eisenstein et al., "Symposium: Caste, Class, Elites, and Revolution," *CRE* (1979); B. Gille, "La société française," in J. Mistler, ed., *Napoléon et l'Empire* (Paris, 1968); C. Gindin, "La rente foncière en France, de l'ancien régime à l'Empire," *AHRF* 54 (1982); W. H. Sewell, *Work and Revolution in France: The Language of Labor from the Old Regime to 1848* (Cambridge and New York, 1980); J. Tulard, "Problèmes sociaux de la France impériale," 17 *RHMC* (1970), and *Napoléon et la noblesse d'Empire* (Paris, 1979).

Harold T. Parker

Related entries: CONSTITUTIONS; CHURCH, ROMAN CATHOLIC; ECONOMY, FRENCH; JEWS; LABOR LEGISLATION; LAW, CODES OF; NOBILITY, IMPERIAL; NOTABLES; PROTESTANTS; WORKERS.

SOLDIER, FRENCH, LIFE OF. The average Napoleonic soldier was a conscript enlisted under the provisions of the Jourdan Law. In theory he was eligible for discharge after five years, though from 1804 on most discharges were for medical reasons only. The normal conscript received little training, learned by doing, and if he survived became a veteran teaching others. Experience taught him to take care of his equipment, and with the supply system usually in shambles, he became a skilled, even ruthless, marauder. His life revolved around his section, six to twelve men, with whom he shared bivouac, cooking, fatigues, and battle. Uniforms were ill fitting and uncomfortable, and boots rarely lasted more than a few weeks. Even so, and burdened with a heavy field pack, his marching performance was extraordinary. Compared with contemporary armies, discipline was loose; corporal punishments already had been abolished by the Revolution, though summary executions in the field were not unknown. No wide social gulf separated officers from the rank and file, and promotions for bravery in the field remained a constant spur to morale. Medical services remained inadequate, and for every soldier who was killed in battle, four died of sickness. At that, conscripts fought well in all campaigns, their fighting spirit crumbling only in 1814.

M. Baldet, *La vie quotidienne dans les armées de Napoléon* (Paris, 1964); M. Choury, *Les grognards et Napoléon* (Paris, 1968); J. Morvan, *Le soldat impérial (1800–1814)*, 2 vols. (Paris, 1904); G. E. Rothenberg, *The Art of Warfare in the Age of Napoleon* (Bloomington, Ind., 1977).

Gunther E. Rothenberg

Related entries: ARMY, FRENCH; CONSCRIPTION; MEDICINE.

SOMO SIERRA, BATTLE OF. See PENINSULAR WAR.

SOULT, NICOLAS-JEAN DE DIEU (1769–1851), duc de Dalmatie, marshal of France. Of the middle class, the son of a notary, his father hoped Soult would study law, but he enlisted (1785) in the Royal Army. A sergeant in 1791, he became an officer after the overthrow of Louis XVI (1792) and by 1799 was a major general. He shared with André Masséna the glory of holding Genoa (1800) against Austrian siege, which allowed Napoleon to cross the Alps and triumph at Marengo. Bonaparte made him, successively, colonel general of the consular guard, commandant of the camp of St. Omer (on the channel, where the future Grande Armée was being trained), and marshal (1804). He commanded a corps in the Austerlitz campaign (1805) and in the Jena-Auerstädt campaign (1806) and in 1808 was created duc de Dalmatie.

Soult led a corps to Spain under Napoleon (1808) to restore Joseph Bonaparte to the throne. In 1809 he became Joseph's chief of staff and in 1810 conquered Andalusia for him. He remained in Andalusia as de facto governor until 1812, when he was forced to withdraw because of Wellington's victories in the north.

In 1813, he joined Napoleon in Germany. After Joseph's defeat at Vitoria (21 June 1813), however, the emperor sent him to take over the king's army. He fought a delaying action against the duke of Wellington in the Pyrenees and southern France and held Toulouse until officially informed of Napoleon's abdication (1814).

In 1815 he rallied to Napoleon and was his chief of staff during the Waterloo campaign. Exiled until 1819, Louis XVIII restored his rank in 1820. Under Louis Philippe he was successively minister of war, minister of foreign affairs, and prime minister. He died marshal general of France.

K. Bleibtreu, *Marschall Soult* (Berlin, 1902); N. J. de Dieu Soult, *Mémoires du maréchal Soult*, 3 vols. (Paris, 1854), and *Mémoires, Espagne et Portugal* (Paris, 1955). *Related entries:* PENINSULAR WAR; WATERLOO CAMPAIGN.

SPAIN, KINGDOM OF (1808–13), Napoleonic satellite state under King Joseph Bonaparte (Jóse Napoleon I), Napoleon's elder brother. The history of the kingdom and of the Peninsular War are almost inseparable. Moreover, there were two Spains in the period, since those who fought the French in the name of the Bourbon king, Ferdinand VII, always held at least an outpost in Cadiz.

The Bonaparte kingdom had its origin in the Junta of Bayonne, May–July 1808. The deputies were not elected but invited by Napoleon—directly or indirectly—but it was a distinguished group, which seemed to represent the traditional leadership of Spain. It included the prince del Castelfranco, the dukes del Parque and d'Infantado, liberals such as Francisco Cabarrus, Gonzalo O'Farrill, Pedro Cevallos, and Don Manuel Romero, two archbishops, and the heads of the Franciscan and Dominican orders. Napoleon was encouraged in his false belief that Spain would welcome a new dynasty. He therefore deposed the Bourbon kings—Charles IV and his son, Ferdinand VII, who had overthrown him—and summoned to Spain his brother Joseph, then king of Naples.

Joseph was enthusiastically received by the members of the Junta and other delegations. He cheerfully swore to uphold the liberal constitution approved by the Junta (if supplied by Napoleon). He was crowned at Burgos on 7 July 1808 by the archbishop of Burgos and departed for Madrid. Accompanying him was an all-Spanish ministry comprising liberals who had been silenced or imprisoned in recent years. Many of the older ones, such as Francisco Cabarrus, had served the reforming monarch Charles III. Joseph traveled to his capital but was in residence only eleven days (20–30 July 1808) before he was forced to withdraw in the face of a nationwide uprising. Napoleon, enraged, built his army in Spain to 300,000 and in November 1808 appeared to command it personally. He easily crushed the Spanish forces, only one-third the number of his own. Marshal Nicolas Soult drove an allied British army to take ship at Coruña. Napoleon restored Joseph to his throne in Madrid and left for Paris (16 January 1809).

Napoleon seemed to have won the war, taught the Spanish a lesson, and left Joseph free to organize his government; however, he had not counted upon the determination of the British or on the persistence of the Spanish and their raging hostility to the French, fanned by the clergy, who considered Napoleon an agent of the devil. Sir Arthur Wellesley (later duke of Wellington) appeared in Portugal with a British army augmented by Anglo-Portuguese contingents, which the French could never dislodge. The remote and mountainous areas of Spain and Portugal swarmed with guerrillas whom the British supplied and encouraged. Similarly, Spanish regular armies, though defeated by the French with monotonous regularity, tended to break, only to disperse and reform. Thus Joseph, though the most well intentioned of men, could accomplish few reforms or give the Spanish the enlightened government he had intended.

Joseph was pleased with the Constitution of Bayonne (1808). It provided for a single-chamber Cortes, partly appointed but with a majority elected indirectly by universal manhood suffrage. The king appointed a Ministry, Council of State, and Senate. There were to be French-style judicial and administrative systems. Equality of taxation and opportunity, equality before the law, and freedom from arbitrary arrest were guaranteed. Feudal rights were declared abolished, as were internal tariffs and guilds. The Catholic church was declared established, but this provision was modified after the rebellion of 1808 by Napoleon himself, who decreed abolition of the monastic orders and the inquisition.

Joseph tried to govern by the constitution and tended to neglect the war, which was a continual source of irritation to Napoleon. Joseph did take the field, however, when he deemed necessary. He fought Wellington in 1809. He and Marshal Soult conquered Andalusia in 1810, but he did not give the conquest (as the war had become) the attention that Napoleon expected. The result was that in mid-1810 Napoleon confined Joseph's direct government to the Madrid area, called the center, and put the rest of Spain under military governments. Catalonia was ruled by Marshal Pierre Augereau and later Marshal Jacques Macdonald; Aragon and Valencia by Marshal Louis Suchet; and others by generals—Navarre by Georges-Joseph Dufour, later Honoré Reille; Biscay by Pierre Thouvenot; Burgos by Jean-M. Dorsenne; and Valladolid and vicinity by Paul Thiébault. This system persisted until 1812 when Napoleon restored Joseph to command of French forces, presumably including the military governors. In 1812–13, however, Joseph was forced to fight for his kingdom and could not execute domestic reforms.

Nevertheless, throughout his five-year reign, Joseph labored to bring Spain such benefits as possible of enlightened government. He organized his ministry, which remained all Spanish, even to the minister of war, Gonzalo O'Farrill. He made elaborate plans, assisted by Don Manuel Romero, minister of interior and justice, to organize Spain into thirty-eight prefectures and to install a new judicial system. He proclaimed the abolition of feudal dues and privileges and enforced his edicts wherever he could.

In an effort to stimulate the economy, he offered the royal industries for sale. (The liberal dogma of the time favored free enterprise.) He also abolished royal monopolies on the manufacture of tobacco, playing cards, wine, liquor, and sealing wax and offered them to private enterprise. Unfortunately, in the midst of the civil war that went on during his entire reign, these measures were not beneficial. Investors could not be found, and the crown had to reverse many of its policies. Joseph's government was always in debt. The issuance of paper money (based on confiscated properties of the church and rebels) made the situation worse since the paper inflated rapidly and was soon worthless.

Despite his financial problems, Joseph remained dedicated to reform and public welfare. He centralized control of innoculation and sanitary measures, of hospitals, orphans' homes, and homes for the aged. As a sanitary measure, he equipped Madrid with a new water system, which terminated in decorative fountains in every major square in the capital. He is remembered even today in the Spanish guidebooks as "king of the fountains." At the same time, however, he is described as "Pepe Bottelas" (a drunkard), which rebel propaganda labeled him. Joseph had plans for a complete public school system but could found only a few secondary schools and a school of geometry in Madrid. He also established the royal botanical gardens, which still exist, and gave Spain its first opera company. He converted the Prado palace into an art museum, now one of the world's most famous. He even had plans to restore the Alhambra of Granada, which was done by the later governments.

The Bonaparte Kingdom of Spain was a failure since Joseph was compelled to remain perpetually at war and eventually was driven out by Wellington in 1813. However, even Joseph's enemies, viewing what he had intended to do, said that if he somehow could have inherited the throne instead of having it conquered for him, he would have gone down in history as a popular and progressive monarch. Surely many of the liberals who supported the rebel government at Cadiz and served in the Cortes regretted that they had not opted for Joseph's government. The rebels' famous Constitution of 1812, later a model for liberal constitutions in Europe, was something of an exercise in one-upmanship—in that the rebels attempted to improve on Joseph's constitution of Bayonne. Ferdinand VII renounced this constitution on his return and persecuted the liberals, many of whom, ironically, fled to France. Although the reign of Joseph ended in catastrophe, it is considered by Spanish historians today to have begun the modern era in Spain.

M. Artola, *Los Origines de la España contemporanea*, 2 vols. (Madrid, 1959); O. Connelly, *The Gentle Bonaparte: A Biography of Joseph, Napoleon's Elder Brother* (New York, 1968); A. Fugier, *Napoléon et l'Espagne, 1799–1808*, 2 vols. (Paris, 1930); G. de Grandmaison, *L'Espagne et Napoléon, 1804-1814*, 3 vols. (Paris, 1908–31); G. Lovett, *Napoleon and the Birth of Modern Spain*, 2 vols. (New York, 1966).

Related entries: AFRANCESADOS; BAYONNE, CONSTITUTION OF ; BAYONNE, JUNTA OF; BONAPARTE, JOSEPH; CHARLES IV; FERDINAND VII DE BOURBON; GUERRILLAS; MARMONT; MASSENA; PENINSULAR WAR; PORTUGUESE CAMPAIGNS; SUCHET; WELLINGTON.

SPAIN, KINGDOM OF: MINISTERS.

Minister Secretary of State	Mariano Luis de Urquijo	1808–13
Finance	Francisco de Cabarrus (Died April 1810)	1808–10
	Francisco Angulo	1810–13
Interior	Gaspar Melchor de Jovellanos (Named 1808; ignored appointment and joined the rebels)	

	Don Manuel Romero	1809–
	Almenara (José Martinez Hervas)	1809–13
Justice	Sebastian Piñuela y Alonso (Retired to monastery November 1808)	1808–
	Don Manuel Romero (and Interior) (Died 1812)	1809–12
	Almenara (and Interior)	1812–13
Foreign Affairs	Pedro Cevallos (Deserted to rebels July 1808)	1808–
	Campo-Alange (Manuel José de Negrette)	1809–11
	Santa Fé (Azanza)	1811–13
War	Gonzalo O'Farrill	1808–13
Police	Pablo de Arribas (de facto minister)	1808–13
Marine	José Mazarredo y Salazar (Died 1812)	1808–12
	O'Farrill (and War)	1812–13
Indies	Azanza (Made duke of Santa Fé, 1810)	1808–13
Ecclesiastical Affairs	Piñuela (and Justice) (Retired to monastery November 1808)	1808

Related entries: PENINSULAR WAR; SPAIN, KINGDOM OF.

STADION, JOHANN PHILIPP VON, COUNT (1763–1824), Austrian foreign minister. Ambassador to Stockholm (1787) and London (1790), Stadion resigned in 1795 in protest against Foreign Minister Franz von Thugut's policy. He returned under Cobenzl to be ambassador to Berlin (1801) and St. Petersburg (1803). In 1805, after Napoleon's victory at Austerlitz and the disastrous (for Austria) Peace of Pressburg, he was made foreign minister. To enable Austria to resist Napoleon's domination, Stadion proposed to breathe new life into corporate institutions, reorganize the army and establish a militia, and promote popular education and German patriotism. But political conflicts at court and in the government, the indecision of the emperor, together with the varied traditions and structures of the multinational state, narrowly circumscribed his attempts. After Austria's defeat in 1809, Stadion resigned in favor of Clemens von Metternich. In 1813, however, he negotiated with Prussia and Russia the entry of the Habsburg monarchy to the anti-Napoleonic alliance. As president of the exchequer after 1814 and as finance minister after 1816, Stadion devoted himself to the restoration of the shaken finances of the state.

A. Brusatti, "Graf Philipp Stadion als Finanzminister," *Österreich und Europa, Festgabe H. Hantsch* (Wien, 1965); H. Rössler, *Graf Johann Philipp Stadion* (Wien, 1966).

Eckhardt Treichel

Related entries: DIPLOMACY; FOREIGN POLICY; PRESSBURG, TREATY OF; SCHÖNBRUNN, TREATY OF (1809); WAGRAM CAMPAIGN.

STAEL-HOLSTEIN, ANNE-LOUISE-GERMAINE NECKER, BARONNE DE (1766–1817), novelist, literary critic, and renowned hostess of a liberal opposition salon in the Consulate (temporarily allied to, but distinct from the *idéologue* circle). Mme. de Staël sympathized with the plight of the Bourbon family in 1792 and advocated constitutional monarchy in her mature political writings. When she returned to France from exile in 1795, however, she and her lover, Benjamin Constant, defended the moderate Republic.

Both welcomed the Brumaire coup, but by early 1800 she was helping to frame Constant's speeches for civil and political liberties in the Tribunate. Her study *De la littérature* (1800) even associated liberty with human perfectibility. Bonaparte's petulant fury at her opposition stemmed from her links in 1802 to the alleged conspirator Jean Moreau, to the hostile pamphleteer Camille Jordan, and to the appearance of the unfriendly memoirs of her father, Jacques Necker. After publication of her novel *Delphine* (1803), with its pro-English and feminist sentiments, the imperial authorities harassed her with enforced exile from Paris, and sometimes from France (see her *Dix années d'exil*, 1820). Even the politically innocuous novel *Corinne* (1807) rankled Napoleon by its success.

Mme. de Staël's stay in Weimar in 1803–4 inspired her to describe glowingly German customs, art, literature, and philosophy (*De l'Allemagne*, 1810). Napoleon's police destroyed the first edition; it was in effect first published in London in 1813. This introduction to German culture awakened French interest in German literary Romanticism and heightened awareness of Immanuel Kant's philosophy. In 1814 Mme. de Staël supported Bernadotte for the French throne before rallying to the Bourbons. The Second Restoration relieved her from the embarrassment of her ambivalent approval of Constant's Additional Act (which liberalized Napoleon's constitution) during the Hundred Days.

S. Balaye, *Mme. de Staël: Lumières et liberté* (Paris, 1979); *Cahiers staëliens* (periodical since 1962); Colloque de Coppet, *Madame de Staël et l'Europe* (Paris, 1970); H. Guillemin, *Madame de Staël, Benjamin Constant, et Napoléon* (Paris, 1959); J. C. Herold, *Mistress to an Age* (London, 1958).

Martin Staum

Related entries: CONSTANT DE REBECQUE; *IDEOLOGUES*; INSTITUT NATIONAL DES SCIENCES ET DES ARTS; WOMEN.

STATISTICS. Under the Bourbons the controller-general's office had long sought quantitative information about the French population and economy. By mid-eighteenth century, it was receiving from the intendant's subdelegates biweekly reports of the market prices of grains, bread, vegetables, meat, wool, linen, and iron and from the inspectors of manufactures semiannual reports on the production of woolen, cotton, and linen cloth. From time to time it also conducted special statistical inquiries on mining, metallurgical industries, paper manufactures, tanneries, forests, and hemp and on population (births, marriages and deaths). After many interruptions during the Revolution, the governments of the Directory, the Consulate, and Empire intensified this statistical effort.

Lucien Bonaparte and Jean Chaptal, Bonaparte's second and third ministers of interior, established the Bureau of Statistics, which lasted until 1812. Under an imaginative minister of interior, Chaptal, and a zealous bureau chief, Alexander de Férrière, it launched a massive statistical description of France in 1801. Prefects of each department were instructed to secure from subprefects, mayors, and local savants and societies of agriculture detailed descriptive (verbal) and quantitative data on the topography, population, agriculture, industry, and commerce of their jurisdiction in 1789 and 1801. This was to be a vast cooperative inquiry with a twofold purpose: to discover what change had occurred during the Revolution and to establish for 1801 a cross-sectional description of France from which later demographic and economic movement could be measured. However, the reports came in slowly or not at all. Only thirty-five were ultimately submitted, and they were uneven in completeness and accuracy. In 1806 Chaptal's successor as minister of interior, J.-B. de Champagny, and his chief of the Bureau of Statistics, Charles-Etienne Coquebert de Montbret, formally terminated the huge project. The bureau, however, continued its work. Having attempted a census in 1801, it tried to conduct another in 1806. It conducted special statistical investigations of manufactures (1806), cotton factories (1806), the cultivation of oranges and olives (1806), mines and forges (1811), the textile industry (1811), tanneries (1811), and paper production. These inquiries and others like them formed the basis of the comprehensive published report of the minister of interior, J.-P. B. de Montalivet, to the Legislative Body, 25 February 1813, entitled *Exposé de la situation de l'Empire*.

Throughout its existence, the bureau maintained the fortnightly reporting of the market prices of grains, vegetables, meat, wood, and coal and the annual reports on the state of crops and crop production. It also requested monthly reports of the movement of French population (births, marriages, deaths). The results of this massive statistical effort were uneven in completeness, accuracy, and usability. The art of phrasing questionnaires to secure precise information was just being developed. The bureau was asking too much of slender prefectoral staffs. Some harried prefects, subprefects, and mayors worked hard and carefully to answer the questionnaires; others did not. Nevertheless, a mass of data was accumulated that has not yet been fully exploited by historians.

Statistical activity in Napoleon's France extended beyond the minister of interior's bureau. Local savants and societies became interested; statistical periodicals were published. For decades French economists and administrators had speculated why the industry of England surpassed that of France. Several French statisticians, including Joseph-Antoine Bosc, separately sought the answer statistically by calculating for each country its national income and the share of each component (agriculture, houses, industry, domestic commerce). They thus advanced the sophistication of reasoning on the subject.

L. Bergeron, *La statistique en France de l'époque napoléonienne* (Brussels, 1981); J.-N. Biraben, "La statistique de population sous le Consulat et l'Empire," *RHMC* 17 (1970); R. Boudard, "La première 'statistique du département de la Creuse' realisée en l'an IX a la demande du gouvernement consulaire,'' *RIN* 137 (1981); B. Desgrey, ''Montalivet et la statistique au temps de l'Empire,'' *RIN* 106 (1968); O. Festy, ''Les essais de statistique économique pendant le Directoire et le Consulat,'' *AHRF* 25 (1953); B. Gille, *Les sources statistiques de l'histoire de France: des enquêtes du 17ᵉ siècle à 1870* (Geneva and Paris, 1964); J. C. Perrot, *L'âge d'or de la statistique régionale française (An IV–1804)* (Paris, 1977); M. Reinhard, *Etude de la population pendant la Révolution et l'Empire* (Paris, 1961) and *Premier supplément* (Paris, 1963); G. Thuillier, ''Aux origines de la comptabilité nationale: les essais de calcul du revenu national de 1800 a 1808,'' *RIN* 132 (1976).

Harold T. Parker

Related entries: BONAPARTE, LUCIEN; CHAPTAL; MONTALIVET.

STEIN, HEINRICH FRIEDRICH KARL VOM UND ZUM, BARON (1757–1831), German statesman, liberal reformer in Prussia, leader in the German liberation movement. Shortly after finishing his law studies at Göttingen, Stein entered the Prussian civil service. After 1804, he was responsible for economy and finances and drafted plans for the reorganization of the upper echelons of state agencies (memorandum of April 1806). He made enemies, however, and in January 1807 King Friedrich Wilhelm III dismissed him. Stein utilized the leisure to give form to his concepts of how the state ought to be constituted (Nassau Memorandum of June 1807).

In July 1807 he was recalled by the king, whose armies had been defeated by the French. Napoleon had taken Prussian territory west of the Elbe and in Poland and had also demanded an indemnity. Stein was entrusted with the difficult negotiations with France concerning the amount and nature of the payment. Simultaneously he endeavored to lay the groundwork for a rebellion against the French, and an incriminating letter of his fell into French hands. Friedrich Wilhelm III was forced to dismiss Stein once again (November 1808). He fled to Bohemia.

During the fourteen months of his second ministry, Stein had initiated fundamental reforms. Their goal was to transform the Prussian monarchy, without revolution, from an absolutist and largely feudal state into one with a moderately liberal constitution. His progam involved the participation of citizens in decision making at municipal and higher levels and the ultimate election of a state parliament. He was not guided by ideals of egalitarian democracy, however. The franchise was tied to the possession of property. Stein's ultimate objective was to free society from the fetters of feudal institutions and the bureaucratic tutelage of the state. His brief tenure, however, permitted the realization of no more than a fragment of his program: the liberation of the peasants and extension to everyone of the right to own land (Edict of 9 October 1807); the establishment of freedom of trade (24 October 1807); the awarding of full property ownership rights to peasants on the royal domains (27 July 1808); and introduction of communal self-administration (19 November 1808). Stein's successors did not continue his plans in their entirety.

In 1809 Stein propagandized in favor of the ill-fated Austrian attempt to lead a war of German liberation. In 1812 he became adviser to Czar Alexander I, was instrumental in forging the alliance between Russia and Prussia (Treaty of Breslau, March 1813), and was named president of the Administrative Council of the Allied Powers for Northern Germany, the purpose of which was preparation for the struggle against Napoleon. In 1814, Stein was placed in charge of the reconquered provinces. His appearance at the Congress of Vienna, where his plan for a restored German empire fell on deaf ears, was his culminating political act. He spent the last decades of his life primarily on his estate in Westphalia. His final legacy was the founding of the *Monumenta Germaniae Historica*, which became the definitive printed collection of German medieval documents.

E. Botzenhart, *Die Staats- und Reformideen des Freiherrn vom Stein* (1927); H. Conrad, *Freiherr vom Stein als Staatsmann im Übergang vom Absolutismus zum Verfassungsstaat* (1958); E. Fehrenbach, "Verfassungs- und sozialpolitische Reformen und Reformprojekte in Deutschland unter dem Einfluss des Napoleonischen Frankreich," *Historische Zeitschrift* 228 (1979); W. Hubatsch, *Die Stein-Hardenbergschen Reformen* (1977); G. Ritter, *Stein*, 2 vols. (1931, 3d ed. 1958); D. Schwab, *Die "Selbstverwaltungsidee" des Freiherrn vom Stein und ihre geistigen Grundlagen* (1971); J. R. Seeley, *Life and Times of Stein*, 3 vols. (1878, reprint 1968).

Dieter Schwab

Related entries: FRIEDRICH WILHELM III; HARDENBERG; PRUSSIA, KINGDOM OF; VIENNA, CONGRESS OF.

SUBSIDIES. See WARFARE, ECONOMIC.

SUCHET, LOUIS-GABRIEL (1770–1826), duc d'Albufera, marshal of France. Of the upper bourgeoisie, son of a silk manufacturer, he entered the army via the National Guard. He fought at Toulon (1793) and under Bonaparte on the first Italian campaign. While Napoleon was in Egypt (1798–99), he served under G.-M.-A. Brune in Holland and in 1799 was a major general.

Suchet's skill at staff work kept him in the background. He brilliantly seconded André Masséna in Italy (1800) and as inspector of the infantry but was not made one of the original marshals. He got no military promotion for his service on the Austerlitz and Jena-Auerstädt campaigns but was made a count.

Between 1808 and 1814 Suchet came into his own in Spain as both a commander and ruler. He conquered Aragon, seized Tarragona (believed impregnable), and subdued Valencia. As military governor of these provinces, he defeated the guerrillas, capturing "The Student," Francisco Xavier Mina, a greatly feared and romantic figure. He utilized Spanish officials, paid his own expenses, and sent money to the chronically bankrupt King Joseph at Madrid. Napoleon made him a marshal (1811) and duc d'Albufera (1812). After Joseph's defeat at Vitoria (1813), he found his position untenable and retreated into France (1814). He returned to support Bonaparte during the Hundred Days and was destituted during the Second Restoration. His rank was restored in 1819, but he never returned to public life. His *Mémoires* are a valuable source on the Peninsular War.

F. Rousseau, *La carrière du maréchal Suchet* (Paris, 1898); L. G. Suchet, *Mémoires du maréchal Suchet,. . .sur ses campagnes en Espagne depuis 1808 jusqu'en 1814*, 2 vols. (Paris, 1828).

Related entries: MARSHALS OF THE EMPIRE; PENINSULAR WAR; SPAIN, KINGDOM OF.

SULKOWSKI, JOZEF (c. 1770–1798), Polish soldier and adjutant of Bonaparte. An illegitimate child adopted by an uncle, he was disinherited because of his republican beliefs. In his *Ostatni głos obywatela polskiego* (Last voice of a Polish citizen) of 1791, he advocated the emancipation of the peasantry and the equality of all classes. He entered the army, and during the war of 1792 against the Russians he won the *Virtuti militari* medal, Poland's highest military order, but went into exile after the Russian victory. He learned Arabic in Paris and was dispatched by the Committee of Public Safety to Istanbul, but heard of the Kosciuszko uprising (1794) and made for Poland, arriving too late to fight. He returned to Paris, was commissioned a captain in the French army, and assigned to Bonaparte's Army of Italy. Napoleon made him his adjutant. On his return he published *La campagne d'Italie 1796 et 1797*. Sułkowski took part in the Egyptian expedition in 1798 and was both a soldier and member of the Institut d'Egypte, under the auspices of which he began compiling an Arabic dictionary. He was killed in a skirmish near Cairo. Sułkowski was regarded by numerous contemporaries as a military genius. Lazare Carnot stated, "If we had no Bonaparte, we would still have Sułkowski." His countrymen rate him as a Polish patriot and democrat who incidentally served Napoleon.

K. Kozminski, *Jozef Sułkowski* (Warsaw, 1935); J. Reychman, *Jozef Sułkowski* (Warsaw, 1952); A. Skałkowski, "Jozef Sułkowski w legendzie i historii," *Przegląd Wielkopolski* (1947).

John Stanley

Related entries: EGYPTIAN CAMPAIGN; ITALIAN CAMPAIGN, FIRST.

SWEDISH-BRITISH TREATY (3 March 1813). Britain promised 1 million rix-dollars to subsidize an army of 30,000 men under Crown Prince Bernadotte, to fight with the Allies. Britain also acceded to the cession of Norway to Sweden. See also FOREIGN POLICY; GERMAN WAR OF LIBERATION.

SWISS CONFEDERATION. See SWITZERLAND.

SWITZERLAND, converted by the French Republic into the Helvetic sister republic (1798), restored to an attenuated confederation by Napoleon (1803), evacuated by the French, 1813. In the late eighteenth century, the Swiss Confederation consisted of a mosaic of thirteen virtually sovereign cantons (Uri, Schwyz, Unterwalden, Lucerne, Zug, Zürich, Glarus, Berne, Appenzell, Fribourg, Solothurn, Basel, and Schaffhausen), other allied states, and independent states. All had different forms of government but shared a growing sense of solidarity stimulated by the common need to defend themselves since there was no federal army. The aristocracy who held political power in the cantons held fast to the status quo of peculiar feudal rights. From Paris, expatriate Swiss liberals, such as Peter Ochs and Frederick Laharpe who wanted a unified state, succeeded in stirring up Revolutionary enthusiasm among the Swiss population. After the Congress of Rastadt in November 1797, General Bonaparte visited Switzerland to test public opinion and was greeted as a hero. By the end of that year, the Directory decided to intervene and ''liberate'' the rich area in order to help defray the costs of maintaining the then-idle Army of Italy. In January and February 1798, uprisings occurred throughout the cantons, and on January 28 General J.-F.-Xavier Ménard with 15,000 French troops became the first foreign army ever to enter the region. As they entered the Vaud, the Diet was dissolved (January 31) and a liberty tree was planted in Aarau. Once Berne fell on March 5, the other states capitulated as well. Both of the Directory's objectives were accomplished: the seizure of the treasure of Berne to finance the forthcoming Egyptian expedition and control of the mountain passes. As Vaud, Berne, and Lucerne fell, the Helvetic Republic was proclaimed. The latter was accompanied by brutal repression of all resistance, some of which, including that of the women of Schwyz, had been quite heroic. From 1798 until the fall of Napoleon, Switzerland, historically the bastion of freedom, became in fact, if not in name, a French protectorate.

Because the liberal constitution, modeled on that of the French Directory, abolished torture and established equality before the law, set up a uniform state, and reduced the twenty-two cantons to administrative units, it satisfied only a minority of the Swiss, who were as yet unready for self-government and democracy. Two parties were bitterly and mutually opposed throughout Switzerland: the Federalists and the Unionists or Centralists. Because of the factions, four coups d'état occurred in the next five years, each generating changes in the constitution. By the spring of 1802 the Centralists were back in power under a united constitution.

Napoleon wanted to disengage from Switzerland, leaving it neutral, but when French troops were withdrawn as a consequence of the Peace of Amiens, political chaos resulted. Napoleon commanded a halt to the civil war and acted as official mediator. He invited delegates of both parties from all regions to Paris and, after hearing them out, decided to adopt a middle course. Napoleon submitted the Act of Mediation, compiled by himself, to the Committee of Consultation (19 February 1803). In place of centralization, it created nineteen quasi-sovereign cantons with a federal Diet, over which Napoleon's *Landammann* presided, keeping it entirely subservient to Paris. The seat of government would rotate annually among the six cities of Fribourg, Berne, Solothurn, Basel, Zürich, and Lucerne. Internally, liberty of the press and popular sovereignty passed away, and the Swiss reverted to such customs as judicial torture. Monastic property was restored, and monasteries were allowed to reopen. Consequently, with this fusion of the new and old, mediation aroused violent irritation on many sides; still, with the exception of the uprising of April 1804, Napoleon's astute diplomatic act produced eleven years of peace, and Switzerland gradually recovered from the Revolution. Benevolent societies helped in national reconciliation, and the study of Swiss history, languages, poetry, and the arts revived. Moreover, forestry, manufacturing, and canal building progressed. The first Swiss normal school was open in 1810. External affairs were another matter, however, since Switzerland was bound to France by a defensive alliance and a military capitulation. The Continental System hurt trade. Then France annexed Valais in order to control the newly constructed road over the Simplon. And Napoleon used Switzerland as a source for troops; about 10,000 Swiss soldiers died in the Russian campaign.

In 1813, Napoleon's overcommitments led him to end French occupation, so Switzerland regained its independence without a struggle. When the Allies announced their plans to invade the country, the Swiss retreated from the frontier without defending their neutrality. Thereafter, the constitution of mediation was abolished and the government resigned (23 December 1813). In the summer of 1814 Lord Castlereagh sent the skillful diplomat Stratford Canning, viscount Stratford de Récliffe, to Zurich as the Allies' representative for the purpose of obtaining Swiss agreement for a new constitution that would create an independent, united, and neutral Switzerland, strong enough to withstand French influence in the future. The reorganization of Switzerland was completed 12 September 1814 by the admission of the former allied states of Geneva, Neuchâtel, and the Valais. British success was only partial, however, since the cantons reacted against Napoleonic centralization and preferred to return to their former particularistic traditions of separate currencies, tariffs, weights and measures, and individual armies. During the Hundred Days, Stratford Canning tried in vain to persuade the Swiss to join the grand coalition against Napoleon. Most of them preferred immediate neutrality, but six days before Waterloo (12 June 1815), when less courage was required, the Swiss formally joined the coalition. After Waterloo, the Swiss army fought its last campaign in history on foreign soil, against the wishes of the government, by invading France (3 July 1815) and joining in the Austrian siege of Huningue. Five days later the mutiny of the regiments of Aargau, St. Gallen, and the Ticino put an end to it.

After prolonged diplomatic negotiations, the Swiss ratified the Federal Compact, a treaty guaranteed by the Great Powers, which could not be revised except by unanimous consent of the twenty-two virtually sovereign states within the frontiers of Switzerland (7 August 1815). A period of reaction disturbed by liberal agitation followed until the revolution of July 1830.

E. Chapuisat, *Le Commerce et l'industrie à Genève pendant la domination française, 1798–1813* (Geneva, Paris, 1908), and *La Suisse et la Révolution française* (Geneva, 1945); J. Courvoisier, *Le maréchal Berthier et sa principauté de Neufchâtel 1806-1814* (Neufchâtel, 1959); A. Custer, *Die zürchen Untertanen und die französische Revolution*

(Zurich, 1942); E. Guillon, *Napoléon et la Suisse, 1803-1815. D'après les documents inédits des affaires étrangères* (Paris, Lausanne, 1910); A. Hunziker, *Der Landammann der Schweiz in der Mediation (1803-1813)* (Zurich, 1942); M. Meylan, *Le grand conseil sous l'acte de Médiation* (Lausanne, 1958); E. Weber, *Pestalozzi, der revolutionäre Patriot* (Zurich, 1946).

June K. Burton

Related entries: FOREIGN POLICY; SISTER REPUBLICS.

SYMBOLISM AND STYLE. Napoleon understood the art of propaganda and the propagandistic possibilities of art. Engravings, paintings, public monuments, and official coinage carried the Napoleonic message in the most direct way: with his own likeness as the focus of attention. During Napoleon's reign the Monnaie de Paris struck more medals than had been issued in the preceding century. One of his pet projects was the *Histoire métallique de Napoléon le Grand* prepared by a commission of the Institut; Napoleon personally inspected the drawings and devoted considerable funds to the work. This collection reflected the two main characteristics of Napoleonic symbolism: neoclassical style and the personalization of power. Even as first consul, Napoleon's profile had quickly replaced the feminine allegory of Liberty as the symbolic representation of state legitimacy. After 1802, all official coins carried the Napoleonic bust, thus reviving the personal image of power so characteristic of the monarchy. In contrast to the monarchs, however, Napoleon's look was ascetic and his hair style obviously Roman. In 1807 coins began to reproduce an image that was even more imperial; the laurel wreath on Napoleon's head recalled Caesar, Augustus, and their successors.

The neoclassical style could be very eclectic; the motif might be Egyptian, Greco-Roman, or even Etruscan in reference. But Napoleonic taste always favored the monumental. Public monuments in particular reflected the imperial fascination with the grandiose. The *style Empire* also invaded interior spaces; beds, cabinets, wardrobes, and desks had sphinxes, columns, or mythological figures serving as legs, and the use of mahogany and bronze made these everyday objects ponderous and pretentious. Geometrical design and monumentality dominated both public and private constructions.

The Liberator, as he was so often portrayed after the Brumaire coup, later developed a liking for distinctive decorations, which culminated in the revival of heraldry. When it was first established, the Legion of Honor carried with it no decoration, insignia, or costumes. But two years later, in 1804, the Legion got its own decoration, and in 1808 the imperial nobility was established complete with titles and coats of arms. Like most other things Napoleonic, however, imperial heraldry was carefully controlled: crowns and helmets were suppressed in favor of the more uniform toque, and only the materials and number of plumes distinguished one rank from another. In addition, the coat of arms carried the insignia of the nobleman's profession, whether minister of state, archbishop, prefect, mayor, or simply landowner or military officer. In this way, Napoleon underlined the subordination of the nobles to his person (there was only one crown, the imperial one) and the importance of function and service for his nobility.

C. Bizot, *Mobilier Directoire Empire* (Paris, n.d.); B. Poindessault, ''Napoléon était-il l'Héritier de César?'' *RIN* (1973); A. Révérend, *Armorial du premier Empire* (Paris, 1974).

Lynn A. Hunt

Related entries: ARCHITECTURE; ART; HERALDRY; PAINTING; SCULPTURE.

SYRIA, INVASION OF. See EGYPTIAN CAMPAIGN.

T

TACTICS, NAPOLEONIC. Napoleon based his tactics on the reforms introduced during the last years of the Old Regime and the innovations of the republican army. The infantry by the 1790s employed firing lines, assault columns, and skirmishers singly or in combination, depending on specific battlefield circumstances. An infantryman learned to fight as part of a line or column and as a light trooper, and he could shift from one tactical mode to another as required. Artillery operated in direct close support of the infantry whenever possible, and the cavalry performed scouting and screening missions and occasionally functioned as a shock formation.

Republican armies traveled with a very small logistical train, thereby improving their mobility. Small units, the battalion, half-brigade, and division, could fight independently or as part of a larger force, and subordinate commanders were encouraged to show initiative by seizing advantage of favorable conditions instead of passively awaiting orders from higher echelons.

While serving the Republic, Napoleon became thoroughly familiar with the French tactical system and fully understood the importance of speed, shock, flexibility, and firepower. During the first years of the Empire, the Grand Armée, which contained many veterans of republican campaigns, reached a high level of tactical proficiency. Napoleon was able to employ his forces with decisive results even against numerically superior enemies. At Austerlitz his 73,000 men defeated an 85,000-man Austro-Russian army, and at Auerstädt a single corps routed the bulk of the Prussian army.

After 1808, Napoleon's tactics became less effective. Veterans died, were wounded or retired, and imperial commitments expanded. More and more, the emperor had to rely on new recruits, and he began to substitute mass for maneuver. Battles involved ever-growing numbers of men and guns, produced higher and higher casualties, and saw less decisive results. After 1808, Napoleon never again shattered an enemy army on the battlefield. Moreover, Napoleon's enemies produced bigger armies and to a degree improved their armies' tactical capabilities, thus reducing further the French tactical advantages that had produced such decisive results between 1805 and 1807. Napoleon retained his strategic ability almost to the end of his career, but after 1808 his tactical instruments became steadily less effective.

Lieutenant Colonel Belhomme, *Histoire de l'infanterie en France*, 5 vols. (Paris, n.d.); J. Brunet, *Histoire générale de l'artillerie*, 2 vols. (Paris, 1842); J. Colin, *L'infanterie au XVIIIe siècle: la tactique* (Paris, 1907), *La tactique et la discipline dans les armées de la Revolution* (Paris, 1902), and *Les transformations de la guerre* (Paris, 1911); T. Denison, *A History of Cavalry* (London, 1877); J. A. H. Guibert, *Essai générale de tactique*, 2 vols. (Liège, 1775); E. M. Lloyd, *A Review of the History of Infantry* (London, 1908); Ministère de la guerre, Etat Major de l'armée, Archives historiques Infanterie organization générale: Cartons $X^{p}5$, $X^{p}81$, $X^{s}4$, $X^{s}6$; *Règlement concernant l'exercice et les manoeuvres de l'infanterie du 1er août 1791* (Paris, 1808); S. Ross, *From Flintlock to Rifle Infantry: Tactics, 1740–1866* (London, 1979); W. Rustow, *Geschichte der Infanterie*, 2 vols. (Gotha, 1857–58); Commandant Thiry, *Histoire de la tactique de l'infanterie française* (Paris, 1905).

Steven T. Ross

Related entry: ARMY, FRENCH.

TALAVERA, BATTLE OF. See PENINSULAR WAR.

TALLEYRAND-PERIGORD, CHARLES-MAURICE, PRINCE DE (1754–1838), foreign minister of Napoleon, instrumental in his downfall. Grand seigneur, bearer of one of the most ancient names in France (a count Adelbert de Périgord had helped elect Hugh Capet king in 987), a clubfooted cripple, a detached observer of life who yet participated, a diplomat extraordinary, Talleyrand served six regimes and betrayed four. He was adept at abandoning sinking ships after slyly opening the scuttles. Talleyrand maintained that his shifts of allegiance always served the interests of France, but his enemies and even his friends observed that they also served the interests of Talleyrand.

He was born in Paris, the son of Charles-Daniel de Talleyrand, who after a half-century of loyal service with the Royal Army attained the rank of lieutenant general. Charles-Maurice was crippled by an accident in infancy (his left foot was deformed, and he had to wear a heavy brace to support his weakened leg). Incapable of a military career, he was compelled by his parents to enter the church. He rose rapidly in the ecclesiastical hierarchy of the Catholic church: subdeacon in 1775, deacon and priest in 1779, in 1780 chosen by the Assembly of the Clergy one of two agents-general to manage its vast ecclesiastical properties and successfully to defend them against royal encroachment, consecrated bishop of Autun in January 1789, and in April elected by his diocesan clergy their deputy to the Estates General. In the Constituent Assembly he proposed on 10 October that "the nation retake" the vast ecclesiastical properties he had once managed, while it provided for the support of the clergy and of public education. He sealed the betrayal of his order by celebrating Mass at the Fete of the Federation of 14 July 1790, which commemorated the first anniversary of the taking of the Bastille, and by consecrating, on 24 February 1791, newly elected bishops who had taken an oath of allegiance to the Civil Constitution. He then renounced his clerical state and became a layman.

He entered the international diplomatic game in 1792, when the French government sent him to London on the futile mission of negotiating an alliance with England. During the Terror, he took refuge in the United States but returned to France in 1797 to become minister of foreign affairs under the Directory (1797–99) and, after helping engineer the coup d'état of Brumaire, under Napoleon (1799–1807). He resumed the post under the Bourbons in 1814 and 1815. In a career that was a flow of interlacing intrigues, he advocated (with a few lapses) a consistent foreign policy for France: moderation in conquests, an *entente cordiale* with the established civilized powers, England and Austria, against the aggressive parvenus Prussia and Russia. He carried it out successfully, however, only under Louis XVIII and Louis Philippe.

Napoleon was charmed by Talleyrand and thought him "so capable, the most capable minister I had." And indeed, as long as Talleyrand was minister of foreign affairs, he served Napoleon well, even in securing what he disapproved, such as the harsh Treaty of Pressburg with Austria (1805), the Continental System (1806), and the Russian alliance at Tilsit (1807). However, Talleyrand also encouraged Napoleon in more nefarious enterprises: the execution of the duc d'Enghien, the establishment of the Empire, and the overthrow of the Spanish Bourbons. And all the while, Talleyrand demanded and received huge sums from the governments with which he negotiated.

But the policies of Talleyrand and Napoleon increasingly diverged. Talleyrand spoke usually for moderation; Napoleon moved from one dizzy, dazzling conquest to another in a career that Talleyrand came to see as dangerous and doomed. After 1807, when Talleyrand left the foreign ministry he began to betray Napoleon—perhaps to save France from the "imperial madman"—and certainly to save himself. And since Napoleon continued to consult him and use him in special missions, he had frequent opportunities to be unfaithful. At the conference between Napoleon and Alexander at Erfurt (1808), Napoleon relied on Talleyrand to win from the czar "guarantees of Russian cooperation in case of an Austrian attack." But in fact Talleyrand privately "advised Alexander to avoid any promise of intervention against Austria" (Whitcomb). Back in Paris (1809) Talleyrand went on the Austrian payroll, and informed the Austrian ambassador, Clemens von Metternich, of the secret orders sent French army commanders. At the end, when the Allied troops occupied Paris in March 1814, Talleyrand administered the coup de grâce by having the Senate vote on 1 April a provisional government with Talleyrand as president and, on the next day, Napoleon's deposition.

C. Brinton, *The Lives of Talleyrand* (New York, 1936); E. Dard, *Napoléon et Talleyrand* (Paris, 1935); L. Madelin, *Talleyrand*... (New York, 1948); M. Schumann, "Talleyrand: prophète de l'entente cordiale," *Nouvelle revue des deux mondes* 12 (1976); C. M. de Talleyrand-Périgord, *Lettres de Talleyrand à Napoléon* (Paris, 1967); E. A. Whitcomb, *Napoleon's Diplomatic Service* (Durham, N.C., 1979).

Harold T. Parker

Related entries: ABDICATION, FIRST; ALEXANDER I; DIPLOMACY; FOREIGN POLICY; FRANZ II; VIENNA, CONGRESS OF.

TALLIEN, MADAME (THERESE CABARRUS) (1773-1835). As she adapted herself to the currently popular regimes, she was successively the wife and/or mistress of the marquess of Fontenay, the Jacobin Jean-Lambert Tallien, the director Paul Barras (Josephine de Beauharnais' lover), the millionaire Julien Ouvrard, and the prince de Chimay. Born in Saragossa in 1773, Jeanne-Marie-Ignace-Thérèse was the daughter of the Spanish financier Cabarrus and a beautiful woman, Mlle. Galabert, daughter of a tradesman, whom he had secretly married in 1772. Little is known about her childhood, but in 1789, the fifteen-year-old girl agreed to marry the marquess of Fontenay. Although he was impoverished and suffered from gout, he did have a title and an illustrious family tree—enough to get his dainty, young wife presented to Queen Marie-Antoinette.

Mme. de Fontenay's salon became the rage of Marais society and was frequented by such liberals as the Marquis de Lafayette and Alexandre and Charles Lameth. When her husband fled to Spain, she remained in Paris and renounced him as a counterrevolutionary. She was among the numerous persons who petitioned the National Assembly.

In 1794 she went to Bordeaux, preparing to emigrate to Spain; however, she became embroiled in the social and political life of the city. She appeared in a festival as the allegorical Liberty, her arms invitingly outstretched and red hair falling loosely over a white gown. Jean Tallien, the representative of the government of Terror, became infatuated with her, and she used her influence to intercede on behalf of various suspects to save them from the Terror. When Maximilien Robespierre recalled Tallien to Paris, his mistress followed him and was arrested as the inspiration for his misconduct at Bordeaux. While she was in La Force prison, Tallien worked to get her released before the expected date of her execution, 10 Thermidor. Thus conspiring with Barras, Tallien became the hero of the day by drawing a dagger against Robespierre during his speech in the Convention on 9 Thermidor. Since it was the good and beautiful Thérèse who had galvanized Tallien into action, the public nicknamed her ''Our Lady of Thermidor.'' Soon she married her savior Tallien.

Under the Directory, Mme. Tallien (now a director's wife) was the reigning empress of fashion and beauty. She lived in Chaillot, where long rows of carettes parked outside all the way to the fields of the Champs Elysée when ''gilded youth,'' politicians, and frivolous women attended her salon. In costume she outdid her rivals, Josephine de Beauharnais and Mme. Récamier, appearing in Greek dresses slit to the hip or see-through dresses with one breast left bare (as if by accident), wearing sandals or only jeweled rings on the toes of her bare feet.

With her eye ever on the swing of the political pendulum, she left Tallien, taking her little daughter Thermidor with her, and moved into Barras' house. Meanwhile Tallien went to Egypt with General Bonaparte (1798). During the next three years, Mme. Tallien produced three children by Barras and/or Ouvrard, the millionaire monopolist who became her next lover. When Tallien returned home, they were divorced on 8 April 1802. Despite the fact that Mme. Tallien had helped Bonaparte buy a new uniform cheaply after the siege of Toulon, she was never invited to the Tuileries. Nor did she ever marry Ouvrard; instead, she ensured her financial security by wedding the comte de Caraman, heir of the prince of Chimay, in 1805. Napoleon sent his congratulations, and Empress Josephine honored her with a visit, but still no invitation came to attend the French court; however, because of her great benevolences during the Terror, King Joseph Bonaparte of Naples allowed her to be presented there.

In 1814, the Catholic church declared that she had never been married to Tallien since her first husband was still alive. After Fontenay's death in 1815, the church failed to recognize her civil marriage to Tallien and declared her to be the legitimate wife of Joseph de Caraman. Returning to Restoration Paris, the countess de Caraman reopened her stylish salon, this time on the rue de Babylon. But only foreigners came to her balls and concerts, not the noble women of the neighborhood who found her socially unacceptable because she was unwelcome at the Tuileries and Brussels. Chimay eventually became her own little court where she spent her last years enjoying the arts, friendship, her family, and the consolation of religion.

Anonymous, *Lettre du diable à la plus grande putain de Paris. La reconnaissez-vous?* (Paris, 1802); ''Chimay, Jeanne-Marie-Ignace-Thérèse de Cabarrus, princesse de,'' *Biographie universelle*, vol. 4 (Brussels, 1843–47); A. Houssaye, *Notre Dame de Thermidor* (Paris, 1866); A. Jal, *Dictionnaire critique* (Paris, 1872); J. Turquan, *Souveraines et grandes dames: la citoyenne Tallien, témoignages des contemporains et documents inédits* (Paris, 1898); G. Osipovna Sokolnikova, *Nine Women* (New York, 1932 and 1969).

June K. Burton

Related entries: *AFRANCESADOS*; CONVENTION; JOSEPHINE; TERROR, THE.

TALMA, FRANCOIS-JOSEPH (1763–1826), protégé of Napoleon; French tragedian whose innovations in acting, costuming, and stage design revolutionized the French theater. Talma was born in Paris, 16 January 1763, where his father was a dentist, later moving to London. He was given a good education and trained in dentistry, although his love of acting soon led him into amateur theatricals. Talma actually practiced dentistry in Paris, but for only eighteen months. He then joined the Théâtre français and made his debut on 21 November 1787 as Seïde in Voltaire's *Mahomet*. Strongly urged by his friend, the painter Jacques-Louis David, Talma made his first innovation by insisting on historically authentic costumes and scenery for each play, a revolutionary idea futilely tried previously by Henri-Louis Lekain, Mlle. Clairon, and Mme. Saint-Huberti. In an era when costumes were usually flowing capes, satin breeches, and long-haired wigs, Talma was derided for appearing in a Roman toga and headdress in the small role of Proculus in *Brutus* by Voltaire. His second break with tradition was to reject the declamatory style of speaking for a more realistic, natural pattern: breaking the sentences with pauses, emphasizing the sense rather than the meter. His goal was always toward the simple and away from the stilted and artificial.

Physically Talma had all the attributes of a leading man; he was handsome, well built, with a resonant, powerful voice, which he had carefully developed. He became famous for the vigor and passion of his acting, which he claimed was "sensibility." For him, sensibility was "that faculty of exaltation which agitates an actor, takes possession of his senses, shakes even his very soul, and enables him to enter into the worst tragic situations, and the most terrible passions as if they were his own." It was said that from his youth he had an actor's high-strung temperament and melancholic disposition through which he could so thoroughly become the tragic character that tears readily flowed. Talma's first opportunity to play a leading role came in 1789 when he was named a *sociétaire* of the Théâtre français. His friend Joseph Chénier had written an antimonarchical play, *Charles IX*, which other actors had turned down fearing political recriminations. Talma took the title role, which was one of his greatest triumphs, but from the resulting manifestations it was obvious that his pro-Republic sentiments were not shared by all of the company. In 1791 he was forced to resign and form a rival troupe, the Théâtre de la République, located at the Palais Royal, the present home of the Comédie française. During this period, he married Julie Carreau, described as an intelligent, rich, pretty, and passionate woman whose salon was very popular with the Girondins. He divorced her in 1801 and in 1802 married Caroline Vanhove, an actress with the Comédie française and daughter of the actor Vanhove.

During the Terror, Talma's troupe performed the plays of Antoine Arnault, J.-F. Ducis, M.-J. de Chénier, and Népomucène Lemercier. After Thermidor Talma had to defend himself against charges of Jacobinism, and it was at this time that he became acquainted with the little-known General Bonaparte. The two men became close friends; in fact, Louis Constant wrote that Talma was one of the few people whom Napoleon took into his confidence. Talma coached Napoleon in oratory, and the two often dined together. Napoleon brought Talma to Erfurt in 1808 to star in *The Death of Caesar* before the czar and assembled kings. He performed for Napoleon again in 1813 at Dresden, when it was the center of operations.

During the Consulate and the Empire, Talma was unquestionably the greatest actor in France. His genius was for tragedy—which Napoleon preferred—and it was in that genre that he and his stage partner, Mlle. Duchenois, dominated the Comédie française. Everyone who heard him was moved by his presence, his speech, the great improvements in costumes and make-up—by the total perfection in every detail of his performance. Mme. de Staël wrote that his talent made him the equal of all the greatest artists, painters, sculptors, and poets, who, according to her, would profit from studying and listening to him. His career continued under the Restoration. It came to an end with his last performance in June 1826 in Delaville's tragedy of *Charles VI*. Death came on 19 October of the same year.

H. F. Collins, *Talma* (New York, 1964); A. Copin, *Talma et la Révolution* (Paris, 1887), and *Talma et l'Empire* (Paris, 1887); E. Denis de Manne, *La troupe de Talma* (Lyon, 1866); A. Dumas, *Mémoires de Talma* (Paris, 1850); E. Duval, *Talma précis historique* (Paris, 1826); M. Moreau, *Mémoires historiques et littéraires sur F. J. Talma* (Paris, 1826); J.-B. Regnault-Warin, *Mémoires historiques et critiques sur F. J. Talma et sur l'art théâtral* (Paris, 1827), and *Mémoires sur Talma avec notes et nombreux documents collationnés par Henri d'Almeras* (Paris, 1904).

Rachel R. Schneider

Related entries: ART; DAVID; THEATER.

TARENTE, DUC DE. See MACDONALD.

TAUROGGEN, CONVENTION OF. See YORCK.

TEPLITZ, TREATY OF (9 September 1813), formalization of the alliance among Russia, Prussia, and Austria against France. Each country promised to provide a minimum of 60,000 troops for the Allied army and not to make separate peace with France. Austria and Prussia were to recover all territories lost since 1805.

Related entries: FOREIGN POLICY; GERMAN WAR OF LIBERATION.

TERNAUX, GUILLAUME-LOUIS (1763–1833), the leading woolens manufacturer in France under Napoleon and during the Restoration. Guillaume Ternaux created the basic structure of his integrated business empire between 1798 and 1810. By 1810, when he was awarded the cross of the Legion of Honor by Napoleon and named as the first vice-president of the Ministry of Interior's Conseil Général des Fabriques et Manufactures, Ternaux's numerous factories at Sedan, Reims, Louviers, and Verviers (Belgium) employed almost 12,000 workers. He had his own sheep herds, wool-washing plants, dyeworks, machine shops, display factory for new machines, commerce houses, retail outlets, and a private bank. Luxury goods of his own invention were Ternaux's specialty. His famous India shawls (*cachemires*) were produced in Reims; Sedan was the center for soft *draps vigogne* made of Spanish merino wool; and the main factory at Louviers specialized in machine-made superfine woolens, *satins-draps*. A key figure in the mechanization of the French woolens industry, Ternaux was among the first to adopt the early machines of William Cockerill and other Britishers, and in 1811–12 at Bazancourt, he established the first factory in France where wool was combed and spun mechanically. Ternaux's business empire reached its height in 1819–20.

R. J. Barker, "Casimir Perier (1777–1832) and William Ternaux (1763–1833): Two French Capitalists" (Ph.D. dissertation, Duke University, 1958); M. Collignon, "Ternaux, 1763–1833,'' *Bulletin de la Société d'études diverses de l'arrondissement de Louviers* 7 (1903); L. Lomuller, *Guillaume Ternaux, Créateur de la première intégration française* (Paris, 1978).

Richard J. Barker

Related entries: CONTINENTAL BLOCKADE; ECONOMY, FRENCH; NOTABLES; SOCIETY; WARFARE, ECONOMIC.

TERROR, THE (June 1793–July 1794), the bloodiest and most famous phase of the Revolution, resulting from the policies of an emergency war government. It was a response to the major crisis of spring 1793, which sprang from military defeats, provincial conservative revolts, peasant insurrection, royalist plots, economic crisis, and radical popular agitation in Paris. France needed to mobilize all resources to fight a war of survival at a time when it was undermined by dissent and by military and administrative chaos. The Terror was aimed at winning the war while repressing opposition of all forms and at all levels.

The Terror came into existence piecemeal between June and September 1793. On the one hand, radical *sans-culotte* pressure in Paris progressively forced the National Convention to decree coercive security measures and regulate the economy. On the other, local republicans in the provinces used repressive measures against dissent and rebellion. After September the national government embraced the Terror as policy, and control eventually became highly centralized. Initiative passed from the Convention to the Committees of Public Safety and of General Security. The former, under the influence of Maximilien Robespierre, coordinated the war effort and formulated policy; the latter centralized the agencies of repression.

The Terror government, operating under a sweeping Law of Suspects, sought by arrest and execution to remove those who, by word or deed, challenged it and thus weakened the Republic's ability to survive. These included both the visibly treasonable (such as the federalist rebels of 1793) and people deemed likely to be treasonable (such as nobles and priests). For ''victory and order,'' it also regulated the economy by fixing prices for almost all commodities (Law of the Maximum) and instituting a massive system of requisitioning of food and other necessities for the cities and the army. Economic measures were enforced by terror; ''endangering the Republic'' applied to economic crimes. Finally the Terror contained distinct overtones of social regeneration. Some attempts were made to redistribute wealth by assigning the property of the executed ''traitors'' and making the rich subsidize the war effort. Moreover, the Terror was based on a theoretical discourse of regeneration and democracy in which great wealth was seen to be corrupting. The dechristianization movement and the establishment of an official non-Christian Cult of the Supreme Being were also expressed in terms of social regeneration.

The Terror was implemented through emergency institutions staffed by Jacobins who were often from a lower social rank than the officials of previous years. At the local level, popular clubs supervised the population, denounced offenders, and stimulated administration, while Revolutionary committees with powers of arrest acted as enforcing agents. Revolutionary armies, directed by radicals, provided mobile repressive and coercive agents in town and country. Traitors were sent for summary trial at Revolutionary tribunals. The local operation of the Terror was supervised by representatives on mission from the Convention selected by the Committee of Public Safety. In 1794 the Revolutionary armies and most provincial Revolutionary tribunals were suppressed in the interests of centralized uniformity.

The victims of the Terror came from all social classes. At least 16,600 people were executed. As many as 100,000 may have been arrested and imprisoned. Measured in terms of the military survival of the Republic—winning the war—the Terror was remarkably successful. Indeed this very success allowed the Convention to dismantle the system after July 1794 when Robespierre was brought down by factional struggles and executed.

Although this period saw major advances in Bonaparte's career and military reputation (notably at the siege of Toulon), he did not play a role in the Terror. Certainly he was always a political animal and adopted a Jacobin tone in 1793–94. He was accused of Robespierrism in 1794 and imprisoned for two weeks. This stemmed essentially, however, from the fact that Augustin Robespierre had patronized him for his military talent. This relationship was briefly used by other members of the Convention attached to the Army of Italy in order to cover themselves from accusations of Robespierrism.

R. C. Cobb, *Les armées révolutionnaires* (Paris, 1961–63); C. Lucas, *The Structure of the Terror* (Oxford, 1973); A. Mathiez, *La vie chère et le mouvement social sous la Terreur* (Paris, 1927); R. R. Palmer, *Twelve who Ruled* (Princeton, 1941); W. Scott, *Terror and Repression in Revolutionary Marseilles* (London, 1973).

Colin Lucas

Related entries: CONVENTION; NAPOLEON I; TOULON, SIEGE OF.

THEATER. The theater under Napoleon shrank rather than grew. This, among other things, was attributed by Alphonse de Lamartine to the fact that Napoleon favored science and mathematics over literature. More truly, it was because Napoleon felt that actors should serve their country by fostering patriotic spirit, just as soldiers faced the nation's enemies. Thus the theater was under severe censorship, and to facilitate this, the government paid great sums to a small number of theaters and suppressed most of the free enterprise operations, which had been the joy of the sidestreets.

In Paris, the subsidized, official theaters were the Théâtre français (or Théâtre de S. M. l'Empereur), the Odéon, the Opéra, the Opéra Comique (the four *grands*), and the Gaieté, Ambigu, Variétés, and Vaudeville. The Théâtre français (or Comédie française) played largely the classics—Jean Racine, Molière (J.-B. Poquelin), and Pierre Corneille—catering to Napoleon's preference for tragedy by frequent stagings of Corneille. It also revived eighteenth-century works, as did the Odéon, such as those of P. A. Caron de Beaumarchais and Pierre de

Marivaux. The most popular new tragedy was *Les templiers* by François Raynouard. Also played frequently were the works of de Belloy (P. L. Buyrette), such as *Le Siège de Calais* and *Gaston et Bayard*. The Comédie française even sent a troupe to Russia during the campaign of 1812, and Napoleon reorganized it by a decree written in Moscow. Among the popular comedies were *La suite de menteur* by François-Guillaume Andrieux, *Petite ville* of Louis Picard, and *Deux gendres* of Charles Etienne.

Melodramatic spectacles also drew great crowds. They featured the standard gothic and romantic trappings: ruined castles, moon-lit forests and wastes, pining and abandoned maidens, melancholy lovers, and phantoms chained and unchained. The master of this genre was Guibert de Pixérécourt.

One should not forget that the marquis de Sade, incarcerated at Charenton at the request of his family (1803–14), wrote and/or directed and acted in various plays performed by the inmates. They were much attended by the people of fashion in Paris.

The major actor of the period was François Talma, who, catering to Napoleon's tastes, specialized in portraying tragic heroes. Among the more prominent actresses were Mademoiselles Mars (Anne Boutet), George (Marguerite Weimer), and Thérèse Burgoin.

The emperor also favored the opera, for which he built a new structure, and at which were featured not only operas, largely Italian, but also ballets.

A. Albert, *Les théâtres des boulevards, 1789-1848* (Paris, 1902); M. Carlson, *The Theatre of the French Revolution* (Ithaca, N.Y., 1966); Ch.-G. Etienne de Martainville, *Histoire du théâtre français depuis le commencement de la Révolution jusqu'à la réunion générale*, 4 vols. (Paris, 1902); J. Fleury, *Mémoires de Fleury, de la Comédie française*, 6 vols. (Brussels, 1835-37); M.-J. George, *Mémoires* (Paris, 1912); Stendhal (H. Beyle), *Journal de Stendhal (1801-1814)* (Paris, 1888), and *La vie de Henri Brulard*, 2 vols. (Paris, 1949); F.-J. Talma, *Mémoires de Talma*, 4 vols. (Paris, 1849-50).

Related entries: GEORGE; LITERATURE; TALMA.

THIBAUDEAU, ANTOINE-CLAIR (1765–1854), councillor of state and prefect under Napoleon. A terrorist and regicide in the Convention, Thibaudeau remained an ardent republican in the Council of Five Hundred of the Directory but supported the coup d'état of 18 Brumaire. In March 1800 Bonaparte appointed him prefect of the Gironde (Bordeaux) but recalled him to Paris to serve in the Council of State in September 1800. He aspired to a ministry but ruined his chances by opposing, in the name of republicanism, the creation of the Legion of Honor, the Concordat, and the Consulate for life. In April 1803 Bonaparte exiled Thibaudeau from Paris by naming him prefect of the Bouches-du-Rhône (Marseilles), where he stayed until April 1814.

Thibaudeau performed ably as prefect, quickly adjusting to the imperial regime. He replaced former Revolutionaries on administrative assemblies with rich merchants and large landed proprietors and accepted nomination to the Legion of Honor (1804) and the title of count (1809). In 1814 he was banished from

France as a regicide and returned only after July 1830. He used his enforced leisure to write his memoirs, which are among the most valuable of the period.

J. Bourdon, *La législation du Consulat et de l'Empire: la réforme judiciaire de l'an VIII* (Rodez, 1942); C. Durand, *Etudes sur le conseil d'état napoléonien* (Paris, 1949); G. Lefebvre, *Napoleon from Tilsit to Waterloo*, trans. J. E. Anderson (New York, 1969); G. Saint-Yves and J. Fournier, *Le département des Bouches-du-Rhône de 1800 à 1815* (Paris, 1899); A.-C. Thibaudeau, *Mémoires sur le Consulat (1799-1804)* (Paris, 1827), and *Mémoires (1799–1815)* (Paris, 1913).

Harold T. Parker

Related entry: ADMINISTRATION.

TILSIT, TREATIES OF (7 and 9 July 1807), Franco-Russian-Prussian peace treaties signed after the French victory at Friedland, 14 June 1807. They comprised four documents. (1) A public Franco-Russian treaty, by which the Duchy of Warsaw was created under the king of Saxony; the free city of Danzig was established; Russia agreed to mediate between France and Britain, to recognize Napoleon's brothers as kings of Naples, Holland, and Westphalia, and to withdraw from Rumania; and France agreed to mediate peace between Russia and Turkey. (2) By secret articles Russia ceded Cattaro and the Ionian Islands to France, and France agreed that Ferdinand IV of Naples would be compensated for the loss of his throne. (3) A Franco-Russian military alliance (9 July), in which the powers agreed that they would make common cause in any future war; that if Britain did not accept Russian mediation before 1 November 1807, Russia would declare war; that Denmark, Sweden, and Portugal would be forced to close their ports to British ships, and Vienna would be forced to adhere to the alliance. In a deliberately vague clause, Napoleon further agreed that if Turkey did not accept French mediation in the Russo-Turkish war within three months, France would help Russia "deliver from the yoke and the vexations of the Turks all the provinces of the [Ottoman] empire in Europe" except the city of Constantinople "and the province of Rumelia." (4) A Franco-Prussian treaty of peace (9 July), which deprived Prussia of about half its territory and by which it was to ally with Russia and France against Britain. A supplementary convention signed at Königsberg, 12 July 1807, provided for French evacuation of troops from Prussia in exchange for payment of an unspecified indemnity. This convention led to much disagreement.

H. Butterfield, *The Peace Tactics of Napoleon, 1806–1808* (Cambridge, Eng., 1929); V. G. Sirotkin, *Duel' dvukh diplomatii, 1801–1812* (Moscow, 1966); E. V. Tarle, *Kontinental'naia blokada* (Moscow, 1913); A. Vandal, *Napoléon et Alexandre I*, 3 vols. (Paris, 1893–96); M. F. Zlotnikov, *Kontinental'naia blokada i Rossiia* (Moscow and Leningrad, 1966).

Hugh Ragsdale

Related entries: ALEXANDER I; DIPLOMACY; FRIEDRICH WILHELM III; FOREIGN POLICY; WARSAW, DUCHY OF; WESTPHALIA, KINGDOM OF.

***TIRAILLEURS*.** See ARMY, FRENCH.

TOLENTINO, BATTLE OF. See ABDICATION, SECOND; MURAT; NAPLES, KINGDOM OF.

TONE, WOLFE (1763–98), founder (with Thomas Russell and Napper Tandy) of the United Irishmen, which sought to unite Catholic and Protestant Irishmen to secure Irish independence. Branded a dangerous revolutionary, he was allowed to emigrate (1795) to America but then traveled to Paris, where he helped persuade the French to dispatch invasion forces to Ireland in 1796 and 1798. In the wake of the latter, he was arrested and committed suicide in prison (1798). See IRELAND.

TORRES VEDRAS, LINES OF (1809–11), defenses at Lisbon that protected the duke of Wellington's army until he was ready to go on the offensive against the French in the peninsula. They were planned by Major Neves Costa and constructed by Wellington's engineers, Lieutenant Colonel R. Fletcher and Captain J. T. Jones, with the aid of Portuguese soldiers and civilians. The lines, extending some twenty-one miles across the peninsula on which Lisbon is situated, ran from the Tagus to the Atlantic Ocean. Maximum use was made of rivers, mountains, and swamps, as well as forts, mills, houses, and other buildings, in the construction of three lines housing 628 guns manned by 39,475 soldiers. During the third invasion of Portugal (1810–11), Marshal André Masséna invaded the kingdom with 65,000 men and drove to within twenty miles of Lisbon, where his army confronted the lines. Unable to breach these positions, whose defenders had been reinforced by Wellington's Anglo-Portuguese army of 60,000 men, Masséna appealed unsuccessfully to Napoleon for men, supplies, and siege equipment. After several sorties and a prolonged wait of 108 days, Masséna retreated from Portugal, pursued by the Allied army (March 1811). The lines of Torres Vedras thus halted the tide of French expansion and became a turning point in the history of the Napoleonic Empire.

D. D. Horward, ed. and trans., *The French Campaign in Portugal, 1810–1811: An Account by Jean Jacques Pelet* (Minneapolis, 1973); J. T. Jones, *Memoranda Relative to the Lines Thrown up to Cover Lisbon in 1810* (London, 1829); S. J. da Luz Soriano, *Historia da Guerra Civil e do estabelecimento do governo parlamentar em Portugal, comprehendendo a historia diplomatica, militar e politica d'este reino deste 1777 ate 1834*, 15 vols. (Lisbon, 1866–92).

Donald D. Horward

Related entries: MASSENA; PORTUGUESE CAMPAIGNS; WELLINGTON.

TOULON, SIEGE OF (September–December 1793), action in which Napoleon Bonaparte first gained fame. This federal city revolted against the government of the Terror in July 1793. Royalists took over, and on 28 August 1793, a British fleet commanded by Admiral Samuel Hood reinforced the rebels, landing 17,000 troops. Nearby Marseille was also in revolt, and the Convention (Committee of Public Safety) elected to subdue it first, but by the end of August, General Jean Carteaux's army approached Toulon from the west. With the army were government representatives on mission, notably Paul Barras, A. Christophe Saliceti, and Augustin Robespierre, brother of the Incorruptible. As the siege began (7 September) the artillery commander, General E.-A. Cousin de Dommartin, was wounded; the representatives gave his place to Napoleon Bonaparte (recommended by his fellow Corsican, Saliceti). Bonaparte recommended the capture of fortifications on the heights above the harbor, which (he said) protected the British fleet. Carteaux rejected the plan but in November was replaced by Jacques Dugommier, who approved. On December 17, after a two-day artillery barrage from Bonaparte's batteries, "Jacobins," "Hommes sans Peur," and "Chasse Coquins," republican forces captured the forts guarding the inner harbor. Admiral Hood realized that his position was untenable and withdrew on 18 December. Toulon fell on 19 December, and the next day the representatives on mission reported to the Convention that vengeance had begun against traitors in *Port de la Montagne*.

A. Aulard, *Recueil des Actes du Comité de Salut Public*, vols. 6, 7 (Paris, 1894); V. Brunn, *Guerres maritimes de la France, Port de Toulon* (Paris, 1861); O. Havard, *Histoire de la Révolution dans les Ports de Guerre* (Toulon, 1912); D. M. Henry, *Histoire de Toulon depuis 1789 jusqu'au Consulat* (Toulon, 1855).

Leonard Macaluso

Related entries: NAPOLEON I; TERROR, THE.

TOUSSAINT L'OUVERTURE, FRANCOIS-DOMINIQUE (1743–1803), Father of the republic of Haiti. Born a slave in French Saint Domingue (Haiti, or the western half of Hispaniola, or Santo Domingo), he acquired an education with the encouragement of his French masters. His literacy and knowledge, together with his extraordinary toughness, tenacity, and charisma, vaulted him into the top ranks of the black rebellion against the French in 1791. (In appearance, he was an unlikely leader: short—5 feet 2 inches, Napoleon's height—very thin, if wiry and muscular, and with a far from handsome face.) He was never a racist, however, believing that the blacks could learn from the French, and vice-versa. Thus he meant—and later attempted—to allow the whites to live, own property, and conduct business in Haiti—but under black majority rule.

In 1793, when Spain went to war with France, Toussaint, among other black leaders, took service in Spanish Santo Domingo, where he was given a colonel's commission. In 1794, however, when the French Convention abolished slavery, Toussaint returned to Haiti, rescued the French governor, Etienne Laveaux, who was besieged in Le Cap by a black army, and declared his loyalty to France, as a free citizen of France. His reward was a French general's commission and the lieutenant governorship of Haiti. It was not quite enough. While still protesting his Frenchness, Toussaint in 1798 expelled all French officials and became governor, which enabled him to negotiate a withdrawal of the British, who had come to aid the rebels against the French when the sides were easier to identify. Toussaint then went on to attack Spanish Santo Domingo and by 1801 was master of the whole island.

Meanwhile, Bonaparte had come to power in France (November 1799). He credited Toussaint publicly with "saving for France a great and important colony" and said he deserved to be governor. Napoleon was persuaded by the planters' (and ex-planters') faction, however, that French authority had to be reasserted and slavery restored in order to make the West Indian islands profitable again. Napoleon restored slavery in the French possessions (May 1802) but avoided statements regarding Haiti, to which he had dispatched a military expedition.

In January 1802, a French force of 23,000 under General Charles Leclerc forced its way ashore at Le Cap (Cap Haitien). The general carried a deceptive letter from Napoleon to Toussaint, promising freedom for the blacks and honors and fortune for their noble leader, "General Toussaint." The canny black governor was not fooled, and initially the blacks resisted the French fiercely. Leclerc had early successes, however, and was able to win over some black generals. Toussaint decided to negotiate, but Leclerc had him arrested. He was dispatched to France, where he died within a year (April 1803) in a dungeon of the Fort de Joux.

Before Toussaint reached France, however, the black leaders had reunited their forces. News that slavery would be restored had arrived, and Toussaint was seen as a martyr. Moreover, tropical fevers began destroying the French army. In September 1802, Leclerc reported that 100 to 120 men were dying daily and that 4,000 had perished in August. In November 1802, Leclerc himself died of the fever. In 1803 Haiti was lost. It had been central to Napoleon's colonial schemes, and its loss induced him to abandon them, and, among other things, to sell Louisiana to the United States.

It is ironic, however, that Napoleon himself, by betraying Toussaint, removed the one black leader who might have kept the French tricolor flying over Santo Domingo.

A. Cesaire, *Toussaint Louverture: La Révolution française et le problème colonial* (Paris, 1982); C. L. R. James, *The Black Jacobins: Toussaint l'Ouverture and the San Domingo Revolution* (New York, 1938); F. Scharon, *Toussaint Louverture et la révolution de Saint Domingue* (Port-au-Prince, 1957).

Related entries: COLONIES, FRENCH; HAITI.

TRAFALGAR, BATTLE OF (21 October 1805). This battle, which brought Admiral Horatio Nelson death and glory on 21 October 1805, neither saved England from invasion, as some suppose, nor was it France's worst naval disaster of the Revolutionary wars. Napoleon had cancelled his invasion plan in August, when he marched against Austria; and France's worst naval losses occurred when the Allies occupied Toulon in 1793.

In his projected invasion of England, Napoleon planned to obtain temporary French naval superiority in the channel by having the Franco-Spanish fleet under Admiral Pierre-Charles de Villeneuve decoy Nelson and his squadron to the Caribbean. At first everything went according to plan. Villeneuve crossed the Atlantic, Nelson followed, and Villeneuve returned. But then knowing the poor quality of his fleet, Villeneuve sought shelter in Cadiz (as his orders permitted), and Nelson with a blockading British squadron was soon outside. At the command of Napoleon and provoked to action by news that Admiral François-Etienne Rosily was to supersede him, Villeneuve led the Franco-Spanish fleet out to meet disaster at the naval battle of Trafalgar. Aside from Spanish losses, of the eighteen French ships in Villeneuve's force, nine were sunk or taken; Admiral Richard Strachan captured four survivors at sea shortly afterward; five escaped into Cadiz but surrendered to the Spaniards there in 1808. To complete the grim picture, one must recall other French losses that soon followed: J. Bertrand de Leissègues's squadron of five destroyed off San Domingo in February 1806 and four more, under E.-T. de Burgues de Missiessy, that never returned from the West Indies in 1806.

The immediate effect of Trafalgar was to thwart Bonaparte's aims in the Mediterranean, and these losses were a long-term setback to his efforts to build a fleet strong enough to overcome the British.

G. Bennett, *Nelson the Commander* (New York, 1972), and *The Battle of Trafalgar* (London, 1977); Sir J. Corbett, *The Campaign of Trafalgar* (London, 1910); A. T. Mahan, *The Influence of Sea Power upon the French Revolution and Empire* (Boston, 1894); R. Maine, *Trafalgar* (1960); G. J. Marcus, *The Age of Nelson: The Royal Navy 1793–1815* (1971); P. Masson and J. Muracciole, *Napoléon et la Marine* (Paris, 1968); C. Oman, *Nelson* (London, 1947).

Richard Glover

Related entries: AUSTERLITZ CAMPAIGN; ENGLAND, ATTEMPTED CONQUEST OF; NAVY, FRENCH.

TREVISE, DUC DE. See MORTIER.

TRIANON TARIFF. See CONTINENTAL BLOCKADE.

TRIBUNATE OF CONSULATE AND EMPIRE. See CONSTITUTIONS.

TUILERIES, CHATEAU OF, palace of French kings in Paris. The chateau was occupied by Revolutionary assemblies, 1792–99, and was the residence of Napoleon as first consul and later emperor, 1799–1814/1815.

TUSCANY, GRAND DUCHY OF (1809–13), satellite state ruled by Napoleon's sister Elisa Bonaparte Bacciochi. Tuscany was ceded to France by Austria at Lunéville (1801) and converted into a Spanish secundogeniture, the Kingdom of Etruria, in return for the retrocession of Louisiana to France. In Napoleon's eyes, the kingdom was a failure and, worse, traded with the British. In 1807 Napoleon forced the Spanish to relinquish it. In 1808 Tuscany was formally annexed to France and divided into departments. The natives resented the loss of Tuscan identity, however. In 1809 Napoleon placated them by creating Tuscany a grand duchy, with his sister Elisa grand duchess, though the state nevertheless remained part of France.

Elisa, thirty-two in 1809, was Napoleon's eldest sister and had been given an aristocratic education at Saint Cyr under the Old Regime. Of all the Bonapartes, she was perhaps most like Napoleon in her ability to lead, persuade, and organize. She abolished feudalism, applied the Code Napoléon, liquidated monastic property, and financed new schools and public works. She remained technically subordinate to Napoleon, but he put no limits on her authority since she usually anticipated what he wanted and because she made Tuscany financially independent. Moreover, she furnished Napoleon with an army of 10,000, which was large for Tuscany. Her court was the most brilliant in Europe. Elisa took a special interest in the Academy of Crusca, the major project of which was the production of an Italian dictionary. When finished, Napoleon specified that it be used by his administrators in all the Italian states, making Tuscan the official language of all Italy. Elisa left her mark on Florence by straightening and widening public streets and restoring public buildings and churches. By creating a French-trained administrative and judicial corps, she made a definite contribution to the future of Italy. She was forced to withdraw from Tuscany in 1813 by Joachim Murat after he joined the Allies and moved north with his Neapolitan army. In 1814 Tuscany reverted to its Austrian ruler.

A. Corsini, *I Bonaparte a Firenza* (Milan, 1961); A. Fugier, *Napoléon et l'Italie* (Paris, 1947); E. Rodocanacchi, *Elisa Bacciochi en Italie* (Paris, 1900).

Related entries: BONAPARTE, ELISA; EMPIRE, FRENCH; FOREIGN POLICY.

U

ULM, BATTLE OF (15–20 October 1805), defeat of the Austrian army, which opened the road for the French march on Vienna. In the opening weeks of the Austerlitz campaign, Napoleon directed the French army from its encampment on the English Channel to the upper Danube between Ulm and Ingolstadt. The Austrian army, commanded by General K. Mack, the Archduke Ferdinand's chief of staff, was in the vicinity of Ulm facing west, expecting the French to emerge from the Black Forest. On October 7, the French army began to cross the Danube some forty miles east of Ulm and to swing to the south and the west. While the corps of L.-N. Davout and Jean Bernadotte faced west in Bavaria, M. Ney, J. Lannes, and J. Murat closed on Ulm from the east. The Austrians were taken completely by surprise. By the time they realized their danger, the entire French army (more than 150,000 men) was between Ulm and Munich. Murat was given temporary command of the attack on Ulm. The first serious fighting took place at Wertingen, on 8 October, where the Austrians were thrown back on Ulm. However, when Ney's Sixth Corps was called south of the Danube by Murat, General Pierre Dupont's division was left on the north side of the river. It was attacked on 11 October by the forces of Mack in overwhelming numbers, and only the timely arrival of Ney with two other divisions saved the isolated Dupont. By 15 October L. Marmont and Nicolas Soult had joined the attack, which was highlighted by Ney's successful attack on Michelsberg. On 17 October, an armistice was signed, followed three days later by Mack's surrender in which 27,000 Austrians laid down their arms. The Archduke Ferdinand escaped into Bohemia with 10,000 men, and another division escaped south into the Tyrol.

C. Manceron, *Austerlitz* (Paris, 1962); F. N. Maude, *The Ulm Campaign, 1805* (London, 1912); J. Thiry, *Ulm, Trafalgar, Austerlitz* (Paris, 1965).

John Gallaher

Related entries: ARMY, FRENCH; ARMY, HABSBURG; AUSTERLITZ CAMPAIGN; MACK VON LEIBERICH.

UNIONS. See LABOR LEGISLATION.

UNITED PROVINCES OF THE NETHERLANDS. See BATAVIAN REPUBLIC; HOLLAND, KINGDOM OF; NETHERLANDS entries.

UNITED STATES. The wars of the French Revolution and Napoleon buffeted the United States and influenced its foreign and domestic policies. The French Revolution reinforced in the new American federal republic the liberal principles of the emerging Republican party, as well as the conservatism of the developing Federalists. The United States achieved a temporary settlement of its differences with England through the Jay Treaty (1794). It was able to settle the undeclared corsair war waged by the French Republic on American shipping in 1800 with the new first consul, Napoleon Bonaparte.

Thomas Jefferson, Democratic-Republican, the spiritual founder of American liberalism, became president of the United States in 1801, while France, the hope of so many Republicans in the 1790s, had fallen under the sway of Napoleon. The retrocession of Louisiana to France (1801) and the creation of the life Consulate (1802) reinforced Republican concern about national security. By 1803, however, Napoleon's dream of an American empire had been shattered by the failure of Charles-Victor-Emmanuel Leclerc's expedition to Santo Domingo and the imminence of hostilities with Great Britain.

As a result, Napoleon sold all of Louisiana to the United States. Britain and France, however, were soon fighting a total war, and the young American Republic, which became the leading neutral carrier, was caught between the British Orders in Council and the Continental System of Napoleon. While suffering from both British and French depredations, Britain, as mistress of the seas after Trafalgar (October 1805), ultimately caused the greater injury, particularly since the former mother country was treating the United States as if it were still its colony and subject to the old colonial system. Impressment was striking evidence of the contempt of British officialdom. In fact, while jealous of the forward child's commerical growth, British officials were primarily concerned with their life-and-death struggle with Napoleon. American concerns were thus incidental.

The extreme Federalists, staunch conservatives who also reflected at times the interests of many American merchants and shippers and some agriculturalists who benefited from trade with Great Britain and its dependencies, castigated Napoleon as a vicious military despot who endangered the world. To them Republicans were Francophiles. Majority Republicans, on the other hand, liberals as they were, who expressed at times the frustrations of many agriculturalists unable to sell their produce in Napoleonic Europe, tended to consider England as their chief enemy and Federalists as Anglophiles. While frequently irritated with Bonaparte's foreign policies, Republicans believed occasionally that he was still defending some of the liberal principles of the French Revolution and spreading them to the backward countries. More frequently, they recognized his usefulness for the implementation of American foreign policy against Great Britain.

Pragmatic President Jefferson attempted to deal with the British (and French) restrictions through the Embargo Act (22 December 1807), but this was abandoned by Congress and replaced by the Non-Intercourse Act (1 March 1809). Under Jefferson's collaborator and successor, James Madison, one weak measure followed another as the Republicans endeavored to avoid war. In the end, the fundamental and only practical choice was submission or war. Although the War of 1812 was vital to American interests, it was inconsequential in the Anglo-French struggle, but the defeat of Napoleon ended the need for Orders in Council and impressment, and therefore peace came to the American Republic in 1815.

The republic had proved its durability and achieved economic independence. After the Hundred Days Jefferson described Napoleon Bonaparte as the "wretch" who had caused "more misery and suffering to the world than any other being who ever lived before him." The struggle for liberty, he wrote, would now take longer and swell "more rivers with blood." The United States, as he had proclaimed earlier, was "the sole depository of the sacred fire of freedom and self-government," whence sparks would emanate to rekindle liberty in other quarters of the globe.

U. Bonnel, *La France, les Etats-Unis et la guerre de course, 1797–1815* (Paris, 1961); A. DeConde, *The Quasi-War: The Politics and Diplomacy of the Undeclared War with France, 1797–1801* (New York, 1966); R. Horsman, *The Causes of the War of 1812* (Philadelphia, 1962); E. W. Lyon, *Louisiana in French Diplomacy, 1759–1804* (Norman, Okla., 1934); B. Perkins, *Prologue to War: England and the United States, 1805–1812* (Berkeley, 1961); J. I. Shulim, *The Old Dominion and Napoleon Bonaparte: A Study in American Opinion* (New York, 1952, 1968), "Thomas Jefferson Views Napoleon," *Virginia Magazine of History and Biography* 60 (1952), and *John Daly Burk: Irish Revolutionist and American Patriot* (Philadelphia, 1964).

Joseph I. Shulim

Related entries: CORSAIR WAR; DIPLOMACY; FOREIGN POLICY.

UNIVERSITY, IMPERIAL. A teaching corporation rather than a university, it theoretically had as its membership all those involved in educating males in France. Proclaimed in principle by a law of 10 May 1806, the university came into being by decree of 17 March 1808. The term *university* was itself in such disrepute that Napoleon dared use it only after Austerlitz, but the idea had circulated for some time and was not an impulsive one of Napoleon's. Napoleon wanted the teachers to be laymen rather than clerics, and he desired an organization modeled on the army's.

The university aimed at a monopoly of public education. Another purpose was to obtain for the lycées the pupils they lacked.

At the head was a grand master chosen by Napoleon and all powerful in his jurisdiction, though theoretically under the minister of the interior. Probably in an attempt to reconcile the Catholics, as he was interested in having religion serve his power, Napoleon appointed as grand master Louis de Fontanes, who not only favored the Catholics but undercut Napoleon in other ways. The teachings of the Catholic religion constituted one base of instruction. A Council of Thirty, ten appointed for life by Napoleon and the rest by various officials for a year, aided Fontanes. Divided into five sections, it functioned actively. A chancellor, a treasurer, and a maximum of thirty inspectors general reported to the council. Schools at all three levels—primary, secondary, and higher—reported to academies, of which there were twenty-seven, each headed by a rector (appointed by the grand master for five years) and a council, with inspectors reporting to the rector. The grand master was himself rector of Paris. Between a rector and the lycée teachers, there were four other hierarchical levels. In May 1809 the university received a Central Bureau to look into the moral and educational qualifications of candidates for teaching posts.

Napoleon did not pay much attention to primary schools. ''Little seminaries,'' lycées, and communal colleges existed at the secondary level. Lycée teachers received special privileges. Universities and the ''Great Schools'' offered higher education. When private schools proliferated, their number was reduced by heavy financial burdens; the university reform of 1811, aimed at making the university monopoly a reality, strictly regulated nonuniversity establishments, and limited ecclesiastical schools to one per department.

Although in the six years before Napoleon's fall it never succeeded in getting the desired monopoly on teaching, for lack of personnel, especially on the primary level, the university did enable the government to have strict control of the schools. It was one of Napoleon's lasting institutions; even today its spirit controls the Ministry of Education.

F. V. A. Aulard, *Napoléon Ier et le monopole universitaire* (Paris, 1911); J. Godechot, *Les institutions de la France sous la Révolution et l'Empire*, 2d ed. (Paris, 1968); R. B. Holtman, *The Napoleonic Revolution* (Baton Rouge, La., 1978); C. Schmidt, *La réforme de l'université impériale en 1811* (Paris, 1905).

Robert B. Holtman

Related entries: ADMINISTRATION; EDUCATION; FONTANES.

V

VALMY, DUC DE. See KELLERMANN.

VAN DER GOES, MAARTEN. See HOLLAND, KINGDOM OF; HOLLAND, KINGDOM OF: MINISTERS.

VAN DER HEIM, G. J. See HOLLAND, KINGDOM OF; HOLLAND, KINGDOM OF: MINISTERS.

VAUCHAMPS, BATTLE OF. See FRANCE, CAMPAIGN OF.

VENDEE, WAR IN THE (1793–1800), counterrevolutionary peasant movement in western coastal departments of France, begun in the Vendée. The war began with a call for conscripts in February 1793. There was formed in the Vendée department a Royal and Catholic army, made up of peasants and initially led by local priests who opposed the anticlerical legislation of the Revolutionary assemblies. An oath to the government was required, which had resulted in a division of the clergy nationwide into patriot and rebel clergy. Most of the priests in the Vendée were not patriots. As the army grew, nobles supplied leadership, and the British fleet delivered *émigrés*, bishops, and nobles to the coast. The movement spread into Brittany and other neighboring provinces.

The poorly armed and half-trained peasants were easy victims, however, for the republican armies sent out from Paris. The organized forces of the rebellion were totally broken at the Battle of Savenay in December 1793. The movement went underground, however, and was kept alive by the *chouans* (''night owls'') who fought as guerrillas and were strongest in Brittany and Normandy. The civil war heated up in 1794 after the fall of Maximilien Robespierre, which enabled many priests who had been hounded into hiding to return to their pulpits. Moreover, leaders arrived from England bringing money, weapons, and the promise of more. The French armies in western France suddenly found themselves on the defensive against hordes of guerrillas.

General Louis Hoche was sent to bring an end to the fighting but found the going very tough, and the war, Frenchman against Frenchman, became bloodier by the day. Hoche discovered, however, by talking to prisoners, that what the peasants wanted most was the restoration of church services under outlawed priests. He secured permission from Paris to make concessions on religion if the peasants would renounce royalism. On this basis he quickly brought an end to the fighting.

This might have been an end to the rebellion except for the assumption of leadership from England by the brother of the late Louis XVI, the comte d'Artois, who with British aid organized an *émigré* army to land in Brittany. Georges Cadoudal, a *chouan* hero of 1793, had been sent ahead to organize the peasants. At the same time the imprisoned boy king, Louis XVII, age ten, died in the Temple in Paris, which helped to work up sentiment for the royal house. The landing was badly planned. It was made by only 4,500 men at Quiberon, at the end of a long, narrow peninsula. Hoche, who had been warned of the action, blocked off the peninsula and killed or captured the invaders and the local rebels who had joined them. The comte d'Artois (later Charles X), who had never landed, and Cadoudal were among those who escaped to England. Although some guerrilla action continued in the Vendée, the movement was no problem to the government until 1798. At that time the authority of the Directory became very shaky, and guerrilla bands again multiplied.

The movement was virulent in 1799 when Napoleon came to power. With his penchant for seeing to the heart of matters, he decided that a permanent solution would have to be rooted in an agreement with the pope. Thus after Marengo he began negotiations for a concordat that would end the schism in the French clergy. He promised to negate all antichurch laws except those confiscating church property, and he offered the pope his states in central Italy in return for his blessing. The result was the Concordat of 1801. Meanwhile Napoleon offered the rebel leaders an amnesty if they would lay down their arms, and most accepted. He appointed the abbé Bernier, an ex-rebel, the chief negotiator for the concordat. Those rebels who did not take Napoleon's amnesty were hounded mercilessly, and the rebellion was soon dead.

The negotiation of the concordat, however, had given hope to the royalists. The Bourbon Pretender, Louis XVIII, wrote Napoleon, whom he addressed as "My General," attempting to persuade him to restore the monarchy. Napoleon refused since he knew the Vendéan rebels had been fighting more for church than crown. The royalists maintained an underground movement in France, however, until late 1803, when Georges Cadoudal and General Pichegru were arrested for plotting to overthrow the first consul. Pichegru died in prison; Cadoudal was executed in 1804. This marked the end of the royalist movement in France until the Restoration in 1814.

A.-M.-V. Billaud, *La guerre de Vendée* (Paris, 1972); H. Chardon, *Les Vendéens dans la Sarthe*, 3 vols. (Paris, 1976); A. Chaudeurge, *La Chouannerie normande* (Paris, 1982); J.-F. Chiappe, *La Vendée en armes*, 2 vols. (Paris, 1982); A. Montagnon, *Guerres de*

Vendée: 1793-1832 (Paris, 1974); P. Paret, *Internal War and Pacification: The Vendée, 1789-1796* (Princeton, N.J., 1961); C. Tilly, *The Vendée* (Cambridge, Mass., 1976).

Related entries: ARTOIS; BERNIER; CADOUDAL; CONCORDAT OF 1801; CHURCH, ROMAN CATHOLIC; LOUIS XVIII; NAPOLEON I.

VENDEMIAIRE, 13, YEAR IV (5 October 1795), date of the last mass insurrection of Revolutionary Paris, stopped by the "whiff of grapeshot" of Napoleon Bonaparte and a turning point in his career. Earlier the National Convention had finally succeeded in drafting the republican Constitution of the Year III, which was overwhelmingly approved by plebiscite. Much anxiety was nevertheless aroused in Paris by a subsidiary measure, the Two-thirds Decrees, by which 500 serving deputies would retain their seats. Although this was intended to ensure that the transition to the constitutional régime would be gradual, Parisians feared that the deputies' real object was to perpetuate their power and begin a new Reign of Terror. The rising that ensued is called royalist since it was instigated by royalists to prevent the establishment of a legitimate republic. Its real causes, however, were fear and the belief that any local assembly could decide which laws it should obey.

Trouble began on 4 October when General Jacques-François Menou made a vain attempt to arrest some leading agitators. The Convention then entrusted its defense to the deputy Paul Barras, placing five generals under his orders. One of these was Bonaparte, and in all probability it was he who really organized and inspired the defense of the Tuileries, where the Convention sat. Cannon were brought up, a strong reserve established, and troops posted to defend every approach to the palace. On 5 October an assault by vast crowds from the north was repulsed; later a column of insurgents, advancing along the southern bank of the Seine toward a vital bridge, the Pont Royal, was decimated by grapeshot and musketry fire, and thereafter patrols easily dispersed the remaining rebels.

Although the army previously had been employed to repress Paris after an insurrection, this was the first time since 1789 that military force had been completely successful. There were about 300 casualties on each side, but Paris did not revolt again for nearly forty years. As for Bonaparte, he had won recognition, promotion, and the patronage of Barras, and he was soon to command the Army of Italy.

P.-J.-F.-N., vicomte de Barras, *Mémoires de Barras, membre du Directoire, publiés avec une introduction générale, des préfaces et des appendices par Georges Durey*, 4 vols. (Paris, 1895–96); J. P. Garnier, *Barras, Le Roi du Directoire* (Paris, 1970); G. Lefebvre, *The Thermidorians and the Directory; Two Phases of the French Revolution* (1964); A. Soboul, *La première République, 1792–1804* (Paris, 1968); M. J. Sydenham, *The First French Republic, 1792–1804* (London, 1974); K. D. Tønnesson, *La défaite des sans-culottes: Mouvement populaire et réaction bourgeoise en l'an III* (Oslo and Paris, 1959).

M. J. Sydenham

Related entries: BARRAS; ITALIAN CAMPAIGN, FIRST; NAPOLEON I.

VERHUELL, KAREL. See HOLLAND, KINGDOM OF; HOLLAND, KINGDOM OF: MINISTERS.

VICTOR, CLAUDE (CLAUDE-VICTOR PERRIN) (1764-1841), duc de Bellune, Marshal of France. Of the lower bourgeoisie, the son of a notary of La Marche, Vosges, he enlisted in the Royal Army at seventeen and became a sergeant but left to be a grocer. In 1791 he reentered the army via the National Guard. In 1793 he was one of the heroes of Toulon and was promoted to *général de brigade*. He fought under Bonaparte in the first Italian campaign (1796–97), in Egypt, and in the second Italian campaign (1800) where he received a saber of honor after Marengo.

Victor was posted to Holland and Denmark and missed the Austerlitz campaign (1805); however, he fought against the Prussians (1806) and displayed exceptional skill against the Russians at Friedland (1807). Napoleon made him a marshal (1807) and duc de Bellune (1808).

In Spain (1808–11), he was a solid and dependable corps commander but had to share responsibility for Joseph's failure (if not defeat) at Talavera. In 1812 he served in Russia, in 1813 at Dresden and Leipzig, and in 1814 in the campaign of France until he was severely wounded at Craonne. In 1815 he did not support Napoleon. Louis XVIII made him a peer of France, major general of the Royal Guard, and minister of war (1821–23). Only one volume, covering 1792–1800, of his *Mémoires* has ever been published.

L. Chardigny, *Les maréchaux de Napoléon* (Paris, 1980); R. F. Delderfield, *The March of the Twenty-six; The Story of Napoleon's Marshals* (London, 1962); C.-V. Perrin, *Mémoires* (Paris, 1847); P. Young, *Napoleon's Marshals* (London, 1974).

Related entries: FRANCE, CAMPAIGN OF; PENINSULAR WAR.

VIENNA, CONGRESS OF (15 September 1814–9 June 1815), meeting of the representatives of European states at Vienna to restructure Europe in the aftermath of the Revolutionary and Napoleonic wars. After the defeat of France in 1814, the victorious Allies determined to create a stable new order in Europe based on the principles of monarchical legitimacy, compensation, and balance of power. This was evidenced in the first Peace of Paris (30 May 1814), which recognized the Bourbon government of France, restored it to the boundaries of 1792, and enacted no punitive measures. Although denied a role in the forthcoming peace conference provided for in article XXXII of the treaty, France remained a major power.

Nevertheless, the former Allied powers were to retain control of the decision-making process at Vienna. Informal meetings of their ministers—Robert Castlereagh (Britain), Clemens von Metternich (Austria), K. A. von Hardenberg (Prussia), and Karl von Nesselrode (Russia)—began on 15 September 1814 and resulted in a protocol (22 September) reaffirming that decision. The representatives of France (Charles Maurice de Talleyrand) and Spain (Don Pedro Gomez Labrador), however, refused to recognize decisions made without them since their nations were signatories of the Peace of Paris, which had summoned the conference. This forced postponement of the formal opening of the conference, scheduled for 1 October, and although delegates' credentials were belatedly verified, no plenary session was ever held. Ultimately a Committee of Eight, signatories of the Peace of Paris (including Portugal and Sweden), formed a directing body, but real power lay in the hands of a Council of Four and later of Five with the inclusion of France (9 January 1815).

The stalemate over organization led to enforced idleness for many representatives. That, combined with the large number of pleasure seekers in Vienna and the desire of the Austrians to be good hosts, has given the congress an undeserved reputation for frivolity. In fact, much hard work took place. Ten committees were established to deal with the major problems facing the delegates, and work proceeded smoothly.

The major crisis threatening the Congress was over the Polish-Saxon question. Czar Alexander desired to reconstitute the Kingdom of Poland (including Prussian territory) in personal union with Russia. The Prussians agreed if compensated by Saxony, whose king had been allied with Napoleon; however, Austria and Britain opposed this intrusion of Russia into central Europe. To the czar's advantage, the Russian army occupied the disputed territories. The impasse was broken, and France assumed a major role at the Congress when Talleyrand negotiated a secret treaty (3 January 1815) with Britain and Austria to support them militarily. Alexander got a smaller Polish state than he wanted and Prussia about two-fifths of Saxony. The remaining problems were settled with dispatch, hastened by the return of Napoleon from Elba (March). The final act of 121 articles was signed on 9 June 1815.

By the terms of this act and collateral treaties, a new conservative status quo emerged. In Western Europe, France, Spain, and Portugal were restored to their former positions. The Kingdom of the Netherlands was established by combining the former Austrian Netherlands (Belgium) with the United Provinces to act as a barrier to French expansion. Sweden, which had lost Finland to Russia in 1809, received Norway, taken from Denmark, as compensation. In Central Europe the German Confederation replaced the Holy Roman Empire. Prussia was given additional territory in western Germany to act as a barrier to France, turning it from an Eastern-oriented state into a Western power. Austria was compensated for losses in the west by territories in central Europe and Italy. In Italy the Bourbons returned to the Kingdom of the Two Sicilies, and the Papal States were restored. The republics of Genoa and Venice disappeared; Genoa went to Sardinia to strengthen it against France, and Venice to Austria, which now dominated the peninsula. In Eastern Europe, Russia emerged as the dominant power. It had been enlarged by Bessarabia (from the Ottoman Empire) and Finland (from Sweden), and the czar was sovereign in the new Kingdom of Poland.

The decisions of the Congress evoked the wrath of nineteenth-century liberals. Yet the conservative status quo established by the peacemakers of 1815 did create a stable European order, one that endured substantially unchanged for a century.

H. Dyroff, ed., *Der Wiener Kongress 1814/15* (Munich, 1966); G. Ferrero, *The Reconstruction of Europe* (New York, 1941); E. Gulick, *Europe's Classical Balance of Power* (Ithaca, 1955); J. Kluber, ed., *Acten des Wiener Kongresses*, 8 vols. (Erlangen, 1815–19); H. Nicolson, *The Congress of Vienna* (London, 1946); H. Spiel, *Der Wiener Kongress* (Düsseldorf, 1966); H. Straus, *The Attitude of the Congress of Vienna toward Nationalism* (New York, 1949); C. K. Webster, *The Congress of Vienna, 1814–1815* (London, 1934).

Ray E. Cubberly

Related entries: ABDICATION, FIRST; ALEXANDER I; CASTLEREAGH; HARDENBERG; HUNDRED DAYS, THE; METTERNICH; PARIS, FIRST TREATY OF; TALLEYRAND.

VIGEE-LEBRUN, ELIZABETH-LOUISE (1755–1842), artist. As she lived through the apex, decline, fall, and replacement of eighteenth-century French aristocratic society, portraitist Elizabeth Vigée broke down the sex barrier for professional women artists. She was born in Paris the daughter of portraitist Louis Vigée, who painted in the style of Watteau and who developed her precocious talent. After his death, she directed all of her energies into her work and became an artist of renown by age fifteen and a member of the Academy of Saint Luke at age nineteen. Throughout her teens she supported her family, including her stepfather, with her commissions. Possibly to escape her home life, she consented to marry Jean-Baptiste Lebrun in 1776. Since Lebrun, whose name she added to her maiden name, was an art dealer and critic, the marriage promised the advantage of being able to study and learn from observing the works of masters; however, it lasted only briefly because her husband was too much like her do-nothing stepfather and, in addition, gambled excessively. The independent and strong-willed artist went through her pregnancy alone, working until hours before the birth of her daughter Julie, her only child.

Vigée attracted the attention of Marie-Antoinette, who called her to Versailles in 1779; subsequently, in 1783, she was presented to the Royal Academy by Claude-Joseph Vernet. Her candidature elicited lively opposition, and opponents alleged that François-Guillaume Menageot did her work for her. She was admitted on the same day as her rival, Adélaïde Labille-Guiard (1749–1803). She was also the subject of much gossip, partly due to her decision to live independently and partly because of her infamous salon. But her loyalty to the Bourbons was indisputable, and she prevailed. As official painter to the queen, she executed more than twenty portraits of her patroness, as well as of men, women, and children in the royal family. Because of her close connections with the monarchical establishment, she wisely fled on the eve of the Revolution.

During her self-imposed exile, she initially went to Rome and joined the Academy. Later she traveled throughout Europe, receiving the special attention of monarchs everywhere and repaying their hospitality by painting the portraits that grace museums today. While Vigée never understood or accepted the French Revolution, she did return to Paris in 1802, but she became associated with Mme. de Staël.

In 1835 Vigée published three volumes of memoirs that mirror her times, unconventional life, and the characters whom she painted, which also include the Neapolitan musician Pasiello, the princess of Lamballe, Lady Emma Hamilton at Naples, and Mme. de Staël.

Although she invented no new style or technique, Vigée's 660 portraits are highy praised. She had an ability to capture fleeting moments and delighted in naturalness, costume, and texture. She could also portray men in a dynamic manner, the portrait of her friend the landscape artist Hubert Robert being a good example. The always flattering manner of her portraits contributed to her financial success. Of all her works, probably her two portraits of herself with her daughter were best loved by contemporaries because they epitomized their preconceptions about the purpose of women's art. Much respected by her pupils, of which Marie-Victoire Lemoine is the most important, Vigée served as a role model to women artists.

W. H. Helm, *Vigée-Lebrun, Her Life, Her Works, and Her Friendships* (London, 1916); E. Kyle, *Portraits of Lisette* (New York, 1963); P. de Nolhac, *Madame Vigée-Lebrun: Painter of Marie Antoinette* (Paris, 1912); K. Peterson and J. J. Wilson, *Women Artists: Recognition and Reappraisal from the Early Middle Ages to the Twentieth Century* (New York, 1976).

June K. Burton

Related entries: ARCHITECTURE; ART; DAVID; DENON; GERARD; GROS; GUERIN; HAMILTON; ISABEY; LOUVRE; STAEL-HOLSTEIN.

VILLENEUVE, PIERRE-CHARLES DE, admiral. See TRAFALGAR, BATTLE OF.

VITORIA, BATTLE OF (21 June 1813), decisive victory of the duke of Wellington over a French army commanded by Joseph Bonaparte and Marshal Jean-Baptiste Jourdan, which effectively ended French rule in Spain. Ordered by Napoleon to retire from Madrid to Valladolid to consolidate his forces and, if necessary, defend southern France, Joseph departed Madrid on 17 March 1813. Forced to retreat by Wellington, he abandoned Valladolid and Burgos in turn, but on 19–20 June prepared to fight at Vitoria. The 50,000-man French army was deployed in three lines, protected on the center and right flank by the Zadorra River. None of the bridges was destroyed, however, or even closely guarded. The French front extended for twelve miles with a dangerous six-mile gap from Tres Puentes to Gamarra Mayor on the right.

Wellington attacked with 75,000 men on 21 June, but his complex plan quickly broke down. A feint on the French left at the Heights of Puebla ran into stiff opposition. The main attack, by two columns, on the French right was seriously delayed when one of the columns got lost. The net effect, however, was to convince the French that the main attack was at Puebla. While their attention was diverted, Wellington crossed the unguarded bridges at Tres Puentes and flanked the French first line, forcing it to retreat.

The French infantry tried to reform about three miles to the rear but was never properly positioned. A general retreat began toward Salvatierra. It was uncoordinated and made through rugged country, but nearly 42,000 French soldiers escaped. The immense treasure left behind proved better than a rear guard; Wellington's army disintegrated into a plundering mob.

Vitoria encouraged the Allies and opened southern France to invasion but was not a brilliant victory. Wellington's tactical plan required coordinated movements through rugged country, the role of the left wing was unclear, and the plan was poorly executed. Outnumbered and seemingly trapped, the bulk of the French army, which should have been eliminated, escaped to fight again in the Pyrenees and southern France.

J. Bonaparte, *Mémoires et correspondance* (Paris, 1854); J. B. Jourdan, *Mémoires militaires* (Paris, 1899); W. F. P. Napier, *History of the War in the Peninsula and in the South of France from the Year 1807 to the Year 1814* (London, 1850); C. W. C. Oman, *A History of the Peninsular War* (Oxford, 1902–30); Wellington, *Dispatches* (London, 1834–39).

Jack Allen Meyer

Related entries: BONAPARTE, JOSEPH; DIPLOMACY; FOREIGN POLICY; GERMAN WAR OF LIBERATION; PENINSULAR WAR; WELLINGTON.

VOLNEY, CONSTANTIN-FRANCOIS CHASSEBOEUF (1757–1820), voyager, geographer, philologist of Oriental languages, historian, *idéologue*, senator, member of the National Institute, and count of the Empire. After sitting in the Constituent Assembly, he became a close friend of Bonaparte in Corsica in 1792 and was actively involved in the coming of 18 Brumaire. He warned Napoleon against trying to reassert control over Santo Domingo and Louisiana, had an altercation with him about the Concordat of 1801, which he vehemently opposed, and courageously joined the abbés Emmanuel Sieyès and Henri Grégoire in voting in the Senate against the hereditary Empire. Volney's reputation as one of the greatest savants of his generation was made by his *Voyage en Egypte et en Syrie* (1787), *Les ruines* (1791), and his *Tableau du sol et du climat des Etats-Unis d'Amérique* (1803), all remarkable for their systematic topographical and ethnographical analysis, which demythologized the Holy Land, the New World, the noble savage, and the primitive American of the late eighteenth century.

G. Chinard, *Volney et l'Amérique d'après des documents inédits et sa correspondance avec Jefferson*. (Paris, 1925); J. Gaulmier, *L'Idéologue Volney (1757–1820), Contribution à l'Etude de l'Orientalisme en France* (Beyrouth, 1951).

Emmet Kennedy

Related entry: IDEOLOGUES.

VOLTA, ALESSANDRO (1745-1827), Italian scientist after whom the volt, unit of electrical force, is named. He was patronized by Napoleon in the Kingdom of Italy.

VOLTIGEURS. See ARMY, FRENCH.

W

WAGRAM, BATTLE OF (5–6 July 1809), victory of Napoleon over Archduke Charles of Austria, which ended the campaign of 1809. Checked in his first attempt to cross the Danube by the battle of Aspern-Essling (21-22 May 1809), Napoleon turned the island of Lobau (in the Danube) into a fortified camp and prepared to try again. In response, the Austrians erected field entrenchments opposite the island's northern side. On the night of 4 July, Napoleon surprised the Austrians by launching his corps from the eastern end of the Lobau onto the north shore, thus outflanking the Austrian entrenchments. In the ensuing two-day battle (173,000 French versus 155,000 Austrians), Napoleon's army was in the shape of an arrowhead, pointing at the Austrian center at Wagram, which gave him the advantage of central position and interior lines. On the other hand, Napoleon's troops for the most part were inexperienced French, German, and Italian levies, the Austrian contingents proved stubborn fighters, and Archduke Charles spent himself bringing up reinforcements at critical moments. In a two-day hammering match, it took all of Napoleon's tactical skill to prevail. He used L. N. Davout on the right to roll up the Austrian left wing; sent in Jacques Macdonald in a massive columnar formation against the Austrian center; and boldly and skillfully marched troops across the front to reinforce the French left under André Masséna. On the morning of 7 July, Napoleon still thought he might have to fight a third day, but Archduke Charles had had enough and had conducted overnight an orderly phased withdrawal. The casualties were heavy: 32,500 soldiers of the Grande Armée, 24 percent of those engaged, lay dead or wounded; 37,146 Austrians, or over one-quarter of their effective strength, were killed, wounded, or taken prisoner.

Harold T. Parker

Related entries: BEAUHARNAIS, E.; BERNADOTTE; DAVOUT; KARL VON HABSBURG; MACDONALD; MASSENA; WAGRAM CAMPAIGN.

WAGRAM, PRINCE DE. See BERTHIER, A.

WAGRAM CAMPAIGN (1809). The success of the Spaniards against Napoleon (merely to continue a revolt was a success) fired the hopes of other discontented nations. Austria, a major power and old enemy, possessed an improved army (300,000 regulars, 200,000 *Landwehr*) reorganized by Archduke Charles, perceived that Napoleon's best troops were pinned down in Spain, and hoped for support from a German national uprising (in vain, as it turned out). Austria attacked the French in south Germany on 9 April 1809; the news, which reached Napoleon in Paris on 12 April, was not unexpected. His army of 170,000, in part new levies and troops of Allies, was already in southern Germany around Augsburg (André Masséna) and Regensburg (Louis Davout). Napoleon left Paris on 13 April and took command at Donauwörth on 17 April. He found that his army corps were separated and spread over a line seventy-five miles long. The Austrian commander, the Archduke Charles, had the advantage of central position between the two corps of Davout and Masséna and the opportunity to crush them separately. However, the archduke, though capable, was slow. In a series of maneuvers, Napoleon ordered Davout to retire and Masséna to advance. Then in five successive days, 19–23 April, he won five victories against the Austrians in the battles of Tengen, Abensberg, Landshut, Eckmühl, and Regensburg. But the Austrian army, though it suffered heavily, was not destroyed. The archduke withdrew it, in orderly fashion, north of the Danube toward Bohemia. Napoleon descended the Danube along the southern bank to Vienna, which capitulated on 13 May. Needing to defeat the archduke and thus force the Austrian monarchy to peace, Napoleon tried to transfer his army across the Danube several miles below Vienna. But the crossing was checked by the Archduke Charles and the Austrian army at the two-day battle of Aspern-Essling (21–22 May) and interrupted by the breaking of the French pontoon bridge over the Danube. Six weeks later, Napoleon placed the French army on the northern bank and in the stubbornly fought two-day Battle of Wagram (5–6 July) forced the Archduke Charles to withdraw from the field. The archduke sued for an armistice, which was granted on 12 July. On 14 October the Austrian emperor, Francis I, signed a peace treaty, which ceded over 3 million of his 16 million subjects to Napoleon and associated states.

H. Camon, *La manoeuvre de Wagram* (Paris, 1926); D. Chandler, *The Campaigns of Napoleon* (London, 1965); M. von Hoen and H. Kerchnewe, *Krieg 1809* (Vienna, 1910); G. Rothenberg, *Napoleon's Great Adversaries: The Archduke Charles* (London, 1982); C. G. Saski, *Campagne de 1809 en Allemagne et en Autriche*, 3 vols. (Paris and Nancy, 1899–1902); S. J. Watson, *By Command of the Emperor: A Life of Marshal Berthier* (London, 1957).

Harold T. Parker

Related entries: ARMY, HABSBURG; BEAUHARNAIS, E.; DAVOUT; JOHANN VON HABSBURG; KARL VON HABSBURG; MACDONALD; WAGRAM CAMPAIGN, ITALIAN PHASE; WALCHEREN, INVASION OF.

WAGRAM CAMPAIGN, ITALIAN PHASE (1809). Austria had planned a surprise offensive against the Napoleonic Kingdom of Italy to coincide with its offenses against other portions of Napoleon's empire. Included in the Kingdom of Italy was the geographically separate province of Dalmatia. The Kingdom of Italy was administered by Prince Eugène de Beauharnais as Napoleon's viceroy. Prince Eugène was also commander in chief of all military forces in Italy. The Army of Italy consisted of 71,000 men and 120 guns, plus 14,000 men and 12 guns in Dalmatia, for a total of 85,000.

The Austrian invasion force commanded by Archduke John consisted of 72,000. Of this force, 12,000 were to attack the Tyrol and 10,000 were to invade Dalmatia; the rest were to move down the valley of the Isonzo and overrun Italy.

The invasion of Italy began on 9 April. In the event of a surprise Austrian attack, the French were to fall back behind the fortified Adige River line to concentrate for a counterattack. Instead, Eugène chose to make a stand east of the Adige at Sacile with only a fraction of his army on 16 April. The French were defeated, and Eugène withdrew to the Adige line to regroup. The Battle of Sacile, however, did not redress the strategic imbalance between the French and Austrian forces. The Austrian army was weakened due to strategic consumption, while the French had gained in strength as they fell back toward their bases and reinforcements. The Austrians closed up along the Adige and remained there observing the French from 28 April to 1 May. Learning of Napoleon's victories at Eckmühl, John realized that his position had become strategically untenable and began a withdrawal eastward with the object of returning to Austria. Eugène pursued John and caught up with him on the Piave River near Conegliano where the French inflicted a smashing defeat on the Austrians on 8 May.

Part of John's forces fled eastward to Croatia, while the rest ascended the Tagliamento toward Austria. Eugène dispatched a corps under Lieutenant General Alexandre Macdonald to invade Croatia and effect a junction with Lieutenant General Auguste Marmont while the rest of the Army of Italy invaded German Austria.

John's rear guard was severely handled at Saint Daniel on 11 May. The Austrian main body commanded by John retreated toward Hungary, leaving a screening force along the frontier. From 15 to 18 May, the Austrian frontier defenses at Malborghetto, Tarvis, and Predil were captured by Eugène. Moving north toward Vienna, Eugène intercepted and destroyed an Austrian division under Franz von Jellachich at Saint Michael on 25 May. Contact was made with the units of Napoleon's army at Bruck on 26 May.

Macdonald had stormed the frontier defenses of Croatia on 20 May and captured Laibach on 23 May.

Marmont had been conducting his own campaign in Dalmatia. He defeated the Austrian forces at Mount Kitta on 13 May, at Gradschatz on 17 May, and at Gospich on 21 May. Marmont drove north, eventually reaching Laibach on 3 June.

The Italian phase had been a disaster for the Austrians. During the operations in April and May, the Austrian army was reduced by 50 percent. French losses averaged about 35 percent of the initial forces.

After a period of rest, Eugène was sent into Hungary to complete the destruction of John's army. A battle was fought at Raab on 14 June in which the Austrians were again defeated but John's army was not destroyed.

E. de Beauharnais, *Mémoires et correspondance politique et militaire du Prince Eugène*, 10 vols., ed. André du Casse (Paris, 1859); Napoleon I, *Correspondance de Napoléon Ier*, 36 vols. (Paris, 1867); J.-J.-G. Pelet, *Mémoires sur la Guerre de 1809*, 4 vols. (Paris, 1825); F. F. Vaudoncourt, *Histoire politique et militaire du Prince Eugène Napoléon*, 2 vols. (Paris, 1828).

Robert Epstein

Related entries: BEAUHARNAIS, E.; JOHANN VON HABSBURG; PIAVE, BATTLE ON; RAAB, BATTLE OF; WAGRAM CAMPAIGN.

WALCHEREN, INVASION OF (28 July-14 September 1809), largest amphibious operation of the Napoleonic wars in which a British army of over 44,000 men commanded by John Pitt, second earl of Chatham, supported by a naval force of 266 ships (including 44 ships of the line and 22 frigates) under the command of Sir Richard Strachan, invaded the estuary of the Scheldt River. The British objectives were to destroy the naval establishments along the river (principally at Flushing on the island of Walcheren and at Antwerp), capture or destroy the French fleet based in the Scheldt, and place obstructions in the river so that it would no longer be navigable for warships. The expedition had been planned to form a diversion for Austria, which was battling Napoleon's armies in central Europe, but came after the Austrians had been beaten at Wagram.

The campaign was a dismal failure. Stormy weather, adverse winds, and the navy's inability to blockade Flushing, the growing dissension between Chatham and Strachan, and Chatham's own inactivity and indecision slowed progress. Finally, the outbreak of "Walcheren fever" (malaria, dysentery, typhus, and typhoid), which incapacitated over 12,000 British soldiers, forced the abandonment of the campaign. Only the destruction of the naval facilities at Flushing (which capitulated 15 August) was accomplished. Walcheren was evacuated 23 December 1809. Austria, which had delayed making peace since July (Battle of Wagram), finally signed the Treaty of Schönbrunn in October 1809.

G. Bond, *The Grand Expedition: The British Invasion of Holland in 1809* (Athens, Ga., 1979); T. Fleischman, *L'Expédition anglaise sur le continent en 1809*, Reprint (Brussels, 1973); R. Glover, *Britain at Bay: Defense against Napoleon, 1803-1814* (London, 1973); T. H. McGuffie, "The Walcheren Expedition and the Walcheren Fever," *EHR* 62 (1947); *A Collection of Papers Relating to the Expedition to the Scheldt Presented to Parliament in 1810,* Comp. by A. Strahan (London, 1811).

Gordon Bond

Related entries: CHATHAM; CASTLEREAGH; GREAT BRITAIN; WAGRAM CAMPAIGN.

WALEWSKA, MARIA Z LACZYNSKICH, COUNTESS (1789–1817), Napoleon's "Polish wife." By family arrangement, she married the older Count Anastazy Walewski in 1804. The eighteen-year-old blonde beauty met Napoleon in January 1807 in Warsaw during his winter campaign against the Russians and Prussians and became his mistress, persuaded that it was her duty to Poland. She resided with him at the chateau of Finkenstein. She returned to Paris with him, and he maintained a residence for her there. In 1810 she returned to Poland to give birth to Napoleon's son (called Alexandre Walewski). After his marriage to Marie-Louise, Napoleon stopped seeing her. Nevertheless, she visited him during his exile on Elba in 1814. After his exile to St. Helena, she married General Philippe Antoine d'Ornano and died in childbirth. Generally regarded as Napoleon's one true love, she was surely more faithful to him than any other woman.

M. Brandys, *Kłopoty z Panią Walewską* (Warsaw, 1974); F. Masson, *Marie Walewska* (Paris, 1897); P. d'Ornano, *Life and Loves of Marie Walewska* (Montreal, 1934); C. Sutherland, *Marie Walewska* (New York, 1979).

John Stanley

Related entries: ELBA; JENA-AUERSTÄDT-FRIEDLAND CAMPAIGN; NAPOLEON I; WALEWSKI.

WALEWSKI, ALEXANDRE FLORIAN JOSEF (1810–68), comte de Colonna, Napoleon's natural son by Countess Marie Walewska, French diplomat. Educated in Geneva, he participated in the Revolution of 1830 in Poland, fled to France, and in 1833 became a French citizen. In the diplomatic corps, he headed legations in Buenos Aires, Florence, Naples, and London and during 1855–60 was foreign minister of Napoleon III. He later served in the corps législatif and Senate and in 1866 was made a prince of the Empire.

F. Bernardy, *Alexandre Walewski (1810–1868)* (Paris, 1976); H. d'Escamps, *Le comte Walewski* (Paris, 1868).

John Stanley

Related entries: NAPOLEON I; WALEWSKA.

WARFARE, ECONOMIC, used by Napoleon and his enemies, especially Britain. Crushing defeats imposed by French armies on Austria, Russia, and Prussia in 1805–6 (Ulm, Austerlitz, and Jena) secured the foundations of Napoleon's Empire and extended its sway to Central Europe. Only the humiliation and submission of Britain were needed to complete his victory. Military invasion of the British isles was impossible after Horatio Nelson's destruction of the Franco-Spanish fleet at Trafalgar (1805). Napoleon's only remaining weapon was economic warfare: to destroy the enemy by cutting off life-giving commerce with Europe. Then Britain would find it impossible to encourage and support his remaining continental foes. Finally, Britain's expulsion from European markets might allow France to take its place as their major supplier.

The campaign opened with the imperial decree of 21 November 1806 (issued from occupied Berlin) closing the ports of the Empire and its dependencies to enemy shipping. London struck back with Orders in Council (January and November 1807) ordering a naval blockade of all continental ports adhering to

Napoleon's decree and requiring neutral shipping bound there to submit to British regulation and licensing: no colonial or overseas goods would reach Europe except through British ports. Napoleon quickly answered with the Milan Decree (December 1807) calling for the seizure and confiscation of such neutral vessels as complied with the British orders.

Victory in this economic duel would go to that power which most effectively enforced its blockade without collapsing under its opponent's commercial blows. (Britain, however, weighted the odds in its favor by giving subsidies to Napoleon's enemies.) Naval supremacy gave Britain advantages: surveillance of enemy harbors and control of neutral shipping bound there. Quarrels with neutrals over maritime rights were inevitable, and that issue contributed to the United States' decision to make war on Britain in 1812. In Europe, adherence to the Continental System was the price of peace Napoleon exacted from both his friends and defeated enemies, and by 1810 virtually all of the coastline (except that of Spain and Portugal) had been closed at least officially to the ''nation of shopkeepers.'' But European dependence on British manufactured goods (especially textiles), and colonial reexports (coffee, sugar, and tobacco) opened holes in the blockade, especially as it became clear that France could not supply these items. British shipping carried contraband to the Baltic and the Mediterranean, where it was eagerly received by smugglers willing to risk capture in order to profit from shortages and high prices. Napoleon battled the smugglers as best he could, but in 1809 all his resources were diverted to war with Austria and the peninsular uprising. As a result British goods valued at more than 18 million pounds poured into the Continent through smuggling depots in the Baltic, the North Sea, and the Mediterranean.

With Austria crushed and the Peninsular War presumably contained, Napoleon in 1810 determined on a policy of strict and sustained enforcement of the Continental System, and in the two years that followed, the blockade against British trade became tighter than before. Special tribunals were created to try violations, informers were rewarded, and smuggled merchandise was seized and destroyed. Absolute enforcement was beyond even the emperor's power, however. Critical shortages and dwindling customs revenues led to experiments to admit small amounts of British goods in exchange for French wines and silks. Necessity compelled Napoleon to obtain military supplies from his enemy in preparation for the 1812 campaign against Russia; the Grand Armée was outfitted with English cloth and boots brought in through Hamburg by imperial officials. On the whole, however, 1810–12 witnessed the most effective enforcement of the Continental System, and the resulting economic stagnation, shortages, and public resentment (at least outside France) heightened dissatisfaction with the Empire.

Although the Continental System failed to ruin Britain's economy, it caused severe damage. The early effects of Napoleon's blockade were somewhat eased by Britain's growing transatlantic trade (especially with the United States), but access to the continental markets remained essential to its prosperity. Exports to northern Europe and France fell from 10.3 million pounds sterling in 1805 to 2.2 million in 1808, and the 1807 U.S. Embargo Act drastically reduced shipments to the best alternate market. Severe depression struck Britain in 1807 and persisted for nearly two years. The opening of the Spanish and Portuguese markets in both Europe and the colonies and the upsurge of contraband shipments to Europe in 1809 combined to bring brief but desperately needed relief. Napoleon's 1810 decision to tighten his blockade began a period of increasing difficulty for Britain, during which it came perilously close to economic disaster. In 1811 exports to northern Europe and France dropped to 1.5 million pounds sterling although Spain, Portugal, and the smuggling depots of the Mediterranean absorbed more than 11 million pounds sterling of British goods. The resulting trade credits and the nation's gold reserves were severely taxed to sustain increasingly heavy overseas war expenses after 1810. The cost of the duke of Wellington's army in the peninsula rose to 13 million by 1812, not including financial aid Britain had pledged to its Spanish and Portuguese allies. Bad harvests at home (1808, 1809) necessitated grain purchases abroad, which had to be paid for by drawing on shrinking trade credits and bullion. In desperation London relied on the nation's industrial resources to meet its commitment to the peninsular allies by sending them guns, military supplies, and equipment in place of the money for which they clamored. At sea the loss of British merchant vessels to enemy privateers reached a high of 619 vessels in 1810, but that danger was reduced by the increasingly effective Royal Navy convoy system. The turning point finally came in 1811 after Russia's decision (31 December 1810) to assert its independence from the Empire and open its harbors to British shipping. The Continental System, once breached, crumbled quickly, and soon Sweden, Prussia, and the north German port cities welcomed British trade. Before 1813 ended, the volume of British exports to Europe rose to the point where London was able to send 7.5 million pounds in subsidies to its ever-growing number of allies, in addition to nearly 1 million muskets for their armies now united in the final campaign against Napoleon. After 1807, British aid to Napoleon's enemies never dropped below 2 million pounds per year; in 1812 it had been almost 4 million pounds; in 1814 it was over 8 million pounds; and in 1815, 9.5 million.

F. Crouzet, *L'Economie Britannique et le Blocus Continental, 1806–1813*, 2 vols. (Paris, 1958); E. Hecksher, *The Continental System: An Economic Interpretation* (Oxford, 1922); G. Marcus, *A Naval History of England*, vol. 2 (London, 1971); J. Sherwig, *Guineas and Gunpowder: British Foreign Aid in the Wars with France, 1793-1815* (Cambridge, Mass., 1969).

John M. Sherwig

Related entries: CONTINENTAL BLOCKADE; CORSAIR WAR; DIPLOMACY; ENGLAND, ATTEMPTED CONQUEST OF; TRAFALGAR, BATTLE OF.

WAR OF 1812. See UNITED STATES.

WARSAW, DUCHY OF, often erroneously called Grand Duchy; formed from Prussian Poland ceded by the Treaty of Tilsit (1807) and placed under the governance of Napoleon's ally Frederick Augustus, king of Saxony. Napoleon personally dictated a constitution for the duchy modeled after the French but with many concessions to Polish traditions. Slavery was abolished and the Code Napoléon was introduced. However, both houses of the *Sejm* (Diet) were dominated by the nobles. The Senate comprised bishops and nobles, and the House of Representatives had sixty members elected by the nobility and forty by communal assemblies. Although the *Sejm* lacked the power of its predecessors in Polish history, it did function. The government always had an active opposition; its bills were sometimes even defeated. In 1811 Feliks Łubieński, minister of justice, had his French-style criminal code rejected. Louis Bignon, the French ambassador, considered the duchy's *Sejm* "the only political tribune on the Continent."

King Frederick Augustus, as duke of Warsaw, had all executive power. Furthermore, he had the right of legislative initiative and appointed both the Council of State and the Council of Ministers, who were responsible only to him. Despite the liberal French provisions of the constitution, the Polish nature of the state was assured by the guarantees that all offices would be filled by citizens of the duchy and that the Polish language would be used in governmental and legal bodies.

Originally the duchy had a territory of 104,000 square kilometers (divided into six departments) with a population of 2.6 million. It was enlarged in 1809 by the addition of western Galicia (from Austria). The duchy then had 151,000 square kilometers, ten departments, and 4,334,000 inhabitants (according to the census of 1810, the first in Polish history). The population was composed of 79 percent Poles, 7 percent Jews, 6 percent Germans, 4 percent Lithuanians, and a small number of Belorussians and Ukrainians. Warsaw (78,000 inhabitants) was the capital and by far the largest city. Cracow (24,000) and Poznan (18,000) were also important.

The duchy was tied to France through its monarch, who was a member of the Confederation of the Rhine. Polish forces served Napoleon everywhere, including Spain (1808) and Russia (1812). The duchy was also financially tied to France by debt (previously owed Prussia), which was increased by constant loans to maintain the Polish army. The duchy also had to submit to the Continental Blockade, while it gave French imports favorable tariff treatment.

The abolition of serfdom, required by the constitution, was carried out by the December decree of 1807. It gave the peasants personal freedom but no rights to the land they tilled. Since there was no other occupation for them but farming, the vast majority of peasants remained totally dependent on their noble lords. It was often said the reform liberated the peasant not only from the chains on his legs but also from his boots. Of greater significance than the counterfeit peasant reform was the introduction of the Code Napoléon. It was pushed through the Council of State against great opposition by Feliks Łubieński,who also installed a French judicial system. Nevertheless, Polish conditions invalidated many of the Code's most revolutionary articles. The justice of the peace, at the lowest level, was invariably the local nobleman, so the lord continued to be the source of the law for the peasant. It was similarly always a clergyman who was civil registrar, so that virtually no civil marriages or divorces took place in the duchy. Despite the constitution and the code, the Jews were deprived of all civil rights. Since the overwhelming majority of landowners were noblemen, the code's emphasis on property rights, ironically, strengthened the feudal social and economic order. The clarity and logic of the code, however, and the efficiency of the new courts impressed the Poles, and though the duchy itself disappeared in 1815, the Code Napoléon was the law of the land until 1846. The code thus became a legal symbol of Poland's ties to Western Europe.

Despite the government's best efforts to improve the duchy's economic health, it was never good. Burdened with debt to France, an army disproportionately large, and the costs of a new complex administrative and judicial system, the government never balanced its budget. Deprived of its natural market—Britain—for its most important export, wheat, and experiencing two bad harvests and three major military campaigns on its territory, the government's small efforts to encourage industry and a modern agriculture disappear into insignificance.

Of lasting importance to Polish nationalism were the changes carried out in the duchy's army. Prince Józef Poniatowski, the minister of war, adopted French reforms, which made the army a training ground for citizenship as well as soldiering. The Polish military served Napoleon from Somosierra to Moscow, but a belief in national service was nevertheless ingrained in soldiery. To the populist, democratic traditions of the Polish Legions, Józef Poniatowski added his own aristocratic notions of honor and glory. This potent combination gives the duchy's army its almost mythic position in Polish history.

Equally important were educational developments. In 1807, Stanisław Potocki organized an Office of Education, and the language of instruction became Polish rather than German. In 1811 there were ten secondary schools at departmental level, twenty-three at the district level, and twelve vocational schools. There were also teachers' colleges in Poznan and Lowicz and military schools at Kalisz and Chelm. Most schools were in secular hands, to the chagrin of the Polish bishops led by Ignacy Raczynski. Elementary schools were more difficult to organize, but by 1813 there were 486 in the cities and 803 in the countryside, with 44,670 students. After the annexation of Western Galicia in 1809, the duchy had a university in Cracow to head its educational system.

The duchy also founded, in Warsaw in 1811, the first theater school in Polish history, under Wojciech Boguslawski, a veteran of the Polish theater. In Polish literature, neoclassicism predominated, and patriotic themes were fully exploited. (Witness J. U. Niemcewicz's *Historical Songs*, 1810). Karol Kurpiński was the major Polish composer of the period; Fryderyk Bacciarelli was the most important painter. Moreover, the first dictionary of the Polish language, compiled by S. B. Linde, was printed during this period.

The Poles were never satisfied that the duchy occupied enough Polish territory. There were demands for the return of Silesia to Polish rule, as well as the Free City of Gdansk (Danzig). The Extraordinary *Sejm* of 1812, called by Napoleon, was seen as preparing the way for a restored Kingdom of Poland, perhaps under Jerome, Napoleon's brother. After the Russian disaster, Warsaw was occupied by the Russians (February 1813), and Czar Alexander installed a provisional government over the duchy. The old government fled to Cracow, and Tadeusz Matuszewicz and other ministers contacted the Russians, hoping to save Poland from obliteration. (Poniatowski, however, with many Polish troops, rejoined the French forces in Saxony). Occupied by Russian forces, the duchy ceased its legal existence only in 1815 by the treaties signed at Vienna.

Although the Duchy of Warsaw existed ultimately by right of conquest, the Poles never saw it as an occupied state but rather a partner of Napoleonic France. The duchy left the Poles a system of government, legal code, and new political and military traditions. If Napoleon's opportunism demanded Polish blood and money the Poles saw Napoleon as the only hope for a resurrected land. Poland was one of the few European countries where the benefits of Napoleonic rule clearly outweighed its burdens. Napoleon's creation of the duchy confirmed for the Poles that Poland still lived and that its disappearance in 1795 had been temporary. Napoleon imposed French institutions and remolded Polish traditions, but he also (unwittingly) strengthened the Polish national cause, giving it a more democratic content. In the Kingdom of Poland created by the Congress of Vienna, the duchy's administrative, legal, and military innovations survived. The duchy's short life changed Poland's future. Much of the next century of Polish history was merely an attempt to recapture and extend the reforms carried out during the duchy's existence. The Duchy of Warsaw thus signifies the beginnings of modern Polish nationhood and statecraft.

B. Grochulska, *Księstwo Warszawskie* (Warsaw, 1966); E. Halicz, *Geneza Księstwa Warszawskiego* (Warsaw, 1962); M. Kallas, *Konstytucja Księstwa Warszawskiego* (Torun, 1970); W. Rostocki, *Korpus w gęsie pióra uzbrojony* (Warsaw, 1972); M. Senkowska-Gluck "Le Duché de Varsovie," *Occupants-occupés, 1792-1815* (Brussels, 1969); J. Stanley, "A Political and Social History of the Duchy of Warsaw, 1807-1813" (Ph.D. dissertation, University of Toronto, 1979).

John Stanley

Related entries: FRIEDRICH AUGUST III; LUBIENSKI; PONIATOWSKI; POTOCKI; RACZYNSKI; TILSIT, TREATIES OF.

WATERLOO CAMPAIGN (1815). When Napoleon returned to France from Elba in March 1815, the Allied leaders of Austria, Great Britain, Prussia, and Russia vowed to overthrow him with six armies totaling almost 1 million men. Two of these armies were in Belgium—an Anglo-Dutch force (110,000) under the duke of Wellington in the neighborhood of Brussels and a Prussian (117,000) under G. L. Blücher near Namur. Napoleon decided to take the offensive with an army of 122,000. His plan for the campaign had his old-time brilliance: drive between the Anglo-Dutch and the Prussian armies and defeat first one and then the other. But a series of mistakes by Napoleon and his subordinates turned potential triumph into disaster. The French right wing under Napoleon badly mauled the Prussian army at the Battle of Ligny (16 June), but Michel Ney procrastinated at Quatre Bras and J.-B. Drouet d'Erlon's corps failed to reinforce Napoleon, so that the Prussians retired in good order north toward Wavre. Having defeated the Prussian army, Napoleon sent Emmanuel Grouchy to pursue it with 33,000 men, while he turned to join Ney at Quatre Bras. Napoleon and Ney were slow in getting underway on the morning of 17 June, however. Wellington withdrew northward along a road parallel to the one taken by the Prussians and occupied a strong defensive position on the ridge near Mont-Saint-Jean, south of Waterloo. On 18 June, Napoleon, unaware of the proximity of the Prussian army to his right and assuming that Grouchy had it well in hand, arrayed 72,000 men against the Anglo-Dutch army of 68,000. At 11:00 A.M. he ordered a frontal attack. (The staff work of Nicolas Soult was indifferent; Alexandre Berthier was missed.) Honoré Reille's corps, on the French left, became almost totally involved with the reduction of the British fortified outpost of Hougoumont. General d'Erlon's corps, on the French right, went up the ridge in column formation, unsupported by cavalry and was repulsed. Ney prematurely squandered the French cavalry in magnificent and futile charges against the Anglo-Dutch squares. Meanwhile, during the afternoon, three Prussian corps, totaling 70,000 men, came onto the field of battle and forced Napoleon to commit his one reserve corps, then part of the Guard. Grouchy, baffled by Prussian movement, never appeared to reinforce Napoleon. At dusk, Napoleon released the Guard infantry to Ney, who led it forward, perhaps prematurely. It was repulsed. The French army dissolved into a crowd of retreating fugitives. Napoleon, surrounded by remaining Guards, went with it. The Battle of Waterloo was one of those affairs that provoke debates over what might have been. But once the battle was over, the result was irretrievable, and a man, even a Napoleon, is sometimes caught in the stream of his activity and the nature of his character.

L. Chalfont, ed., *Waterloo* (New York, 1980); D. Chandler, *Waterloo: The Hundred Days* (New York, 1980); L. Canler, *Mémoires du Canler* (Paris, 1968); D. Howarth, *Waterloo: Day of Battle* (New York, 1968); J. D. O. Keegan, *The Face of Battle* (London, 1976); H. Lachouque, *Waterloo* (London, 1975), and *Waterloo, ''la fin d'un monde''* (Paris, 1968); H. T. Parker, *Three Napoleonic Battles* (Durham, N.C., 1983).

Harold T. Parker

Related entries: ABDICATION, SECOND; BLÜCHER VON WAHLSTATT; BONAPARTE, JEROME; ELBA; HUNDRED DAYS; NEY; WELLINGTON.

WEAPONS. See ARMY, FRENCH.

WELLESLEY, RICHARD COWLEY, FIRST MARQUESS (1760-1842), ambassador to Spain, 1809, and foreign secretary in the Perceval cabinet, 1809–12. Wellesley's assignment to Spain was an interim appointment, intended to last only until he could be included in the cabinet. His stay in Spain was brief, but he took real interest in the Anglo-Spanish alliance. The marquess arrived in

Spain just after the Battle of Talavera (1809), in which the Spanish, under G. Garcia de la Cuesta, had given the British questionable support. The British commander, Sir Arthur Wellesley (the marquess' brother), had retreated into Portugal, and there were mutual accusations of desertion and betrayal. As ambassador, Wellesley successfully reestablished harmony within the alliance but failed to persuade the Spanish to undertake the extensive military and governmental reforms he felt necessary for Spain to expel Napoleon's armies.

In November 1809 Lord Wellesley returned to London to enter the cabinet. As foreign secretary, he acted on a long-held conviction that the Peninsular War was the key to ultimate victory over France. Nonetheless, until Wellington embarked on his victorious march through Spain in 1812, many thought his efforts could end only in disaster. Wellesley, almost alone, insisted that Britain must persevere in its efforts and even extend them. Lord Wellesley directed his attentions as foreign secretary primarily toward Spain. Despite Spanish refusal to grant trade concessions to Britain, he kept up aid to the Spanish and tried to mediate between Spain and its rebellious American colonies. He quarreled with Spencer Perceval, the prime minister, who opposed his plans to expand the war effort and resigned. But by 1812 his brother, now duke of Wellington, had turned the tide of war against the French.

Following Perceval's assassination in May 1812, the prince regent commissioned Wellesley to form a cabinet. He was too alienated from his own party and too stubborn to form a coalition, however, and he failed. Lord Wellesley would never again hold a cabinet post. Before his death in 1842, however, Wellesley twice served as lord lieutenant of Ireland.

I. Butler, *The Eldest Brother: The Marquess Wellesley, 1760-1842* (London, 1973); G. Lovett, *Napoleon and the Birth of Modern Spain* (New York, 1965); M. Wellesley, *The Despatches and Correspondence of the Marquess Wellesley, K.G., during His Lordship's Mission to Spain as Ambassador Extraordinary to the Supreme Junta in 1809* (London, 1838).

John K. Severn

Related entries: GREAT BRITAIN AND SPAIN; PENINSULAR WAR; SPAIN, KINGDOM OF; WELLINGTON.

WELLINGTON, ARTHUR WELLESLEY, FIRST DUKE OF (1769–1852). Arthur Wellesley, the fourth son of Garrett Wellesley, first earl of Mornington, was born in Ireland in 1769. He was educated at Eton and, since his mother considered him fit only for the army, at a French military school. He purchased a commission as ensign in the Seventy-third (Highland) Regiment in 1787 and by 1793 had become lieutenant colonel of the Thirty-third Regiment of Foot, without seeing active service.

Wellesley's initial combat experience was in 1794, when he served in the duke of York's expedition to the Low Countries. It was at this time, he said, that he learned ''what one ought not to do.'' In 1797 he joined the Thirty-third in India, where he gained distinction at Seringapatam and Assaye and as governor of Mysore. By the time he left India in 1805, he was a major general, a knight of the bath, and the possessor of a modest fortune.

Between 1805 and 1808 Wellesley was engaged almost exclusively in politics. Promoted to lieutenant general in April 1808, he accepted command of the British expedition to the Iberian Peninsula and defeated the French under Andoche Junot at Roliça and Vimiero (21 August 1808). The furor over the generous terms given Junot by the Convention of Cintra temporarily tarnished Wellesley's image, but a court of inquiry cleared him.

Wellesley returned to command in Portugal after the death of Sir John Moore at Coruña. Once he had forced Nicholas Soult out of Oporto (12 May 1809), Wellesley advanced into Spain. He fought the French under King Joseph Bonaparte to a draw at Talavera (27–28 July 1809) but subsequently had to retreat due to poor Spanish support and overwhelming French numerical superiority. In September he was created Viscount Wellington of Talavera.

In 1810–11 Wellington defeated André Masséna at Bussaco and at the lines of Torres Vedras, near Lisbon, pursued him out of Portugal, and laid siege to Almeida and Badajoz. At Fuentes de Oñoro (3–5 May 1811) he again defeated Masséna in a hard-fought battle and thwarted the French attempt to relieve Almeida. W. Carr, Viscount Beresford, meanwhile, checked Soult's attempt to relieve Badajoz and defeated him at Albuera (16 May 1811), but the French finally managed to concentrate sufficient forces to push the British back into Portugal.

The campaign of 1812 was more successful. Wellington took Ciudad Rodrigo on 19 January, for which he was made an earl. Badajoz fell on 6 April. With these keys to the invasion routes into Portugal in his possession, Wellington advanced into central Spain. Following a month of maneuvering around Salamanca, he caught Louis Marmont's army overextended and shattered it in a brilliantly handled battle on 22 July. The Battle of Salamanca opened the way to Madrid, which Wellington's army entered on 12 August. Six days later he was created a marquis. His attempt to capture Burgos, however, was repulsed with considerable loss. Concentration of the French armies, achieved at the expense of losing Andalusia, once more forced Wellington to retreat into Portugal at year's end.

On 22 May 1813 Wellington, now a knight of the garter, advanced into Spain. Meanwhile, in March, Joseph had been ordered to concentrate French forces at Valladolid to protect southern France. However, Wellington, in a series of brilliant flanking maneuvers, forced the French army back to Vitoria, where he routed it on 21 June. The French counterattack in the Pyrenees at Maya and Roncesvalles was contained, but only after heavy fighting.

Wellington took San Sebastian on 31 August and Pamplona on 31 October, defeated Soult at Nivelle on 10 November, and forced a passage across the Nive on 9 December. In 1814, Wellington again defeated Soult at Orthez (27 February) and Toulouse (10 April), by which time the war was over. Wellington was created a duke in May and ambassador to Paris in July. He was participating in the Congress of Vienna when news reached there on 7 March 1815 of Napoleon's return.

As part of the Allied response, Wellington was made commander in chief of the Anglo-Hanoverian and Dutch armies. On 16 June 1815 he successfully held off Ney at Quatre Bras but retired to Waterloo the next day. He established defensive positions there and on the following day succeeded in containing repeated French attacks until the approach of the Prussians on the French flank gave the Allies overwhelming superiority, and the French army collapsed.

Waterloo was Wellington's last battle. He commanded the army of occupation until November 1818, when he returned to England. His remaining years were spent in a wide variety of political posts, from master-general of ordnance to prime minister. He died at Walmer Castle on 14 September 1852 and was buried with great ceremony in St. Paul's on 18 November.

R. Aldington, *The Duke* (Wellington); E. Costello, *The Peninsular and Waterloo Campaigns* (New York, 1968); R. Glover, *Britain at Bay: Defense against Bonaparte, 1803–1814* (New York, 1973), and *Peninsular Preparation: The Reform of the British Army, 1795–1809* (1963); D. D. Horward, *The Battle of Bussaco: Masséna vs Wellington* (Tallahassee, 1965); H. Lachouque, *Napoleon's War in Spain, 1807–1814* (London, 1982); E. Longford, *Wellington*, 2 vols. (New York, 1969–72); C. W. C. Oman, *A History of the Peninsular War*, 7 vols. (Oxford, 1902-30); J. J. Pelet, *French Campaign in Portugal, 1810-1811* (Minneapolis, 1973).

Jack Allen Meyer

Related entries: PENINSULAR WAR; PORTUGUESE CAMPAIGNS; WATERLOO CAMPAIGN.

WESTPHALIA, KINGDOM OF, German state ruled by Jerome Bonaparte, 1807–13. The Kingdom of Westphalia was the largest state founded by Napoleon on German territory, with an area of 14,615 square miles and 2 million inhabitants. It comprised the states of Hesse-Kassel, Braunschweig (Brunswick), and Wolfenbüttel, Prussian territory west of the Elbe River, southern Hanover, and smaller secular and ecclesiastical principalities, and was a member of the Confederation of the Rhine.

It was given a constitution (15 November 1807) written to Napoleon's order. It proclaimed equality before the law, equality of religions, the dissolution of guilds and similar associations, the abrogation of noble privilege, the abolition of serfdom, and the adoption of the Code Napoléon. Napoleon's objective was to transform Westphalia into a modern state that would serve as the advanced bastion of France and assure it hegemony in Germany and security against Prussia. Thus Napoleon's military conquests were to be consolidated through moral conquest.

Until the arrival of Jerome in 1807, a regency governed from the capital at Kassel. It was composed of such experienced French administrators as J. J. Siméon, J.-C. Beugnot, J. B. M. Jollivet, and J. Lagrange. When the king arrived, the foundations of the model state were already in place. Jerome installed (after some false starts) a reform ministry, headed by P. A. Le Camus (count von Fürstenstein) as chief minister and foreign minister, Siméon as minister of justice, L. F. V. H. von Bülow as minister of finance, and G. A. von Wolffradt as minister of the interior. But constitutional and social improvement did not result. The Diet, by the constitution supposed to participate in the formulation of laws, was convoked only twice (1808 and 1810). Agrarian and manorial conditions were hardly altered. Although the last vestiges of serfdom were abolished, manorial dependency survived because the reform laws provided for compensation to the lords for feudal dues and obligations. The aristocracy had obtained redemption laws that worked to its advantage. In this effort they had been supported by those—principally generals of the Grande Armée or high officials of the Empire—who had received large grants of land in Westphalia from Napoleon. The transfer of these domains, indemnity payments, the supporting of French troops in the kingdom, and the maintenance of an army contingent of 25,000 men drained the kingdom financially.

As Napoleon was driven to engage in continuing military campaigns, the government became dictatorial and exploitative, abandoning most of the model state plans. When in 1813 Napoleon was defeated in Germany, the Kingdom of Westphalia fell apart. The majority of the population greeted the end of foreign domination with relief.

For German history, the Kingdom of Westphalia had long-term importance. In many respects, it served the Prussian reformers as an example; many of its modern institutions were copied by other states of the Confederation of the Rhine, and some of the successor states, especially Prussia, allowed reform legislation of the royal Westphalian era to remain in effect.

H. Berding, *Napoleonische Herrschafts- und Gesellschaftspolitik im Königreich Westfalen 1807–1813* (1973); O. Connelly, *Napoleon's Satellite Kingdoms* (1965); A. Kleinschmidt, *Geschichte des Königreichs Westfalen* (1893, reprint 1970); F. Thimme, *Die inneren Zustände des Kurfürstentums Hannover unter der französisch-westfälischen Herrschaft 1806–1813*, 2 vols. (1893–95).

Helmut Berding

Related entries: BONAPARTE, JEROME; CONFEDERATION OF THE RHINE; GRIMM; MÜLLER.

WESTPHALIA, KINGDOM OF: MINISTERS.

Justice	Siméon, J.-J.	1807–13
Interior	Siméon, J.-J.	1807–8
	Wolffradt, G. A. von	1808–13
Finance	Beugnot, J.-C. and Jollivet, J.-B.-M.	1807–8
	Bülow, L.F.V.H. von	1808–11
	Malchus, K. A.	1811–13
War	Lagrange, J.	1807
	Morio, J.	1807–8

	Eblé, J.-B.	1808–10
	D'Albignac, P.-F.-M.	1810
	Siméon, J.-J. (interim)	1810
	Salha, V.	1810–13
Staatssekretär (Secretary of the Cabinet)	Marinville, C. de	1807–08
	Le Camus, P.-A.	1808–1813

"WHIFF OF GRAPESHOT." See VENDEMIAIRE.

WOMEN. History's image of imperial women reflects the minority who were showcased by the regime gracing the court and attending social gatherings attired in transparent gauze, silk, and rich velour Empire-style dresses: high-waisted gowns with puffed sleeves and décolleté necklines worn with elegant necklaces of gemstones or pearls and matching eardrops. The spectacles, operas, and costume balls they attended were calculated to dazzle the populace. They attracted comment and the artist's brush, which served to compound a misleading impression. The conditions of daily life for most women were harsh before the development of modern medicine, sanitation, and energy sources, not to mention notions about women's rights.

The Civil Code of 1804 protected women, who had no political rights. Husbands were bound to care for their wives' needs. Wives, in turn, had to reside with their husbands (unless they installed concubines in the home) and could be forced by the police to return home. Marriage, a secular matter, was prohibited before age fifteen for girls and eighteen for boys and only with parental consent before majority (twenty-one for females and twenty-five for males). Forced marriage was illegal. Widows had to wait ten months after their spouses' deaths before remarrying. Community property existed, but dotal rights and separate debts could also be established by prenuptial contract. Divorce was permitted, with alimony if needed, on grounds of determined cause (excesses, cruelty, or grievous injury) and by mutual consent only when the marriage was of less than twenty years' duration and the wife was under forty-five. Hence, Napoleon's divorce from the forty-six-year-old Josephine was a singular instance. As protection against momentary weakness, the effect of dissolution was a three-year waiting period before women could remarry.

Further indication of women's legal status is the fact that the great majority of subject areas of medicolegal investigation concerned childbirth, adultery, infanticide, and other matters in which the accused was inevitably a woman. Rape was a worse crime than adultery, but law professors taught that it was rarely real because women were strong enough to resist, wound, or disconcert the rapist if they wished.

Despite inequality, women were venerated for their superior emotional qualities. This cast them for different roles in society. Their place was in the home, where they had three jobs: mistress to the servants to teach religion; wife, lover, and companion to offer advice and listen; and mother, to instill virtues and provide early childhood education to all their children and normally to educate their daughters. Women thereby contributed more to peoples' happiness and public manners than did men. Moreover, women received recognition for their contribution to agriculture, especially in areas like the Vendée where they did all the farm labor while their husbands fished. There were some successful, even famous, career women, such as the painter Marie-Louise Vigée Lebrun, the educator Henriette Genest Campan, the balloonist Marie Armant Blanchard, and Marie-Louise Duges Lachapelle, the midwife-in-chief at La Maternité. Some men claimed that young women almost always dominated their husbands and kept them in slavery until the husbands rebelled and assumed their rightful status.

Marriage was considered the cure for women's emotional and physical need for love since the uterus governed the female body. It was mandatory that women marry between ages twenty and twenty-five to extinguish desire, preserve the stomach, keep body fluids from stagnating, and prevent general physical deterioration. Female fertility lasted from puberty, which normally occurred between ages fourteen and sixteen, through menopause at forty-five to fifty, whereas male fertility was said to cease at age sixty-three. A manual for midwives officially used throughout the Empire stated that conception was more likely shortly before and after menstruation than in the middle of the cycle—something that must have helped the population explosion. In procreation women transmitted their traits to the interior qualities of the offspring and were largely responsible for a couple's sterility and determining a child's sex. How purposefully to procreate one sex was an art receiving consideration because of military losses, but popular theories were rejected by the best physicians who admitted being puzzled. Childbirth was seen as a natural process, not an illness, and rarely was assisted by the application of forceps. There was opposition to murderous Caesarian section and episiotomy, but a few of these were performed successfully while wrapping was still the method for surgical closure. Lesbianism had identifiable physical and mental sources and was accompanied by nervous diseases. Nymphomania was considered fatal unless cured because it went against nature for a woman to be sexually aggressive; Antoine Dubois, the accoucheur of Marie-Louise, publicized the appropriate treatment when he successfully performed a clitoridectomy on a young girl. Intercourse was the prescription for several types of hysteria since this relieved blood pressure in a woman's genitals and was, besides, a harmless act for women unless they were nursing infants. Then, it should be brief and infrequent because lengthy orgasms removed the nourishing sweetness from breast milk. In any case, women had a duty to the nation to nurse infants until they had twenty teeth in order to preserve their own bodies against puerperal fever and to reduce infant mortality. Thus sex manuals and medical journals reveal a curious mentality regarding sex and marriage that incorporated folklore, superstition, and male chauvinism.

Attempts to ameliorate the misery of destitute women were made through Christian charity and public assistance. Napoleon reorganized the Société de

Charité Maternelle to provide layettes for the indigent in Paris and forty major cities. The national system of midwifery education initiated by Chaptal was multipurpose, providing free lying-in for poor and unwed mothers, nursing for foundlings and orphans, training for a cadre of literate women willing to practice this profession in every department of the Empire, and medical research. To prevent infanticide, the emperor installed *tours*, the revolving receptacle of St. Vincent de Paul for the anonymous reception of abandoned infants. All of these efforts, however, failed to meet women's real needs.

Jean Imbert, *Le droit hospitalier de la Révolution et de l'Empire* (Paris, 1954).

June K. Burton

Related entries: ART; BONAPARTE entries; EDUCATION; *IDEOLOGUES*; LAW, CODES OF; LITERATURE; MUSIC; PUBLIC WELFARE; THEATER; WOMEN, EDUCATION OF; WORKERS.

WOMEN, EDUCATION OF. Because Napoleon believed that women should be wives and mothers, he excluded female education from the Imperial University, the government monopoly of secondary and postsecondary education. Nevertheless, there was a flurry of pedagogical activity in this regard. Men were usually better advocates than women for developing the intellectual potential of women. In their books Marc-Antoine Jullien, Louis Dubroca, Catherine-Joseph Girard de Propriac, George Jouard, Hubert Wandelcourt, and J. P. Gasc advanced feminist arguments in an effort to draw state attention to this aspect of social policy. But the fact that male and female educators disagreed about the purpose of women's education justified the emperor's limited action. An official journal of education, *Annales d'éducation*, did appear from 1811 to 1814, edited by François Guizot and Pauline de Meulan, which advised parents to ignore Jean-Jacques Rousseau's opinion about suppressing all female desires lest slothfulness result. Furthermore, upper-class adult women were encouraged to study harmless subjects to alleviate their boredom and "excessive vigor." A few women were given the opportunity to attend special public institutions such as abbé Sicard's school for the hearing impaired and Mme. Campan's Ecouen.

At the elementary level, mothers were able to teach their girls the basics by adapting the methods demonstrated in textbooks written as imaginary lessons being given by a mother to her child. Such reading manuals usually taught the vowels, consonants, syllables, grammatical rules, and exceptions to rules. The form of writing manuals varied from being organized as an exchange of letters between two little girls to songs that girls could sing to learn about orthography and grammar. Special arithmetic books taught the operations of addition, subtraction, multiplication, and division, complex numbers, progressions, square roots, interest and annuities, and comparison of the metric system with the former system of weights and measures.

Although in general girls' curricula were in keeping with the emperor's goals of keeping women dependent and submissive while useful, industrious, and frugal, an examination of the sexually segregated textbooks designed for school and home use indicates that there was some interest in teaching girls foreign languages to develop reasoning ability. Textbooks on women's history enhanced self-image and provided heroic role models; however, the study of history itself was not deemed essential to the performance of housewifely duties.

Manuals that taught home economics and sex education provided literate women with scientific and practical knowledge that was especially useful in remote or rural areas. These expressed the view that female identity was defined by nature and limited by sexuality. Although they inculcated the bourgeois value of hard work, this was tempered with emphasis on the need for love, beauty, and both intellectual and physical satisfaction in women's lives. Also, they taught women how to perform necessary tasks such as animal husbandry, shearing sheep, training a dog, drying herbs, even reforestation, as well as how to feed, clothe, and bathe a baby.

Napoleon's greatest achievement in the field of women's education was the creation of the first national system of midwifery education. Regulations for this were drawn up by the minister of interior in 1807, after Napoleon had sent the note on the provisional organization of Ecouen from Germany. By 1808, the functioning of these schools was operative under the direction of the prefects. At the national normal school of midwifery in Paris, La Maternité, and in the departmental branches the prescribed curriculum incorporated four distinct elements: theory and practice of accouchement, vaccination, phlebotomy, and study of medicinal plants. The use of three official textbooks written by Jean-Louis Baudelocque and Anne-Marie Boivin plus a five-piece instrument kit also aimed at creating uniformity between the capital and the Empire. The textbooks contained illustrated lessons on the ways infants present themselves for delivery and, when labor failed to proceed safely, how the midwife was supposed to assist nature. The use of pregnant mannikins with trap doors in their abdomens to enable positioning replicas of one fetus or twins obviated the use of cadavers for amphitheater equipment without encountering risk to human subjects. The outstanding imperial midwifery teachers were doctors Jean-Louis Baudelocque (1746–1810), Antoine Dubois (1756–1837), and François Chaussier (1746–1828), as well as Marie Lachapelle (1769–1822) and Marie Boivin (1773–1841). The 1,500 poor women who graduated from these schools improved obstetrical care, discouraged infanticide, treated syphilitic women and infants, and nursed foundlings as they delivered future generations of Frenchmen and women.

M.-A. Gacon-Dufour, *Manuel de la ménagère* (Paris, 1805) and *De la necessité de l'instruction pour les femmes* (Paris, 1805); J. Gasc, *Discours sur l'éducation des femmes* (Paris, 1810); A. Legroing-la-Maissoneuve, *Essai sur le genre d'instruction qui paraît le plus analogue à la destination des femmes* (Paris, 1800); J. F. Montain, *Le guide des bonnes mères* (Lyon, 1807); C.-E. Pastoret, *Rapport fait au Conseil Général des Hospices. . .depuis ler janvier 1804 jusqu'au Ier janvier 1814* (Paris, 1816); P. Rougeron, *L'historien des Jeunes Demoiselles* (Paris, 1810).

June K. Burton

Related entries: CAMPAN; ECOUEN, CHATEAU OF; EDUCATION; LACHAPELLE; MEDICINE; PUBLIC WELFARE; WOMEN.

WORKERS. In Napoleonic France, *worker* (*ouvrier*) still referred generally to anyone who worked with his hands. However, the term was beginning to take on the more restricted meaning of an urban wage earner, and it is so used here. The authorities made a clear legal distinction between shopkeepers and master artisans, obliged to take out an annual trade license (*patente*), and workers, who were required to register with the police and carry a passbook (*livret*) or, in certain trades, wear a numbered badge. Workers as a group included such disparate elements as journeymen in the traditional skilled crafts, wage earners in the few large-scale factories, and unskilled day laborers who often sold their services in the streets. *Chambrelans* (home workers) received their raw materials from merchant-manufacturers and made the finished product—whether shoes, nails, or cotton thread—to order in their own homes. Domestic servants and house porters were also workers in the broadest sense of the word.

Excluding agricultural wage earners, workers constituted about 6 to 7 percent of the French population and perhaps half of the inhabitants of the largest cities. The only significant concentrations were in Paris and Lyon. In large centers, the native working population was reinforced by waves of temporary or permanent migrants from the countryside. Some trades, such as building, were dominated by seasonal migrants who traditionally left their villages at fixed times of the year to earn the cash they needed at home. The masons of the Creuse department are the most notable example.

Wages showed wide variation. A highly skilled man could earn as much as 3 to 5 francs a day, while an unskilled man might make between 1 franc, 50 centimes and 2 francs, and a woman's wage rarely exceeded 50 centimes. On the whole, workers were better off than before the Revolution, partly because of a war-induced labor shortage. They made significant gains in nominal wages in the 1790s, although these were eaten away by inflation. It seems certain, however, that real wages were moderately higher in 1804 than in 1789 and that the rise continued until about 1810. The only scientific study of wages and prices in this period, by Alexandre Chabert, suggests that between the Directory and the Restoration, nominal wages rose faster than the cost of living. A period of falling wages began in 1817, so that in retrospect the Napoleonic era must have seemed a golden age to most workers. But the gains were unevenly shared. Skilled workers benefited most, the unskilled hardly at all, and real wages may actually have declined in the textile industry.

Any improvement was, of course, relative. Poverty stalked all wage earners, for even the best paid feared seasonal unemployment, irregular periods of economic crises (1806–7, 1810–11, 1812–15), and poor harvests, which sent the price of bread soaring (1801–2, 1811–13). A worker's lodgings were usually crowded and unsanitary, his minimal clothing shabby and dirty. The basis of the popular diet was bread supplemented with dried legumes and fresh vegetables in season. However, the consumption of meat (especially pork) did increase after 1789, in Paris more than in other cities. Cheap wine was the usual drink for men; women and children made do with water. The regime did its best to allay the discontent caused by poverty. It distributed year-round poor relief (there were at least 90,000 recipients in Paris alone), provided public works in winter and during periods of high unemployment, and sought to assure a steady supply of bread at controlled prices.

Although there is no evidence of class consciousness among French workers at this time, they were not unaware of their economic interests. Many workers belonged to mutual aid societies, which, in return for monthly dues, guaranteed them a small income when sick and a modest pension in old age. There were at least eighty such societies in Paris by 1815 and hundreds more in other cities of the Empire. Some were sponsored by the Catholic church; others were encouraged by private philanthropy or local authorities. Skilled workers joined mutual aid societies more frequently than did the unskilled. Skilled workers in certain crafts found aid and companionship in illegal *compagnonnages*, traditional journeymen's associations, which, driven underground in the Revolution, reemerged in the late 1790s. They gave members lodging and financial support when needed and sought to maintain high wages through control of the labor market. There were two rival federations of *compagnonnages*, and violent brawls between their members were common on work sites and highways across France.

Authorities were always concerned that such associations promoted workers' combinations (primitive unions) and strikes. Collective action of this kind was strictly illegal but frequent nonetheless. There were ninety workers' organizations in Paris between 1800 and 1814, according to incomplete police records, which probably leave many uncounted. Some involved only a handful of workers in a single workshop, but others were considerably larger. For example, in October 1806, thousands of building workers went on strike for one week against a government regulation that increased their workday by one hour. To judge from the case of Paris, most combinations (at least sixty-nine of ninety) sought higher wages, although some demanded shorter hours or the revocation of wage cuts. The most militant workers were those in the traditional skilled crafts. Construction workers (especially stonemasons and carpenters) headed the list, followed by hatters, printers, and weavers. There is no statistical analysis of strikes in other cities, but police reports suggest a pattern similar to that of Paris. Certainly, provincial strikes could be equally well organized and threatening. In July 1808, the shoemakers of Toulouse struck for higher wages, set up a strike fund, and invited other trades to join them before the municipal government repressed the movement with forty-nine arrests.

Workers had no distinct political consciousness. Rather, they tended to share the ideology of the shopkeepers and master artisans. This had been true in the heyday of the *sans-culotte* movement, which, however, had been destroyed under the Directory; the few surviving radical leaders conspired ineffectually against the new regime. The continual war seems to have worn down workers' early enthusiasm for Napoleon, from whom they had expected peace and prosperity. But there was no organized opposition from them, merely occasional grumbling over conscription or unemployment. Despite the historical orthodoxy, there is no real evidence that Napoleon enjoyed an extraordinary popularity among French workers, at least not prior to 1814. The Napoleonic legend was primarily a development of the First Restoration and the Hundred Days, which revived Revolutionary nationalism in opposition to the Bourbon monarchy and fused it with Bonapartism. Napoleon was seen henceforth as the embodiment of the French Revolution and became a popular folk hero.

A. Chabert, *Essai sur les mouvements des revenus et de l'activité économique en France de 1798 à 1820* (Paris, n.d.); M. D. Sibalis, "The Workers of Napoleonic Paris, 1800–1815" (Ph.D. dissertation, Concordia University, 1979); G. Vauthier, "Les ouvriers de Paris sous l'Empire," *REN* 2 (1913).

Michael D. Sibalis

Related entries: ECONOMY, FRENCH; LABOR LEGISLATION; LAW, CODES OF; SOCIETY.

WURMSER, DAGOBERT SIGMUND VON, COUNT (1724–97), Austrian field marshal. Born in Strasbourg, Wurmser first served in the French army and during the Seven Years War (1756–63) became a general. In 1763, with the consent of the French king, Wurmser and his army corps entered Austrian service. During the War of the Bavarian Succession, he was promoted to major general, in 1787 to general of cavalry, and in 1790 made commanding general in Galicia. During the War of the First Coalition against France, he commanded the imperial army in the Rhineland and in 1793 breached the Weissenburg defenses, which had been regarded as impregnable. But differences between the Austrian and Prussian headquarters prevented further successes, and Wurmser was recalled. In 1795 he again was placed in charge of the Rhine army and seized Mannheim. In 1796 Wurmser was promoted to field marshal and given command of the Austrian army in Italy, where his opponent was Napoleon Bonaparte. There he proved unable to contend with the twenty-six-year-old Corsican. Bonaparte attacked his forces before he could unite them, defeated them in detail, and drove Wurmser into the fortress of Mantua. With a garrison of 24,000, of whom 7,000 were effective at the end, Wurmser held Mantua for seven months and surrendered only after other Austrian armies proved incapable of rescuing him. That was in February 1797; he died before the end of the year.

Brigitte Holl

Related entry: ITALIAN CAMPAIGN, FIRST.

WÜRTTEMBERG, a *Rheinbund* ally of Napoleon, 1806–13. A political entity since the seventh century, its medieval counts had concentrated their power around Stuttgart. Its Parliament, established in 1457, was one of the oldest in Europe. In 1514, the Poor Conrad Uprising had led to granting the first constitution, the *Tübingen Vertrag*, which recognized individual liberties. The Reformation was introduced in 1535 and consolidated by Christoph I (1515–68), who established a state church (Lutheran), with a separate financial administration, and a free educational system for training the clergy. After 1648, many reigning dukes attempted to impose stricter centralization and heavy taxes, but the estates usually were in opposition, especially in 1764 and 1797–1805. The parliament represented only the bourgeoisie, Lutheran prelates, and peasants, not the nobles. Only after the Napoleonic cessions did the mediatized knights form a House of Lords.

Württemberg had joined the war against France in 1792 but made a separate peace in 1796. The parliament was sympathetic to France, even to forming a French-style republic. Duke Frederick II (I) negotiated a secret alliance with Austria (1799) and then suppressed the parliamentary reform movement. In 1803 the French annexed Montbelliard, on the left bank of the Rhine, but Württemberg was compensated by territory on the right bank by the *Reichsdeputationshauptschluss* of 25 February 1803. The Reichstag further made the duke an elector and granted the annexation of Ellwangen and Zweifalten abbeys and of free towns such as Reutlingen, Rottweil, and Hall.

Napoleon forced an alliance on Frederick at Ludwigsburg on 5 October 1805. The reward, after the defeat of Austria, was a king's crown (1806). King Frederick I remained Napoleon's faithful ally in the *Rheinbund* from 1806 to 1813. The annexation of large territories from the "mediatized" lords (Hohenlohe, Limburg, Mergentheim) and of free towns like Ulm, Heilbronn, and Crailsheim increased the size of Württemberg from 9,500 to 19,500 square kilometers and the population from 600,000 to 1.35 million. Frederick's daughter Katharina was married to Jerome Bonaparte to seal the alliance. Between 1806 and 1815 a centralized, absolutist government was introduced in Württemberg by Philip C. F. von Normann, the prime minister. It provided for a French-style ministerial system, which presided over twelve departments (*Landvogteien*), which in turn supervised sixty-five counties (*Oberämter*). Frederick I joined the Allied coalition at Fulda in 1813 and preserved his kingdom and authority, despite the attempts of the Congress of Vienna to force a parliament on him.

O. Borst, *Württemberg. Geschichte u. Gestalt eines Landes* (Konstanz, 1978); K. Weller, *Württembergische Geschichte* (Stuttgart, 1975).

Helen P. Liebel-Weckowicz

Related entries: AUSTERLITZ CAMPAIGN; BONAPARTE, JEROME; CONFEDERATION OF THE RHINE; GERMAN WAR OF LIBERATION.

Y

YORCK VON WARTENBURG, JOHANN DAVID LUDWIG, COUNT (1759–1830), Prussian general. As a young officer Yorck (or York) was court-martialed for insubordination and cashiered. After serving with a regiment of the Dutch East India Company in South Africa, he reentered the Prussian army in 1787. In the Jena campaign he gained one of the few Prussian successes in the rearguard action at Altenzaun (26 October 1806). At Lübeck he was wounded and taken prisoner. He was exchanged the following spring and became an important figure in the regeneration of the Prussian army.

Yorck was not among the inner circle of reformers, and his brusque criticisms of H. F. K. vom Stein and of social change are often cited as exemplifying the Prussian reactionary. In reality he was too independent-minded to fit any category. He married a commoner, advocated conscription, and helped lead the fight for tactical reform, which was inseparable from improving treatment of the rank and file.

In the invasion of Russia he commanded the Prussian contingent, assigned to the left wing under Marshal Jacques Macdonald. Intermittently during the campaign, he received Russian appeals to quit the French. When Macdonald began to retreat in December, Yorck resumed negotiations with the Russians. On 30 December, acting on his own responsibility, he signed the Convention of Tauroggen, which neutralized his force for two months, an act of great strategic and political significance. It not only prevented Macdonald from making a stand on the Niemen but led to the rising of the East Prussian estates and provided a strong impetus to Prussia's declaring war on France in March 1813.

In the campaigns of 1813 and 1814, Yorck commanded the First Prussian Corps, winning successes at the Katzbach, Wartenburg, Möckern, Laon, La Chaussée near Vitry, and Athies. The inadequate support he gave Fabien von Sacken at Montmirail proved his most serious failure. He was made a count in 1814. In 1815 he did not see action.

Yorck lacked sweeping idealism, but in his professionalism, tenacity, and pronounced sense of independence, he represents one significant element of the Prussian military effort during the reform era and the Wars of Liberation.

J. G. Droysen, *Das Leben des Feldmarschalls Grafen York von Wartenburg* (Berlin, 1851–52); W. Elze, *Der Streit um Tauroggen* (Breslau, 1926); P. Paret, *Yorck and the Era of Prussian Reform* (Princeton, 1966).

Peter Paret

Related entries: GERMAN WAR OF LIBERATION; PRUSSIA, KINGDOM OF; RUSSIAN CAMPAIGN; SCHARNHORST; STEIN.

Z

ZAJACZEK, JOZEF (1752–1826), Polish general. An army officer from an early age, Zajączek served in the war of 1792 against the Russians as a major general. When King Stanisłas Augustus abandoned the patriotic cause, he went into exile. During the Kosciuszko uprising of 1794, he held Warsaw against the Prussians but was made a prisoner when the revolution failed. Freed in 1795, he went to France, where he published *Histoire de la révolution de Pologne en 1794 par un témoin oculaire* (1796). He took part in Napoleon's Egyptian expedition (1798) as a French brigadier general and in the campaigns of 1805 and 1806–7.

After the Battle of Jena (1806), he commanded a Polish legion in Napoleon's service and hoped for a restored Kingdom of Poland. In two memorials to Napoleon, he recommended that Poland be given a constitution similar to that of France, a Bonaparte king, and French-style laws eliminating noble privilege. After the creation of the Duchy of Warsaw, he served under Józef Poniatowski, although he felt that his service entitled him to head the Polish army. He fought in the campaigns of 1809 and 1812 (Russia) and lost a leg at the crossing of the Berezina during the retreat from Moscow.

Taken prisoner by the Russians at Vilnius, he soon agreed, however, to help the Grand Duke Constantine organize the army of the new Russian-sponsored Polish kingdom. In 1815 he was appointed military governor of Poland and in 1818 made a prince. He was as loyal to the Russians as he had been to the French. Though he had been a "Jacobin" until middle age, he is remembered as a conservative in the Congress Kingdom of Poland.

M. Chojnacki, "Z dziejów polskiej Legii Połnocnej 1806-1808," *Wojskowy Przegląd Historyczny* 1 (1960); J. Nadzieja, *General Józef Zajączek* (Warsaw, 1975); A. Reiss, "Z Napoleonem na Warmii i Mazurach," Wojskowa Akademia Polityczna, *Biuletyn* 8 (1962); F. Skarbek, *Dzieje Polski*, vol. 2: *Królestwo Polskie* (Poznan, 1877).

John Stanley

Related entries: ARMY, FRENCH; PONIATOWSKI; RUSSIAN CAMPAIGN; WARSAW, DUCHY OF.

ZINZENDORF UND POTTENDORF, KARL VON, COUNT (1739–1813), Austrian finance minister and state councillor. As comptroller general of Joseph

II, he began abolition of labor services, sought to implement Joseph's unsuccessful single tax reform, and financed the Turkish war. He was a physiocrat and free trade advocate. In 1801 he became Teutonic commander in Austria and in 1803 had to negotiate transfers of Teutonic Knight lands to lords in Germany. He helped formulate Austrian financial policy during the wars against Napoleon. As Francis II's financial adviser, he stabilized the currency and improved tax collections. The *Klassensteuer* financed Austrian wars and raised 16 million to 20 million gulden but could not deal with paper money inflation. He retired in 1809, before the Austrian state bankruptcy of 1811. He is best remembered as an indefatigable leader in agricultural reform and a zealous advocate of the rights of the estates. He is famous for his multivolume diary, which describes Vienna's salons and social life, as well as his economic ideas.

E. G. von Pettenegg, *Ludwig und Karl von Zinzendorf* (Vienna, 1879); H. Wagner, ed., *Wien von Maria Theresia bis zur Franzosenzeit* (Vienna, 1972).

Helen Liebel-Weckowicz

Related entries: ARMY, HABSBURG; FRANZ II; WAGRAM CAMPAIGN.

Chronology of Napoleonic France

1768

15 May — France acquires Corsica from Genoa.

1769

15 August — Birth of Napoleone Buonaparte at Ajaccio, Corsica

1778

15 December — Napoleone leaves Corsica for France.

1779

1 January — Napoleone and his elder brother Giuseppe (Joseph) enter school at Autun. Napoleone changes first name to Napoleon but remains Buonaparte.

April — Napoleon enters Brienne.

1784

30 October — Napoleon enters Ecole Militaire in Paris.

1785

1 September — He graduates from Ecole Militaire as a sublieutenant.

30 October — Napoleon assigned to La Fère Artillery Regiment at Valence.

1788

June — He is attached to the School of Artillery at Auxonne.

1789

5 May — Estates General Meets.

14 July — Storming of Bastille. French Revolution begins.

1790

July — Paoli returns from exile to Corsica as royal governor.

1791

10 February	Napoleon returns to duty at Auxonne.
1 April	Promoted to first lieutenant.
1 October	Constitution of 1791. Constitutional monarchy under Louis XVI, September 1791-August 1792.

1792

February	First coalition against France initiated with alliance of Prussia and Austria.
1 April	Buonaparte elected lieutenant colonel, 2nd Battalion, Corsican Volunteers (National Guard).
8–12 April	Riot at Ajaccio, in part provoked by Napoleon's battalion.
20 April	France declares war on Austria.
28 May	Napoleon in Paris; promoted to captain.
10 August	Louis XVI overthrown.
15 September	Napoleon returns to Corsica, where he and his brother Lucien are active in Jacobin clubs.
21 September	National Convention, September 1792-October 1795.
22 September	French Republic is proclaimed. "First Day of Liberty," later becomes first day of Year I of Revolutionary calendar, not put into effect until September 1793.

1793

March	Corsica in revolt against France. Buonapartes outlawed.
13 June	Napoleon and Buonaparte family arrive in France.
July	The Terror begins.
27 August	British reinforce royalists at Toulon.
16 September	Napoleon commands artillery of French army besieging Toulon.

YEAR II OF THE REPUBLIC

22 September (1 Vendémiaire)	Revolutionary Calendar in effect. First day of Year II.
17–19 December (27-29 Frimaire)	French recapture Toulon from British and royalists.
22 December (2 Nivôse)	Napoleon Buonparte promoted to *général de brigade*.

1794

6 February (18 Pluviôse)	Napoleon assigned to staff of (French) Army of Italy.
July 28 (10 Thermidor)	End of Terror. Execution of Robespierre.
9–20 August (22 Thermidor–3 Fructidor)	Buonaparte jailed at Antibes as a Jacobin after fall of Robespierre.

YEAR III OF THE REPUBLIC

1795

2 May (14 Floréal)	Napoleon transferred to Paris: he rejects assignment to the Vendée.
16 May	Batavian (Dutch) Republic founded.
21 August (4 Fructidor)	Napoleon assigned to Bureau topographique.

YEAR IV OF THE REPUBLIC

1 October (9 Vendémiaire)	Belgium annexed to France.
5 October (13 Vendémiaire)	Buonaparte suppresses revolt in Paris with the "Whiff of Grapeshot."
16 October (24 Vendémiaire)	Buonaparte promoted to *général de division*.
26 October (4 Brumaire)	Napoleon commander of Armée de l'Intérieur.
3 November (12 Brumaire)	Government of Directory, November 1795–November 1799.

1796

2 March (12 Ventôse)	Napoleon commander of (French) Army of Italy.
9 March (19 Ventôse)	Napoleon marries Josephine de Beauharnais.
March	Enroute to Nice to assume command of Army of Italy he changes his last name from Buonaparte to Bonaparte.
6 April (17 Germinal)	First Italian Campaign (1796–97) begins.

12 April (23 Germinal)	Battle of Montenotte.
13 April (24 Germinal)	Battle of Millesimo.
14–15 April (25–26 Germinal)	Battle of Dego.
21 April (2 Floréal)	Battle of Mondovi.
28 April (9 Floréal)	Armistice of Cherasco (Piedmont).
10 May (21 Floréal)	Battle of Lodi.
15 May (26 Floréal)	Bonaparte enters Milan.
5 August (18 Thermidor)	Battle of Castiglione.
8 September (22 Fructidor)	Battle of Bassano.

YEAR V OF THE REPUBLIC

15–17 November (25–27 Brumaire)	Battle of Arcola.

1797

14 January (25 Nivôse)	Battle of Rivoli.
2 February (14 Pluviôse)	Surrender of Mantua.
18 April (29 Germinal)	Preliminary Peace of Leoben. End of First Italian Campaign.
9 July (21 Messidor)	Cisalpine Republic created.
4 September (18 Fructidor)	Coup d'état of 18 Fructidor.

YEAR VI OF THE REPUBLIC

17 October (26 Vendémiaire)	Treaty of Campo Formio. First Coalition against France dissolved. (Only Britain still at war.)
27 October (6 Brumaire)	Bonaparte given command of Army of England while still in Italy.

10 December (20 Frimaire)	Bonaparte in Paris; recommends against expedition to England.

1798

January–February	Napoleon and Talleyrand push for expedition to Egypt.
15 February (27 Pluviôse)	Roman Republic created by French. Pope imprisoned.
29 March (9 Germinal)	Helvetic (Swiss) Republic created. Republic of Geneva annexed to France.
19 May (30 Floréal)	Expedition sails for Egypt from Toulon. Egyptian Campaign (1798–99) begins.
1–2 July (13–14 Messidor)	Landing/capture of Alexandria.
21 July (3 Thermidor)	Battle of Pyramids (at Embabeh).
1 August (14 Thermidor)	Battle of Nile.
5 September (19 Fructidor)	France reformulates conscription laws (Jourdan-Delbrel decrees).

YEAR VII OF THE REPUBLIC

29 December (9 Nivôse)	Second Coalition against France (Britain, the Ottoman Empire, Russia, Austria, and lesser European powers).

1799

20 February (2 Ventôse)	Napoleon captures El Arish and invades Syria.
7 March (17 Ventôse)	Napoleon captures Jaffa.
19 March–20 May (29 Ventôse to 1 Prairial)	Siege of Acre.
16 April (27 Germinal)	Battle of Mount Tabor.
18 June (30 Prairial)	In Paris: coup d'état of 30 Prairial. (Directory purged except for Barras. Sieyès, Ducos, Gohier, and Moulin added).
25 July (17 Thermidor)	Battle of Aboukir.
24 August (6 Fructidor)	Bonaparte sails for France.

YEAR VIII OF THE REPUBLIC

9 October (17 Vendémiaire)	Napoleon lands at Fréjus.
16 October (24 Vendémiaire)	Napoleon in Paris.
9–10 November (18–19 Brumaire)	Coup d'état of 18 Brumaire. End of Directory. Bonaparte, Sieyès, and Ducos appointed temporary consuls.
12 December (21 Frimaire)	Constitution of the year VIII. Bonaparte first consul, Cambacérès and Lebrun second and third consuls, the Consulate, December 1799–May 1804.
22 December (1 Nivôse)	Council of State installed.
27 December (6 Nivôse)	Senate installed.

1800

1 January (11 Nivôse)	Installation of Tribunate and *Corps Législatif*.
7 February (18 Pluviôse)	Plebiscite results published; Constitution of Year VIII approved.
13 February (24 Pluviôse)	Bank of France founded.
17 February (28 Pluviôse)	Law reorganizes administration of France.
2 March (11 Ventôse)	Prefects appointed for departments.
3 March (12 Ventôse)	Closure of list of *émigrés*.
5 April (15 Germinal)	Austrians attack Masséna at Genoa.
15–23 May (25 Floréal–3 Prairial)	Napoleon crosses Alps; Second Italian campaign begins.
2 June (13 Prairial)	Napoleon enters Milan.
4 June (15 Prairial)	Masséna capitulates at Genoa.
14 June (25 Prairial)	Battle of Marengo. Death of Desaix; End of Second Italian campaign.
12 August (24 Thermidor)	Commission appointed for drafting Civil Law Code.

YEAR IX OF THE REPUBLIC

7 October (15 Vendémiaire)	Spain cedes Louisiana to France.
20 October (28 Vendémiaire)	*Emigré* list modified to allow more to return to France.
5 November (14 Brumaire)	Negotiations for concordat open with papacy.
3 December (12 Frimaire)	Battle of Hohenlinden.
24 December (3 Nivôse)	Bomb (Infernal Machine) attempt on Bonaparte's life in rue Saint-Nicaise.

1801

9 February (20 Pluviôse)	Treaty of Lunéville with Austria.
23 March (2 Germinal)	Alexander I becomes czar of Russia.
2 April (12 Germinal)	Nelson destroys Danish fleet at Copenhagen.
April (Germinal)	Napoleon establishes camp at Boulogne for invasion of England.
15 July (26 Messidor)	Concordat of 1801 with Pius VII signed.
30 August (12 Fructidor)	French army left by Napoleon in Egypt surrenders to British.

YEAR X OF THE REPUBLIC

13 December (22 Frimaire)	French expedition sails from Brest for Santo Domingo.

1802

26 January (6 Pluviôse)	Bonaparte president of Cisalpine Republic (renamed Republic of Italy).
5 February (16 Pluviôse)	French expedition arrives at Santo Domingo.
25 March (4 Germinal)	Treaty of Amiens with Britain.
26 April (6 Floréal)	*Emigré* list reduced to one thousand.

1 May (11 Floréal)	Creation of *lycées*; new system of education launched.
19 May (29 Floréal)	Legion of Honor established.
2 August (14 Thermidor)	Bonaparte named consul for life.
4 August (16 Thermidor)	Constitution of year X. Elba annexed to France.
11 September (25 Fructidor)	Piedmont annexed to France.

YEAR XI OF THE REPUBLIC

23 September (1 Vendémiaire)	Construction begins of Ourcq canal to bring fresh water to Paris.
15 October (23 Vendémiaire)	French troops enter Switzerland.
24 December (3 Nivôse)	Twenty-two *chambres de commerce* created in France.

1803

4 January (14 Nivôse)	Senatoriates established.
23 January (3 Pluviôse)	Institut National reorganized.
19 February (30 Pluviôse)	Act of Mediation institutes the Swiss Confederation.
11 March (20 Ventôse)	Napoleon establishes the Boulogne camps to train army for the invasion of England.
3 May (13 Floréal)	Louisiana ceded to United States.
18 May (28 Floréal)	Rupture of the Treaty of Amiens. War resumes between France and Britain.
1 June (12 Prairial)	French troops occupy Hanover (Mortier).

YEAR XII OF THE REPUBLIC

1 December (9 Frimaire)	*Livret ouvrier* (work pass) introduced.

1804

13 February (23 Pluviôse)	Discovery of royalist plot to kidnap Bonaparte.
19 February (29 Pluviôse)	General Moreau arrested.
28 February (8 Ventôse)	General Pichegru arrested.
9 March (18 Ventôse)	Cadoudal arrested.
21 March (30 Ventôse)	Execution of duc d'Enghien; Civil Law Code proclaimed.
18 May (28 Floréal)	French Empire proclaimed.
19 May (29 Floréal)	Marshals of the Empire created (eighteen of twenty-six total).
28 June (9 Messidor)	Execution of Cadoudal; banishment of Moreau.

YEAR XIII OF THE REPUBLIC

2 December (11 Frimaire)	Coronation of Napoleon I.

1805

26 May (6 Prairial)	Napoleon king of Italy.
4 June (15 Prairial)	Genoa annexed to France.
7 June (18 Prairial)	Eugène de Beauharnais, viceroy of Italy.
9 August (21 Thermidor)	Third Coalition against France. Austria joins Britain and Russia.
25 August (7 Fructidor)	Grande Armée leaves Boulogne for Germany. Ulm-Austerlitz campaign begins.

YEAR XIV OF THE REPUBLIC

14 October (22 Vendémiaire)	Battle of Elchingen (Ney).

20 October (28 Vendémiaire)	Mack surrenders at Ulm.
21 October (29 Vendémiaire)	Battle of Trafalgar. Nelson annihilates Franco-Spanish fleet.
14 November (23 Brumaire)	Bonaparte enters Vienna.
2 December (11 Frimaire)	Battle of Austerlitz (end of Austerlitz campaign).
15 December (24 Frimaire)	Convention of Schönbrunn (with Prussia).
26 December (5 Nivôse)	Treaty of Pressburg (with Austria).
31 December (10 Nivôse)	End of the Republican Calendar.

1806

1 January	France returns to Gregorian calendar.
23 January	Death of William Pitt.
30 March	Kingdom of Naples. Joseph Bonaparte king.
4 April	Imperial Catechism is published.
22 April	Governor appointed for the Bank of France.
10 May	Imperial University established.
26 May	Kingdom of Holland created.
5 June	Louis Bonaparte king of Holland.
12 July	Napoleon establishes Confederation of the Rhine.
July	Fourth Coalition against France: Prussia, Russia, Great Britain, lesser powers.
6 August	Holy Roman Empire dissolved: Emperor Francis II becomes Emperor Francis I of Austria.
9 August	Prussian army mobilizes.
25 September	Prussian army invades Confederation of the Rhine.
6 October	Napoleon takes command of Grande Armée of Germany. Jena-Auerstädt-Friedland campaign begins.
14 October	Napoleon defeats Prince Hohenlohe at Jena. Davout defeats Duke of Brunswick at Auerstädt.
27 October	Bonaparte enters Berlin.
21 November	Continental Blockade inaugurated by Berlin Decree.
10 December	Grand Sanhedrin is opened to determine policies on Jews.
18 December	Bonaparte enters Warsaw.

1807

1 January	Napoleon meets Countess Walewska in Warsaw.
7 February	Battle of Eylau.
2 March	Decrees on civil status of Jews.
24 May	Danzig (Gdansk) surrendered to French.
14 June	Battle of Friedland; end of Jena-Auerstädt-Friedland campaign.
25 June	Napoleon and Alexander meet on a raft anchored in the Niemen River.
7–9 July	Treaties of Tilsit between France, Russia, and Prussia.
19 August	Tribunate is suppressed.
11 September	Commercial Law Code is proclaimed.
27 October	Secret Treaty of Fontainebleau between Napoleon and Charles IV of Spain (actually First Minister Manuel Godoy).
30 November	General Junot occupies Lisbon. Peninsular War, November 1807–June 1813.
13 December	Milan Decree extends Continental System to neutrals.

1808

20 February	Murat appointed lieutenant-general of the emperor in Spain.
1 March	Senatus Consultum organizes the Imperial nobility.
7 March	Fontanes named grand master of the Imperial University.
18 March	Spanish coup at Aranjuez. Charles IV abdicates and his son proclaimed king Ferdinand VII.
24 March	Murat enters Madrid.
2 May	*Dos de Mayo*
May	Bayonne Conference.
7 July	Joseph Bonaparte crowned king of Spain. Murat and Caroline Bonaparte king and queen of Naples.
14 July	Battle of Medina de Rio Seco (Bessières).
19 July	Battle of Baylen (Castaños/Dupont).
30 July	Joseph evacuates Madrid.
21 August	Wellesley defeats J.-A. Junot at Vimeiro.
30 August	Convention of Cintra; French army evacuates Portugal in British transports.
17 September	Imperial University organized.
8 October	Napoleon meets Czar Alexander at Erfurt.
15 October	Much of Grande Armée ordered from Germany to Spain.

5 November	Napoleon assumes personal command of the Army of Spain.
30 November	Battle of Somo Sierra.
13 December	Madrid capitulates.

1809

16 January	Battle of Coruña. Napoleon leaves Spain.
29 March	Soult captures Oporto.
6 April	Austria proclaims war of Liberation of Germany. Fifth Coalition against France (Britain, Austria, rebel Spain).
9 April	Archduke Karl von Habsburg invades Bavaria.
April	Wagram campaign begins.
19–23 April	Battles of Abensberg, Landshut, Eckmühl, and Regensburg.
26 April	Wellesley lands at Lisbon with British army.
12 May	Battle of Oporto (Wellesley/Soult).
13 May	French occupy Vienna.
17 May	France annexes the Papal States.
21–22 May	Battle of Aspern-Essling. Marshal Lannes killed.
11 June	Pope Pius VII excommunicates Bonaparte.
5–6 July	Battle of Wagram; end of Wagram campaign.
6 July	Pius VII arrested and taken to Savona.
27–28 July	Battle of Talavera.
14 October	Treaty of Schönbrunn (France and Austria).
30 November	Napoleon announces intention to divorce Josephine.
15 December	Senatus Consultum pronounces the divorce.

1810

January	Continental Blockade modified: Some prohibited goods allowed admittance with tariff payment.
14 January	Church court in Paris annuls marriage of Napoleon and Josephine.
17 February	Rome annexed to French Empire, Napoleon's heir to bear title of king of Rome.
30 March	Ecole Normale Supérieure revived and reorganized.
1 April	Napoleon marries Marie-Louise of Austria.
17 April	Masséna given command of French Army of Portugal.
May	Marshal Bernadotte elected crown prince of Sweden.
1 July	Louis abdicates throne of Holland. Holland annexed to France.
9 July	Masséna captures Ciudad Rodrigo.
5 August	Continental Blockade modified by Trianon tariff decree.
15 August	Inauguration of the Vendôme column.

27 August	Masséna captures Almeida and invades Portugal.
29 September	Battle of Bussaco.
October–March 1811	Siege of Torres Vedras lines (Lisbon).
18–25 October	Fontainebleau Decrees again modify Continental Blockade.
13 December	Annexation of north German territories to French Empire.
31 December	Czar Alexander breaks with Continental Blockade.

1811

January	Preparations begin for Russian campaign.
March	Masséna abandons siege of Torres Vedras.
20 March	Birth of Napoleon II, king of Rome.
10 May	Marmont replaces Masséna in command of Army of Portugal.
December	Napoleon intensifies preparations for Russian campaign.

1812

19 January	Spain: British take Ciudad Rodrigo.
16 March	Joseph Bonaparte again commander of French troops in Spain.
24 March	Secret alliance between Russia and Sweden. Sixth Coalition against France (Russia, Sweden, supported by Britain; indirect support from rebel Spain).
6 April	Spain: British take Badajoz.
8 May	Spain: Rebel Cortes issues Constitution of 1812.
May	Grande Armée assembling in East Prussia and Poland.
16 May	Napoleon received at Dresden by Austrian emperor, German kings, and others.
30 May	Napoleon takes command of Grande Armée.
18 June	War of 1812, United States declares war on Great Britain.
24–25 June	Grande Armée crosses Niemen and invades Russia. Russian campaign begins.
26 June	Napoleon takes Vilna.
22 July	Spain: Battle of Salamanca (Wellington over Marmont).
28 July	Napoleon reaches Vitebsk.
August	Spain: Wellington occupies Madrid (recovered by Joseph in November).
17–19 August	Battle of Smolensk.
7 September	Battle of Borodino.
14 September	Napoleon enters Moscow.
October	Spain: Wellington made Allied commander.
19 October	Retreat from Moscow begins.
23 October	Malet conspiracy in Paris.

24 October	Battle of Maloyaroslavets.
6 November	Napoleon hears of Malet conspiracy.
10–12 November	Grande Armée in Smolensk.
18–19 November	Ney extricates rear guard.
26–28 November	Crossing of the Berezina.
5 December	Napoleon leaves army at Smorgoni. Murat given command.
9 December	Murat evacuates Vilna.
14 December	Ney commands rear guard at Niemen.
16 December	Twenty-ninth bulletin issued in Paris.
19 December	Napoleon in Paris.
30 December	Convention of Tauroggen: Corps of Prussian General Yorck joins Russians.

1813

17 January	Posen: Remnants of Grande Armée end retreat from Russia. Murat departs for Naples, leaving command of army to Eugène de Beauharnais.
January–April	Eugène withdraws army to line of the Elbe.
25 January	Napoleon signs new concordat with Pope Pius VII, who later renounces it.
26 February	Treaty of Kalisch, Prussia and Russia ally against France.
16 March	Prussia declares war on France (Austria assumes role of armed mediator). German war of liberation begins.
25 March	Death of Field Marshal Kutuzov.
25 April	Napoleon assumes command of Grande Armée at Erfurt.
1 May	Marshal Bessières killed near Lützen.
2 May	Battle of Lützen.
18 May	Bernadotte lands at Stralsund to join Allies.
21 May	Battle of Bautzen.
30 May	Davout occupies Hamburg (until after Napoleon's fall).
4 June–10 August	Armistice in Germany.
21 June	Battle of Vitoria (Wellington over Joseph Bonaparte).
26 June	Allied peace offer to Napoleon.
27 June	Secret Treaty of Reichenbach between Austria and Allies.
12 August	Austria joins Allies, declares war on France. Final Grand Alliance of Allies against France complete.
26–27 August	Battle of Dresden (Napoleon over Schwarzenberg).
7 October	Wellington crosses Bidassoa. Second front opened against France.
16–19 October	Leipzig, ''Battle of the Nations''; Saxony, Baden to Allies. Napoleon begins retreat to Rhine.

October–November	Collapse of Confederation of the Rhine and Kingdom of Westphalia.
9 November	Allies offer Napoleon peace with natural frontiers for France.
November	Holland to prince of Orange.
12 November	Wellington crosses Nivelle.
13 December	Wellington crosses Nive.

1814

1 January	Allies cross Rhine.
January–March	Campaign of France.
11 January	Murat, king of Naples, defects to Allies.
24 January	Joseph Bonaparte named lieutenant-general of Empire.
25 January	Napoleon leaves Paris for Chalôns-sur-Marne.
1 February	Blücher and Schwarzenberg defeat Napoleon at La Rothière.
5 February	Congress of Châtillon opens. Allies offer Napoleon peace with boundaries of 1792 for France.
10 February	Napoleon defeats Russians at Champaubert.
11 February	Napoleon defeats Russians at Montmirail and Prussians at Château-Thierry.
14 February	Napoleon defeats Blücher at Vauchamps.
18 February	Napoleon defeats Schwarzenberg at Montereau.
1 March	Treaty of Chaumont between Allies.
7 March	Napoleon defeats Blücher at Craonne.
9 March	Blücher defeats Marmont at Laon.
12 March	Wellington enters Bordeaux.
31 March	Paris is surrendered to Allies by Marmont and Mortier.
2 April	Senate proclaims deposition of Bonaparte. (Corps Législatif does same the next day.)
3 April	Marmont defects to Allies.
4 April	Napoleon's marshals refuse to march at Fontainebleau.
6 April	Napoleon abdicates in favor of Napoleon II.
11 April	Napoleon abdicates unconditionally. Treaty of Fontainebleau signed. Marie-Louise and Napoleon II in custody of Francis I of Austria.
16 April	Eugène makes terms in Italy.
1 May	Treaty of Paris, Louis XVIII restored. France of 1792.
3 May	Louis XVIII enters Paris.
4 May	Napoleon in exile on Isle of Elba.
29 May	Death of Josephine at Malmaison.
September 1814–June 1815	Congress of Vienna.

1815

25 February	"Vol de l'Aigle" (Napoleon sails from Elba).
1 March	Napoleon lands near Cannes.
7 March	Napoleon confronts Fifth Regiment at Grenoble.
13 March	Allies at Vienna outlaw Napoleon.
15 March	Murat attacks Austrians in Italy.
18 March	Marshal Ney supports Napoleon.
20 March	Napoleon in Paris. Hundred Days begin (20 March–22 June 1815).
28 March	Allies renew Treaty of Chaumont.
3 May	Austrians defeat Murat's army at Tolentino.
15 June	Napoleon's army crosses Sambre at Charleroi (Belgium).
16 June	Battles of Ligny and Quatre-Bras.
18 June	Battle of Waterloo.
22 June	Napoleon's second abdication.
7 July	Allies enter Paris.
8 July	Napoleon at Rochefort.
14 July	Napoleon surrenders to Captain Maitland aboard *Bellerophon*.
23 July–4 August	Napoleon aboard ship at Plymouth.
2 August	Allies declare Napoleon prisoner. Custody to Britain.
7 August	Napoleon leaves Plymouth aboard HMS *Northumberland* for St. Helena.
13 October	Murat court-martialled and shot at Pizzo, in Naples.
16 October	Napoleon begins exile on St. Helena.
20 November	Second Treaty of Paris.
7 December	Execution of Marshal Ney.

1821

5 May	Napoleon dies on St. Helena.
1822–1840	Growth of Napoleonic Legend.

1840

December	Napoleon's remains returned to Paris; interred in Invalides on 15 December.

General Bibliography

The titles here are of general works, bibliographies, dictionaries, and similar compilations. Monographs, specialized works, and articles are listed with appropriate dictionary articles, as is some primary material. The bibliographies will serve as a key to the primary source collections and archives, as well as the enormous volume of Napoleonic historical literature.

BIBLIOGRAPHIES

Godechot, Jacques. *L'Europe et l'Amérique à l'époque napoléonienne (1800–1815)*. Paris, 1967.

———. "La période révolutionnaire et impériale." In *Revue Historique* 504 (October–December 1972), 507 (July–September 1973), 516 (October–December 1975), 533 (January–March 1980), 536 (October–December 1980).

Kircheisen, Friedrich M. *Bibliographie Napoleons*. 2 vols. Berlin, 1902.

———. *Bibliographie du temps de Napoléon comprenant l'histoire des Etats Unis*. 2 vols. Paris, 1908–1912.

Monglond, André. *La France révolutionnaire et impériale: Annales de bibliographie méthodique et description des livres illustrés*. 10 vols. Grenoble, 1930–1978.

Tulard, Jean. *Bibliographie critique des mémoires sur le Consulat et l'Empire écrits ou traduits en français*. Geneva, 1971.

Villat, Louis. *La Révolution et l'Empire*. 2 vols. Vol. 2: *Napoléon (1799–1815)*. 3d ed. Paris, 1949.

BIOGRAPHIES

Bainville, Jacques. *Napoléon*. Paris, 1931. New ed., edited by Jean Tulard. Paris, 1976.

Kircheisen, Friedrich M. *Napoleon: Sein Leben und seine Zeit*. 9 vols. Stuttgart, 1911–1934.

Manfred, Albert Zakharovich. *Napoleon Bonaparte*. Moscow, 1972. In Russian and French.

Markham, Felix. *Napoleon*. New York, 1963.

Rose, J. Holland. *The Life of Napoleon I*. 11th ed. 2 vols. London, 1934.

Tarlé, Evgenii. *Napoleon*. 1st Russian ed. Moscow, 1933. French and English ed. Paris and London, 1937.

Thompson, J. M. *Napoleon Bonaparte, His Rise and Fall*. London, 1952.

Tulard, Jean. *Napoléon: Ou le mythe du sauveur*. 2d ed. Paris, 1979.

LIFE AND TIMES

Bergeron, Louis. *France under Napoleon*. Translated by R. R. Palmer. Princeton, 1981.

———. *L'Episode napoléonien: Aspects intérieurs*. Vol. 4 of Seuil (pub.), *Nouvelle histoire de la France*. Paris, 1972; and Jacques Lovie and André Palluel-Guillard. *L'épisode napoléonien: Aspects extérieurs*. Vol. 5 of same series. Paris, 1972.

Bignon, Louis, Baron. *Histoire de France sous Napoléon*. 14 vols. Paris, 1838–1850.

Braudel, Fernand, and Ernest Labrousse, eds. *Histoire économique et sociale de la France*. Vol. 3. Paris, 1976.

Connelly, Owen. *The Epoch of Napoleon*. New York, 1972, repr. 1978.

———. *French Revolution/Napoleonic Era*. New York, 1979.

Crawley, C. W., ed. *New Cambridge Modern History*. Vol. 9. London, 1965.

Driault, Edouard. *Napoléon et l'Europe*. 5 vols. Paris, 1910–1927.

Godechot, Jacques, B. Hyslop, and D. Dowd. *The Napoleonic Era in Europe*. New York, 1970.

Göhring, Martin. *Napoleon: Vom alten zum neuen Europa*. 2d ed. Göttingen, 1965.

Herold, J. Christopher. *The Age of Napoleon*. New York, 1965.

Latreille, André. *L'ère napoléonienne*. Paris, 1974.

Lefebvre, Georges. *Napoléon*. 4th ed. Paris, 1953. 5th ed. by Albert Soboul. Paris, 1965.

———. *Napoleon*. 2 vols. Translated by Henry Stockhold. London, 1969.

Madelin, Louis. *Histoire du Consulat et de l'Empire*. 16 vols. Paris, 1937–1954.

———. *History of the Consulate and Empire*. 2 vols. London, 1932; New York, 1934–1936.

Mistler, Jean, ed. *Napoléon et l'Empire*. 2 vols. Paris, 1968.

Sieburg, Heinz Otto, ed. *Napoleon und Europa*. Cologne, 1971.

Soboul, Albert. *Premier Empire*. Paris, 1973.

Thiers, L. Adolphe. *Histoire du Consulat et de l'Empire*. 21 vols. Paris, 1845–1874.

Zaghi, Carlo. *Napoleone e l'Europa*. Naples, 1969.

INTERNATIONAL

Aretin, Karl Otmar, Freiherr von. *Vom Deutschen Reich zum Deutschen Bund*. Göttingen, 1980.

Bourgeois, Emile. *Les révolutions (1789–1830)*. Vol. 2 of *Manuel historique de politique étrangère*. 4 vols. Paris, 1893–1926.

Butterfield, Herbert. *The Peace Tactics of Napoleon, 1806–1808*. Cambridge, England, 1929.

Connelly, Owen. *Napoleon's Satellite Kingdoms*. New York, 1969.

Crouzet, François. *L'économie britannique et le blocus continental*. 2 vols. Paris, 1958.

Deutsch, H. C. *Genesis of Napoleonic Imperialism*. Cambridge, Mass., 1938.

Dunan, Marcel, ed. *Napoléon et l'Europe*. Paris, 1961.

Fehrenbach, Elisabeth. *Vom Ancien Regime zum Wiener Kongress*. Munich, 1981.

Fugier, André. *La révolution française et l'empire napoléonienne*. Vol. 4 of *Histoire des relations internationales*. Edited by Pierre Renouvin. Paris, 1954.

Hales, E.E.Y. *Napoleon and the Pope*. New York, 1961.

Heckscher, Eli F. *The Continental System: An Economic Interpretation*. Oxford, 1922.

Helleiner, Karl F. *The Imperial Loans: A Study in Financial and Diplomatic History*. Oxford, 1965.

Lefebvre, Armand. *Histoire des cabinets de l'Europe pendant le Consulat et l'Empire*. 3 vols. Paris, 1847.

Mahan, Alfred T. *The Influence of Sea Power upon the French Revolution and Empire, 1793–1812*. 2 vols. 14th ed. New York, 1919.

Meinecke, Friedrich. *Das Zeitalter der deutschen Erhebung, 1795–1815*. 6th ed. Göttingen, 1957.

Mowat, R. B. *The Diplomacy of Napoleon*. London, 1924.

Raumer, Kurt von, and Manfred Botzenhart. *Deutsche Geschichte im 19. Jahrhundert*. Vol. 3: *Deutschland um 1800. Krise und Neugestaltung. Von 1789 bis 1815*. Wiesbaden, 1980.

Sorel, Albert. *L'Europe et la Révolution française*. 8 vols. Paris, 1885–1904.

Weis, Eberhard. *Propyläen Geschichte Europas*. Vol. 4: *Der Durchbruch des Bürgertums, 1776–1847*. Berlin, 1978.

Zaghi, Carlo. *Napoleone e l'Italia*. Naples, 1966.

WAR

Blond, Georges. *Grande Armée, 1804–1815*. Paris, 1979.

Chandler, David G. *The Campaigns of Napoleon: The Mind and Method of History's Greatest Soldier*. New York, 1966.

Chardigny, Louis. *Les maréchaux de Napoléon*. Paris, 1980.

Dodge, T. A. *Napoleon: A History of the Art of War*. 4 vols. London, 1904–1907.

Esposito, V. J., and J. R. Elting. *Military History and Atlas of the Napoleonic Wars*. Reprint ed. New York, 1978.

Farrère, Claude. *Histoire de la marine française*. Paris, 1962.

Lachouque, Henry. *Anatomy of Glory: Napoleon and His Guard*. New ed. London, 1978.

———. *Napoléon et la garde impériale*. Paris, 1957.

———. *Napoléon, 20 ans de campagnes*. Paris, 1964.

———. *Napoleon's Battles: A History of His Campaigns*. Translated by Roy Monkcorn. New York, 1967.

Oman, Sir Charles. *History of the Peninsular War*. 7 vols. London, 1902–1930.

Phipps, Ramsay Weston. *The Armies of the First French Republic and the Rise of Napoleon's Marshals*. 5 vols. Reprint ed. Westport, Conn., 1980.

Quennevat, J.-C. *Atlas de la Grande Armée. Napoléon et ses campagnes (1803–1815)*. Paris, 1966.

Rogers, Hugh Cuthbert Basset. *Napoleon's Army*. London, 1974.

REFERENCE WORKS

Allgemeine deutsche Biographie. Edited by R. von Lilliencron et al. 56 vols. Leipzig, 1875–1912.

Bercenay, Babie de, and L. Beaumont. *Galerie militaire, ou Notices historiques sur les Généraux en chef*. 7 vols. N.p., n.d.

Bergeron, Louis, and Guy Chaussinand-Nogaret. *Les "masses de granit": Cent mille notables du Premier Empire*. Paris, 1979.

———, eds. *Grands notables du premier empire: Notices de biographie sociale*. Vol. 1: *Vaucluse*, by Alain Maureau, *Ardèche*, by Germaine Peyron-Montagnon. Paris, 1978. Vol. 2: *Mont-Blanc, Léman*, by André Palluel-Guillard. Paris, 1978. Vol. 3: *Bas-Rhin*, by Michel Richard, *Sarre, Mont-Tonnerre, Rhin et Moselle, Roër*, by R. Dufraisse. Paris, 1978. Vol. 4: *Jura, Haute-Saone, Doubs*, by Claude-Isabelle Brelot. Paris, 1978. Vol. 5: *Gard*, by Armand Cosson, *Hérault*, by Henri Michel, *Drôme*, by Gérard-Albert Roch. Paris, 1980. Vol. 6: *Alpes-Maritimes, Corse*, by Jean-Yves Coppolani, *Aude*, by Jean-Claude Gegot, *Pyrénées-Orientales*, by Geneviève Gavignaud, *Bouches-du-Rhône*, by l'abbé Paul Gueyraud. Paris, 1980. Vol. 7: *Aube, Marne*, by George Clause, *Haute-Marne*, by George Viard. Paris, 1981. Vol. 8: *Loir-et-Cher, Indre-et-Loire*, by Jeanine Labussière, *Loire-inférieure*, by Béatrix Guillet. Paris, 1982.

A Biographical Dictionary of Eminent Scotsmen. Edited by Robert Chambers. Rev. and enlarged ed. Edited by Thomas Thomson. 3 vols. Facsimile of 1876 London edition. Hildesheim, N.Y., 1971.

Boylan, Henry, ed. *Dictionary of Irish Biography*. Dublin, 1978.

Chaunu, Pierre, and J.-P. Bardet, eds. *Paroisses et communes de France. Dictionnaire d'histoire administrative et demographique*. Paris, 1980.

The Complete Peerage of England, Scotland, Ireland, Great Britain, and the United Kingdom, Extant, Extinct, or Dormant. Edited by George Edward Cokayne. New rev. and enlarged ed. Edited by V. Gibbes. 13 vols. in 14. London, 1910–1959.

A Critical Bibliography of French Literature. Edited by Richard A. Brooks. 6 vols. to date. Syracuse, N.Y., 1979–1983.

Dictionary of National Biography. Edited by Sir Leslie Stephen and Sir Sidney Lee. 22 vols. London and Oxford, 1949–1950, with supplements 1951–1981.

Dictionary of Scientific Biography. Edited by Charles Coulstow. 14 vols. New York, 1970–1976.

Dizionario biografico degli Italiani. Rome, 1960–.

Enciclopedia italiana di scienza, lettero ed arti. 36 vols. Rome, 1929–1939.

The Gentleman's and Connoisseur's Dictionary of Painters. Edited by Matthew Pilkington. London, 1798.

Godechot, Jacques. *Institutions de la France sous la Révolution et l'Empire*. 2d ed. Paris, 1968.

Jal, Auguste. *Dictionnaire critique de biographie et d'histoire*. 2 vols. Geneva, 1970.

La Chenaye-Desbois, F. A. de. *Dictionnaire de la noblesse de la France*. 19 vols. 3d ed. Paris, 1863–1877.

Lalanne, Ludovic. *Dictionnaire historique de la France*. Reprint of 1872 ed. Geneva, 1977.

Marion, Marcel. *Dictionnaire des institutions de la France aux XVIIe et XVIIIe siècles*. Paris, 1923.

Melchior-Bonnet, Bernardine. *Dictionnaire de la Révolution et de l'Empire*. Paris, 1965.

Neue deutsche Biographie. 12 vols. Berlin, 1953–.

Nouvelle biographie generale. Edited by J.C.F. Hoefer. 46 vols. Paris, 1852–1877.

Palluel, André. *Dictionnaire de l'empereur*. Paris, 1969.

Perrot, Jean-Claude. *Age d'or de la statistique regionale française (an IV–1804)*. Paris, 1977.

Prévost, M., et al. *Dictionnaire de biographie française*. 2 vols. Paris, 1933–1956.

Polski Slownik Biograficzny. Cracow, 1935–.

Robinet, Jean François Eugène. *Dictionnaire historique et biographique de la Révolution et de l'Empire*. Reprint of 1899 ed. Nendeln, 1975.

Tulard, Jean. *Napoléon et la noblesse d'empire: avec la liste complète des membres de la noblesse impériale (1808–1815)*. Paris, 1979.

Savant, Jean. *Les ministres de Napoléon*. Paris, 1959.

Les sénateurs du Consulat et de l'Empire. Edited by Leonce de Bretonne. Reprint of 1895 ed. Geneva, 1974.

Sirjean, Gaston. *Encyclopédie généalogique des maisons souveraines du monde*. Vol. 7: *Bonaparte*. Boulogne-sur-Seine, 1963.

Six, Georges. *Dictionnaire biographique des généraux et amiraux français de la Révolution et de l'Empire (1792–1814)*. 2 vols. Paris, 1934–1935.

Valynseele, Joseph. *La descendance naturelle de Napoléon ler: Le Comte Léon, Le Comte Walewsky*. Paris, 1964.

———. *Les maréchaux de la Restauration et de la Monarchie de Juillet, leur famille et leur descendance*. Paris, 1962.

———. *Les princes et ducs du Premier Empire, non maréchaux; leur famille et leur descendance*. Paris, 1959.

Winkler Prins encyclopaedie. 20 vols. Amsterdam, 1947–1960.

Wurzbach, Constantin von. *Biographisches Lexikon des Kaiserthums Oesterreich*. 60 vols. Vienna, 1856–1891.

Index

Note: French accents have been omitted in this index.

About the Editor

OWEN CONNELLY is Professor of History and Director of Graduate Studies in History at the University of South Carolina. His other books include: *Napoleon's Satellite Kingdoms; The Gentle Bonaparte: A Biography of Joseph, Napoleon's Elder Brother; The Epoch of Napoleon;* and *French Revolution/Napoleonic Era*.